World History

World History: Journeys from Past to Present uses common themes to present an integrated and comprehensive survey of human history from its origins to the present day. By weaving together thematic and regional perspectives in coherent chronological narratives, Goucher and Walton transform the overwhelming sweep of the human past into a truly global story that is relevant to the contemporary issues of our time.

Revised and updated throughout, the second edition of this innovative textbook combines clear chronological progression with thematically focused chapters divided into three parts as follows:

- Part I. Emergence (human origins to 500 CE)
- Part II. Order (1 CE to 1500 CE)
- Part III. Connections (500–1600 CE)

The expanded new edition features an impressive full-color design with a host of illustrations, maps and primary source excerpts integrated throughout. Chapter opening timelines supply context for the material ahead, while end-of-chapter questions and annotated additional resources provide students with the tools for independent study. Each chapter and part boasts introductory and summary essays that guide the reader in comprehending the relevant theme.

In addition, the companion website offers a range of resources including an interactive historical timeline, an indispensable study skills section for students, tips for teaching and learning thematically, and PowerPoint slides, lecture material, and discussion questions in a password-protected area for instructors. This textbook provides a basic introduction for all students of World History, incorporating thematic perspectives that encourage critical thinking, link to globally relevant contemporary issues, and stimulate further study.

Candice Goucher is Professor of History at Washington State University, Vancouver.

Linda Walton is Professor of History at Portland State University, Oregon.

'I know of no other textbook so successful in complementing chronology with in-depth attention to the major historical processes essential to thematic approaches to world history. It grounds global processes and patterns in the lives of a range of local actors whose collective experiences reveal to us a vivid history of global interaction. This textbook is essential reading for anyone interested in teaching and learning both the content and practice of world history.'

Clif Stratton, *Washington State University*, USA

'This is a terrific text. I am amazed at the breadth and balance of its coverage and at the authors' ability to find telling details in a wide variety of cultures. It will inspire students to look at the world in historical terms and at history as human experience rather than "national" experience.'

Stephen Ruzicka, *University of North Carolina*, USA

'The strength of *World History: Journeys from Past to Present* is use of narrative to support each theme. The authors' perspectives flavor the narratives and themes with modern influences. This text provides a balanced and detailed approach to the world story.'

Greg Ryder, *Radford University*, USA

'This textbook for undergraduates is encyclopaedic and entirely successful in its ambition to cover major themes and events in human history from today to the beginning of time.'

Patrick O'Brien, *London School of Economics*, UK

'An engaging and lucidly written survey of world history. This deftly interwoven thematic approach provides a refreshing and illuminating narrative of the global human past. It should be required reading in colleges and universities.'

Joseph M. Fernando, *University of Malaya, Malaysia*

World History

Journeys from Past to Present

Second Edition

Candice Goucher and Linda Walton

Volume 1

Routledge
Taylor & Francis Group

LONDON AND NEW YORK

First published 2008 by Routledge
This edition published 2013
by Routledge
2 Park Square, Milton Park, Abingdon, Oxon OX14 4RN

Simultaneously published in the USA and Canada
by Routledge
711 Third Avenue, New York, NY 10017

Routledge is an imprint of the Taylor & Francis Group, an informa business

British Library Cataloguing in Publication Data
A catalogue record for this book is available from the British Library

Library of Congress Cataloging-in-Publication Data
Goucher, Candice Lee.
    World history : journeys from past to present / Candice Goucher and
    Linda Walton. — 2nd ed., combined ed.
        p. cm.
    Includes bibliographical references and index.
    ISBN 978-0-415-66999-3 (hardback) -- ISBN 978-0-415-67000-5 (pbk.)
    1. World history—Textbooks. I. Walton, Linda A. II. Title.
    D21.G7185 2012   909—dc23

ISBN: 978-0-415-67001-2 (hbk)
ISBN: 978-0-415-67002-9 (pbk)
ISBN: 978-0-203-06972-1 (ebk)

Typeset and designed
by Keystroke, Station Road, Codsall, Wolverhampton

Printed in Canada

Contents

Pages 347–693 can be found in Volume 2 of *World History*.

Plates

Maps

Figure credits

10.1 Bibliotheque Nationale de France

10.2 Object reg. no: CM 1878,0301.384 © The Trustees of the British Museum

10.3 Courtesy of Special Collections, Fine Arts Library, Harvard University

10.4 Scala/Art Resource, NY

11.1 © Luke Daniek/iStock

11.2 Courtesy of the Iris & B. Gerald Cantor Center for Visual Arts at Stanford University

11.3 http://en/wikipedia.org/wiki/Quipu

11.4 From Heinrich Zimmer, *Art of Asia* (New York: Pantheon 1955), plate 345. Photo: Gunvor Moitessier

11.5 Courtesy of the Trustees of the British Library, OR2784, fol.96r

11.6 Photo: Linda Walton

11.7 Escorial Monastery Library/Oronoz

12.1 © Ali Meyer/Corbis

12.2 McGee, David, ed., The Book of Michael of Rhodes, Volume 1 – Facsimile: A Fifteenth-Century Maritime Manuscript, figure 107a, page 244, © 2009 Massachusetts Institute of Technology, by permission of The MIT Press

12.3 Courtesy of the Trustees of the British Library

12.4 Gift of Labelle Prussin, Ph.D. 1973. Yale University Art Gallery

12.5 National Palace Museum, Taiwan, Republic of China

12.6 © Bettmann/Corbis

Part I opener NASA Goddard Space Flight Center Image by Reto Stöckli (land surface, shallow water, clouds). Enhancements by Robert Simmon (ocean color, compositing, 3D globes, animation). Data and technical support: MODIS Land Group; MODIS Science Data Support Team; MODIS Atmosphere Group; MODIS Ocean Group Additional data: USGS EROS Data Center (topography); USGS Terrestrial Remote Sensing Flagstaff Field Center (Antarctica); Defense Meteorological Satellite Program (city lights)

Part I summary Bridgeman Art Library

Part II opener © The Art Archive / Alamy

Part II summary Courtesy of the Trustees of the British Library

Part III opener Danish Royal Library (Det Kongelige Bibliotek)

Part III summary Metropolitan Museum of Art, Marquand Collection, Gift of Henry G. Marquand, 1889 (89.15.19)/ © 2011. Image © The Metropolitan Museum of Art/Art Resource/Scala, Florence

Preface to the Second Edition

World history identifies the patterns and processes of the historical journey shared in common by all the planet's peoples. *World History: Journeys from Past to Present* uses essential themes of the human experience to present an integrated and comprehensive survey of world history from its origins to the present day. This new edition marks a significant step in the field of world history. Whereas the First Edition used selected themes to narrate all of human history in each of its chapters, the revised Second Edition fully integrates the thematic perspectives into the unfolding story of the global past, beginning with the earliest human journeys of Part I and concluding with the contemporary issues of Part VI. By weaving together thematic and regional perspectives in coherent chronological narratives, the approach transforms the overwhelming sweep of the human past into a truly global story that is relevant to the contemporary issues of our time. Twenty-four themes in human history provide a dynamic framework for the study of the vast reaches of our common past. These themes can also shape our understanding of differences that emerge from change over time and help us discover insights into what connects past and present.

This book's journey reflects the theme of collaboration. The original collaboration began over two decades ago and culminated in a two-volume work, *In the Balance: Themes in Global History* (Boston: McGraw-Hill, 1998), co-authored by Candice L. Goucher, Linda A. Walton, and Charles A. LeGuin. Now out-of-print, *In the Balance* nonetheless inspired and helped to develop a thematic framework for the multimedia project *Bridging World History* [Annenberg/Corporation for Public Broadcasting (2004) accessible at www.learner.org/resources/series197.html], for which Goucher and Walton were lead scholars. And it has inspired the book you read today, a grandchild of the world history field, reflecting significant advances in the scholarship and teaching of world history in the intervening years since we began our collaboration.

Like all world histories, the Second Edition of this book is selective in tracing the journey of the human past from the earliest prehistory of human origins to the present age of globalization. Our starting point for the human journey is the origin of the human species, and as we follow the many thematic pathways of that journey we rely on a variety of evidence and multidisciplinary interpretations. We make use of archaeology and allied sciences throughout the book, and include in each chapter primary sources, maps, and visual images that enrich the textual content and encourage critical thinking.

From the humans who conquered the planet through a multitude of movements and moments that carry us to the present, the six parts of this book portray through combined thematic, chronological, and regional lenses both the diversity and the commonality of the human experience. Each chapter explains a key theme as the principal framing device used to navigate a single portion of the human journey. The selection of critical themes relevant to past and present and to all parts of the globe creates a truly global history. The chapters together focus on multiple themes that best illuminate the journey: on the mobility and interrelationship of peoples; on their connections with the environment; on the patterns of inequality and justice embedded in the ways people organize themselves politically, economically, and socially; how people constructed and expressed cultures through ideas, religion, and art; and how technologies both defined societies and responded to the needs and visions of people in those societies.

Revised and updated throughout, this new edition combines clear chronological progression with thematically focused chapters divided into six parts as follows:

PART I: EMERGENCE (Human origins to 500 CE) Individual chapters trace the themes of migration, technology and environment, urbanization, and religion, demonstrating their fundamental importance to the emergence of human communities across the globe. The chronological framework for this narrative embraces the earliest human history to the emergence of stratified societies and political order.

PART II: ORDER (500–1500 CE) Order is a broad theme that encompasses the construction of social, economic, and political orders from thematic and comparative perspectives. Chapters explore the spread of world religions; the diversity of economic systems as responses to environments; the building of communities through levels of social interaction – families, kinship groups, and social categories such as caste; and finally, empires, the largest-scale political orders before 1500.

PART III: CONNECTIONS (500–1600 CE) This is the umbrella theme that draws attention both to the variety of connections across space that linked peoples and cultures and to the construction of connections over time that reflected attempts to interpret and transmit the past. Individual chapters present the connecting themes most relevant to the period 500–1600 extending from trade along the Silk Roads to the global voyages that created a new global system.

PART IV: BRIDGING WORLDS (1300–1800 CE) This part explores the thematic elements of a newly interconnected global reality. Chapters use the themes of commerce and change, the transmission of traditions, maritime worlds, and the boundaries, frontiers, and encounters on land that redrew the contours of communities during this critical period of globalization.

PART V: TRANSFORMING LIVES (1500–1900) This part focuses on themes that reflect the global impact of transformations between the sixteenth and nineteenth centuries. Individual chapters examine the themes of crucibles of change in the material, social, and economic lives of people everywhere and the world created by revolutionary developments of nationalism and the global Industrial Revolution.

PART VI: FORGING A GLOBAL COMMUNITY (1800–present) The concluding part approaches the complex processes of globalization in the modern world through the thematic lens of accelerating difference and increasing integration, reflected in the twin poles of conflict and community. The human story is viewed through global wars juxtaposed with common concerns for the survival of life on the planet shared by people everywhere. Chapter themes of imperialism, colonialism, and resistance and revolution are included here, along with a return to the earliest themes of technology, environment, migration, and identity.

The expanded new edition boasts an impressive full-color design with a host of illustrations, maps, and primary source excerpts integrated throughout. Chapter opening timelines supply context for the material ahead, while end-of-chapter questions and annotated additional resources provide students with the tools for independent study. Each part features introductory and summary essays built around visual images that orient the reader to the big picture. Each individual chapter also begins with an opening vignette that employs the theme of the chapter, followed by a concise introduction to the chapter theme and its importance in world history. Images and primary sources throughout have been selected to provide balanced global coverage among the peoples and places of the world.

In addition, the companion website offers a range of resources including an interactive historical timeline, an indispensable study skills section for students, tips for teaching and learning thematically, and PowerPoint slides, lecture material, and discussion questions in a password protected area for teaching and learning. This textbook provides a basic introduction for all students of world history, incorporating thematic perspectives that encourage critical thinking, link to globally relevant contemporary issues, and stimulate further study.

There is arguably no more challenging or critical field of history needed to prepare the educated global citizen facing the twenty-first century. Thinking, teaching, and learning thematically offers particular advantages by presenting readers with the chance to bridge the familiar and new, the past and the present. This volume's bold thematic approach and its recursive elements reinforce learning, making it possible to build pathways of complex learning by returning to view the past through multiple thematic and chronological lenses. From beginning to end, the themes of shared humanity and human purpose have guided our journey through world history just as surely as they did the journeys of our ancestors, when they moved out from the prehistoric African forests and savannas to create new worlds.

Abbreviations in dating system

BCE	Before the Common Era
BYR	Billions of Years ago
ca.	*circa*
CE	Common Era
MYR	Millions of Years ago
ya	years ago

A visual tour of *World History: Journeys from Past to Present*

Pedagogical features

World History offers a number of features specifically designed to enhance the teaching and learning experience.

HISTORICAL TIMELINES   Each chapter opens with a timeline, identifying key people and events relevant to the chapter and providing a chronological context for the material ahead.

FIGURES AND MAPS   The text uses a wide range of visual materials, including maps, photographs, and reproductions of paintings. Such resources bring history to life, making it easier to understand and apply concepts and trends in world history.

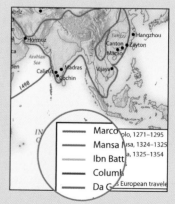

PART OPENING AND CLOSING PAGES   Each part boasts introductory and summary essays that effectively introduce and conclude the relevant theme.

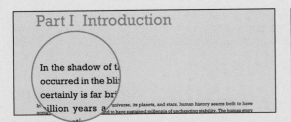

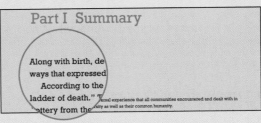

DEFINITIONS OF KEY TERMS   Key vocabulary is highlighted in the text and defined in a complete glossary at the end of the book. This reinforces students' knowledge and understanding of key historical terms.

FURTHER READING   Each chapter concludes with an annotated list of key scholarly books, articles and websites for independent study. Students will find this list particularly helpful for developing and researching papers and other assignments.

STUDY QUESTIONS   At the end of each chapter there are a number of key discussion questions, which deal with the most important themes and events and encourage students to think critically about the material. Sample answers to these questions are available for lecturers on the companion website, making them easily assignable as home-study tasks.

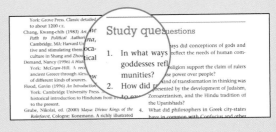

Companion website

www.routledge.com/cw/goucher

Visit the companion website for a whole host of student and instructor resources that both support and enhance the textbook, including:

Instructor resources:

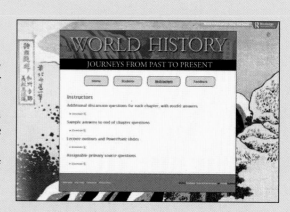

- Sample answers to end of chapter questions, making the questions in the book perfect for home study assignments
- Additional discussion questions for each chapter, again with sample answers for ease of marking
- Template lecture outlines, in the form of PowerPoint slides, ready prepared for each chapter
- Assignable questions for your class based on important primary source material

Student resources:

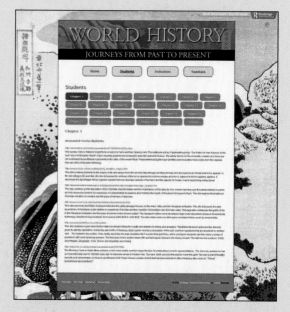

- Interactive Wikipedia-style timeline, containing an array of interactive material and information to complement the themes in the book
- An annotated list of useful web links for each chapter, to further your studies
- Vital links to primary source material for each chapter
- Essential study skills section, with advice on how to read historical documents, approach history exams and write history essays

Part I
Emergence
Human origins to 500 CE

Planet Earth
from space

Part I Introduction

In the shadow of the history of the universe, its planets, and stars, human history seems both to have occurred in the blink of an eye and to have sustained millennia of unchanging stability. The human story certainly is far briefer than the history of the cosmos. Even our planet, which was formed more than 4 billion years ago, dwarfs the history of humankind in terms of its duration. Regardless of one's perspective – that of the cosmos or that of the human species – the era covered in Part I is conceivably the most significant and dynamic period of world history. During a period of dramatic climatic change on the Earth, our species (*Homo sapiens*) evolved in Africa and then spread worldwide. The biological evolution of modern humans provided the intellectual and cultural capacity to dominate the planet. However unique humans were, their survival relied on the successful adaptations in the biosphere they shared with other living things. Global migrations spread our ancestors to most parts of the planet, where they began to adapt to and alter their environments. For most of human history, communities were small, foraging and hunting groups. As members of the planet's dominant species, some humans made the fateful decision to adopt agriculture and they began to genetically modify the plants and animals in the world around them.

The beginnings of agriculture during and after the Holocene coincided with a process of settling down, successfully increasing the available food supplies and swelling local populations. Marking the emergence of settled agricultural communities around the world was an unprecedented degree of complexity. Being settled allowed individuals to accumulate the stuff of life, from pottery to metal tools and permanent structures. The human experience constitutes much more than its material realms. During this same era, an internal life emerges, as do systems of communication that facilitate the transmission of traditions. The human experience thus is uniquely comprised of both material and non-material realms of beliefs and ideas. Surely part of the successful human journey has been the transfer of knowledge across generations, spinning a web of past and present dreams and endeavors.

Part I covers most of human history, beginning more than 4 million years ago. Anatomically modern humans emerged in Africa around 200,000 years ago. By about 500 CE, city life and complex religious and social orders thrived in most parts of the world. The overarching theme of Part I explores the emergence of the essential components of the human journey, emphasizing both changes and continuities and demonstrating the importance of human migration, relationships between technology and the environment, the impulse towards building community, and the role of ideas and beliefs in understanding our place in the cosmos.

Chapter 1: Human migration: World history in motion explores the emergence of anatomically modern humans with their extraordinary mobility that enabled them to dominate the planet. Human migrations have shaped the genetic and cultural diversity of the human experience. We examine the most significant migration event of world prehistory: the colonization of the planet. **Chapter 2: Technology and environment: Transformations in world history** examines the physical and material worlds to which human societies have had to adapt as they spread around the world. Changing landscapes have been a feature of the human experience since the beginning. The planet has undergone and continues to undergo significant geological, climatic, and environmental changes. Humans have also induced environmental change as a consequence of their technology. In this chapter, we explore early human ecologies and focus on technological changes related to food and survival strategies. Humans have adapted to nearly every environment on planet Earth, making the human species the most dominant and destructive. The beginnings of agriculture triggered the most significant transformation in the planet's history. The technologies related to water control, food storage, and the beginnings of metallurgy also had a profound impact on the environment and on population dynamics. **Chapter 3: Cities and city life in world history** looks at the process of settling down into an urban lifestyle, a process still underway. From the earliest cities up to the present, urban life increasingly marked the common experience of being human around the globe. People constructed communities, whether they lived in cities or in relation to cities. The urban experience brought new opportunities and distinctive challenges, from greater cultural interaction and complexity to health and wealth disparities. Finally, **Chapter 4: Ideas and power: Goddesses, kings, and sages** examines early systems of belief. It presents the earliest city-states as they appeared in Eurasia, Africa, and the Americas, showing how the growth of organized religions such as Hinduism and Judaism was intertwined with the increasing complexity of social and political orders. It traces the expansion of early city-states into kingdoms and empires and follows the accompanying changes in the nature of religious beliefs and practices.

Exploration of the themes in Part I provides the building blocks for understanding what follows: the human journey from past to present. Emerging from the stories of migration, adaptation, community, and ideas are the patterns of world history. These patterns reveal the increasing complexity and accelerating differences contained in the human experience.

13.7 BYR	4.5 BYR	3.5 BYR	600 MYR	220–67 MYR	65 MYR	6 MYR
Cosmic origins ("The Big Bang")	Our Sun and planets	First living organisms	First multi-celled eukaryotic organisms	Dinosaurs	Earliest true mammals	First hominins (human ancestors)

TIMELINE

1 Human migration

World history in motion

The history of human mobility took a giant leap forward in 1978, when the archaeologist Mary Leakey and her assistant found a remarkable trail of 3.6-million-year-old footprints in the volcanic tuffs at Laetoli, a prehistoric site in Tanzania, East Africa. On a relatively flat surface, early **hominins** had walked in the freshly littered shower of ash from a nearby volcano, leaving behind their footprints millions of years ago. The subsequent onset of the region's annual rainy season then created a cement of water and ash that preserved

1.1 Trail of hominid footprints fossilized in volcanic ash. This trail was found by Mary Leakey's expedition at Laetoli, Tanzania in 1976. It dates from 3.6 million years ago and shows that hominids (probably *Australopithecus afarensis*) had acquired the upright, bipedal, free-striding gait of modern man by this time. The footprints show a well developed arch to the foot and no divergence of the big toe. The prints are from two adults, and possibly a third set belonging to a child who walked in the footsteps of one of the adults. The prints to the far right belong to a hipparion, an extinct three-toed horse.

3.5 MYR	2 MYR	500,000 ya	116–75,000 ya	35–12,000 ya	8000 ya	5000 ya
Laetoli footprints made	*Homo erectus* moves out of Africa to Eurasia, including Java and China	Neanderthals flourished	Earliest settlement of Australia, Oceania, and the Pacific	Settlement of the Americas	Indo-European migration begins	Bantu expansion underway in sub-Saharan Africa

the footprints. These early hominins, whose footprints preserved a moment in prehistory, most likely were tree-dwelling creatures. Becoming bipedal and walking upright on two legs freed the hands, led to increased brain size, and provided a distinct advantage for mobility and survival. The earliest evidence for bipedalism now appears to come from the even earlier journey of yet another species of human ancestors, *Sahelanthropus*, who may have walked through African grasslands and forests millions of years before the hominins at Laetoli.

More than 6 million years separate the earliest evidence of human footsteps and the moment when humans first walked on the moon, leaving an American flag and their footprints behind (see Figure 1.4 at the end of the chapter). What these events share in common is their global reach. The earliest travelers out of Africa are genetically related to every human being who ever walked on this Earth, while the early astronauts recorded their astonishment in first viewing the big, blue planet from space. This book is about that human journey, from the most distant past of our human ancestors to the present. Most narratives of the human past examine change over time, rather than a single-moment event of the past as the Laetoli footprints represent. **World history** is different in that it seeks a global perspective on the past, one that acknowledges and integrates the historical experiences of all of the world's peoples. Only by examining humanity's shared past is it possible to view today's world in meaningful historical context. Like all historians, world historians create narratives of the past from records of individual and collective experiences, and they interpret the past in response to ques-

tions shaped by the world they live in. Viewing change over time requires world historians to distance themselves from the single moment and to view instead the broader patterns and processes that emerge. The processes that led to the point in time when modern human ancestors actually came down from the trees to walk through African savannas permanently triggered routine **bipedalism**. Walking upright on two feet was a strategy that allowed these human ancestors the distinctive advantage of seeing over the tall grasses that replaced forests during an era of climatic change. This terrestrial locomotion occurred first in Africa and it began the long march of human history.

Introduction to the theme of migration

Today we take for granted the amazing mobility of humans. With ever-increasing speed, humans travel from one side of the globe to the other. Since their origins, human migrations have had important consequences for the planet and all species. While historians rarely have the actual footprints left by humans on the move, they do rely on a staggering variety of historical and scientific evidence to trace the history of human migrations that began long before the development of writing. For example, biology and paleontology study the history of life on Earth. Paleontological research is based on fossil records and focuses only on selected chapters in our biological evolution, such as the major adaptation of bipedalism between about 6 and 4 million years ago or the significant changes in brain capacity

300 BCE	1519–22 CE	1924	1961	1969	1998–2012
Hohokam migration in the Americas	First maritime circumnavigation of the globe	First aerial circumnavigation of the globe	First human space travel (Yuri Gagarin)	First walk on the moon	International Space Station

between 800,000 and 200,000 years ago. Other important chapters in prehistory, such as the development of omnivorous behavior (consuming both animals and plants) or the emergence of **culture** (distinct patterns or styles of behavior), are less well documented because such evidence is less tangible and permanent. The history of human migration points to the single place of origin and the many destinations of the human journey. Migration is also one of the main forces that have shaped the genetic commonalities and the cultural diversity of human populations. How did early human migrations out of Africa people the planet? What are the varied sources for studying the patterns and impact of human migrations? How did later migrations shape the human experience? Finally, what are the causes and consequences of a world history continuously in motion? Studying migration in human history allows us to answer these questions within the widest possible lens: the place of humans in the history of the cosmos.

Evolutionary footprints: Human origins in Africa

World historians now situate the emergence of the unique human species within the larger story of cosmic history. Called "Big History," the timeline of everything from the origins of the solar system about 13 billion years ago (written as 13 BYR) to the more recent appearance of life on the planet Earth about 3.5 BYR, the cosmic perspective reminds us that the human story constitutes a relatively recent and unique moment in time on our planet. Scientists continue to make

new discoveries of hominin fossils that are used to understand the human evolutionary group of species needed to reconstruct our origins. In order to trace the evolutionary past, scientists use an empirical approach and rely on physical evidence. Not all archaeologists agree on the details of the human species family tree and each new fossil is debated in terms of where it fits with the existing evidence, but they do agree on the evolutionary pattern of the past. Classification systems are used to develop models for the appearance of the species *Homo* (humans or their ancestors), an event that has pushed back human origins and human prehistory to more than a million years ago. Since the early discovery of "Lucy" (the famous fossil of the bipedal, but small-brained *Australopithecus afarensis*) on the Afar plain of Ethiopia, the fossils of many more hominins, or human ancestors, have been uncovered.

The fossil evidence now suggests that at least 12 distinct species, including our own *Homo sapiens sapiens*, split from a common ancestor with the African ape and walked on the Earth over the course of the past 7 or 8 million years. Some species, such as the *Australopithecines*, became extinct and others were more successful in making adaptations to the changing environments of the planet. Walking upright preceded the development of brain capacity. Only one species, *Homo sapiens sapiens*, which was fully evolved by about 100,000 years ago, remains worldwide. These discoveries have caused world historians to reconsider what makes the human experience unique. They have also reminded us how what we know about the past is dependent upon a range of supporting evidence, from oral traditions that describe ancient landscapes to the geology that documents change over thousands or even millions of years.

Another major site of human evolutionary research in East Africa has been the Great Rift Valley, including Olduvai Gorge in Tanzania, investigated over two generations by a family of scientists: Louis Leakey (1903–72), Mary Leakey (1913–96, his British wife), their son, Richard, and their daughter-in-law, Meave. In the sand, gravel, and other detrital material deposited by running water in the Olduvai Gorge, the Leakeys discovered stone tools and other evidence from about 2.6 million years ago. The stone tools excavated at Olduvai Gorge by the Leakeys and others provide part of the long chain of evidence of stone tool use that marked early human behavior and continued to several thousand years before the present. Other species may have used (but not necessarily have made) stone tools to butcher animals as early as 3.4 million years ago. Early bipedal hominin species have also been found recently in Chad in Central Africa, and they may have roamed across West Africa, too.

Tracing migration routes

Eventually the movements of hominins connected continents as they traveled beyond Africa to Eurasia. The first intercontinental travel occurred nearly 2 million years ago (written as 2 MYR), when upright and bipedal hominins (probably *Homo erectus*) moved out of Africa. Bigger brains and long limbs, once thought to have spurred the exodus, were likely not needed for those early journeys. Walking upright on two legs freed the hands of these hominins and led to increasingly specialized tool use and expanding minds.

Sometime around 2 million years ago, some of the early hominins may have taken up running, an activity that the genus *Homo* uniquely developed and is still developing. The endurance ability of human ancestors to run long distances not only helped early hunters and scavengers but also led to changes in the balancing mechanism of the

inner ears, wide sturdy knee-joints, and prominent buttocks. About this same time, one or another species of hominins could be found across Afro-Eurasia. Eventually hominins spread to Southeast Asia and to China, where stone tools have been found dating to between 1.66 and 1.32 MYR. Finally they reached Southeastern Australia by about 50,000 to 46,000 years ago. Most of the continental area encompassing Africa, Europe, and Asia received migrants from East Africa by about 1.5 MYR, some even earlier. Fossils dated to about 1.8 MYR have been found in ex-Soviet Georgia, where the species would have encountered cool seasonal grasslands. Two Eurasian sites associated with the species that spread out of Africa (usually identified as *Homo erectus*), one in Israel and one in the Caucasus Mountains of Central Asia, are dated to about 1.6 MYR. By about 780,000 years ago, stone tools in Britain attest to the ability of humans to migrate to and survive in colder, forested environments. Elsewhere, on the Deccan Plateau of the Indian subcontinent, locally produced stone hand axes dating to about the same time of the *Homo erectus* finds in the Caucasus have been discovered, while in Central Asia, locally manufactured pebble tools attest to human occupation after 750,000 years ago. Recent discoveries on the island of Flores in Indonesia have revealed a third species of *Homo*, a small hominin standing about three-feet tall and still surviving 18,000 years ago. Although relatively little archaeological evidence of early human habitation in tropical parts of Asia has not been discovered, it is possible that hominins there would have used perishable material such as bamboo rather than stone for their tools, thus making it much more difficult for archaeologists to locate sites.

The most famous fossils found in East Asia are those of the *Homo erectus* "Peking Man," first discovered in the 1920s in the cave complex at Zhoukoudian near Beijing in north China. Dated to as early as half a million years ago, the original collection of fossils from this site disappeared in the turmoil of World War II and have never been

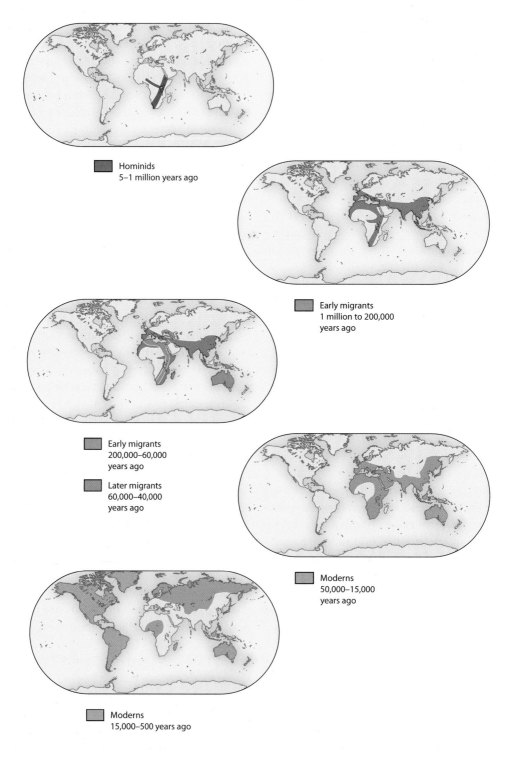

Map 1.1 Global migrations out of Africa.

recovered. Working from excellent casts of the fossils, and with additional remains recovered up through the 1960s, Chinese and international paleoanthropologists have continued to refine their understanding of the various layers of this site. Peking Man (and Woman) ate the meat of wild animals, whether as scavengers or hunters, and used stone tools. It was initially believed that they also knew how to use fire, but recent testing of the ash indicates that humans may not have intentionally made the fire. More recently discovered fossil fragments of *Homo erectus* from several other sites spread geographically from far northeast to far southwest present-day China have been dated to almost 2 MYR. Recent revised dating of "Java Man" fossils in Southeast Asia demonstrates that these *Homo erectus* ancestors lived around the Solo River and at Sangiran on the island of Java in present-day Indonesia from 1.8–1.6 MYR. Pushing back the original dates of these remains by 800,000 years indicates that *Homo erectus* was in Southeast Asia, as well as East Asia, as early as in Africa, and that the move out of Africa may have begun about 2 million years ago, far earlier than originally believed.

Due to the slow retreat of the glaciers, the environment of Europe 2 million years ago was less inviting to the African migrants than that of Asia. As the glaciers retreated around 500,000 years ago, Europe became more attractive to migrating species. As the climate improved, so did the food supplies: animal life underwent significant changes, and new species of deer, bovid, rhino, and horse appeared as more favorable foraging conditions emerged. The earliest, most widely distributed European hominin species are not those of *Homo erectus* but those of the more recent Neanderthal, a name derived from discoveries made at a site in the Neander Valley in modern Germany. Once thought to be an evolutionary "dead end," the Neanderthal now is believed to have interbred with *Homo sapiens* migrants from Africa about 60,000 years ago. Genetic mapping has demonstrated that most Eurasians have a small number of Neanderthal genes in common. Available evidence suggests that the second wave of migration out of Africa accounts for the appearance of anatomically modern humans elsewhere. Other Late Stone Age peoples, including the anatomically modern *Homo sapiens*, appear to have moved into Europe from West Asia during the earliest retreat of what is called the Wurm glaciation, about 35,000 years ago. These migrants, called Cro-Magnon after a site in the Dordogne Valley in France, eventually displaced earlier ones. However, for more than 15,000 years after modern *Homo sapiens* appeared in Europe, the more northern parts of the continent remained unoccupied because of its uncertain climate and unpredictable food resources.

Evidence of our genetic past

The origins and spread of anatomically modern humans from Africa is supported by new evidence from paleoanthropology (the study of fossil human remains), recent dating techniques, computer simulations that model human differences, and genetic studies. One of the most significant scientific projects of the twenty-first century, the Human Genome Project (1990–2003), has demonstrated the similarity (down to 99.9 percent) of all genetic patterns across the human species. Genetic evidence from DNA analysis of blood samples collected from peoples around the world show tiny variations compared to other species. The genetic evidence from studying mitochondrial DNA (found in cells and inherited from the mother) also confirms the tracing of a single lineage back to the African homeland. The peoples within Africa show the greatest genetic variability compared to insignificant variation across the rest of the world's racial groupings, demonstrating that there is no genetic basis for classifying humans into racial types. Today what we call "race" is actually a very complicated and subjective categorization of inherited physical attributes and historical identities. Not only is there is a single species worldwide, but each of us carries the genetic history of our common and very mobile human past in the DNA of our own cells.

The migratory routes that interconnect the planet also have been scientifically tracked by studying the genetic similarities and differences among modern populations and tracing them back to a common ancestor in Africa. The genetic evidence confirms that the original out-of-Africa movement began as early as about 2 MYR. Sites with anatomically modern human remains are common in Africa during the Middle Stone Age (200,000–40,000 years ago), confirming the second migratory wave out of Africa after about 100,000 years ago. Genetic evidence has also recently suggested that about 70,000 years ago, harsh environmental events reduced the number of humans to thousands living mostly in Southern Africa. Many questions remain about our origins. Even if these human ancestors were anatomically modern, did they possess fully modern human characteristics such as culture? Did a genetic mutation or some other event trigger the changes that enabled the sudden appearance of the capability to produce tools and art? At what point did the species obtain uniquely human consciousness?

Science is not the only way of explaining the world and the way it came to be. Not all scientists agree on the complicated interpretations of each bit of evidence. While most historians now regard prehistory as a legitimate part of the reconstruction of the past, some people continue to find the scientific explanations troubling or incomplete. Many more have been able to reconcile their own beliefs and traditions with the scientific facts of human evolution and the origins of the world. Evidence for the systematic study of world prehistory extends beyond science. It relies on the stories told by stones and bones, changing environments, the scientific record of human fossils, the human genome, and archaeology, as well as myth and legends. The earliest evidence for the human experience is material and oral rather than written. Explaining our human origins has its own history since it has been a preoccupation of many different cultural traditions across time and space. Yet we can all agree that explaining the origin point of the human journey is the necessary first step to tracing the migrations that followed.

Origin myths: The creation of the world

World history, like other subfields of the discipline of history, relies on standards for historical reconstruction, which were set in the nineteenth century. Oral history and legend – a source of the earliest remembered or imagined beginnings of human life – were customarily excluded from historical writing. Professional historians considered such sources to be dubious and unscientific, to belong to literature or folklore, much as they assigned "stones and bones" to the realm of archaeologists. It was not until the twentieth century that historians generally began to accept oral tradition and myth as recent attempts to explain and comment on, rather than merely remember, the much longer past of human life on the planet. Accepted as explanation and commentary, oral accounts, like archaeological evidence, became useful in reconstructing the past 10,000 or 20,000 years. The intriguing issue is that various cultures in different places and different times share a similar concern about their journeys in the past. Incorporating into history oral evidence that has been written down or transmitted across many generations via storytelling is especially important to the global understanding of human origins.

Creation legends or myths explain how people believed the world began, and origin myths tell how and where human beings came to be a part of the world. There are varying versions of what people believed or imagined about what happened at the beginning of the human story. They reveal much that is common, as well as much that is unique, about how the past is perceived. By doing so, they are powerful sources of cultural identity, not only telling us how early people understood the world but also giving some sense of important aspects of their cultures and experience, such as social and political organization, family life, gender and ecological relationships, spiritual life and values. Oral history, like other kinds of history, frames events, lives, and processes through culturally specific points of view.

Australian

Versions of their origins unique to Australian Aboriginals reflect archaeologically proven migrations that took place perhaps 50,000 years ago. The legends refer to the era of creation as the "Dreamtime," and they explain the migration of their ancestors to Australia in terms of beliefs about superhuman spirit ancestors who lived during the Dreamtime. The Kakadu people of Australia believe that the arrival of Imberombera, the Great Earth Mother ancestress, was by canoe, a mythical version of an event, which archaeologists and prehistorians accept, even though no canoes – since they are perishable artifacts – have survived. Kakadu legend further explains the populating of Australia by the fact that when Imberombera came to Australia, she was pregnant, her womb filled with children. Once on the continent, she created the natural landscape – hills, creeks, plants, and animals – and peopled it with her children. According to one Aboriginal storyteller, Wandjuk Marika, myths about origins are recounted in different versions, according to stories learned from their ancestors:

> The truth is, of course, that my own people, the Rirajingu, are descended from the great Djankawu who came from the island of Baralku far across the sea. Our spirits return to Baralku when we die. Djankawu came in his canoe with his two sisters, following the morning star, which guided them to the

shores of Yelangbara on the eastern coast of Arnhem Land. They walked far across the country following rain clouds.[1]

South Asian

The people of the Indus Valley **civilization** of South Asia (ca. 1600–3000 BCE) left little indication of their beliefs about their origins other than some archaeological evidence of a fertility cult, which, like many others, centered on a mother or Earth goddess. The earliest South Asian creation texts date from the period of the Indo-European invasions (ca. 1500–500 BCE) and represent much more recent ideas introduced by the invaders. The texts are collectively known as the Vedas (literally, "knowledge") and include hymns, ritual texts, and philosophical works. The central narrative in the oldest of these texts, the Rig-Veda, concerns the deity Indra, who slew a serpent demon and by this act created cosmic order:

> Indra's heroic deeds, indeed, will I proclaim, the first ones which the wielder of the thunderbolt accomplished. He killed the dragon, released the waters, and split open the sides of the mountains.
>
> When you, O Indra, killed the first-born among the dragons and further overpowered the wily tricks of the tricksters, bringing forth, at that very moment, the sun, the heavens, and the dawn – since then, indeed, have you not come across another enemy.
>
> Indra, who wields the thunderbolt in his hand, is the lord of what moves and what remains rested, of what is peaceful and what is horned [aggressive]. He alone rules over their tribes as their king; he encloses them as does a rim the spokes.

Other scriptures in the Vedic tradition present the idea that the creation of the universe was the product of the sacrifice of the primeval man,

Purusha, who was sacrificed by his children and from whose body the universe was created. One of the later scriptures in the Rig-Veda, the "Hymn of Creation," displays a questioning attitude toward the idea of creation, implicitly expressing doubt about various theories that existed, such as the suggestion that creation was the result of a sexual act or the product of a "cosmic egg." This text exhibits a high level of abstract thinking and is one of the earliest examples of philosophic doubt:

> Then even nothingness was not, nor existence.
> There was no air then, nor the heavens beyond it.
> What covered it? Where was it? In whose keeping?
> Was there then cosmic water, in depths unfathomed?
> Then there were neither death nor immortality,
> nor was there then the torch of night and day.
> The One breathed windlessly and self-sustaining.
> There was that One then, and there was no other.
> But, after all, who knows, and who can say whence it all came, and how creation happened?
> The gods themselves are later than creation, so who knows truly whence it has arisen?
> Whence all creation had its origin,
> he, whether he fashioned it or whether he did not,
> he, who surveys it all from highest heaven,
> he knows – or maybe even he does not know.

West Asian: Judeo-Christian

The role of a creator god is present in the Judeo-Christian tradition as reflected in the story of creation in the Book of Genesis, found in the Bible and Torah, the product of many stories origi-

nating in the first millennium BCE. This story attributes the act of creation to one god, who forms human beings in his own image:

> In the beginning God created the heaven and the earth. . . .
> And God said, Let there be light: and there was light. . . .
> And God made the firmament, and divided the waters. . . .
> And God called the dry land Earth; and the gathering together of the waters called he Seas. . . .
> And God said, Let the earth bring forth grass, the herb yielding seeds, and the fruit tree yielding fruit. . . .
> So God created man in his own image. . . .

Chinese

In contrast to this, an early Chinese account (second century BCE) offers an account of creation without a creator:

> When heaven and earth were joined in emptiness and all was unwrought simplicity, then without having been created, things came into being. This was the Great Oneness. All things issued from this oneness but all became different, being divided into the various species of fish, birds, and beasts.

The creation of the world is often seen as a process of separating the heavens from the Earth or the waters from the heavens, either by a creative force or without an agent.

Native American

A Cherokee myth from North America described the primal environment as a watery one. An image of primeval water covering a not-yet-created Earth was found among almost all

American peoples with the exception of the Inuit in the farthest Northern Arctic region.

Another people of North America, the Hopi, connect the emergence of humans with the beginnings of migration:

> Way back in the distant past, the ancestors of humans were living down below in a world under the earth. They weren't humans yet [because] they lived in darkness, behaving like bugs. Now there was a Great Spirit watching over everything; some people say he was the sun. He saw how things were down under the earth, so he sent his messenger, Spider Old Woman, to talk to them. She said, "You creatures, the Sun Spirit doesn't want you living like this. He is going to transform you into something better, and I will lead you to another world." When they came out on the surface of the earth, that's when they became humans. In the journeys that followed, they were looking for a place of harmony where they could follow good teachings and a good way of life.[2]

Yoruba

In the Yoruba myth from Nigeria in West Africa, the Earth was created from the beginning of heavens and primeval waters. The creator deities are fully humanized, with characteristics that are recognizably fallible. One of the deities even falls asleep, having drunk too much palm wine, and misses his chance to create land.

Sumerian

In the region of Sumer in ancient West Asia, the Earth sat upon a vast primordial sea of sweet water, and creation was a matter of differentiating the raw matter of Earth, Heaven, and air into specific things. There was an assumed prior existence of a god and goddess, from which sprang the gods of the Sumerian pantheon:

> When on high the heaven had not been named,
> Firm ground below had not yet been called by name,
> Naught but primordial Apsu, their begetter,
> And Mummu Tiamat, she who bore them all,
> Their waters commingling as a single body:
> No reed hut had been matted, no marsh land had appeared,
> When no gods whatever had been brought into being,
> Uncalled by name, their destinies undetermined –
> Then it was that the gods were formed within them.

The god Apsu was killed by his offspring because they feared he would kill them. The sea was then made from the body of the father; the sky was made from the body of the mother, Tiamat, who tried to destroy the children who had murdered her husband but was herself killed by them. There is a sequence of the acts of creation carried out by the gods – light, day and night, earth and sky, sun, moon, and stars, and with them the ordering of time. Then humanity was created, with its obligations and duties to the gods.

Greek

There are striking parallels between the Sumerian and Greek traditions, since those of Sumer influenced those of Greece. The anthropomorphic gods of the Greek tradition showed a similar pattern of human and superhuman behavior as they created the world. Heaven and Earth gave birth to numerous gods and goddesses. The youngest, who attacked and castrated his father, married his sister and devoured their children, with the exception of Zeus. When Zeus grew up, he was able to disgorge his brothers and sisters alive from his father's body. Zeus thus became the leader of the Olympian gods, deities held in common by all Greeks, and had the capacity to mate with humans. The Olympian gods exhibited human passions and failings, just like the mortals over whom they ruled.

Nordic

The gods of northeastern Eurasia were divided into two families of deities, one connected with war, one with peace. There was a struggle between the two groups of gods that was resolved in favor of the warlike deities, chief of whom was Odin. Odin presided over Valhalla, where human heroes are received after death. Odin gave his name to the English day, Wednesday ("Odin's day"), as other gods and goddesses did to other days, for example, Thor to Thursday ("Thor's day").

Japanese

Gods also play a central role in the creation of the world described in the Kojiki, the earliest textual source of native Japanese beliefs, compiled in 712 CE. Like Apsu and Tiamat in West Asia, a pair of gods, Izanami and Izanagi, gave birth to the Japanese islands and a host of deities:

> When the primeval matter had congealed but breath and form had not yet appeared, there were no names and no action. Who can know its form? However, when heaven and earth were first divided, the three deities became the first of all creation. The Male and Female here began, and the two spirits (Izanagi and Izanami) were the ancestors of all creation.

The progeny of these two gods included Amaterasu, the Sun Goddess, who became the central deity of Shinto (literally, "Way of the Gods"), the native belief system of Japan. The Sun Goddess of Shinto is only one example of a solar deity. Solar deities were present in many early societies that were dependent on **agriculture**, since the sun was vital to their welfare. The

Egyptians worshiped Ra, a solar deity. The Aztecs of Mesoamerica, the area between the United States and South America, believed that the sun ordered and structured the universe. For them, the sun and moon were dualities of masculine and feminine, darkness and light, life and death. An eclipse was viewed as an upsetting of the necessary equilibrium between the two, leading to a collapse of the world order. Eclipses were depicted in drawings as mythical animals "eating" or "biting" the sun. In early China, an eclipse was explained as an archer shooting the sun. The Incas of South America believed that the sun created the first Incas, a brother and sister, who set out on a journey to be tested and founded the Incan empire. Among the Aztec, the sun and moon engaged in a daily cosmic battle in the sky above.

China: Origins of human culture

Chinese records, which are thought to reflect a historical memory of community leaders in the fifth or sixth millennium BCE, portray the rulers of antiquity as wise rulers who bequeathed to their subjects the knowledge of agriculture, writing, and medicine. Although ideas about the creation of the world can be identified in early Chinese thought, there was no dominant creation myth. It was the origins of human culture and society, not the creation of the world that concerned early thinkers in China. The recorded bequests of agriculture and writing illustrate definitive elements of Chinese culture: an agrarian economy with an elaborate textual tradition in which the farmer and the scholar are both idealized. The importance of agriculture, and grain in particular, was reinforced in the account of the birth of the progenitor of the Zhou (pronounced "Joe") people, "Lord Millet," in the Book of Songs, the earliest poetic anthology in China (sixth century BCE):

> She who in the beginning gave birth to the people,

This was Jiang Yuan.

How did she give birth to the people?

Well she sacrificed and prayed

That she might no longer be childless.

She trod on the big toe of God's footprint,

Was accepted and got what she desired. . . .

She gave birth, she nurtured;

And this was Houji [Lord Millet]. . . .

He planted large beans;

His beans grew fat and tall.

His paddy lines were close set,

His hemp and wheat grew thick,

His young gourds teemed.

Truly Houji's husbandry followed the way
    that had been shown.

Certain commonalities are apparent in the creation stories discussed here: the creative act by which earth was separated from sea and air; the anthropomorphic struggle among deities; the tangible connection between gods and humans; and the role of gods in originating cultural knowledge, including knowledge of the past. Most peoples also tell stories of their arrival in the world, either by an act of creation or a journey, in order to provide legitimacy for political rule or cultural identity. These various versions of the distant human past suggest that all myths, despite unique cultural features, reflect common human experiences, curiosities, and concerns.

Colonization of the planet

Whatever the origins of the human community, the most significant migration event of world prehistory is the colonization of the planet: humans are the only animals to have achieved near-global distribution. Prehistorians had long considered that the movement of humans in prehistory reflects their purposefulness, but how did this sense of purpose arise? Understanding the process of global colonization raises the questions of how and where humans emerged as a species and how and why humans moved across the

Earth's landscapes to occupy all environments found on this planet. After leaving Africa, anatomically modern humans eventually spread by land and by sea to all the inhabitable parts of the planet. Why these earliest migrants left Africa to colonize the world is a complex, important question. The answer is likely to be found in a web of interrelated factors centered on human behavior, specifically behavior selected to reduce risk and increase the individuals' fitness for adaptation and survival. Calculated migration must have resulted from information sharing, alliance building, memory, and the ability to negotiate – all skills that necessarily accompanied increasingly complex social and cultural groups. The increasing complexity of existence inevitably led our human ancestors out of Africa, resulting in a global distribution of diverse human groups worldwide. Sometime around 70,000 years ago, the population of *Homo erectus* went extinct and *Homo sapiens* themselves (totaling perhaps only 10,000 to 15,000 individuals worldwide) were threatened by extinction. It is believed that more individuals survived in tropical Africa, which accounts for the greater genetic variability of ancient populations there and of African populations now. At about this time (about 70,000 years ago), the range of distinctive human appearances, including skin color, rapidly appeared as the species interbred and certain mutations allowed their DNA carriers and their descendants to adapt to new environments. Human populations soon recovered from the brink of extinction and began to reclaim a natural trajectory of expansion. Increasing population may have prodded the migration of some groups. Armed with the attributes of **culture**, the distinctive, complex patterns of behavior shared by human groups, humans eventually adapted to and conquered virtually every global environment. Developing an understanding of their origins and commonly shared features included explanations about the journeys that led them to their homelands.

Whenever or wherever human societies and cultures first appeared, the peopling of our globe has been a product of migration from place to place. Given the small numbers of people and the vast distances they traversed, and considering their technologically limited modes of transportation, the movement of people around the globe seems miraculous. It was undertaken entirely by people who walked on foot and perhaps floated on rafts, who gathered and hunted food, and who thrived in diverse and difficult environments.

Most historians agree that symbolic cultural expression helps make the human species unique.

Recent evidence of early symbols, including a red piece of iron oxide (ochre) incised with cross-hatchings, has been found at a site in Southern Africa dated to the critical era of African migrations. Interpreted as information rather than decoration, the evidence of markings supports the theory that the second wave of African ancestors left the continent with the cultural advantages that would have furthered their migration. Some researchers believe that the key cultural roots included the development of widespread use of social networks, an important human marker.

PRIMARY SOURCE: THE ORIGIN OF HUMAN CONSCIOUSNESS

World historians agree that one of the defining characteristics of being human is the expanded capacity of the human brain: the ability to ponder an awareness of ourselves in the cosmos, accumulate that understanding and knowledge, and communicate the collected cultural memory from one generation to the next. When does the evolution of human consciousness come into focus? The engraved ochre from Blombos dated to about 77,000 years ago is the earliest evidence of abstract, symbolic thought. Many scientists look to the use of symbols as evidence of this key human trait that emerges among the *Homo* species. By about 40,000 years ago, musical instruments, painting, and sculpture can be added to the list of human accomplishments.

Making tools required a mental template for the fashioning of patterned shapes. Rock art similarly reflected the ability to inscribe inner thoughts and beliefs on the outside world. But it was the discovery of a small piece of iron oxide at the site of Blombos Cave, South Africa, that marked a new stage in research of human capabilities and symbolic thinking. Scientists don't

1.2 Engraved red ochre, Blombos Cave, South Africa (ca. 70,000 BP). Cross-hatchings are believed to be the oldest "art," engraved with "tally" marks.

agree on whether the hatchings represent the "tally marks" of reckoning or record some other measurement of action or observation. We likely will never know with any certainty how the object was used. Regardless of its specific function, the object's obvious employment of visual communication conveys a distinct advantage useful for adaptation and survival. Artistic expression through making symbols was the first means by which our early human ancestors sought meanings beyond the visible world of nature. Ancient objects like the engraved ochre from Blombos simply began the long journey of human self-awareness.

Successful adaptations enabled these populations to survive in different ecological zones and, competing with Neanderthal populations, to eventually win out as the sole surviving human species in Afro-Eurasia.

Many examples of global colonization depended on interactions between people, and between people and their environments. Gradually, sometime during the Middle Stone Age (perhaps 100,000 to 200,000 years ago), distinct patterns of interaction emerged among humans and between them and the landscapes in which they lived. Because the distinctive physical and social environments to which humans adapted were themselves constantly changing, cultures too continually changed. That early humans acquired technological and social skills can be inferred from widespread evidence of their material culture – stone tools and utensils, carved figurines, rock and cave art, and the like, dating from about 40,000 years ago – which has been found in most parts of the globe.

Language and communication

Humans also developed language and language sharing, the highest level of communication skill and one still regarded as unique to humans. As they spread around the globe, our human ancestors developed efficient and various languages as the means of remembering and transmitting information within shared social contexts. Some scientists believe this social interaction occurred with the first systematic use of fire for cooking foods. Exactly how or when languages emerged remains obscure, but when they did, language and the ability to reason abstractly separated humans from their hominin ancestors, and both reinforced the uniqueness of the species and confirmed its humanity.

Language would have been critical to communicating ideas, planning itineraries, and transmitting culture across the approximately 5,000 generations that separate us from our common human ancestor. The key physical adaptation, which may have occurred only about 200,000 years ago, was the lowering of the larynx in the human throat, enabling us to produce speech by modifying passing air. No other species is capable of modifying and reinventing its behavior through speech. Scientists also use the changes in language to trace the evolution of speech and the movements of speakers across the landscape.

All human languages are similar in being capable of expressing the needs, desires, and history of their speakers. Few would disagree that the ability to communicate verbally and symbolically is at the core of the behaviors and increasingly complex social structures of human beings. Communication has extended the impact of collective human learning across multiple generations. Humans are distinctive as a species because of their ability to inherit knowledge. The development of language unquestionably furthered the social and technological evolution of humans and facilitated systems of reciprocity and social exchange. For example, the division of labor in food production and the exchange and transportation of goods and products were greatly expedited by speech. Being able to assign different tasks to different individuals furthered co-operation and fueled the processes of social and cultural evolution. Sharing information greatly accelerated the adaptation and ultimate impact of the human species on the planet.

The evolution of increasing specialization in language and technology were parallel and likely interrelated developments. From the available evidence of stone technology worldwide about 500,000 years ago, tool types would have seemed very similar. By about 50,000 years ago, distinctive differences had appeared: regional specialization in tool making reflected cultural evolution and the occupation of different environments requiring different tools. On the basis of available evidence and its chronological pattern, the soundest judgment seems to be that continuous migration from the African continent peopled the adjacent landmass of West Asia and there created an ancient crossroads of cultural interaction. Scattered temporary settlements of Stone Age culture appeared in West Asia as they did in most of the habitable world. Evidence of human societies in West Asia dating to about 35,000 BCE[3] is well established. Since there is no evidence of a significant migration of new peoples into West Asia between 1.5 MYR and 35,000 BCE, the people who settled there were probably descendants of the early migrants from Africa. After about 10,000 years ago, their descendants gathered and later planted wild grain, and they were soon building the first West Asian cities.

Long after the first global migration of humans from Africa to Australia beginning about 50,000 years ago, the continuity of cultural style suggests the endurance of a population made up of only two or three language groups related to African languages. The development of West Asian culture and social structures was a product of slow change from within rather than an influx of new people coming from without. The early movement of people likely followed the fringe of the Indian Ocean into the tropical areas of the Pacific world. Movements into northern (and colder) lands occurred over time.

Demography, animals, rock art, and climate

As prehistoric cultures evolved, peoples moved into previously uninhabited areas. It is likely that human population increases were largely responsible for these migrations, although severe climatic fluctuations or natural catastrophes might also have triggered migration. Demographic changes, increases or decreases in population size or characteristics, interacted with other aspects of **ecology**, including cultural and environmental events, to encourage people to move. Population pressures on scarce or limited resources forced people into ever more restrictive environments that, in turn, required adaptive strategies. Early

humans, armed with effective tools, food storage, and social cooperation, could colonize deserts, snow-covered tundra, and arid lands.

We have already seen that the earliest African migrations extended the achievements of human evolution to other parts of the globe. Since these migrations, more than a million years ago, no part of the globe has ever been truly isolated. Not all migration was permanent, and descendants of early migrants sometimes returned to Africa, resulting in an interchange of peoples, products, and ideas between Africa, West Asia, and the lands bordering the Mediterranean and the Red Sea. The Indian Ocean coast of East Africa and Eurasia was also an entry point for peoples and their cultures, creatures, and crops, such as bananas (beginning sometime before about 6,000 years ago). Descendants of Africans themselves also ventured on voyages across the Indian Ocean to the Indian subcontinent and ultimately connected the story of human migration to China, Australia, and New Guinea. Humans were not the only populations to spread across the landscape. For example, the highly variable climate of the Sahara, the world's largest desert covering almost one-third of the African continent, has experienced severe drying conditions between roughly 8,000 and 7,000 years ago and again after about 5,000 years ago, leading to today's parched environment. The dramatic shift from lakes and humid climate to dry conditions led to the migration of animal species such as the elephant, as well as to human migration. After the last dry period, humans made further adaptations, sometimes by developing irrigation and farming.

The domestication of animals further increased human mobility. On foot, mobility was estimated to be about 72 kilometers (45 miles) per century, meaning that few individuals traveled more than a few days away from where they were born and the spread of humans was extremely gradual. Earlier animal migrations had spread the species most useful to human movements – the camelid (including camel, alpaca, and llama) and the equid (including horse, ass, onager, and zebra) families from North America to Eurasia some 13

PRIMARY SOURCE: INTERVIEWING ANCIENT ROCK ART

In 1869, a young African hunter named /A!kunta was sent to prison for "cattle raiding" in a region of the southwestern Cape of South Africa that had once belonged to his San-speaking ancestors. In a remarkable sequence of events, the young man was released to the linguist Wilhelm Bleek, who with his sister-in-law Lucy Lloyd began a series of interviews with /A!kunta, one of the last /Xam San speakers.[4] Called "Hottentots" or "Bushmen," pejorative terms used by the Dutch settlers, groups of these hunters and gatherers had been made nearly extinct by the processes of colonization and resettlement. Speaking to Lucy Lloyd on 22 July 1871, /A!kunta says:

> The weather is fine. I stay the two years, I go in the path, I return to my house. I return to my wife, for my wife sits waiting for me in the house. She cannot eat the springbok's flesh, for she waits for me in my house.

Over the several years of being interviewed, /A!kunta revealed his knowledge of the language, stories, and rituals that had been transmitted to him. Lloyd later published these stories, including the creation myths of the first beings, the mantis, his wife and daughter, the porcupine.

On the area farms, Bleek and Lloyd had noticed ancient and intricately skilled rock paintings, which they observed to be about the things that "most deeply moved the Bushman mind." In his interviews, /A!kunta also provided historians and archaeologists with windows through which the rock art of the surrounding mountains and valley could be viewed. The images recorded the ancient journeys of San and others, who entered the region. He says:

> No more do we Bushmen hunt in these hills, the fire is cold. Our songs are quiet . . . But listen carefully: You will hear us in the water . . . Look carefully: You will see us in the rock.

Despite the questionable way in which they were obtained, many historians and archaeologists believe that these interviews helped transform the study of rock paintings from pure speculation to interpretations informed by the understanding of the San worldview. The paintings of eland were testimony to the activities of

1.3 Cave painting at Tassili-n-Ajjer in the Sahara Desert of Algeria. This painting is from the Hunter or Bubalus Period, ca. 7000–3500 BCE.

shamans, who harness the spiritual energy of the spirit world through trance. The analysis of painted images over the millennia took place in the cultural contexts of generations of hunters and gatherers, who occupied the landscape seasonally for more than 10,000 years. Without the conversations recorded and transcribed on 12,000 manuscript pages by Bleek and Lloyd, the meanings of the San past inscribed in their rock art would have been completely lost to future generations.

MYR. The harnessing of the Asian camel, the South American llama, and the Eurasian horse or donkey occurred much later (tamed in the wild by about 6000 BCE), when they expanded the migratory activity of early human groups just as humans were settling down. Their use was costly but sped up journeys and made contacts between increasingly settled regions of the world more frequent.

For more recent eras, world historians rely on evidence as diverse as language and archaeology to trace human movements. Social networks, defined by the communication between individuals and groups, probably shaped the earliest human migrations and they have constituted the single most important factor shaping all migration ever since.

Linguistic evidence of migration

The earliest beginnings of language help make humans distinct from other animals. The study of language can also offer important clues about the historic migration of peoples around the world. All human languages can be divided into approximately 12 classificatory groupings: Nilo-Saharan, Niger-Congo, Khoisan, Afro-Asiatic, Dravidian, Dene-Caucasian, Austric, Indo-Pacific, Australian, Eurasiatic, Kartvelian, and Amerind. There is disagreement over exactly when each of these groupings emerged. Most historians would place their emergence between about 10,000 and 20,000 years before the present, based on the current distribution of descendent speakers of related languages. The oldest and widest spread of language groups also suggests two key periods

of migrations. The first was from Africa to the Pacific along water-borne routes and through tropical locales between 80,000 and 50,000 years ago. The subsequent human migration identifies dispersions through temperate zones between 40,000 and 30,000 years ago, reaching the more extreme environmental zones. This later distribution also suggests that human groups differentiated into subgroups more rapidly and even before the great Ice Age.

Distinctive linguistic features, such as click sounds, can reveal patterns of movement if they are found in geographically distant populations. For example, clicks can be found in Southern African and Southeast Asian languages today. Also, similar words in different languages can demonstrate common origins. Substantial movements from the savanna areas of Eastern and Southern Africa are reflected in the distribution and history of Khoisan languages sometime after 80,000 years ago. Speakers of Nilo-Saharan languages who moved eastwards into the Indian Ocean world may eventually account for the similarities between African, tropical Asian, and Oceanic language groups.

The Bantu migrations in Africa demonstrate ways the study of language can help scholars trace human movement in the distant past. Between 6,000 and 1,000 years ago, Bantu speakers from the Lake Chad region slowly spread across most of sub-Saharan Africa. By about 1000 BCE, the pace of their migrations quickened. They may have been aided in this process by their ability to make and use iron tools and weapons, which could have given them an advantage over other human communities. The incorporation of words from other language groups into Bantu languages, including words related to agriculture and herding, both provide evidence of other groups Bantu speakers encountered and indicates that they may have acquired knowledge of these processes from non-Bantu speakers.

The Bantu expansion involved speakers of related languages that now make up the populations of the southern half of the African continent. This largest and longest of recent African migrations also accounts for the shared cultural and political patterns that have helped to mitigate that continent's environmental and cultural diversity. The movement of Bantu speakers, like the spread of Asian peoples into the Pacific, may initially have been the result of dramatic climatic fluctuation. Both the Bantu and Asian migrations have been documented by archaeological and linguistic evidence, including the similar styles of and decoration on excavated pottery and the shared vocabulary of distant peoples.

One day it may be possible to trace in greater detail the pattern of all early human migrations using linguistic evidence. For the present time, historians have limited and fragmentary evidence of how (and when) the world's 12 or more language groups emerged and whether those groups are related ancestrally. For example, the speakers of early Indo-European languages appear to belong to one large super-family of languages (Eurasiatic) that emerged sometime after about 40,000 years ago. Historians do not agree on the exact location of their homeland. Later migrations can be traced between the areas occupied by the ancestors of Celtic groups and Central Asian peoples and likely resulted in shared physical and cultural characteristics. For example, by about 4,000 years ago, a community in the Tarim Basin buried their dead in dry and sometimes salty soils, which preserved and mummified the bodies. Archaeologists have been able to detect distinctively Caucasian features, fair skin and light-colored hair from the remains of these Indo-European migrants, who once lived near the modern Chinese city of Urumchi. Much later migrations can be studied by examining the

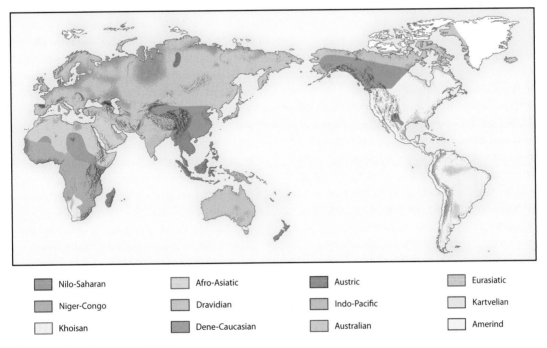

Nilo-Saharan	Afro-Asiatic	Austric	Eurasiatic
Niger-Congo	Dravidian	Indo-Pacific	Kartvelian
Khoisan	Dene-Caucasian	Australian	Amerind

Map 1.2 World language groups.

similarities and differences in language groups. The Late Stone Age migration of the Celtic people who inhabited the trans-Alpine area north of the Mediterranean basin and west of the Urals was one of the most widespread movements of peoples in Europe. Better conditions and the lure of other cultures drew the Celts south to the Mediterranean and West Asia and west toward the Atlantic and the British Isles, where they settled during the first millennium BCE.

The end of the Ice Age

The recession of glaciation permitted migration and settlement from West Asia to Europe, and by the time the Ice Age ended (ca. 10,000 BCE) distinctive societies and cultures had evolved there. The end of the Ice Age was of similar significance in East Asia, where it allowed early humans to develop a more complex array of subsistence strategies that included hunting, fishing, gathering, and the use of diversified and specialized tools. For these and other early migrations, historians have only the most general chronological outlines for thousands of people over the generations.

All migrations have in common the evidence each provides for the extraordinary success story of early human populations. From East Africa to other continents, human populations after the end of the Ice Age steadily increased in number, and human groups increased in size and complexity. Expanding populations sent new migrants into the next valley or across the sea to the next port, to occupy virtually every conceivable environmental niche on this planet. Population increase has been the single most critical factor shaping the human story.

The peopling of the landmasses we now call Africa and Eurasia was largely accomplished mostly on foot across land, over hundreds of centuries, and by hundreds of generations. Some migrations to other parts of Asia, the Pacific, and the Americas required long-distance travel across water, either by boats or across the temporary land bridges that appeared in various parts of the world during the glacial lowering of the world's sea levels, approximately 50,000 years ago. For some parts of the world – Australia and New Guinea, for example – both land bridges and rafts or boats would have been necessary for successful human migrations.

REACHING THE AMERICAS It is generally recognized that the earliest inhabitants of the Americas were immigrants from Asia, though the picture of migration to the Americas is less clear than elsewhere. Biological evidence from blood types and dental patterns indicates that the nearest relatives of the earliest Americans are found in Northeast Asia. Disagreement over dating has resulted in debate about who exactly the immigrants were and how and when they arrived. It has long been hypothesized that people came from Eurasia (Siberia) to the northernmost reaches of North America. Pebble tools discovered at a Siberian site only tentatively dated to between 1.5 and 2 million years ago suggest hominin inhabitants in Asia at that date, far earlier than the appearance of humans in Beringia, the area of the connecting bridge between Asia and North America. There is also a lack of evidence south of the ice sheet in the Americas. Consequently, informed opinion places migration from Eurasia across Beringia to the Americas during the period between 35,000 and 12,000 years ago.

The traditionally accepted dates for the peopling of the Americas, 11,000–11,500 years ago, are based on evidence of human habitation far to the south of Beringia, at a Clovis, New Mexico, site. Recently the lithic assemblages underlying Clovis points (and therefore predating their makers) were excavated in Texas and dated to about 13,200 to 15,500 years ago. There are possibly earlier sites of human habitation, which may date back as far as 19,000 years ago in North America and to 33,000 years ago in South America. This evidence includes sites that some historians speculate may have been reached by migrants across the North Atlantic from Europe west to the Americas. Although some of the dates remain controversial, widely accepted evidence indicates that the Americas were most likely inhabited by humans around 15,000 years ago. Widespread evidence of occupation in the eastern Arctic regions of Greenland, Canada, and Northeast Asia also supports this dating. Colonization of the Arctic took place as ice sheets retreated at the end of what is known as the Wisconsin glaciation about 10,000 years ago.

The Beringian theory of the arrival of Eurasians in the Americas holds that at the time of the migration to the Americas, Siberia and central Alaska were connected by a land bridge across what is now the Bering Sea. Having crossed this bridge into the Americas, people found that there were two great fluctuating ice sheets, one covering the area around and south from Hudson Bay, and another flowing down the Rockies. Between the two was an ice-free corridor, a route south roughly from the Yukon down through Montana, which humans and animals took as they occupied what had been a land without people.

Another theory of settlement of the Americas is that the Eurasian migrants might have sailed south along an ice-free Pacific Coast. The close connection of the culture of Pacific Coast peoples with marine resources might lend credence to the idea that migration to the Americas was by sea. Important adaptive strategies were developed by Pacific Coast peoples to utilize marine resources: specialized harpoons have been discovered that, with seaworthy canoes, allowed Pacific Coast peoples to kill sea mammals. Some historians have gone as far as suggesting that migration from Asia to the Americas was entirely by boat, across the Pacific Ocean. Similar theories of migration to the Americas across the Atlantic from Africa have also been proposed. None has found general acceptance.

REACHING THE PACIFIC ISLANDS Human settlement of the Pacific island world, Australia, and New Guinea may have begun as early as 50,000 years ago, although recently excavated Australian rock-shelter sites may testify to human presence there earlier than 60,000 years ago. This was a period of fluctuating glaciation when the sea level was temporarily low. Even so, as much as 50 kilometers (31 miles) of open sea would have had to be crossed to reach Australia, since at no time in the last 3 million years was there a complete land bridge between the Asian and Australian continents. Whether humans arrived as castaways, adrift on logs or other vegetation, or on boats or canoes deliberately constructed for intended voyages, they would have found themselves isolated once the glaciers retreated and the sea returned to its former levels. Along with the human inhabitants of Australia, the fauna and flora were also isolated, each to evolve in ways unique to its isolated environment: kangaroos, for example, are one product of the separation and isolated evolution of species. Recent dating of discoveries of rock engravings, red ochre, and stone artifacts at a site called Jinmium in north-western Australia may push back the dates of the earliest migrations to between 75,000 and 116,000 years ago, suggesting to some researchers that the first artists were not modern humans at all but rather an earlier, archaic species of *Homo sapiens*. Perhaps art may not be a defining characteristic of human behavior.

Though scattered Early Stone Age sites have been found across much of Australia and New Guinea, full-scale and continuous occupation of these difficult environments began as a result of later migrations during the last glacial age, around 12,000 BCE, when Indonesia, Malaya, and Borneo were once again attached to one another and to the Asian mainland. Bands of gathering and hunting people moved steadily eastward and southward. From Indonesia, some crossed by canoe or raft to the continent of New Guinea–Australia–Tasmania. The presence of these new migrants can be documented by linguists, who have studied the distribution and relatedness of Australian Aboriginal languages. Both the expansion of land created by the lowering sea levels and the eventual restriction of lands as the sea rose again effected demographic changes and the movement of peoples.

A much more recent migration of people culturally related to the Southeast Asian mainland has been dated to 7,000 years ago. This Late Stone Age migration is divided into four distinct groups, and it is clear that people from both the islands and the mainland of Southeast Asia participated. Were they pushed south by the cold of the extended glaciers or by other northern peoples fleeing harsh environmental changes? Were they propelled by the pressures of expanding populations? The evidence is insufficient to provide an answer. As was the case for most coastal and island settlements, early sites dating to the period of actual migration have been destroyed by the changing sea level.

The rise and fall of global sea levels had a significant impact on the migrations into the Pacific and Americas. The Earth's last dramatic climate change was a glacial retreat ending about 10,000 years ago and placing us in an interglacial period. The glaciers melted significantly and the oceans rose to the present level of shorelines (although global warming has subsequently produced continued glacial melting). The previous land bridges were submerged, and today's archipelagos and islands were created. Until recently it was thought that not long afterward, another wave of migrants, mainland Malays, moved by canoe into Indonesia, the Philippines, Melanesia, and finally Micronesia. There only the easternmost Pacific island world of Polynesia remained unpeopled, to be settled during the last 3,000 years. These late dates have recently been questioned by archaeological finds dated to about 30,000 BCE in Melanesia, on the islands of New Britain and New Ireland, and in the East China Sea on Okinawa.

Crossing boundaries: Later migrations

The earliest human migrations that populated the planet involved travel across both land and sea, expanding the boundaries of human interaction and human settlement. The genetic, environmental, and linguistic evidence of these early migrations have helped identify patterns in both the large-scale and the brief movements of many individuals and groups. Historians often have been able to identify and document migration only once small-scale movements accumulated from a significant number of individuals and groups of migrants and were observed over long periods of time.

Once the planet was colonized and humans settled in one place, the human urge to migrate was undiminished. Migrations continued to create historical patterns that were complex and varied. What distinguishes later movements from the earliest colonization is that all of them can be characterized as crossing boundaries – boundaries that were geographic, environmental, linguistic, cultural, and political. From about 12,000 years ago, the earliest human settlements distinguished boundaries between the natural and human realms. After cities arose in all parts of the world, urban–rural boundaries were crossed by migrants attracted to cities for their amazing array of opportunities, where larger concentrations of populations could interact and exchange goods, genes, and ideas. The establishment of polities – such as city-states and empires – depended upon the boundaries of trade and territory being protected from the threat of invasion, often by standing armies. The expansion of empires created new opportunities for migration. Increasing mobility meant leaving one's familiar birthplace and native language for a vastly different and possibly more complicated grouping of communities.

Technology also played a role in enabling migrations on both land and water. The available mode of transport and the reason for moving have changed ever more rapidly. The introduction of the camel to West Africa, the domestication or use of load-bearing animals such as the horse, llama, donkey, and elephant, were critical changes in human–animal relations that regularized contacts between communities and created systematic networks that furthered migration to and between sites. Whereas the llama could easily climb the steps of fifteenth-century CE Incan roads, the Spanish horses (in 1532) could not. These technological adaptations were specific to the cultural and environmental contexts in which they occurred and they helped determine the direction and motivations of willing migrants. Intercontinental migrations relied on maritime and other technologies – eventually including horses, guns, ships, and sails. The eventual harnessing of wind, steam, and other kinds of energy allowed sailing and steamships, airplanes, railroads, and automobiles to serve migratory interests of human populations with ever-increasing speed. Today, in the terminology of the "information superhighway," the worldwide web users conjure up a metaphor of migratory interconnectedness to describe the virtual communities of the Digital Age.

As connections by land and sea began to be constructed in all parts of the globe, they provided new limitations and opportunities for individuals and groups to participate in migration. Not all members of the human community participated equally. Women usually migrated shorter distances and men migrated longer distances. In some societies the access to distant destinations translated into access to power and wealth. Indeed, trade was one of the most powerful motivating forces in luring humans on to roads and waterways. The pull of trade, the push and pull of war, the expansion of polities, pandemic disease, and persistent exploration of new communities – all contributed to the continuing role of migration in shaping human history.

Creating diaspora

All migrations share a common feature of displacement. People leave their homeland community and travel to a new location some distance away. Most travelers – whether as settlers, conquerors, or refugees – were absorbed gradually by their new communities, bringing changes to the languages and cultures of both the migrants and those that received them. A distinctive type of community formed when migrants came in sufficient numbers to enable them to retain their original culture and language. The term "**diaspora**," comes from the Greek word meaning "a sowing or scattering of seeds" and refers to a dispersal of people who survive as a community. The common features of a diaspora persisted whether the migrants were victims, laborers, traders, cultural travelers, or participants in empires. For example, the Jewish diaspora was created by the successive movements of Jews out of Palestine, to Babylonia after the Assyrian invasion in 722 BCE, and eventually to the Iberian peninsula after the defeat by the Romans in 70 CE. Jews, who were later expelled from Iberia (1492–97 CE), settled in eastern Europe; finally the **Nazi** era (during World War II) led to subsequent migrations, extending their religious and cultural diaspora to the Americas and the modern state of Israel. Sequences of migrations created a South Asian trading diaspora, as early as the second century CE, connecting the Indian Ocean maritime trade with the Southeast Asian network of ports. People known as "Roma" were laborers on the fringes of the caste system, sent as slaves to other parts of West Asia between the eighth and eleventh centuries CE and, after about 1300 CE, on to Europe, where Romani-speaking "gypsies," who, by keeping their distinctive language and culture intact, maintained a separate identity. Later migrations of South Asian and East Asian indentured and contract laborers after the fourteenth century CE created diaspora communities extending to Australia, Africa, Europe, and the Americas, especially in the Caribbean between about 1834 and 1924.

The opportunities provided by the expansion of trade, empire, and religion furthered the number of travelers and increased the likelihood of large-scale and permanent migration – relocating in the faraway trade ports. Trading diasporas accounted for the gradual dispersal of peoples, sometimes aided by the territorial extent of large empires such as the Mongol or Mali. For example, Muslim merchants spread from Saudi Arabia to Egypt and across North Africa after the seventh century CE. As Islam penetrated the trans-Saharan trading networks in the thirteenth and fourteenth centuries, Muslim merchants created a trading diaspora through the cultural connections of the Mali empire. Merchant diasporas had their own life cycles, contracting and expanding as trade opportunities were won or lost. Other merchant diasporas eventually connected the traders of Yemen, the West African Hausa, South Asians, Chinese, and Lebanese Christians, among the many groups over the past 2,000 years whose trading activities led to migrations across land. Trade also accounted for the movements of many human groups who lived along waterways, notably the Pacific Islanders and the Vikings, whose continuous migration eventually led to long-term changes in language and culture.

Crossing the seas: The Vikings and Polynesians

Colonization usually replaced, absorbed, or displaced earlier groups in their control of communities and only rarely established new communities. Viking migrations created diasporas or dispersals that reached from North Russia to Newfoundland and south to North Africa. According to written accounts and archaeology, their incursions were both peaceful and violent. During the ninth century CE, the harshness of the Scandinavian environment and the pressure of an increased population on lands of limited productivity, along with the lure of profit and adventure, stimulated ambitious Norse or Viking

rulers to set their people into motion. As immigrants, conquerors, and traders, Vikings left their northern homelands in open boats of 21–24 meters (70–80 feet) in length. Long and narrow, elegant and efficient, these were primarily rowed ships with a supplementary square sail, with high sides but a shallow draft. They could carry as many as 60 or 70 people across the open sea as well as down the quieter waters of inland rivers.

They first appeared as plunderers and adventurers; they stayed as traders and mercenaries and encompassed many cultural groups, not just the Norse. In their remarkable boats, they followed river routes further south to the Black Sea and imposed their control over the various disunited Slavic peoples among whom they appeared. By 850 CE, they had gained control of Novgorod and soon thereafter Kiev in present-day Ukraine.

Other Vikings, principally from Norway and Denmark, went west and south. Before the end of the eighth century, they were skirting and raiding Scotland and Ireland. By 830, they were establishing villages there and on the offshore islands; they used these small colonies as bases from which to raid and plunder the rich monastic establishments on the fringes of Christian Europe. From their stations in Ireland and the North Sea islands, the Vikings sailed westward across the open North Atlantic.

Shortly after the middle of the ninth century, they reached Iceland and settled there permanently; from Iceland they were lured on to Greenland, where Erik the Red set up a colony in 981. From there, Erik's son, Thorvald Eriksson, who had been told about a place called "Vinland" (an Old Norse term for "grassland" or "pasture") by his brother Leif, who had reached this land (actually thought to be Nova Scotia) about the year 1000, pushed westward to Labrador and southward to Newfoundland, on whose northernmost point, at L'Anse aux Meadows, the first known "European" colony in North America was established. Vikings may also have sailed further south to Massachusetts and Martha's Vineyard, but their colony at L'Anse aux Meadows lasted scarcely a year and their connection with the eastern shores of North America was not permanent.

On the opposite side of the Americas, both in contrast to the western expansion of the Vikings and much earlier, Polynesian migrations moved from west to east across the Pacific Ocean. Evidence from linguistics and archaeology suggest that the thousands of islands that lay scattered over the face of Pacific Oceania remained isolated from the connections that had been established between Africans, Asians, and Europeans before 1250 CE. The crossing and settling of the Pacific were no more extraordinary than crossing the ice and drifting snow of Beringia to reach the Americas. Both movements are impressive evidence of the wide range of potential human response to environmental change. The final settlement of Polynesia testifies to this flexibility: Polynesians moved from an equatorial tropical zone that had no winter to the cool, seasonal world of New Zealand and eventually to the semi-tropics of the Hawaiian Islands. Thousands of miles separated these colonies, and 1,000 years or more separated their initial settlements. Each colony developed different material cultures in response to different environments. Yet today, as a result of continuous migration, all the Polynesian settlements share related languages and systems of belief.

Pacific Oceania is divided into Melanesia, Polynesia, and Micronesia. Later migrations colonized these distant habitats, creating new communities. The peoples who inhabited these islands established their own regional connections across the Pacific as early as the first and second millennia BCE, when maritime traders identified with the Lapita cultural tradition began to settle in Melanesia, the islands south of the equator from Papua New Guinea to the west to Fiji to the east. The Lapita culture, named for an archaeological site in New Caledonia, was

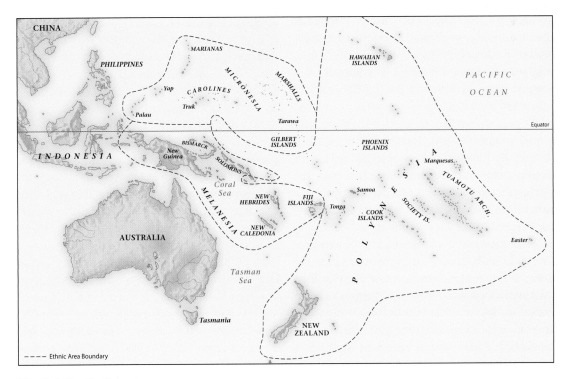

Map 1.3 Pacific Oceania.

probably an extension of much earlier migrations to Pacific Islands from Southeast Asia. As sedentary agriculturalists, the Lapita brought with them domesticated plants and animals along with a distinctive pottery style. They cultivated crops such as taro, yams, bananas, breadfruit, and coconuts, which were spread by occasional voyages among the islands. By 1300 BCE, these people had reached the outer boundary of Fiji and soon after made their way to Polynesia by way of Tonga and Samoa. Regional exchange networks accounted for the spread of Lapita culture to Vanuatu, one of the major island groups in central Melanesia. Polynesia, bounded by Hawaii, New Zealand, and Easter Island, was subject to changes brought about by fluctuations in contact as well as by migration of peoples across extensive sea routes.

The Polynesians who settled in New Zealand, the Maori, provide a well-documented example of how Polynesians explored and settled the Pacific in decked vessels capable of carrying 100–200 persons, with water and stores sufficient for voyages of some weeks. They had knowledge of the stars and were able to determine favorable seasons for voyages. They were keen navigators, setting their courses from familiar landmarks and steering by the sun and stars and the direction of winds and waves.

Polynesian settlement of New Zealand presented an enormous ecological challenge, since most of the domesticated plants and animals from the Marquesas either failed to survive the long voyage or died out soon after in the different climate. Polynesian settlers adapted to the new environment by becoming hunter-farmers, which led to environmental changes and to the necessity to adopt new strategies for survival that were no longer linked to their Marquesan origins. Exploits over such distances produced daring sailors and skilled navigators. To maintain the connections among their islands, Micronesians mastered the intricacies of seasons, currents, and winds, and even developed representational charts to guide them on their long voyages.

Summary

Since the spread of *Homo sapiens*, human beings have remained mobile creatures. The mobility of the earliest humans was one of their most astounding achievements, as they covered vast areas without the benefit of horse power or the wheel, much less the benefits of jet-propelled, air-conditioned comfort and speed. Throughout their history, people have continued to move about. Migration, variously occurring from no fixed locales, was the product of many things: the need for food and work; the need for protection; and because of population pressures, conflict with others, or the sense of adventure.

Migration was the result of and sometimes the catalyst for major shifts in population throughout world history. United Nations sources have estimated approximately 14–16 million refugees, 20–25 million displaced people, and 35 million "economic migrants" in the Northern Hemisphere at the beginning of the twenty-first

1.4 Footprint from moon landing by astronaut Neil Armstrong. More than 3 million years after the hominin footprints preserved at Laetolil (see Figure 1.1) the human species took their first steps to colonize other parts of the solar system.

century. Modern migration is not only fueled by war and conflict. It has been as frequently the quest for educational gain, or the consequence of desire, poverty, hunger, terrorism, and environmental destruction. The modern condition of mobility reflects the most glaring and widening gaps between wealthy and impoverished groups. Most modern migration reflects the systematic ways that societies fail to meet basic human needs, even while it is perceived as providing opportunities for self-betterment. Most recently, international space programs have extended human migration into outer space, with the first landing on the moon in 1969 and the first permanent community on the International Space Station, a joint project of the United States, Russian Federation, Japan, Canada, and Europe, since 2000. How a world history in motion has balanced the dual needs for mobility and staying put, for continuity and change, underlies many of the most compelling themes connecting our global past, present, and future.

Notes

1   Quoted in Josephine Flood, *The Archaeology of Dreamtime: The Story of Prehistoric Australia and Her People* (Honolulu: University of Hawaii Press, 1983), p29.
2   Glenn Welker, compiler. Creation/Migration/Origin Stories <www.indigenouspeople.net/legend.htm> Accessed 11 September 2010.
3   BCE (Before the Common Era) and CE (Common Era) refer to the system of dating recent eras from the present (2012 CE) back 2,012 years to the "zero" of a timeline that then extends further back in time beginning in the year 1 BCE, 2 BCE, and so on.
4   See www.akuntaproject.org for the two interviews quoted.

Suggested readings

Chang, Kwang-chih (1986) *The Archaeology of Ancient China*, New Haven, CO: Yale University Press. Revised fourth edition of a classic work by a leading anthropologist-archaeologist. Detailed illustrations and account of human beginnings in China.

Christian, David (2003) *Maps of Time: An Introduction to Big History*, Berkeley, CA: University of California Press. An integrative approach to world history framed by placing human history within the context of the history of life, the Earth, and the universe.

Crosby, Alfred W. (2004) *Ecological Imperialism: The Biological Expansion of Europe, 900–1900*, Cambridge: Cambridge University Press. Investigates the roots of European domination in the transformation of ecological relationships.

Ehret, Christopher (2002) *The Civilizations of Africa: A History to 1800*, Charlottesville, VA: University Press of Virginia. Emphasizes linguistic mapping of migrations.

Eltis, David, ed. (2002) *Coerced and Free Migration: Global Perspectives*, Palo Alto: Stanford University Press. Examines the peoples, values, cultures of post-1500 CE migrations, emphasizing similarities between free and coerced migration.

Hoerder, Dirk (2002) *Cultures in Contact: World Migrations in the Second Millennium*, Durham, NC, and London: Duke University Press. Explores the roles of power and perspective in human migration, with emphasis on the last 500 years.

Jones, Steve, Robert Martin, and David Pilbeam, eds (1992) *The Cambridge Encyclopedia of Human Evolution*, Cambridge: Cambridge University Press. Presents the major issues in human evolution.

Manning, Patrick (2005) *Migration in World History*, New York: Routledge. Uses human migration as a single thematic lens through which to view world history.

Olson, Steve (2003) *Mapping Human History: Genes, Race, and Our Common Origins*, Boston: Houghton Mifflin. Synthesizes human origins and early migrations.

Stringer, Christopher and Robin McKie (1996) *African Exodus: The Origins of Modern Humanity*, New York: Henry Holt. Surveys the genetic and archaeological interpretation of human evolution and migration.

Online resources

Annenberg/CPB, *Bridging World History* (2004) <www.learner.org/channel/courses/worldhistory> Multimedia project with interactive website and videos on demand; see especially Units 3 Human Migrations and 26 World History and Identity.

The National Geographic Society, *The Genographic Project: Atlas of the Human Journey* (2006) <www3.nationalgeographic.com/genographic/index.html>

The site maps genetic markers and journey highlights of the migrations out of Africa and around the globe between about 200,000 and 10,000 BCE.

PBS, *Nova Program: Evolution* (2001) <www.pbs.org/wgbh/evolution/index.html> One episode and supporting site investigates human origins.

Smithsonian Institution, *Human Origins Program* <humanorigins.si.edu> Provides up-to-date essays, short videos, and interactive timelines that scientifically trace the journey of our human origins, including genetic and other human evolution evidence.

Migration DRC (University of Sussex) *The World Migration Map* (Updated 2007) <www.migrationdrc.org/research/typesofmigration/global_migrant_origin_database.html> Provides access to data from the Global Migrant Origin Database, developed by the University of Sussex's Development Research Centre on Migration, Globalisation and Poverty, allowing users to see the origins and destinations of migrants to and from nearly every country in the world.

Study questions

1. What characteristics are uniquely human? Which was most important in the development of human behavior – physical or intellectual changes?

2. Which sources provide the most valuable evidence for the migrations of early humans and why?

3. What do creation stories share in common? What are some differences that reflect cultural preoccupations?

4. Compare the importance of early migrations on land and on water.

5. What was the impact of environment on early migrations?

6. What was the role of technology on the successful peopling of the planet?

14–7000 BCE	14,000	10,000	9–7000	9000	8500	8–5000
Domestication of dog	Jomon pottery, Japan	Holocene era	Intensification of cereal use, West Asia	Jericho site occupied	Domestication of animals	Potato domesticated in South America

2 Technology and environment

Transformations in world history

The Roman writer Pliny the Younger described the eruption of Mount Vesuvius on the Italian peninsula on 24 August 79 CE, a natural event that destroyed and buried the towns of Pompeii and Herculaneum. After reporting his uncle's heroic efforts to rescue people with ships of the fleet he commanded off the coast, Pliny records his own escape:

> . . . [that] the flames remained some distance off; then darkness came on once more and ashes began to fall again, this time in heavy showers. We rose from time to time and shook them off, otherwise we should have been buried and crushed beneath their weight. I could boast that not a groan or cry of fear escaped me in these perils, but I admit that I derived some poor consolation in my mortal lot from the belief that the whole world was dying with me and I with it . . . At last the darkness thinned and dispersed like smoke or cloud; then there was genuine daylight, and the sun actually shone out, but yellowish as it is during an eclipse. We were terrified to see everything changed, buried deep in ashes like snowdrifts. We returned to Misenum where we attended to our physical needs as best we could and then spent an anxious night alternating between hope and fear. Fear predominated, for the earthquakes went on, and several hysterical individuals made their own and other people's calamities seem ludicrous in comparison with their frightful predictions.

Source: Pliny the Younger, "The Eruption of Vesuvius, 24 August, AD 79," in John Carey, ed., *Eyewitness to History* (New York: Avon Books, 1987), pp19–20

Not all interactions between humans and their landscapes were as terrifyingly dramatic as either the volcanic eruption of Mount Vesuvius described by Pliny the Younger or the recent tsunami that devastated the Indian Ocean region

31

8000	7000	7000	7–4000	6700	5700	5500
Rice domesticated in South Asia	Gradual emergence of agriculture (wheat, barley, and herding) at Mehrgarh, Pakistan	Early agricultural drainage and taro cultivations, Kuk, New Guinea	Hunter-gatherers replaced by farmers in Europe	Maize domesticated in Mesoamerica	Rice paddy fields, China	Central European Neolithic transition underway at Brzesc Kujawski, Poland

Ein antikes Relief, den Einsturz eines Tempels in Pompeji bei dem Erdbeben des Jahres 63 n. Chr. darstellend. (Nach de Rossi.) Vgl. Text, S. 138.

2.1 Woodcut: damage to Temple of Jupiter, Pompeii (ca. 62 CE). The Roman banker Lucius Caecilius Lucundis commissioned this relief for his household shrine in Pompeii, Italy, following the devastating 6.4 magnitude earthquake of 62 CE. The frieze depicts the collapse of the Temple of Jupiter. Seventeen years later, a major volcano buried the town.

almost 2,000 years later, but all such interactions were characteristic of one important theme in world history: the changing relationships between humans and their environment.

Introduction to the theme of environment

Global migration and colonization of the planet by early humans presented a sequence of changing landscapes and eventually brought people into intimate contact with every natural environment the globe offers. The planet has undergone great geological, climatic, and envi-

ronmental change in the past and continues to do so today. Relatively little of the past 4 billion years of environmental change was human-induced. Astronomical and geological events, such as the eruption of Mount Vesuvius, account for the most dramatic impacts to date.

Humans also created technologies that wrought unprecedented processes of environmental change, unmatched by other species. The human story intensifies the scope and scale of its impact on ecological change in the last century. In this chapter, we examine a major theme in human history: the different ways in which humans have been part of ecosystems and the patterns by which environmental and human

4700 BCE	3300	2500	1600–1045	1300	1000	1000
Long-distance copper trade, Eurasia	Eurasian Bronze Age	Millet domesticated in West Africa	Bronze vessels in Shang dynasty, China	Iron Age underway	Rice agriculture, metallurgy, and weaving, Japan	Domestication of reindeer in Siberia

2.2 Eruption of Mount Fuji. The eruption of Mount Fuji on the Japanese island of Honshu occurred in 1707, before the artist Katsushika Hokusai was born. The volcano's plume is depicted as a dragon, a symbol of supernatural powers and the mythical animal whose active energy "yang" was thought to reign over the universe. The Japanese borrowed the concept of yin and yang as balancing forces from China.

histories are intricately woven together. Key eras in human environmental history can be identified with significant changes in four areas of human life: food, metals, towns, and energy systems. We ask the interrelated questions of how environments have shaped world history and how humans have shaped the environment. What has been the impact of changing world environments on human societies? In what ways has the course of technological change been shaped by the environment? And how has technology also transformed the environment?

Technology defines human culture

Technology is a defining feature of the human cultural experience. **Culture** is the patterned behaviors, which a social group develops to understand, use, and survive in their environment. Both humans and natural forces shape culture; it encompasses both ideas and artifacts and includes such things as technology, language, beliefs, and values. Transmitted both consciously and unintentionally, culture perpetuates itself as learned behavior, molding the ways societies behave across generations. Though individuals make use of inherited cultural knowledge to guide their actions and interpret their experiences, cultures are not permanently fixed. They undergo change as members of a society learn new things and encounter and respond to new experiences, ideas, and peoples. In this way, cultures reproduce themselves.

The earliest cultures have been identified by studying archaeological finds; patterned cultural variations called style can be observed in the evidence of material culture, such as 2-million-year-old stone tools or the stunning rock art that began to appear about 40,000 years ago. Anthropologists believe that about 250,000 years ago, wild swings in global climate forced most of the hominin species to adapt or become extinct. So human evolution – especially the evolution of brains and advanced human cognition – has operated as an adaptation to a challenging environment. The use of cultural memory systems helped our human ancestors adapt to change itself rather than to any specific environmental niche. Cultural variation or style helped ensure continuity of peoples and their groups, and it enabled groups to retain the memory of valuable information, such as the manufacturing process to create a hand ax, by transmitting it beyond a single lifetime. As groups spread out across the globe, this communication and its historical memory became critical to the community's survival.

No aspect of culture had a greater impact on human history than did **technology**, the totality of means used to create objects necessary for human survival and comfort. Even in the case of the earliest stone tools, it has been estimated that more than 100 separate, precise blows were needed to shape an individual stone into a useful biface tool, and thousands of intricate stitches created a single basket. Technology includes ideas as well as tools because it relies on human memory. The continuity of technological styles required the communication of complex processes from one generation to the next. Technological change became the cutting edge, so to speak, of human history, as tools replaced biological evolution as the main source of change. The transformation of the "big history" into human history may be measured by the names of periods assigned to the past. These eras are not defined by environmental or climatic changes, but rather by their technological characteristics. Beyond their cultural styles, technologies have contributed to defining the significant periods from the "Stone Age" to the "Nuclear Age."

Tools have always required the control of knowledge. Between about 100,000 and 20,000 years ago, some of the earliest human artifacts appear to be associated with the control of specialized information. The incised iron oxide ore from Blombos Cave may have functioned as an object for reckoning or counting, an interpretation that attests to fully human consciousness. Some of these magical objects of carved antler or bone are called batons by archaeologists, who interpret their use as devices for extending human memory. Engraved markings on many of these objects, like the paintings and engravings on cave and rock shelter walls, refer to observed patterns of nature, such as lunar phases or seasonal migrations of animals. Possession of batons would have enabled those skilled in their translation to predict changes in the landscape. Such tools also created and altered people's inner landscapes, how humans perceived the world around themselves. Symbols that could be used and reused to manipulate the world constituted a source of power. Specialists accumulated the power. Flint knappers, shamans, healers – like later pottery makers and metallurgists – all recognized the imagined possibilities of technology and were able to express them successfully in the physical world, whether in the identification of seasons or the shaping of stone tools. No further biological adaptations were necessary for human expansion into new environments. Cultural innovations would be needed and their evolution eventually enabled the successful human career. Using tools, human communities began to thrive in the new environments into which they expanded, and they altered the physical landscape as they conquered the globe.

Environment and technology

Important among the determinants of cultural variation, including technologies, are the environmental contexts or landscapes in which people lived. Throughout history, cultures have been influenced by the natural worlds in which they are rooted. Although humans moved from place to place – collectively, at an average of about 200 miles per year in their earliest migrations – they also became attached to specific landscapes. Environment thus plays a major role in the construction of culture and in cultural variation. For example, Inuit technology and culture, shaped by its Arctic environment, allowed adaptation to the extremely cold temperatures of a world of ice and snow and provided specialized tools of bone and stone for fishing and hunting seals. The stable freshwater lakes of East Africa, on the other hand, provided vastly different conditions for establishing scavenging, hunting, and fishing technologies in its warm, prehistoric wooded savanna and grassland environment.

Cross-cultural interaction, the contacts with other societies, resulted in continuous cultural readjustment, adaptation, and change. Ancient environmental change also quickened the pace of cultural change. For example, the **desiccation** (drying up) of the Sahara occurred recently, sometime after about 15,000 years ago, losing the region's great lakes and rivers and creating a vast desert in which hippopotamus and elephant could no longer survive. The dramatic environmental shift caused major changes in early African cultures and required equally dramatic shifts in lifestyles and technologies, even the forced migration of populations. Archaeologists have identified tool kits among the artifacts carried by the early emigrants in their global colonization, suggesting the importance of retaining technological information in times of changing environments.

Early human ecologies

Ecology is the relationship between organisms and their environments. The cultural relationship between humans and their environment varied according to people's perceptions of the landscape. In this way, technology and culture altered both the inner landscape of the individual and the physical landscape of the natural world. Though in the modern world, influenced by the powerful impact of industrialization, we tend to see nature inevitably as something to be dominated and controlled by human effort, early human cultures were shaped and informed by an awareness of the power of nature. Even in modern times, many peoples, such as the Fang in Central Africa, believe that humans must seek a balance between themselves and the natural world, rather than trying to dominate or control the natural world. The human-built ordering of the Fang village used organizing principles to arrange house structures using symmetry and then separate them from the invasive forest environment. Yet their dependence on the surrounding Central African rainforest was a balancing act shaping the Fang culture and requiring both built and natural realms. Modern ecology similarly derives its core notion of the essential relationship between human society and nature from this kind of thinking.

Although concern with the order of human society and the arts of human culture became predominant characteristics of Chinese thought, the school of thought in early China known as Daoism displayed a sharp sensitivity to the need for humans to live in harmony with nature, to acknowledge and appreciate the patterns of human birth, life, and death as part of the constant transformations of nature. Based on a belief in the oneness of all things – humans, stones, trees, water, animals – Native American cultures were shaped by the environments in which they took form. Native Americans of the northwest coast regulated their activities around the natural life patterns of the salmon; the pattern of Inuit life was determined by the seasons: caribou hunts and fishing in the summer, seal hunts and ice fishing in the winter. Even their homes were seasonally determined: tent-like structures in the summer, ice structures in the winter. Such societies minimized their demands on their ecosystems by moving their settlements in accordance with natural patterns. For these societies, cultural activity and the cycle of environmental change were interdependent.

Human views regarding their place in the natural world have in common an acknowledgment that any relationship between human society and the environment is fundamental to survival. The influence of nature on human societies and the ways different cultures have responded to their places in the natural world are crucial elements of historical understanding and basic to the ways in which cultures explain their pasts. Studying these relationships also increases our understanding of the past as process. Seeing human historical events in the context of long-term ecological or geological time produces a perspective on human history and a set of historical concerns very different from one based on single historical events or the accomplishments of individuals. Approaches to the human past that focus on the related history of the lands and oceans have had a profound influence on contemporary world historians, encouraging them to set the study of historical events into the context of slow geological time that unfolds across millennia and stressing the relationship between human history and the environment.

Awareness of the relationship between environment and historical cultures has also been heightened and intensified by current ecological concerns and the rise of systems science in the past century. How the Romans polluted their water sources, the extent to which West African iron smelters deforested their environment, the relationship between population and resources in Chinese history – these historical problems echo familiarly in recent times. The roles of environment and technology were intertwined and provided both limits and opportunities to the human experience.

Subsistence and environment

Technological changes related to food strategies were fundamental in forming relationships between humans and their environment. Until food storage and trade altered the subsistence equation by making some reliant on others, the food that early hunters and gatherers consumed was limited to what was available locally. For most of human history, people lived in relatively small groups, gathering, fishing, and hunting what they needed from their immediate environments. Success was ultimately measured by the group's survival. Sometimes effective subsistence strategies depended on people's seasonal movements, sometimes on their cooperation, and sometimes on the occasional sharing, storage, and exchange of foods. For tens of thousands of years and, in some parts of the world throughout the twentieth century, such subsistence patterns supported human populations. Gathering, hunting, and fishing were essential activities of the earliest world cultures, as they provided the basic food supplies.

Dramatic climatic changes made adjustments in the relationship between humans and their environments desirable and even necessary. The climatic changes were often slow, natural processes, as for example, the gradual process through which the African Sahara became a vast, dry desert. They could also be sudden, catastrophic occurrences. Long before the eruption of Mount Vesuvius, described at the beginning of this chapter, major volcanic events contributed to the ever-changing landscape of the planet's natural world. For example, scientists believe that about 75,000 years ago, a massive volcanic eruption of Mount Toba on the island of Sumatra may have threatened the human species with extinction. It is possible that the gigantic plumes of ash and smoke from this eruption triggered six days of darkness and years of winter, creating a sort of ice age. Human populations struggled to survive and may have dipped as low as about 10,000 individuals worldwide. It is thought that some of the best chances of survival favored populations in tropical Africa, thus giving them a much greater genetic variability.

Change may also have been the result of human intervention, sustained manipulation of the natural world, and over-exploitation of natural resources: such environmental abuse is not confined to the present day. Extensive alteration of the environment, whether of natural or human origin, sometimes made it essential that humans change their subsistence patterns. For example, evidence indicates that prehistoric peoples in the Western Cape region of Southern Africa exploited marine resources part of the year and then moved inland, where they followed territorial herds of small mammals and intensively collected plants and tubers in other seasons. Beginning 20,000 years ago, the culture of these peoples was based on a complex, interactive pattern of land use and technology adapted to their region.

Beyond the recurring seasonal cycles were larger global climate patterns. Daily and seasonal weather are the products of interlocking systems of cycles that are created by the Earth's movement and the fact that the Earth is globe-shaped. Because

there is an inherent difference in the way the sun heats the closer middle (equator) and the more distant ends (poles) of the Earth, the poles are colder than the tropics and an exchange of warming and cooling air sets off pathways of movement that we call wind and weather. Scientists are beginning to identify cycles that track the movements linked to corresponding areas of warm water in the Pacific. The formation of each mass of warm water or "El Niño" produces a countervailing pattern before reverting back. These shifts correspond to some of the most challenging environmental crises in world history and helped to integrate large parts of the planet even before they were connected by human interactions.

Strategies needed for gathering, fishing, and hunting were less vulnerable to climatic change than were systems of agriculture. The traditions of earlier gathering-fishing-hunting peoples were retained rather than abandoned by succeeding agriculturalists. Once agriculture was fully

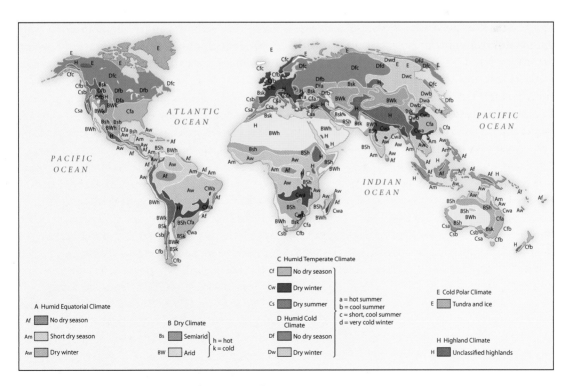

Map 2.1 Modern world climates. After Köppen-Geiger.

adopted by individuals, their societies rarely reverted to foraging plants, while fishing and hunting continued. Nonetheless, during famines and droughts, farmers retained and used the knowledge of flora and fauna that were not normally a part of later agricultural diets (such as edible insects, grubs, and wild plants). Although they can seem to be archaeologically "invisible" next to the splendor of later villages, towns, and **monumental architecture**, the gathering-fishing-hunting populations and their unique patterns of relationships between environment and society remained important to the herders, sedentary farmers, and townsfolk who succeeded them.

The earliest gathering-fishing-hunting societies had a profound effect on their environments. Even though early humans had no more than stone or bone tools at their disposal, they altered the environment more significantly than did the other species with which they shared the planet. These early societies, which might be expected to have been less destructive of their environments than later agricultural and sedentary societies – with their greater potential for ecological abuse – did not enjoy an unchanging relationship with nature.

Both the persistence of the nomadic lifestyle and the successful increase in societies in which hunters, fishers, and gatherers settled more permanently in a favored locale were dependent on continuous cultural innovations. Technology was especially significant in negotiating the changing environmental conditions. The relationship between demographic change and technical innovation has led some scholars to suggest that constant population increase should be considered one defining characteristic of human achievement. While neither demography nor any other single factor can explain human history, the increasing size of human communities has challenged their members throughout world history by providing both an impetus for change and a reminder that humans live within the context and limits of a natural world.

From early stone tools to pyrotechnology

Even the earliest human communities were dependent on tools that enabled them to sustain themselves by exploiting their environments

2.3 Cave paintings of people with cattle at Tassili-n-Ajjer, in the Sahara Desert of Algeria. These paintings are from the Cattle Period, ca. 4000–2000 BCE.

more efficiently. Appropriate technology was basic to the ways humans organized themselves to utilize the natural resources available to them. Gathering-fishing-hunting communities relied on stone tools ranging from crude stone pounders for crushing grain, seed, and nuts to intricate, refined small stone instruments, or microliths, such as fish hooks, scrapers, and knives, in addition to wooden digging sticks and implements fashioned from bone and other organic materials. The technology involved in tool production became increasingly proficient with experience and need. It is clear, for example, that a well-fashioned, polished Late Stone Age tool involves greater technological expertise than a stone whose intrinsic size and shape enabled it to be used as a tool without much modification. Technology continually developed as it kept up with the changing environments and changing demands of various cultures around the world and, as both accompaniment and cause, its impact reached revolutionary proportions during the global transitions from gathering-fishing-hunting to sedentary agrarian lifestyles.

THE HOME-COOKED MEAL   The application of fire was one of the earliest tools that transformed the physical landscape. Fire produced dramatic changes in the lives of early humans, staving off predators, keeping people warm and safe. Fire also permitted the transformation of foods and other materials through heat treatment. The evening cooked meal was a universally shared experience. Cooking food transformed many plants to edible status and also captured more nutrients and proteins, assuring greater rates of survival. The application of fire eventually created the sciences of cooking and fermentation, which altered mental landscapes, as the many examples of early alcoholic drinks attest. The modern scientific study of the dregs of ancient Egyptian beer has made it possible to identify the sophisticated technology of brewing used by the Egyptians. As the role of technology in transforming society continues to be studied and debated, there is little doubt that technology also helped fuel the lively social interactions of ancient peoples around the globe.

THE DREGS OF HISTORY   The relative merits and pitfalls of the products of technology have been debated throughout history. Greek legend claims that the god Dionysus left Mesopotamia in disgust because its people were so addicted to the local barley beer or ale. About 40 percent of the grain produced locally went for the production of

2.4 Egyptian tomb model of baking and brewing. In ancient Egypt domesticated barley and emmer were used for brewing a popular beverage drunk through tubes from ceramic cups.

Sumerian beer. In ancient Egypt, both emmer and barley were used for brewing a popular beverage drunk through tubes from ceramic cups. As early as 1400 BCE, the beer of **pharaohs** and workers alike was consumed in taverns, where one risked the dangers of loose talk while drinking a beverage called "Joy Bringer." Early rice beers in India, palm wines in West Africa, and the fermented juice of cactus in Mesoamerica intoxicated peoples throughout history.

Scientists have examined beer residues in vessels found in Egyptian tombs and workers' villages to determine the technology and reproduce the beer-making recipe. They found that ancient brewers used a complex two-part process: first sprouting and heating a batch of grains to increase their susceptibility to attack by enzymes that increase the sugar content; then mixing this batch with sprouted and unheated grains in water. Yeast was added to the combination of sugar and starch, and this concoction was fermented to make beer.

TRANSFORMING THE HUMAN LANDSCAPE
Fire allowed human groups to conquer new environments and probably encouraged the development of social networks and advances in communication through the sharing of food and shelter. The ability to cook foods altered and expanded the diets and improved the health of early populations. Yet the simplest levels of technology were also capable of altering the environment and adversely affecting users' health. Smoke from fires in small, closed, poorly ventilated houses would have caused chronic pulmonary disease in Stone Age humans. Human-built fires, especially the burning of forests and fields, left a residue of pollutants that can be found in the past 100,000 years of polar ice strata. Pollutants such as lead aerosols, produced by ancient metallurgical technologies, have been detected in polar strata dating to periods as early as 800 BCE.

The botanical evidence available in lake-bottom sediments in Asia and East Africa suggests that significant modifications in plant and animal communities took place there as a result of pre-historic human activities such as the manufacture and use of substances that turned out to be poisonous to plants and fish. Intensive resource collecting, even ancient over-hunting, and over-grazing also created disequilibrium and change in early ecologies. For example, the hunting to extinction of the Australian marsupial lion or the over-exploitation of marine mammals in the Northern Pacific argue for significant human-induced changes. The loss of primary forest cover and destruction of the world's rainforests, currently a major global ecological concern, first began as a result of the systematic application of fire as an aid to hunting and food preparation with the spread of *Homo erectus* from around 500,000 years ago.

Agricultural beginnings

Today, scholars and the public debate the wisdom of the genetic modification and manipulation of world flora and fauna. That process of modification began with the domestication of species and the rise of agriculture. Agricultural change is only one way in which increasingly populated societies adapted their cultural lifestyles to the changing landscape. Agriculture is defined as the domestication of plants and animals to make them more productive and human-dependent. The development of agriculture began about 15,000 years ago, following the late stages of the last Ice Age and the onset of the Holocene epoch (about 12,000 years ago). No single model for agricultural origins explains the great variation in the Neolithic "revolution" or transformation on a global scale. First identified from archaeological evidence in West Asia, agricultural technology was an adaptation of forager-hunters some 4,000 years before, who had begun first to harvest wild varieties of cereals, including wheat and barley. Their descendants established semi-permanent villages. Striking out from their settlements, early food producers gathered useful grains such as emmer, einkorn, barley and rye, leading to long-term genetic changes that made the plants dependent on human interference. They similarly intensified their involvement with keeping animals, especially grazing cattle, sheep, goats, and pigs. The processes of deforestation accelerated with the introduction of agricultural practices and the intensified use and genetic manipulation of plants and animals to make them more productive. Other new technologies, such as pottery making and metallurgy, utilized fire and brought about even more severe changes in the landscape. Pollution and deforestation have been the seemingly inevitable artifacts of human technological history from ancient to contemporary times.

Transitional societies: Pre-agricultural communities

Complex, settled human communities that existed before the emergence of sedentary agriculture are known as transitional societies. They have multiplied in number and complexity since scientists began studying the transformations to agriculture around the world. Settled groups sometimes experimented with food production and often appear to have opted for continuous foraging strategies even when agricultural techniques were known. Vastly different models for the spread of the Neolithic, and even for its abandonment, now appear alongside the linear passage from foraging to settled farming.

Skara Brae, in the Orkney Islands off the northwest coast of Scotland, is a splendidly preserved example of such a community. Around 2500 BCE, various populations that practiced agriculture were migrating to Britain from the European continent. They brought with them livestock and seed and destroyed Britain's forests to clear the land for cultivation and herding, beginning a change that would permanently alter the landscape of the British Isles. While this process was underway, the gathering-fishing-hunting community of Skara Brae flourished, isolated from and resistant to the new people who had moved onto the mainland to the south and the practices they had brought with them.

When the sands of the shore that had covered Skara Brae three millennia before shifted, an unmatched picture of the life of a transitional British community that existed without agriculture was revealed. The inhabitants of Skara Brae were isolated from all intercourse with the outside world and forced to rely on what their limited and rather bleak environment provided for them. Lacking metals and having almost no imported objects, they exclusively used locally manufactured implements of stone and bone. The community was supported by an abundant supply of shellfish, seabirds, fish, and venison, which apparently were so plentiful that specialized fishing and hunting equipment was not required. Crops were not planted, but, in addition to hunting, the community kept herds of sheep and cattle. Life in this isolated, self-supporting, and independent hunting-herding community may have been hard, but it was relatively peaceful: no armaments were found.

The hamlet of Skara Brae consisted of a communal workshop and about a half-dozen houses, several times rebuilt, some of which were about 40 square meters (430 square feet) in size. Each had a central hearth, on either side of which were fixed beds. There were dressers and cupboards and an efficient sewage system of slate-slab drains. The dwellings and the furniture, as well as the implements, were all manufactured of stone. All the structures were huddled together and connected by narrow, roofed alleyways, for mutual warmth and shelter. The indications are that life was not neat and orderly. Shells and bones were scattered haphazardly over floors, beds, and cupboards. The pendants, pins, and beads made in the community, together with its equipment and tools, exhibit a certain aesthetic sense as well as providing an impressive example of environmental accommodation.

Sedentism (settling down in one place) was easier in environments rich in resources not easily depleted than it was at Skara Brae. In other transitional societies, the environment for hunting and gathering was often lush and more bountiful and could sustain ever-higher population levels without the group's having to resort to agriculture and its labor-intensive practices. The Pacific Northwest of the North American continent and the "aquatic" civilizations of West-Central Africa are two such examples. In both, marine resources and fishing were abundant enough to support sizable villages. Pre-agrarian settled communities had their own individual technologies, some of which were also used by sedentary agricultural societies. Grinding slabs and stones in West Asia dating from about 15,000 years ago were used to process gathered seeds, nuts, and berries. The sickles of Ethiopian harvesters cut wild, not domesticated, grains. Pottery, once principally associated with agriculture, has been widely found in transitional villages without domesticated crops.

Sedentism itself required both cultural continuity and change. Disease control was a new requirement of larger populations aggregated in permanent settlements, whose complexity included management of water resources, parasites, and infectious diseases previously unknown to more mobile populations. Much later agricultural communities continued the use of gathering-hunting tools, such as stone hammers and scrapers. Given this continuity, agriculture appears not to have been technologically revolutionary in all instances; it was, however, a successful response to and contributing factor in the needs of increasing populations around the world.

Early agricultural models

Since sedentary agriculture entails more consistent effort and less flexible labor requirements and patterns of settlement than hunting and gathering, why did early peoples take up this more demanding way of life? Among the possible explanations are stress or crisis, the effect of a demographic change, such as overpopulation, or an environmental change, such as an alteration in climate. By endangering previously successful subsistence strategies or creating opportunities for new, more productive ones, both could act as catalysts to induce modifications in ways of life. Agricultural practices might require greater effort, but they had the potential to sustain larger populations on smaller areas than gathering-hunting practices did. Most revolutionary were the increasing levels of energy use that characterized the beginnings of agriculture.

SCENARIOS FOR THE BEGINNINGS OF AGRICULTURE   The emergence of various agricultural systems and sedentary societies occurred mostly independently and followed different scenarios in many different parts of the world. Until quite recently, it had been assumed that agricultural origins were limited to several centers: the river valleys of Africa and Asia (the Nile, Tigris-Euphrates, Indus, and Yellow Rivers). From these centers, it was supposed that the "idea" of agriculture diffused to other regions of the world. But the pattern of agricultural origins as now understood is far more complicated than this fairly simplistic model would suggest. Much of the focus has been on cereals, but bananas, yams, and taro were also important early domesticates (domesticated varieties that become agricultural crops) from tropical parts of Africa and Asia. Potatoes, cassava, beans, and squash were domesticated in the Americas. There were also numerous pre-agricultural centers, indicating the possibility of multiple agrarian origins: for example, some West Asian sites, exceptionally well suited to preserving botanical and archaeological evidence of early cultivation, were not in river valleys but in dry, temperate, upland areas or savannas.

West Asian agricultural beginnings

Sometime between 14,000 and 6000 BCE, the mostly gathering and hunting peoples in West Asia gradually became both sedentary and eventually also reliant on domesticated plants and animals that they had previously collected or hunted wild. At the Dederiyeh Cave, in northwest Syria, people lived in permanent stone structures. Plant remains dated between 14,000 and 13,000 years ago indicated that residents collected wild wheat, pistachios, and almonds. Based on evidence of food storage at the site of Gilgal in the Jordan Valley, about 11,300 years ago, granaries for storing wild barley came before actual plant domestication. The emergence of agriculture in West Asia sometimes followed the creation of permanent settlements. The earliest such settlements found thus far are in Iran, Iraq, Syria, and Turkey, located in hill country between mountains and plains, near but not on rivers and streams. These are regions of complex ecology that offer a changing variety of wild food sources throughout the year. The people of these early settlements are called "Natufian," after the name of the earliest identified site. They lived on collected wild foods: grains such as emmer, einkorn, barley, and rye. They also exploited gazelle, cattle, sheep, goats, birds, fish, and mollusks.

A few of the early Natufian sites show some indication of small round wood-and-clay huts. At one such site, Ain Mellaha near Palestine, people lived in about 50 houses, one or two of them painted with red ochre. At all the sites, polished stones were used to grind the collected grains. The grain was stored in pits lined with clay that had been hardened by fire. Such storage techniques, which allowed the preservation and the gradual biological evolution of more productive grains, are thought to be a necessary first step to grain domestication.

Staying in one place through the seasons year after year allowed for the effect of accidents; a spillage of gathered barley germinating near the settlement, for example, might have been the inspiration for habitual "spillage," or sowing, of seed in a nearby field. In this fashion, the development of agriculture sometimes took generations of trial and error. The Natufians weathered major climatic shifts until a warming period provided conditions that may have encouraged farming after about 9450 BCE. The evidence from West Asia suggests that it could have taken another 1,500 years or more before settled generations produced an unmistakable pattern of deliberate planting of wheat and barley around settlements wherein there also lived domesticated dogs, sheep, and goats.

Domestication of animals

The beginnings of agriculture included both the domestication of animals (**pastoralism**) and the cultivation of plants (arable agriculture). Pastoralism is even more difficult to identify in the prehistoric archaeological record than is the cultivation of plants, largely because it was not dependent on either sedentism or the use of pottery. Consequently, far less has been understood about the historical importance of pastoralists. Many early pastoralist societies were nomadic. The seasonal movements of peoples with their herds precluded the kind of material accumulation reflected in the historical records of cultivators and even sedentary, non-agricultural fishing populations. The early herding of some animals, such as the Siberian reindeer, may have begun with semi-domesticated animals. Domesticated animals varied widely from one part of the world to another: from dogs to camelids to horses, chickens, pigs, cattle, sheep, and goats. A number of farming communities also had significant pastoral components, which provided a productive mosaic of subsistence strategies that would ultimately ensure the community's survival. Some early pastoralists appear to have used only live animals for dairy and not meat products.

Animal products, including milk, fur, and skins, eventually provided essential trade and subsistence items around the world and reduced the reliance on hunting.

Domestication of plants

It has been suggested that the preliminary period of habitat management, or experimentation and selection, that evolved out of gathering activities marked the transition to arable agriculture. If this scenario is correct, then women, who were the primary gatherers, played a critical role in the transformation of early societies from gathering-hunting to agriculture. In the Late Stone Age, tools associated with the domestic activities of women, such as grindstones and grinding hollows, indicate the intensive use of plant foods and suggest that supplies may have come from domesticated as well as gathered plants. In many places, domestication of both plants and animals was a slow process involving both human skills and long-term genetic changes in wild species.

Crop domestication occurred in regions in which cultigens (wild varieties) of the crop were native. Cultivated rice could and did appear everywhere from East Asia to West Africa, where varieties of wild rice were available to be exploited, while ensete, a banana-like plant whose cultigens were unique to Ethiopia, was first domesticated there. The search for agricultural origins has required the cooperative efforts of botanists and archaeologists, who examine the current and past patterns of plant distribution and the potential patterns of agricultural origins.

The transport model

It is possible that agriculture emerged in some places without conscious human intent. Another model for the emergence of agriculture, the transport model, has supposed that systematically harvested and stored wild plants will evolve biologically over time. In this model, the ease by which cereal grain could be transported served as a selective factor in domestication. That is, plants with desirable characteristics, such as grains that stay longer on the stalk (and thus can survive the journey from field to village), those that thrive under disturbed circumstances, and those that reproduce more effectively after storage will be the majority genetic sample planted and reproduced. The transport model has particularly been used for evidence of early agriculture in West Asia.

The hydraulic model

Another historical explanation for the beginnings of agriculture was a theory associated with the belief that the earliest agricultural societies occurred in river valleys. The theory of "hydraulic civilization" connects water-related technology – terracing, dams, canals, waterwheels, wells – with successful cultivation and surplus agricultural production. At the site of Kuk, in New Guinea, the early drainage agriculture of taro (9,000 years ago) and banana (6,950 years ago) has demonstrated the importance of specific agricultural models in tropical regions. The linkage of technology to the transition to agriculture and the growth of complex organization in sedentary societies were based on examples from more temperate environments around the Nile and Indus Valleys, Mesopotamia, China, and the Valley of Mexico. Though river valleys are no longer considered the original sites of sedentary agrarian cultures or "cradles of civilizations" (as they were once called), domestication did, of course, occur in river valleys scattered around the world. The earliest widely accepted evidence of Nile agriculture, carbonized grain found at village sites, dates from between 6000 and 5000 BCE. This evidence suggests that the transition to agriculture in the Nile Valley occurred at approximately the same time that it did in other river valleys and somewhat later than the 7500 BCE dates for the upland areas of West Asia or the Pacific.

Early agricultural societies

What characterized the earliest societies based on agriculture? Although the crops varied around the globe and across vastly different environmental regions, agricultural societies provided early peoples with the opportunity to settle in one place, be committed to a single geographic location, and intensively exploit local resources in order to support their expanding populations. Without exception, early agricultural societies became socially and materially complex communities.

China and Japan

By at least the sixth millennium BCE, people who inhabited various regions of what we now know as China practiced sedentary agriculture, ceramic technology, social stratification observable in burial forms, human and animal sacrifices, and systems of notation or protowriting, including oracle bones. The traditional Chinese view of the origins of agriculture attributed it to a sage-king called the "Heavenly Husbandman," who taught the people how to cultivate the land:

> In the time of the Heavenly Husbandman, millet fell as rain from the heavens. The Heavenly Husbandman then tilled the land and planted the millet . . . he fashioned plows and hoes with which he opened up the wasteland.
>
> Source: Francesca Bray, "Swords into Plowshares: A Study of Agricultural Technology and Society in Early China," *Technology and Culture*, 19 (1978), p3

At least two, and perhaps three, major culture complexes dominated the sixth and fifth millennia BCE in China. One was centered in northwest China, represented by a reconstructed village site, Banpo, of the Yellow River Valley Yangshao pottery culture. The other was located along the east coast, at the Qinglian'gang site of the Longshan pottery culture in the Yangzi River delta. Some scholars believe that yet another culture complex, located along the southeastern coast and Taiwan, called Dapenkeng, was roughly contemporaneous. To a large extent, the cultures of the south and east represented adaptations to an environment that was substantially different from that of the north. The cultivation of rice began in the wet, marshy lowlands of the Yangzi Valley, an area dramatically unlike the arid northern plains, where millet was the primary crop. The cultivation of rice required well-irrigated fields and intensive labor, which encouraged cooperative efforts among the members of a settled community.

Rather than seeing the Yellow River Valley as the East Asian "cradle of civilization" like the Nile in North Africa, the Tigris-Euphrates in West Asia, and the Indus in South Asia, where the practice of agriculture developed and from which it radiated outward, it seems now, given the explosion of archaeological discoveries over the past few

2.5 Chinese Neolithic pottery types of the Yangshao culture, Chinese Neolithic, 3000–2000 BCE.

decades, that there were multiple centers of agriculture that flourished before 5000 BCE. There were certainly two distinct ways of farming that developed in the north and the south, and they remain characteristic today of a basic ecological division in China: between the steamed bread and noodle-eating north and the rice-eating south. Similarly, early sites for both horticulture, the cultivation of plants without systematically planting them, and agriculture have been identified in Southeast Asia, evidence of a contemporary and independent evolution of agriculture there. It was once thought that the earliest human cultures identified in the Japanese archipelago (dating to 16,000 years ago) did not practice agriculture until it was diffused there from Southeast or East Asia late in the first millennium BCE. However, now there is evidence of horticulture as well as extensive tool kits associated with sophisticated gathering and hunting cultures. Foraging replaced large game hunting and sedentary villages with ceramics (called Jomon) housed large populations engaged in exchange networks, while exploiting marine resources. Domesticated rice appears only in the first century of the first millennium BCE, along with metallurgy and weaving. As in West Asia and Africa, it seems likely that there were several East and Southeast Asian paths to the substitution of sedentary agriculture for hunting and gathering. Agriculture should be seen as one ecosystem manipulation strategy among many, including horticulture, gathering and hunting, and pastoralism.

Africa

Elsewhere, subsistence patterns of early sedentary peoples altered with shifts in ecological systems. An African site of environmental disequilibrium and crisis, Dhar Tichitt in Mauritania, witnessed the successful transition from the use of wild to domesticated cereals. There, between about 1100 and 1000 BCE, the use of millet and sorghum was incorporated into pre-agricultural subsistence

strategies when the lakes around which large, settled populations lived began to dry up. Solid, direct evidence of the domestication of plants has been established by the dating of carbonized grains and seeds, but there is also much indirect and speculative evidence of the slow transition to agriculture that reveals much about the process. Such things as seed impressions on the bottoms of storage pots or "sickle sheen," the gloss produced on stone tools by the polishing effect of the silica contained in plant stalks as they were cut and harvested in fields, are indicators of agricultural beginnings. Such evidence has been found in archaeological sites from West Asia and Africa that date back to thousands of years before the earliest domesticated plants. For some types of early domesticates, such as yams, there is also the fact that direct physical evidence is unlikely to have been preserved, since the tuber itself becomes the "seed" that propagates a new generation. There is early African evidence of the cultivation of rice along the Niger River in West Africa, and at the site of Jenné-Jeno in Mali, evidence of domesticated rice (by about 500 BCE) exists alongside that of exploitation of other resources in the inland Niger delta, an area of periodic flooding. People fished and hunted, using their abundant resources to support increasingly complex societies. Their mud-walled houses multiplied, and the increase in population led to greater social complexity over time.

Western Eurasia

The study of the emergence of agriculture in the region we now call Europe has centered on the historical issue of diffusion: the transfer from one society to another of complex or small traits associated with a technology, in this case sedentary agriculture. The pattern of the spread of agriculture to the Balkans suggests diffusion. Despite the evidence of an indigenous Neolithic transition (a period of gradual settling down, intensive plant exploitation, and widespread use of pottery), for many years historians believed that the Neolithic agricultural revolution came to the European continent from West Asia, spreading first to neighboring Greece and eastern Europe, and then in a series of waves westward and northward. However, as archaeologists and historians working in other parts of the world began to examine the role played by topographical, climatic, and ecological conditions in the emergence of agriculture, their perspectives suggested that diffusion was a questionable and too-simple explanation for the transition to agriculture. Ecological conditions – climate, soil quality, rainfall – varied as widely in Europe as elsewhere, and the areas in which agriculture developed were widely separated: the Mediterranean basin was separated by the Alps from the Danube and Rhine River basins, each of which was distinct, and they were all unlike the rocky fringe lands of Scandinavia and the northern British Isles. Despite the effect of such variety on the development of European agriculture, a common European transformation from gathering-hunting to sedentary agrarian culture has been identified. Evidence of scattered and divergent transitions to agriculture dates from the mid- to late Neolithic era (after 5000 BCE) and seems to be related to the introduction of pottery and exploitation of indigenous grains and fruits, which were domesticated. These remains suggest that the transition to agriculture appeared in some places independently and was not necessarily the result of diffusion. However, recent genetic evidence seems to confirm the arrival of invading farming populations at several specific sites that record the rapid transition to agriculture.

Though western Eurasian agrarian societies emerged somewhat later than those in West Asia and elsewhere, the region was endowed with good resources and conditions for animal and plant domestication: there were widely scattered but large areas of arable land, and the climatic conditions – temperature and rainfall – in most of them are suitable for agriculture. The model suggests that generic agricultural concepts, such as cultivation, and certain specific fruits and grains emerged independently in various regions while particular agrarian practices and products, such as tools and seeds not indigenous to the continent, appeared eventually as a result of diffusion from elsewhere.

The transition to a sedentary agrarian culture has been connected with the pottery that accompanied it. An early ceramic ware, known as Linear Pottery I, was in use between 4700 and 3700 BCE in central and eastern European regions, in an area stretching from the North Sea coast and the Rhine Valley to the vast regions north of the Black Sea. Evidence found at Linear Pottery sites indicates that a number of varieties of grains, including wheat, barley, millet, flax, and peas, were cultivated during this period. Recent genetic studies have suggested that the movement of a relatively small number of farmers may have altered subsistence patterns rapidly with their introduction of domesticates.

DOMESTICATION OF ANIMALS   Among the earliest innovations suggesting the emergence of agrarian life is the domestication of animals. Local people domesticated the dog, probably as an aid to hunting, between 8000 and 5000 BCE. Evidence of domestic dogs has been found in western European coastal regions, where people lived as hunters and shellfish gatherers, as well as in sites in northern and central Europe. Many of these sites are contemporary with Neolithic communities whose culture extended over a long period. Domestication of animals may have spread across western Eurasia before the cultivation of plants, and the advent of cultivation contributed to the sorts of animals domesticated. Sheep, which were domesticated in Asia as early as 9000 BCE, along with cattle, goats, and pigs, were a part of the transition to agriculture as early as the fourth millennium BCE. By 2500 BCE, the horse was domesticated in the southwestern portion of the Eurasian steppes, when it spread further westward and northward. The domestication of the dog and horse suggests that not all inhabitants were sedentary agrarians and that early populations continued to be mobile.

While northern peoples were domesticating dogs, peoples in the Balkan area and southeast of the Balkans were beginning to plant and cultivate seeds. There, evidence of plant cultivation, domestication of animals other than dogs, and pottery date from as early as 6000 to 5000 BCE The spread northward and westward was apparently rapid: by 4000 BCE, similar evidence exists for trans-Alpine Europe.

EARLY AGRICULTURAL TECHNIQUES Domestication of grains and other plants depended on the use of the hoe and the digging stick, a tool also used around the world by gatherers. In some areas, particularly the heavily wooded parts of today's northwestern trans-Alpine Europe such as modern Germany, it was necessary to use slash-and-burn techniques in order to make the transition to agriculture. Dense forests were cleared and burned, and the cleared area was cultivated until the soil was exhausted. Without properly spaced fallow periods or fertilizer, cultivation caused soil to lose its fertility rapidly. This resulted in frequent relocation, which meant, in essence, repeating the slash-and-burn techniques in a new area.

The transition to sedentary agrarian cultures was accompanied by continuing gathering, hunting, and fishing activities, though they were adjusted to life in permanent settlements of sturdy dwellings fixed to a single site. The earliest evidence of such communities, dating from about 6,000 years ago, has been found in the Balkan Peninsula of southeastern Europe. Elsewhere, in northern and western Eurasia, temporary settlements and horticulture, combined with gathering and hunting, continued for a millennium or so. The establishment of permanent agrarian communities, in which wheat, millet, and other grains were cultivated in combination with livestock breeding and herding, was the final stage of the agricultural transition. It was, however, only the beginning of technological changes in agriculture,

which would benefit greatly from the application of horse power to the plowing of fields after about 800 CE, the introduction of the harness from the nomadic peoples of Central Asia, or the even earlier (ca. 100 BCE) use of water and wind power for grinding grain. The expansion of plowing caused soils to wash off to bedrock and hillsides to become eroded, a high environmental cost of the increased food production.

The Americas

The emergence of agriculture in the Americas follows patterns similar to those found elsewhere and raises similar questions of diffusion and variation. The Americas encompass a variety of climates and ecologies, ranging from frigid to tropical, wet to arid. Despite some claims that certain plants domesticated in the Americas suggest African origins for Western Hemisphere agriculture, it is accepted that the transition to agriculture there was a separate process, not a product of diffusion from Africa, Asia, or Europe.

THE LONG DROUGHT The separate origin of agriculture in the Americas has an ecological consideration in the evidence for desiccation or extended drought. A dramatic crisis, often referred to as the Long Drought, affected the region of the southwest of the present United States and northern Mexico; it began around 8000 BCE, reached a peak about 5500 BCE, and lasted until around 2000 BCE. The Long Drought was very likely the major impetus for the emergence of agriculture in North America and suggests that the transition to agriculture in parts of the Western Hemisphere is chronologically comparable to the development of agrarian practices in other parts of the world. Both the maize culture of Mesoamerica and the root culture of northwestern South America were well established by the mid-sixth millennium BCE. A corollary to drought, maize culture emerged as an alternative or supplement to poor gathering-hunting conditions. At

2.6 Mesoamerican maize: 5000 years of evolution (*from left to right*). 5000 years of maize evolution from tiny wild corn to a modern example ca. 1500 CE.

the time of this transition to plant cultivation, animals were also being domesticated, but not for food; it appears that the essential American diet as agriculture emerged was largely vegetarian, supplemented by hunting and fishing.

MESOAMERICAN MAIZE CULTURE   Even given the emphasis on plant foods in the Americas, the development of agrarian societies, as elsewhere, was gradual. Following the initial ventures into planting and domestication, cultivation improved and became more structured. The earliest model of such development occurred in the Valley of Mexico. The climate of this area alternated between wet and dry spells, with the rains being brought by east winds from the Gulf of Mexico to modify the effects of drought. Early grain cultivation included a large variety of plants with edible seeds; archaeologists are debating precisely how long it took for maize to develop as the primary crop is currently. Until recently, it was thought that maize, supplemented by beans and squash, was established as the pattern for agriculture between 5000 and 4000 BCE, but recent excavations in the Central Balsas Valley of Mexico have pushed the dates back to about 8,700 years

ago, without, however, altering the factors that caused the shift to agriculture. One thing is obvious: it took a long time to transform the indigenous plant ancestors of corn (maize) and squash into productive food sources and even longer to spread their cultivation across sharply differing climates.

SOUTH AMERICAN ROOT CULTURE   Other American centers developed both root and grain crops. The potato, an Andean domesticate, was developed from wild varieties that grew on mountain slopes from modern Colombia south to Bolivia. Here, too, desiccation had pushed peoples into the valleys fed by the annual Andes snow melts. Andean grain agriculture may possibly be an example of diffusion within the Americas; it is uncertain whether the cultivation of corn and cassava (both among the world's most difficult plants to domesticate) in Peru was learned from Mesoamerican peoples or was indigenous to South America. Incan cultural explanations exist but do not resolve the issue of diffusion as a source of agricultural practices. Corn and cassava, a tuberous root from which bread flour is made, were believed by the Incas of Peru to have their origins in a dramatic time of crisis.

The Incan legend of Pachacamac explains this adaptation:

Pachacamac, who was a son of the sun, made a man and a woman in the dunes of Lurin. There was nothing to eat, and the man died of hunger. When the women bent over searching for roots, the sun entered her and made a child. Jealous, Pachacamac caught the newborn baby and chopped it to pieces. But suddenly he repented, or was scared of the anger of his father, the sun, and scattered about the world the pieces of his murdered brother. From the teeth of the dead baby, corn grew, and from the ribs and bones, cassava. The blood made the land fertile, and fruit trees and shade trees rose from the sown flesh. Thus the women and men born on these shores, where it never rains, find food.

The Pachacamac legend suggests that interrelated forces believed to be both natural and supernatural were central to Incan culture and survival.

NORTH AMERICAN AGRICULTURE The question of the diffusion of maize agriculture is not limited to South America. Diffusion is also considered a possible explanation of the origins of North American agriculture, where the oldest corn found (in New Mexico's Bat Cave) dates from about 7500 BCE. In the manner of the Incan cultural explanation of the origins of corn and cassava, the following legend of the Hopi people of the American Southwest offers an explanation of agriculture in North America:

> Moing'iima makes corn. Everything grows on his body. Every summer he becomes heavy, his body full of vegetables: watermelon, corn, squash. They grow in his body. When the Hopi plant, they invariably ask him to make the crop flourish; then their things come up, whether vegetables or fruit. When he shaves his body, the seeds come out, and afterwards his body is thin. He used to live on this earth and go with the Hopi. When things grow ripe, he becomes thin and is unhappy. He stays in the west.

In some parts of North America, agriculture emerged tentatively or made no headway at all. In the Pacific Northwest, an abundance of nourishing plants and fish allowed gathering-hunting lifestyles to persist long after agriculture emerged elsewhere. The Mississippian culture, which reached from Appalachia to the Great Plains and from the Great Lakes to the Gulf of Mexico, turned to sedentary agriculture only gradually, between 2000 and 800 BCE; the Mississippians retained their gathering-hunting patterns alongside part-time farming, in which domesticates were exploited but not necessarily

relied upon. It is noteworthy that diverse peoples scattered throughout the Americas all turned to agriculture at about the same time. Whether directly or indirectly resulting from factors such as environmental change or population growth, agricultural development was never a designed, sudden process but a slow and uncertain drift.

Technology and environment

The movement from hunting and gathering to agriculture followed many different and seemingly independent paths around the world in response to a variety of specific environments. Embracing an agricultural life was usually more difficult and labor intensive than hunting and gathering. Once established, however, agricultural societies could support larger and more complex societies than hunter-gatherer societies. As settled societies grew larger, they became stratified, revealing greater social inequality, and a propensity to be more destructive of their environments.

The far-flung foraging and hunting peoples and their farming and herding descendants were impelled toward a new, intensive approach to food production. Wherever settled agricultural communities eventually appeared, so did population increases, environmental stresses, and technological innovations. While this change in the course of human history – sometimes referred to as the Neolithic Revolution – was indeed momentous, it was neither sudden nor straightforward. Rather, the "revolution" took place over generations and sometimes thousands of years. It occurred independently in different world regions and relied heavily on the character of specific environments. Indeed, for many parts of the world, early agricultural practices were grafted on to existing lifestyles in diverse ways, suggesting that the distinction between hunter-gatherers was not always sharply drawn.

Efforts to pinpoint the earliest plant domesticates are complicated by characteristics of the plants themselves. Cereal grains, with their hard-shelled seeds, were often burned (carbonized)

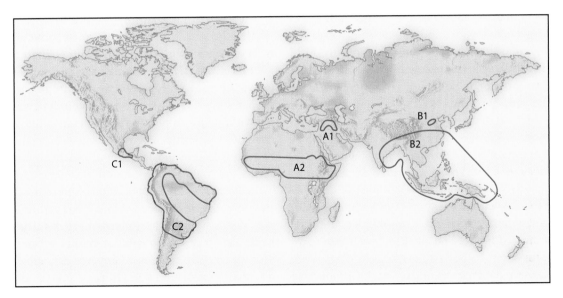

Map 2.2 Early food crops. A1: wheat, peas; A2: yams, coffee, melons; B1: rice; B2: rice, bananas, sugar cane, yams; C1: maize, beans; C2: potatoes, peanuts.

during preparation and thereby preserved for archaeological discovery and analysis. In contrast, domesticated root crops lack hard, burnable parts and are otherwise difficult to distinguish from their wild ancestors. Consequently, such root crops as potatoes, yams, and manioc in the Americas, Africa, and Asia could have been domesticated even earlier than the cereals and grasses, for which there is good evidence.

Western Eurasian hunter-gatherers and the farmers who gradually replaced them relied on the use of the hoe, the digging stick, and the use of fire to clear lands for crops. Elsewhere, temporary settlements and horticulture, combined with gathering and hunting, continued for a millennium or so. The introduction of the plough was significant only in working certain soils. Technological changes in agriculture would benefit greatly from the application of oxen or horse power to the plowing of fields, using iron ploughshares around the third century BCE in China, and after about 800 CE in Europe, where the plough was combined with other innovations such as the introduction of the harness from the nomadic peoples of Asia, or the even earlier (ca.

100 BCE) use of water and wind power for grinding grain that also had an impact on productivity.

Water control and the role of environment

What role did the environment play in the rise of agriculture? Was environment more critical than cultural innovations? Clearly the environment provided an array of available plant and animal species for possible domestication. What factors led humans to select and invest intensively in specific species? Part of the answer rests in the attachment of human societies to the cultural memories associated with the landscapes of birth and death. Agriculture often required an investment in a single environment and sometimes in a single species. The intimate knowledge of a landscape was transmitted from one generation to the next generation, whose survival depended on it.

The success of early civilizations depended on the ability of societies to ensure their stability by adapting to changing environmental conditions and by controlling them when possible. As in

Egypt and Mesopotamia, the control of water in early China was an important factor in increasing technological and political complexity. Did the demands of water control always lead to a concentration of power and authority? In China, the need for dikes – built to prevent the Yellow River from flooding its banks and for irrigation to support wet rice agriculture – brought about the growth of a centralized bureaucratic state. While the concept of a hydraulic society may be overly deterministic, water control did play a role in dynastic changes by undermining political stability when dikes ruptured and floods destroyed homes and fields. China's two main waterways, the Yellow and Yangzi Rivers, were connected by the Grand Canal, a product of human engineering in the sixth century CE that enabled grain, especially rice grown in the fertile Yangzi delta area, to be transported to the capital area. Other smaller river systems, canals and waterways enabled the expansion of markets and a commercial economy from the eighth century onward.

The history of agriculture in West Asia during the Holocene and in the Americas after 8000 BCE suggests the importance of an ecological consideration for the list of possible explanations for the rise of farming. There is little doubt that reliance on a narrowed territory and familiar range of plants and animals made societies more susceptible to the vagaries of droughts and unpredictable weather than did the options offered by a wider range of foraging and hunting. The dramatic crisis, often referred to as the Long Drought, may be linked to the spread of maize culture of Mesoamerica and the root culture of northwestern South America, which were well established by the mid-sixth millennium BCE. The emergence of "maize culture" as an alternative or supplement to poor gathering-hunting conditions was a corollary to drought. In contrast, the adaptability of the Natufians responded to both drought and increasingly moist conditions that followed, suggesting that cultural innovations provided the necessary tools for flexibility and survival.

From local to global food sources

Archaeological work in the highland Tehuacan Valley suggests that the intentional cultivation of maize first took place sometime after 6000 BCE, though the primitive maize of this early era was not yet a dietary staple. The earliest cultivators of maize were probably driven by extended droughts that had diminished the supply of wild foods across the highland region. Still, these people, living in small bands, remained primarily foragers and hunters, occupying various camps during their seasonal rounds in search of meat and other foods. Later excavation levels at Tehuacan begin to show a different picture. After 5000 BCE, a growing, somewhat less mobile Tehuacan population increased the proportion of both wild *and* domesticated plant foods in their diet while the proportion of meat decreased.

The Aztec called the domesticated plant *teocintli* meaning "God's ear of corn." The potency of corn was believed by the early Mesoamericans to be both spiritual and physical. According to Aztec beliefs, the first human couple cast kernels of maize to divine their future. With corn and other selected plants, the vision of that future would include the eventual creation of permanent, settled communities and large ceremonial complexes. Yet as the eventual staple of Mesoamerica and much of North and South America, corn initially did not necessarily have a great immediate impact wherever it appeared. Archaeologists have been able to measure the carbon atoms in human bone excavated from sites in the Americas in order to identify how much corn ancient people did eat, whether this corn was eaten in combination with other particular foods such as marine resources, and whether those populations were mobile, thus adding another scientific means of determining the dates, diffusion, and impact of the crop. The exchange of world foods began after Columbus brought corn to other parts of the world, where the impact on population growth was significant.

Today the post-Columbian processes of globalization have brought people into contact with the foods of new continents. Plants such as the chili pepper, native to the Americas, have conquered the cuisines of the planet. Peanuts, maize, soy, and improved strains of rice have supported dramatic population changes and altered the destinies of world societies. The eventual reliance of humans on global rather than local food has been debated since at least the time of the eighteenth-century French philosopher Jean-Jacques Rousseau, who expressed suspicion regarding foods that were imported from faraway lands. The transfer of foods from their original habitats to new ones was accelerated by the processes some historians have identified as ecological imperialism, acknowledging the impact of the political domination in the transfer of plants, animals, and diseases from one world region to another. Even in ancient times, the storage and redistribution of food and the role of trade were essential parts of the variety of human strategies for feeding the growing populations around the world.

Villages, towns, and environment

The entrenchment and spread of agricultural systems in the millennia between 14,000 and 2000 BCE set off explosions in both food production and population. Deliberate agriculture in most world regions fostered impressive increases in population, which in turn gave rise to the spread of early agricultural peoples to new areas of the globe. However, as agricultural peoples overtook foraging and hunting peoples, the relationship of humans to their environment began to change dramatically. Nonetheless, the transition to agriculture worldwide presents such a range of examples that no single explanatory model satisfies. The emergence of various agricultural systems and sedentary societies occurred quite independently at vastly different times and followed different scenarios in many different parts of the world, ranging from river valleys to dry, temperate, upland areas.

Greater numbers of people living together in relatively stable communities, with domesticated animals also living close by, gave rise to infectious diseases and other illnesses that were easily spread by settled peoples and rare among the mobile forager-hunters. For example, because of its long urban tradition, China soon developed populations with some immunity to diseases that flourished in crowded conditions, such as measles and smallpox. Once animal husbandry was adopted, China, unlike the Americas, had experience with diseases shared with animals, such as influenza. The peoples of the Americas were devastated by their first contact with Eurasian diseases carried by pigs introduced during the European conquest. The greater concentrations of sedentary human communities, geared to an *intensive* relationship with their environment rather than an *extensive* one, also resulted in frequent cases of environmental degradation: polluted wells, contaminated rivers and streams, and defoliated landscapes. So, while birth rates rose (in part because of changes in weaning, nursing, and birth spacing) among the settled agricultural populations, local diets became narrower, labor became more routine, and life expectancies fell.

From pyrotechnology to the age of metals

The second major area of human impact on the environment resulted from the use of metals, long indicative of technological "advances" synonymous with definitions of civilization. The use of fire had been an essential tool for the expanding human populations, who reached less temperate environments around the planet. The intentional use of fire as a tool (**pyrotechnology**) had many consequences. Cooking food provided the signature human diet with more energy through altered proteins, starches, and structures of food, not to mention the rich opportunities for sharing, communication, and cooperation. The impact of the increasingly complex material culture was visible even in the earliest communities: the cutting down of trees for firewood contributed to the early evidence of deforestation that has continued until today. Wood fueled the firing of pottery used to store food, the heat for cooking meals, and the working of metals to be made into implements. The heat treatment of materials eventually became specialist activities. About the time fired pottery generally came into widespread use (ca. 14,000–6000 BCE), technologies for working metal were developed. Metallurgical technologies were used to produce tools that had a great effect on agriculture – and commerce and war as well – at the time the transition to sedentary societies was occurring in many parts of the world.

The "age of metals" varied from place to place and came earlier to some places than others. Not all societies developed technologies for the same metals. In West Asia, the Balkans, Spain, and the Aegean, for instance, copper metallurgy was the first to develop (between 9000 and 2500 BCE). In Africa, iron metallurgy was developed (at least as early as ca. 2500 BCE, both with the working of meteoritic iron and by smelting iron ores). It began to supersede all others in areas where iron ore was available. Iron, being a harder, stronger metal able to retain sharp edges, could be used to create more durable and useful tools. As the demand for metal tools increased, the uneven distribution of ores around the globe endowed some societies with riches and others with the need to trade. Tin-bronzes, alloys or mixtures of copper and tin (or lead or antimony) are found at Velikent in Daghestan (in the Caucasus region) in the third millennium BCE. By about 1500 BCE, the demand for superior bronze, metals harder than copper (though not as hard as iron), resulted in the importation of tin from as far away as Cornwall (in West England) or Central Asia to West and Southeast Asia for use in bronze metallurgy. Unlike the working of stone, a material that remained essentially unchanged except in shape, metalworking represented a fundamental **alchemy**: the very nature of matter was changed by human skill and technology.

Metallurgy had a devastating impact on the environment everywhere it was employed. Mining activities themselves were destructive, as

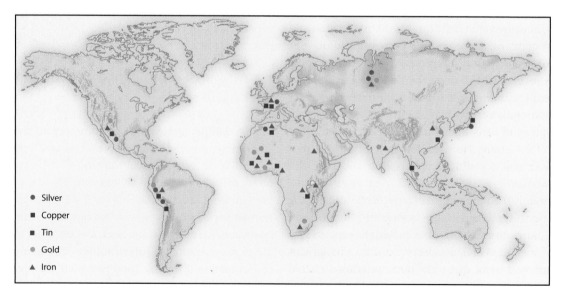

- ● Silver
- ■ Copper
- ■ Tin
- ● Gold
- ▲ Iron

Map 2.3 Early metal sources before 1500 CE.

Neolithic miners of silex (chalk), flint, and obsidian demonstrated around the world. Digging resources out of the earth changed the landscape and contributed to erosion of hillsides, often the places in which new ores were observed. The first use of native copper required no underground extraction, but soon afterward the copper and tin of most ancient workings began to be found in veins or lodes in older, harder rock. Its extraction required the use of fire and specialized stone hammers, and ultimately the construction of shafts, supporting architecture, and drainage systems. Deforestation and soil erosion were common consequences of mining and working of metals.

METALLURGY IN AFRICA AND THE AMERICAS   In West Africa, metallurgists conceptualized the production of iron and steel (probably after 3000 BCE) as the harnessing of both technical and spiritual forces. Adept in changing the very nature of matter, specialists emerged as powerful members of the community. Their powers depended on the most powerful deities: those controlling the manufacture of iron tools and weapons. The site of Meroe (ca. 400 BCE) in the middle Nile is an example of the intensive exploitation of pyrotechnological knowledge, including pottery and metals. Substantial quantities of slag, the waste product of iron smelting, together with surviving tools, including spears, tweezers, adzes, axes, hoe blades, and shears, suggest an impressive industry. The fuel consumption of major African metallurgical centers, such as found at Meroe, created serious problems of deforestation, and industries eventually declined or shifted as forests disappeared. The specialists – workers in iron, copper, gold, and glass – who altered the environment with such devastating impact were held in awe, both revered and feared. Control over technology, in Africa as elsewhere, served as a vehicle for the expression of social and political dominance and subordination. Metals acquired symbolic importance as expressions of power and social distinctions.

In the Andean zone of western South America (modern Peru, Bolivia, Ecuador, and Colombia), metals played only a minor role in warfare: there were no Andean bronze- or steel-tipped weapons, and cloth and worked fibers also provided weaponry (slings for projectiles) and protective armor. Obsidian, a naturally formed volcanic glass, was highly prized and widely traded in its raw form, which was shaped into arrowheads and spear points. The role of metals was relegated to non-utilitarian realms. In the Andean region, copper, gold, and silver were used decoratively and artistically to convey both secular and religious status and power. The Andean craft worker was interested in a metal's color and appearance, not in its strength or durability. Sophisticated techniques of alloying, gilding, and silvering that used electrochemical methods of surface alteration dominated the repertoire of metalsmiths in Andean societies during the first millennium CE.

Complex copper metallurgies helped to shape South American societies. As early as 500 BCE, peoples on the northern Peruvian coast worked copper and gold. Later artisans also produced

2.7 Iron smelting furnace, Bassari region, Togo (West Africa). The study of recent technological practices has aided the interpretation of archaeological remains of metalworking. Tall, natural-draft furnaces produced high-carbon iron and steel, and widespread deforestation. Specialist knowledge required for their operation was restricted to the men in certain lineages.

2.8 Gold figure of a jaguar, Chiriqui, Panama.

a copper-gold alloy well suited to sheet-metal working. At a reconstructed Peruvian site dating to between 900 and 1500 CE, archaeologists have excavated the earliest evidence in the world of intensive smelting of copper-arsenic alloys. The furnace openings revealed elaborate sacrificial offerings of llamas and food. Ceramic-tipped cane blowing tubes were used to raise the furnace temperatures, and additives were used to help remove impurities so that nearly pure copper could be produced. Each smelting would have produced only about 0.3–0.6 kilogram (0.66 to 1.32 pounds) of metallic copper, yet used enormous quantities of fuel. Accordingly, the burial of a leader with about 500 kilograms (1100 pounds) of copper objects was an ostentatious statement of power and wealth.

Copper-silver and copper-gold alloys expressed significant cultural aspects of Andean value systems. For example, when copper encased or was alloyed with pure gold, the hidden or disguised gold was thought to represent the divine quality of a seemingly human ruler. In South America as elsewhere, technology reflected cultural preoccupations and provides critical evidence for understanding gender and status in early societies and cultures. Ironically, South American silver would play a major role in globalization and environmental loss after 1500 CE.

METALLURGY IN EURASIA   This pattern of metallurgical development in Africa and the Americas stands in contrast to Eurasia, where the Copper Age preceded the Bronze Age and the Iron Age. The technology that dominated in each of these new eras was defined by the inevitable replacement of the older metal by the newer one. By the third millennium BCE, communities in China, the Indus Valley, and the western Mediterranean basin constituted examples of Bronze Age culture as a result of their significant advances in metallurgical expertise. Bronze (an alloy combining copper and tin) was an elaboration of the earliest copper metallurgy, which had developed in areas adjacent to abundant ancient copper sources such as those near the Balkans, in the Sinai, and in East and Southeast Asia. In Thailand, where the earliest evidence of a tin and copper alloy was once thought to predate the third millennium, development of bronze is not thought to have begun before 2000 BCE. The Egyptians had previously added arsenic to copper (probably around 3000 BCE) to produce silvered bronze mirrors with reflective surfaces; they did not alloy copper with tin before about 2000 BCE. In China, bronze weapons were used by the founders of the first historic dynasty, the Shang (ca. 1600–1045 BCE), which emerged on the north China plain in the early part of the second millennium BCE. In addition to weapons, bronze ritual vessels were cast for use in ceremonies sanctioning the political legitimacy of the Shang kings.

The transition from bronze to iron in the Mediterranean basin and Europe was late and sporadic. Bronze metallurgy there dates variously from the second millennium BCE; it was accompanied by the rise of increasingly hierarchical communities with growing populations. Eurasian metallurgy and deforestation in the early Bronze Age may contribute to quantifying and understanding human interactions with the climate system over time. Bronze fulfilled Europeans' needs for perhaps 1,000 years before it was superseded by iron. From the sixth century BCE,

Greek and Roman societies relied on iron for tools and weapons, but as early as the eighth century BCE, the Greek poet Hesiod (fl. ca. 776 BCE) had lamented the new Iron Age: "I wish that I were not any part of the fifth generation of men. . . . For here now is the age of iron." Hesiod's doubts about the effects of iron weapons on Greek culture may have rested on the belief that iron was implicated in ending the heroic age that preceded this warring, competitive generation; his words were hardly an enthusiastic endorsement of inevitable or progressive change. Technological innovations have always produced mixed responses throughout history.

One important factor in the adoption of iron for use in weapons was its relatively widespread availability. The environmental costs were high because of the dense woods required to produce

PRIMARY SOURCE: LAMENTING TECHNOLOGY

In imperial China, mining continued to be a lucrative and essential enterprise controlled by the state, which licensed the production of iron and other metals. An eighteenth-century poem reveals something of the unwaveringly harsh conditions experienced by mine workers:

Lament for the Copper-bearing Hills
   By Wang Taiyue
They gather, at dawn, by the mouth of the shaft,
Standing there naked, their garments stripped off,
Lamps strapped to their heads in carrying-baskets,
To probe in the darkness the fathomless bottom. . .

In the chill of the winter, their bodies will tremble,
Hands blistered with chilblains. Their feet will be chapped.
Down the mine, for this reason, they huddle together,
But hardly revive, life-force at a standstill. . .

The wood they must hunt is no longer available.
The woods are shaved bald, like a convict's head. Blighted,
Only now they regret – felling day after day
Has left them no way to provide for their firewood.

> Source: Mark Elvin, "Introduction," Mark Elvin and Liu Ts'ui-jung,
> eds, *Sediments of Time: Environment and Society in Chinese History*
> (Cambridge: Cambridge University Press, 1998), pp10–11

Everywhere metallurgy was practiced, the impact on the environment was visible. Wang Taiyue's poem suggests the human and ecological dimensions of exploitation. Chinese miners' livelihoods grew increasingly difficult as the ore became scarce and the wood needed for smelting was used up.

consistently high temperatures inside the smelting furnaces. Though iron ore was difficult to extract and purify, once successful metallurgical techniques could produce useful amounts, iron superseded all previous metals for weapons and tools. It was the principal form of iron produced in Europe until the nineteenth century, when new techniques revolutionized iron metallurgy there.

In China, the preferred iron products were cast iron and steel, high-carbon alloys that were much harder. Chinese artisans were producing cast iron and steel by the fourth century BCE. Both were widely used in the era known as the Warring States (481–221 BCE). The introduction and widespread use of iron were related to the dramatic social and economic changes that resulted from conflict and frequent shifts of power during this period. Iron was used for weapons, and warfare created conditions in which those with access to iron technology were at an advantage. It is likely that iron artifacts spread before iron technology was known in Korea and Japan. A third-century BCE text refers to "spearheads of steel . . . sharp as a bee's sting." Iron was also used by the time of the Warring States for the share, or blade, of the ox-drawn plow, probably based on wooden plows used by Chinese farmers in wet ricelands. The Eurasian use of the plow altered and even interfered with the earth's natural processes of soil formation, thus contributing to severe erosion even while food production dramatically increased.

Despite the chaotic conditions in China resulting from war, or perhaps in part because of them, iron acquired great value and even commercial exchange utilized iron currency. Merchants grew rich on its profits and agriculture prospered, aided by the use of iron tools. After the unification of the empire in the third century BCE, the government quickly grasped the importance of controlling iron production as a source of revenue. In the second century BCE, Emperor Wu of the Han dynasty (202 BCE–220 CE) created government monopolies of salt and iron. Criticisms by Confucian scholars such as those preserved in the *Debates on Salt and Iron* (81 BCE), did not succeed in ending the monopolies and later dynasties continued to control the production and sale of salt and iron (along with other metals such as tin, copper, lead).

By the first millennium BCE, cast-iron technology was commonly used to manufacture household items, such as scissors, and to build temples, pagodas, and bridges. But the environmental costs were great: before the end of the first millennium, north China was deforested. The expansion of iron production after this depended on the use of coal or **coke**. By the Song dynasty (960–1279) the technological and production levels of the iron industry in north China equaled that of the early stages of the **Industrial Revolution** in England more than 500 years later.

Summary

Since the beginning of human history, technology and ideas have been intertwined in their impact on landscapes. World historians link changes in human ecology and the most significant rise in complexity to the origins of agriculture. Agricultural innovations allowed early human populations to assume a dominant role on the planet. These and other technological transformations have not produced an unquestioned improvement in the quality of life. Technological innovations have had a profound impact on the consumption of energy and resources, while transforming the physical landscape. Though humans have altered their landscapes since prehistoric times through the use of fire and other manipulations of the environment, the human impact on the landscape has intensified dramatically since the advent of food production. With agriculture came the steady increase in population and ever more complex adaptations of subsistence, trade, and exchange. This complexity was registered in technological and cultural transformations that initiated a long period of increasing inequality against the backdrop of the environmental consequences of expanded energy use.

The two greatest environmental changes in the last 3,000 years have been the destruction of forests (with its accompanying reduction of global biodiversity) and the reorganization of surface waters (water control systems, irrigation, dams, etc.). Both of these changes began with the Neolithic Revolution and the age of metals and have been accelerated after the Industrial Revolution. The recent period between 1800 and 1914 witnessed an unprecedented expansion of agriculture and population growth throughout the world, both of which had continued devastating effects on world resources and the physical landscape. These forces can be held directly responsible for the increasing pressures of global deforestation, destructive forms of increased energy consumption, and global warming. Ecological destruction in the twenty-first century may make nomads of us all again, while reducing alternative possibilities of habitation and survival of the world's environmental diversity.

Suggested readings

Barker, Graeme (2006) *The Agricultural Revolution in Prehistory: Why did Foragers become Farmers?* London: Oxford University Press. Provides global coverage of the process of agricultural origins and spread by using a regional comparative approach to archaeological research.

Diamond, Jared (1997) *Guns, Germs, and Steel: The Fates of Human Societies*, New York: W.W. Norton. Debates the roles of environment and culture in determining historical developments in different parts of the world since about 11,000 BCE.

Elvin, Mark (2004) *The Retreat of the Elephants: An Environmental History of China*. New Haven and London: Yale University Press. Examines China's past and potential future impacts on the environment since the extinction of the elephant over 4,000 years through the changing understanding of relationships between nature and culture.

Elvin, Mark and Liu Ts'ui-jung, eds (1998) *Sediments of Time: Environment and Society in Chinese History*. Cambridge: Cambridge University Press. Selected articles on the environmental history of China, including demography, climate, water, and forest resources.

Fagan, Brian (1999) *Floods, Famines, and Emperors: El Nino and the Fate of Civilizations*, New York: Basic Books. Explores some of the unusual weather events and climatic shifts in human history and considers their causes and consequences.

Keightley, David N., ed. (1983) *The Origins of Chinese Civilization*, Berkeley, CA: University of California Press. Articles by specialists on such topics as environment and agriculture, Neolithic cultures and peoples, metallurgy, writing, and early political organization.

McNeill, J.R. (2000) *Something New Under the Sun: An Environmental History of the Twentieth-Century World*, New York: W.W. Norton and Company. An environmental history of the modern world emphasizing the impact of the industrialized world on deforestation and pollution.

McNeill, William H. (1977) *Plagues and People*, Garden City, NY: Doubleday. A provocative study of the relationship of disease to demography and its effect on global history.

Montgomery, David R. (2007) *Dirt: The Erosion of Civilizations*, Berkeley, CA: University of California Press. A scientist's compelling look at the history of soil and the impact of civilization.

Radkau, Joachim (2008) *Nature and Power: A Global History of the Environment*, Cambridge and New York: Cambridge University Press. Explores the changing relationships between humanity and the natural environment from prehistoric times to the present.

Schmidt, Peter R., ed. (1996) *The Culture and Technology of African Iron Production*, Gainesville: University of Florida Press. Good introduction to current issues in African Iron Age studies.

Wertime, Theodore A. and James E. Muhly (1980) *The Coming of the Age of Iron*, New Haven, CO: Yale University Press. Although somewhat outdated, presents a comparative look at the age of iron in various cultural settings of world regions.

Williams, Michael (2003) *Deforesting the Earth: From Prehistory to Global Crisis*, Chicago: University of Chicago Press. Examines 10,000 years of human impact on the Earth's forests.

Worster, Donald (1977) *Nature's Economy: A History of Ecological Ideas*, New York: Cambridge University Press. An essential history of human relationship with the natural world and how this has been expressed in human thought.

Online resources

Annenberg/CPB, *Bridging World History* (2004) <www.learner.org/channel/courses/worldhistory> Multimedia project with interactive website and free, downloadable videos; see especially Unit 4 Agricultural and Urban Revolutions.

PBS Nova Program: Tracking El Nino (1998) <www.pbs.org/wgbh/nova/elnino> Examines the current and historical impact of meteorological events.

Study questions

1. How do world historians define culture?
2. Describe the evidence historians use to study cultural adaptations by early human populations.
3. How did technology and culture alter both the inner landscape of the individual and the physical landscape of the natural world?
4. Identify some common characteristics of early agricultural societies. Did sedentism always precede resource control?
5. Why did pastoralism alter the human use of the natural world?
6. How did the early appearance of agriculture vary across Afro-Eurasia and the Americas?
7. What was the impact of pyrotechnology?
8. Why would some people have lamented the Iron Age?
9. How did ancient metallurgy further the process of increasing complexity and inequality?

10–2000 BCE	9000–6500	8000	5800	5000	4–3000	2300–1500	2200–1085
Increased populations live in dense, crowded villages	Jericho, West Asian urbanism	Delphi oracle	Çatalhöyük, in central Turkey	Sumerian cities	Nile cities	Harappan culture, Indus Valley	Thebes

TIMELINE

3 Cities and city life in world history

The diversity and variety of life increased dramatically with the rise of urban centers. Ever since the earliest village, larger communities of people were themselves magnets of population growth and they drew the keen interest of travelers. In the third century CE, a poet-traveler recounted his visit to the city of Madurai, vividly portraying the social, economic, and religious life of this city on the southern tip of the South Asian subcontinent:

> The poet enters the city by its great gate, the posts of which are carved with the images of the goddess Lakshmi. It is a festival day, and the city is gay with flags; some, presented by the king to commemorate brave deeds, fly over the houses of captains; others wave over the shops which sell toddy [a fermented drink made from blossoms of the palm tree]. The streets are broad rivers of people of every race, buying and selling in the market place or singing to the music of wandering minstrels.
>
> The drum beats and a royal procession passes down the street, with elephants leading and the sound of conches [shell trumpets]
>
> ... Stall keepers ply their trade, selling sweet cakes, garlands of flowers, scented powder, and rolls of betel nut [to chew]. Old women go from house to house selling nosegays and trinkets. Noblemen drive through the streets in their chariots, their gold-sheathed swords flashing, wearing brightly dyed garments and wreaths of flowers. The jewels of the perfumed women watching from balconies and turrets flash in the sun ... Craftsmen work in their shops, bangle-makers, goldsmiths, cloth weavers, coppersmiths, flower sellers, wood carvers, and painters. Food shops are busily selling mangoes, sugar candy, cooked rice, and chunks of cooked meat. In the evening, the city's prostitutes entertain their patrons with dancing and singing to the accompaniment of the lute. The streets are filled with music. Drunken villagers, in town for the festival, reel about in the streets. Respectable women visit the temples in the evening with their children and friends, carrying lighted lamps as offerings. They dance in the temple courts, which resound with their singing and chatter. At last the city

1500	1600–1027	1200–900	1000–100	671 BCE–present	333 BCE	322–ca.100 BCE
Urban origins near Athens	Shang dynasty, China	Olmec culture	Chavín de Huántar, Peru	Constantinople, capital of Roman empire	Alexander the Great defeats the Persian army	Pataliputra, largest city in the world

sleeps . . . all but the ghosts and goblins who haunt the dark and the housebreakers, armed with rope ladders, swords, and chisels. But the watchmen are also vigilant, and the city passes the night in peace. Morning comes with the sounds of brahmins intoning their sacred verses. The wandering bands renew their singing, and the shopkeepers open their booths. The toddy-sellers ply their trade for thirsty early morning travelers. The drunkards stagger to their feet. All over the city the sound is heard of doors opening. Women sweep the faded flowers of the festival from their courtyards. The busy everyday life of the city is resumed.

Source: A.L. Basham, *The Wonder that Was India* (New York: Grove Press, 1954), pp203–4]

3.1 Temple facade at Madurai. The temple tower is still surrounded by small vendors selling foods for the temple shrines.

In many ways, Madurai strikes us as being much like any modern city. Food and goods in dizzying amounts and varieties can be bought, day and night. Craftsmen, noblemen, prostitutes, shopkeepers, minstrels, captains, royalty – all are thrust together in the fabric of city life. At night, a different world emerges, that of "ghosts and goblins" but also of well-provisioned thieves and the watchmen who safeguard the city while it sleeps. Because it is a festival day, there is a vibrant religious atmosphere. But religion is also more deeply and permanently present, from the images of the goddess carved into the posts of the city gate to the temples that dot the urban landscape. The atmosphere of a festival day is striking and characteristic even of some modern Indian cities. We might say that the particular religious cast of these festivities is something culturally distinctive to South Asian society, although not unique to urban sites. But what is common to the origins of cities throughout the world, and what is distinctive about cities as they evolve in different cultural settings and change over time? Why do people congregate in cities, and what benefits and drawbacks are there to urban life?

250 BCE–present	206 BCE–907 CE	100 BCE–750 CE	200 CE	250–900	324–1453	700–1400	750
Jenné-Jeno	Chang'an	Teotihuacán	Madurai flourished	Classic Mayan cities	Constantinople capital of Roman and Byzantine empires until captured by Ottomans	Mississippians	Baghdad capital of Islamic Abbasid Empire

Introduction to the theme of cities

Human population increase on a global scale has been a constant factor in changing community forms and evolving relationships between humans and their environments, despite dramatic, though usually short-term and regionally limited, decreases due to war or disease. The city is one particular form of human organization emerging where sedentary peoples were concentrated in densely populated, complex settlements. Complexity was both a necessary condition for and a consequence of large, growing communities. Complexity appeared in the form of bureaucracies that registered populations, taxed them, and maintained order, as well as in the form of systems of trade, communication, and defense. No less important were rituals of public order, both religious and secular, and aspects of everyday life such as going to the market to buy food or taking part in an annual festival. In this chapter, we explore a wide array of forces and circumstances that encouraged human settlement in early urban forms. What were the relationships between early urban communities and their environments? How were the changing structures of more recent urban communities shaped by the forces of global industrialization and colonialism? As we consider the creation of early cities, we examine the human experience of city life, its benefits and the global challenges created by dramatic demographic change.

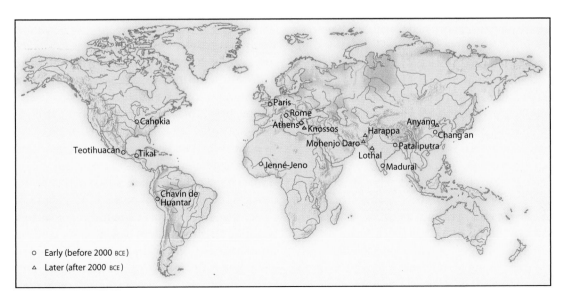

Map 3.1 Early cities.

1000–1200	1200–1400	1350–1400	1798
Muslim invasions of Delhi	Cairo flourished	"Black Death" plague in Eurasia peaks	Essay on Population by Thomas Malthus

World demography: Crowded daily lives

The creation of a sedentary community relied on groups of people who found a common purpose in staying in one place. Settling down may have eventually occurred around the world, but what were the dynamic forces that set the process of urbanization in motion? The interplay of population increase and agricultural innovations reinforced continuity and created the conditions for a revolutionary change in the patterns of subsistence and in the shifting concentrations and locations of early communities. Above all, agriculture both created and sustained increasing populations around the world. Reliance on agriculture made necessary the commitment to staying in one place. Disease control became a new requirement of larger populations aggregated in permanent settlements, whose complexity included management of water resources, parasites, and infectious diseases previously unknown to more mobile populations. And wherever cities came into being, they did not do so in isolation from rural hinterlands, which continued to feed the city folk.

The major feature of world populations through time has been their increasing numbers, in spite of disease, famine, and warfare. Historical demography is the study of changes in population throughout history. The natural biological increase of early human populations reflected the initial success of the species in adapting to a variety of changing environments. It is likely that many early human migrations resulted from the pressure of such demographic increases on limited food resources. Although the long-term, cumulative trend of human populations has been in the direction of a regular increase over time, increases were not always possible or desirable in the shorter-term historical experience of individual groups and societies. Disease, drought, famine, war, and natural disasters figure among the causes of temporary declines of populations in parts of the world, but they did not alter the basic overall trend of population increase.

From a global perspective, the biggest consequence of the establishment of sedentary farming communities (villages) between 4,000 and 12,000 years ago was the increased rate of population growth. Larger, denser village settlements were common to every continent. Agricultural peoples experienced more than the annoyances of crowded circumstances. Focused reliance on single agricultural crops resulted in resource consumption that was less diverse and often this led to less well-balanced diets, tooth decay due to the increased consumption of processed foods, especially carbohydrates (such as grain porridges and breads), and more susceptibility to contagious diseases, possibly as a result of their closer association with domesticated animals and animal viruses. Despite these downsides to crowded daily lives, the early inhabitants of villages, towns, and cities occasionally had longer life spans.

According to historical demographers studying changes in population through history, most of the demographic increases common to prehistory were also not the result of migrations or shifts in mortality rates but rather appear to have been associated with higher fertility rates. The reasons settled agriculturalists gave birth to more children is a matter of speculation. Demographic studies of contemporary gathering and hunting peoples provide a possible clue. Although many factors can affect the number of births to each female during her lifetime, birth spacing as a result of breast-feeding has been observed in many populations. Nursing a child stimulates hormones that suppress ovulation and menstruation (called lactational amenorrhea) with the consequence of producing a birth-spacing pattern that reduces fertility rates. Because infant formulas (high-carbohydrate, easy-to-digest cereals, and animal milk) were more readily available in the diets of agriculturalists than those of gatherers and hunters, infants were weaned from mother's milk at an earlier age, and the space between births became considerably shorter. The result was a trend in population growth that has characterized a more crowded human history ever since.

Emerging complexity

Increasing economic, social, and political complexity also accompanied the formation of settlements we can identify as cities. This complexity meant that many peoples, occupations, goods, and ideas came together into a single settlement that satisfied diverse needs. Though cities appear around the world, they were not a universal stage in the development of civilization, a term derived from the Latin word for "city," *civitas*, nor were they the logical and necessary culmination of earlier forms of community. For a long time, historians debated whether ancient Egypt was a civilization without cities. While agriculture was common to many cities, it didn't automatically lead to urbanization. In some parts of the world (Mexico, Panama, and Ecuador, for example) plant domestication was around for almost 5,000 years before people began to settle in cities. The most common definitions of "civilization" include the presence of some or all of the traits commonly found in the large-scale, complex communities we call cities: monumental architecture, usually religious in nature; writing

or other formal systems of record keeping and communication; trade; formal governmental structures; social stratification; and representational art. What forces brought together these factors and the people they served in large communities? What encouraged the particular form of complex social and economic organization characteristic of the city?

Ancient settlements become cities

Urbanism was no accident. It was clearly a preferred form of human community as populations increased and then sought the variety, stimulus, and security of large settlements. Urbanism has been more extensively studied in West Asia than in almost any other part of the world. This is partly due to the abundant and well-preserved evidence, the product of dry conditions and less-acidic soils, and partly the result of scholarly interest in studying what were thought to have been the world's first cities. The earliest West Asian cities were based on gathering and hunting as well as on the cultivation of domesticated crops by sedentary farmers. Hunting and gathering continued to supply needs after groups became sedentary. By around 6500 BCE, West Asian settlements such as Jericho in ancient Palestine, were large enough to be considered small cities. They initially served their hinterlands, the surrounding rural areas, as exchange centers for goods and services, culture, and ideology. In turn, the strategic control of the hinterland's resources was necessary for urban survival, giving rise to specialization, including urban elites and standing armies.

Jericho was an older, year-round settlement, dating back to as early as 9000 BCE, when the site was established as a sanctuary beside a spring for hunter-gatherers. Over the next millennium, their descendants made the transition from a wandering to a settled existence. By the eighth millennium BCE, Jericho had an estimated population of about 2,000. The community was surrounded by defensive and protective walls to which were attached such monumental architectural features as a heavy stone tower. Jericho seems to have been only incidentally a farming community. It perhaps drew its wealth from trade, the exchange of goods that traveled from the Red Sea to Anatolia. Around 7000 BCE, Jericho was abandoned and replaced by a more modest and straightforward farming community with houses and walls built of sun-dried mud brick, a material widely used throughout West Asia at this time. The decline and replacement of Jericho seem indicative of a pattern in West Asia. Like Jericho, there were many other settlements that appeared and declined, expanded and contracted, as cities eventually became more closely connected with the agricultural development of their hinterlands.

Agriculture and the development of urban life

The development of agriculture was important to the rise of most cities across the world, since agriculture supported the population growth that cities housed (see Chapter 2). Surplus food produced as a result of technological innovations in the intensive cultivation of plants or specialization in herding animals allowed people to settle in communities that grew in size and density and became cities. Reliable food supplies were essential to the emergence and survival of cities. The resources needed for expanding densely settled populations could be obtained by trade or by other means, such as war, as well as by integrating agricultural hinterlands with the concentration of population in an urban center.

The size of later cities reflected, in most cases, the agricultural potential of the immediately surrounding region. One of these cities, Çatalhöyük, in central Turkey, is an example of a complex urban society that developed without agriculture. By 5800 BCE, the city had a population estimated at between about 5,000 and 8,000 people settled in a thousand densely built houses surrounded by a well-watered plain. The houses were so crowded together that no streets or walkways existed. Instead people moved around

3.2 Cahokia Mounds.

on the rooftops and then gained access to living space below through crawl holes in the ceilings. The interior spaces were extremely clean and well maintained, although the community was surrounded by refuse areas and unhygienic accumulations of human and animal fecal remains. Yet people there maintained relatively healthy lives and exploited wild plants and animals. Unlike many early cities, the site of Çatalhöyük lacks any indication of a central authority and little if any social stratification. There is evidence from elaborate murals, clay figurines, and burials that the people of this community had constructed a complex religious and social life. A few houses are more elaborate with richer burials.

The activities associated with religious specialists were commonly found in cities. Other specialists were skilled laborers or artisans, some of whom passed on the valuable secrets of their trade through family or household relationships. At Çatalhöyük, for example, there was a specialized labor force producing stone implements and excellent woolen textiles, metal goods, and pottery for the marketplace. Like other city dwellers, specialists were dependent on their rural counterparts, who remained full-time food producers, and it is likely that trade and exchange sustained the community over its 1,000-year history.

Çatalhöyük's society and culture, taken together with that of the earlier and smaller Jericho, underlines the difficulty of making a unilinear connection between agriculture and the emergence of cities. The process of urbanization was a slow one of trial and error, complicated by environmental and other accidental factors. The interplay of environment, food supply, and the establishment of cities was a dynamic social process. No "first city" emerged in this or any part of the world during this earliest period, only many towns, each in its own way seeking to sustain a society that became more densely settled and complex. Some were successful and some were not; success, in some cases, meant building larger, even more complex urban systems and political orders. Elsewhere, success meant survival of

populations in smaller human communities and the disappearance of urban centers.

By about 5000 BCE, during the Ubaid period, a fully urban project was underway in southern Mesopotamia. Walled cities were so densely positioned along the region's waterways that they were in sight of each other. More than 80 percent of Sumerians lived in cities, which were characterized by a common layout of inner city (with a palace and residences), an outer city, and the harbor, a hub of commercial activities. Although this pattern of community contained an extremely large number of urban dwellers, only about one out of five persons living in Sumerian cities were specialists and not food producers. In other words, the vast majority of city dwellers were also engaged in agriculture.

Environmental factors and urban growth

Environmental factors also offer clues to the process by which some people established cities. Situated in the shifting environmental context of southern Mesopotamia, Sumer was an attractive area for settlement in the fifth and late fourth millennium BCE. Although rainfall was limited, the region's lands were made fertile by silt deposited by the Tigris and Euphrates Rivers. Established populations had cultivated the marshes for 1,000 years and developed small town settlements scattered along the Persian/Arabian gulf coast. Farming and irrigation techniques supported canals, dikes, and reservoirs that greatly increased agricultural production, which in turn attracted more people and created denser settlements. Uruk was one of several cities that emerged in Sumer following the climatic changes that occurred with the end of the Holocene and the onset of a dry period after about 3500 BCE, when its population reached about 50,000.

Ensuring a water supply became a major activity in Uruk. As the years of drying continued, major projects were undertaken to straighten and clean river courses and canals, which were cut away from the rivers to the fields in ever more complex patterns. Uruk provides an example of the complex relationships between environment and the emergence of cities. By 2800 BCE, the plains of Sumer were no longer profusely dotted with small settlements. Instead, there were lines of cities – Uruk, Lagash, Nippur, Kish – each with its hinterland of associated settlements that followed the lines of the rivers and main canals. These later cities used complex irrigation methods to adapt to the increasingly dry conditions and scarcity of food. Full-time urban specialists such as scribes, priests, and artisans were supported by rations of barley and other foods. The organization of these cities represented the communal strategies for coping with potential adversity through the collection and redistribution of agricultural surpluses. The hierarchical organization also confirms the essential aspects of urban growth: specialization and interactive engagement with a rural network.

NORTHEAST AFRICA   Northeast Africa (Egypt) was settled rather slowly, probably at first by peoples who moved in from areas in East-Central Africa, perhaps as early as 13,000 BCE. These peoples domesticated and raised barley and wheat in communities scattered along the Nile Valley. Arable land was found only along the narrow confines of the riverbanks. As in Sumer, with the climatic changes brought on by the end of the last glaciation, desiccation and changes in the Nile delta intensified the land problem in the Nile Valley. As people were forced on to smaller pieces of irrigable land near water sources, they were forced to live in denser settlements, which survived only by intensively exploiting resources and controlling their distribution. By the end of the fourth millennium BCE, whenever and wherever cities developed, the new urban forms were sustained by the relationships between those situated on the river and those in the hinterland of the earlier agricultural-herding communities. The formation of dynastic settlements appears to

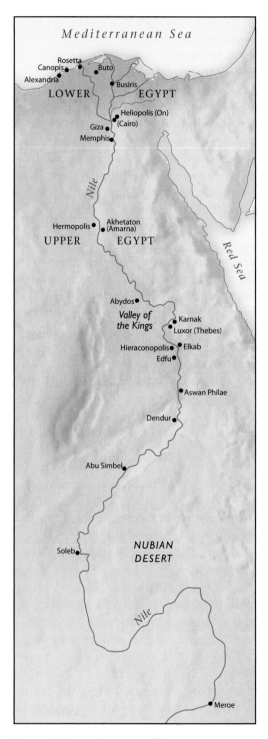

Map 3.2 Early cities of the Nile.

confirm the importance of the interrelationship between city, state, and the cosmos.

The settlement of Thebes in Upper Egypt and Memphis in the Lower Egypt delta were also the consequence of religious and political developments that centered on the remarkable environmental conditions of the Nile itself. One of the characteristic features of a city was monumental architecture. In Thebes, which succeeded Memphis as the capital of Egypt in about 2200 BCE, following the disintegration of the Old Kingdom, inscriptions, funerary monuments, and great buildings record the achievements of Theban rulers of the New Kingdom (ca. 1575–1085 BCE). These inscriptions, monuments, and buildings were also physical reminders to city residents of the spiritual or divine realms. As at Memphis, among the most impressive architectural achievements are those found in the necropolis. One mortuary temple consisted of a long, unroofed causeway leading to a court with a platform on which was a giant altar. To the rear of this was the temple proper; the burial chamber was hewn out of the rock of the cliff against which the temple abutted and was entered from a concealed place in the pavement of the temple floor.

Temples remained a key monumental feature of state ideology. The principal deity of Thebes was Amon-Ra, chief of the gods, and Egyptians sometimes referred to Thebes as "No-Amon," or "City of Amon." Sections of the city were devoted to lesser local gods. Initially, the necropolis, a vast city of temples and tombs along with the dwellings of priests, was on the west bank and the living city on the east bank of the Nile. As the city grew in size, eventually covering an area of eight square kilometers (three square miles), royal palaces and their accompaniments were added to the necropolis as individual rulers died and were reborn into the afterlife. The city of the dead stretched back from the western shore of the river as far as the desert hills. Each of the city's many temples collected its own community of living members, too; one of the oldest of these com-

munities was around the temple of Karnak. New temples were constantly being built, and a long series of royal tombs and funerary monuments extended far into the desert in the Valley of the Kings.

By the end of the fourth millennium BCE, responses to environmental factors had helped shape a stable agricultural society in the Nile Valley, based on irrigated farming in the natural floodplains and delta of the Nile. Variation in regional rainfall and the short- and long-term trends of Nile flooding required systematic responses. Community efforts to control water required the organization of labor, responses that reflected the growing complexity of activity in Egyptian cities. Supported by their agricultural hinterlands to the south, cities became centers of both exchange and a distinctive culture. Settlements were also loci for exercising power. Establishing successful agricultural systems and being able to predict Nile flooding became vital to effective religious and political leadership. One of the pharaoh's most important tasks was feeding the people. Famine and plenty were seen as indicative of a cosmic order, from the flooding of the Nile to the growth of vegetation and the increase of flocks. As settlements became more crowded, living space was expanded upward to city rooftops and sometimes to second stories. Traders traveled up and down the Nile, carrying on their transactions from boats that defined cities as land-based as well as floating hubs of activity. Never far from the Nile waters, the ancient Egyptians lived as part of an elaborate system that linked the river, land, and labor to a world of belief.

SOUTH ASIA   The earliest South Asian cities, like those of Sumer and the Nile, appeared in a river valley, the valley of the Indus, in the area that is now Pakistan. The Harappan culture of the Indus Valley flourished from around 2300 to around 1500 BCE. The Harappan culture emerged as a network of communities based on herding and the limited practice of grain cultivation, not unlike the Tigris-Euphrates region. Sites indicate numerous village communities of mud brick scattered along the Indus and its tributaries and along the shores of the Arabian Sea. The eventual appearance of large cities, some of which housed populations estimated at more than 35,000, suggests that the sort of desiccation that contributed to urbanization in Sumer and Egypt may also have been a factor in the development of urban settlements in the Indus Valley.

Mohenjo-Daro, the best-documented site, was located midway along the Indus River, and Harappa lay about 6,500 kilometers (4,000 miles) to the northeast on a tributary of the Indus. The annual inundation of the Indus Valley, along with simple irrigation techniques, made possible the settling of relatively large communities in the region by the third millennium BCE. Harappan cities were part of systems of local trade and economy linking rural producers to urban centers of occupational specialists. They also became centers of long-distance trade, establishing contacts with the Persian Gulf and Mesopotamia, Persia, Afghanistan, and areas to the south of the Indus River on the Indian subcontinent. The social and political complexity of urban life sometimes dictated the emergence of a government with bureaucracy and strict rules and laws, transforming the city into an ordered city-state.

Shortly after 1750 BCE, the character of this civilization was disrupted by a series of floods and the changing course of the river, which contributed to the depletion of resources. When the Indus River changed its course, the patterning of irrigation strategies was altered, destroying the food surplus, and commercial activity. Successive waves of migrations may have included squatters from neighboring villages, nomadic communities replacing the urban population, and crumbling walls replacing the glorious citadels. Other chariot-riding peoples laid claim to the remains of Harappan culture, bringing their semi-nomadic way of life, new languages, and vastly different ideas about food, social organization, and religion. These newcomers gradually settled the region in much smaller communities, including some that surrounded the other great river system of northern India, the Ganges. By the sixth century BCE, the Ganges Valley was the primary center of population, productivity, cities, and commerce in South Asia.

Cities as ceremonial and commercial centers

Many early cities were ceremonial or religious centers, as remarkable for their monumental structures as for the technology of city planning employed by the people who built them. Monumental architecture helped sustain knowledge of past rulers and their accomplishments for future generations, protecting the legitimacy of dynasties. Trade could be both a catalyst for urbanization and also its consequence. As regional systems of trade and exchange developed, they included larger concentrations of activity and settlement. Centers that were ceremonial might also lead to the growth of commercial activity serving large populations. In general, once material needs of large populations were being satisfied, one characteristic urban form that emerged was the ceremonial complex.

INDUS VALLEY   Indus cities were among those early centers boasting monumental architecture. Temple sites are found in each urban center, where worshipers gathered to conduct rituals. Water purification rites, still found in modern Indian culture, were an important part of ancient rituals, and evidence of public baths has been excavated. The urban societies of the Indus were literate. Their script, dated to about 2500 BCE, is unlike any early West Asian script and remains mostly undeciphered. As symbols of cosmic, social, and moral order, public ceremonial structures such as pyramids, mounds, and temples were centers of political, social, and sacred space. Staffed by priests in service to rulers, these monuments suggest the essential redistribution of resources embedded therein. Sustaining the economic relationships that supported elites relied on protecting the connections between an urban center and its agricultural hinterland. Religious practices often served as a symbolic means of redistributing resources, providing strategic access without resorting to the use of armies.

THE AMERICAS   Urban processes could be triggered by the attraction of large populations to sacred sites. One of the earliest cities in South America was Chavín de Huántar, located in the northern highlands of modern Peru from about 1000–1100 BCE. Substantial stone buildings, probably used for ceremonial or religious purposes, were erected on temple platforms. Outside the city center and surrounding its religious core were the inhabited dwellings, which were made of perishable materials. Here is where people traded and practiced their crafts. The specialists of Chavín produced a distinctive pottery: "Chavín" has become the name attached to culture associated with a style of pottery that portrayed snarling jaguars and birds of prey. Evidence indicates that there were contacts and trade between the people of Chavín and other pilgrimage sites that included the Mochica, Nazca, and Chimu coastal kingdoms and the highland empires of Tiahuanaco and Huari.

Along the coasts of and inland from the Gulf of Mexico are the important archaeological remains – monumental stone architecture and sculpture – from the urban society of the Olmec people (1500–400 BCE). As elsewhere in the Americas, buildings were primarily ceremonial in nature – temple-crowned pyramids facing vast plazas – and they were generally set outside the city sites. Evidence of irrigation systems that suggest reliance on an agricultural hinterland has been found, and both artifacts and the widespread influence of Olmec artistic style and motifs suggest that the Olmecs engaged in long-distance trade in raw materials such as shells, stone, and obsidian.

In the Valley of Mexico, Teotihuacán was a sacred ceremonial center founded around 100 BCE and lasted until around 750 CE, when the city was burned to the ground. Approximately 2,600 buildings have been excavated at its site not far from present-day Mexico City. Its earliest phases may be associated with a sacred cave shrine, which attracted a coalescence of small hamlets into a larger sacred center. The palaces, temples, apartment compounds, ceremonial plazas, and markets of Teotihuacán at its height were laid out in an orderly grid pattern, which was occupied by at least 100,000 city dwellers. Clan groups or guilds may have inhabited the uniform large apartment compounds organized around patios, each with its own drainage system. Quarters for priests and storehouses flanked the Pyramid of the Sun.

Life in the city of Teotihuacán was crowded and animated by the constant arrival of daily visitors. Brightly colored parrot and quetzal feathers, foods from rural fields, prisoners of war to be sacrificed in the urban capital – all manner of ordinary and exotic goods and peoples entered the city. The inner city's residents were mainly the wealthy elite and their servants who lived in luxurious dwellings that consisted of rooms around a common courtyard. Laborers and specialists lived on the outskirts of the city, but daily markets must have brought many of them to the city center for trade and exchange. Life inside the city probably also included many masked performers in splendid costumes. The mural art of these and other activities shows a rich vocabulary of images, masked figures, and deities. The laws of the city were embodiments of the natural order of the universe, as harsh and demanding, as it was a lush and bountiful paradise. Supporting a population of more than 100,000 meant that overcrowding, problems of sanitation, and poverty were ever-present.

Other classic Mayan (250–900 CE) cities include the southern sites of Tikal, Palenque, Copán, and Calakmul, in addition to a network of cities in the northern lowlands. Some sites are marked by pyramids or palaces, evidence of religious and ceremonial importance. Other sites used natural features (such as caves or hills) to command a presence. Carved stone slabs called "**stelae**" depict rulers and describe the accomplishments of war and trade. In the lowlands of the Yucatán peninsula, where the Maya (classic Maya fl. ca. 250–900 CE) were concentrated, there were around 50 cities, ceremonial centers for the practice of religious ritual on graduated-platform mounds. Tikal, one of the main Mayan cities, boasted a population of nearly 50,000. Mayan cities controlled outlying territories and extracted the resources of these areas to support the rich material life of the urban centers. Mayan cities vied for religious prestige as well as resources. The economy of the Maya was based on the cultivation of maize, and most of the urban population was supported by the labor of farmers. Other resources were gathered through coercion, and warfare conducted by shaman-kings had a distinctive ritual basis.

CHINA   The earliest cities in East Asia were also ceremonial centers. The rise of urbanism in China was directly related to the formation of early political orders, in particular the first dynastic state, the Shang (ca. 1600–1045 BCE). Shang kings based their political authority on their claim of descent from ancestors who were able to intercede with the central deity of Shang religion. Because political authority was legitimized by religion, the royal capital where the ruler lived was a sacred ceremonial center that embodied the close relationship between kingship and urbanism in early China. Shang rulers moved their capitals several times during the course of the dynasty, possibly in response to shifting defense needs or access to resources.

Like earlier Shang capitals, Anyang was a ceremonial center, including royal tombs containing evidence of human sacrifices as well as a rich material culture, such as bronze vessels, chariots, and jade. Near the modern city of Anyang on the north China plain lie the ruins of the late Shang capital, which was excavated in the early twentieth century. The "palace" itself, like other buildings at the Anyang complex, was made of daub-and-wattle (mud-and-thatch) construction on a pounded-earth foundation, creating a dirt floor that would become polished by use over time. Storage pits and drainage ditches fulfilled the practical needs of the concentrated population, many of whom lived in subterranean "pit" dwellings built into the ground. Social stratification was evident in the distinction between the nobility's ground-level dwellings with their pounded-earth floors and the four-meter-deep (13-foot-deep) pit dwellings of urban commoners, which resembled those of their social status who lived in the countryside.

The ability of a relative few – the Shang king and nobility – to claim the right to the fruits of labor of the many – farmers and producers – made possible the settlement of urban sites by allowing ruling elites to be fed and supported by the labor of those subject to their political control. Not only the evidence of rich material culture displayed in tomb artifacts, but also articles and foodstuffs that supported daily life, were produced by artisans and farmers, whose labor was controlled by a small elite.

After the unification of the empire in the third century BCE, the Chinese capital cities retained their earlier ceremonial functions. Imperial capitals and other urban sites were administrative and political centers rather than primarily centers of settlement, production, and trade. Sites were chosen using principles of **geomancy**: landscapes were selected with topographical properties believed to confer benefits on the residents of the city. In the imperial capital, the ruler's palace and other important buildings were built in a south-facing direction, to take advantage of the benevolent southern winds. Chang'an, the imperial capital during the Han (206 BCE–220 CE) and Tang (618–907 CE) dynasties, located in northwest China, was also the eastern terminus of the Silk Road. The city itself was laid out in a regular square, with thoroughfares running north–south and east–west, embodying symmetry and order as the imperial capital manifested the patterned order of the empire.

In the mid-eighth century CE, Chang'an was probably the largest city in the world, with a population of more than 1 million enclosed within the city walls and immediate suburban surroundings. As the terminus of the Silk Road, the city received goods from the great caravan route across Central Asia, which also carried Chinese silks and spices to other parts of the Eurasian continent. Thus Chang'an was both an imperial capital – a ceremonial political center – and a center of international trade. Beginning in the late Tang dynasty, towns and cities increasingly grew up as centers of commerce, but these commercial cities existed side by side with administrative towns that were walled enclaves of political authority. Impressive feats of urban planning, the cities of China reflected the stability of cultural influence and centralized political power.

Urbanization, conquest, and commercial growth

While cities sometimes emerged as commercial centers in response to the stimulus of external trade, the origins of other cities are found in local urban systems that slowly expanded over time. Slower evolutionary development of urban systems integrated a hierarchy of interlinked sites. The presence of established commercial networks attracted merchants, beckoned artisans, created patterns of urban growth, and sometimes invited conquest.

WEST AFRICA Evidence from the archaeological excavations of Jenné-Jeno, in modern-day Mali, confirmed an indigenous growth of urbanism in the western Sudan. Radiocarbon dates document the continuous settlement of Jenné-Jeno from before 250 BCE. In the early phases of the site, its inhabitants fished, hunted, used pottery, and had domesticated the cow. By the first century CE, they were cultivating African rice. About the same time, people began to build more permanent mud structures and the size of the settlement increased to an area of more than 10 hectares (approximately 25 acres); at the height

of the settlement (400–900 CE), Jenné-Jeno had spread to more than three times that size. Its population reached between 7000 and 10,000 inhabitants. Finds of pottery and terracotta sculpture, copper, iron slag, and gold indicate a rich material culture, craft specialization, and the involvement of the city in long-distance trade.

The early Jenné-Jeno was a commercial city without monumental architecture. A large wall, however, that measured about three meters (ten feet) across was built around the city. As was characteristic of West African urban wall-building traditions, the Jenné-Jeno wall was probably not built for defensive purposes. Jenné's walls served to define the settlement's identity and allow the city's elite to protect and tax the flow of goods, caravans, and people, thus sharing in common with other early cities the distinction between town and countryside. Sometime before the twelfth century, Islamic merchant clerics joined the trading caravans plying the Saharan trade. In Islamic West Africa, the need for protection of the long-distance trade routes connecting cities also led to the creation of military states, which grew powerful through their strategic access to resources. Eventually West African Islamic cities like Jenné acquired the defining urban feature – the mosque.

Like a number of other West African urban centers, Jenné-Jeno was located at the intersection of major trade routes. The city was an important collecting point for gold and other goods and was critical to the development of West African commercial relations. Like other centers of social, economic, and political complexity, Jenné-Jeno enjoyed a stable agricultural base. Farmers on the rich floodplains of the inland Niger delta produced a considerable surplus in rice, sorghum, and millet and produced these and other foodstuffs, such as smoked and dried fish, for trade. Well placed on the axis between the savanna and the region of the edge of the desert, called the Sahel, and situated at the highest point for reliable transport by canoe along the Niger River, Jenné played an important role in regional trade networks. This in turn made possible the rapid expansion of trade with Arabs in later centuries.

The example of Jenné-Jeno suggests that a city should be thought of together with its countryside. Indigenous trade and independent urban development effectively related to the city's relationship with its own hinterland in an integrated regional system. Archaeologists have surveyed a 100-square-kilometer (62-square-mile) area of Jenné-Jeno's rural hinterland and sampled some 42 contemporary sites. On the basis of their size and diversity, it is clear that these sites functioned in a hierarchical relationship to Jenné-Jeno, with Jenné-Jeno as their center and increasingly smaller settlements spaced at further distances as though along spokes on a wheel. Their patterning further supports the presence of a high degree of urbanism and an intraregional economy with Jenné-Jeno as its center point. Jenné-Jeno flourished not in isolation but within a rich and ancient urban system.

NORTH AMERICA   Complex agricultural systems and urban centers of trade comparable to those that developed in other world regions also appeared in North America in an area that is now the southeastern United States, between the Atlantic and the Great Plains, the Mississippi and Ohio Valleys, and the Gulf of Mexico. This is the area of the Mississippian culture, in which the largest cities emerged as attempts to integrate the region's economy.

Mississippian culture began developing before 700 CE and spanned the next 700 years. A pattern of cultivation of beans, corn, and squash similar to that of Mesoamerica made it possible for full-time agriculture to sustain an increasing population. The Mississippians – a general name for many different peoples and cultures scattered over thousands of square kilometers – lived on farms and in villages, towns, and cities. None can compare, however, with Cahokia, clearly the principal center of Mississippian culture, which was located in present-day southern Illinois just across the river from the modern city of Saint

Louis, Missouri. About 25,000 people lived in Cahokia at its peak around 1100 CE, and it was the focus of a much larger group of people who lived in the hamlets and villages that constituted its hinterland. With the increasing complexity of the urban center at Cahokia, these smaller hinterland settlements adapted to meet the demands of increasingly structured obligations and opportunities by altering their production of goods, provision of services, and participation in ceremonies that linked them ritually to the urban center. Urban development thus affected not only the people living in cities but also the people outside the cities.

Cahokia, like other Mississippian towns, was part of a trading network that stretched from Hudson Bay to the Gulf of Mexico and probably on into Mesoamerica, and from the Atlantic to the Rocky Mountains (see Chapter 6). Graves at Cahokia reveal the extent of the trade that centered there. In them, copper from Lake Superior, flints from the areas of Oklahoma and North Carolina, and many art objects from afar have been found. Cahokia covered almost 16 square kilometers (6 square miles) and was protected by a series of stockades and bastions. It contained more than 100 human-made earthen mounds, dominated by the largest earthen mound in North America, Monks Mound, the base of which covers six hectares (15 acres). Standing around 30 meters (100 feet) high, Monks Mound was one of the largest human-made structures in the Americas before the European conquest. Mounds, which were common to Mississippian towns, account for the description of the Mississippians as "Mound Builders." As in Mesoamerica and South America, the mounds were used for ritual and ceremonial purposes, as temple or burial mounds, but they also served a key economic role by visibly integrating the countryside. They were built with great effort of the most readily available local material: dirt, every grain of which was carried and put into place by humans. The Mississippian culture reached its peak sometime between 1200 and 1300 CE, after which its populations began to decline and cities were abandoned. The cause of Cahokia's demise is not fully understood, but regional competition for economic and political power led to the development of other centers.

MEDITERRANEAN CITIES Cities in the Mediterranean region also reflected the rise of complex political orders that integrated the commercial wealth of urban centers. Early urban development in the Mediterranean can be seen in Athens, where the remains of walls, early fortifications, pieces of a tower, and tomb, suggest a settlement as early as 1500 BCE. These remains indicate a small place of minor significance, a settlement primarily of local importance. The Greek poet Homer (ca. 800 BCE) made scant mention of Attica or the abrupt hill – the Acropolis – on which Athenians erected their earliest settlement. Eventually it was the city's role as the reserved precinct of the goddesses and gods of Attica that distinguished Athens as the urban center for the farmland and villages that made up its hinterland.

The most important festival in ancient Athens was the Panathenaia, the annual state festival honoring the city's patron deity, the goddess Athena Polias ("of the city"). Every four years the festival was celebrated on a grand scale, including musical competitions, recitations of Homer's epic poetry, gymnastic and equestrian contests, and a long, colorful procession through the city to the goddess Athena's shrine on the Acropolis. The culmination of this spectacle was the presentation of a peplos, a richly woven robe, to the cult statue of Athena. Spinning and weaving occupied most of women's time, even that of elite Athenian women.

The **agora**, or market, where everyone had a right to trade agricultural surplus or manufactured articles, was the focus of commercial life. No elites controlled the access to or distribution of valuable goods. The agora was a civic forum too, where, after worship and marketing, property owners might discuss common community issues – such as customs duties or the issues of government or war – in a sort of open-air town council. It

was accepted in Athens that decisions made in common were preferable to any made by a single person.

Small farmers were always of decisive importance to Athens, as they provided the connection between independent agrarian village life and urban society. As infantrymen they protected the city. Farmers went to the urban center on market days, for religious occasions, or to attend the town council. The first Athenians to abandon this pattern and become permanent residents in the city were artisans and craftspeople, blacksmiths, potters, weavers, and tanners. These skilled workers held both rural laborers and the urban poor in contempt. Between 750 and 550 BCE, the number of city dwellers swelled as the result of a population explosion, which lessened the already sparse amount of arable land in Attica. Increasing urbanization led to expanding trade beyond the city as well as increasing complexity and inequalities within it.

Athenians looked to the sea. Trade and entrepreneurship resulted in overseas connections and expansion. Commerce and values associated with commerce became triumphant. Merchants who traded across the Mediterranean made enormous fortunes, and by the fifth century BCE, numerous commercial middlemen had begun to share in the profits of that trade. Athens began to develop specialties and, as it did so, to import much of its raw materials and food: two-thirds of the grain consumed by Athenians was imported from beyond the city's borders. Early city planners recognized that the success of the complex public and political functions of Athens, a city-state with its distinctive participatory government, relied on limiting the population growth or expanding beyond its borders. The Greek city-state was called a *polis*, the origin of the word "politics."

GREEK CITY-STATES Ancient cities in Southwest Asia and the Mediterranean sometimes became political centers and none was more characteristic of this conceptualization of centrality than Delphi, located at the ancient place of

PRIMARY SOURCE: THEOGNIS ON TYRANNY AND SOCIAL DISCORD

The Greek poet Theognis of Megara (fl. ca. sixth century BCE) wrote poetry that addressed the fierce politics of life in his city-state, a contentious zone for ethical and civic development in the ancient world. An aristocrat, Theognis was concerned with social hierarchy and economic changes that pitted the rich against the poor and brought individual desires and collective good into conflict. This poem is addressed to Kyrnos, son of Polypais, a wealthy citizen. Kyrnos also means "illegitimate."

> Kyrnos, this city is pregnant, and I fear she may bear a man
> Who will correct our wicked presumption [hybris].
> For even if her citizens are still prudent, her leaders
> Have descended to great wickedness.
> Good men, Kyrnos, have not yet destroyed a city;
> But when it pleases the base to be insolent
> And they corrupt the people and give judgment in favor of the unjust
> For the sake of their own gains and advancement,
> Do not hope that that city will remain untroubled.
> Not even if it now lies in great tranquility,
> When these things become dear to base men,
> Gains which bring with them public misfortune.
> For from such come discords and kindred murder
> And sole rulers [mounarchoi]; may they never be pleasing to this city!

Source: Matthew Dillon and Lynda Gailand, *Ancient Greece: Social and Historical Documents from Archaic Times to the Death of Socrates.* (London and New York: Routledge, 2010), p46.

omphalos, the name of which meant literally the navel of the cosmos. It is the place where Zeus released two eagles to fly in opposite directions. They eventually circled the Earth and met again on the actual spot of Delphi. A community established as early as the eleventh–ninth centuries BCE, Delphi became a sanctuary and the site of an oracle by the eighth century BCE. Many cities in ancient Greece set their sights on colonization as a means of expansion. As a consequence of their having developed laws and bureaucracies, they expanded into city-states. Any overseas colonization required approval from the Delphic Apollo. Like Olympia, Delphi was also a location

of Pan-Hellenic Games, which included contests in poetry, athletics, music, and equestrian events. The city was a site for political display and for other cities to show off their spoils of war. These included the monument commemorating victory in the Greek–Persian wars of 480–479 BCE. The victory monument was a giant bronze column with serpent coils and snakeheads topped by a golden cauldron. Inscribed were the names of the 31 (out of 700) Greek cities that had fought against the Persians.

ROME   Rome was another Mediterranean city that claimed imperial origins in the story of its growth from the eighth century BCE. From early beginnings as a pastoral community to a string of palisade hill forts, the urban center eventually claimed dominance over the culture and politics of the entire Mediterranean region. A legendary series of stone walls, bridges, and aqueducts were built as the community gradually grew in size. Pliny referred to the Roman sewers as "the most noteworthy things of all." The water system flushed water through its sewers and served public baths and latrines that had bench-like seats. The complex water supply system had both cultural and political meanings. Situated in a strategic location on the Tiber River, Rome was called by some a Greek city in the fourth century BCE, but only a few centuries later came to conquer Macedonia and eventually Carthage.

SOUTH ASIA Greeks may have been aware of flourishing cities as far away as the South Asian subcontinent. In 331 BCE, Alexander the Great defeated the main Persian army, eventually turning his attention to the Indian subcontinent. A fourth-century BCE account by the Greek Megasthenes (ca. 350–290 BCE) describes the city of Pataliputra, a political and economic center strategically located along the Ganges River trade route. Pataliputra was the capital of the Mauryan empire founded by Chandragupta Maurya in 322 BCE. At the time Megasthenes' account was written and for perhaps two centuries afterward, Pataliputra was probably the largest, most sophisticated city in the world, with as many as 300,000 inhabitants. Surrounded by large wooden walls with 570 towers and 64 gates, Pataliputra was the center of a wealthy, highly organized economic system that included farms, granaries, textile industries, and shipyards that built ships for seaborne trade. Pataliputra was also the seat of a famous university and library, along with palaces, temples, gardens, and parks.

Several centuries later, in the third century CE, the city of Madurai, capital of a southern Indian state, flourished as a cultural, economic, religious, and political center. Like other south Indian cities

of the time, Madurai was enriched by maritime trade, largely with Southeast Asia, and dominated by a temple complex. As described in the introduction to this chapter, Madurai displayed the social, economic, and cultural complexity characteristic of other cities found throughout the world in the first centuries CE.

Urban culture on the Indian subcontinent was greatly affected by repeated conquests. Traditional Indian cities of all sizes had two focuses: the palace and the temple. The homes of the urban poor were humble huts of wood, reed, and mud brick, thatched with straw. Many urban poor had no shelter and slept in the open in the city. Large, open areas that featured trees and expanses of water – lakes, pools, and basins – often surrounded temples and palaces. Fortified cities were encircled by moats, some of which contained earthworks covered with spiny shrubs, and by high walls with numerous towers and balconies for defending troops.

THE ISLAMIC WORLD The vast interactive sphere of the Islamic world depended on the existence of large cities, which served as centers for faith and commercial activity. The flourishing trade in turn often relied on conquest for its expansion. The ancient Hindu city of Delhi was the site of Muslim invasions between 1000 and 1200 CE and became a capital during the Muslim sultanate (1206–1526). One of the most noticeable alterations of the city was the destruction of Hindu temples, the materials of which were used to build the mosque and the citadel. Buddhist monasteries and nunneries on the northwest frontier of India also became the target of the politically ambitious sultans between the thirteenth and sixteenth centuries.

Not only on the South Asian subcontinent, but elsewhere in Eurasia and Africa, the creation of Muslim empires led to the growth of large cities. The complexities and demands of urban life gave direction and impetus to long-distance trade that served the populations of Islamic cities. The great Islamic cities such as Baghdad or Constantinople were centers of trade and manufacturing. Surrounding the stable urban population of merchants, shopkeepers, and craftsmen was a larger population of unskilled workers, peddlers, street cleaners, and the semi-employed, a stratum that included a large proportion of rural immigrants. Market gardens were situated on the outskirts of the cities and attracted a fluctuating labor force from the countryside.

The structure of Islamic cities reflected economic and other roles: trade and manufacturing, religion and scholarship, government and justice. Two or more complexes of major buildings were part of every Islamic city. One complex was the main mosque, surrounded by the chief courts, schools of higher learning, shops that sold objects of piety, and possibly the shrine of a saint identified with the life of the city. Another complex included the central marketplace (the main point of exchange), offices of money-changers, storehouses, and shops that sold locally made or imported goods. A third complex might be government offices. The power of government was present in everyday urban life (as watchmen, market supervisors, and police), but it was expressed as well in large and sometimes ostentatious public buildings.

Wealthy traders, merchants, and craftsmen resided near their buildings, and scholars and religious leaders near theirs, but most of the urban population lived outside the center in quarters that were a tangle of small streets and cul-de-sacs. Each quarter had its mosque (or shrine or church or synagogue), local market, and public baths. The tendency was for each quarter to house specific religious or ethnic groups. Farthest from the center, near or beyond the walls of the city, were the poorer quarters of rural immigrants and the workshops of noisy or malodorous crafts (such as tanning or butchering). Also outside the city walls were cemeteries.

Non-Muslims in Islamic cities were set apart from the families of believers. They paid a special tax (*jizya*), and Islamic law required that they show signs of their difference by dressing in special ways and avoiding colors (especially green)

associated with Islam. They were prohibited from carrying weapons or riding horses (much as native populations in Spanish America were) and could not build new places of worship or repair pre-Islamic ones without permission. Laws about marriage were strictly enforced: non-Muslims could not marry or inherit from Muslims. And though Christians or Jews might occupy positions of importance in certain economic activities, such as the arts, they were virtually excluded from others, such as food preparation.

While all Islamic cities shared a commercial role, some originated as imperial administrative centers. Baghdad was founded from about 750 CE, as the capital of the Islamic Abbasid Empire and the home of the caliph ("successor" of Muhammad). For more than five centuries, the city was a world center of education and culture. Under Abbasid rule, Baghdad became a city of museums, hospitals, libraries, mosques, and baths:

> The baths in the city cannot be counted, but one of the town's sheikhs told us that, in the eastern and western parts together, there are about two thousand. Most of them are faced with bitumen, so that the beholder might conceive them to be of black, polished marble; and almost all the baths of these parts are of this type because of the large amount of bitumen they have . . . The ordinary mosques in both the eastern and the western parts cannot be estimated, much less counted. The colleges are about thirty, and all in the eastern part; and there is not one of them that does not outdo the finest palace. The greatest and most famous of them is the Nizamiya, which was built by Nizam Al-Mulk and restored in 504 AH (the Islamic calendar, 1110–11 CE). These colleges have large endowments and tied properties that give sustenance to the faqihs who teach in them, and are dispensed on the scholars.
>
> Source: R.J.C. Broadhurst, Ibn Jubayr, *The Travels of Ibn Jubayr, 1184* (London: Cape, 1952)

The rise and decline of empires had an impact on the fortunes of cities. Constantinople was the capital city of the Byzantine Empire after the fall of the Roman Empire. It was also the western terminus of the Silk Road, and in 1453 it became Istanbul, the capital of the Ottoman Empire. Baghdad was conquered and destroyed by the Mongols in 1258. The new rulers established the Il-Khan Empire in Persia and Iraq with its new capital at Tabriz in northern Persia. Baghdad was reduced to a secondary city in the new Mongol empire and its role as the leading city of the Muslim world was overtaken by Cairo, where the caliphate was restored and through which most trade then passed from the Mediterranean to the Indian Ocean.

As noted by Ibn Battuta in the fourteenth century, Cairo was a lively, prosperous city. Called by some the "mother [city] of the world," Cairo flourished in the thirteenth, fourteenth, and even early fifteenth centuries, though its population peaked at half a million in the first half of the fourteenth century. Well before Cairo's elevation to its key role in east–west trade during the thirteenth century, prosperous merchants were part of a vital commercial life in the city. Like Constantinople or Istanbul, the capital of the Ottoman empire and a city as large as any in Europe, Cairo's importance increased as a result of Muslim conquest. By the fourteenth century, when the Ottomans gained control of Egypt, Cairo had become a major world city with 250,000 inhabitants. Its population would climb to an estimated 300,000 by the end of the seventeenth century, when it continued to be a major center of trade and cultural exchange among Africa, West Asia, and Europe.

Later expansion of commercial cities

In 1000 CE, Europe's population was approximately the same as it had been during the heyday of imperial Rome, a millennium earlier, approx-

imately 36 million. During the twelfth and thirteenth centuries, the population rose rapidly as a result of expanded cultivation of marginal lands and technological innovation, reaching about 80 million. But the demographic climb in most cities was also punctuated by periods of disease and decline. The Black Death, as it came to be known, devastatingly reduced populations across Eurasia as it spread rapidly through large cities. The disease probably erupted from the Yunnan region of southwestern China and was spread first through the military incursions of the Mongols and later through Afro-Eurasian trade routes. In the Hebei Province (near the modern city of Beijing) about 90 percent of the population died. The plague affected vast areas across pre-modern Eurasia. In Europe, where the plague killed an estimated 25 million people, or as much as half the population, numbers continued to decline until about 1400 CE.

Not only disease, but also hunger plagued the poor in cities. Compared to the grandeur and luxury of some Islamic and South Asian cities, early Paris had suffered the growing pains of many expanding population centers. Sometime before the fourth century BCE, the settlement of Paris was established on an island in the Seine much smaller than the present Ile de la Cité, both a central and a defensible location. From this location, its people navigated the lower course of the Seine and perhaps reached the coast of Britain. As Paris expanded its river commerce and grew in wealth, it also became a religious center. Romans built a temple to Jupiter there, and subsequently Christians located one of their earliest north European bishops there, probably in the third century CE. By becoming the seat of a bishop, Paris, as Christians reckoned it, became a city. It took another 1,000 years for it to become a major urban center – of secular government, commerce, industry, and culture.

The divisions between countryside and urban life were often blurred. Streets were muddy pastureland where sheep and pigs grazed on grass and garbage. A twelfth-century CE Parisian "traffic jam" caused a pig to run between the legs of a horse, upsetting his rider, the heir to the royal throne. Individual households sometimes had gardens and vineyards (on the other side of town walls) to supplement the availability and offset the high cost of foods. Still, there were many poor and many hungry. Even the wealthy Parisian could not escape the unpleasantness and pollution that was the consequence of an increasing urban population.

The concentration of specialists such as leatherworkers, metalworkers, weavers, and other craftsmen, who flocked to cities to produce and sell their wares in the great city markets contributed to a significant decline in the quality of water and hygiene, even as it helped develop the city's trade and economy. The city government in Paris faced enormous problems and complaints about activities it tried to regulate and control. Blood and carcasses from slaughterhouses and the urine, alkalines, and salts used in tanneries, waste products from smelting, choking smoke from the burning of coal and other fuels, noisy industrial activities – all created undesirable living conditions for city residents. Disease and vermin, such as rats, were rampant. Filth was everywhere a condition of

urban existence. Public baths – in contrast to Baghdad, there were only 32 in all of Paris in 1268 CE – were eventually banned by the Church because of their noted contribution to rampant promiscuity. By the time of the plague, the urban concentration in Paris was especially vulnerable to the spread of disease, which likely killed about one-third of its inhabitants in a single year. Ties between cities and their surrounding countryside remained close, especially where, as in Italy and the Netherlands, cities were numerous, and the balance of power and dominance slowly shifted from the countryside to the city, from the land to the markets increasingly linked to maritime worlds.

Despite major setbacks like plagues, epidemics, and famines, by 1500 CE, the world population had reached roughly 450 million. These levels would double in the following 300 years – meaning that the planet would be home to about 900 million humans in 1800 CE. Shifting demographic centers brought new cities into being, rebuilt and enlarged others, and left obsolete locales abandoned on the margins of the new maritime power. The globalization of trade from about 1500 CE would also bring about commercial and technological changes that had their most powerful

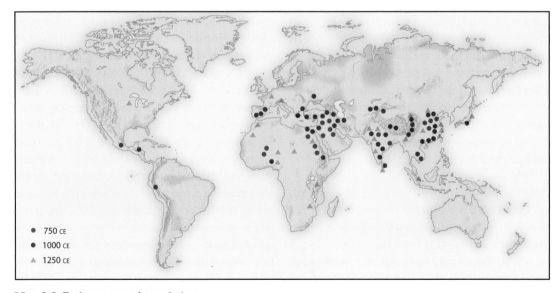

750 CE
1000 CE
1250 CE

Map 3.3 Early centres of population.

impact in cities. As centers of population, production, and consumption of material goods, cities were sites of transformation.

Cities and population growth

Both the size and scale of cities have changed dramatically over time. With a population estimated at more than 450,000 in 100 CE, Rome was once the largest city on the planet. More than 1,000 years later, its size was surpassed by other great cities of Eurasia, including Beijing. Today more than 4 million tourists visit the city of Rome annually, suggesting its legacy may outweigh its contemporary importance. Urbanization led to significantly larger concentrations of population and a proliferation of human achievements. Cities also became the focus for questioning the global impact of population growth. After all, cities have absorbed two-thirds of the world's population growth since the mid-twentieth century. The increased rates of population growth themselves have long drawn public scrutiny. The effect of human population growth has been debated at least since the eighteenth century. Thomas Malthus, in his influential *Essay on Population* (1798), expressed the belief that population grew at a rate exceeding that of resources; this theory led many to conclude that surplus population means too many people and not enough resources. Others attributed the perception of overpopulation to the inequitable division of resources in society. Nineteenth-century capitalists, in contrast, welcomed increased numbers of laborers and consumers, who created the expanded markets necessary for capitalist industrial growth.

Tremendous postwar population increases were noted with alarm by many in the twentieth century, including the biologist Paul Ehrlich, who described the "problem" of growth in his book *The Population Bomb* (1968), at a time when there were 3.5 billion human beings, five times the population of Malthus's world. More than 90 percent of the current population growth occurs in the poorest countries of the world, and a billion of the current 6.6 billion inhabitants of the world, the "bottom billion," live in poverty, a fact that suggests that a large part of the crisis at the crossroads is political and economic.

This global crisis has altered the character of world cities, which now house about half the world's population. Urban slums have become home to more than one billion people, who live in dangerous and crowded conditions. What it means to be a world city today (controlling capital and information flows) may not hold true in the next generation.

Summary

This chapter has provided examples of the transition from early settled communities to urban centers beginning as early as the sixth millennium BCE. Some, like Memphis, which became Cairo, have survived the millennia, while others have declined and disappeared. The early cities were concentrations of increasingly diverse and highly stratified populations. Many originated as or became ceremonial centers, drawing large numbers of people to participate in rituals that were believed to propitiate deities, to encourage good agricultural harvests, or to request the support of the gods in war against their enemies.

Cities, since their origin, existed on a continuum of urban–rural relationships. Gradually they transcended their original primary functions. They were the centers from which ideology, institutions, material goods, and other urban "products" were transmitted to their hinterlands, on which they in turn depended. Such systems were also recipients of goods, peoples, and ideas from areas beyond their radii. The degree of urbanism in any part of the world was dependent on the ability of each large community to maintain an integrative system between itself and its hinterland. Though cities flourished around the world, most people still did not live in cities before the nineteenth century; most did, however, live in intricate relationship with them, visiting them, trading with them, and supporting them with food and other necessary and valued goods and services. The commercial revolution and global industrialization resulted in the further pull of populations towards urban centers in the past few centuries.

Wherever urban systems appeared, they had common characteristics. Urban society became more complex. It involved larger numbers of people and greater management and control of resources and environments, resulting in a wider variety of economic activity and a more rigid structuring and organization of the city's inhabitants. In addition to more opportunities and the availability of more goods and services, urban life often meant the intensification of inequality and rigid divisions along lines of class, status, and gender. The systems of authority and relationships of inequality found in urban settings grew out of earlier patterns of larger social groupings and evolved to suit the conditions of urban life: complex and large communities of varied, interdependent parts required the mechanisms of control and centralized decision-making to negotiate these differences. For example, gender differences and relations became more clearly defined. Even in early agricultural communities, male dominance was more accentuated than it had been in gathering-hunting societies, an accentuation that was powerfully confirmed and perpetuated in urban societies. Sometimes male gods were credited with the growth of cities, and male warriors and rulers protected the trade routes that connected cities with their supporting hinterlands. Increasingly the specialist occupations found in cities (including the activities of metalworkers, tanners, scribes, and priests) were reserved for men.

As later cities became centers for capital accumulation, they also wielded political power and furthered divisions based on gender and class. A combination of ecological factors, the mobility of elites, logistical considerations, and ideological considerations both constrained and encouraged the directions of urban growth around the world. Overcrowded and polluted cities would become sites of instability and tremendous social and economic change. Only today do more people live in cities than in rural areas for the first time in human history.

It is impossible to understand the historical rise of urbanism without taking into account the functional relationship between the urban center and its surrounding area. The process of successful integration of city and countryside, of constructing a larger political or community identity from increasingly diverse and divergent parts, while supporting specialists, including political elites, who build exploitative relations in a hierarchical fashion – is common to all the urban societies described in this chapter. These connections are explored further in Part III. Cities remain a constant throughout history after their appearance in the sixth millennium BCE, and both cultural and historical circumstances determine the changing nature of cities and their variety.

Today, in the twenty-first century, the process of urbanization is escalating, with the sharpest growth in cities in less-developed parts of the world. In 1950, fewer than 30 percent of the world's people lived in cities; now at the beginning of the twenty-first century, more than half do, and the number is steadily increasing. Tokyo is currently the only world city with a population of more than 20 million, but it likely will be joined by Mumbai, Lagos, Shanghai, Jakarta, São Paulo, and Karachi, with Beijing, Dhaka, and Mexico City close behind. By the year 2025, it is estimated that more than two-thirds of the world's population will be city dwellers, making the urban experience one of the few truly common denominators among humankind.

Suggested readings

Allchin, F.R. (1995) *The Archaeology of Early South Asia: The Emergence of Cities and States*, Cambridge:

Cambridge University Press. Useful source on South Asian urbanism.

Balter, Michael (2006) *The Goddess and the Bull, Çatalhöyük: An Archaeological Journey to the Dawn of Civilization*, Walnut Creek, CA: Left Coast Press. Highly readable case study of how archaeologists study how and why people settled down in the first cities.

Chandler, Tertius (1987) *Four Thousand Years of Urban Growth: An Historical Census*, Lewiston, NY: St David's University Press. Identifies the top ten cities at different points in history.

Cipolla, Carlo M. (1967) *The Economic History of World Population*, Harmondsworth: Penguin. Brief, stimulating view of demographic and economic development tracing the history of the great trends in population and wealth that have affected global societies as a whole.

McEvedy, Colin and Richard Jones (1978) *Atlas of World Population*, London: Allan Lane/Penguin. Fully illustrated (with graphs, maps, and diagrams) history of world demography.

McIntosh, Roderick J. (2005) *Ancient Middle Niger: Urbanism and the Self-organizing Landscape*, Cambridge: Cambridge University Press. Summarizes key research on early West African urbanism at one site, exploring concepts of settlement hierarchy in a global context.

Morris, A.E.J. (1994) *History of Urban Form: Before the Industrial Revolution*, New York: Longman Scientific and Technical. Third edition of the classic introduction to the historical evolution of cities.

Roberts, Allen F., et al. (2003) *A Saint in the City: Sufi Arts of Urban Senegal*, Los Angeles: University of California, Fowler Museum. Places the visual culture of urban Senegal in the longer history of Islamic arts in Africa

UN-Habitat (2003) *The Challenge of the Slums: Global Report on Human Settlements*, London: United Nations. United Nations study on twenty-first century trends in urban poverty.

Whitfield, Peter (2005) *Cities of the World: A History in Maps*, Berkeley, CA: University of California Press. An illustrated overview of more than 60 world cities.

Online resources

Annenberg/CPB, *Bridging World History* (2004) <www.learner.org/channel/courses/worldhistory> Multimedia project with interactive website and videos on demand; see especially Unit 4 Agricultural and Urban Origins.

Hodder, Ian, *Çatalhöyük Research Project* (2007) <www.catalhoyuk.com> The official site of the ongoing excavations of the Neolithic village in Anatolia

UNESCO, *World Heritage Site* (2007) <whc.unesco.org/en/list> Documents the most valuable of known sites, including the remains of most early cities and their monuments and other symbols of cultural heritage.

Waugh, Daniel, *Silk Road Seattle Project* (Simpson Center for the Humanities, University of Washington) (2007) <depts.washington.edu/silkroad/cities/cities.html> Cities along the Silk Road.

Wentworth-Rinne, Katherine, *Aquae Urbis Romae: The Waters of the City of Rome* (2007) <www3.iath.virginia.edu/waters/first.html> A cartographic series that traces the importance of water in the history of this city and the changes in the water infrastructure over time.

Study questions

1. What are the features of an ancient city? How do they differ from those of a modern city?
2. How were agricultural developments related to the growth of urbanism?
3. What were the causes and consequences of population increases?
4. What was the role of trade and exchange at Çatalhöyük and other settlements?
5. What was the impact of the environment on cities?
6. Why do cities begin to have an impact on state development?
7. Describe the kinds of evidence historians use to understand cities as either commercial or ceremonial centers.
8. Classify the following early sites of urbanization as ceremonial or commercial centers: Chauvin de Huantar, Nile Valley, China, Jenné-Jeno, Athens, Mohenjo Daro, and Çatalhöyük.
9. Compare the rise of urbanism in West Africa and the Mediterranean. How does the need for social and political order in complex societies also have the potential to create inequalities?

10. What does the Greek poet Theognis of Megara think about the social and political hierarchies of his world? What experiences might have shaped his views?

11. Compare the importance of economic, religious, and administrative functions in early Islamic cities.

12. What are the reasons for an increasing reliance of urban centers on trade?

13. Why might most world populations have declined to live in ancient cities?

3500 BCE	3200 BCE	2570 BCE	2300 BCE	2000 BCE	1900 BCE	1750 BCE	1500 BCE
Uruk and other urban centers begin to flourish in Mesopotamia	Hieroglyphics used in inscriptions	First of great pyramids built at Giza	Sargon I rules Akkadian Empire	Indus Valley civilization flourishes	Palace at Knossos built	Code of Hammurabi	Indo-European migrations into Indus Valley

4 Ideas and power

Goddesses, kings, and sages

In the mid-seventh century BCE, the ancient city of Thebes was the religious center of the unified realm of Upper and Lower Egypt. The founder of the 26th dynasty, King Psammetichus I, ruled from the dynastic capital of Saïs in the western Nile delta. But in order to consolidate his rule, he needed to gain the support of the religious leaders in Thebes, so the king sent his eldest daughter, Nitocris, to join the powerful sisterhood of attendants of the Theban god Amun. Her father negotiated a position for Nitocris within this sisterhood that placed her in direct succession to the highest position as God's Wife of Amun. An extraordinary stone pillar carved at the time records this event in 656 BCE:

> I have given to him [the god Amun] my daughter to be a god's wife and have endowed her better than those who were before her. Surely he will be gratified with her worship and protect the land of him who gave her to him . . . [The god's wife departs from the king's apartment.] Her attendants about her were many in number . . . They set

forth happily to the quay in order to head southwards to the Theban nome [administrative district]. The ships about her were in great numbers . . . all being laden up to their gunwales with every good thing of the palace . . . Putting to land at the quay of the city of the gods Thebes. Her front hawser was taken, and she found Thebes with throngs of men and crowds of women standing and jubilating to meet her . . . Now after she came to the god's wife Shepenwepe, the latter saw her and was pleased with her.

> Source: Gay Robins, *Women in Ancient Egypt* (London: British Museum Press, 1993), pp154–55

A fleet of richly outfitted vessels escorted Nitocris to Thebes, and she brought with her a huge dowry of lands and other goods, recorded in detail on the pillar inscription. Although we do not know when Nitocris ascended to the position of God's Wife, she died in 586 BCE, so she must have been very young when her father sent her to Thebes. Nitocris's eventual position as God's Wife ensured

1375 BCE	1200 BCE	1200 BCE	1045 BCE	753 BCE	550 BCE	515 BCE	500 BCE
Amenhotep IV adopts name of Akhenaten and introduces monotheistic religion of sun god Aten in Egypt	Maya establish themselves in Yucatan and Central America	Life of Zoroaster?	Zhou conquest of Shang in China	Traditional founding of Rome by Romulus	Founding of Persian Achaemenid Empire under Cyrus	Building of Second Temple in Jerusalem	Lifetimes of Mahavira, Buddha, and Confucius

for her father the support of the Theban priesthood, and thus secured his political authority over Upper and Lower Egypt. The institution of God's Wife provides vivid testimony to the inseparability of the spheres of politics and religion in the ancient world.

Shared beliefs in gods and goddesses created the basis for a common identity among early peoples, but these beliefs could also sanction political authority when rulers claimed powers conferred on them through special relationships to gods or goddesses. Whether male or female,

4.1 Male and female figures carved on wall in Luxor (Thebes), Egypt.

human consorts acted as liaisons between gods and goddesses and the human community. The relationship between gods and humans was central to the development of religion throughout the world. How did people in increasingly complex societies around the world understand and interpret their place in the cosmos? How did religion help to construct, and to make sense of, the social and political worlds people inhabited?

Introduction to the theme of ideas and power

The expansion of human communities both by growth in numbers and by the concentration of the population in cities, shown in Chapter 3, brought about changes in the scale and complexity of society. As populations increased, competition for resources transformed how communities related to their gods and how people related to each other. In response to these changes, early community-centered religions either adapted or were forced to give way to new ideas. When military leaders sought to strengthen their control over expanding territories, they often bolstered their authority by claiming to have powers conferred on them by gods or goddesses: they became god-kings. Gods and goddesses were thus seen not only as creators of the cosmos, but also as partners or progenitors of human rulers. Seeking the protection of deities through rituals and sacrifice to ensure the fertility of fields or success in war, people began to venerate rulers as god-kings.

Over time, challenges to the authority of god-kings and the priesthoods that supported their

399 BCE	331 BCE	250 BCE	221 BCE	100 BCE	100 CE	410 CE
Death of Socrates	Founding of Alexandria by Alexander the Great	Height of Ashoka's reign in Mauryan Empire	First unification of China under the Qin state	Teotihuacán becomes dominant city in highlands of Central America	Height of Roman and Han Empires	Sack of Rome by Visigoths

rule arose from prophets and reformers who proposed new conceptions of spirituality and new forms of religious practice. Some rulers of empires were able to harness the religious movements that grew from these challenges and use them to expand their power. Other imperial rulers saw these new religions as threats and tried to suppress them, sometimes successfully and sometimes not. In this chapter we will explore the variety of gods, goddesses, and god-kings that emerged around the globe, and the challenges that arose both from new religions and from new ideas as sources of political authority. Ideas and power were closely intertwined in the ancient world.

From goddesses and gods to god-kings

The transformation from community-based worship of cosmic gods and goddesses to the veneration of urban deities tied to rulers of city-states took place earliest in ancient West Asia. Variations on this theme can be seen in North Africa (Egypt), East Asia (China), and Mesoamerica (Teotihuacán and Maya), where pharaohs and kings also sought the sanction of gods and goddesses to rule. As rulers enlarged their territories and expanded the scope of their political authority to vast empires, the powers of their gods and goddesses also spread across cultural and geographic boundaries and were transformed.

West Asia: Urban goddesses and gods of empire

In West Asia during the mid-fourth through the mid-third millennia BCE, the concentration and expansion of military power in the region of Mesopotamia ("between the two rivers") led to the formation of a series of dynastic states (in which rule was inherited through families) in the watershed of the Tigris and Euphrates Rivers in modern Iraq. The foundation of these lay in the southern Mesopotamian region of Sumer, where city-states provided the earliest forms of political organization enabling the exploitation of economic resources through military control. The transition from urban center to territorial (or dynastic) state was closely tied to religious ideas and practices. In the early urban centers of West Asia, residents chose one of their members to become the consort of the city god or goddess.

The goddess Inanna first appears in the late fourth millennium BCE as the tutelary deity of Uruk, one of the most important urban centers in Sumer. She was the deity of the city's central storehouse, suggesting the connection between the rise of urban life dependent on the storage of food and the protection of those resources. Like other deities in the region, she had a human consort, a priest-king who ruled through the favor of the goddess. By the mid-second millennium BCE, Inanna had merged with her northern Mesopotamian counterpart, Ishtar, the tutelary deity of the city-state of Akkad, and exhibited a multifaceted, androgynous character. Already by the third millennium BCE, the central Sumerian city of Nippur seems to have acquired a uniquely sacred status, thus elevating its city deity, the warrior god Enlil, to a position of dominance over other gods. Later conquerors claimed to rule with the sanction of Enlil.

Although both Sumerian and Akkadian settlements coexisted in the watershed of the Tigris and Euphrates during the third millennium BCE, it was the Akkadians who began to con-centrate political authority and to create the first unified empire in this region. In the late third millennium BCE, Sargon I (ca. 2334–2279 BCE.) brought the region of Sumer under his control and claimed power over a territory that stretched from the Mediterranean to the Persian Gulf. The Akkadians depended on military force to control and redistribute resources and on writing as

PRIMARY SOURCE: THE CODE OF HAMMURABI (ca. 1750 BCE)

The Code of Hammurabi is a collection of case law, consisting of decisions handed down by Hammurabi that could be used as precedents for other cases. These cases reveal much about Babylonian life, such as a belief in sorcery, ideas of female chastity, contractual obligations, the principle of reciprocity in punishment, and fair repayment for services and restitution for property (including family members, servants, and slaves, as well as material property). The prologue to the Code invokes the god Marduk and his lineage of cosmic deities as sanction for the rule of Hammurabi the lawgiver.

When the lofty Anu,[1] king of the Anunnaki,[2] and Enlil,[3] lord of heaven and earth, who determines the destiny of the land, committed the rule of all mankind to Marduk, the first-born son of Ea, and made him great among the Igigi,[4] when they pronounced the lofty name of Babylon, made it great among the quarters of the world and in its midst established for him an everlasting kingdom whose foundations were firm as heaven and earth – at that time Anu and Enlil named me, Hammurabi, the exalted prince, the worshiper of the gods, to cause righteousness to prevail in the land, to destroy the wicked and the evil, to prevent the strong from plundering the weak, to go forth like the sun over the black-headed race, to enlighten the land and to further the welfare of the people. Hammurabi, the shepherd named by Enlil am I, who increased plenty and abundance; who made everything complete . . . The ancient seed of royalty, the powerful king, the sun of Babylon, who caused light to go forth over the lands of Sumer and Akkad; the king who caused the four quarters of the world to render obedience; the favorite of Inanna am I. When Marduk sent me to rule the people and to bring help to the land, I established law and justice in the language of the land and promoted the welfare of the people.

1   father and king of the gods
2   gods of the Earth
3   god of wind
4   gods of the heavens

Source: Sanders, Thomas, et al., *Encounters in World History*,
Vol. I (Boston: McGraw-Hill, 2006), pp65–66.

an essential tool in the accounting and record keeping necessary to the administration of their state. The earliest known and identified script had been created in Sumer before 3000 BCE. The **cuneiform** (from the Latin *cuneus*, meaning "wedge") script, formed with a wedge-shaped reed stylus on unbaked clay tablets, was adopted by both the Sumerians and Akkadians, as well as by later peoples in West Asia. Religious inscriptions from the time of Sargon I, written in both Sumerian and Akkadian, promoted the notion that he had been appointed to rule by the Sumerian god Enlil.

Invasions of Semitic peoples from Syria on the eastern end of the Mediterranean brought about the collapse of the Akkadian Empire. These invaders established in succession two dynastic states, Babylonia and Assyria. The Babylonian ruler Hammurabi (ca. 1792–1750 BCE) issued the earliest extant codification of legal and administrative regulations. Hammurabi claimed that the god Marduk had sent him to rule and commanded him to use the laws to bring justice to the people of Babylonia.

The Hittites, invaders from central Eurasia, sacked Babylon in 1595 BCE, and Babylonia gradually succumbed to continuing waves of migration by nomadic peoples. In the fourteenth century BCE, a new kingdom rose in the northern part of Mesopotamia that eventually took the place of the Babylonian empire: Assyria. The sacred city of the Assyrians was Assur, located on the banks of the Tigris, and the Assyrian ruler was also the chief priest of the cult of the god Ashur. Assyrian priests replaced the Babylonian deity Marduk with Ashur as king of the gods.

Religion supported the rule of kings by linking political authority with the power of gods, such as Enlil with the Akkadian ruler Sargon or Marduk with the Babylonian ruler Hammurabi. The Code of Hammurabi and later law codes like it provided rules to order society that were sanctioned by religion – thus Hammurabi's claim that Marduk had commanded him to bring justice to the people he ruled through his laws. Writing was an important corollary to both religion and law, as it enabled the recording of myths and laws, subjecting both to the permanence of clay, or

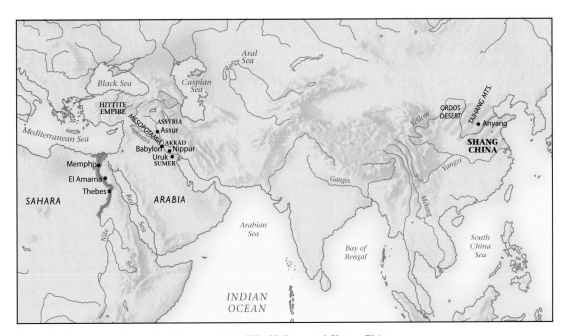

Map 4.1 Mesopotamian cities, Egypt and the Nile Valley, and Shang China.

even stone, and conferring status on those who commanded scribal skills. When new empires rose, their rulers replaced the gods of the defeated with their own, as the Assyrians replaced the Babylonian deity Marduk with their own god, Ashur.

North Africa: Egyptian gods and pharaohs

At approximately the same time as West Asian dynastic states were expanding (in the fourth and third millennia BCE), religion and politics were becoming closely allied in the emergence of Egypt in North Africa. Terracotta female figurines fashioned of Nile mud suggest the existence of fertility beliefs and possibly goddess worship in this region of North Africa during Neolithic times, but by the third millennium BCE, there was a multitude of both gods and goddesses with anthropomorphic qualities.

The Egyptian ruler, the pharaoh, was wor-shiped as a living god who was the point of contact between the human and divine realms. It was the pharaoh's responsibility to preserve and maintain *ma'at*, the order of the universe and the harmony of human society. Three principal deities reflected the ecological conditions of the Nile Valley essential to human survival in that region: Osiris represented the fertilizing power of the annual Nile floods; Isis, the fertility of the Earth; and Horus, the vital force of vegetation resulting from the union of Isis and Osiris. The pharaoh was believed to be the embodiment of Horus, the "living Horus," and thus a son of Osiris. Osiris was also associated with the dead and the afterlife, an important component of Egyptian religion that led to the building of elaborate pyramids filled with treasures for pharaohs to use in the afterlife. Both murals on tomb chambers in the pyramids and accompany-ing hieroglyphic ("sacred carving") inscriptions portray an array of deities and describe the after-life in the underworld, presided over by Osiris.

Amun, originally the local deity of Thebes, began to acquire wider significance after about 2000 BCE, as the power of Thebes grew. The Theban god Amun and Re, the sun god of Heliopolis, a city near the apex of the Nile delta, began to be fused together in the deity Amun-Re, representing the unification of Upper and Lower Egypt. One of the few women to rule as pharaoh, Hatshepsut (r. ca. 1479–1458 BCE), supported her right to rule by claiming to be the daughter of Amun-Re.

Just as religion could be used to support political authority, attempts to change religious beliefs and practices were resisted by powerful priesthoods with vested interests in the status quo. The pharaoh Amenhotep IV (r. ca. 1353–1335 BCE) tried to transform the polytheistic Egyptian religion to a monotheistic focus on one god, Aten, who was represented as a solar disk. Amenhotep moved the capital from Thebes to Amarna in order to escape the power of the Theban priesthood loyal to Amun-Re and renamed himself Akhenaten, "beneficial to Aten." The new religion, however, did not survive Akhenaten's reign. His son Tutankhamen (r. ca. 1334–1323 BCE) returned to Thebes and restored the Theban priests of Amun-Re to power.

East Asia: Gods and kings in Shang China

Slightly later than states in West Asia and North Africa, the Shang dynastic state in the Yellow River Valley of East Asia emerged in the early second millennium BCE. Its rise from Neolithic centers in the north China plain was linked to the introduction of bronze technology. Control of this new technology enabled warriors to use more powerful weapons and subdue larger numbers of people and territory. In addition to weapons, bronze was also used for the equally important purpose of rituals to legitimize the power of newly risen kings, who claimed access to a central deity, Di, through their royal ancestors. Elaborate bronze vessels held sacrifices of food and wine offered to the ancestors of the Shang kings, and oracle bones were used in **divination** rituals to communicate with ancestral deities and with Di.

Oracle bones, the shoulder blades of oxen or sheep or turtle plastrons (the flat underside of turtle shells), were inscribed with questions to the gods in archaic Chinese script. Questions such as "Will there be a good harvest?" or "Will we [the Shang] be successful in battle against our enemies?" were addressed to Di, and the answers were read by interpreting cracks made in the bones when heated over a fire. These divination, or fortune-telling, practices were under the control of priestly scribes, and the ritual value of writing in early China foreshadowed the sacred character of written texts and the power associated with literacy in later Chinese history.

Shang society was dominated by chariot-riding warriors organized according to lineages identified with **totemistic** figures, such as the black bird that was the ancestor of the Shang ruling family. Evidence from a royal tomb suggests that women could hold military power virtually on a par with men. The tomb of Fu Hao, consort of a king who ruled about 1400 BCE, has yielded evidence that she controlled a large army in her own right. Still, male kings were regarded as the intercessors with Shang gods. Although female goddess images have been found in Neolithic sites in northeastern China, the lack of similar figures in Shang and later sites suggests that whatever beliefs these images represented had disappeared by Shang times.

Mesoamerica: Divine kings of the rainforest

On the opposite side of the globe, the Mesoamerican cultural world included the area of modern central and southern Mexico, Guatemala, Belize, El Salvador, and much of Honduras. The relatively late Mayan culture (ca. 300–900 CE) in the Mesoamerican lowland rainforests of the tropical Yucatán peninsula was heir to traditions transmitted from much earlier cultures in the region, such as the Olmecs (ca. 1500–400 BCE).

While many aspects of the Olmecs' culture remain a mystery, we know that they irrigated their farmlands, produced monumental sculptures in basalt, introduced both calendrical and writing systems, and, like the Shang Chinese, practiced totemism – belief in clan descent from an animal or natural object – as part of a complex set of religious beliefs. The Olmecs have been referred to as the "mother civilization" of Mesoamerica, since their legacy provided the foundation for later cultures in that region. Their calendar, in particular, became the basis of all later Mesoamerican calendar systems, one of the most highly developed aspects of Mesoamerican cultures.

Heirs to the Olmecs, the rulers of the city-state of Teotihuacán by around 100 CE controlled the largest urban site in the Valley of Mexico and probably in all of Mesoamerica. By 500 CE, it had reached a peak population of 200,000, but it was gradually eclipsed by other cultural centers in Mesoamerica and in decline by the mid-eighth century. For the more than seven centuries of its

4.2 Teotihuacán mural of the Great Goddess. Murals such as this were painted on thinly plastered walls of apartment compounds throughout the city of Teotihuacán. Their flat, linear style and primary colors depict images associated with male and female deities.

existence, Teotihuacán unified the population and culture of the Valley of Mexico through its religion.

The rulers of Teotihuacán associated their rule with the Feathered Serpent, Quetzalcoatl, whose temple lay near one end of the ceremonial plaza at the center of the city, and also with the primal deity, Tlaloc, whose shrine was the Pyramid of the Sun. Extant images of a powerful goddess, perhaps associated with the Pyramid of the Moon at the other end of the ceremonial plaza, convey aspects of war and fertility, both central to Teotihuacán's identity as a dominant power in the region until the sixth century CE. Although the power of Teotihuacán extended over a fairly wide territory and its military might was formidable, it remained primarily a city-state, as did other Mesoamerican cultural centers.

Rulers of Mayan kingdoms that coexisted with Teotihuacán in the Mesoamerican lowland rainforests of the tropical Yucatán peninsula warred over control of territory but shared each other's gods. The Mayan pantheon included numerous deities, manifestations of the cosmic breath that animated the natural and human worlds. The names of Mayan gods and goddesses, as well as events aligned with the complex Mayan calendrical system, were recorded in a hieroglyphic script inscribed on the walls of temples and monuments. Blood sacrifice was believed to be required to nourish the gods, either through self-inflicted blood-letting (earlobes and tongues) or the sacrifice of prisoners of war.

A series of remarkable murals (ca. 800 CE) in Bonampak, Mexico, relates a single narrative of a battle and its aftermath. Magnificently adorned Mayan warriors are accompanied by musicians blowing long war trumpets of wood or bark. At a stepped platform, the prisoners of war have been stripped and are having their nails torn from their fingers. A captive rests on the steps; nearby a severed head lies on a cluster of leaves. A great lord in jaguar-skin battle dress is accompanied by other noble spectators, including women in white robes. In the final ceremonies, sacrificial dancers wear towering headdresses of quetzal plumes and

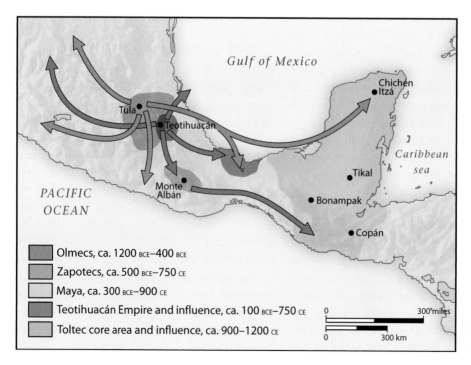

Map 4.2

Mesoamerica.

performers disguised as water gods are accompanied by an orchestra of trumpets, rattles, drums, and turtle shells struck with antlers. The Mayan social hierarchy, based on beliefs in the primacy and sacredness of warfare, is above all recorded in the colorful and dramatic wall paintings.

Unlike god-kings such as the Egyptian pharaohs, Mesoamerican rulers, including the Maya, were believed to rule for the gods but were not themselves gods. However, like the ancestors of Shang kings in China, deceased royal ancestors could share the realm of the gods. Mayan gods and ancestors of Mayan kings often are portrayed as hovering in the same realm, and at times share common attributes. A major deity associated with Mayan rulers is the Maize God, who cyclically dies and is reborn as corn is harvested and planted. A vessel from the Mayan city-state of Tikal dated to ca. 250–600 CE depicting King "Great Jaguar Paw" as the Maize God is inscribed with titles that link the ruler to the god as his protector deity.

Divine encounters: Transformations in religion and society

As states and empires expanded and contracted, the power of deities that sanctioned their rule similarly waxed and waned. Conquering armies carried their gods with them, and when they encountered other gods and goddesses they either replaced them with their own or, more commonly, hybrid deities that shared features of both appeared. Political expansion thus produced religious change, and religions also shaped transformations in both social and political orders among conquerors and conquered.

South Asia: Indus Valley and Vedic religion

The Indus Valley civilization (ca. 2500–1500 BCE) in South Asia shared beliefs, such as goddess worship, with other parts of the world. Terracotta figurines of female fertility deities have been found in sites at the Indus Valley centers of Harappa and Mohenjo-Daro. Animal figures molded in clay indicate that, like the ancient Egyptians and Shang Chinese, the Indus Valley peoples attributed special powers to animals, and animal imagery was a prominent artistic motif. The cow held a position of special importance, like the cat did in Egypt and the bull in the Mediterranean world.

Beginning around 1500 BCE, nomadic cattle herders and warriors from Southwest Asia moved into the realm of the Indus Valley civilization. Equipped with horse-drawn chariots, they rode into battle, led by their warrior god, Indra. As they encountered the remnants of the Indus Valley civilization and settled there, the invaders assimilated indigenous ideas and gradually integrated early Indus Valley goddess beliefs with their own.

The new social and political order was sanctioned by a pantheon of deities, who were manifestations of cosmic forces. The original triumvirate of central deities included Brahma, the creator, Shiva the destroyer, and Vishnu the preserver. Goddesses figure in the Vedic pantheon only in relatively minor ways until much later (ca. 400–800 CE), when female divine power (**shakti**) was recognized and the image of the mother goddess as a supreme being became important. The consorts of Shiva and Vishnu, for example, are incarnations of Devi, the great goddess. Durga is the warrior form of Shiva's consort, and Kali is the demonic version, a grim goddess associated with death and destruction. As in the Indus Valley culture, animals continued to be important in the pantheon of gods and goddesses. For example, Ganesh is the benevolent elephant-headed son of Shiva, and Hanuman, the monkey god, symbolizes loyalty and strength.

The blending of Indus Valley and Indo-European religious culture was also represented in the Vedas ("knowledge"), a collection of orally transmitted ritual hymns that were compiled as written texts between around 1200 and 600 BCE.

Vedic texts were transcribed in the phonetic script of Sanskrit. A hymn in the Rig-Veda, one of the earliest texts, describes the creation of four social groups from the ritual sacrifice of a cosmic being, Purusha, a composite of deities. Purusha's body is cut into different parts, each of which represents a caste: **brahman** (priest), **kshatriya** (warrior), **vaishya** (merchant), and **shudra** (slave). In this way the idea of caste was given a cosmic sanction. Those beyond or outside the caste system were "untouchables" whose occupations (grave digging, hide tanning) made them too impure or unclean to associate with others.

The concept of caste was transmitted as part of Brahmanism, the name given to the belief system and ritual practices of early India associated with the priestly tradition of the Brahmanas (sacred utterances), Vedic texts dating from the ninth to seventh centuries BCE. These texts emphasize the importance of ritual in regulating social relationships, including ranking by caste, and in preserving **dharma**, the divine order and sacred law of the cosmos reflected in the notion of human duty to fulfill one's obligations according to caste. Brahmans ("those who chant sacred utterances," or priests) who carried out the rituals were in a position of superiority to even warrior rulers because they controlled the ritual link between the cosmic order, personified in the numerous deities of the Vedic pantheon, and the human social order.

The Mediterranean world

Contemporary with migrations into the Indus Valley, various Indo-European peoples moved into the Aegean basin, where they encountered centers of earlier (third to first millennium BCE) Mediterranean culture represented by the Minoan palace at Knossos on the island of Crete and the citadel of Mycenae on the Greek mainland. Figurines from the palace at Knossos wearing dresses that expose and emphasize the breasts represent priestesses of Minoan religion, or per-

haps images of a goddess with power over nature, shown in her grasp of writhing snakes in both hands. Shrines on Crete dated to 1400 BCE contain terracotta goddess statues, and by the second millennium BCE, the Myceneans had an elaborate pantheon of gods and goddesses. This pantheon included the later Greek gods Zeus, Poseidon, and Dionysus, all of whom dwelt on the sacred Mount Olympus.

The Greek poets Homer and Hesiod (ca. eighth century BCE) described the gods and goddesses of the Olympic pantheon as anthropomorphic figures who both controlled the forces of nature and interacted with human beings. By the sixth century BCE, the *polis* (city-state) of Athens could boast of a full-fledged civic religion, centered on the Olympian goddess Athena Polias, the patron deity of Athens, at her temple on the Acropolis. The Pananthenaia festival celebrated the goddess with a public procession, sacrifices, hymns, and dances.

4.3 Calyx krater portraying Greek gods Niké and Poseidon. Named for their low handles shaped like the calyx of a flower, calyx kraters were ceramic vessels used for mixing water and wine in ceremonial community settings.

Contemporary with the practice of civic religion that was communal and public, mystery religions that prized secret knowledge known only to initiates also flourished. Mystery religions promised rebirth or regeneration, demanding secrecy of their initiates in exchange for benefits in life or after death. The shrine to the Olympian goddess of crops and fertile earth, Demeter, at Eleusis near Athens became the center of the Eleusinian mysteries, which focused on life, death, and the sprouting of the new crop. Like Demeter, the Egyptian goddess Isis was also associated with the renewal of life. Although Isis was known to the Greeks as early as the fifth century BCE, a mystery religion dedicated to her appeared only in the last two centuries BCE when it spread throughout the eastern end of the Mediterranean.

Even more popular than the cult to Isis, worship of the great mother goddess Cybele originated during the early first millennium BCE in Anatolia (modern Turkey) and later spread throughout the Greco-Roman world. Known as Meter (mother) in Greece, Cybele was officially venerated in Rome by the end of the third century BCE as *Magna Mater*, Latin for "Great Mother". Her worshipers participated in ecstatic dancing, and bull slaughtering was part of a ritual performance that produced blood with which initiates were sprinkled. Followers of both Cybele and Isis were found all over the Greco-Roman world, and the two goddesses were often conflated.

The dualism of mystery cults and the Olympic pantheon in the early Mediterranean world indicates that there was a variety of ritual practices and beliefs held by those who inhabited the Greek mainland and the surrounding islands by the beginning of the Dark Age (ca. 1200–800 BCE) ushered in by the invasions of Indo-Europeans. By the end of this period, a people known by their Greek name of Phoenicians appeared and helped to reconnect the inhabitants of Greece to the rest of the Mediterranean. A maritime trading people who originally lived along the Lebanese coast of the eastern Mediterranean, the Phoenicians introduced a writing system based on alphabetic characters to peoples across the Mediterranean. The advantages of an alphabetic script over earlier systems such as cuneiform and hieroglyphics are great: there are relatively few symbols to learn, and they are easily adaptable to different languages. The development of an alphabetic script for writing Greek contributed to the cultural integration of the Greek world over the next three centuries, and to the sharing of religious ideas and practices throughout the Mediterranean world.

From god-kings to prophets and preachers

In Eurasia and North Africa as early as the third millennium BCE, similar belief systems developed that were focused on gods who sanctioned the power of kings to rule. In Egypt, the pharaohs were considered to be "living gods," while elsewhere kings ruled with the divine sanction of gods, as in Sumer, where goddesses or gods were consorts of rulers, or in Shang China, where royal ancestors interceded with a supreme deity. Drawing on earlier animistic and shamanistic beliefs, as in Mayan Mesoamerica, priests and scribes played important roles in confirming the authority of rulers by claiming to communicate with gods and ensuring the legitimacy of rulers. Sacred scripts aided rulers in preserving the records of their relationships with deities and thus sanctioning their rule.

By the end of the first millennium BCE, smaller, diverse religions distinct from civic or state religions appealed to people at all levels of society and flourished throughout the world. Religions dedicated to the goddesses Isis and Cybele, at times appropriated by rulers and at times subversive of the state, spread throughout the Mediterranean world from Spain to Anatolia (modern Turkey) and from North Africa to Europe (as far as modern Germany). Around the world, from Mesoamerica to the Mediterranean, visions of the afterlife provided solace in the face of the universal experience of death and vividly portrayed realms of the dead, often furnished with material goods offered up by the living. In the proliferation of local traditions, peoples everywhere sought to gain security in the face of change.

As early as the second millennium BCE, new religious ideas arose that did not focus on goddesses, gods, or god-kings. New belief systems promoted by prophets and preachers challenged the power of shamans, priests, and god-kings and focused instead on ethical questions of right and wrong or good and evil and on the meaning of human existence and suffering. These new religions evolved in the context of earlier religious traditions and gradually brought about transformations in societies and states across Afro-Eurasia.

West Asia: Judaism

The roots of Judaism can be traced among the semi-pastoral peoples of Mesopotamia as early as the second millennium BCE. One group among these peoples, later known as the Hebrews, moved westward early in the second millennium BCE under the leadership of the patriarch Abraham. According to the Biblical account, Abraham abhorred the idol worship found in his birthplace, Ur, in Mesopotamia, and moved his family and herds through the Syrian desert to a new home in Canaan at the eastern end of the Mediterranean, where they continued to worship their ancestral clan divinity.

Around the middle of the second millennium BCE, the Hebrews moved to Egypt, probably as part of the Hyksos ("rulers of foreign lands") army that invaded Egypt at that time. After the Hyksos were forced out of Egypt, the Hebrews were enslaved there. About 1250 BCE, following a leader named Moses, the Hebrews fled Egypt and resettled in Palestine. Under the guidance of Moses, Yahweh, originally the most powerful of numerous gods, emerged as the favored god of the Hebrew tribes. Moses claimed that God (Yahweh) had transmitted to him the sacred laws by which

the community should live. These were the Ten Commandments, and they were inscribed on tablets of stone and sealed up in a box called the "Ark of the Covenant," reflecting the covenant, or pact, with God made by the Hebrew people.

Under Moses' successor, Joshua, the 12 Hebrew tribes that traced their descent from Abraham and his sons staked out territory in Palestine. In the eleventh century BCE, Saul became the first king of Israel. Under the rule of his son David (r. ca. 1000–960 BCE), the transition from a tribal confederacy to a unified monarchy was completed. The Ark of the Covenant was brought to David's new capital of Jerusalem, which became the political and religious center of the kingdom of Israel. The First Temple was built by David's son and successor, Solomon (r. ca. 960–920 BCE).

Although questioning the Bible as a historical document is not new, recent archaeology has shown that much of the familiar Biblical account of the origins of the Hebrew people related here, beginning with the patriarch Abraham, his son Isaac and Issac's son Jacob, and including their enslavement in Egypt, exodus, and the foundation of the kingdom of Israel under David and Solomon are narratives composed in the ninth–seventh centuries BCE. Although based at least in part on much older oral traditions, the composition of these Biblical texts in a much later time period than the events they record makes them unreliable as historical documents. Israel was at that time ruled by Josiah, a descendant of David, who sought through these historical narratives to create a common past and thus identity for his people. The people the Bible calls "Israelites" were but one among many peoples who inhabited the land of Canaan, and their experiences were part of the shared history of these peoples. The kingdoms of David and Solomon were probably in reality small chiefdoms with limited power, and Jerusalem as a unified capital only gained its central position in the late eighth century BCE, shortly before the Assyrians destroyed Israel in 720 BCE. Inscriptions from the eighth century BCE that contain references to a pair of gods, Jehovah and his consort Asherah, suggest that monotheism may have been a product of the kingdom of Judea that followed the destruction of Israel.

In 597 BCE, when the Babylonians plundered Jerusalem and destroyed the First Temple, they deported many leading Israelite families to Babylon. This was the origin of the diaspora (Greek for "scattering" or "dispersal") in which Israelites were forcibly deported or fled their homelands to settle elsewhere and establish communities. One of the most important steps in setting up a new community was the establishment of a synagogue (Greek for "bringing together"), a communal meeting place that served educational and social, as well as religious, functions.

In addition to religious ritual focused on the Temple in Jerusalem or on a synagogue elsewhere, a central issue of Hebrew belief became just and moral behavior among human beings. Such behavior was the result of obeying Yahweh's laws, while transgression of his laws led to punishment. The eighth-century conquest of Israel by Assyria and the sixth-century captivity of Hebrews in Babylon were interpreted as examples of Yahweh's punishment for the Hebrews' misbehavior. Modern archaeology dates the expansion of Judah's territory into the former kingdom of Israel to the reign of Josiah in the sixth century BCE, and identifies his reign also with the adoption of monotheism and the codification of religious law. In around 515 BCE, the Second Temple was built by exiles returning from captivity in Babylonia and the Deuteronomic Code was introduced, embodying the laws to be followed by the Hebrew people so that they would not err again. By the sixth century BCE, Judaism was a religion based on one god, who was the creator and lawgiver, and on humans, who ideally ruled the Earth justly, guided by God's laws.

South Asia: Hinduism

During the sixth century BCE, as the Israelites were claiming their god, Yahweh, to be the only God

and his laws to be the only laws, new ideas rose in India to challenge both the domination of Brahman priests and the emphasis on rituals characteristic of Vedic religion. Although some secular rulers resisted priestly power and in this way challenged Brahman priests, newer texts expressed critical reflection on Vedic ideas and practices from within the tradition itself. The internal critical tradition is represented by the Upanishads ("sessions"), which refer to esoteric knowledge gained from sitting at the feet of a master. Chronologically the last of the Vedic tests, the Upanishads were compiled between the seventh and third centuries BCE and represent a speculative and ascetic (contemplation and self-denial for religious purposes) tradition. The Upanishads focus on the meaning of ritual rather than ritual itself, demythologize the Vedic pantheon, and raise questions concerning the meaning of human existence.

Concepts such as **karma**, meaning "law of causality," and **samsara**, "wheel of life," were used differently in the Upanishads than in previous Vedic texts. Karma, for example, in earlier contexts had meant "ritually prescribed behavior," as emphasized in the priestly tradition; in the Upanishads its meaning was transformed to "cumulative causality determined by human actions." The goal of human existence, according to the Upanishads, should be to escape the endless cause–effect sequence of the continuous cycles of existence and achieve individual identification with a unified cosmic essence. The concern of these texts with metaphysical questions rather than with ritual practice reduced the importance of priests and thus their position in society.

The reformulation of traditional Vedic ideas and practices between the second century BCE and the second century CE contributed to the development of religious traditions later known as Hinduism ("of the Indus"). One of the important texts composed during this era contains instructions of the creator of the universe to the first man and king, Manu, and was used as a guide to creating the ideal social order. The Book of Manu was the first text to use the Sanskrit term *varna* (color, rank) to describe the four categories of humans, and it explained the caste system as a consequence of *karma* (actions) accumulated in earlier incarnations.

Ideas about both social and spiritual life were further developed in other religious and philosophical literature, including the Sanskrit epics, the Mahabharata and Ramayana, both completed in their final written form in the first centuries CE. The latter work, the Ramayana, tells of the heroic exploits of Prince Rama, while the Mahabharata focuses on a great battle fought among descendants of Rama's brother, King Bharata. Although not an integral part of the epic, the sacred poem Bhagavad Gita ("Song of God"), composed in the second century CE, was inserted into the Mahabharata and became one of the most influential scriptures of Hinduism.

In the Bhagavad Gita, the god Krishna, an incarnation of the solar deity Vishnu, takes human form as a charioteer who befriends and counsels Arjuna the warrior. Arjuna, a representative of the warrior caste, faces a battle in which he must slay his own relatives. As Arjuna wrestles with the moral dilemma this presents, Krishna recites the Bhagavad Gita. Krishna counsels Arjuna that he must fulfill his duty as a warrior and that he is not to worry about his role in the deaths of his friends and relatives because their deaths in battle will allow their souls to move on to the next life. Arjuna, he says, is merely an agent of a cosmic process, and his own salvation depends on his carrying out his duty. He must act, without attachment and without personal ambition, to fulfill his role in society, as must every individual according to his caste. The moving and eloquent injunction on how to live one's life expressed here says that, like Arjuna, one must live and act according to what is expected of one's place and role in the world, without the interference of personal ambition or even human emotional attachments to kin and friends. The Bhagavad Gita can be regarded as the main ethical text of Hinduism, showing how carrying out the faithful execution of one's duty (*dharma*) results in good *karma*.

South Asia: Jainism and Buddhism

By the sixth century BCE, an era of commercial expansion, social conflict, and religious turmoil on the Indian subcontinent, the rich Ganges River plain of northern India was dotted with more than a dozen kingdoms. In this setting, Jainism and Buddhism rose as challenges to the Vedic establishment. Both were rooted in a "wandering ascetic" movement that opposed the power of Brahman priests; both also rejected caste ideology and the sacrificial rituals of the Vedic religion, drawing on the critical intellectual tradition associated with the Upanishads.

Mahavira (ca. 540–468 BCE), whose name means "Great Conqueror," was the founder of Jainism (followers of *jina*, the "conqueror"). He abandoned his comfortable life as the son of a

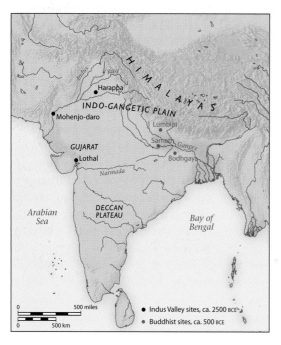

Map 4.3 Early Indus Valley sites and Ganges Valley Buddhist sites.

tribal chief to become a wandering ascetic at about the age of 30. He reacted to priestly ritualism by promoting ascetic practices for his followers and taught the annihilation of *karma* by penance and disciplined conduct. Jains believe that everything in nature is alive and endowed with a form of spiritual essence; they also believe in the doctrine of non-violence, which has had a profound influence on Indian culture and society into modern times.

Like Mahavira, the man later known as Buddha was born in the sixth century BCE to the ruler of a kingdom in the Himalayan foothills and grew up amid the luxurious surroundings of palace life. As he became an adult he began to recognize the existence of suffering, sickness, and death. He sought an understanding of the causes of human suffering by following the teachings of various ascetics and holy men. Dissatisfied with their teachings, Buddha eventually achieved **nirvana** (the extinction of forces that cause rebirth), "enlightenment," or the realization of the true nature of existence through a combination of meditation and ascetic practices.

The Four Noble Truths, taught by Buddha in a famous sermon at the Deer Park at Sarnath, contain the basic precepts of Buddhist belief: that life is suffering; that the cause of suffering is desire; that in order to stop suffering, one must stop desire; and that the way to accomplish this is through the Eightfold Path, which includes ascetic practices and mental disciplines followed by monks, holy men who live apart from society and have committed their lives to religious practice. The debt of Buddhism to earlier Indian **cosmology** and thought, particularly that of the Upanishads, is evident in fundamental concepts such as *samsara*, the cycle and bondage of rebirth, and *karma*, the cumulative causality of actions that propels humans through life after life.

In contrast to Jainism, which remained confined to India, Buddhism was later transmitted to East and Southeast Asia to become one of the great world religions. By the sixth century BCE, when both Buddhism and Jainism took shape in South

Asia as reformist challenges to the dominant Brahman tradition, a new system of religious belief that challenged prevailing ideas and was similarly concerned with ethical questions began to form in the setting of the Persian Empire in West Asia: Zoroastrianism.

Southwest Asia: Zoroastrianism

Indo-European language and culture were shared by peoples who moved into the highlands of modern Iran in the late second millennium BCE with those who migrated into the Indus River Valley around the same time. These peoples also shared common religious ideas that we know as Vedic religion in South Asia, later transformed into Hinduism. In the territory west of the Indus Valley and south of the Hindu Kush that became Persia, the religious ideas Indo-European migrants

4.4 Buddha preaching, Sarnath, fifth century CE. Sarnath, near the modern city of Varanasi, was the place where Buddha gave his first sermon to five disciples and formed the *sangha*, the community of monks.

carried with them – belief in multiple deities, often associated with tribal divisions, purification by fire – were challenged by a self-proclaimed prophet named Zarathustra (Zoroaster in Greek). Much mystery surrounds both Zoroaster himself and the origins of the religion that bears his name. Scholars still disagree as to when Zoroaster lived, either in the late second millennium BCE (around the time of the migrations of his people) or centuries later in the sixth century BCE, a contemporary of Mahavira and Buddha. Whenever he lived, he began preaching to farmers and semi-sedentary herders who lived south of the Aral Sea in what is now northeastern Iran. This traditional borderland between settled farmers and the wide-ranging nomads of the Central Asian steppe was subject to frequent border raids and wars, and the perennial instability of this area provided fertile ground for a prophet's preaching. By the seventh century BCE, first the Medes, then the Persians,

began to establish control over this area, and it was under the Persians that Zoroaster's ideas began to spread.

In place of the numerous Indo-Iranian gods and goddesses, Zoroaster proposed a dualistic pairing of gods: Ahura Mazda, the "Wise Lord," who represented the ethical good, and Angra Mainyu or Ahriman, the embodiment of darkness and falsehood. Life was a constant moral war between two forces, and human beings had to choose between lies and truth, darkness and light. Unlike the eternal turning of the Hindu Wheel of Life, there was in Zoroaster's preaching a certain end to the war, when all humans would be called to account for their actions here on Earth and rewarded with either eternal paradise or hell. The teachings and principles of Zoroaster are found in the Avesta, a collection of hymns and sayings written down long after his lifetime. Although there were opponents of Zoroaster's ideas,

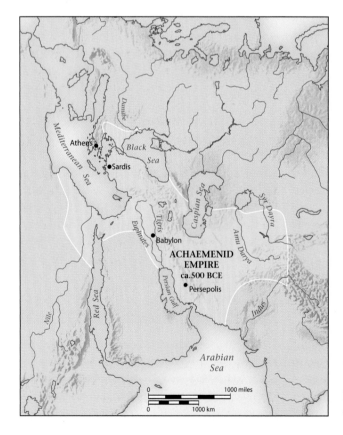

Map 4.4 Persian Achaemenid Empire ca. 500 BCE.

Zoroastrianism gained enough support among the powerful to become the state religion of a succession of Persian empires.

The Achaemenid rulers of Persia claimed sovereignty based on rights granted them by the principal Zoroastrian deity, Ahura Mazda. Kingship was thus both semi-divine and universal. The Achaemenid (named for a common ancestor, Achaemenes) founder, Cyrus the Great (r. ca. 550–530 BCE), conquered the Mesopotamian kingdom of Babylon in 539 BCE; under one of his successors, Darius I (r. 521–486 BCE), the frontiers of the Persian Empire were expanded from Egypt in the west to Central Asia and the Indus River in the east. Darius built a ceremonial capital at Persepolis that was designed to display his wealth and power, bolstered by Zoroastrian religious imagery. After the fall of the Achaemenids in 330 BCE, until the rise of Islam in the seventh century CE (see Chapter 5), some variation of Zoroastrianism continued to find followers in Persia, especially under the Parthians (ca. 200 BCE–225 CE) and the Sassanians (225–636 CE) when it was the official religion of the empire.

Sages and society: Philosophy and politics in early China and Greece

In the sixth century BCE, as Judaism's cosmology took shape in West Asia, Buddha searched for the meaning of life in India, and Zoroastrianism began to flourish in the Persian Empire, in both China and Greece philosophers (those who love knowledge or wisdom) began to construct visions of society and politics that would shape their worlds for the next two millennia. In contrast to the monotheism of the Hebrews and the metaphysical orientation of early Buddhist cosmology, both of which sought to explain the purpose of human existence and the meaning of human suffering, philosophers in Greece and China were more concerned with the nature of reality, human knowledge, and the ordering of society.

The concerns of early Greek and Chinese thinkers were also distinct from animism, shamanism, or theocracy, which viewed nature with a sense of mystery and awe and deities as powerful forces to be feared and propitiated. In contrast to these, the systems of thought that developed in sixth-century Greece and China were human-centered and built on rationalist explanations of the cosmos not dependent on the intervention or favor of gods. In contrast to the integrative relationship between humans and cosmic or spiritual forces found in theocratic states, such as those of Shang China and ancient West Asia, the humanistic and rationalistic ways of thinking developed in early China and Greece were based on an oppositional relationship between humans and the cosmos. Unlike the integration of the human and natural worlds in theocracies, whose rulers were identified with a deity or some cosmic force, in classical China and Greece philosophers saw the human world and the cosmos as two distinct realms.

The flowering of ideas in China during the fifth century BCE was paralleled by the development of philosophy in the Greek city-states at about the same time. In both the Chinese world and the Greek world, the growth of new ideas and debates among thinkers took place in an unstable political and social environment that provided fertile ground for conceiving new ways of achieving and maintaining social and political order. In China, the "Hundred Schools of Thought" flourished in an arena of competing states that rose against the background of the breakdown of the central authority of the Zhou kings; in Greece, the ferment of ideas was associated with the political form of the city-state and the practice of **democracy**.

China: From shamanism to the Mandate of Heaven

The religion of the Shang people in early China was shamanistic, dependent on the ability of individuals with spiritual powers (shamans) to communicate with the world of gods. Shang

China was a theocracy because the ancestors of the Shang kings were believed to be deities who served the principal god, Di. When the Shang dynastic state was replaced by the Zhou people, who invaded their territory and conquered them in the mid-eleventh century BCE, there was a corresponding transformation of concepts that sanctioned kingship. The Shang anthropomorphic supreme deity, Di, was gradually replaced by a far more abstract concept of Heaven, which represented an idea of order imposed on the human world through the person of the ruler, who held the "Mandate of Heaven."

The Zhou king exercised power by appointing his kin to rule over territories within the Zhou realm. The king's relatives were conferred with titles and ranks that gave them status as an aristocracy with the right to rule in the name of the Zhou king. The relationship between this titled nobility and the Zhou king was symbolized and confirmed by the transfer of a mound of earth from the central altar of the Zhou king to altars in each of the territories. This decentralized form of government worked well for about two centuries. As the blood ties that were the basis of bonds between the king and the territorial lords grew thinner with each generation, the authority of the Zhou king gradually eroded. By the sixth century BCE, there was warfare among the independent states that had formerly been part of the Zhou realm.

The emergence of Confucianism, Legalism, and Daoism

The ideas that are labeled "Confucian," "Legalist," and "Daoist" took root in a common cultural background known as the era of the "Hundred Schools of Thought" in the sixth to third centuries BCE. This was a period of great intellectual ferment, as old social and political structures crumbled. New concepts were generated in a flood of "schools of thought" related to power struggles among the states that controlled parts of what would later be known as China.

CONFUCIANISM The man we know as Confucius (551–479 BCE) was born into this chaotic age. Like many of his contemporaries, Confucius was greatly troubled by the disorder of his time and sought answers to the question of how to restore order to society. He unsuccessfully sought a post as adviser to the ruler of a state, but gained a following of devoted disciples who transcribed his teachings in a work known as the *Analects*. Confucius looked to the early days of the Zhou as a golden age, and he idealized the institutions of the sage-kings of antiquity as models for his own society.

Confucius challenged the social order of his time by redefining the basis of elite status. He argued that exemplary conduct, rather than aristocratic birth, entitled individuals to high social status. The scholar, not the warrior or the administrator, should be at the pinnacle of the social hierarchy. The aristocratic code of ceremonial behavior, *li* ("ritual"), became in Confucius's thinking the social forms that structured the five core human relationships, including everything from proper etiquette to the performance of ancestral sacrifices. Three of these five relationships were family bonds (father–son, husband-wife, elder brother–younger brother), reflecting the importance Confucius assigned to the family as a model for the rest of society; two of the relationships (ruler–subject, friend–friend) applied to government and to society outside the ties of kinship.

Warfare intensified in the generation after his death, ushering in a period known as the Warring States (ca. 480–250 BCE). Approximately a century after Confucius's death, Mencius (ca. 372–289 BCE) expounded the theory of the Mandate of Heaven, giving full expression to a concept that was used in ancient texts to justify the conquest of the Shang by the Zhou. According to this theory, Heaven confers the right to rule on the person who is morally qualified; the sanction for rule thus depends on moral character, not on military strength or on the power of gods.

LEGALISM   An alternative to Confucian ideas that rose in the ferment of the Warring States period, Legalism presented a utilitarian set of ideas designed to ensure the unchallenged power of the state and the ruler. Like Confucian thinkers, those associated with Legalism were also searching for solutions to disorder of the times, but their answers were profoundly different. Han Feizi (d. 233 BCE), the principal philosopher of the Legalist school, argued that human nature was bad, Han Feizi believed that it was necessary to control people by the use of "strict laws and harsh punishments" and thus to manipulate individual self-interest to serve state power.

One of the early Legalist figures was Shang Yang (fl. ca. 356–338 BCE), whose views were articulated in the *Book of Lord Shang*, a manual on how to administer a state, and who served as adviser to the ruler of the Qin state in north-western China. Shang Yang was concerned with how to maintain the ruler's power and authority in a setting of competing states. According to the *Book of Lord Shang*, the primary functions of the state are agriculture and war, emphasizing the necessity of both an economic base and the maintenance and extension of the power of the state through military means.

DAOISM   In contrast to Confucian concerns with human nature and social order, and Legalist concerns with the state and political order, Daoist thinkers of the Warring States period argued that people should aspire to live in harmony with nature and take nature as the model for human behavior. The *Daodejing*, a text commonly attributed to a mythical figure, Laozi, contains a complex variety of ideas that convey a mystical approach to knowledge. Both this text and the *Zhuangzi*, parables attributed to the philosopher Zhuang Zi (fourth–third centuries BCE), promote the notion of the transformations of nature as the only certainty in the world of experience. People should accept change as the only constant, following a path revealed in the transformations of nature. The ideas articulated in these early texts were later associated with a school of thought known as Daoism. The term *dao* ("path") was also used by Confucian thinkers to refer to the "path of humanity," meaning ethical social behavior; in Daoism, the path to be followed is that of nature, not that of human society.

The Athenian polis and democracy

Between about 800 and 500 BCE, both Greek society and Greek beliefs were transformed by the emergence of city-states, the expansion of the Greek world resulting from colonization and trade, and the introduction of influences from West Asia and North Africa. By the fifth century BCE, Greek thought and society were closely intertwined with the development of the *polis*, the city-state. Athens, based on its hinterland, Attica, was one of the independent city-states that flourished on the Greek mainland at this time. The Olympian deity Athena, goddess of wisdom, was the focus of the public cult that gave unity and harmony to the city-state, and mystery cults continued to flourish as well. However, the fame of the Athenian city-state has less to do with its religious practices, whether the Olympian civic or mystery cults, than with two developments that grew out of changing patterns of Greek life after the eighth century BCE: democracy (*demos* = people, *kratos* = rule) and the emergence of rational and humanistic thought.

Through the seventh century, like other Greek city-states, Athens was ruled by aristocratic clans, whose power was rooted in petty kingships of earlier times. These aristocratic clans provided the membership of the **areopagus**, the council, which they joined after being elected one of nine **archons**, or magistrates. During the seventh century, Athens began to experience social and economic conflict among aristocrats, wealthy merchants, and farmers. In 594 BCE, an aristocrat named Solon (ca. 630–560 BCE) was elected chief *archon* with authority to restructure the government of the city-state. Solon may have sympathized with the desire of those outside his own social class to exercise political rights and instituted a series of reforms. He broke the aristocracy's monopoly on power by opening up membership in the governing council to those with wealth as well as aristocratic ancestry, and by forbidding the enslavement of free citizens for the repayment of debts, he secured the basis of a free peasantry.

A further step toward democracy took place under the leadership of Cleisthenes (fl. ca. 507 BCE), whose reforms changed the basis of selection to the governing council in such a way as to further undermine aristocratic power. He reorganized the units, or "tribes," from which council members were selected using the *deme*, or place of residence, to determine membership in a territorial unit rather than the previous criterion of ancestry. To the general assembly of citizens, the basic arena of political activity, Cleisthenes added new institutions, including popular courts. Athenian justice, like Athenian politics, became a matter of popular participation; citizens made the laws and pronounced the judgments as well. Each person appearing before the court argued his own case, and decisions were made on the basis of the will of the majority of citizens.

Athenian democracy reached its peak under the leadership of Pericles (ca. 495–429 BCE), a skilled orator and military commander. But even at this period of its fullest development, participation in the politics of the Athenian city-state was limited to a minority. Periclean Athens (including Attica, its hinterland) had a population of more than 300,000, of whom perhaps 10 percent qualified as legal citizens. Other Athenians – slaves, resident aliens (metics), and women – were denied participation in the political process. Only native-born Athenian males aged 18 and older had the right to vote on matters in the public assembly and only those male citizens over the age of 30 were eligible to serve in public office. Despite its limitations, Athenian democracy represented a sharp break from previous forms of government everywhere that were dependent on military force and the sanction of gods or goddesses.

WAR AND THE ATHENIAN EMPIRE During what became known as the Persian Wars (ca. 494–445 BCE), Athens, along with Sparta, a city-state on the Peloponnesian peninsula, thwarted the designs of the Achaemenid Persian emperors Darius and Xerxes to drive the Greeks out of Anatolia and to invade the Greek homeland. The Delian League (named for the island of Delos, where the League met) had been formed by Greek city-states during the Persian Wars but came under Athenian control in 478 BCE. After the wars, using the Delian League as a base, Athens expanded its power throughout the Aegean and created an empire based on the strength of its fleet and its armies. The creation of the Athenian Empire, which extended political, economic, religious, and judicial control over a wide region, alarmed other Greek city-states, especially Sparta.

Sparta, unlike Athens, was a city-state based on war, and its social and political organization reflected this. Male citizens were reared and trained by the state to serve in the military. Having made important contributions to the defeat of the Persians and dominating the Peloponnesus, Sparta assumed the leading role in challenging Athens in the fifth-century BCE Peloponnesian War. This conflict, begun when Pericles was still in power and Athenian democracy was at its height, lasted nearly three decades (431–404 BCE) and resulted in widespread destruction and loss of life. It ended with the defeat of Athens and the end of the golden age of Athenian democracy, which anti-democratic forces blamed for the loss of the war.

POLITICS AND PHILOSOPHY IN ATHENS The evolution of Athenian political democracy was accompanied by an explosion of creativity in ideas. By the time of Pericles, questions about the natural world and the origin and essence of things led some to reject both civic and cult religious beliefs to seek understanding of the world in *philosophia*, or wisdom. The fundamental question that exercised Greek thinkers of the sixth and fifth centuries BCE was: How do we know what we know?

The intellectual differences and cosmic debates among the Greeks were a reflection of the conflicts that went on within and between the Greek city-states during their "warring states" period (fifth to fourth centuries BCE), roughly concurrent with the Warring States period in China and the flourishing of various schools of thought there. During this uncertain time, skepticism and relativism were introduced into Athenian thought by a group of professional teachers of rhetoric who became known as Sophists. Sophists argued both sides of a given idea or thesis, an exercise that fostered a relativistic view of things. The Sophists' skepticism led them to reject the traditional religious and political guidelines for society. For them it was not the community, with its religious and political sanctions, but the rational individual that was the source of truth and knowledge.

Socrates (ca. 469–399 BCE), one of the most influential Athenian thinkers, sought to go beyond skepticism and to establish acceptable moral and ethical codes, much as Confucius had some years earlier in China. Unlike Confucius, however, Socrates used an intellectual rather than a traditional historical basis for his views. According to Socrates, all ideas are preconceptions and true knowledge is to be arrived at by questioning them. As a result of his suggestion that all knowledge is relative and final truths are unattainable, Socrates was found guilty of impiety and corrupting youth and put to death in 399 BCE. His ideas were viewed as particularly dangerous because he espoused them during the collapse of Athens in the war against Sparta, a time when certainty, not questioning, was demanded.

Socrates' most famous pupil was Plato (427–347 BCE), who continued his teacher's philosophical quest. In his *Republic*, Plato described the ideal state as a commonwealth ruled by a class of philosopher-kings. The world of phenomena, Plato believed, is a shadow world dimly reflecting the real world of ideas. It is this world of ideas that philosopher-kings understand and what qualifies them to govern. Beyond the world of things and experiences, apprehended by the senses, there is another, more fundamental world of eternal forms and types. On the basis of his observation of Athenian democracy, which had brought about the death of his mentor, Socrates, Plato believed that the people (**demos**) were an unruly lot, incapable of governing properly.

Plato's most famous student was Aristotle (384–322 BCE), who ultimately rejected his teacher's idealistic view of knowledge in favor of the systematic study and investigation of nature as the source of knowledge.

The idea of empire

Ancient empires built from the expansion of city-states appeared as early as the Akkadians, whose empire in the late third millennium BCE stretched from the Mediterranean to the Persian Gulf. Like the Akkadian ruler Sargon, who claimed a mandate from the Sumerian god Enlil, rulers of the Babylonian and Assyrian empires also drew on the religious sanction of gods to legitimize their authority. The Athenian Empire rose from the needs of defense against a common enemy, and did not seek to legitimize its dominance through religion. However, all other early empires did employ religion to support the authority of rulers. As religions evolved from the worship of urban gods and goddesses, to ritual practices controlled by priesthoods, to ethical systems and political ideologies, religion was used in new ways to sanction the rulers of new and powerful empires.

The Hellenistic Empire

Both a weakened Athens and its competitor city-state, Sparta, were among the many Greek city-states that were overcome in the fourth century BCE by the rising power of Macedon, a region in the northernmost part of Greece. Under Philip II (r. 359–336 BCE) and his son Alexander the Great (356–323 BCE), Macedon was unified and gained control of the Greek world along with much of West Asia and North Africa. The Persian Achaemenid Empire was conquered by Alexander the Great, whose Hellenistic (Greek-like) Empire built directly on the experience of its Persian predecessor. After his first victory over the Persians, he advanced along the eastern Mediterranean seacoast and southward into North Africa, where he was welcomed as pharaoh by the Egyptians, who were resentful of Persian rule.

In 331 BCE, Alexander founded the city of Alexandria at a strategic location with a good harbor that served both military and commercial purposes. City temples were dedicated both to Greek gods and to the Egyptian goddess Isis, reflecting Alexander's policy of accommodating local religious beliefs along with Greek ones. During his stay in Egypt, Alexander also visited the oracle of the Egyptian god Amun at Siwah, along the Libyan border. This oracle was known and respected in the Greek world as a place of pilgrimage and homage to a god regarded by the Greeks as a manifestation of the Greek Zeus. Alexander consulted the oracle about his ancestry: Was he the son of a god, Zeus Amun? The oracle supposedly confirmed Alexander's belief that he was indeed the son of Zeus Amun. Though the Greeks believed that the offspring of mortals and divinities were human heroes, not gods, the Egyptians believed in the divinity of their rulers, a notion to which Alexander easily adapted.

Completing his conquest of Persia and acquiring the riches of cities such as Babylon and Persepolis, Alexander turned his armies toward India. In 326 BCE, he crossed the Indus River and pressed on until his army refused to go farther. After Alexander's premature death, such centralized authority as he had been able to maintain was replaced by a loose confederation of Greco-Asian states administered by his generals and their successor dynasties. The post-Alexandrine Hellenistic world was an empire only in the sense that it was united by a common culture with varied political centers. By around 300 BCE, a relatively stable system had emerged: the Macedonian general Seleucus and his successors gained control of Persia and its Central, South, and West Asian (the region of modern Iraq and Syria) possessions. The Seleucids were pushed out of Persia in around 250 BCE by the Parthians, who in turn were replaced by the Sassanids (224–651 CE). The Iranian plateau and much of Mesopotamia were thus ruled for almost 900 years by these heirs of the Persian Achaemenid Empire.

Ptolemy, another Macedonian general, and his successors took Egypt, Palestine, and Phoenicia. Others controlled Anatolia, Thrace, and the "home" territories of Macedonia and Greece. These successor states dominated West Asia for more than two centuries. Following his death, the remnants of Alexander's empire shared a common law, language, trade, and cosmology. Rulers such as the Ptolemies in Egypt or the Seleucids and their heirs in Persia presented themselves as gods, just as Alexander had in Egypt and elsewhere. As religion continued to be used to support political authority and could be manipulated to sanction new rulers, there was a rich blending of religious traditions; some cults, such as that of Isis, spread throughout the Hellenistic world.

South Asia: The Mauryan and Gupta empires

Influenced by and contemporary with the Hellenistic Empire created by Alexander, the Mauryan Empire was founded in South Asia by Chandragupta Maurya (r. ca. 324–301 BCE). A statecraft manual called the *Arthashastra*, commonly attributed to Kautilya, an adviser of the Mauryan founder, described a system of small states and prescribed how the rulers of these states should act. The author of the *Arthashastra* also provided a philosophical basis for the practice of politics. Like his Chinese contemporary, Shang Yang, Kautilya emphasized both the science of politics or statecraft, especially strategies designed to expand and strengthen the king's power, and the exploitation of material resources necessary to support the consolidation of his rule.

The Mauryan Empire reached its height during the reign of Ashoka (r. ca. 272–232 BCE), when Buddhism was adopted as the official religion. Although the empire fragmented shortly after the death of Ashoka, an essential element that contributed to the sustenance of imperial unity under the Mauryans was the use of Buddhism as a universal religion joining disparate ethnic and linguistic groups. Inscriptions of edicts issued by Ashoka during his reign are the oldest extant written records of Indian history, and they illustrate the use of Buddhism as a sanction for rule. They also show the influence of the Hellenistic states and the contact between northern India and the Mediterranean that was established by the successors of Alexander.

In these inscriptions, Ashoka is called "Beloved of the Gods," he is described as regretting the death and destruction that accompanied his conquests and looking on to the next life rather than taking pleasure in the power and luxury of his role as king. Unlike his grandfather, Chandragupta Maurya, who had renounced his throne to become a Jain monk, Ashoka established legitimacy for his rule over many different peoples on the Indian subcontinent by claiming to be the first true *chakravartin* ("he for whom the wheel of the law turns"), or universal monarch.

Waves of Greek and other Indo-European invaders into northwestern India brought about the fragmentation of the Mauryan Empire, but the model of the Hellenistic Empire continued to exercise an influence on the Indian subcontinent for later rulers, such as the Kushana, a nomadic people commanding a large steppe empire in southwestern Asia and northwestern India during the first centuries CE. After the disintegration of the Kushan Empire, the Guptas (ca. 320–500 CE) succeeded in uniting northern India. The Ganges city of Pataliputra was the Gupta capital, serving as a

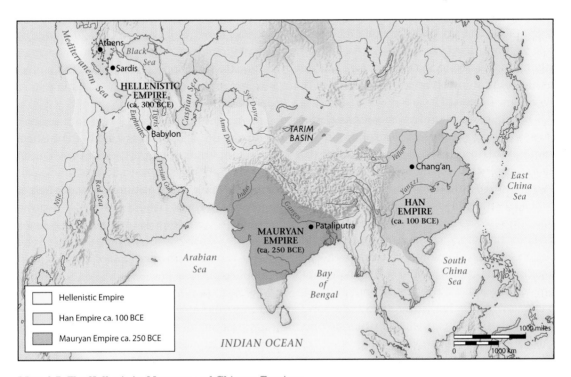

Map 4.5 The Hellenistic, Mauryan and Chinese Empires.

center of the monumental architecture and literary culture that flourished under the Guptas. Although the Guptas supported the Brahman priesthood, they nonetheless practiced religious tolerance and Buddhists were free to practice their own religion.

East Asia: The Chinese Empire

Contemporary with the Mauryan Empire in South Asia and the Hellenistic Empire of Alexander the Great in West Asia, the Chinese Empire was created in East Asia. In the mid-third century BCE, the northwest state of Qin (pronounced "chin") established its dominance over other states and molded these previously independent political units into a centralized administrative structure under the rule of an emperor (*huangdi*). Qin Shihuangdi (r. 221–210 BCE), the "first emperor of Qin," took the title of emperor for the first time and ruled through a central government that included civil, military, and censorial branches. The empire was administered through military commands, each of which was subdivided into counties, used as the basic structure of imperial rule well into the twentieth century. Both the administrative system and the tripartite structure of the central government were adopted by succeeding dynasties.

The Qin state's triumph over its adversaries was directly related to the political philosophy of Legalism. Legalism was adopted by the Qin state as the ideological apparatus of rule, and other ideas, most significantly Confucian ones, were banned. In the states brought under Qin control, imperial officials imposed centralized controls such as standardization of weights, measures, and currencies. The adoption of a formal legal code and the unification of various written scripts into one made possible the relatively uniform implementation of government legislation over a wide geographical area that included vastly different cultural and linguistic regions.

The Han dynasty (206 BCE–220 CE) followed the fall of the short-lived Qin. In contrast to "Qin," which is identified with the geographical territory of China, "Han" is used to refer to the Chinese people and their culture. The Han Empire was built on the foundations laid by the Qin, but the Han founders rode to power on a tide of rebellion against the tyranny of the Qin. The Han rejection of Legalist ideas associated with Qin rule and the adoption of Confucianism as state ideology obscured the reality that Legalist institutions of centralized rule formed the basis of Han imperial government.

The authority of the Han founder and his successors was supported by the Confucian Mandate of Heaven. This doctrine, first expressed by the Confucian philosopher Mencius, provided a cosmological sanction for political authority by identifying the ruler as the link between Heaven and the order of human society. Han Confucianism infused the idea of the Mandate of Heaven with elements of Daoism and other early cosmologies. Human society and the natural world were understood to be part of an organic whole, so that patterns of human society resonated in nature and vice versa. Imperial misrule, it was believed, would be manifested in nature by negative phenomena, such as solar eclipses or earthquakes. In contrast, benevolent and correct government would resonate in nature as a supernova or a comet.

Apart from the imperial religion of Han Confucianism, many deity cults flourished. Prominent among such deities was the Queen Mother of the West, a Daoist deity who was part of the emerging Daoist pantheon. Practitioners of popular or religious Daoism performed rituals to seek good fortune from deities, practiced alchemy (attempts to turn one element into another), and sought ways of achieving immortality through potions or physical practices.

The Mandate of Heaven that legitimized Han imperial rule also provided sanction to rebel leaders calling for the overthrow of the dynasty. Even in the early Han, the Confucian philosopher Dong Zhongshu (ca. 179–104 BCE) pointed out to Emperor Wu the hardships of the peasantry in the face of wealth and extravagance among the aristocracy. According to Dong, because the rich had such large estates, the poor were "left without enough land to stick an awl into" and "reduced to eating the food of dogs and swine." By the latter Han, such conditions led many peasants to join a messianic (promising deliverance or salvation) religion called the "Way of Great Peace," a combination of popular beliefs and religious Daoism. Donning yellow scarves and calling themselves "Yellow Turbans," these rebels adopted the color yellow as a symbol of their overthrowing the color white, which was associated with the Han. Undermined by rebellion within, and prey to foreign invaders from beyond the Great Wall, the Han dynasty fell in the mid-third century CE. Domestic unrest coupled with foreign invasion became a recurrent pattern in the dynastic cycle, explaining the Han loss of the Mandate of Heaven and setting the stage for a new dynasty to replace it. Religion could be used to undermine rulers as well as to support them.

The Mediterranean and Europe: The Roman Empire

The Latin peoples who settled on the banks of the Tiber River in central Italy as early as the eighth century BCE began an expansion that created a vast empire encompassing large parts of Europe, West Asia, and North Africa by the first century BCE. The Romans were quick to acculturate, to accept new influences and ideas from peoples with whom they came into contact, such as the Etruscans and the Greeks.

Early Roman religion was an animistic cult of personified spirits or **_numina_**, ranged in a hierarchy of good and evil. Religious rites were connected with the family, with attempts to

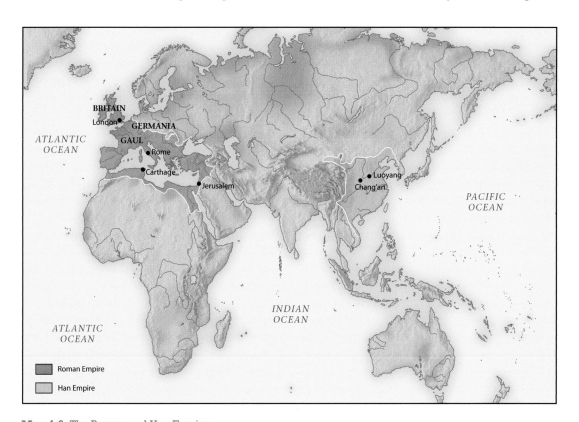

Map 4.6 The Roman and Han Empires.

secure protection from *numina* for domestic life and livelihood, and each family had its protective spirit, or **genius**, who inhabited the home. In each home there were sacred spots: for example, in the hearth dwelt Vesta, the spirit of fire; in the store-room dwelt a guardian spirit. Rites to keep good spirits in the home and evil ones away were plentiful. The practice of throwing spilled salt over the left shoulder, for example, which many people still do today to ward off bad luck, originated in such early Roman rites.

By the third century BCE, even before they expanded eastward into Greece and West Asia, the Romans incorporated into their practical agricultural animism many anthropomorphic deities they appropriated from the Greeks. The process continued as Rome became an empire. The newer gods were generally communal rather than familial, worshiped publicly rather than privately in the home, and their organization and ritual practices were controlled by the state. By the time Rome expanded beyond Italy, cults centering around Apollo and Hercules and the great mother goddess, Cybele, had taken root in Rome. Great temples were built to public deities such as Jupiter and Juno, the Roman name for the Greek Zeus and Hera, his wife; to Mars (the Greek Aries), god of war; and to Neptune (the Greek Poseidon), god of the sea. Along with the newer deities, the early Roman *numina* remained important but took anthropomorphic form: Vesta, the spirit of fire, became identified with Rome itself, and priestesses known as vestal virgins were responsible for maintaining and protecting her sacred flame.

The Hellenistic influences on Rome were accelerated as the Romans expanded eastward to impose their control over the post-Alexandrine eastern Mediterranean and North African coastline; at the same time, Rome extended its sway into northern and western Europe. Roman expansion beyond the Italian peninsula began with three Punic Wars (between 264 and 146 BCE) with the North African state of Carthage, Rome's major competitor for power in the western Mediterranean. Carthage was defeated, and its territories became the Roman province of Africa.

At the beginning of the second century BCE, the Romans turned to Greece and then to the successor states of Alexander's empire in West Asia and Egypt. By the middle of the first century BCE, Roman armies had also conquered much of western Europe south of the Rhine and Danube Rivers, along with England. Military campaigns under the leaderships of generals such as Julius Caesar (100–44 BCE) and his great-nephew Augustus (63 BCE–14 CE) created a Roman empire that stretched from Spain to Syria and from Britain to North Africa.

The expansion of Roman territory created political and social tensions. Having expelled its last king in 509 BCE, Rome became a republic in which decisions were nominally made by assemblies of citizens. But the Roman Republic was, like Athens, neither egalitarian nor democratic. Property ownership and gender were both criteria for participation in government. During the Punic Wars, the freedom of even upper-class Roman women, who had previously been allowed to attend public ceremonies and to move about openly in the city, was curtailed. The divisions between the poor and the well-to-do became increasingly aggravated rather than ameliorated by Roman expansion and, by the first century BCE, conflict between rich and poor was a major problem in Rome, as it had been in Han China.

The Roman Republic was ruled by an oligarchy in the form of the Senate, the members of which were males from wealthy and powerful families. From the late second century BCE, oligarchic control in Rome was challenged by popular discontent. Power eventually fell into the hands of a succession of military leaders, culminating in the dictatorship of Julius Caesar (r. 49–44 BCE) and the transformation of the Roman Republic into the Roman Empire by his great-nephew Octavian, who ruled as Emperor Augustus Caesar (r. 31 BCE–14 CE).

Augustus based the bureaucratic structures of his empire on the models of the Roman Republic and the Hellenistic states that succeeded the empire of Alexander the Great. For the European portions of the Roman Empire, Augustus shaped to his purposes institutions such as the Senate. Similarly, he modified and used the administrative personnel and practices of the Hellenistic successor states, such as Ptolemaic Egypt, in the eastern portions of the empire, at least until he found it necessary to annex and rule these areas directly. By employing a common language (Latin), common law, and common ideology, Augustus created a loyal and efficient bureaucracy throughout the vast reaches of the Roman Empire and thereby "Romanized" the empire.

Asia Minor (modern Turkey), previously under the domination of Persia, Athens, and the Hellenistic Empire of Alexander and his successors, provides an example of how Augustus used ideology to support imperial control. Under Roman rule, this network of Greek-speaking city-states and Hellenistic kingdoms was divided into several provinces, each administered by a governor who was appointed by Rome. But Roman rule was necessarily superficial, and the peoples of Asia Minor continued to identify primarily with their cities.

Emperor-venerating rituals formed the basis of an imperial cult, which took shape during the reign of Augustus. The imperial cult became an important means of establishing Roman authority in a region long familiar with such ritual practices. Residents of cities in Asia Minor had little difficulty accommodating the Roman imperial cult to local traditions venerating other deities. The imperial cult coexisted with other earlier, indigenous religious cults, such as that of the great mother goddess Cybele, who was possessed of the same sort of life-giving, creative powers associated with the Neolithic fertility goddesses.

Beginning about 180 CE and lasting a century, Rome was gripped by a period of internal dissent and external pressures resulting from economic instability, continuing social tension between the wealthy and the poor, and problems with imperial succession resulting in a series of emperors who were incompetent to cope with pressing prob-lems. When Diocletian (r. 285–305 CE) came to the throne, he attempted to restore and reinvigorate the empire, and he split the administration of the empire into eastern and western halves with the dividing line at the Adriatic Sea.

Association of the rituals of the imperial cult with imperial power was enhanced during Diocletian's rule. Augustus had allowed temples to be built to "Rome and the emperor" and sacrifices to be made to the *genius*, or spirit, of the emperor. But it was customary for emperors to be deified only after their deaths until Diocletian assumed the role of emperor-god during his lifetime and thus brought Roman practices into conformity with those of the West Asian theocracies conquered by Rome. Neither Diocletian's innovations nor the vigorous efforts of his successor, Constantine, were able to defer the fate of the Roman Empire. In the year 410, the Visigoths, a Germanic people, invaded Italy and sacked Rome, an event generally taken to signal the decline of the Roman Empire in western Europe, although the idea of the empire persisted in a variety of forms for many decades thereafter.

Summary

Politics and religion are both ways of systematically constructing power, and the expression of symbolic systems through religious ritual has been as effective and important a means of imposing order on the world as administrative systems or military force. Early dynastic states in West Asia, North Africa, East Asia, and Mesoamerica expanded their territorial control through military means and used religious ideas to sanction the exercise of power by central rulers. In East Asia, Shang kings asserted their right to rule through claiming that their ancestors held the power to mediate with the supreme deity worshiped by the Shang people. The ability to transmit knowledge through writing was also an important aspect of power related to religion. Priests with the ability to read and write the archaic script commanded status and authority in Shang society because they held the key to interpreting the will of the supreme deity. This was equally true for Egyptian pharaohs and their priests, who had knowledge of hieroglyphics; for the kings of Sumer and Akkad, whose priests and administrators used cuneiform script for both sacred and secular purposes; and for Mayan rulers in Mesoamerica, where scribes employed hieroglyphics in the service of the state cult.

In contrast to the use of ideas to further power, as in early theocracies, religious ideas could also be used to contest the established order of things and to challenge the power of rulers and states. Both Buddhism and Jainism, for example, emerged from but also challenged the Vedic tradition and its priesthood. Rejecting the Vedic priests' emphasis on ritual, Buddhism posed questions having to do with the meaning of human existence and suffering; its answers drew on Indian cosmology. The Hebrew prophets sought an explanation of human existence and suffering in the special relationship of the Hebrew people with a transcendent God, and Judaism drew on other West Asian cosmologies, including Zoroastrianism. Zoroastrianism grew out of ancient Indo-Iranian religious traditions in West Asia and taught a doctrine of ethical reform rooted in the cosmological dualisms of good and evil, light and dark.

As Buddha, Abraham, and Zoroaster challenged the dominant religious traditions of their times, thinkers in Greece and China envisioned new social and political orders. In the decentralized, competitive political environment of the Greek city-states and the Warring States in late Zhou China, new visions of political community were created by thinkers compelled by circumstances – the absence of either centralized rule or community structures that ensured some degree of order – to consider how best to achieve social and political order. The political form of democracy was worked out in the institutions of the Athenian city-state, and the philosophical underpinnings of this and other ideals were expressed by thinkers such as Socrates and Plato.

In China during the same period, Confucius and his followers envisioned an ideal society rooted in the institutions of the past, the rule of the sage-kings of antiquity, much like the philosopher-king idealized by Plato. In China, Legalists rejected Confucian emphasis on ethical values and on ritual as the means to achieve a harmonious society, arguing that only "strict laws and harsh punishments" could ensure social and political order.

Legalism provided the ideological underpinnings for the first unified empire in China, the Qin. Its successor, the Han, rejected the harshest ideas of Legalism in favor of the ideals of Confucianism but adopted the form of the Legalist state with central authority vested in the emperor. Han emperors then made use of cosmological notions related to early Daoism to support their right to rule. Unlike Roman emperors, Han rulers were not deified; rather, they were seen as standing at the pinnacle of human society, a crucial link between the cosmos and humanity.

After the demise of Alexander and his empire in West Asia, the imperial tradition was extended by his successors in various forms throughout West, Central, and South Asia, as well as North Africa. While they drew on the legacy of Alexander to sanction their rule, they also made use of local beliefs to reinforce their power, just as Roman emperors did in the imperial cult. In South Asia, Hellenistic influence provided a powerful model for the Mauryan and Gupta Empires, whose rulers were also god-kings, manifestations of cosmic order associated with either Buddhism or Hinduism. No less than Egyptian pharaohs, whose role was to maintain cosmic order, or *ma'at*, and Chinese emperors, who claimed the Mandate of Heaven to order the world, the Mauryan ruler Ashoka relied on a Buddhist sanction to rule, taking the title of *chakravartin*, "he for whom the wheel of the [Buddhist] law turns," to reflect his central role in promoting *dharma*, the law of the universe.

Alongside, and sometimes subsumed by, the official belief systems of dynastic states and empires were popular beliefs that celebrated the spiritual values of the individual within the larger community. These spiritual and ethical values almost certainly existed on a widespread and popular scale, preserved only through private and household ritual practice, often in the shadow of the magnificent displays associated with state cults.

Suggested readings

Basham, A.L. (1954) *The Wonder that Was India*, New York: Grove Press. Classic detailed survey of India up to about 1200 CE.

Chang, Kwang-chih (1983) *Art, Myth, and Ritual: The Path to Political Authority in Ancient China*, Cambridge, MA: Harvard University Press. A provocative and stimulating thematic approach to political culture in Shang and Zhou China.

Demand, Nancy (1996) *A History of Ancient Greece*, New York: McGraw-Hill. A recent textbook survey of ancient Greece through Alexander, stressing analysis of different kinds of sources.

Flood, Gavin (1996) *An Introduction to Hinduism*, New York: Cambridge University Press. A thematic and historical introduction to Hinduism from its origins to the present.

Grube, Nikolai, ed. (2000) *Maya: Divine Kings of the Rainforest*, Cologne: Konemann. A richly illustrated overview of recent research on the Maya, including religion, with contributions from many different scholars.

Hall, David and Roger Ames (1987) *Thinking Through Confucius*, Albany, NY: State University Press of New York Press. Comparative examination of key concepts in Confucius's thought by one specialist in Chinese philosophy and one in Greek philosophy.

Iles Johnston, Sarah, ed. (2003) *Religions of the Ancient World: A Guide*, Cambridge, MA: The Belknap Press of Harvard University Press. Topical and historical guide to religions in the ancient Mediterranean world.

Schwartz, Benjamin (1985) *The World of Thought in Ancient China*, Cambridge, MA: Harvard University Press. Thoughtful and provocative survey of the classical period of Chinese philosophy, covering Confucianism, Daoism, and Legalism.

Online resources

Bridging World History, units 5 and 6 <www.learner.org/courses/worldhistory/unit_main_5.html> <www.learner.org/courses/worldhistory/unit_main_6.html>

Study questions

1. In what ways did conceptions of gods and goddesses reflect the needs of human communities?

2. How did religion support the claims of rulers to exercise power over people?

3. What kind of transformation in thinking was represented by the development of Judaism, Zoroastrianism, and the Hindu tradition of the Upanishads?

4. What did philosophers in Greek city-states have in common with Confucius and other thinkers in China during the fifth century BCE?

5. How did rulers such as Alexander or Augustus adapt local religious traditions to serve the interests of imperial power?

6. What were mystery religions and what role did they play in the relationship between communities and state power?

Part I Summary

Along with birth, death was a universal experience that all communities encountered and dealt with in ways that expressed their diversity as well as their common humanity.

According to the Akan (Ghana, West Africa) proverb, "it is the destiny of every human to climb the ladder of death." This proverb was represented by the ancient symbol of a ladder on Akan funerary pottery from the Late Iron Age, but its truth echoes in cultures around the world. Artistic expression became the universal medium for communicating beliefs, fears, questions, and longings about the mysteries and meanings of human life and death.

Ancient Egyptians envisioned the departure to the afterlife as a boat trip down the waters of the Nile. Egyptian stone inscriptions, wall and coffin paintings, and illustrated manuscripts on papyrus depict the transition as a rather frightful trip to the underworld; others portray preparations for the deceased's travels. Commissioned by private individuals, Egyptian coffin paintings often were personal, autobiographical laments, such as "The Dialogue of a Man with his Soul" (2255–2035 BCE), a debate on suicide. Egyptian funerary beliefs were collected in the Book of the Dead, dating to the time of the New Kingdom (ca. 1570–1070 BCE) and containing an illustrated set of hymns, prayers, and magic formulas to guide and protect the soul in its journey.

Funerary arts from around the world share the common concern that the deceased person's life after death be materially comfortable if not better than their lifetime had been. Furniture, food, and sometimes people accompanied the deceased person, as in Mayan, Egyptian, or Chinese society, where tombs were filled with elaborate grave goods for use after death. At the site of Mawangdui in south central China a mid-second-century tomb has yielded such items of daily use as red and black lacquer dishes, ladles, and food containers along with the mummified body of a woman known as Lady Dai, who was entombed there with her husband and son. Among the artifacts retrieved from this tomb is a painted silk funerary banner that was draped over Lady Dai's coffin. Its figures and symbols attest to the practice described in literary texts as the "summons of the soul." Chinese of the Han period (206 BCE–220 CE) believed that the soul had a dual aspect: one part was earthly and returned to the earth at death, and another was spirit, which left the body at death. Mourners performed a ritual by waving a banner on the rooftop to plead with the departed spirit to return.

By the fifth century BCE in the Mediterranean, temples were dedicated to Ceres, a Roman goddess of birth and death associated with the agricultural seasons and the transformations of nature. The continuous link between fertility and returning the dead to the earth was basic to the concept of death as part of the life cycle. Roman women were responsible for preparing and mourning the corpse and thus also played an important role in funerary rites. Societies around the world used burial sites as places

Illustration from the Book of the Dead (Egypt, New Kingdom ca. 1310 BCE), showing the deceased scribe Hu-Nefer, being led to his hour of judgment with Osiris, God of the Dead (seated right).

in which to remember the past. These could be individual graves of family members buried beneath the earthen floor of a household or monumental mounds and temples that paid homage to dead rulers. The concepts of reincarnation and rebirth would link generations to their ancestors. Whether physical or metaphysical, primarily verbal or visual, remembrance was a common and comforting human attempt at immortality.

The themes that emerged in the chapters of Part I are central to world history and they appear to shape the successful journey on every continent. Migration and adaptation were responses to the task of community-building and the elaboration of belonging that helped to foster both change and stability. The increasing complexity of human societies depended on the successful forging of relationships between humans and the natural world and between urban and rural, while ideas of power connected the visible and invisible realms. Although Part I has explored these themes from earliest human consciousness, we may find that the thematic threads that emerged in the first eras continue to weave together the patterns of the human experience through the twenty-first century and beyond.

Part II

Order

1 CE to 1500 CE

Isabelle of Angouleme and Eleanor of Aquitaine, Royal Hunting Scene. Fresco in St. Radegund's Chapel, Chinon, twelfth to thirteenth century.

Part II Introduction

Eleanor of Aquitaine (ca. 1122–1204) was by all accounts an extraordinary woman: heir to lands that made her the most important vassal of the king of France, queen of France and later England, the first queen to go on crusade in the Holy Land, and the mother of ten children. One of her sons by the English king was Richard the Lionheart, whose fortunes she protected throughout the political struggles between England and France during his captivity in the Holy Land. She was also a generous benefactor to the abbey of Fontevraud, and like many other aristocratic women of her time, she retired to the convent there at the end of her life. The wealth and status Eleanor gained through her father created exceptional opportunities for this dynamic woman, who took advantage of them to explode medieval European expectations of gender roles and social behavior by using family fortunes in the pursuit of power. Her story highlights the multiple prisms through which individual lives are refracted: personal experiences of gender and family, and the religious, social, economic, and political worlds in which these experiences are embedded.

Part II addresses the broad theme of order: how did human beings create increasingly complex social, political, and economic orders? Building on the themes of migration, adaptation, community, and ideas and power developed in Part I, this section examines the ways in which the spread of religions was interwoven with the expansion of empire, and tracks continuities and changes in economic, social, and political orders across the globe between the first century CE and 1500.

Chapter 5: The spread of world religions: Missionaries, merchants, and monarchs begins with the spread of Buddhism following its origins in a sixth-century-BCE Himalayan kingdom, tracing its paths across Asia along the routes traversed by missionaries, monks, and merchants. Christianity and Islam both emerged from common roots in West Asia, to spread across Afro-Eurasia in the period before 1500. Buddhism, Christianity, and Islam all built on earlier religions in Asia, but are called "world religions" because they spread far beyond the societies in which they emerged. As these world religions expanded across both political and geographical boundaries in Afro-Eurasia before 1500, they were transformed by the cultures and peoples they encountered as much as they altered beliefs and practices around the world.

Chapter 6: Making a living: World economies focuses on the basic and universal question of how people made a living in the past. How did they gain access to what they needed to survive, and even to prosper? How did societies create systems of exchange based on differing concepts of value? What was considered valuable – land, labor, or commodities such as grain, gold, silk, and salt? Diverse environmental and ecological settings provide the context for the development of different economies. As systems that provided access to, and control over, both material and human resources (labor) and their distribution, economies were closely intertwined with political power.

Chapter 7: Family matters: Gender, family, and household considers the familiar and intimate world of the family and household in relation to gender roles. The building block of all human societies is the biological family, but the biologically determined family varies greatly in its importance across cultures and over time. The role of the biological family depends on its place within a web of relationships defined in culturally specific ways. Gender is also based on observed biological differences, but is equally a cultural and social construct. Transformations in gender, family, and household were brought about by influences from religion, changing economies, and regulation by the state.

Chapter 8: Ties that bind: Lineage, clientage, and caste explores the roles played by lineage societies in world history, from West Asia to West Africa. It also traces patterns of patron–client relations, including those commonly called "feudalism" in both Europe and Japan. The concept and practice of caste is examined in both South Asian and West African contexts. Slavery is treated in its worldwide context as both an economic and a social system based on the institutionalization of difference.

Chapter 9: Early empires draws on material presented in the previous chapters in this section to focus on the political aspect of order by examining both common and diverse characteristics of empires in Eurasia, Africa, and the Americas: Srivijayan and Khmer Empires in Southeast Asia, the Mongol Empire, the Mali Empire, and the Mexica-Aztec and Incan Empires. What features are shared by empires in the pre-1500 period? What differences can be identified in the creation and collapse of these empires?

TIMELINE

35 CE	30–100	ca. 100	216–277	224–651	312	315
Crucifiixion of Jesus	Compilation of Christian Gospels	Buddhism transmitted to China	Lifetime of Mani	Persian Sassanid Empire	Constantine declares for Christian god	Frumentius converts King Ezana of Axum

5 The spread of world religions

Missionaries, merchants, and monarchs

In 836 CE, the Japanese Buddhist monk Ennin joined an embassy from the Japanese court to China, hoping to visit Chinese centers of Buddhist learning and enrich his understanding of the faith and its practice. After two abortive attempts to cross the sea, the embassy finally reached China in 838 CE. When embassy officials departed for the Tang capital of Chang'an, Ennin stayed behind awaiting Chinese government permission to travel to Mount Tiantai, the center of the Tiantai (Jpn. Tendai) sect of Buddhism. Tendai Buddhism had taken root in Japan after its teachings were transmitted from China by Ennin's predecessor and mentor, Saichō, at the beginning of the ninth century. Denied permission to go to Mount Tiantai, Ennin desperately tried to find ways to stay in China. During one of these attempts, he and his companions were helped by Korean coal merchants after being shipwrecked along the coast. But Ennin was eventually ordered to depart with an embassy ship. Fortunately for him, bad weather intervened and the Japanese ship was forced back to the tip of the Shandong peninsula, where Ennin and his companions were put ashore and sought shelter at a small Korean monastery. After enjoying the hospitality of the Korean monks, Ennin and his followers were convinced to travel to nearby Mount Wutai, one of the greatest centers of Buddhism in Tang China, rather than the more distant Mount Tiantai in the southeast. Aided by their Korean colleagues, Ennin's group received official permission to make this journey before proceeding to the imperial capital. One of the first encounters described by Ennin was with the learned monk Zhiyuan:

Monk Zhiyuan said, "In the twentieth year of Zhenyuan [804] I saw Saichō of Japan go to

351–430	380	450	ca. 550	ca. 570–632	622	651
Lifetime of St. Augustine	Christianity offiicially becomes religion of Roman Empire	Council of Chalcedon	Buddhism transmitted to Japan	Lifetime of Muhammad	Muhammad's fllight from Mecca (hejira)	Compilation of Qur'an

Tiantai in search of the Law. The prefect of Taizhou [site of Mount Tiantai], himself provided him with paper, ink, and scribes, and they copied several hundred scrolls, which he gave to Saichō, who obtained seals for them and then returned to his homeland." Then he asked about the prosperity of the Tendai sect in Japan. Accordingly, I related in brief about the rebirth of Huisi [515–77, the second patriarch of the Tiantai sect, believed to have been reincarnated as Prince Shōtoku in early sixth century Japan] and the spread of Buddhism. Zhiyuan and the group were extremely happy.

Adapted from Edwin O. Reischauer, trans., *Ennin's Diary: The Record of a Pilgrimage to China in Search of the Law* (New York: Ronald Press, 1955), 229–30.

The remarkable account left by Ennin of his travels in Tang China in search of Buddhist teachings illustrates key features of the dynamic and complex environment in which world religions spread: pilgrims seeking to visit sacred sites related to their faiths, the role of government officials in facilitating or prohibiting access to religious sites and institutions, and the multicultural and multilingual setting of the transmission of religious doctrines and practices. In Ennin's case alone, he was navigating among Sanskrit, Chinese, and Japanese languages and texts, and in the course of his own journey, he engaged with Korean merchants and monks, as well as Chinese monks and officials.

The spread of world religions encompasses pilgrims such as Ennin, missionaries who first brought Buddhism to Korea and Japan, and merchants who carried their beliefs with them as they traveled and traded. Rulers of states and empires converted to these world religions and in turn promoted them through their patronage – sometimes even through forcible conversions of their subjects. Although all three world religions became intertwined with politics, in the case of Christianity and Islam the spread of these world religions was closely connected with imperial expansion. The story of the spread of world religions is also one of the transformation of these religions as they encountered new beliefs and practices across the cultural frontiers they traveled. Buddhism adopted new ideas and practices as it spread from India to China, Korea, and Japan, and Christianity and Islam were similarly transformed as they migrated from their places of origin across the globe.

Introduction to the theme of the spread of religions

Buddhism, Christianity, and Islam are often referred to as universal or world religions because they expanded beyond their places of origin in South and West Asia and spread across vast regions of the globe. All three were proselytizing religions: Buddhists, Christians, and Muslims all tried to convert others to their beliefs. Buddhism, Christianity, and Islam were at different times and in varying degrees patronized by rulers who donated their wealth and power to promote the faiths, sometimes as a devotional act and sometimes as a political strategy. Patronage, however

656	668	711	712–84	715	750	751
Founding of Umayyad Caliphate at Damascus	Unifiication of Korean peninsula under Silla and promotion of Buddhism	Muslim invasion of Iberian peninsula	Nara period in Japan and state patronage of Buddhism	Muslim armies cross Indus	Founding of Abbasid Caliphate at Baghdad	Defeat of Chinese at Talas River by Arabs and Turks

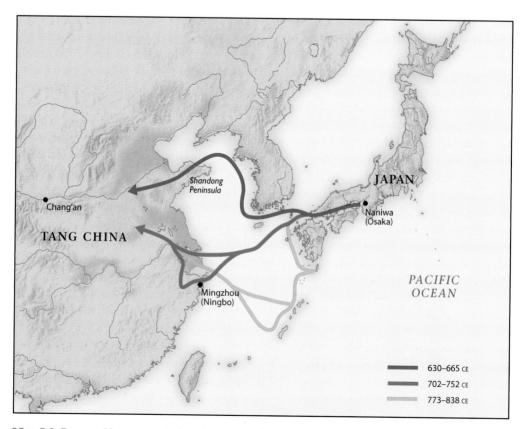

Map 5.1 Routes of Japanese missions to China at the time of Ennin's travels.

valuable to the spread of religions, also had consequences, as Buddhism, Christianity, and Islam were drawn into the politics of states in Asia, Africa, and Europe.

Buddhism originated in a Himalayan kingdom in what is now Nepal during the sixth century BCE. Its founding figure, Buddha, was a contemporary of Confucius in China and the early Greek philosophers, antedating Jesus by 500 years and Muhammad by a millennium. The foundations of Buddhism were deeply rooted in early Indian cosmology, drawing on concepts such as *dharma*, which meant "duty" in the Upanishads, but became the "law of the universe" in Buddhism. By the beginning of the first millennium CE, however, the influence of Buddhism waned in its South Asian homeland as it began to spread from India to East and Southeast Asia, where it gained many followers and became a potent cultural, social, and even political force.

800	988	1095	1198–1216	1324–5	1453	1492
Charlemagne crowned Holy Roman Emperor	Conversion of Vladimir and Kievan Rus'	First Crusade launched by Pope Urban	Reign of Pope Innocent III	Pilgrimage to Mecca of Mali ruler Mansa Musa	Conquest of Constantinople by Turks	Christian reconquest of Iberian peninsula

Christianity and Islam arose in the same geographic and cultural setting of West Asia. Both drew from the ancient traditions of that region, particularly that of the Jewish people and Judaism. Despite the dispersal of the Jewish people, their religion survived both in its own right and as a profound influence on the development of Christianity and Islam. Christianity was inspired by the life and death of its founder, the Jewish prophet Jesus of Nazareth (d. ca. 35 CE). His death and resurrection became the mythic center of Christianity, as it symbolized the eternal life of those who followed the Christian faith. The name of the religion is drawn from the appellation Christ, Greek for the Hebrew **messiah** ("anointed"). Five hundred years later, Islam ("submission to the will of God"), was founded by the prophet Muhammad (ca. 570–632 CE). Believers in Islam also regarded Jesus as a prophet, although Muhammad was believed to be the ultimate prophet of God, known in Islam as Allah.

As they spread through Africa and Eurasia, Christianity and Islam encountered other belief systems and cultures, which were variously absorbed and adapted by Christian and Islamic rulers. Buddhism similarly engaged the religious beliefs and cultural ideals of the societies its missionaries penetrated. In contrast to the monotheistic background of Christianity and Islam, Buddhism grew in a cultural and philosophical environment that recognized the coexistence of many deities, even many different pantheons. As it spread from India to China, Korea, Japan, and Southeast Asia, it encountered and adapted to many different cultures, changing them as

Buddhism itself was transformed by exposure to these cultures.

Buddhism

By the beginning of the first century CE, Buddhist missionaries were carrying their beliefs and practices beyond India to Central, East, and Southeast Asia, along the **Silk Roads** and over maritime routes. Before its transmission beyond the frontiers of India, Buddhism had divided into Mahayana ("Greater Vehicle") and Theravada ("Doctrine of the Elders") traditions. Mahayana Buddhists emphasized universal salvation through devotional practices accessible to lay believers. This contrasted with the Theravada (also known pejoratively as Hinayana, or "Lesser Vehicle") concentration on the discipline of renunciation, spiritual self-cultivation, and meditation characteristic of monastic life, and the belief that only those who devoted their lives to Buddhist practice could attain enlightenment. As the goal shifted from enlightenment, at the heart of early Buddhism, to salvation in Mahayana Buddhism, there was a profound change in the fundamental orientation of Buddhist believers.

The central religious goal of Mahayana belief was that of the **bodhisattva**, one who seeks enlightenment for the purpose of aiding other beings in the pursuit of awakening, in contrast to the Theravada *arhat,* who was concerned with individual spiritual liberation. The *bodhisattva* ideal was rooted in the altruism of Buddha in his former lives, when he sought to help other living beings. It was represented in Mahayana Buddhism by the Buddhas and *bodhisattvas* who became the focus of worship by Mahayana believers. The *bodhisattva* Avalokiteshvara and the Buddha Amitabha became the center of Mahayana Buddhist beliefs and practice. As Buddhism was transmitted from India across Asia, the Mahayana tradition came to dominate Central and East Asia, while Theravada became dominant in Southeast Asia, and these differences continue to the present day.

Buddhism in China

When the Han dynasty fell in 220 CE, China entered a long period of political turmoil and social disorder. The Buddhist belief that life is suffering and that the world of the senses is impermanent and illusory held great appeal for people living in chaotic conditions of frequent warfare and political, social, and economic instability, making them easily susceptible to conversion. Central Asian monks translated the **sutras**, the sacred scriptures of Buddhism, from Sanskrit and Pali (the classical languages of South Asia) into Chinese and transmitted Indian Buddhism to an elite Chinese audience. Often these monks were patronized by non-Chinese rulers of nomadic peoples who invaded and conquered north China during the three centuries following the fall of the Han dynasty and who were attracted to Buddhism for political as well as spiritual reasons. Merchants who traveled the Silk Roads were also active transmitters of Buddhism, carrying their faith with them as they plied their trade across Central Asia.

The career of Kumarajiva illustrates both the difficulties and complexities of the transmission of Buddhism. Born in the Central Asian oasis state of Kucha in 343, Kumarajiva became one of the most prolific and important translators of Buddhist texts into Chinese. As a young boy he took monastic vows, and his scholarly accomplishments in the study of Buddhist scriptures soon brought fame that spread as far as China. When

the ruler of the Eastern Jin dynasty heard about him, he sent a delegation to bring Kumarajiva to his court at Chang'an. But before Kumarajiva could reach the Jin capital, he was kidnapped by a rebel general and held in captivity for 17 years. Despite the circumstances, Kumarajiva was able to use this time to learn Chinese, and when he finally arrived in Chang'an in 401, he immediately began translating Buddhist sutras into Chinese.

Transferring Buddhist ideas across the vast cultural frontier between India and China required translators to search for native vocabulary that could at least vaguely suggest the concepts they were trying to convey. But ultimately they were restricted to terminology that might be quite distant in meaning from what they began with. The translation of texts, however skillful, meant the transformation of ideas. For example, the concept of *nirvana* (literally, "extinction," meaning the extinction of the illusion of permanence) was rendered by the Daoist term, *wuwei*, literally "non-action."

Buddhist missionaries in China were challenged to teach this new religion in the context of indigenous beliefs and practices, especially what we know as Confucianism and Daoism. The teachings of Confucius (551–479 BCE), recorded by his disciples in the *Analects*, exhorted people to follow the models of the sage kings of antiquity and to bring order to both family and society through the practice of ritual. Confucius paid little attention to the spiritual realm, preferring to deal with what he could know through experience. The Buddhist monastic ideal rejected family, and focused entirely on cultivating spiritual life. Daoist teachings and practices aimed at knowing how to correlate one's life with *qi*, the "vital breath" of the cosmos that animates nature, humans, and gods, and so was more easily accommodated by Buddhism.

CHINESE BUDDHIST SECTS All sutras were supposed to represent the teachings of Buddha, but in fact the doctrines they transmitted were not consistent. These differences gave rise to scholastic traditions within Chinese Buddhism that sought to systematize and reconcile the diverse teachings found in the sutras. The Tiantai ("Heavenly Platform") school, which the Japanese monk Ennin followed, dated from the latter sixth century and attempted to synthesize Buddhist teachings by a system of doctrinal classification. Tiantai followers believed foremost in the efficacy of the *Lotus Sutra*, one of the earliest sutras and one that espoused a relatively straightforward path to Buddhahood, aided by the compassionate *bodhisattva* Avalokiteshvara. This sutra became the most important text in East Asian Buddhism, with a popular appeal that transcended sectarian differences. Somewhat later, the Huayan school (Kor. Hwa'ŏm, Jpn. Kegon) developed another method for doctrinal classification, although it took its name from a single sutra that was regarded as the pinnacle of Buddhist teaching.

One of the most important sectarian developments was the Pure Land school, said to have originated with a devotional cult to the Buddha Amitabha established by the learned cleric Huiyuan (334–416 CE). The Pure Land school preaches the efficacy of complete faith in the precepts of Buddhism to attain salvation and worships the Buddha Amitabha and the *bodhisattva* Avalokiteshvara. These two deities preside over the Western Paradise, the "Pure Land," where believers seek to go to attain enlightenment with the aid of the Buddha Amitabha and *bodhisattva* Avalokiteshvara. Both of these were Sanskrit names indicating their Indian origin. Known as Guanyin ("one who embraces the world") in Chinese (Kor. Kwan'um, Jpn. Kannon), the *bodhisattva* Avalokiteshvara became the most popular Buddhist deity in China and eventually in both Korea and Japan.

Chan (Skt. *Dhyāna*, "meditation"), is a distinctly Chinese sect that originated during this early period and was premised on the notion that every living being contained the Buddha-nature. Chan rejected scriptural study in favor of practices such as meditation that could bring about the realization of the Buddha nature and thus enlightenment. The development of the Chan sect in China was heavily influenced by Daoism and is better known in the modern West by its Japanese name, Zen (Kor. Sŏn).

IMPERIAL PATRONAGE OF BUDDHISM   By the sixth century CE, Buddhism was thoroughly integrated into Chinese culture, and believers could be found at all levels of society. When China was reunified in the latter sixth century by Yang Jian, founder of the Sui dynasty (589–617 CE), he made use of both Buddhist and Confucian sources of legitimacy for claiming the right to rule. He declared that he had received the Confucian Mandate of Heaven, but he also laid claim to the Buddhist ideal of the *chakravartin* ruler. The Sui was swiftly displaced by a new dynasty, the Tang (618–907 CE), which inaugurated an era of great cultural flourishing and imperial expansion. Like their predecessors, the founding emperors of Tang claimed the Mandate of Heaven, but they also made use of Buddhism to support their rule. One of the most famous ruler patrons of Buddhism was the Empress Wu (r. 690–705 CE), who claimed power after the death of her husband and who used Buddhism to promote her political interests. Called "Imperial Bodhisattva" by those who sought to win her favor, she had Buddhist images carved into mountains in north China to demonstrate her devotion to the faith and thus to gain the goodwill of powerful Buddhist clergy and aristocratic lay believers.

Both the imperial house and wealthy aristocratic families made donations to Buddhist monasteries and temples, and devout individuals took vows as monks or nuns. The Buddhist church acquired great wealth and power as both the size and number of monastic estates and the population of monks and nuns soared during the seventh and eighth centuries. Later emperors attacked the wealth of monastic Buddhism, reclaiming lands and forcing monks and nuns to return to lay life. The suppression of Buddhism in 845 CE caused thousands of temples and monasteries to be razed and restored hundreds of thousands of monks and nuns to lay status. Despite the withdrawal of state patronage and support signaled by the mid-ninth century attacks on Buddhism, in subsequent centuries, lay and popular forms of Buddhist belief and practice took hold at all levels of Chinese society and Buddhism continued to flourish, influencing arts and literary culture as well as religious life.

The spread of Buddhism to Korea and Japan

At the height of its power in the seventh and eighth centuries, when Tang China influenced all of East Asia, Buddhism became an important conduit of Chinese cultural influence. Buddhist missionaries went out from China to other parts of East Asia, especially Korea and, later, Japan. In the mid-sixth century CE, the Korean peninsula was divided among three kingdoms concentrated in the north (Koguryo), southwest (Paekche), and southeast (Silla). Inhabitants of the peninsula learned of Buddhist teachings by the late fourth and early fifth centuries. Buddhism became the official religion of Silla in the sixth century, helping to consolidate the new institution of kingship there and subsequently for Silla's unification of the peninsula in 668. Silla was a thoroughly Buddhist state, although Buddhism incorporated elements of indigenous shamanistic religion. Buddhism continued to flourish in Koryŏ (918–1392 CE), along with Confucianism, which provided both ideological and institutional support for the government.

In the mid-sixth century, a delegation from the kingdom of Paekche brought a Buddha image and some scriptures to Japan, and this is traditionally seen as the first official notice of Buddhism there. Sixth-century Japan was in the process of transforming a confederation of clans into a centrally organized dynastic state. Buddhism played a role in this process by presenting an alternative to indigenous religious beliefs, later known as Shinto, or "Way of the Gods." Both animism and shamanism were part of early Shinto, as were totemistic clan ancestors who were venerated as progenitor deities of clans. The "Way of the Gods" was that of both the deities and spirits found in nature and the anthropomorphic deities that populated the Japanese creation myths.

Like the term Hinduism, which came into use long after the ideas and practices associated with it were formed, the term "Shinto" was created to refer to indigenous beliefs and practices associated with the clan-based society of early Japan only after the advent of Buddhism. The new religion of Buddhism was championed by one of these clans, the Soga, as a means of promoting its own interests in power struggles at the "court" of the Sun line, the imperial family who claimed descent from the central Shinto deity, the sun goddess. The son of a Soga mother and imperial father, Prince Shōtoku (574–622 CE) served as regent for his young empress aunt at the Japanese court during the late sixth and early seventh centuries and was a devout patron of Buddhism. He encouraged the copying of Buddhist scriptures in classical Chinese and supported the building of temples. Patronage by the imperial court through the actions of Prince Shōtoku helped the Buddhist faith gain adherents among the aristocracy.

The transmission of Buddhism to Japan from China and Korea also served as a means of transmitting other aspects of Chinese civilization, such as political institutions, literature (poetry and history), and Confucian thought. In 604 CE, Prince Shōtoku issued a series of moral injunctions designed to promote loyalty to the sovereign; these injunctions reflect Confucian influence as well as Shinto and Buddhist ideas, woven together to provide sanction for imperial authority over powerful clans. The era of the Taika reforms, beginning in 645 CE, saw the adoption of administrative rules and institutions directly modeled on those of Tang China and designed to further centralize power in the imperial court. The formal literary language of classical Chinese was used for government documents, historical records, and poetry and other writings.

By the beginning of the Nara period (712–84 CE), named for the imperial Japanese city modeled on the Chinese capital, Chang'an, Buddhist sects established monasteries and temples in the new city, resplendent with Buddhist images produced by Korean and Japanese artisans. Buddhist priests became powerful figures in the society of the new state, which was modeled on the imperial government of Tang China. In the 770s, one of these priests even made an unsuccessful play for the throne, relying on the favor of a reigning empress. In the subsequent Heian period (794–1185), although the capital moved to the new city of Heian (modern Kyoto) to escape the power of Buddhist priests, Buddhism flourished among both the aristocracy and the common people.

By around 1000 CE, Buddhism was deeply rooted in East Asia and had undergone profound changes with the development of sectarian traditions distinctive to East Asia. These new sects were transmitted from China to Korea and Japan, and monks and priests like Ennin traveled back and forth between Korea, Japan, and China seeking teaching and scriptures. The entire Buddhist canon was published in Korea in the early thirteenth century, and when the woodblocks from this edition were destroyed by the Mongols, they were redone in the mid-thirteenth century. More than 80,000 of these woodblocks are still housed at a monastery in southern Korea. Both the Pure Land and Chan sects gained large followings in Korea and Japan by the thirteenth century. With the development of popular salvational sects such as Pure Land, Buddhism penetrated all levels of society, from ruling aristocracies to the common people. The Buddhist church played a role of economic, social, and political importance, and Buddhist priests were members of the educated establishment in China, Korea, and Japan. Buddhist monks engaged in welfare activities, providing charity for the poor, while the large estates that belonged to some temples and monasteries made them among the wealthiest landholders in Tang China, Silla Korea, and Heian Japan.

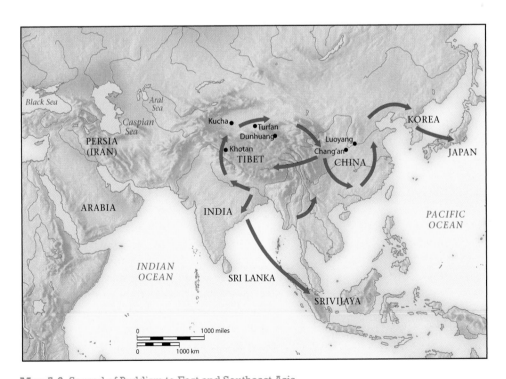

Map 5.2 Spread of Buddism to East and Southeast Asia.

Buddhism and Hinduism in Southeast Asia

Both Hinduism and Buddhism were transmitted to Southeast Asia by sea routes as early as the first and second centuries CE, and by the seventh century, Buddhism had penetrated the Southeast Asian archipelago. Early stone inscriptions at Palembang, the capital of the Srivijayan Empire (ca. 683–1085) on the Malay peninsula and the island of Sumatra testify to state patronage of Buddhism, showing how local imagery of the sacred mountain and sea and the traditional veneration of ancestors were blended together with Buddhist ideas. Buddhist themes imposed upon indigenous traditions provided a common set of ideas that transcended local communities. To build regional prestige, Srivijayan rulers became major builders of Buddhist temples and patrons of Buddhist scholarship in their territories. In the late eighth century, rulers of Java constructed Borobudur, the largest Buddhist monument ever built.

Shortly thereafter, on the mainland of Southeast Asia, the Khmer state gained control over the Mekong River Valley and delta. Both Hinduism and Buddhism provided sanction for the authority of rulers and built common cultural and religious bonds among the Khmer people.

Khmer rulers initially blended Hinduism with indigenous beliefs to consolidate their power over expanding territory, and the Sanskrit language was adopted by the Khmer court. Worship of the Hindu god Shiva, who was identified as the "Lord of the Mountain," was connected with indigenous beliefs in the sanctity of mountains, the home of ancestral spirits. Shiva was also associated with fertility, and similarly worship of Shiva was merged with local fertility beliefs in Shiva's representation by the stone or metal "phallus," the *lingam*, inserted upright into the circular "vulva," or *yoni*, at shrines dedicated to him in the Khmer

5.1 Meditating Buddha on Stupa Terrace at Borobudur, Java, eighth century CE.

state. The twelfth-century Hindu temple complex, Angkor Wat, eventually incorporated Buddhist images, as rulers aligned themselves with both Hindu, and later Buddhist, deities. On the walls of the Khmer capital Angkor Thom, also built in the twelfth century, are huge Buddhist images of whom the Khmer ruler was said to be a manifestation.

In the fourteenth century, the newly consolidated Sinhalese (Sri Lankan) form of Theravada Buddhism was spread by missionary monks into continental Southeast Asia (modern Burma, Thailand, Laos, and Cambodia). The strong monastic tradition that developed here shared a common canon of scriptures with Sri Lanka written in the sacred Pali language. Monks were the keepers of literary culture, and monasteries were centers of learning as well as religious life.

A vigorous sea trade linking South and Southeast Asia in the early centuries CE brought Buddhism to the Southeast Asian archipelago, and the patronage of rulers there helped to spread it among the people. Buddhism was also transmitted overland from north India into continental Southeast Asia, where it mingled with local beliefs as well as Hinduism and was also patronized by rulers of emerging states and empires. Merchants, monks, and kings all contributed to the spread of Buddhism to Southeast Asia.

Christianity

At the beginning of the first millennium CE in Palestine, then a province of the Roman Empire, a Jew named Jesus was born in the town of Bethlehem. Palestine had come under Roman control about 65 BCE, but some Jewish groups continued to resist the Roman occupation. Jewish political activists, called "Zealots," a small minority of the Jewish population, carried out guerrilla attacks against the Roman government. Another group of Jews, the Essenes, chose to withdraw from the tensions of everyday life under Roman occupation and settle in communities to await the imminent end of the world that would usher in a new age. The Essenes held baptisms in their communities to commemorate the repentance of sins and entry into the Army of God.

Mystery cults, based on secret rites or doctrines known only to the initiated, flourished in Palestine as they did throughout the Roman Empire. The dominant mystery cult was that of **Mithra**, an Indo-Iranian solar deity who, by slaughtering a mythical bull, fertilized the earth. Mithraism was a militant cult that was especially popular with the Roman military, although it was attributed to Zoroaster and thrived in the Persian Empire. It may have been particularly attractive to soldiers because it preached the virtues of courage and fraternity. As part of the religious context in which Christianity took root, its practices reveal similarities to those followed by Christians. The ritual of baptism to cleanse away previous sins was carried out before a large mural that portrayed Mithra slaying the bull, and the celebrants ate a sacred meal of bread and wine. The sacred day of Mithraism was 25 December, the winter solstice.

When he was about 30 years old, Jesus set out to preach reform in this Palestinian milieu of many diverse religious beliefs and practices. He spoke against narrow reliance on ritual, attacked the legalistic and too-worldly character of community religious leaders. He warned of the imminent end of the world, the resurrection of the dead, judgment, and the establishment of the kingdom of God. After three years of preaching to increasingly receptive audiences, the Romans tried Jesus on two counts: for blasphemy and for claims of being "king of the Jews." Jesus did not deny the claim of kingship, although he had never asserted it. Given the combination of armed Jewish Zealots hostile to Rome and the popular belief that the "kingdom of God" would result from the apocalyptic struggle between good and evil, Jesus seemed very much a political danger to Roman authority in Palestine. He was convicted of the charges and executed by crucifixion around 35 CE.

The small community Jesus left behind could easily have collapsed or become just another separatist community like the Essenes. The issue that tested it was the question of the acceptability of **Gentile** (non-Jewish) membership in the community of Jesus's followers. A number of Jesus's early followers in Jerusalem refused to accept Gentiles into their community, feeling that a Gentile presence would defile what they considered Jewish worship. As a result, a division developed among the followers of Jesus, and those who would not accept the Gentiles into common worship, as they believed that Jesus's message had been meant primarily or exclusively for the Jews, withdrew to worship separately from those who admitted Gentiles to worship. Following the Roman occupation of Jerusalem in 70 CE, the separate Jewish Christian community disappeared. Under the leadership of Paul, the strongest supporter of joint worship, Christianity became increasingly Gentile and expanded rapidly.

Between 70 and 100 CE, the sacred texts of Christianity were established through a complex process of selection and editing. What emerged from this process were the four Gospels, or "Good News," written in Greek by four of Jesus's apostles. They describe the sayings and deeds of Jesus and spell out collectively how these sayings and deeds were to be understood. To these Gospels was added the Epistles of Paul, couched in the form of advisory letters and sermons written by him to early Christian communities in need of advice. In contrast to the more formal biographical approach of the Gospels, Paul's Epistles described his experience with Jesus and were a highly personalized and spiritual account. These texts (the "New Testament") were attached to the Judaic sacred scriptures (the "Old Testament") to comprise the Christian Bible.

Within a century after the death of Jesus, there were small communities of Christians strewn across western Eurasia and North Africa. These communities developed from the efforts of Jesus's disciples and their followers. As Christian believers spread geographically, Christianity began to adapt to and absorb both the ideas and the practices of different cultures. The number of Christians expanded through the second and third centuries, and by the fourth century Christianity rivaled both Persian Zoroastrianism and its later manifestation, **Manichaeism**, in influence in West Asia.

Manichaeism

The Zoroastrian concept of an ongoing war between good and evil, light and dark, provided crucial background for the development of Manichaeism, named after its founder, Mani (ca. 216–77 CE), an itinerant preacher and physician from southern Iraq. Mani served at court in Iran in the early years of the Persian Sassanid dynasty (224–651 CE). Mani developed a fully detailed cosmology based on Zoroastrianism. The war between good and evil, light and dark, he said, would go on throughout eternity. According to Mani, humanity was created to be soldiers on the side of light but through defeats and setbacks had become hopelessly entangled in the material dark world. All humans had a spark of divine light in them. Every child born took from that spark, however, diluting light further in dark matter. A series of messengers and prophets had been sent down to Earth to offer salvation from the swamp of evil darkness that is Earth; Buddha had been one of them, Zoroaster another, and Jesus had been one of the greatest of them. Following him, Mani came as the "seal of the prophet," the "apostle of Jesus Christ," to enlighten humanity on how to identify and venerate its spark of light. Mani was executed as a heretic but, through its learned priesthood, Manichaeism gained many adherents in the Roman and Persian empires, eventually spreading as far east as China.

The adoption and spread of Christianity in the Roman Empire

Despite rivals such as Manichaeism and official opposition and persecution by Roman rulers, Christianity continued to spread. Augustine (354–430 CE), one of the great Christian thinkers and a "Church Father," was a North African who professed Manichaean beliefs before his conversion to Christianity. Although the Roman emperor Diocletian carried out a major persecution of Christians in 303 CE, his successor Constantine (r. 306–37), whose mother was a Christian, became a champion of the religion. In 312, on the eve of a major battle, Constantine promised to declare for the Christian god in the event he won. The victorious Constantine was true to his pledge, sanctioning Christianity by giving it legal status and favoring Christians for the rest of his life. In 380, Christianity became the imperial state religion. By the fifth century, the secure position Christianity had achieved tended to supplement and increase imperial authority, as emperors, now resident in Constantinople, were supported by an increasingly institutionalized and powerful Christianity.

The social values of early Christianity also contributed to its success. Although from the formative years of the Christian movement women were regarded as inferior members of Christian society – denied the right to become priests, for example – they were accepted as members of the church. This was not the case among other contemporary religions. And, whereas membership in some of the Gnostic cults was socially exclusive, confined to elite males, Christians came from all segments of society. Because Christianity was neither elitist nor socially exclusive, many of its adherents were poor laborers. Christian communities practiced mutual support, providing both practical and spiritual help for each other.

Moreover, Christians quickly showed exceptional organizational skills. During the second century, the distinction between clergy and laity was made clear and as the movement expanded, the clergy increased in numbers and developed hierarchical structures. This administrative organization enabled the Church to recruit new members efficiently and to support and integrate them into the community. In the fourth century, as Christianity became the imperial religion of Rome, its organization became a mirror image of Roman imperial structures, and state and Church became dependent upon each other, partners in power.

The unity of the Roman world was split in two within a century of the recognition of Christianity as the official religion of the empire in 380 CE. The political capital of the Roman Empire had already been moved east to Constantinople, the new imperial city built by the Emperor Constantine at the site of Byzantium, an ancient Greek settlement on the Bosporus, which connects the Black Sea and the Mediterranean and links Europe to West Asia. The vast bureaucratic apparatus of imperial Rome reconstituted itself at Constantinople, the "Second Rome," where highly trained cadres of clerks, inspectors, and spies kept close scrutiny over the lives and possessions of the city's inhabitants. In the fourth century, as emperors became Christian, the bureaucracy served as both a support and a model for Christianity. The eastern Roman, or Byzantine, empire produced a rich synthesis of Greek culture, Roman institutions, and Christianity. Its Christian character was expressed in the sixth-century church of Hagia Sophia ("Holy Wisdom") with its rich mosaics and elegant architecture.

A series of ecumenical councils in the fourth and fifth centuries wrestled with the question of how both divinity and humanity were combined in the figure of Christ. Two doctrines branded as heresies by the last of these councils in 451 were those of **Nestorianism** and Monophysitism. Named for a patriarch of Constantinople who upheld the doctrine of the dual nature of Christ (both human and divine), Nestorianism gained followers in Persia and later made its way as far east as China. Monophysitism (*monos* = one +

5.2 Mosaic from Hagia Sophia, showing Madonna with Byzantine Emperor Constantine and Roman Emperor Justinian.

physis = nature), a reaction against the emphasis of Nestorians on the humanity of Christ, stressed the unitary nature of Christ's divinity. Its supporters were based in Alexandria, rather than Constantinople, and Monophysitism found a following in Syria and Armenia, as well as Egypt and elsewhere in northeast Africa.

Christianity in Africa

In northeast Africa, Christianity reached the Nile Valley during Roman times and the region of the middle Nile, Nubia, early in the first millennium, probably through trade and missionary connections. Evidence along the Nile suggests that Christian communities may have survived there

in secrecy for many of their early years. Murals painted on walls reflect local interpretations of Monophysite doctrine, which held that Christ had only one (divine) nature, rather than two (both human and divine). Monophysite Christianity in Egypt became known as the Coptic Church because the Coptic language, rather than the Greek of the elites, had been used to preach to the masses. When Monophysitism was declared a heresy by the Council of Chalcedon (451 CE), a division was created between the Coptic church and Constantinople.

In the middle Nile, Christianity encountered the Kingdom of Kush (ca. 900 BCE–400 CE). Pharaonic gods continued to dominate Kushite ideology until the demise of the kingdom, surviving in Kush much longer than they did in

Egypt itself. Isis and Amun-Re were most prominent of these pharaonic gods; the rulers of Napata and Meroe, the centers of Nubia's Kushite kingdom, even took the name of Amun-Re as an element of their throne names. Rulers were personifications of gods and thus expressions of divine and secular authority.

With the advent of Christianity, the ruler was no longer divine, but conversion likely gave him trading advantages. Archaeological remains from this time no longer include royal tombs, a change suggesting that rulers' access to material wealth and spiritual power had been reduced. Instead, the Christian states of Nubia were ruled by both the local political authority and the Church, which was represented by its links to the larger, international Christian community. The Christian cross appears on buildings and coinage from this era. Replacing the early signs of divine kingship, the cross was considered an emblem of human authority and sanctioned the ruler's control over people. This control did not necessarily extend to their beliefs. The continuing use of pre-Christian cities as ceremonial and political centers in Christian times suggested how tenuous the foreign religion was and how necessary traditional links were for gaining local acceptance by later political rulers.

By the end of the sixth century CE, a substantial Christian community existed in the middle Nile, divided into three distinct kingdoms: Nobadia, Makuria, and Alodia. Excavations at the sites of Dongola and Faras have revealed multiple churches and cathedrals, as well as a Christian royal palace.

Farther east, toward the Ethiopian highlands, the state of Axum was also reached by the dispersion of Eastern Orthodox Christianity, this time through the Red Sea port cities. The official introduction of Christianity has been attributed to the first consecrated bishop of Axum, Frumentius of Constantinople, in 315 CE. Frumentius received the support of the two brother kings, Abraha (Ezana in the only surviving inscription of the time) and Atsbaha.

One of the primary motivations for the fourth-century conversion to Christianity by Axum's King Ezana was the trading advantage offered to Axum as a result of religious connections with the Byzantine world; status as a Christian polity conferred certain guarantees of prices and trading partners. Axum was renowned as a center of gold and other luxury-good production. Some notice of the Axumite kingdom's wealth and power was taken by classical authors such as Pliny the Elder, who mentioned the trade port of Adulis on the Red Sea around 60 CE. The *Periplus of the Erythraean Sea*, a sailing guide to the Mediterranean, Red Sea, and Indian Ocean, also from the first century CE, mentions both Adulis and the city of Axum. From the time of Ezana, pilgrimages of Ethiopians to holy places in Jerusalem and Rome became common and continuous.

By the sixth century CE, Axum stood at the axis of a giant web of trade routes reaching from the interior of the African continent to Asia and the Mediterranean. Pre-Axumite and early Axumite religions included the moon god, of south Arabian origin, and Mahrem, a god of war. Their associated symbols, the crescent moon and disc, eventually gave way to the cross, which appeared exclusively on stone stelae and coins minted from the time of Ezana. Like the inscriptions from the time of the Mauryan ruler Ashoka in the third century BCE, who claimed the support of Buddha for his kingship, inscriptions carved into stone monuments and appearing on coins during King Ezana's reign proclaimed his reliance on the new Christian religion: "I will rule the people with righteousness and justice, and will not oppress them, and may they preserve this Throne which I have set up for the Lord of Heaven." From its beginnings at Axum, the Christian state of Ethiopia survived throughout much of the second millennium CE, in part because the mountainous terrain permitted the isolation of the Christian communities and their defense against hostile neighbors.

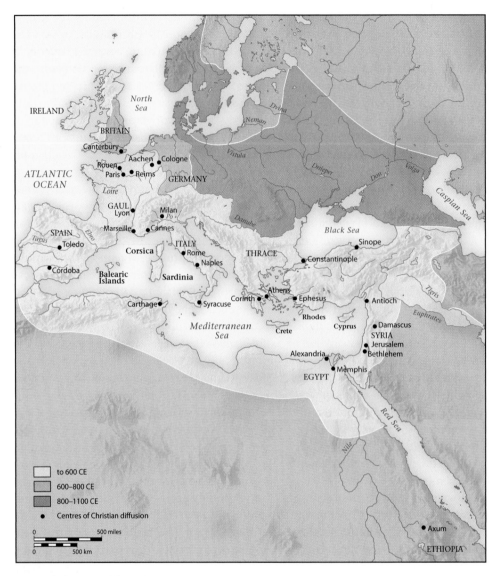

Map 5.3 Spread of Christianity.

Christianity in western Europe

Beginning in the 380s CE, the western half of the Roman Empire, including the old imperial capital of Rome, was occupied by successive waves of Germanic invaders. As the Germans settled into the western portions of the empire, they replaced imperial political control with their own, in the forms of the Visigothic kingdom on the Iberian peninsula and the Ostrogothic kingdom in Italy.

But Roman Christianity was not displaced, even though the Germans were either non-Christians or heretical Christians. The Roman Church, under the leadership of popes, quickly and effectively stepped into the vacuum left in western Europe by the removal of imperial control there. In the absence of Roman imperial authority, the organization and ideology of Christianity provided western Europe with its major unifying force, and once the Germans were converted, the alliance of the Christian Church with Germanic states made it a major force in western Europe.

Only one of the Germanic successor kingdoms persisted: that of the Franks, whose territories occupied the area from the Rhine River south toward the Pyrenees and the Mediterranean, the area that today is known as France. The Frankish chieftain Clovis (r. 481–511 CE) succeeded in establishing dominance over other Germanic peoples in Gaul by ousting his rivals and by allying with Roman Christianity. The Frankish state fused Greco-Roman (Mediterranean), Germanic, and Christian influences, laying the foundations of later European culture.

When Islamic armies crossed the Pyrenees and pressed northward into the heartland of the Frankish kingdom, Charles Martel, a Frankish official, defeated the invaders at the Battle of Poitiers in 732. Martel's success assured that Europe north of the Mediterranean basin would continue to develop along Latin–Christian–German, rather than Islamic, lines. It also led to placement of the Frankish kingdom into his own family's hands. His descendants furthered the development of close relations with the Roman Church. His son Pépin protected the pope in return for papal support of his right to rule. In 756, Pépin assigned a girdle of lands stretching across central Italy to the **papacy**. These "Papal States" remained the temporal possession of popes until 1870, and today's 32-hectare (13-acre) Vatican City is the last vestige of Pépin's donation. Pépin's successor, Charles (r. 768–814), continued his father's support of the papacy, and was crowned emperor as Charles the Great (or Charlemagne) of the Holy Roman (Carolingian) Empire by Pope Leo III in 800.

Latin Christendom, which looked to the authority of the pope in Rome, however, did not represent the entire Christian world. Another Christianity was centered at Constantinople, which became the seat of the Eastern Orthodox Church and the capital of the Byzantine Empire. Constantinople was a cosmopolitan and prosperous city, a major trading center that connected east and west. Until its capture by the Turks in 1453, Constantinople was a bulwark against Islam in the east and a center for the propagation of Christianity to lands and peoples to the east, such as the Slavs.

The conversion of the Rus' to Christianity

In the ninth century, the city of Kiev was transformed from a commercial center for Viking trade into the political capital of Kievan Rus'. Indigenous people called the Norse invaders "Varangians" or "Rus'," and when the Norsemen imposed their control over the Slavic peoples in that region, the name Rus' was adopted for the new state. The rulers of Kievan Rus' looked to the wealthy and powerful Byzantine Empire as a source of culture and religion to consolidate their own political authority. In 978, Prince Vladimir (ca. 958–1015) became ruler of all the Rus', having expanded the territory of Kievan Rus' well beyond that held by both his father and grandfather.

Although Christianity was not unknown in Kiev, the people of Rus' were predominantly followers of both Norse and Slavic gods, such as the thunder-lightning god, Perun. Vladimir's interest in Christianity was influenced by the Christian beliefs of his grandmother Olga, who had been baptized in Constantinople in 955 while on a diplomatic mission there. Her grandson Vladimir later forged an alliance with Byzantium, pledging military aid to the Byzantines against both the Vikings and encroaching Muslim forces. He sealed the alliance by taking the sister of the Byzantine emperor as his wife. Since she was a Christian, he was required to convert in order to wed her, and so was baptized in 988. In the same year, according to later accounts, Vladimir marched the entire population of Kiev to the banks of the Dnieper River to be baptized. Apocryphal or not, this story led to the eventual canonization of Vladimir by the Russian Orthodox Church. The conversion of Vladimir to Eastern

PRIMARY SOURCE: PRINCE VLADIMIR'S SEARCH FOR A RELIGION

The *Tale of Bygone Times*, also known as the *Russian Primary Chronicle*, is a history of Kievan Rus' from about 850 to 1100, compiled around 1115 at the Kievan Caves Monastery. Among the events chronicled in this work is the conversion of Vladimir, his baptism, and that of the Kievan Rus' in 988. Prior to this, the account describes Vladimir's appointment in 987 of a mission to investigate various religions in order to help him decide which to follow. Although we can be certain that the chroniclers embellished this account to serve political ends, it nonetheless reflects not only the variety of religions that flourished then in the borderlands surrounding Kievan Rus', but also the importance ascribed to religion as a force to supplement arms in the maintenance of political authority.

Vladimir summoned together his boyars and the city elders, and said to them: "Behold, the Bulgarians came before me urging me to accept their religion. Then came the Germans and praised their own faith; and after them came the Jews. Finally the Greeks appeared, criticizing all other faiths but commending their own, and they spoke at length, telling the history of the whole world from its beginning. Their words were artful, and it was wondrous to listen and pleasant to hear them. They preach the existence of another world. 'Whoever adopts our religion and then dies shall arise and live forever. But whosoever embraces another faith, shall be consumed with fire in the next world.' What is your opinion on this subject, and what do you answer?" The boyars and the elders replied: "You know, O prince, that no man condemns his own possessions, but praises them instead. If you desire to make certain, you have servants at your disposal. Send them to inquire about the ritual of each and how he worships God."

Their counsel pleased the prince and all the people, so that they chose good and wise men to the number of ten, and directed them to go first among the Bulgarians and inspect their faith. The emissaries went their way, and when they arrived at their destination they beheld the disgraceful actions of the Bulgarians and their worship in the mosque; then they returned to their own country. Vladimir then instructed them to go likewise among the Germans, and examine their faith, and finally to visit the Greeks. They thus went into Germany, and after viewing the German ceremonial, they proceeded to Constantinople where they appeared before the emperor. He inquired on what mission they had come, and they reported to him all that had occurred. When the emperor heard their words, he rejoiced, and did them great honor on that very day.

On the morrow, the emperor sent a message to the patriarch to inform him that a Russian delegation had arrived to examine the Greek faith, and directed him to prepare the church and the clergy, and to array himself in his sacerdotal robes, so that the Russians might behold the glory of the God of the Greeks. When the patriarch received these commands, he bade the clergy assemble, and they performed the customary rites. They burned incense, and the choirs sang hymns. The emperor accompanied the Russians to the church, and placed them in a wide space, calling their attention to the beauty of the edifice, the chanting, and the offices of the archpriest and the ministry of the deacons, while he explained to them the worship of his God. The Russians were astonished, and in their wonder praised the Greek ceremonial. Then the Emperors Basil and Constantine invited the envoys to their presence, and said: "Go hence to your native country," and thus dismissed them with valuable presents and great honor.

Thus they returned to their own country, and the prince called together his boyars and the elders. Vladimir then announced the return of the envoys who had been sent out, and suggested that their report be heard. He thus commanded them to speak out before his vassals. The envoys reported: "When we journeyed among the Bulgarians, we beheld how they worship in their temple, called a mosque, while they stand ungirt. The Bulgarian bows, sits down, looks hither and thither like one possessed, and there is no happiness among them, but instead only sorrow and a dreadful stench. Their religion is not good. Then we went among the Germans, and saw them performing many ceremonies in their temples; but we beheld no glory there. Then we went on to Greece, and the Greeks led us to the edifices where they worship their God, and we knew not whether we were in heaven or on earth. For on earth there is no such splendor or such beauty, and we are at a loss how to describe it. We know only that God dwells there among men, and their service is fairer than the ceremonies of other nations. For we cannot forget that beauty. Every man, after tasting something sweet, is afterward unwilling to accept that which is bitter, and therefore we cannot dwell longer here." Then the boyars spoke and said: "If the Greek faith were evil, it would not have been adopted by your grandmother Olga, who was wiser than all other men." Vladimir then inquired where they should all accept baptism, and they replied that the decision rested with him.

Source: Serge A. Zenkovsky, *Medieval Russia's Epics, Chronicles, and Tales*. Revised and Enlarged Edition (NY: Meridian Books, 1974), pp66–8.

Christianity through Byzantium ensured that the Russian Church would belong to the Eastern Orthodox Church, not the Latin Church of the West. In the fifteenth century, the veneration of St. Vladimir became a state cult and when Mongol power was finally overthrown with the rise of Muscovy under Ivan III, Moscow was declared the "Third Rome."

Islam

Islam, the third universal religion, provides an even more powerful example of the interaction between religion and empire. Islam appeared in the seventh century CE in Mecca, a flourishing trade city located halfway up the Red Sea coast between Egypt and the Indian Ocean. The people of Mecca traded heavily in Indian spices, Chinese silks, and Yemeni incense with both the Byzantine and Sassanid Persian Empires in the north. They were well aware of world politics. They were also aware of the main belief systems of West Asia. They knew of Zoroastrianism through trading contacts in Mesopotamia and the Persian Gulf, and of Christianity through trading trips north to Syria and Egypt or across to Christian Ethiopia. They knew something of Judaism, not only because of business but also because large numbers of Jews lived in Yemen and even closer in the agricultural town that would later be known as Medina. The Meccans were themselves believers in a south Arabian pantheon of gods and goddesses. Little is known of these early beliefs other than that they centered on the sun and moon; there were also local sacred places that were pilgrimage sites.

Muhammad and the founding of Islam

In the year 610, one of the businessmen of Mecca, Muhammad, experienced what he later described as a vision on an evening walk in the hills outside the city. In it he was enjoined by the angel Gabriel to speak God's word, to warn humanity of the imminent coming of the day of judgment and the need to correct greedy and immoral ways. Persuaded that he had been chosen to be a messenger of God, he dedicated the rest of his life to exhortation and action: exhortation to lead a just and moral life, action to establish a godly community in which all members accepted, or submitted to, God's plan and laws. Islam is the Arabic word for "acceptance" or "submission." A Muslim is one who follows Islam. The community of Muslims was to include all of humanity, not just Arabs.

In the first years, Muhammad's street-corner preaching of the coming apocalypse was ignored by most of the citizens of Mecca. His attacks, however, on the morals of the wealthy and powerful and on the false gods of Mecca and the evils of polytheism led to his persecution. Ultimately, in 622, persecution led to the migration (*hejira*) of Muhammad and his now fairly sizable group of followers to the town that would later be known as Medina ("city of the prophet"), 300 miles north of Mecca. There the first Muslim community was formally established. To commemorate this event, the Muslim calendar, one calculated in lunar months, begins in 622.

Within two years, Muhammad had begun a vigorous policy of bringing the people of Mecca to God's path. Since Medina was on the caravan routes to Mecca, Muslims could interfere with trade, which was a serious threat to the primacy of Mecca in the Arab world. The leading families of Mecca gathered armies to destroy Medina and the Muslims, but their attacks failed. In 629, during the pilgrimage season, the victorious Muslims of Medina moved toward Mecca as a group, ostensibly on a pilgrimage to perform the religious rite of making a circuit around the sacred stone, the Black Stone of Ka'aba, which had become part of Muslim worship. The Meccan leadership came halfway out to meet them, and a postponement of the pilgrimage until the next year was negotiated "to ready the city for the large crowd." In 630, Muhammad and his supporters returned to Mecca unchallenged, and the city rapidly became Muslim. Muhammad lived only two more years, but during those years the community expanded to include the whole of the Arabian peninsula and part of southern Syria as well. After Muhammad's death in 632, the expansion of Islam continued even more rapidly.

Like Christianity, the religion of Islam bears much resemblance to those of earlier traditions in the region. As preached by Muhammad, Islam conceived of a universe unfolding, with a beginning, God's creation, and an end, a cataclysmic war between good and evil and a day of judgment. Like Christianity and Judaism, Islam also has a sacred book. This similarity is openly recognized: Islam is called by Muslims "the religion of Abraham." This is because it is believed that the same laws of God were previously revealed by prophets to both Jews and Christians and that Muhammad was the last of a long line of prophets. Jews and Christians, along with Zoroastrians, are considered by Muslims to be "People of the Book" and are held in higher regard than those of other beliefs. As in Judaism, all the prophets, including Muhammad, were human and mortal. The divinity of Jesus is not recognized in Islamic theology, although the ideas of his conception by the Virgin Mary and his resurrection are.

The Qur'an and Muslim life

The Qur'an is the sacred book of the Muslims. This book, a collection made in 651 of Muhammad's revelations written down by followers as he uttered them, contains all the principles and precepts necessary to live life according to God's plan. Considered to be God's word and eternal, the Qur'an was revealed and copied down in Arabic. The effect has been to make Arabic the official, if not sacred, language of Islam, learned to some degree by all Muslims.

In addition to the Qur'an and its language, Islamic law and daily ritual held the Islamic community together in faith as it rapidly expanded to include many diverse cultures. *Shari'a*, or Islamic law, took its final shape in the ninth century. Like the Jewish Talmud, it is comprehensive, dealing with dietary laws and prayer ritual as well as with building codes and punishment for murder. The *shari'a* is based on the Qur'an, which functions in effect as the constitution of God. For cases not clearly addressed by the Qur'an, local customs, *hadith* (stories about the sayings and actions of Muhammad), general consensus, and analogy were used to modify and extend the *shari'a*, which became the law of the land wherever Muslim governments held sway.

While the *shari'a* defined legal relations in the Islamic world, the "Five Pillars of Islam" guided everyday individual practice of Islam. To be a Muslim, one must follow the five primary rules spelled out in the Qur'an. The first is that Muslims must bear witness or testify that they believe in the one and only God and that Muhammad was his last prophet. The second is that they must pray daily. Five times per day is specified in the Qur'an, and they must pray especially on Friday, when the whole community gathers to hear a sermon. Third, Muslims must voluntarily give a tenth of their annual income to provide for the poor of the community. Fourth, during one month of the year, Ramadan, all Muslims must fast during daylight hours. Finally, at least once in their lives, they should go to Mecca on pilgrimage. Today,

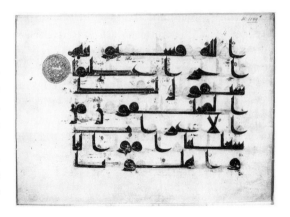

5.3 Verse from the Qur'an written in *kufic* script, an angular form named for the city of Kufa in southern Iraq. This verse is from *sura* (chapter) 38, verses 87–8, and says: "This is a message to the world. And you will certainly know the truth"; and *sura* 39, verse 1: "This is a revelation of the scripture, from God, the almighty, the wise."

millions of pilgrims from all over the world visit Mecca each year.

These factors – the Qur'an and its Arabic language, the Five Pillars of Islam, and the *shari'a* – together provided a set of principles to guide people's lives that would become the basis for a multicultural community reaching from West Africa to China. From the beginning of Islamic expansion, efforts were made to hold this multicultural community together under a single imperial government. These attempts proved unsuccessful, even though Islam remained the official state ideology of component parts of the Muslim world just as Judaism had been in the Jewish Palestinian state and Christianity was in the Roman Empire after 380. As with Judaism and Christianity, there was pressure from rulers to create and maintain an orthodoxy, an "official" Islamic credo and ritual.

Divisions in Islam

Because Islam, like later Judaism, has no ordained priesthood, religious authority was invoked by scholars and judges. Informal councils, and conferences of scholars and judges produced over time the standard positions on free will, revelation, and the role of reason in law and theology. The close association of political and religious authority made opposition to established government an issue that had to be justified on theological grounds. Similarly, theological differences became political issues. Both theological and political differences caused long-standing and profound divisions in Islam.

One such division is the split between **Sunni** and **Shi'i** Islam. This originated as a political dispute over government succession following the death of Muhammad. Some felt that a member of his family should succeed him, while others

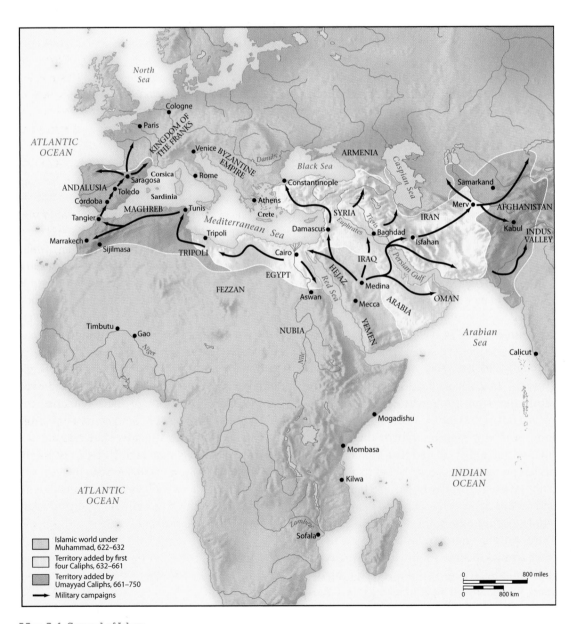

Map 5.4 Spread of Islam.

thought it should be someone elected by and from the general council of community leaders. The latter was the Sunni, or "traditional" way, and it won out. The other was the way of the Shi'is, or "partisans" of the Prophet's family and their descendants. Initially, there was little theology involved in this. After 200 years of underground resistance, however, the majority Shi'i position evolved into a messianic doctrine by the ninth century, a time of political turmoil in the Islamic Empire. According to this doctrine, the seventh (some say the twelfth) descendant of Muhammad through his son-in-law Ali did not die but rather was lifted up by God as the Mahdi, or Messiah, and waits in Heaven for judgment day. While waiting, he guides the Shi'i leaders on Earth below, making those leaders in turn very powerful figures in the Shi'i community. Other political disagreements produced theological differences, but only the Sunni/Shi'i split resulted in significant division.

Over the centuries, both Sunni and Shi'i faced the challenge of popular mysticism, Sufism, which coexisted uneasily with Sunni orthodoxy for several centuries after the rise of Islam. It developed out of an ascetic movement that appeared in the first Muslim century in reaction to the great material wealth generated by the Arab conquests. **Sufi** mysticism emphasized a special spiritual love of God and, above all, provided the means for direct personal religious experience of the divine, which held great appeal for the common believer.

Early Islamic empires and the spread of Islam

The Islamic state that expanded out of Arabia in the mid-seventh century looked at first to be nothing more than a series of raids by the rural farming and nomadic Arabs of the peninsula. It was anything but that. Rapidly seizing Palestine, Syria, and Mesopotamia by 640, the armies moved steadily west through Egypt and across north Africa into Spain, east through Iran, and south into India. By 730, an Arab Islamic empire stretched across West Asia into continents beyond, well-established and functioning much as other empires did to provide order to the world. The functions were the same; the ideology behind them was, however, different.

The Islamic government that was established by Muhammad in Mecca in 630 began as an expression of the revealed word of God. Islamic ideology called on all people, including government leaders, to return to God's path for humanity. This path spelled out how individuals were to relate to God and to others in society. Its political dimension focused on the ordering of the community according to God's plan. The Muslim community rested on the assumed universality of membership in Islam. Membership was determined not by birth but rather by an individual's professed faith in God and ethical behavior according to God's laws. Accordingly, the expansion of the Muslim community was potentially limitless. The role of Islamic government was to maintain God's law and order as described in God's book, the Qur'an, which functioned as a constitution for Muslim society. Islamic rulers, and their laws and decrees, were as subject to the Qur'an as were ordinary citizens.

The role of the Muslim ruler and the principles of succession to rule were established in the first decades of the Islamic state's history. As long as Muhammad was alive (up to 632), his power as ruler was unchallenged. Upon Muhammad's death, however, the choice of his successor, or caliph, triggered controversy. Despite the problems of succession, the early Islamic state was well served by experienced leaders supported by the sophisticated merchant aristocracy of Mecca, who were well aware of the political and economic systems of West Asia. With the rapid conversion and recruitment of large numbers of nomadic lineage groups throughout Arabia into its army, Islam expanded by conquering Roman Syria and Egypt, and by defeating the Sassanid Persian Empire in the east.

In 656, the caliphate was assumed by Muawiyah, son of the aristocratic Bani Umayyah family of Mecca. Muawiyah moved the Islamic Empire's capital to Damascus, where it remained until 750, when the dynasty he founded, the Umayyads, was overthrown. In Damascus the institutional foundations of Islamic imperial administration were established as further expansion of the state took place.

The success of this expansion was astonishing. By 650, Syria, Mesopotamia, and Egypt had fallen to Muslim armies, and the Sassanid Persian Empire as well. North Africa was brought under Islamic governmental control in the following decades. Spain was invaded in 711; by 730, nearly all of it was governed by Muslim administration and would remain so for another 700 years. By the end of the eighth century, the city of Córdoba on the Iberian peninsula was the leading city west of Constantinople, housing a population of perhaps half a million Muslims, Christians, and Jews. For at least 400 years "al-Andalus," as Islamic Spain became known, flourished as a rich multicultural society where Muslims, Christians, and Jews lived, worked, studied, and prayed in close proximity to each other. But from the beginning of the Crusades in the late eleventh century until the fall of Granada to Christian forces in 1492, tensions grew under the pressure of this threat and Muslim rulers of al-Andalus attempted to tighten their control of the non-Muslim population.

The same course of rapid conquest was followed in the east as it had been in the west. By 715, Muslim armies had crossed the Indus River and moved north to occupy much of its huge river basin in northwestern India. The Muslim invaders of India encountered fragmented political authority in the form of regional kingdoms that had unsuccessfully attempted to unite north India. In the mid-seventh century, the ruler of one of these kingdoms had established control over the Ganges plain, but this political unity had not survived his death. The Muslim invaders also encountered Hinduism and Buddhism among the populations they conquered in north India, as well as the strict social hierarchy shaped by the caste system. Previous invaders had been absorbed by the

ancient civilization of the subcontinent, but the Muslims were bearers of a proselytizing religious faith with a powerful social and political ideology that sharply challenged the cultural and social, as well as political, orders of India. After the Muslim invasions that began in the eighth century, India became a land where Muslim mosques (places of worship) and Hindu temples stood side by side.

By the twelfth century, several Sufi orders had migrated from West Asia into the Indian subcontinent. Sufism found many parallels in Hindu *bhakti*, which was focused on devotion to a personal god, through common language, imagery, and motifs. Sufism in India provided a means of establishing contact between Muslims and Hindus, was responsible for many conversions to Islam, and contributed to Hindu–Islam syncretic movements. In Hindu *bhakti*, God was seen as having three forms: Vishnu (generally in the incarnation of either Rama or Krishna); Shiva; and *shakti*, the female form. No caste or social distinctions were made among people in *bhakti*, although the movement was typically led by brahmans. *Bhakti* can be seen as a reaction against the highly ritualized, exclusive Brahmanism of the period.

Afghanistan and Central Asia were integrated into the caliphate through a series of campaigns between 699 and 740. When Kashgar fell to an Arab general in 738, the Islamic Empire had reached the Chinese border. Chinese forces were defeated at the Talas River near Lake Balkhash in 751, and Tashkent fell in the same year. China itself, however, was never invaded: the distance was too great and the terrain too difficult. By 750, manpower to administer the enormous empire, let alone to expand its boundaries, had grown very scarce. There would be more conquests after 750 under the Abbasid dynasty, which followed the Umayyad, but nothing comparable to those carried out by the Umayyads.

UMAYYAD CALIPHATE The Umayyad caliphate in Damascus (656–750) was a time of empire-building, in administration as well as conquest. The centuries of Roman and other imperial administrative experience in Syria contributed to the transformation of provincial West Asian rule. To many of the original Muslims of Mecca and Medina, the caliphate centered in Damascus looked like a secular Syrian kingdom. Though Muawiyah, the first Umayyad caliph, and most of his court were from Mecca or Medina, by 700, their successors had been away long enough and were so engrossed in empire-building that they and their government had grown away from their west Arabian beginnings.

Under the Umayyads, the process of aligning the dynasty with powerful lineage groups was achieved by borrowing heavily from the Roman administrative practices with which they came into contact in Syria and on the basis of which they succeeded in extending Islamic and Arab influences throughout the lands they conquered and ruled. As had been true of Roman law in the Roman empire, Islamic law was an additional source of the unity and control the Umayyads sought, although it took a century after they came to power before sufficient precedent and scholarship had built a full legal structure.

By 700, all Umayyad coinage was standardized with Arabic letters and the declaration "In the Name of God." By that time also, Arabic was the language of administration throughout the empire, from Spain to India. The use of Arabic was greatly reinforced throughout the empire by the conversion of large numbers of its population to Islam and hence their need of Arabic to read the Qur'an. By the end of Umayyad rule, even certain aspects of Islamic architecture had become standardized throughout the empire as well, most obviously the mosque with its attached minaret (tower) for calling the community to prayers.

According to Islamic policy, in addition to normal taxes, non-Muslim subjects were obliged to pay a special poll, or head, tax, as well as higher land taxes than Muslims. Avoidance of these taxes – along with the natural inclination to become part of the group in power – had a great deal to do with the rapid conversion of the conquered popu-

lations. Few if any forced conversions took place during the Islamic expansion. Converts expected their tax liabilities to be lifted immediately upon conversion, but they found the government to be very slow to do so.

By 700, the government could not at once maintain its armies of conquest and cut taxes. There were a few efforts at tax reform over the next several decades. The Umayyad court clearly favored Arabs and Arab culture, particularly Arabs of the peninsula, over other peoples and cultures for official governmental and military positions within their state. Arab historians today speak of this period as one of "Arabism." This ethnic bias reinforced the growing feeling that the Umayyads were using Islam only as a tool for power, and this view increasingly undermined them. In 750, the Umayyads were overthrown by a well-organized popular uprising mobilized under the ideological banner of Shi'ism. The army that marched successfully against the Umayyads came mostly from Persia, but there were many Arabs who fought along with them. The Abbasid revolution, so called after the dynasty that took over from the Umayyads, represented a shift from Arabism and the resurgence of a key element in Islam, the equality of all in the faith.

ABBASID CALIPHATE   The Abbasid capital was almost immediately moved east to Iraq, where a city called Baghdad, or "City of Peace," was planned and built in the following decades. By 800, Baghdad's population was close to 1 million, comparable to that of the Tang Chinese capital at Chang'an in 750. This shift to the east was paralleled by the full integration of Persian and other new Muslim subjects into the state administration. While the Umayyad state had claimed to be Islamic in ideology, it had in fact functioned as an Arab empire; the empire created by the Abbasids was Islamic in practice as well as in theory. This equalization of ethnic status among subjects greatly accelerated the process of Islamization of West Asia and increased the incentive for conversion.

For a little more than 100 years after it replaced the Umayyad dynasty, there was no significant opposition to the Abbasid government, nor was there any significant new expansion of the empire. These were years of relative peace, used to develop the institutions of Islamic government further. Just as the Umayyads had utilized the Roman institutions they found in Syria, the Abbasid caliphate incorporated many of the institutions and rituals of the Persian Empire, the center of its territory. The position of caliph grew to share many of the trappings of the old Persian emperor. Though not divine, the Abbasid caliph's title became "Prince of the Believers" and even "Shadow of God on Earth."

In order to reinforce their power, the Abbasids endowed their caliphs with a greater degree of religious authority than had previously been the case. Scholars were called upon to clarify and establish an orthodox credo and ritual, and the Abbasids enforced it with threats of imprisonment or worse. Heresy was a violation of state policy. The authority of the caliphate was further increased by additions to Islamic law. Scholars under Abbasid patronage developed a legal theory that the caliph held absolute power. Thanks to this and other standardizations of both content and procedure, the *shari'a* took its final orthodox form in the eighth and ninth centuries.

In all of these developments of the Abbasid imperial government, there is a pattern common to other early empires: a common language, common systems of belief, and an empire-wide legal system and bureaucracy. Arabic was the language of administration across the Abbasid Empire and also the language of sacred knowledge, the Qur'an. As many Persians as Arabs were bureaucrats in the Abbasid government, but they all used Arabic. The law itself, fully developed to cover every possible source of litigation whether in India or North Africa, was also a critical factor in holding the empire together in the eighth and ninth centuries. The weak point of the imperial structure was the legitimacy of the Abbasid caliphate. Having displaced the Umayyads, the Abbasids themselves were liable to being over-turned. Abbasid legitimacy, like that of any Islamic government, was measured by its ability to provide ethically correct Islamic governance and equitable policies for the distribution of wealth. With its vast accumulation of capital, the Abbasid government was especially vulnerable on the charge of inequity of wealth. In 867, a slave revolt spread through southern Iraq, touching off a series of revolts throughout the empire from northeast Persia to Syria, Yemen, and North Africa. Within 100 years, the Abbasid caliphate's power was confined to Iraq. Elsewhere, new governments had sprung up, Islamic to be sure but independent of the central imperial government.

Abbasid caliphs continued to exist as figureheads for the Seljuk Turks, who succeeded them in actual power in 1055 while continuing the dynasty in name. In 1258, a Mongol army sacked Baghdad and killed the last Abbasid caliph; so ended the first and largest Islamic empire, culturally distinctive yet in function very much like other early empires of the world.

"Holy wars": Christianity, Islam, and the Crusades

Since the origins of Islam and the subsequent creation of Islamic empires beginning in the late seventh century, sites of Christian pilgrimage in the Holy Land at the eastern end of the Mediterranean had been under Muslim control. In 1095, Pope Urban II (1088–99) called for a crusade to restore the Holy Land of Palestine and the holy city of Jerusalem to Christian control. Supported by European Christian monarchs, a series of eight crusades were carried out over the next two centuries to restore Palestine to Christian control. They were initially successful and established Christian kingdoms in Palestine, but by the end of the thirteenth century, the kingdoms had been lost to the Muslims. The Crusades absorbed the attention of Muslim rulers such as the sultan of Egypt and Syria, Saladin (ca. 1137–93), who vigorously battled Christian forces over control of the Holy Land.

Both Christianity and Islam at the time of the Crusades included notions of holy war, and used images of both spiritual renewal and personal struggle to encourage the faithful to devote themselves to the cause of battle against the unbelievers. The militant enthusiasm of the Crusaders to fight for the Christian faith was matched by the equally zealous fervor of the Muslims, whose war against the infidels was justified by the idea of *jihad* ("struggle") as defined in the Qur'an. But in the long term, the most important consequences of the Crusades were economic, rather than religious. The provisioning of large numbers of crusaders and their retinues helped to revive trade between East and West, and by the thirteenth century Venice had become the pivot of international trade in the Mediterranean.

Merchants, Mongols, and the spread of Islam

Following the expansion of Islam through the creation of Islamic empires that stretched from the Iberian peninsula to northern India, Arab traders carried the faith across the Indian Ocean to southern coasts of India, the east coast of Africa, and Southeast Asia. Caravan traders who moved along the Gold Roads of Africa and the Silk Roads of Eurasia transported Islam along with gold, silk, and other commodities. By unifying a vast swath of Eurasia in the thirteenth century, the Mongols helped to spread Islam through Central and into East Asia. A combination of conquest, commerce, and conversion brought Islam to the farthest reaches of Africa and Asia.

After the invasions of Egypt and North Africa beginning in the seventh century, Islam gradually began to penetrate further into the African

5.4 Dome of the Rock. The Dome of the Rock in Jerusalem is one of the most contested religious sites in the world, sacred to both Muslims and Jews. Site of the Jewish Second Temple that was destroyed by the Romans, Muslims believed it to be the place where Muhammad ascended to heaven and erected the building in 691 CE as a shrine for Muslim pilgrims. When Crusaders captured Jerusalem in the twelfth century, it was turned into a church, and then restored as a Muslim site under Saladin at the end of the twelfth century.

continent through the influence of traders and clerics. On the East African coast, Islam arrived as early as the eighth century, coinciding with the increasing urbanization of the coast connected to Indian Ocean trade. **Syncretism** characterized the early spread of Islam in both East and West Africa. Trade with Arab merchants who traveled the caravan routes across the Sahara appealed to rulers of states in West Africa, who converted to Islam while retaining local religious beliefs and practices. By the twelfth century, the influence of Sunni and Sufi traditions had overtaken that of earlier Shi'i converts. Sunni orthodoxy was largely dominant in towns where centers of Islamic learning, madrasas, were built. The more mystical Sufi tradition dominated in rural areas, spread largely through long-distance trade and by independent Sufi scholars.

Originating as an oasis market town for trans-Saharan trade before the twelfth century, from the fourteenth through eighteenth centuries Timbuktu was a center for the transmission of Islam in West Africa and had its own madrasa. Islam flourished in West Africa, though indigenous religious beliefs continued to dominate the lives of people outside the scholarly and commercial elites of urban centers such as Timbuktu. The influence of Islam was manifested in the flamboyant pilgrimage of the Mali ruler Mansa Musa to Mecca in 1324–25.

The slow diffusion of Islam across the Sahara through commerce and the cultural influence of Muslim clerics compares well to the expansion of Islam across the Indian Ocean and into Indonesia. Arab and Indian Muslim traders were active in Southeast Asian waters as early as the eighth century. During the late thirteenth century, Marco Polo visited Sumatra and noted that many residents of towns and cities had converted to Islam, while those living in the countryside and the hills continued to follow earlier traditions – likely a combination of native, Hindu, and Buddhist practices. By the time Marco Polo made his observation, Sufi saints were traveling the same roads and in the same ships as Muslim merchants, prepared to seek followers of their own version of Islam in the region.

Evidence of the conversion of local rulers in Southeast Asia to Islam begins in the late thirteenth century with the ruler of Samudra-Pasai. The first state in the region to convert officially to Islam, by the fourteenth century it was a center of Islamic studies. The legendary founder of the Muslim sultanate of Melaka, known by his Hindu title, Parameswara ("prince-consort"), married a princess of the ruling dynasty of Samudra-Pasai across the Strait of Melaka, converted to Islam, and changed his name to Iskandar Shah. By 1420, he had parlayed his marriage alliance into full control of both sides of the strait and all of the trade flowing through it. By 1500, Melaka was the largest and most populous commercial emporium in the international trade world of Southeast Asia.

The great success of Muslim Melaka did much to spread the new Islamic religion through the islands, first to the main trading ports and then to the people of the hinterlands. By 1500, nearly all of the port city-states of the island world from Java to the Philippines were ruled by Muslim sultans. By the end of the fifteenth century, Islam was to be found throughout maritime Southeast Asia, though not on the Southeast Asian mainland, where Buddhism and Hinduism continued as the dominant cultural and religious influences along with indigenous beliefs.

Summary

Buddhism, Christianity, and Islam are world religions because they were able to transcend ethnic, cultural, and geographic divisions and draw followers from many different backgrounds and ways of life. Modes of transmission varied, ranging from missionaries, to political converts, to merchants, to imperial expansion. The core beliefs of Buddhism, Christianity, and Islam were adaptable to many different peoples and cultures and all three were used at times to provide religious sanction for the authority of rulers. Unlike

Buddhism, however, both Christianity and Islam used military power to conquer and convert peoples and created their own governments. Despite the evolution of diverse practices and doctrines over time and across geographical space in a wide range of different cultural settings, people still identified themselves as Buddhists, Christians, or Muslims.

From its origins in sixth-century BCE India, Buddhism was transmitted through Central to East Asia by the beginning of the first millennium CE to become the first world religion. Emerging from the Sumerian and Judaic traditions of early West Asia, both Christianity and Islam were, by the close of the first millennium CE, institutionalized world religions with large populations of adherents in lands that stretched from northern Europe to North Africa and from the Mediterranean to East Africa and the Himalayas. As all three of these religions were introduced into different cultures and societies, they underwent significant adaptations to indigenous belief systems at the same time that they dramatically altered the religious ideals and values of peoples around the globe.

All three of the world religions – Buddhism, Christianity, and Islam – were further expanded by those who held the reins of power in the areas where they took root. Although Buddhism interacted with political authority in various cultural settings, lending its sanction to some rulers, it did not become the engine of empire that Christianity and Islam did. Just as political forces shaped the growth and spread of these religions, so Christianity and Islam both played powerful roles in legitimizing political authority.

Religious beliefs, practices, and institutions can be a means of articulating and consolidating relations of power, as well as a source of personal, community, and state or larger political identities. As Buddhism expanded into Southeast Asia, it interacted with both Hinduism and indigenous beliefs in varying political contexts, from empires to city-states. Christianity spread into many different lands, from the eastern end of the Mediterranean westward to the Iberian peninsula and the British Isles, and eastward to the Slavic lands. Islam spread beyond its birthplace into Africa, where it flourished alongside African belief systems in the West African Mali Empire and in East African coastal port cities. World religions were able to spread far and wide not only because they transcended local identities, but also because they assimilated and adapted many of the beliefs and practices they encountered as they expanded around the globe.

Suggested readings

Berkey, Jonathan P. (2005 [2003]) *The Formation of Islam: Religion and Society in the Near East, 600–1800*, New York: Cambridge University Press. A recent survey of the development of Islam in historical context.

Buswell, Robert (2004) *Encyclopedia of Buddhism*, New York: Macmillan. A very useful reference work with hundreds of articles on key concepts, figures, and events in the history of Buddhism and its contemporary practice.

Elverskog, Johan (2010) *Buddhism and Islam on the Silk Road*, Philadelphia: University of Pennsylvania Press. A study of the harmonious interaction between these two world religions along the Silk Road in premodern times.

MacCulloch, Diarmaid (2010) *Christianity: The First Three Thousand Years*, New York: Viking. A provocative narrative from a global perspective of the history of Christianity, embedded in the complex of religious traditions that constituted the world in which Christianity evolved and that shaped its growth over three millennia.

Online resources

Annenberg/CPB, *Bridging World History* (2004) Unit 7 The Spread of Religions <www.learner.org/courses/worldhistory/unit_main_7.html>

Buddhism in China <depts.washington.edu/chinaciv/bud/5buddhism.htm> Part of *A Visual Sourcebook of Chinese Civilization*, this website portrays the impact of Buddhism on Chinese society and the Chinese transformation of Buddhist belief and practice.

PBS, *Islam: Empire of Faith* <www.pbs.org/empires/islam> Companion website to this PBS film on Islam.

Study questions

1. How did Buddhism, Christianity, and Islam challenge the beliefs of the societies in which they arose?

2. How did Buddhism, Christianity, and Islam gain followers, and by what means did they spread beyond their places of origin?

3. Why are Buddhism, Christianity, and Islam referred to as "world religions"?

4. Compare how Buddhism, Christianity, and Islam each interacted with political power.

5. In what ways did Buddhism, Christianity, and Islam adapt to the religious and cultural environments of the places where they spread?

6. How did Buddhism, Christianity, and Islam alter the societies and cultures they penetrated?

ca. 50 CE	ca. 500	ca. 700	ca. 500–1000	670–1025	794–1185	ca. 880
Founding of Funan Kingdom in Southeast Asia	Iroquoian semi-permanent settlements	First *waqf* established	Emergence of Central African kingdoms	Srivijayan Empire in Southeast Asia	Heian period in Japan	Founding of Kievan Rus'

6 | Making a living

World economies

On Christmas Day, 1085, William the Conqueror, king of England, deliberated with his advisers about the people and the land of the kingdom he ruled. A contemporary chronicler recounts the outcome of these discussions:

> Then he sent his men over all England into every shire and had them find out how many hundred hides there were in the shire, or what land and cattle the king himself had in the country, or what dues he ought to have in twelve months from the shire. Also he had a record made of how much land his archbishops had, and his bishops and his abbots and his earls . . . what or how much everyone had who was occupying land in England, in land or cattle, and how much money it was worth.
>
> Source: Quoted in David Roffe, *Domesday: The Inquest and the Book* (Oxford: Oxford University Press, 2000), p1.

This survey was recorded in what later became known as the *"Domesday Book,"* named for the Day of Judgment because of its unparalleled importance in the eyes of the inhabitants of England at the time. A rich portrait of economic life in late eleventh-century England can be drawn from the data recorded in the pages of the *Domesday Book*. A precise and detailed account of wealth and property held by the king, his lords, the church, and everyone else, the *Domesday Book* provides a snapshot of the distribution of wealth in England at one point in time.

In this chapter we focus on the basic and universal question of how people made a living in the past. How did they gain access to what they needed to survive, and even prosper? How did societies create systems of exchange based on differing concepts of value? What was considered valuable: land, labor, or commodities such as grain, gold, and salt?

Introduction to the theme of world economies

After the spread of agriculture throughout much of the world, many people settled in villages and

960–1279	900–1400	ca. 900	ca. 1000	ca. 1000	1086	1258
Song dynasty in China	Mississippian culture in North America	Beginning of Plains Village period in North America	Eastern Woodland Iroquois farming maize, beans, squash	Large permanent settlements of Pacific Northwest Coast peoples in North America	Completion of the *Domesday Book* in England	Mongol sack of Baghdad

6.1 Peasants reaping the harvest under the supervision of the lord's official (ca.1300–1325). The labor of peasants tilling the fields and harvesting the crops belonged in part to the lord, whose officials were responsible for ensuring that the land produced as rich a harvest as possible.

became farmers. The concentration of population in larger settlements led to the development of cities, which became dependent on food supplied by farmers in rural areas surrounding urban sites. Others, however, did not adopt a sedentary way of life in either cities or their hinterlands and continued to live as nomads, following animal herds as they moved across steppes, grasslands, and tundra. Pastoral peoples also often fished and hunted, and frequently combined horticulture – and even agriculture – with herding. Both pastoralism and agriculture were practiced in common and diverse ways shaped by the environments people inhabited and by the technologies they employed. People who lived along inland

rivers or along the coastlines of the world's seas and oceans depended on these waters for their economic survival. Their environment required that they fish or gather seaweed and other maritime products. This same environment also provided the means for inhabitants to make a living through trade, either domestically with inland or riverine populations or – depending on their mastery of navigational technology – across the seas by long-distance voyages.

Through detailed case studies of key economic systems in combination with synthetic regional overviews, this chapter will explore the variety of ways people have structured their economic lives – how they have sought to survive, and beyond

1348	1381	ca. 1400–1532	1430–1520
Spread of plague in England and Scotland	Peasants' Revolt in England	Inca Empire	Mexica-Aztec Empire

that, how they have found ways to trade, make profits, and enrich themselves. As economies developed surpluses, people began to trade products they gathered or produced, expanding the range of foods they ate, clothes they wore, or things they used. Merchants – those whose trade was "trade" – appeared in many societies, altering social orders and creating new relationships between producers and political authorities. This chapter thus incorporates trade as an essential aspect of economic life, but does not focus on the important role played by interregional trade through such long-distance routes of commercial and cultural exchange as the Silk Roads (see Chapter 10). Keeping in mind the ways that environments shape economies, and technologies enable them, we will examine the relationships between economic systems, social orders, and political power as they changed over time. Who provides the labor that produces goods? What are the mechanisms by which a society's resources are distributed to the population? Who or what determines the allocation of resources, and how is equality or inequality in the distribution of resources related to configurations of political power and social status?

Manorial economies in medieval England and Japan

Before about 1200, in both agricultural and pastoral economies across the globe, kinship relations defined the basic unit of production and consumption. In many parts of the world where agriculture predominated, households made up largely (though not exclusively) of individuals related by blood were organized into larger scale units known as **manors**.

England

England in the late eleventh century, at the time of William the Conqueror's survey, was an agrarian society in which more than 90 percent of the population made their living from the land, and the majority of these people resided on manors. The inhabitants of the manor were the landlord and his family, along with the people whose labor sustained the manorial economy by farming the land: the peasants. They owed service to the landlord in return for use of the land, and they lived in villages in close proximity to the manor house or on the lands they tilled. There would also be an overseer who managed the lands on behalf of the lord, and a priest who ministered to the religious lives of the residents of the manor.

According to the *Domesday Book*, fewer than 200 laymen and roughly 100 major churches (including bishoprics, abbeys, and priories) together possessed about 75 percent of the assessed value of the entire country. Powerful lords rented out parcels of their estates to tenants who were often described as knights and thus belonged to the same social circles as the lord. Somewhere between a half and three-quarters of the estate was kept *in demesne* to provision the lord directly with the needs of his personal household with food and income. Most **demesnes** were leased for money rent, and the lessees constituted a landowning middle class, a gentry.

But by far the largest number of people were either *villeins*, who held or rented some amount of land, or serfs, who were bound to the soil and labored at the behest of the landlord. **Serfdom** in western Europe emerged in the chaotic conditions that prevailed in the aftermath of the collapse of the Roman Empire, when security provided by lords was exchanged for labor on their lands. Unlike slaves, serfs could not be bought and sold as individuals or families, but they were bound to the land and transferred along with ownership of the land.

All arable land was normally laid out into two types of fields, with rotation of crops based on seasonal planting and half the fields commonly left idle or fallow. Fields under cultivation were divided into long, narrow strips, which were divided among the various claimants to land rights: the landlord, knight tenants, *villeins*, and serfs. To maintain tenure of even the modest strips assigned to them, serfs owed more than labor service to the landlord. Along with customary dues and rents, they were obliged to give a percentage of all they harvested to the lord, a tithe to the manor or village priest, and perhaps a share to the steward who oversaw and managed the lands of the estate. There were also extra obligations, such as gifts made to the landlord on certain holidays and other special occasions, and there was additional labor owed, called *boonwork*, such as collecting the lord's firewood or doing other errands for him and maintaining roads and bridges on the manor.

The landlord also had control of certain products of the manor, known as *banalities*. These included products of the manorial winepress, gristmill, and oven, which belonged to the lord and which the residents of the manor had no choice but to use. Common land was held collectively by the village community, whereas forests, meadows, and waterways were controlled by the lords. Lords held hunting privileges, which were denied the peasants, and hunting rights included riding roughshod through fields in pursuit of prey.

Beginning in the eleventh century, there was an increase in agricultural productivity, boosted by further technological improvements such as the horseshoe and horse collar, which made it easier to harness horses to plow the fields. Combined with the proliferation of watermills to provide power for grinding grains and the clearing of additional lands for cultivation, technological innovations helped to speed demographic growth. As the population grew, so did towns and cities. Urban centers offered opportunities to peasants from the countryside to engage in trade, handicrafts, and other jobs as the development of a commercial economy surged. But the manor persisted as the primary basis of agriculture, even though some lords began to shift their crops to production for the market.

Over the next two centuries, there was overall growth in the population and some expansion of the economy through increased volume of trade in such goods as wool, cloth, and timber, but no agricultural or commercial revolution. Nor were there significant advances in industrial technology, and the major industries remained essentially the same: mining, salt production, shipbuilding, sea fishing. England's foreign trade in the thirteenth century was controlled by Italian merchants operating out of the ports of Venice and Genoa. The Crusades of the eleventh–thirteenth centuries had reconnected north-western Europe to the trading networks of the eastern Mediterranean and Afro-Eurasian land routes, but England remained on the periphery. Demands for English wool, however, did help to preserve the balance of trade and ensure that bullion flowed into England to maintain the coinage – the silver penny – at a consistent standard. And population growth between the late eleventh and thirteenth centuries meant the expansion at least of settlement and cultivation and the growth of towns. Between 1100 and 1300 approximately 140 new towns can be documented.

But the expansion of cultivation to marginal lands did not necessarily provide the productivity needed. By the thirteenth century, attempts to farm arable land more intensively led to the widespread adoption of the **three-field system** in place of the two-field one. A pattern of cultivation that promoted "sustainable agriculture" by rotating crops among either two or three fields and leaving one field idle or fallow, both systems were designed to replenish the soil and maintain productivity. The transition to a three-field system was a response to the need to feed a growing population by increasing food production. To preserve soil quality under more intensive cultivation – the effect of the shift from a two-field to a three-field system – necessitated more use of fertilizer, which in turn was dependent on livestock. And livestock pasturage was reduced as pastures and woodlands were both brought under cultivation.

There is some evidence that economic conditions were tightening up for the English peasant by the end of the thirteenth century, as population growth outpaced agricultural productivity. Estate records of the time indicate that at least the average size of tenant holdings was shrinking. And, although slavery had all but disappeared, perhaps as many as half the population were serfs subject to the demands of the lords on whose estates they labored. In the twelfth century, the labor services owed by many serfs were converted to the payment of money rents. Around 1200 – and certainly with the impact of the Magna Carta (1215) in promoting the rule of law – the king's judges began to decide who had the right as a "free man" to be heard in court and who did not. The effect of this was to establish a two-tiered classification of society: half enserfed as unfree and half regarded as free. Whereas in the past, lords were able to freely manipulate customary services owed by tenants, as a legalistic way of addressing disputes gained ground, the arbitrary exactions of lords became more difficult to enforce. The bottom line, however, remained that people with or without land, free or unfree, often barely survived. Living on the margins of existence meant that even a relatively minor drop in

harvest might have a major impact on mortality, either through starvation or diseases that were rooted in malnutrition.

Growth in population meant an increasing demand for food, an often devastating consequence for the poor but a rewarding development for the rich when prices rose, as they did around 1200 and again in the late thirteenth century. A related result of the population increase was the plentiful labor supply, which meant that money wages did not grow in tandem with the rise in prices. Wealthy landowners made large profits by selling their excess produce at markets, which were proliferating throughout the countryside. The increasing importance of production for the market led many landlords to take over management of their estates directly rather than leasing lands to tenants. For example, Abbot Samson of Bury St Edmonds took his estates into his own hands around 1200 and appointed managers to run them in order to produce a surplus for sale on the open market. This managerial revolution and accompanying interest in agricultural technology benefited only some of England's inhabitants at the time. By the end of the thirteenth century, population pressures were straining the traditional agricultural economy and heightening divisions between rich and poor.

By 1300, English peasants were living in a world where land was scarce, alternatives to farming were few – wages were low even if jobs could be found – and prices were high. England's population boom had reached its peak by 1300, and by the mid-fourteenth century, lowered living standards for much of society – produced by too many people trying to eke out a living on too little land – resulted in high mortality rates that brought a stop to demographic growth. A series of poor harvests due to bad weather and natural disasters in the first half of the fourteenth century showed the fragility and vulnerability of the economy and people's livelihoods and produced a temporary dip in the population. But it was the epidemic known as the Black Death that had the greatest impact on the population and on all levels of English society in the mid-fourteenth century.

Beginning in 1348, the plague spread throughout England and into Scotland, swiftly reducing population by about a third. The catastrophic decline in population did improve conditions for labor by raising demand and therefore wages, but the human physical and psychological cost was enormous. In the face of labor shortages, English landowners attempted to exert control over the peasantry, and the Crown likewise supported their efforts by rulings that tried to stabilize wages and return them to pre-plague levels. Peasant frustrations accumulated and erupted finally in the Peasants' Revolt in 1381, precipitated by yet another increase in the poll tax, a three-fold increase in as many years. Opposition to this brought together a wide range of English society, from agricultural workers to townsmen, who finally converged on London to demand that King Richard II essentially dismantle serfdom. But the spontaneity that spawned the insurrection was unable to sustain its hold and the rebels quickly dispersed to their homes in the towns and countryside. Ultimately, the growth of commerce and urbanization would have the effect of breaking down the old manorial system and, to some extent at least, freeing the peasant.

Like their counterparts in continental Europe who experienced similar changes, both lords and peasants were subject to the swift ravages of plagues such as the Black Death as well as to long-term economic changes that took place in response to demographic shifts, developments in technology, and the expansion of trade networks.

Japan

Halfway around the world from medieval England, the economy of another island society exhibited many of the same characteristics as the English and European manorial economy. When William the Conqueror ordered the compilation of the *Domesday Book* to record the wealth of his kingdom, peasants in Japan were laboring on landed estates called *shōen*. These manors were held by the imperial family, by aristocratic families, or by powerful religious institutions, much like the ownership of properties recorded in the *Domesday Book* for medieval England. Also like the manorial economy of medieval England, that of eleventh-century Japan had developed over several centuries, emerging from the collapse of a centralized state in the eighth century. In the increasingly decentralized polity of Heian Japan (794–1185), an aristocratic elite residing in the capital depended on estates in the countryside that were run by estate managers and protected by hired warriors.

Although we might use the same English term, "manor," for the Japanese estate known as the *shōen*, the latter differed substantially from a European manor. *Shōen* lands, like manor lands, were not necessarily contiguous; the *shōen* was often made up of a group of scattered plots. Unlike their European counterparts, however, the Japanese estate did not center on a manor house, and it had no seigniorial demesne (lord's land) farmed by the boonwork of the peasantry, as on the European manor. The economic base of the Japanese estate was irrigated rice agriculture, which demanded cooperative labor from cultivators, in contrast to the rainfall-dependent agriculture of Europe, in which individual cultivators and their families worked the land. It was also probably more profitable. Though the Roman state existed only as a ghostly remnant through scattered practices that continued under the European monarchies and the Church, in Japan the edifice of imperial government created on the model of the centralized bureaucratic state of Tang China remained in formal structures and institutions, if not so much in practice.

Like the imperial family and Buddhist temples and monasteries, wealthy noble families held title to properties scattered throughout Japan and relied on the income generated by these estates to support their luxurious lives and cultural pursuits in the elegant capital. Landholdings could be anywhere from a few acres to several thousand acres, and might be divided among irrigated rice fields and forested mountain valleys. For example, according to a register of holdings drawn up in 1325, the Saishoko-in Temple owned 20 estates in 16 provinces, so these properties needed to be structured into a smoothly functioning system to be viable economically, and thus an effective means of transportation and distribution was essential.

Estates produced more than simply agricultural products. Along with rice, estate workers made textiles such as silk and linen, and were sources of salt and cooking oil as well as iron and lacquer wares produced by village craftsmen. The more land in the hands of powerful and socially prominent families, the less income went into the coffers of the state. In 1068, Emperor Go-Sanjo tried to curtail the growth of estates by issuing an edict to regulate them. But by issuing this edict, he implicitly recognized the existence of private estates, and thereby validated them to some degree. The trend toward privately held estates continued, and by the twelfth century, only about one-tenth of all land remained in the public domain, despite the fact that the original premise of the imperial state was that all the land of Japan was "owned" by the emperor, who had the right to distribute the lands as he wished.

Everyone who lived on an estate had certain rights and obligations no matter what their social status, ranging from the managers who represented the interests of the absentee landlord, the owner of the estate, down to the tenant farmers who tilled the land and make a bare living from their labor or independent farmers who rented land to farm. Japanese peasants were not serfs, bonded to the soil, so they had a certain degree of mobility that enabled them to move from place to place. Nonetheless, they did rise up in protest when they felt they were being oppressed by estate owners and managers. They could and did present their landlords with petitions listing their grievances. Sometimes these petitions even invoked Shinto deities to support their claims: "If

we have uttered untruths or falsehoods, may the vengeance of . . . the Great Buddha, Hachiman and the guardian deities of the estate, and of all the deities, great and small, of Greater Japan be visited upon us."[1]

By the fourteenth century, economic changes were underway in Japanese society, which was now dominated by a warrior elite, the samurai, rather than the courtly aristocrats of the Heian period. Merchants and trade were playing a larger role in the economy, and money was increasingly used in payment for goods and services rather than barter. Regions became more specialized in the production of certain goods, and markets expanded. As the social and political landscape changed, opportunities for mobility increased and Japanese peasants could take advantage of these opportunities either to participate in the diversification and specialization of agricultural production or to engage themselves in trade as merchants in rural marketplaces and at temple fairs.

Markets and money in medieval China

By the time that commercial changes were beginning to undermine the manorial systems in England and Japan, Chinese peasants had already experienced a commercial revolution. The commercial revolution in China, however, was slowed and eventually halted by the invasions of nomadic peoples on their borders that culminated in the Mongol conquest in the late thirteenth century. Although debates continue to swirl around the precise nature of landholding in China during the Song dynasty (960–1279), the era of the "commercial revolution," two things are certain: there was great regional variation in modes of landholding, and there was no widespread "manorial" system that generally bound peasants to the land. With a population of about 100 million in the year 1000, China began to experience a series of changes that catapulted its economy into rapid growth and the commercial revolution was well underway.

By the beginning of the eleventh century, the introduction of new early-ripening and drought-resistant strains of rice from Southeast Asia began to increase the supply of food. These imported strains of rice either allowed planting and harvesting more than one crop a year, because the rice plants matured quickly, or enabled farmers to plant rice in places that were not well irrigated and where it had not been possible to plant before. At the same time, improvements in dam technology allowed the reclamation of lowland swampy areas to open up new land for farming. The resulting increases in food production contributed to population expansion. Population growth, in turn, contributed to the expansion of markets for products. An expanded marketplace, coupled with efficient transportation networks facilitated by stable political conditions in the eleventh century, encouraged regional specialization of production for the market. Regions began to specialize in the production of textiles, such as silk – which required the cultivation of mulberry bushes and the feeding of silkworms as well as the skill of weavers – or in agricultural products such as oranges or tea. Tea, for example, was produced in the southeastern coastal province of Fujian, but was marketed to regions all over China.

Trade with nomadic neighbors provided Chinese with markets for their own products and access to commodities they needed. They imported silver, hemp cloth, sheep, horses, and slaves from the north, and eventually exported tea, rice, porcelain, sugar, silk, and other goods in exchange for medicines, horses, and other items. Maritime trade had begun to prosper under the earlier Tang dynasty, when Indian and Arab merchants traveling Indian Ocean maritime routes established permanent communities at the southern port of Canton. With the commercial revolution of the Song dynasty, maritime trade was recognized as a vital part of the economy and received official patronage and supervision. By the mid-twelfth century, profits from maritime commerce were about one-fifth of the state's total cash revenues.

In the eleventh century, state revenues from commercial taxes and state monopolies (principally iron and salt) equaled the yield from agrarian taxes; by the twelfth century, commercial revenues far exceeded the income from agrarian taxes. The increasing use of both metal and paper currency and the development of institutions of banking and credit that took place in the Song era were both key aspects of the commercial revolution of the period. Between the eighth and eleventh centuries, for example, the output of currency quadrupled, while the population grew much more slowly.

The shift from localized economies based on barter or exchange of goods to an increasingly monetized economy of scale that integrated regional economies was aided by the use of paper currency and credit. The round bronze coin with a square hole, called "cash," which was strung in units of 1,000, was the basic unit of currency minted by the Song state, but it was heavy and cumbersome to use and transport in any great quantity. Innovations such as the use of certificates of credit or bills of exchange – documents showing that money deposited in one place could be exchanged for a receipt that could be used to pay for goods in another – made it possible for merchants to carry on trade across regions with ease. Paper had been invented in China by the beginning of the first millennium, and the use of paper currency also began in China among regional entrepreneurs in the tenth century. By the eleventh century, the Song government was printing official paper currency.

The development of printing technology – both movable type printing and woodblock printing – and a commercial printing industry facilitated the spread of other technologies by making available cheap books, for example, which instructed farmers in new agricultural methods. Advances in the textile industry improved production, the scale of which is suggested by an early fourteenth-century account of a mechanical spinning wheel that could spin 130 pounds of thread in 24 hours. Along with cotton and silk textiles, the production of ceramics expanded, with both imperial and private commercial kilns scattered throughout the empire. The technique of making porcelain was perfected in the twelfth century, and a variety of ceramic art was produced.

For many centuries Chinese craftsmen had produced cast iron, and they also made steel, utilizing smelting techniques well in advance of Europe. By the early twelfth century, the production of crude iron concentrated in north China ranged between 35,000 and 125,000 tons, a level comparing favorably with that of England several centuries later on the eve of the Industrial Revolution. Since the north China plain was already deforested by the Tang, and therefore access to charcoal was limited, growth in the production of iron during the eleventh century was dependent on the use of coal, an innovation that Europe did not employ until the eighteenth century. Wang Ge, a twelfth-century industrial entrepreneur, prospered in this environment. With a small capital investment, Wang acquired a timber-covered mountain where he began to produce charcoal by employing local farmers in the slack agricultural season. Local iron ore deposits enabled him to set up two iron foundries that employed as many as 500 workers. Wang himself ran one of the foundries, and the other was supervised by a manager. With the profits

6.2 Along the river during the Qingming Festival, Qing dynasty (1644–1911). Completed by a group of court painters in 1736, this painting was based on a famous scroll from the twelfth century depicting the lively commerce and other urban activities of that era in the Northern Song (960–1126) capital city of Kaifeng. Many now regard the original scroll as representative of an idealized generic city, rather than specifically Kaifeng, and this much later copy is colored inevitably by the eighteenth century milieu of its artists.

from the foundries, he acquired two more assets, a wine shop and a lake, where he employed several hundred families in the fishing trade.

Laborers such as those who worked for Wang Ge in the twelfth century might also have tried their luck in the cities. Cities grew and prospered as both marketplaces and centers of population, offering opportunities for employment in a wide array of different commercial enterprises. An account of the southern capital, Hangzhou, written in 1235, describes the vibrant commercial atmosphere of the urban markets there:

> During the morning hours, markets extend from Tranquility Gate of the palace all the way to the north and south sides of the New Boulevard. Here we find pearl, jade, talismans, exotic plants and fruits, seasonal catches from the sea, wild game – all the rarities of the world seem to be gathered here. The food and commodity markets . . . are all crowded and full of traffic . . . Various businesses are designated by the word "company" . . . even physicians and fortunetellers are included . . . artisans sometimes call their businesses "workshops," such as a comb workshop, belt workshop, gold and silver-plating workshop.
>
> Source: Patricia B. Ebrey, ed., *Chinese Civilization: A Sourcebook* (New York: Free Press, 1993), p178.

Cities such as Hangzhou became destinations for people from the countryside because the restaurants, shops, and entertainment houses offered jobs that seemed attractive in comparison with rural life. The populations of Hangzhou and other cities grew and the social life in urban areas created new cultural opportunities and brought about changes in gender roles and social status. Even though China's population was still overwhelmingly rural, by 1200, when the manorial system in England was at its peak, the commercial revolution of the eleventh century had substantially altered the Chinese landscape – physically, socially, and, above all, economically.

Slavic peoples and the economy of Rus': Trade and agriculture

To the north and west of China lay the lands of the Rus', whose economy combined agriculture and trade, along with hunting and fishing. As early as the fifth and sixth centuries, Slavic peoples from the Carpathian Mountains and the Danube Basin began to move into the region of the Dnieper River, where they lived by hunting, fishing and gathering in the forested river valleys. They gradually moved southward where they were able to find land suitable for agriculture and animal husbandry. These territories abutted steppe lands near the Black Sea, where nomadic pastoralists migrated and made their homelands.

The rivers of the Rus', as the Slavic peoples and others who joined them from the Baltic and Scandinavia came to be called, provided a transportation network where trading posts were set up for furs and other goods produced in the region. The traders who operated along this network were called Varangians (later Vikings), and the route itself was called the Varangian Road. A combination of trade in forest goods and products along with agriculture (grain crops such as wheat, barley, and rye) and animal husbandry (largely cattle) formed the basis of the economy of the region as the rise of the state of Rus' took place in the ninth century.

The practice of agriculture among the Rus' shared much in common with the rest of Europe, including a shift from the two-field to three-field system of crop rotation. The agricultural economy was also organized into a manorial system, with communal villages and larger settlement towns that served as trading centers. Novgorod, far to the north of the Rus' capital of Kiev, flourished as a hub of long-distance trade from the ninth through the sixteenth centuries, exchanging goods transported on Viking ships with those brought along riverine routes up from the south and across to German trading cities on the Baltic.

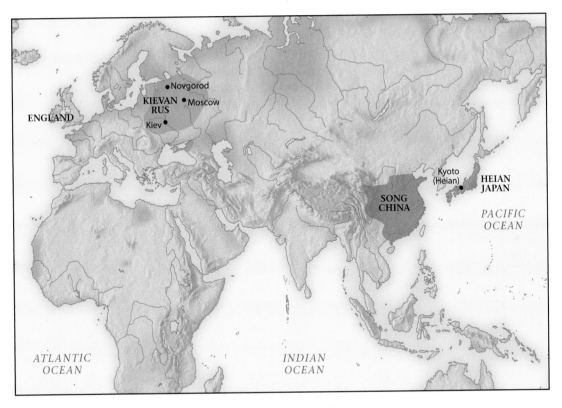

Map 6.1 England, Kievan Rus', Song China and Japan in ca. 1100.

Beginning in the mid-twelfth century, Kiev gradually lost ground to a federation of principalities, foremost among them Moscow, and trading routes shifted accordingly eastward. After the conquest of Kiev by the Mongols in 1240, Moscow's princes emerged as the leaders of the Rus'. Artisans and merchants were carried off by the Mongols, while cultivators were increasingly subject to control by the nobility to produce tribute for their Mongol overlords.

Pastoral economies: Herders and horsemen

By the early first millennium CE, a regular pattern of relationships developed in many parts of the world between nomadic pastoral economies and sedentary agrarian ones, like that between neighboring steppe peoples and the people of Rus'. Across the frontiers that divided these two different ways of life, trading relationships and warfare were both common. Dwelling in the steppes of Mongolia during the early second millennium CE, the Mongols had a pastoral economy based on sheep, goats, and yaks for sustenance (food, clothing, and shelter), camels for trade-related transportation, and horses for hunting, herding, communication, and warfare. Like farmers, whose crops were at the mercy of weather, disease, and predators, pastoralists shifted their pastures according not only to the seasons, but also to the vagaries of drought and climatic shifts, as well as other potentially devastating problems such as animal diseases. The Mongols traded with their sedentary agriculturalist neighbors, the Chinese, for grain, textiles, tea, and other goods. The Chinese likewise had need of goods, especially horses, from their pastoralist neighbors. Horses were a necessity for warfare, and they were also used for transportation, but the Chinese had very limited pastureland, and so depended on obtaining horses through trade. But trade relations between neighboring states periodically disintegrated into warfare, with Chinese raids on Mongol camps or Mongol raids on Chinese communities.

The success of the Mongols in their expansion across Eurasia in the thirteenth century relied heavily on the adaptation to the environment of the traditional technology of horse breeding. Mongol horse breeders had preserved an early form of domesticated horse, with a stocky body and thick, coarse mane that helped it to survive in the extremely cold and dry temperatures of Mongolia. When the Mongols created their empire, they became nomadic rulers of largely agrarian peoples, and exacted tribute from – or taxed – the population of conquered states. The Mongol empire illustrates key aspects of economic life: the role of environment and technology in shaping economic systems (agriculture, pastoralism); the control and distribution of material resources by rulers and states through tribute and taxation systems; the role of trade in connecting different economies, as well as in exchanging goods within economies.

PRIMARY SOURCE: MAKING A LIVING IN BADAKHSHAN

Marco Polo is best known for his descriptions of life in China under the rule of the Mongol emperor Khubilai Khan, but his writings also include detailed accounts of places from Central Asia to Japan. One of these records his observations of the peoples of Badakhshan, in what is now a province in northeastern Afghanistan that borders Tajikistan and Pakistan. His account highlights the mineral riches of the region that were a source of wealth and power for the ruler and a means to eke out a living for those who labored to extract the minerals from the earth. Like others across the globe, the peoples of Badakhshan exploited the natural wealth of their environment, but they also grew crops, hunted animals, and traded the minerals they mined for goods they needed from both nearby and more distant neighbors.

It is in this province that those fine and valuable gems the Balas Rubies are found. They are got in certain rocks among the mountains, and in the search for them the people dig great caves underground, just as is done by miners for silver . . . The stones are dug on the king's account, and no one else dares dig in that mountain on pain of forfeiture of life as well as goods; nor may any one carry the stones out of the kingdom. But the king amasses them all, and sends them to other kings when he has tribute to render, or when he desires to offer a friendly present; and such only as he pleases he causes to be sold. Thus he acts in order to keep the Balas at a high value; for if he were to allow everybody to dig, they would extract so many that the world would be glutted with them, and they would cease to bear any value. Hence it is that he allows so few to be taken out, and is so strict in the matter.

There is also in the same country another mountain, in which azure is found; 'tis the finest in the world, and is got in a vein like silver. There are also other mountains which contain a great amount of silver ore, so that the country is a very rich one; but it is also (it must be said) a very cold one. It produces numbers of excellent horses, remarkable for their speed.

They are not shod at all, although constantly used in mountainous country, and on very bad roads. . .

The mountains of this country also supply Saker falcons of excellent flight, and plenty of Lanners [another kind of falcon] likewise. Beasts and birds for the chase there are in great abundance. Good wheat is grown, and also barley without husk. They have no olive oil, but make oil from sesame, and also from walnuts.

In the mountains there are vast numbers of sheep – 400, 500, or 600 in a single flock, and all of them wild; and though many of them are taken, they never seem to get aught the scarcer.

In this kingdom there are many strait and perilous passes, so difficult to force that the people have no fear of invasion. Their towns and villages also are on lofty hills, and in very strong positions. They are excellent archers, and much given to the chase; indeed, most of them are dependent for clothing on the skins of beasts, for stuffs are very dear among them. . .

Source: From *The Travels of Marco Polo*, translated by Henry Yule, Book 1, Chapter 29; <en.wikisource.org/wiki/The_Travels_of_Marco_Polo/Book_1/Chapter_29>

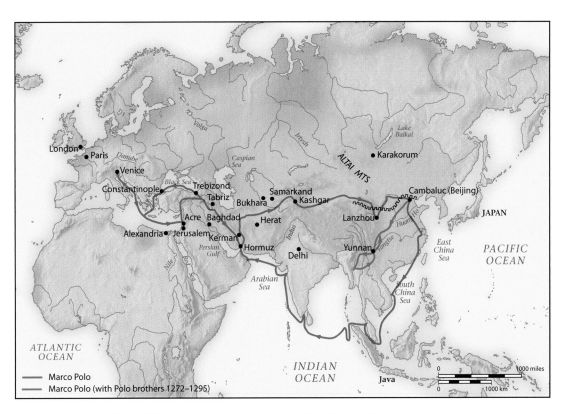

Map 6.2 Eurasian Mongol Empire, showing route traveled by Marco Polo.

Farmers and traders in Southeast Asia

The Mongols spread into mainland Southeast Asia, and they attempted to invade Java, but the climate and difficulty of moving through jungle terrain on horseback prevented its incorporation into the Mongol Empire. In this part of Asia, commerce and agriculture were historically intertwined, in part because of regional physical geography that supported both riverine and maritime trade. By the end of the first century CE, the area of present-day Vietnam, Cambodia, Laos, Thailand, and Burma – the great river plains of mainland Southeast Asia – was divided among a number of regional polities. Made fertile by the silts of regular and relatively gentle monsoon flooding, these plains were very productive for rain-fed and increasingly irrigated rice farming. They were, moreover, quite large and capable of supporting sizable and concentrated populations. The plains were also easy to dominate politically, in contrast to mountainous regions, where communication and transportation were more difficult. Sometime around 50 CE, what later Chinese sources would describe as the "Kingdom of Funan" emerged on the lower Mekong delta and along the coastline of Thailand to the west.

Early Funan was composed of a number of communities, each with its own ruler, linked loosely together by a common culture and by a shared economic pattern of rice farming supplemented with participation in the regional coastal trade. Funan's population was made up primarily of farming people in the hinterland and maritime traders in the coastal towns, who were economically interdependent. Surplus rice production found a ready market at the ports, where ships passing along the coast supplied themselves. Ship traders in turn had no difficulty paying for the rice and other agricultural products with goods brought from foreign ports. This nicely balanced exchange system, which may have been in place 100 years or more previously, underwent a significant change between about 50 and 150 CE. The

change was brought about by external factors and reinforced internally by ambitious rulers, who transformed Funan into an empire. The catalyst for this transformation was a boom in the India–China maritime trade, which intensified the importance of exchange.

Funan, which began as a group of autonomous agricultural communities on the lower Mekong and Tonle Sap Rivers, found that the growth of maritime shipping passing through the region brought enough profit through trade to support a larger population base. With an increased population, the leaders of Funan expanded their land's agricultural productivity by investing in more intensive irrigation, and they began to conquer neighboring communities. They also sought to monopolize the region's maritime trade by conquering rival coastal emporiums, or trading centers.

While Funan's origins lay in agriculture-based communities transformed into an empire by wealth and power that came from control of the international coastal trading networks, Srivijaya emerged from river-based coastal trading communities which were joined together to form a maritime empire (see Chapter 9). By developing good relations with the agricultural hinterland in order to gain a dependable supply of commodities for trade, the founders of Srivijaya were able to support a larger maritime trade zone and thus to establish an empire that dominated the region from about 670 to 1025. Srivijaya's capital, Palembang, on the island of Sumatra in modern-day Indonesia, was strategically situated near the southern entrance of the Strait of Melaka. With its fleets and armies, it gradually established dominance of the coastlines and built a major coastal emporium on the southeast coast of Sumatra.

In Java during the declining years of Srivijaya, the east coast maritime trading region became unified under the government of Majapahit, a dynastic city-state and trading confederation. By the end of the thirteenth century, Majapahit had developed its own extensive and tightly controlled trade network with the Malay peninsula

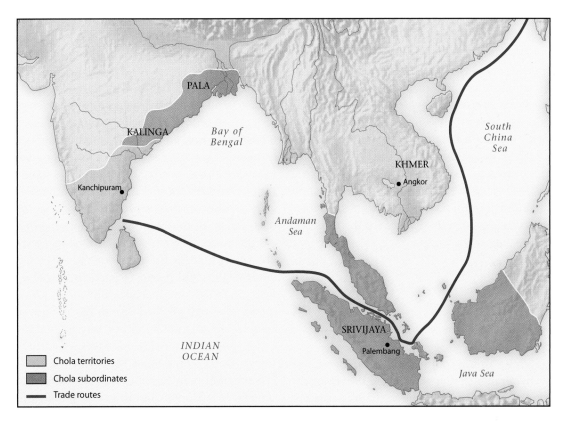

Map 6.3 The World of the Chola in South and Southeast Asia, ca. 1025.

and islands to the north, including Sumatra, Borneo, Sulawesi, and the Moluccas.

Rulers and regional economies in South Asia

Between the ninth and thirteenth centuries, regional dynasties across the landscape of South Asia built their political authority on the ability to exploit the wealth and command the labor of agrarian communities from the Himalayas to the Indian Ocean. In the wake of earlier empires in the north such as the Mauryans and the Guptas, regional rulers laid claim to territories in both the northern and southern parts of the subcontinent. The Chola dynasty, for example, extended its influence from its home territory of Tamil Nadu to Sri Lanka and even Southeast Asia. Agricultural

growth was stimulated by state development of irrigation projects, but agricultural surpluses were funneled into the ruler's treasury or the hands of powerful local lords who owned lands and commandeered the labor of peasants. Smaller landowners likewise owed substantial portions of what they produced to support the military and bureaucratic apparatus of the state.

Coastal port cities expanded opportunities to trade goods produced in the hinterland, such as cotton. Kanchipuram, a city in Tamil Nadu, was both the seat of the Pallava dynasty in the region from the seventh to the tenth centuries and a center of textile production. The city was also the site of numerous religious shrines for Hindu, Jain, and Buddhist faiths, and religious pilgrims, who were shoppers and traders contributing to the commercial activities of the city and region. Along with regional dynastic rulers, temples and monasteries throughout northern and southern India held large estates where peasants labored to support Hindu, Jain, and Buddhist priesthoods. There were many diverse and complex regional variations in landholding patterns, but overall a key feature of economic systems in South Asia was the relationship between agriculture and commerce that shifted according to the dynamics of warfare, invasions from the north, shifting political regimes, and contact with traders along the Indian Ocean coasts. Both agrarian expansion and commercialization continued within the framework of regional polities well into the fifteenth century.

Environmental diversity and ecological adaptation in Africa

Across the African continent, an enormous range of environmental diversity created the ecological conditions for hunting and gathering, pastoral nomadism, agriculture, animal husbandry, and trade as ways of making a living. Long-term environmental changes forced both human and animal populations to adapt, either creating new technologies or migrating to new places. The sahel (from Arabic for "border" or "shore") formed an ecological boundary zone between the arid Sahara Desert to the north and the watered grasslands of the savanna to the south that stretched from the Atlantic to the Indian Ocean. The sahel became a zone of nomadic pastoralism and mixed agriculture and pastoralism. Herders and farmers traded with each other, exchanging goods such as grain and cloth (farmers) for hides, milk, and salt (herders). But these peaceful trading relationships could erupt into conflict, and when farmers organized into larger and more defensible communities they were able to protect their goods from expropriation by nomads. The earliest states in West Africa were formed in this zone of interaction between farmers and pastoralists. By the tenth century, cities such as Gao and Timbuktu emerged as centers of economic specialization and trade.

Complex political systems had emerged to the west and north of Lake Victoria in East-Central Africa by the early first millennium CE. Central African farmers practiced **vegeculture** (cultivation of corms and tubers of tropical carbohydrate-rich foods) in the rainforests, along with hunting and gathering. They adapted their farming techniques to diverse environmental conditions. In savanna regions, farmers pursued vegeculture in the river valleys, while cereal crops were grown on the open lands. Beginning around 500 CE, herders pastured cattle in areas of the savanna that were not susceptible to the tsetse fly, which could destroy herds and people by spreading sleeping sickness. By this time, banana cultivation – which produced a high yield relative to the amount of labor – led to food surpluses throughout the region, and iron-smelting was widespread in the Congo basin. From about 800 CE in the Great Lakes region, political centralization was tied to centers of economic growth and population increases from surplus food production and long-distance or regional trade. The success of banana cultivation and herding led to environmental pressures and conflicts over scarce land, which in turn created conditions for the rise of territorial chiefdoms to protect and defend rights to land. The spread of cowrie shell and bead currencies suggests that trade became an increasingly important part of economies in this region.

East Africa (modern Kenya, Uganda, Tanzania) shared the cultivation of bananas and the development of iron production during the first millennium CE, but also depended on trade through its coastal port cities, where a mercantile Swahili civilization emerged. Some coastal city-states such as Kilwa and Zanzibar even minted their own coins by at least the eleventh century, and were centers of long-distance trade, exchanging goods from the hinterland with Indian Ocean traders.

Northeast Africa gave rise to early states, an abundance of agricultural and pastoral societies and a steady stream of merchants. Trading textiles, glassware, precious stones, iron, woods, ivory and other goods from the port city of Adulis on the Red Sea, the state of Aksum controlled the export of inland products out of the Sudan. Beginning in the first century CE, Adulis was part of the Red Sea trading network that linked the Roman Empire and the Mediterranean with the Indian Ocean.

In North Africa, imperial agricultural estates were established during the period of Roman rule, and commodities such as olive oil were produced for distribution all over the Mediterranean region. This agricultural economic base persisted after the advent of Islam to the region in the eighth century, but Islam brought traders who connected North African products to regions beyond the Mediterranean.

By around 500 CE, diverse economies were established in different environmental zones across Southern Africa. A nomadic pastoral economy was found in the drier central and western regions. Farmers began to establish villages in the eastern zone coastal regions and river valleys of present-day Zambia, Zimbabwe, and Mozambique, while herders of cattle and sheep sought the drier western regions. Hunter-gatherers continued to follow their much older ways of life, coexisting and bartering with farmers and herders. By the early twelfth century, urbanization was evident in place such as the Limpopo River Valley. The site of Mapungubwe exhibits features of the urban and economic development of this time, with both social stratification and specialization of production evident. Mapungubwe was superseded by Great Zimbabwe, which was larger and more complex than the regional centers, but exhibited similar features, simply on a larger scale. Evidence of trade with far-flung regions shows that these Southern African sites were part of a much larger trading network.

Land, labor, and markets in the Mexica-Aztec economy

The economy of the Mexica-Aztec Empire in the Valley of Mexico, contemporaneous with the Incan Empire, was based on a system of highly intensive agriculture. Rights to land were controlled by the ruler and distributed according to either an institution or the social rank of a person. In addition to the lands held directly by the ruler, other lands were assigned to support the holders

6.3 Stone wall at Great Zimbabwe, Southern Africa. Trade goods from as far away as China have been found at this site, which flourished around 1250 CE.

of certain offices, or to individuals of noble rank. The latter were held during a person's lifetime and transmitted by inheritance, while the land attached to offices was inherited by newly appointed officials.

Agricultural workers were attached to large rural estates, where they labored in fields belonging to the nobility and warrior classes. These laborers fell into different categories according to their degree of attachment to the land and their status as citizens of the Mexica-Aztec Empire. The lands of the ruler and nobility were cultivated by commoners, who in some cases were provided with land as tenant farmers and were then required to supply labor for the lord's estate. Peasants who served noble landlords are sometimes described as a special class called **mayeque**. Another type of labor was provided by slaves, some who had been prisoners of war and others who were required to labor but were otherwise free. Some people had no rights to land and hired themselves out to work as field hands or, in the case of women, as weavers.

Artisans practiced their crafts within the household, producing goods for the market. Masons, carpenters, potters, basket makers, and other craftsmen were found in most villages, while more highly specialized and skilled artisans such as goldsmiths were attached to the ruler's palace or the houses of the nobility. Farmers, artisans, and merchants all paid tribute to their political superiors – the ruler or noble families – with a portion of what they produced. The exact amount varied according to whether land was used as the basis for tribute, or whether tribute was assessed on a per capita basis. In central Mexico, land was predominantly used as the basis for assessment.

Between the basic economic unit of the household, which might include several related families as well as servants or slaves, and the larger community, was the **barrio**. A barrio was a group of households – or even several villages – that cooperated in ceremonial, political, and economic activities. Since households jointly bore the responsibility to pay tribute to the state from the land they farmed, the barrio provided the framework for the joint administration of the land and collective responsibility for the payment of tribute. Although the barrio was usually identified with a territory, it was also built around kinship ties, ethnicity, occupation, or patron–client relations within a lord's household.

Irrigation works, effectively controlled rural labor, and an elaborate series of canals, dams, and terraces helped to feed the population of the Mexica-Aztec Empire. To support the city of Tenochtitlan, built on a swampy island, the Mexica-Aztec constructed **chinampas**, raised fields, where the water table could support multiple crops per year. Equally important were the complex systems of roads and waterways that brought goods and peoples to central markets. While tribute goods from throughout the empire flowed into the palaces of the rulers of Tenochtitlan, Tetzcoco, and Tlacopan, reflecting the political relationships and social status of different groups, the market was also an important component of economic life. Marketplaces were located at specified places within towns and commercial activity was supervised by market authorities. Money was not used; rather goods were either bartered or paid for by using cacao beans or other proxy currencies.

Professional merchants known as *pochteca* were organized as members of certain *barrios*, and their chiefs oversaw disputes within the marketplace. *Pochteca* who were allowed to engage in long-distance trade were also sometimes deputed to act on behalf of the ruler as a representative to foreign rulers in presenting or accepting gifts or in exchanging goods. Regional markets served largely regional exchange networks, but the central marketplace in Tenochtitlan on the eve of Spanish conquest drew as many as 50,000 people on market days, and half as many on regular days, and offered a variety of goods brought to the Aztec capital in the Valley of Mexico from as far away as present-day Guatemala.

Long-term changes in economic systems could be brought about by agrarian cycles, such as that identified by scholars in the evolution of the Mexica-Aztec economy. Around 1100 CE in the Valley of Mexico, abundant rainfall and plentiful land coupled with a relatively low population level provided the basis for rising prosperity, with the cultivation of new lands, urbanization, and population growth in a commercialized economy. But during the height of the Mexica-Aztec Empire, labor was abundant, while land was in short supply, and despite intensive agriculture that made use of sophisticated irrigation technology as well as coerced labor, standards of living declined and famines were a constant threat. Economic instability may thus have contributed to the collapse of the Mexica-Aztec Empire when the Spanish appeared in the sixteenth century.

Trade and tribute in the Incan Empire

As ecologically diverse as the varied landscapes of Africa and Eurasia were, dramatic environmental differences were concentrated in a much smaller area in the Andean region of South America where the Inca Empire rose early in the fifteenth century. Verticality was the defining characteristic of the environmental constraints on making a living here. Only 2 percent of the land is arable, compared with about 25 percent of the mountainous volcanic archipelago of Japan. The topography rises and falls many thousands of feet in short distances, creating many microclimates and ecological niches that produce different products and are home to various animals on which the human

Map 6.4 Mexica-Aztec and Incan Empires.

inhabitants depend. Andean tubers – more than 470 different varieties of these "potatoes" have been identified today – and camelids such as the llama and alpaca are found on the **altiplano** (high plateau) 4,260 meters (14,000 feet) up. Maize and peppers are grown in the high valleys, 1,830–3,050 meters (6,000–10,000 feet) above sea level; coca, in the "eyebrow of the jungle" valleys 915 meters (3,000 feet) up. Honey, nuts, and birds are found in the Amazon rainforest, and salt and fish in the dry deserts and the Pacific coast. Access to a full range of these ecological niches is necessary to consume a complete basket of goods.

Gaining control of the varied regional economies of the numerous ecozones found along the Andean coast of South America, the Incas built on the experiences and institutions of their predecessors to craft an empire that ruled more than 10 million people by commandeering both labor and material resources of communities scattered throughout the region. In order to do this, the Incas had to construct an economic system that integrated and utilized the wealth and productive capacities of ecologically and ethnically distinct communities that stretched for nearly 4,830 kilometers (3,000 miles) along the western coast of South America. The ability to transport goods from one part of the empire to another was vital. The 40,000-kilometer (24,850-mile) Incan highway system was a vast network of roads that constituted both an essential achievement of the Inca rulers and a remarkable engineering feat. A Spanish observer commented:

> In human memory, I believe that there is no account of a road as great as this, running through deep valleys, high mountains, banks of snow, torrents of water, living rock, and wild rivers . . . In all places it was clean and swept free of refuse, with lodgings, storehouses, Sun temples, and posts along the route.
>
> Source: Terence N. D'Altroy, *The Incas* (Oxford: Blackwell, 2003 [2002]), p3 (quoting Pedro Cieza de Leon).

The storehouses mentioned here played a similarly crucial role in the ability of the Inca state to extract wealth from the peoples it conquered and redistribute it. Storage is essential to maintain a stable supply of food through the uneven cycles of planting and harvest in agricultural subsistence economies. Storage facilities are equally important in political economies such as that of the Incan Empire. The Inca rulers commandeered resources through an elaborate system of reciprocity, in which provincial leaders (*kuraka*) supplied labor and goods in return for their local authority being recognized by the Incan state. Although labor services were regarded as the basic obligation in this reciprocal relationship and the main source of wealth for the Inca state, commodities such as coca were also supplied by local communities and stored for redistribution in the large storehouses that dotted the Incan landscape.

When the Incas conquered a region, they claimed all resources and allocated them among the state, the state religion, and the subject communities. By then reapportioning farming and grazing land back to the community, the Incan state demanded labor service (*mit'a*) in return. In Peru's Huánuco region, for example, people there were assigned as many as 31 different duties for the state: farming, herding, masonry, military service or guard duty, mining, portage, and artisanry. At the level of the local community, the key unit was the **ayllu**, a corporate kin group that organized households and was the basis for the distribution of access to farmlands, pastures, and other resources. Elite members of the *ayllu* had rights to farm and pastoral labor, personal services, and some craft products, in return for their ceremonial, political, and military leadership, and for sponsoring festive events. They established their authority in part by distributing material goods and food to their people, including cloth, maize beer, and coca. This relationship – economic, political, and social – was mirrored in that between the provincial elites (especially their leaders, the *kuraka*) and the Incan state. As the diverse ecozones mandated, the regional economies varied greatly and so did the products they supplied, ranging from marine or farm products, to textiles, ceramics, and sandals.

Recognizing the great diversity of the peoples and economies controlled by the Incas, how might one region have functioned within the structure of the Inca state economy? The Wanka people of the Upper Mantaro Valley of the Peruvian central highlands were conquered by the Incas around 1460. The main Inca highway from the imperial capital Cuzco to Quito in the north ran through this valley. The total Wanka population was probably close to 200,000, and after the Inca conquest, Wanka communities moved down from hilltop locations to reside in a more dispersed settlement pattern along the valley margins. As elsewhere, Wanka elites were drawn into the state administration as local representatives of the Inca rulers, and labor taxes were assessed on the local population. Wanka informants to the Spanish later revealed that they had, in effect, been required to produce staples for the state:

> . . . they [the Wankas] were sent to tend fields of food and [to make] clothing and maids were named for their wives; and native clothing and all [things] that they could produce were ordered put into storehouses, from which gifts were made to soldiers and to the lords and to the valiant Indians and to whomever appeared; and similarly, it was ordered that those who worked in their fields and houses receive something from the storehouses.
>
> Source: Terence D'Altroy and Timothy K. Earle, "Staple Finance, Wealth Finance, and Storage in the Inca Political Economy," *Current Anthropology*, 26.2 (April, 1985), p193.

In addition to the staples supplied by conquered peoples such as the Wanka, the Incan state continued earlier practices of the circulation of prestige goods such as gold and silver, shells,

feathers, and semi-precious stones. The Incan state demanded "gifts" from local elites that could include shell beads and gold, silver, or copper objects. Alternatively, staples collected from communities as tribute could be converted into the support of artisans at the capital who produced prestige goods. One of the most important of these goods was the fine cloth used for giving as **bridewealth**, buried in mummy bundles, sacrificed in rituals, and used as a status marker. Cloth was produced for state use either by craft specialists – through their labor service, using wool provided by the state – or by displaced colonists and female weavers who were employed on a full-time basis by the Incan state. Colonies of craft producers included weavers, such as the inhabitants of a town near Cuzco, where a Wanka master-weaver reported later to a Spanish

6.4 Felipe Huaman Poma de Ayala, Incan woman making cloth and thread (1615).

chronicler that his father had held the position of head of 500 households there. Fine cloth, in effect, functioned as a unit of value that could be exchanged for other goods and services.

As the Incan state expanded, resources were brought under the control of royal and aristocratic kin groups at the center. Some of these resources were lands that were converted into private estates for living and dead kings, their descendent kin groups, and other aristocratic lineages. The most imposing of these royal estates lay in what was called the Sacred Valley of the Incas, between Pisac (near Cuzco) and Machu Picchu. Inca rulers and elite carved out estates from virgin territory, commandeered lands that had already been developed, or increased their holdings by accepting "gifts" from subjects (voluntary or otherwise). Royal estates were spread across the landscape to provide access to a wide range of resources. For

example, the estate of one ruler contained croplands, pastures, settlements, forests, parks, a pond and a marsh, a hunting range, and salt fields. The workers that maintained this estate numbered 2,400 men and their families. Because of the ecological heterogeneity of the Andes, estates were spread across different zones and are therefore difficult to measure in size, but some imperial holdings probably covered thousands of hectares. As expansive and impressive as these royal estates may have been, and as diverse as their holdings, they were concentrated at the heart of the empire. Throughout the farthest reaches of the Incan empire, however, it was the combined productive forces – both labor and goods – exploited by the Inca rulers that fueled the engine of the Incan state and characterized the distinctive Incan political economy.

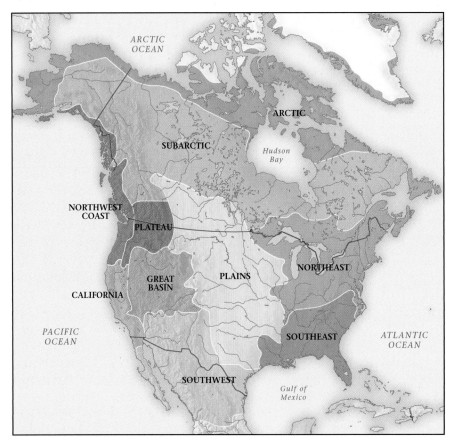

Map 6.5
Regional distribution of native peoples in North America, ca. 1000–1500.

Economy and environment in North American landscapes

Like the diversity of the environments included in the Incan Empire, or the variety of economic systems that evolved across the African continent, North America encompassed a wide range of different environmental zones in which many different peoples made their livings.

The earliest peoples on the Great Plains of North America banded together in their joint search for sustenance, based primarily on hunting bison. After about 900 CE, during what is called the Plains Village period, influences and migrants from the east led to the development of substantial Plains Village communities that were at least semi-permanent. Sometimes they were fortified by dry ditches and stockades, and they were usually equipped with underground storage pits. Village sites reveal a larger and more complex inventory of stone, bone, and wooden tools and a more varied pottery. Farming was restricted to the alluvial bottomlands of larger rivers, and the horticulture of the Plains Village sites indicates the use of advanced strains of maize and beans along with other domesticates.

Mississippian culture flourished between 900 and 1400 CE in the Midwest and centered on the urban site of Cahokia with a population of between 15,000 and 38,000 at its height (see Chapter 3). Mississippians practiced agriculture, but also engaged in long-distance trade in goods they produced, such as finished blades, sculptures, furs, and foodstuffs. The Mississippian economy was specialized, and the division of labor was set against the background of a hierarchical political order that commanded labor resources and invested in large-scale public works evident even today. As Cahokia declined in the thirteenth and fourteenth centuries, other Mississippian communities in the southeast began to emerge as new centers. These chiefdoms were the precursors of later agriculture-based southeastern tribes such as the Choctaws, Chickasees, Creeks, and Cherokees.

Archaeological evidence shows that between about 1250 and 1500, Pueblo peoples of the southwestern part of North America moved often and in large numbers, likely due to changes in the ecological niches they inhabited. Dwellings were built, occupied, abandoned, and later reoccupied. By the sixteenth century, the Pueblo peoples were a total population of fewer than 250,000 horticulturalists who resided in modest-sized towns and villages scattered throughout present-day New Mexico and Arizona.

The Iroquois, who dwelled on the northern fringes of the Mississippian culture in the Eastern Woodlands, lived by a combination of hunting, gathering, fishing, and subsistence agriculture in semi-permanent settlements dating from about 500 CE. By around 1000, the Eastern Woodland Iroquois had adopted improved hardy strains of the "three sisters" crops – beans, maize, and squash – which enabled them to shift toward a greater dependence on agriculture, rather than horticulture. Pueblo peoples in the arid southwest practiced irrigated agriculture, also cultivating beans, maize, and squash, along with cotton and tobacco. Like the Eastern Woodlands Iroquois, surplus production enabled them to build towns with higher population densities.

The bounty of nature provided a rich surplus for Pacific Northwest Coast peoples without practicing agriculture. As a result of the mountain ranges that parallel it, the entire Pacific Northwest coastal area from the Alaska panhandle to northern California is a temperate rainforest. Ocean currents and relatively warm air masses encourage natural food production, and rivers that descend from the mountains are filled with migratory fish during spring and summer. This environmentally rich area was home to dense populations settled in scattered sites. Because of the plentiful natural food sources, these people lived relatively easy lives characterized by elaborate ceremonialism, with an emphasis on material wealth and distinct social ranks based on wealth.

Subsistence patterns over the last two millennia depended on the exploitation of fish runs, sea mammal hunting, shellfish gathering, and other forms of fishing, gathering, and hunting. Intensive foraging for nature's bounty allowed for scattered, basically permanent settlements. Giant cedar trees in the region were used to create dugout boats and – with the aid of only wedges and mauls – were split into planks that became the principal building material for northwest coast homes. By about 1000, large, permanent settlements of several hundred people appeared, despite the absence of agriculture.

The wealth provided by nature resulted in huge surpluses, but the uniformity of the environment in virtually every locale was so great that trade and redistribution of subsistence goods were never developed much, except between the upstream (interior) and downstream (coastal) communities. Even here, exchange was not important enough to lead to the emergence of more centralized or complex political orders.

Because of the rich natural sources of food, Pacific Northwest Coast peoples were able to live in settled communities and subsist by gathering, fishing, and hunting, with little evidence of trade. In contrast, before the beginning of the Plains Village period around 900, inhabitants of the Great Plains were nomadic hunter-fisher-gatherers who needed to move frequently to find new sources of food. But after about 1000, both Plains peoples and Eastern Woodlands peoples such as the Iroquois were practicing agriculture, expanding their populations, and living in permanent or semi-permanent settlements. The Mississippians also practiced agriculture, depended on both riverine and overland trade, and built one of the largest known urban settlements in North America.

Religion and the economy in the Islamic world

Because of the vast reach of Islamic empires, from the steppes of Central Asia to the Iberian peninsula and North Africa, it is impossible to encapsulate the ways of making a living found in these diverse landscapes into a few generalizations. Islam, nonetheless, has frequently been associated with a variety of economic institutions that were established by Islamic rulers across Afro-Eurasia. These institutions were imposed as part of imperial government, but inevitably they were also inflected by local customs and conditions wherever they were implemented.

Whether or not the fact that the founder of Islam was a merchant played a role in the economic institutions that evolved in the Islamic world, it is true that Islam as a faith was certainly not hostile to commerce. The commercial prominence of Mecca, where Muhammad began to spread his message in the early seventh century, may well have provided a positive environment for merchants, but the power of leading commercial families on the Arabian peninsula undoubtedly influenced the nature of Islamic law in its favorable attitude toward merchants and commerce.

A key institution in Islamic law as it applies to the economy is the commercial partnership, *mudaraba*. This is an agreement between a sedentary investor and a traveling merchant through which the two parties split the profits of the commercial venture. This kind of partnership drew on earlier forms of agreements and is similar to commercial partnerships found in western Europe, but the *mudaraba* is usually regarded as considerably more flexible than its European counterpart because it took into consideration both the potential riskiness of the venture and the reputation of the merchant. Because of its flexibility, even non-Muslim traders in the Islamic world chose to make use of this arrangement, as documents from the famous Cairo Geniza relating to Jewish, Coptic, and Muslim merchants testify. For example, Old Cairo (Fustat) was famous for its glass production, and traders from all over the Mediterranean were involved in partnerships with local glassmakers.

Like Christianity, which condemned interest, Islamic law also banned the practice of charging interest on loans. But just as the condemnation of interest in the Christian West was honored as much in the breach as in practice, there is plentiful evidence of debt contracts based on interest found in societies under Islam in the premodern world. In addition to the annual pilgrimage to Mecca, devout Muslims were also supposed to pay the tithe known as **zakat**. This payment was to be used by rulers at least in part for the benefit of the needy, but in fact this was a source of revenue for Islamic states that could be used as the rulers determined. First conceived as a wealth tax, the granting of broad exemptions transformed the *zakat* into what was effectively a tax on livestock and agricultural production. Non-Muslims were subject to a special poll tax, *jizya*, which was levied in return for protection, along with a special land tax higher than that paid by Muslims.

One of the most important economic institutions found throughout the Islamic world is the **waqf**, a charitable land endowment. The earliest example dates to the eighth century, when the center of the Islamic empire was Damascus, but it spread along with the empire over the following centuries to all parts of the Islamic world. A wealthy individual donated property as an income-producing endowment for a specific purpose: to build and maintain a mosque, a school, or a hospital, among other services for the poor. In fact, urban services that might otherwise be regarded as essential municipal responsibilities were provided by the *waqf* in the Islamic world before modern times. But the *waqf* had another dimension besides the alleviation of poverty: it could serve as a kind of tax shelter for the donor, who could compensate himself for his services from the *waqf* funds, or hire his relatives.

Urbanization was widespread throughout the Islamic world, and cities generally provided hospitable environments for trade, as well as a variety of opportunities for rural immigrants to find work. Many such cities where merchants congregated were found along the trade routes known as the Silk Roads. In Persian cities like Isfahan and Nishapur, communal organizations known as *futuwwa* drew together people from different religious groups according to their professions, usually a craft they practiced. Agricultural technology, especially underground irrigation systems known as **qanat**, literally made the desert bloom, providing not only sustenance for landlords and farmers but also surplus agricultural goods to trade. The invasions of Mongols in the thirteenth century not only laid waste to cities such as Baghdad, but also destroyed much of the *qanat* system and thus depleted the agricultural riches of the Persian heartlands. Economic systems, however sophisticated and productive, were prey to military invasions as well as to climatic changes, shifts in trade patterns, and demographic stresses such as the Black Death.

Regional systems and the impact of long-distance trade

Well before the Roman and Han Empires dominated western and eastern ends of Eurasia, long-distance trade connected regional economic systems, often operating in cyclical patterns of rise and decline. World historical transformations such as the expansion of Islam in the seventh century (see Chapter 5) and the creation of the Mongol Empire in the thirteenth (see Chapter 9) clearly had major impacts on regional economies throughout Afro-Eurasia. Much earlier connections forged by the Silk Roads from the first and second centuries BCE also continued over more than a millennium to facilitate long-distance trade as well as the flow of cultures and religions across Eurasia. Religious (Islamic empires), political (Mongol Empire), and commercial (Silk Roads) purposes drove these connections, which brought not only commodities such as silks, gold, salt, ceramics, and medicines, but also new foods, ideas, and diseases across long distances. The Silk Roads are only the best known of several complex cross-regional routes. Others include the Gold Roads in West Africa, and the Turquoise Roads in the Americas (see Chapter 10).

Janet Abu-Lughod has traced eight circuits of trading networks that linked parts of Afro-Eurasia during the thirteenth century, to create what she called "a thirteenth-century world system." Such ongoing market centers as the Champagne Fairs in northwestern Europe were only one of the sites where long-distance traders converged. Cities such as Constantinople and later Venice were centers of long-distance trade due to their prime locations astride the convergence of land and sea routes. From the late eleventh century to the mid-thirteenth century, the Crusades unintentionally fostered economic relations between Europe, West Asia, and North Africa as a by-product of religious conflict. The Hanseatic League, formed by an alliance of German cities in 1241, promoted trade across Europe. Long-distance trade routes across Eurasia were relatively secure and safe during the *pax Mongolica* when the Mongol Empire was at its height. When overland routes began to decline after the fall of the Mongol Empire, maritime routes were unaffected and continued to provide means for long-distance trade across Afro-Eurasia. Both overland and sea highways also operated within the Americas, connecting peoples and cultures in North and South America through trade.

Summary

Peasants working in the fields on manors in England and Japan, Chinese merchants using paper money to carry out transactions, and Wanka weavers producing fine cloth for their Inca rulers were all engaged in making a living. They shared the common goal of laboring to produce goods or services that would enable them to feed and shelter themselves and their families. But the ability to obtain these basic human needs was determined by where these individuals stood in the food chain – by their place in a complex web of economic relationships framed by distinct political structures. In many cases examined in this chapter, ways of making a living were

circumscribed by both economic and political systems that limited the ability of individuals to benefit from their own labor. Even though their economic systems were far from identical, it is clear in the cases of England, Japan, and China that the development of markets and a money economy by the fourteenth century had begun to break down barriers between urban and rural and between lord and peasant. In contrast, Incan rulers, for example, oversaw a distinctly non-market economy, tightly controlled by the center, which exacted tribute from the people and territories it controlled. The Mexica-Aztec economy was also a tribute economy, but incorporated markets and merchant entrepreneurs along with the tribute delivered from various regions of the empire.

Across the African continent, societies exhibited a wide range of adaptations to different environments, incorporating trade along with agriculture and herding, and using iron technology to increase agricultural production. Pastoral economies of the peoples who inhabited the steppes of Central Asia had their own distinctive rhythm and structure based on the environmental conditions characteristic of that region. Seasonal migration was a natural part of economic life, moving camps as animals were herded to new pasturelands with the change of seasons.

The development of both agriculture and commerce amid the regional political diversity characteristic of both South and Southeast Asia provided subsistence for many and wealth for a few. In parts of Afro-Eurasia where Islamic law held sway, economic life was shaped by religion as well as political authorities.

Peoples of North America inhabited a variety of terrains, ranging from the abundant forests and rivers of the Pacific Northwest to the arid plains of the Midwest, the woodlands of the East Coast, and the swamps and forests of the southeast. Their ways of making a living were shaped by these differing environments, and like their counterparts in the steppes, tundras, and taigas of Asia, they were flexible in adapting to the places where they lived and creative in their uses of technologies to sustain and enhance their ways of life.

Note

1   In Thomas Keirstead, *The Geography of Power in Medieval Japan* (Princeton: Princeton University Press, 1992), p86.

Suggested readings

D'Altroy, Terence N. (2002) *The Incas*, Oxford: Oxford University Press. A comprehensive study of Incan society, politics, and economy, focusing on the political economy of the empire.

Dyer, Christopher (2002) *Making a Living in the Middle Ages: The People of Britain, 850–1520*, New Haven, CN: Yale University Press. A thorough study of the ways in which people at all levels of society in medieval Britain provided for themselves and their families amid changing economic circumstances.

Hassig, Ross (1985) *Trade, Tribute, and Transportation*, Norman, OK: University of Oklahoma Press. This study focuses on systems of economic exchange in Central Mexico.

Khazanov, Anatoly (1984) *Nomads and the Outside World*, Cambridge: Cambridge University Press. Approaching the study of nomadic peoples from the perspective of their relationships with the "outside world," this study sheds light on important aspects of economic life within nomadic societies as well as the role played by trade with other states and peoples.

Reid, Anthony (1988) *Southeast Asia in the Age of Commerce, 1450–1680, Volume One: The Lands Below the Winds*, New Haven and London: Yale University Press.

Shiba, Yoshinobu (trans. Mark Elvin) (1992 [1970, first translation; 1968, original Japanese publication]) *Commerce and Society in Sung China*, Ann Arbor, MI: University of Michigan Center for Chinese Studies. A study of transportation, agricultural and handicraft products, markets, cities, and the organization of commerce in China between the tenth and thirteenth centuries.

Online resources

Annenberg/CPB, *Bridging World History* (2004) Unit 8 Early Economies <www.learner.org/courses/world history/unit_main_8.html>

Asia for Educators, *The Song Dynasty in China (960–1279)* <afe.easia.columbia.edu/song> This interactive website makes use of the famous twelfth-century scroll, "Spring Festival on the River," to portray aspects of urban life and the economy in Song China.

Study questions

1.   What are some of the ways that environment has shaped economic systems?
2.   How have political authorities – states – exercised control over people's economic lives?
3.   How has technology brought about changes in economic systems?
4.   Does religion play a role in economic life? How?
5.   How does a manorial economy work?
6.   Compare a tribute economy to a market economy.
7.   What are some of the causes of economic growth?

18 BCE–9 BCE	45–118 CE	ca. 55–118 CE	307–337	354–430	ca. 650	ca. 750
Roman emperor Augustus' legislation to promote childbearing	Ban Zhao, author of *Admonitions for Women*	Tacitus writes on German family life	Constantine's rule and spread of Christianity in Roman Empire	Augustine, author of *The City of God*, writes on ideal family	Qur'an compiled	Dunhuang documents

7 Family matters

Gender, family, and household

In the early 1250s, a Flemish Franciscan friar named William of Rubruck made a long and arduous journey from his homeland across Eurasia to the Mongol capital, Karakorum. While in the Holy Land on crusade, William had learned about the Mongols, whose conquest of Eurasia had threatened Europe in 1241, but who were now being sought by Christian rulers as allies against the Muslims. William decided to go to Mongolia to see for himself, and to try to convert the Mongols to Christianity. He was the first European to visit Karakorum on the Orkhon River in Mongolia and return to write about it. The Latin account of his journey, the *Itinerarium*, provides not only descriptions of the Mongol court and capital, but also detailed observations of Mongol life that naturally reflect his own cultural background. Nowhere is this more evident than in his depiction of marriage as it casts light on gender relations, family, and household in Mongol society:

As to their marriages, you must know that no one among them has a wife unless he buys her; so it sometimes happens that girls are well past marriageable age before they marry, for their parents always keep them until they sell them. They observe the first and second degrees of consanguinity, but no degree of affinity; thus (one person) will have at the same time or successively two sisters. Among them no widow marries, for the following reason: they believe that all who serve them in this life shall serve them in the next, so as regards a widow they believe that she will always return to her first husband after death. Hence this shameful custom prevails among them, that sometimes a son takes to wife all his father's wives, except his own mother; for the *ordu* of the father and mother always belongs to the youngest son, so it is he who must provide for all his father's wives who come to him with the paternal household, and if he wishes it he uses them as wives, for he esteems not himself injured if they return to his father after death. When then anyone has made a bargain with another to take his daughter, the father of the girl gives a feast,

794–1185	ca. 978–1016	1085–ca. 1151	ca. 1140–1195	1056–1111	1157–1225	ca. 1100–1300
Heian period in Japan flourishing of elite women's literary culture and "marriage politics"	Murasaki Shikibu, author of *The Tale of Genji*	Li Qingzhao, poet and wife	Yuan Cai, Chinese author of guidebook for family life	al-Ghazali, Muslim author of *Book on the Etiquette of Marriage*	Hojo Masako, wife of founder of Kamakura shogunate	Cairo Geniza documents

and the girl flees to her relatives and hides there. Then the father says: "Here, my daughter is yours: take her wheresoever you find her." Then he searches for her with his friends till he finds her, and he must take her by force and carry her off with a semblance of violence to his house.

Source: William of Rubruck, *The Journey of William of Rubruck to the Eastern Parts of the World, 1253–55*, translated and edited by W.W. Rockhill (London: Hakluyt Society, 1900), <depts.washington.edu/silkroad/texts/rubruck.html#customs>

Seen through the eyes of a Christian cleric, Mongol marriage customs were strange, and some were even offensive. No doubt Mongols would

have found Christian European marriage customs and relations between women and men equally bizarre and perplexing. In the most intimate realm of human social life, both ideals and practices of marriage, family, and household varied greatly over time within cultures as well as between cultures. How were gender identities and the basic social institutions of marriage, family and household constructed and experienced differently across cultures before 1500, and what can this tell us about patterns and processes in world history?

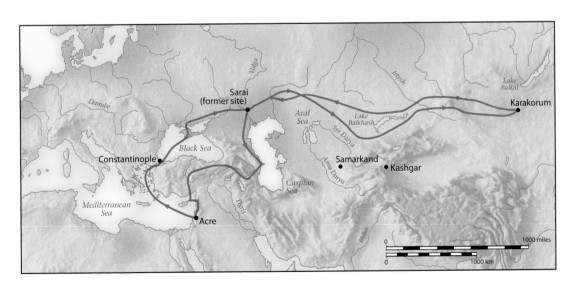

Map 7.1 Travel route of William of Rubruck.

1253–55	ca. 1300	1325
Journey of William of Rubruck to the Mongols	West African forest states	Founding of Tenochtitlan

Introduction to the theme of gender, family, and household in world history

Family and household comprise the most basic level of human social interaction and historical meaning. But it has not been easy for historians to piece together the history of families and family life from textual sources because even when such sources do exist, they often treat the family either as an object of state control for taxation purposes or as the target of moral rulings from religious authorities. However, historians can also look to a multitude of sources beyond standard historical documents that illuminate gender, family, and household in world history: oral testimony, mythology, genealogies, life histories, legal codes, archaeological finds, language, and literature.

Different linguistic terms for family and household reveal something of the variety of ways societies have conceived these institutions. For example, the modern Chinese word *jia*, usually translated as "family," refers more properly to what English speakers would call a household, a corporate unit with a common residence and shared economy. The term *zong* refers to the patri-line (those who trace common descent through the father), a multigenerational group that links kin over time, while *zu* refers to the same-generation group of kin who share a common surname and descent, such as aunts, uncles, cousins, and so on. Customarily, *zong* and *zu* are used together to mean both ancestral line and the extended kinship group, which is sometimes

referred to as a lineage or clan. Thus, in Chinese there is a distinction between the corporate household unit and the broader connections of the extended kin group, traced through both lineal descent and the lateral community of shared surname.

In contrast to the principle of patrilineal descent enshrined in the Chinese family system, among the Akan of West Africa, the word for "family" is **abusua**, a matriline (matrilineal descent group) that traces common descent through its female relatives. Within the *abusua*, the sense of shared belonging and the rights and protections afforded to members could only be acquired by both men and women through birth ties to a mother or aunt. Among the Sioux peoples of North America, the word for "family" or "relatives" included all living things, from ants to aunts.

Throughout history and across cultures, the distinction between public and private has marked differing spheres of responsibility and control according to gender. The realm of domestic interiors – both physical and social – was relegated to women, as indicated by the term "the inner quarters" in imperial China. Like family and household, and intimately related to both, the concept of gender is socially and cul-turally constructed, not biologically determined. Constructions of gender, family, and household both vary across cultures and change over time. Agents of economic production as well as biolog-ical reproduction, families and households were shaped by social, cultural, political, economic, and ideological forces, as were the roles of men and women and shifting relations between them. Every aspect of gender, family, and household – from the most intimate and personal to the most public and formal – intersects with and reflects larger patterns of historical change: migration, urbanization, the spread of religions, and the rise and fall of states and empires. Understanding continuities as well as changes in gender, family, and household over time and across cultures illuminates the dynamic relationship between broader processes of historical change and the most private realms of human interaction.

Gender, family, and household in Roman law and society

Throughout the vast Roman Empire, stretching at its height from North Africa to the British Isles and from the Black Sea to the Iberian peninsula, there was enormous variety in the structures of family and household. Viewed even from the limited perspective of the urban center, Rome, however, we can identify aspects of family institutions that continued to influence Mediterranean and later European societies long after the fall of the Roman Empire.

The English word "family" comes directly from the Latin word *familia*, but the meanings of the two words are almost completely different. In its broadest usage, *familia* referred to all persons and property under the control (*patria potestas*) of the head of the family (**paterfamilias**), including servants and slaves as well as kin. Although Romans had no term for the conjugal unit of father–mother–children, this triad was central to Roman family life, even in situations of extended and multigenerational families. The key relationships were those of husband and wife, and parents and children, even though elite households also included numerous servants and slaves who attended the master and mistress, cared for their children as wetnurses, nannies, and foster mothers, and managed the estates and businesses

belonging to the *paterfamilias*. Although slaves were not legally free to marry, they often did form unions within the *familia*; freed slaves also tended to marry within the *familia* and took the family name (*nomen*) of their former owners. The **domus**, the Roman house and household, was for elite Romans a public space as well as a domain of family intimacy and privacy. The atrium, the main public area of the house, was the place where rites of passage were marked and celebrated, and births and deaths were announced to the outside world by decorations on the threshold. Both the location of the house and the house itself were the physical expression of a family's place in society.

The Roman government implemented policies to encourage childbearing and to discourage celibacy or childless marriages among the elite. Julius Caesar's law of 59 BCE, for example, made land available to fathers of three or more children. In 18 BCE and again in 9 CE, Emperor Augustus issued legislation to promote childbearing. Political preference was given to fathers of three or more children and women who had borne three children were exempted from the need for a male guardian. The encouragement of childbearing emphasized in legislation under Augustus continued throughout the later Roman Empire. Roman coinage of the second century CE, for example, was used to advertise ideals of Roman motherhood, often in association with women of the imperial family.

Roman women enjoyed a relatively high degree of independence in marriage. Upon marriage, a woman transferred from her father's authority to that of her husband, and her dowry went along with her to become part of her husband's property. But on the death of her husband, the wife was entitled to an equal share of her husband's property along with her children. A wife could also divorce her husband and take much of her dowry with her, giving a wealthy wife a good deal of independence.

Apart from legal prescriptions over divorce and property rights, however, there is plentiful evidence of companionate marriages in which husbands and wives shared mutual respect and affection for each other and for their children. The valediction of a letter written from exile in 58–57 BCE by the Roman orator Cicero to his wife, Terentia, expresses the emotional attachment he felt for her and their children: "My dear Terentia, most faithful and best of wives, and my darling little daughter, and that last hope of my race, Cicero, goodbye!"[1]

However, Cicero's devotion to Terentia did not prevent him from divorcing her about ten years after he wrote this letter. Cicero was not a wealthy man, and he had great difficulty in repaying Terentia's dowry, as he was required to do upon divorce. Both Cicero and Terentia remarried, also a common occurrence among the Roman elite, due either to the death of a spouse or to divorce. Remarriage led to the proliferation of complicated households of step-parents, step-siblings, half-siblings, and other relatives.

Roman leaders and authors often promoted an idealized view of the Roman family under the firm authority of the *paterfamilias* in which wives were faithful, children were obedient, and slaves were submissive. The satirist Juvenal (ca. 60–140), for example, described exemplary virtuous women of archaic Rome in contrast to the decadent, adulterous women of his own day. Youth, too, were seen as disrespectful and disobedient, unlike those of earlier times under the domination of patriarchs who could determine life or death. The disruption of patriarchal order in the family and the violation of family bonds were linked by many commentators to social breakdown. Laments of moral decay within the family echoed throughout the later Roman Empire, to be exploited by early Christian communities who criticized the decadence of Roman life.

Beyond Rome itself, families and households were less subject to the interference of the state. Much of what we know about the social structures and habits of northern peoples such as the Celts and the Germans comes from observations written down by Romans. As in Mediterranean Europe, women in northern Europe were subject to male dominance and were primarily valued as mothers and household managers. In Celtic society, described by Julius Caesar (100–44 BCE) as belligerent, lives bordered on extreme forms of domination and submission, and people were afraid to act independently, living in utter dependence on the few dominant male warriors.

The Roman historian Tacitus (ca. 55–118 CE) presented an admiring portrait of Germanic family life as a moral lesson to the Romans, whom he felt were growing decadent. Germanic males were reportedly monogamous warriors, and the wife was the warrior's partner in all things, although care of the household and cultivation of the fields was left to women, who in turn were expected to live in "impregnable" chastity. From birth, care of children was also the woman's responsibility. The greater the number of a man's offspring and relations, the greater his influence and security when he was old. Old women were highly regarded, apparently being considered to have prophetic or spiritual powers.

Christianity, family, and household in medieval Europe

With the conversion of the Roman emperor Constantine (r. 306–37) to Christianity, this new religion gained the support of the state. Spreading throughout the realms of the Roman Empire – and later the Byzantine Empire – Christianity gradually transformed society, including ideas about family and household. Although another well-known convert to Christianity, the North African Augustine (354–430), wrote extensively in his *Confessions* and in *The City of God* about the family as a unit of society based on the conjugal union of husband and wife, in other ways Christianity challenged the model of the conjugal family by offering alternatives to marriage and procreation for both men and women. By the time of Augustine, monasticism provided opportunities to live outside the structures of family and household within a religious community. The early Christian community thus created bonds of fellowship that transcended and replaced family bonds. But Christians also drew on the social symbolism of kinship relations and family life in creating their new religious communities. Beginning with the concept of Jesus as the "son of God" and the idea of "God the father," the symbolism of the family was a powerful model in Christian ideology.

In the centuries between the fall of the Roman Empire and the crowning of Charlemagne as Holy Roman Emperor by the pope in 800, Christianity penetrated beyond urban centers such as Rome and Constantinople to the countryside. Along with Christianity, economic changes began to transform rural society. The peasant household replaced Roman slave-based agriculture as the means of economic production. The head of the household, much like the Roman *paterfamilias*, exercised control over the household members, and was the link between the household and the

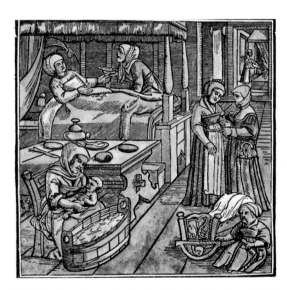

7.1 Medieval woodcut showing birth of a child. Medieval childbirth was difficult and dangerous, and required the help of a community of women beyond the immediate household to care for the mother and the child.

world beyond the house and fields. The dwellings and diet of the rural poor were spare and simple, a mud-and-thatch hut shared with animals, built around an open fire for heat, with turnips, beer, bread, and perhaps some cheese to eat. The bed was the most important item of furniture, and even the poorest peasant household had at least a mattress, if not a bedstead, which would often be shared by both adults and children.

By the ninth century, the establishment of Christian parishes throughout the European countryside transformed the daily lives of peasants who labored on the manors and estates of landlords and attended church regularly in local parish churches. Although marriage did not officially become a sacrament of the Church until the twelfth century, eventually parish registers recorded the births, deaths, and marriages of both the aristocracy and the peasantry. According to the Church, marriage was a matter of consent affirmed through the exchange of vows between bride and groom; once a conjugal union was formed, it was regarded as indissoluble. The Church's intrusion into family life went beyond its control of the marriage sacrament. The practice of regular confession to a priest who prescribed penance meant that, through its clergy, the Church exercised control over family behavior. In addition to mandating celibacy for the priesthood and idealizing the religious life of chastity, poverty, and obedience, the Church excluded women from the priesthood.

With the gradual disappearance of serfdom in the eleventh and twelfth centuries, towns and cities increased in size and number. Migration from rural areas accounted for much of this growth, as rural laborers sought work in urban businesses and industries. Families and households adapted to new opportunities for work offered in urban settings, sending their sons and daughters to work as domestic servants or as apprentices. In fourteenth- and fifteenth-century Toulouse in southern France, for example, more than half of the apprentices and young male servants came from outside the city, including many as young as 8 to 12 years old. Sending children to work in the cities was an economic strategy adopted by many rural families that enabled them to survive the uncertainties of dependence on agriculture. But urban life also took its toll, since mortality rates were high. Dense populations and poor sanitation created conditions for disease that were absent in rural villages. Whether as long-term urban residents or newly arrived immigrants, urban women worked in large numbers at a variety of occupations – from weaving wool to hawking food – that provided important sources of income for themselves and their families.

Both women and men who migrated to cities left behind whatever network of family support they had. Some of these migrants remained single, and some married and established their own households. But many were left on their own to seek help in times of crisis. Children were the most vulnerable, both infants and orphans. The earliest foundling hospitals for abandoned infants were established in Italy during the thirteenth century, and the institution spread over the next two centuries through Spain, Portugal and France. Other charitable institutions developed as well to provide food, clothing, and health care. Many of these institutions were the product of religious charity and funded by donations made to churches, monasteries, and convents.

Confucianism, family, and household in Imperial China

Like Christianity in Europe, Confucianism profoundly shaped families and households as well as relations between women and men in China and throughout East Asia. Born into an age of political and social disorder in the sixth century BCE, Confucius considered the family to be the foundation of society. He encouraged families to venerate their ancestors, so the performance of ancestral rites became an important activity of the Confucian family. Each generation was obliged to produce male heirs so that succeeding generations could continue to honor their ancestors.

State and society were modeled on the family. The ruler was to treat his subjects as a father treats his sons, and vice versa. The virtue of filial piety ideally characterized this relationship: the father had absolute authority within the family and absolute obedience was required from the son. In addition to the relationship between ruler and subject, the father–son relationship, along with that between elder brother and younger brother and between husband and wife were among the five fundamental human relationships (the fifth was between friends). Certain aspects of these relationships as prescribed by Confucius are apparent: the dominance of age over youth, and male over female. Age and gender determined hierarchy within the family. Women, no matter how old they became, could not escape the authority of men. As daughters, they were dependents and subordinates of their fathers; as wives, of their husbands; and as widows, of their sons.

One of the most influential interpreters of Confucian ideals with regard to the roles of women in the family was Ban Zhao (ca. 45–115 CE), the daughter of a famous scholarly family of the time and a noted scholar in her own right. She compiled the *Admonitions for Women*, a treatise concerning the moral and ethical principles by which women should order their lives. This work also provided guidance for the practical concerns of everyday life for daughters, wives, and mothers. Some of the chapter titles of this work suggest Ban Zhao's themes: humility, respect and caution, devotion, obedience, harmony. She urged women to yield to others, respect others, and to put others first. Among other things, she addressed the role of women and men within the family: "If a wife does not serve her husband, then the proper relationship between men and women and the natural order of things are neglected and destroyed."[2]

Apart from prescribed behavior written about in classical texts, we know relatively little from standard sources about the intimate details of family life or about the practical operation of households in early imperial China of roughly the first millennium CE. But in part due to the remarkable finds made in the early twentieth century at Dunhuang in the arid northwest of China, we have some household registration records compiled by government officials around 750 for the purpose of taxation. These records tell us something of family members, their ages, and the generations that comprise a household. One household includes the head, whose age is given as 56; a widowed stepmother, 60; wife, 58; two younger brothers (of the household head), 28, 42; son, 18; one younger brother's wife, 25; five daughters, ranging in age from 13 to 31; two sons of a deceased elder brother, 23 and 17; and a younger sister (of the household head), 43.[3] There were altogether three generations in the household, including children of the head's deceased sibling as well as the head's widowed stepmother and unmarried sister and daughters. Women who lacked their own conjugal units had no recourse but to live with their male relatives, whether widowed or never married.

By around 1000 CE, we begin to have much more documentation available to reconstruct the Chinese family and household, and literary sources, especially poetry, provide personal and private perspectives that greatly enhance what we can learn from official records. Literary sources can open a different kind of window on family life in the past, documenting emotional and psychological dimensions of family relationships and suggesting how stated ideals were lived in practice. Despite the apparently rigid demarcation of gender roles in marriage suggested in Ban Zhao's *Admonitions for Women*, emotional ties between husband and wife could often be deep.

A profound emotional and intellectual tie existed between a woman poet named Li Qingzhao (ca. 1084–1151) and her husband. Like other women of her time, she married at a young age, 16 or 17. After her husband's death, she wrote a moving recollection of their marriage as an intimate scholarly partnership. Li Qingzhao and her husband lived in an era when marriage ties were often used as a strategy to enhance a family's political, social, or economic status. Wealth was an important factor, but even more important was the status achieved by those who passed the imperial civil service examinations. For example, a wealthy family with no sons might marry their daughter to the son of a relatively poor family who had passed the examinations and thus had prospects of both wealth and power. Adoption could also be used as a means to gain a son with potential to achieve status through the examinations, particularly if a family had no male offspring. By the thirteenth century, the economic exchange involved in marriage shifted from brideprice (the transfer of wealth and property from the groom's family to the bride's) to dowry (wealth and property brought by the bride to the marriage), suggesting a relatively equal balance in terms of the exchange of property between the families of the bride and groom.

Marriage was more than simply a means to enhanced social or economic status, and families were more than units for the production of examination candidates or marriageable daughters. Marriage and family life reflected a complex of notions about the role and position of women and their relationships with men, and created complicated emotional ties that were often denied or thwarted by social custom and practice. Yuan Cai's guide for family life written in the twelfth century gave practical advice on how to deal with problems that affected family harmony, such as the treatment of women (as wives, concubines, servants, unmarried relatives, or widows) and how to maintain status.

Confucianism idealized the extended family, consisting of multiple generations and branches. Bearing children to continue the ancestral line was a Confucian obligation, but for poor families it was often an economically disastrous burden. Infanticide, particularly female infanticide, was practiced out of economic desperation. We know about the practice of infanticide in the twelfth century, for example, from written sources

PRIMARY SOURCE: HOW TO MANAGE A FAMILY IN TWELFTH-CENTURY CHINA

An upper-class man in twelfth-century China, Yuan Cai (ca. 1140–95), wrote a book of advice for managing a family and household that tells us much about how people viewed the role of women and their position in the household. In contrast to the idealization of family life portrayed in Confucian texts such as Ban Zhao's *Admonitions for Women*, this guidebook was written from the perspective of the day-to-day concerns of family life, displaying a more pragmatic view of human behavior along with a more flexible and tolerant attitude toward women. Yuan's work also makes clear the corporate nature of the household as an economic unit.

Women should not take part in affairs outside the home

Women do not take part in extrafamilial affairs. The reason is that worthy husbands and sons take care of everything for them, while unworthy ones can always find ways to hide their deeds from the women.

Many men today indulge in pleasure and gambling; some end up mortgaging their lands, and even go so far as to mortgage their houses without their wives' knowledge. Therefore, when husbands are bad, even if wives try to handle outside matters, it is of no use. Sons must have their mothers' signatures to mortgage their family properties, but there are sons who falsify papers and forge signatures, sometimes borrowing money at high interest from people who would not hesitate to bring their claim to court. Other sons sell illicit tea and salt to get money, which, if discovered by the authorities, results in fines.

Mothers have no control in such matters. Therefore, when sons are bad, it is useless for mothers to try to handle matters relating to the outside world.

For women, these are grave misfortunes, but what can they do? If husbands and sons could only remember that their wives and mothers are helpless and suddenly repent, wouldn't that be best?

Women's sympathies should be indulged

Without going overboard, people should marry their daughters with dowries appropriate to their family's wealth. Rich families should not consider their daughters outsiders but should give them a share of the property. Sometimes people have incapable sons and so have to entrust their affairs to their daughters' families; even after their deaths, their burials and sacrifices are performed by their daughters. So how can people say that daughters are not as good as sons?

Generally speaking, a woman's heart is very sympathetic. If her parents' family is wealthy and her husband's family is poor, then she wants to take her parents' wealth to help her husband's family prosper. . .

It is difficult for widows to entrust their financial affairs to others

Some wives with stupid husbands are able to manage the family's finances, calculating the outlays and receipts of money and grain, without being cheated by anyone. Of those with degenerate husbands, there are also some who are able to manage the finances with the help of their sons without ending in bankruptcy. Even among those whose husbands have died and whose sons are young, there are occasionally women able to raise and educate their sons, keep the affection of all their relatives, manage the family business, and even prosper. All of these are wise and worthy women. But the most remarkable are the women who manage a household after their husbands have died leaving them with young children. Such women could entrust their finances to their husbands' kinsmen or their own kinsmen, but not all relatives are honorable, and the honorable ones are not necessarily willing to look after other people's business.

When wives themselves can read and do arithmetic, and those they entrust with their affairs have some sense of fairness and duty with regard to food, clothing, and support, then things will usually work out all right. But in most of the rest of the cases, bankruptcy is what happens.

Source: Patricia B. Ebrey, *Chinese Civilization: A Sourcebook* (New York: Macmillan Free Press, 1993), pp166–68.

that document state officials' efforts to establish orphanages to alleviate the problem of infanticide, which was viewed as a great social evil by Confucian authorities. Children of poor families were often sold as servants. In more desperate circumstances, children were abandoned – left to die or be cared for by others.

Although its origins are veiled in legend, we do know that the practice of footbinding became established sometime around 1000. The binding of a female child's foot with the toes turned under so that the foot would be malformed and stunted, shaped into the desired tiny "lily foot," possibly began with a style of dancing with bound feet not unlike that of modern ballet dancers, who wear toe shoes. The practice of binding feet apparently spread from the court as a fashion; it was appealing to men because it caused women to walk with a mincing, dainty step and may have caused physical changes that heightened male sexual pleasure. The spread of the practice was also related to economic prosperity brought about by the commercial revolution of Song times, as only

wealthier households could support women whose feet were bound and therefore were unable to perform physical labor. Bound feet also gave women a languid, passive appearance that contrasted with a masculine image of strength, virility, and activity. Gradually, footbinding came to be seen as essential to the marriageability of young girls, and literary appreciations of the "lily foot" enhanced the aesthetic appeal of this cultural practice.

In China, as in other societies, ideals of family life and gender roles were often in conflict with the realities of daily life for much of the population. Although Confucian piety demanded the strictest standards of moral behavior within the family and in society, prostitution, homosexuality, and other practices frowned upon by Confucianism flourished. Homosexuality, both male and female, was not widely acknowledged but was practiced at all levels of society. By the Tang and Song dynasties, there is anecdotal literature about Buddhist priests and their young male paramours, both male and female prostitutes, and other such practices that flaunted Confucian conventions but were to be found flourishing in the prosperous urban areas of Song China.

During the Mongol rule of China in the thirteenth and fourteenth centuries, Neo-Confucian ideas that celebrated chaste widows – prohibiting widows to remarry – and other restrictions on women were codified in law. As before, women's lives continued to be shaped by their economic status, by where they lived – rural, urban, coastal, inland – and by their education. But above all, Confucian and Neo-Confucian attitudes dictated the place of women in Chinese society and their essential role as mothers and wives or concubines.

Women, family, and household in Northeast Asia: Korea and Japan

Korea and Japan were closely connected in early history, populated by migrations of people from northern Eurasia. Societies on the Korean peninsula and the Japanese archipelago were transformed by waves of influences from China that brought Buddhism and Confucianism, along with Chinese political ideas and institutions.

Korea

In early Korea, before the unification of the peninsula under the state of Silla (668–935) and the accompanying influx of Confucian patriarchal notions, women had a high degree of autonomy and relative equality with men, and these customs continued to influence society even after the advent of Confucianism. Uxorilocal (in which the bridegroom resides in the bride's home) marriages were practiced, and descent was traced bilaterally – through both female and male lines. Even in Koryŏ (918–1392), as Confucianism made further inroads into Korean society, women inherited equally with their brothers. Together, uxorilocal marriage and equal inheritance made it possible

for women to exercise a good deal of independence and to divorce and remarry with relative ease. In certifying status for the state civil service examinations, modeled on those of China, candidates had to demonstrate the appropriate status of four ancestors, one of which was the maternal grandfather. This makes it clear that, despite the influence of Chinese thought, the maternal link remained important in Koryŏ Korea. The importance of maternal relatives can also be seen in mourning rituals, which tended to follow Chinese Confucian norms, but gave much more weight to maternal relatives.

Elite women in both Silla and Koryŏ were granted high positions and respected for their learning as well as for their roles as wives and mothers. Three Silla monarchs were women, but there were no more female rulers after the ninth century. Very little is known about the lives of commoners, beyond their role as subjects of the state. Ironically, somewhat more is known about both male and female slaves, who were owned by the king and his family, by other government agencies, as well as by private families. According to a law of 1039, slave status was inherited through the mother, so the father's status had no effect.

The Choson dynasty (1392–1910) imposed Confucian values on Korean society, most explicitly by instituting a Confucian-style patrilineal descent system with its attendant negative impact on the status of women. What has been called "the Confucian transformation" of Korea substantially altered gender relations and the place of women in society. In much the same way that Neo-Confucianism contributed to a decline in the status of women in China, beginning in the fourteenth century, its adoption in Choson Korea similarly subjected women to strict male authority through a patriarchal and patrilineal family system. Laws were enacted to regulate marriage and inheritance, distinguishing carefully, for example, between the offspring of the primary wife and those of secondary wives.

Japan

Although by the twelfth century at the latest, Confucian patriarchal norms had imprinted themselves on Japanese society, early Japan displays features of a matriarchal society in which women exercised a good deal of power. Chinese records from the third century tell of a shaman-queen, Himiko, who together with her consort brother ruled over a confederacy of clans in early Japan, although it is not clear to what extent she actually ruled beyond communicating with the gods. Evidence from tombs of the third to fifth centuries suggests that both women and men were engaged in military affairs and religious ritual as well as economic activities, including trade.

Indigenous religious beliefs that became the foundation of Shinto, as the native religion was known after the introduction of Buddhism in the sixth century, also reflect the power of women: the central solar deity, Amaterasu, is female, and priestesses continue to play an important role in rites at Shinto shrines even in the present. The imperial family was known as the Sun line because they claimed descent from Amaterasu, the Sun Goddess, and the emperor (or empress) was her chief priest. Six female monarchs reigned during the seventh century.

Successive waves of influence from China introduced Buddhism, the structure of a bureaucratic, centralized state, and other new ideas and institutions that profoundly shaped Japanese society during the Nara period (710–84). One important change introduced was the recognition by the state of private property, and women as well as men were able to buy and sell land and engage in other economic activities such as sake production. A bilateral system of descent – traced through both mother's and father's lineage – prevailed in early Japan as in Korea. Marriages were temporary and, among the aristocracy, spouses retained their own independent residences. After the death of her husband-brother and siblings, Empress Suiko (r. 592–628) ruled

together with her nephew, Prince Shotoku. The influence of Confucianism may have contributed to the eventual prohibition on women rulers after the end of the eighth century.

Powerful families such as the Fujiwara in the Heian period (794–1185) entrenched themselves at court in part through marrying into the imperial family. Women were barred from succession to the throne after the eighth century, but they retained political importance as pawns in the practice of "marriage politics." By marrying his daughter to the heir to the throne, a Fujiwara male, for example, could become the father-in-law of the emperor. If his daughter gave birth to a son, he would become the grandfather of the new heir and hence a powerful and influential member of the court.

Women in the Heian period were more than daughters to be married and wives to bear children. They could hold and inherit property, and thus their legal position was relatively strong, although they depended on male protectors, fathers, or husbands. The flowering of native Japanese literature – especially the novel and the poetic diary – in this era was largely a product of women writers. Denied the possibility to hold government office and conduct affairs in the weighty official language of classical Chinese, Heian women wrote in *kana*, the phonetic syllabary for Japanese developed in the ninth century. Court ladies such as Murasaki Shikibu (ca. 978–1016), the author of *The Tale of Genji*, described their world, the Heian court, and the emotional and psychological background of the social relations that occupied their daily lives.

Heian social mores, while seeming in some ways to allow great sexual freedom, were precise and highly regulated. Prince Genji, the hero of Murasaki's famous novel, was married to Lady Aoi, the daughter of an important court minister and thus an appropriate spouse for the emperor's son. By Heian convention, Lady Aoi continued to reside with her parents, and her husband visited her there. It was acknowledged and expected that men such as Genji would have relations with other women. In Genji's case, tragedy was brought about by the spiteful jealousy of one of his lovers, whose malevolent bewitching caused the death of his wife in childbirth. Women did not have the same sexual freedom as men, but they did engage in amorous affairs and intrigues. Commoner women at the lower rungs of society faced a far more difficult set of circumstances, since they had neither wealth nor social standing to provide support.

The only alternative open to women without families was to enter a nunnery or become a courtesan. Buddhism, by its very nature, provided an alternative to family in which individuals severed all ties to family and society outside the religious community.

Although Buddhism taught that women were inferior to men, and that they would have to be reborn as men in order to achieve enlightenment, orders of mendicant nuns still provided a place for women with no home or family. The rise of salvationist sects of Buddhism in the late Heian also offered women opportunities to participate more freely in the pursuit of enlightenment (see Chapter 5).

In subsequent centuries, the status of women changed dramatically as Japanese society came to be dominated by military values, and changes in inheritance practices – from division of property among sons and daughters to a single male heir – further contributed to a decline in the economic independence of women. By the late twelfth century, the court-centered cultural world of the Heian aristocracy had given way to a society ordered by warriors and animated by martial values. Although Hojo Masako (1157–1225), the wife of the founder of the first **shogunate**, took the Buddhist tonsure as expected after her husband's early death, she continued to speak with the authority of being her husband's widow while her father and brothers ruled the country. Apart from the weakened court nobility, who exercised less and less control over the country, military strength and skill were what determined political power and social status.

Women, however, held the power of reproduction. The family provided a mechanism to produce heirs to "**fiefs**," and the role of women was to bear the heirs. A woman was expected to exhibit loyalty to her husband's lord, even to the extent of allowing her own offspring to die in place of the lord's heir. She was also expected to aid her husband in carrying out the final act of honor and loyalty to the samurai ethic: assisting her husband in ritual suicide and joining him in death by her own hand. Women widowed by warfare might take Buddhist vows and enter a nunnery.

Beginning in the fourteenth century, with the growth of a commercial economy, non-elite women were active purveyors of fish, rice, beans, tofu, and worked at sake brewing and cloth dyeing. They also traded textiles, ceramics, and other goods. Because of the limited sources that survive, however, we still know relatively little about commoner women and their families and households in Japan before the sixteenth century.

Women, family, and household in Inner Asia

The relative lack of written sources for the ethnically diverse and complex societies of Inner Asia makes it more difficult to trace historical change in the patterns and structures of family and household. Even accounts by observers such as that by William of Rubruck are rare. Inner Asian nomadic societies were patrilineal and patrilocal. Property – the herds – was normally divided among the sons of a family, with a share reserved for the parents. In contrast to many societies, where primogeniture (inheritance by the eldest son) prevailed, the youngest son ultimately inherited the paternal household's share along with his own. The household, measured in numbers of tents, was the basic social unit among steppe nomads. As in China, where patrilineal relatives might share common lands and residences, patrilineal kin in nomadic societies often shared common pastures and camps. The labor of an extended family was very useful in pastoral nomadism, which depended on the management of animal herds. Efficiency was increased by the combining of smaller herds, made possible by extended family ties; and women's work in milk processing or felt making was similarly improved by cooperation. The extended family, however, as in China, was a cultural ideal and had some economic advantages, as suggested; but it was also difficult to maintain, due to the inherent instability of large groups.

Although the position of women among nomadic pastoral peoples was certainly lower than that of men, women were able to fraternize with men more freely and openly than in the more sedentary agricultural societies of Asia. Women could own, manage, and dispose of property. They managed the households, and often the camps while men herded, although women sometimes also managed the herds. In the thirteenth century, the pope's envoy to the Mongols, Johann de Plano Carpini, made the following observation about men's and women's work in the Mongol camps:

> The men do nothing but occupy themselves with their arrows and to a small extent look after their herds; for the rest they go hunting and practice archery . . . Both men and women stay in the saddle for a long time . . . All the work rests on the shoulders of the women; they make the fur coats, clothes, shoes, bootlegs, and everything else made from leather. They also drive the carts and mend them, load the camels, and are very quick and efficient in all their work. All the women wear trousers, and some of them shoot with the bow as accurately as the men.
>
> Source: Berthold Spuler, *History of the Mongols: Based on Eastern and Western Accounts of the Thirteenth and Fourteenth Centuries* (Berkeley, CA: University of California Press, 1972), pp80–81.

The man would bring to a marriage his share of his family's herd, and the woman would bring a tent. But it was often not economically feasible for a newly married couple to form an independent household, and so they would remain with the husband's family, participating in the cooperative management of the herds. Marriage bonded two kin groups or even two tribal groups together, and thus daughters could be an important political asset. For example, the clan of Chinggis Khan's wife claimed that their marriage alliances, not their military strength, were the source of their political power: "Since days of old we . . . have been protected by the beauty of our daughters, by the loveliness of our granddaughters, and so we've stayed out of battles and wars. . . We don't challenge empires; we don't go to war with our neighbors. We just bring up our daughters . . . to sit by the Khan . . . as [our] shields."[4] **Polygyny** (one man with multiple wives) was practiced, and each wife had her own yurt, or tent.

As in many other societies, marriage could be an important political strategy for families seeking power and status. After the death of her husband, a woman might retain considerable power through her sons and sometimes even in her own right. When a crisis in the succession of political leadership occurred, the wife of a former chief could wield power as a regent until a new successor was chosen. One example of this was the selection of the senior wife of Chinggis Khan's son and successor, Ögödei, to serve as regent for five years following his death in 1241. In such instances, the strategies of elite Mongol women differed little from those of thirteenth-century elite women in other cultures.

The impact of Islam on women, family, and household in West Asia

Despite the great impact of Islam on West Asia, in terms of both codified religious law and social custom, there was a strong element of continuity between pre- and post-Islamic society in this region of the world. Division into tribal or lineage-based society, village-based farmers and herders, and urban merchants both predated the coming of Islam and continued in post-Islamic West Asia. The critical change that did accompany the introduction of Islam to the region was the imposition of a written religious text, the Qur'an, as a guide to social and political order and the use of this text to create a law code, the *shari'a*. The foundations of the *shari'a* were the unambiguous commands and prohibitions found in the Qur'an. This encapsulation of systematic codes of behavior began in the eighth and ninth centuries, with the work of several schools of legal scholars. The legal code regulated individual and family life within the community, which was defined as consisting of those who were "true believers."

Written codes, by their very nature, changed social customs because they removed practices common to members of a society from their everyday context and transformed them into general principles to be applied across the Islamic world without regard to context. But there was also another source of wisdom known as *hadith*, or oral sayings. The intersection of these two authorities, written and fixed, oral and fluid, required varying degrees of personal reasoning and interpretation. The written laws in general tended to deal with the public level of the Islamic community, particularly stressing its patriarchal structure, rather than with the domestic world of the conjugal family unit, which was dominated by women.

In early Islam, as in early Christianity, a new religious ideology demanded both a break from previous social customs and continuity with them. As they rejected pre-Islamic and pagan practices, both Muslim and Christian believers drew on the social symbolism of kinship relations and family life in creating their new religious communities. For example, when the apostle Paul, a Hellenized Jew, called upon "elders" and "brothers" as leaders of the Christian community, he gave new meaning to these terms: they no longer identified status dependent on seniority and blood ties but leaders of a community of faith that cut across ethnic and kinship groups. Similarly, in Islam, this group was defined as the "community of true believers." Kinship models were retained to describe relationships within the faith. In Muslim brotherhoods, members addressed one another as "brother," suggesting the strength and permanence of the bonds of faith.

Emerging out of the clan lineage society of Mecca, the Islamic family was portrayed in the Qur'an and in the *shari'a* as a highly valued institution and the primary social, economic, and political unit of the community. Women were described by some Islamic writers as inferior to men by nature and thus as owing men obedience, while for others the pivotal duties of Islam applied equally to men and women. In the urban settings of Mecca and Medina, as in Damascus and Byzantium, women could exercise some limited power in their own as well as their husbands' affairs. And like Judaism and Christianity, Islam offered equal access to Heaven for both men and women.

The introduction of Islamic inheritance laws made custom one of the guiding principles of the law. Overall, the family was strengthened by these laws and the patriarchal authority of senior male family members was constrained, but social and economic practice in some regions and some periods found loopholes: the ideals of Islamic law could be – and often were – modified to allow individuals to benefit at the expense of family, for example, or to permit societies to ignore the rights of women to the advantage of patriarchy. Thus, the eventual codification of an Islamic concept of family and household relied on both the written ideal and the flexibility to deviate from that ideal in practice.

Despite these changes, there is little evidence that Islam significantly curtailed women's property rights. As before, under Islamic law, women were entitled to a settlement by their husband or parents at the time of marriage. Although descent was reckoned patrilineally (through the father's line), authority within the family was patriarchal and residence was patrilocal, that is, the family would reside with the husband's family; women were entitled to a share of the parental property. Unlike in East and South Asia, where adoption was one strategy for passing on property within the family – that is, a male would be adopted into the family of his bride – in Islamic West Asia, adoption was prohibited, and close-kin marriage (which was not absent but often prohibited in East and South Asia) was a means of preserving family property.

Early West Asian society also included significant numbers of slaves, who were largely integrated into free Muslim family units. Slaves, mostly captured in war, were used almost exclusively as domestic servants or, by some governments, as soldiers. By law, Muslims could not be enslaved; slaves were drawn from the surrounding non-Muslim populations. Under Islamic law, a slave was a person whose rights had been severely restricted but not totally lost by enslavement. Manumission, or release from the condition of slavery, was encouraged. Many female slaves became concubines, and their children were accorded the same rights as children born within marriage contracts. One of the purposes of *shari'a* law was to establish rules to integrate persons into the family unit and into Islam.

Housing varied throughout the Islamic world, depending on the pre-Islamic culture, climate, available building materials, and geography. However, two household concerns were widely shared: the right of the family to keep its affairs private and the impact of Islamic law and religious practice on women. Households looked inward for strength and satisfaction. Wealth, social interactions, and the intimate areas of family life remained hidden inside the household. Nothing of a house's façade revealed the inner workings or material comfort of the group. The family lived around a courtyard often ornamented with trees and fountains.

According to the Qur'an, believers should "not enter the dwellings of other men until [they] have asked their owners' permission and wished them peace." If visitors were entertained, they were admitted only as far as a men's reception area. Women remained secluded in their own separate area (harem) with apartments. The extent to which women might be permitted to leave the house varied across time and class. Strict Muslims in tenth-century Baghdad, for example, felt that women should never be seen on public streets.

Jews, Moslems, and Christians coexisted in medieval Cairo of the eleventh century, each group having a distinctive religious and ethnic heritage but also sharing some common regional and cultural identity with the others. For example, love was recognized as part of the marriage relationship, and conjugal sex was regulated according to different religious customs: on Thursday for Moslems, Friday for Jews, and Saturday for Christians. All such activity was to occur before bathing in preparation for attending the mosque, synagogue, or church. Mosques, synagogues, and churches all provided charity for indigents, and especially for widows and orphans, thus supplanting the family when necessary. Donations to such charitable enterprises by women from their dowry wealth have been documented. Wives were regarded as companions of their husbands, and they were independently involved in commercial business activities as well as able to go to court for the resolution of legal disputes.

According to the Cairo Geniza documents, which provide an intimate portrait of Jewish, Muslim, and Christian society in medieval Cairo, marriages were conceived as partnerships, with mutual, if not equal, obligations between spouses; both partners had the right to terminate a marriage (although women's rights were more limited), with protection of property rights for women as well as men upon dissolution of the union. By the eleventh to thirteenth centuries, divorce was common – 45 percent of all women married a second or third time – but not always amicable. One husband, an India trader whose long absence from Cairo strained his marriage, reluctantly agreed to free his wife from their marriage if she so desired. In a letter he wrote to her, he said: "Now the matter is in your hand. If you wish separation from me, accept the bill of repudiation and you are free. But if this is not your decision and not your desire, do not lose these long years of waiting."[5]

In his *Book on the Etiquette of Marriage*, the eleventh-century Muslim religious scholar al-Ghazali wrote that there were five advantages to marriage: procreation, satisfying sexual desire, ordering the household, providing companionship, and disciplining the self. Marriage in Islam was based on mutual consent and was therefore a contractual relationship that involved both economic and social obligations. The legal contract of marriage, whether written or not, linked the resources of two families and was the single most important event in an individual's life. It required at least two witnesses, and if a court lay within a reasonable distance, it was recorded there. The contract might specify gifts of land or other family property to the woman or her family. Muslim women could marry only Muslim men, a restriction that prevented the flow of property and population from the Muslim community to other groups. Depending on what the contract stipulated, a woman might retain control of her dowry. A man was required to provide maintenance for his wife, and he could have more than one wife – up to four – as long as he treated them all equally as the Qur'an dictated.

Unlike Christianity, which regarded marriage as a sacrament and thus indissoluble, the contractual basis of Islamic marriage meant that if the obligations were not met, the marriage could be dissolved. Divorce was relatively easy for men: they had only to repudiate their wives three times in order to divorce them. It was more difficult and complicated for women, who could only initiate divorce by appeal to a court judge and only for specific reasons. Both divorce and remarriage were common throughout the Islamic world, among both elite and commoners.

The relative ease of divorce and remarriage, even for those at the bottom rungs of the social ladder, can be glimpsed in three consecutive marriage contracts preserved in a court archive for a freed slave-girl named Zumurrud, a resident of Jerusalem in the late fourteenth century. In early 1389, she married a milkman who was obliged by the terms of the contract to provide as a marriage

7.2 Divorcing husband and wife accuse each other before a judge (*qadi*). Here a scribe listens and records the complaints. Most divorces took place without the intervention of a judge.

gift to her three gold coins, payable in install-ments. He divorced Zumurrud a little over a year later, and she forfeited the remainder of her marriage gift. She soon wed another freed slave, Sabīh, though without waiting for three months as divorced women were required to do before remarrying. In addition to a modest monetary marriage gift, he pledged to support Zumurrud's son by her previous husband, who had legal custodial rights which he apparently chose not to exercise. Six months later, Sabīh divorced Zumurrud, and shortly thereafter she was once again remarried, this time to a weaver who also pledged a marriage gift to be paid in installments.[6] Evident from the tale of Zumurrud's marriages is not only the ease with which the marriage contracts were made and revoked, but also the complicated financial negotiations that under-pinned the contracts.

African women, families, and households: Matrilineality and motherhood

For centuries, from the lively urban center of Cairo to al-Andalus on the Iberian peninsula, Islamic law provided a degree of coherence in regulating family and household practices across culturally diverse societies that rimmed the Mediterranean and beyond. The degree to which Islamic ideas about family and household varied according to local custom and tradition can be seen in the Muslim traveler Ibn Battuta's obser-vations of **matriliny** (in which both descent and property were transmitted through females) in fourteenth-century Mali:

> Their women are of surpassing beauty, and are shown more respect than the men. The state of affairs amongst these people is indeed extraordinary. Their men show no signs of jealousy whatever; no one claims descent from his father, but on the contrary from his mother's brother. A person's heirs are his

sister's sons, not his own sons. This is a thing which I have seen nowhere in the world except among the Indians of Malabar. But those are heathens; these people are Muslims, punctilious in observing the hours of prayer, studying books of law, and memorizing the Qur'an. Yet their women show no bashful-ness before men and do not veil themselves, though they are assiduous in attending the prayers.
> Source: Quoted in Erik Gilbert and Jonathan R. Reynolds, *Africa in World History: From Prehistory to the Present* (Upper Saddle River, NJ: Pearson Prentice Hall, 2004), p93.

Ibn Battuta was startled by these matrilineal customs, which were typical of many African societies, even those which had converted to Islam. Both matriliny and the prominent role of women in society surprised this Islamic traveler because such customs turned upside down the Islamic patrilineal and patriarchal order with which Ibn Battuta was most familiar.

As elsewhere throughout the world, a pervasive concern of African societies throughout history was continuity, the ability of the family and group to reproduce itself. An adult's sense of social com-pleteness was dependent on his or her ability to sire or bear children. Motherhood was an essential aspect of female identity in most societies. Children guaranteed the well-being of an indi-vidual in old age and ensured the transition of the parent's spirit to the community of the ancestors, who would be honored by their descendants. The prevalent belief in reincarnation of ancestors as newborn members of the lineage meant that children were highly valued as visible symbols of the continuity of life. The pragmatic concern of many African women and men regarding fertility ensured a large and productive household labor force.

Among the Batammaliba of northern Togo and Benin, who lived in dispersed, stateless settle-ments in the fifteenth century, the same word designated both the extended family and the house in which its members lived. The meaning of household (those sharing physical space) and family (those sharing social space) formed a continuum. Lacking a household, an individual would be without social and spiritual support. The house was dressed in human clothes, and its parts were identified with parts of the human body as well as with specific human ancestors in its lineage.

The Batammaliba house also reflected the importance of historical ancestors in the identity of the family's compound. Every house served to symbolize a tomb; without the death of an elder, there was believed to be no new life. The arrangement of a settlement's cemetery was identical to the placement of family houses within the village, reinforcing the complementarity of house and tomb, present and past. In the house, family history was evoked and manipulated through daily contact between living family members and their ancestors.

The Akan people who lived in what is now Ghana created some of West Africa's most powerful forest states and empires, beginning around the fourteenth century. Central to Akan identity was the matrilineal structure of society centered on the *abusua* (which referred to family or matrilineage, as well as clan). Matrilineal descent in Akan society refers to the pattern by which Akan men and women marked their place in the continuum of ancestors, by reference to the female side of the family. It had no special connotations for the distribution of political power, which – as elsewhere in large-scale states – worked in favor of men.

The Akan concern with fertility and bearing children was a recognition of the importance of the *abusua* in acquiring individual and community identity. Individuals had recognized rights only through their positions within an *abusua*. Without the protection afforded to members, they were considered without ancestors and without sexual identity. The uncertainty and ambiguity inherent in the lack of ancestry and status are best exemplified by the fact that enemies captured by

the expanding Akan state became permanent slaves unless they were integrated into an *abusua* through adoption or marriage. During the expansion of the Akan state during and after the fourteenth and fifteenth centuries, neither women nor children gained position or power. The emphasis on warfare resulted in men gaining status, and the increased numbers of slaves available to perform household tasks generally

7.3 *Akuaba* fertility figure. The idealized image reflects the desirability of children believed to be the reincarnation of ancestors.

devalued women's labor and diminished their influence even further.

One of the best-known sculptural traditions from the Akan region is the small, abstracted carving of a human figure known as *akuaba*, literally "Akua's child." Oral traditions claim that a woman named Akua, desperate to produce children, once approached a local priest. He consulted the spirit world and then instructed Akua to commission the carving of a small wooden child. She was told to carry the child on her back, feed it, and care for it as if it were real. The whole village laughed at her until she succeeded in her quest to become pregnant and gave birth to a beautiful daughter. The tradition illustrates the high status and importance associated with motherhood in matrilineal societies, even ones in which women are politically subordinated. Children had relatively few rights, since knowledge and power, considered to be the basis of rights, were thought to accumulate with age. Still, children were accorded respect because they were believed to be the reincarnation of ancestors. The *akuaba* fertility figures suggest the important role of children in reflecting spiritual harmony, ideals of individual beauty, and the well-being of the family order.

The extent to which such a unit as the household-family was mediated by the Akan state or local political authority varied according to the status of its members. Typically, interference in the creation of marriage alliances allowed a patriarchy to control the labor of women and their children and thus the accumulation of any household surplus. Even when wealth was inherited through the female line, most women were excluded from most political offices. Exceptions were made for elite Akan women who were beyond their childbearing years. The female office of queen mother was secondary to that of the king, but she was omnipresent and consulted in the ascension of the head of state. Women acted as priestesses and even diplomats who could find themselves making significant contributions to statecraft and foreign policy.

Caste, marriage, and family in South Asia

In his disapproving description of matrilineal society in fourteenth-century Mali, the Muslim traveler Ibn Battuta mentioned that he knew of only one other similar instance and that was "among the Indians of Malabar." Ibn Battuta was referring to a system of marriage practiced along the Malabar coast of India in which *shudra* (the lowest caste) women of one ethnic group who lived in matrilineal and matrilocal joint families married with *brahman* (the highest caste) men who lived in patrilineal and patrilocal joint families. This custom entailed a complicated series of arrangements that ultimately resulted in the joint family being formed around the mother and her children under the authority of the eldest male member of the matrilineage. But this regional tradition is also clearly an exception to the patterns of patriarchy, patriliny, and caste boundaries that predominated throughout most of the South Asian subcontinent.

Inherited divisions of society based on corporate membership, common descent, and **endogamy**, meant that caste determined what people should do with their lives, whom they should marry, whom they should eat with and work with, and where they should live (see also Chapter 8). Caste helped to shape families since it determined the boundaries of group membership and placed restrictions on marriage, though families were shaped by other factors as well. The patriarchal and patrilineal extended joint family – sons or brothers, their wives and children, grandsons, and their wives and children – was the basic structure of family life. The family was bound together by rites of ancestral commemoration, in which three generations of descendants of the deceased participated. This group formed the core of the joint family, and the head of the family managed its property on behalf of all.

Marriages were arranged by families, and sons brought their wives into the parental home and reared their children there. Women were usually married at a very early age – before puberty – in theory to protect them from engaging in sexual activity before marriage and humiliating both themselves and their families. Polygamy (having multiple spouses, especially wives) was customary, although there were many variations, even polyandry (having multiple husbands). Widows were expected to follow a harsh regimen of daily life to honor their dead husbands and, in some upper classes, widows even threw themselves onto their husbands' funeral pyres to demonstrate their fidelity to their husbands.

The three purposes of marriage were religious (the performance of ancestral rites), continuation of the family line, and sexual pleasure. Marriage practices varied greatly according to region as well as caste. For example, in south India, cross-cousin marriage (marriage of a son to his father's brother's daughter) was not only permitted but encouraged. For Hindus in north India, such marriages were generally prohibited, while Muslims in the north often chose spouses from within the patrilineal clan or lineage and thus married a cross-cousin.

As in many other societies, marriage was often a means of establishing alliances between families and of balancing economic against political or social status; for example, a wealthy family might form an alliance with a politically powerful family by contracting a marriage for their daughter with a son of that family. These goals in marrying, however, were always tempered in the case of India by the caste system. In most castes, inheritance was through the male line, but in some castes family property was inherited through the female line. In both north and south India, however, and for Muslims as well as Hindus, marriage as economic exchange involved both bride-price and dowry. The custom of *purdah* (Urdu for "curtain") – the rigorous seclusion of women and the requirement that they cover their faces in all company except that of the immediate family – came to India following the Muslim invasions beginning in the eighth century and appears to have spread over northern India by the fifteenth

and sixteenth centuries. Although this practice may have primarily affected elite women, and lower-class women may have never observed complete *purdah*, women did tend to keep out of sight when men were present.

Another category of person existed in Indian society from at least the thirteenth century and probably well before. This was the *hijra*, literally "neither male nor female," individuals who were castrated males (eunuchs) and cross-dressed as females. According to the late thirteenth-century Venetian traveler Marco Polo, Bengal province was the center of a trade in slaves who were castrated prisoners of war. As early as the second century, castration was also a punishment for adultery or for certain other crimes of the lower castes. Homosexuality was acknowledged in the *Kama Sutra*, (ca. third–fourth century BCE), a guide to erotic love that devoted a chapter to eunuch courtesans. Gender ambiguity provided individuals with the opportunity to cross other boundaries of acceptable behavior and protocol.

Women, family, and household in Southeast Asia

The mythical account of the founding of Funan (in the south of modern Cambodia and Vietnam) reflects the importance of women in society, politics, and religion at the time of Funan's rise as a regional power around 150 CE. According to this story, sometime in the early first century CE, a woman ruler of the lower Mekong delta region led an attack on a passing merchant ship. Successfully defending themselves, the merchants made their way ashore. Their leader, an Indian upper-caste scholar named Kaundinya, "drank water from the land" and married the woman ruler, who is described as the daughter of the ruler of the Realm of Water. Kaundinya then became king of the region, which is described as a number of settlements, each with its own ruler. Seven of the largest of these settlements were assigned to the children of this marriage, while the remainder were held directly by the new king.

By all accounts, before Indian influences became prevalent in Southeast Asia, women had considerable access to positions of public power. Matrilineage, tracing descent through the maternal line, appears to have been characteristic of social structure there. Indian influences to this region were patrilineal, tracing descent through the male line, and strongly patriarchal. In the original story, a woman ruler represented the land of Funan; but after the marriage, the Indian husband took over as king. Although the regimented patriarchy and caste system seen in India did not overtake Funan's culture, it did affect the ruling class structures, and for the next several hundred years Funan's empire was ruled only by men.

Throughout Southeast Asia, women were regarded as the most effective diplomats, perhaps because they were believed to be more persuasive than men due to their role as mothers. Women also were active as military leaders, depicted in sculptures holding swords and shields. The Trung sisters of the Viet kingdom (modern northern Vietnam) led a rebellion against Chinese domination in the first century CE, that was widely celebrated into modern times. As elsewhere in the world, palace women fulfilled a number of roles that set them apart from others of their gender outside the walls of the royal enclosures. There is little material or textual evidence about the activities of everyday folk in the marketplace or in the fields, but both men and women must have labored at both. Male and female slaves – prisoners of war, indentured for debt, or of inherited status – served their owners at a variety of household tasks as well as working in the fields and orchards.

Commercial contacts from as early as the first century CE engendered marriage partnerships between traders from South Asia and China with local women. Foreign traders relied on the local knowledge of their wives to help them conduct business. Women's role in commerce persisted into early modern times. Marriage alliances were extremely important among the elite, and plentiful evidence shows that matrilineal succession was even followed in political dynasties, such as the Khmer Empire (see Chapter 9). Queens also ruled without male consorts. Jayadevi (r. ca. 685–720), for example, ruled one of the polities that predated the Khmer Empire.

Women rulers and aristocrats donated to religious establishments, both Hindu and Buddhist, and women served as religious attendants at temples to Brahmanic gods. With the growing dominance of Theravada Buddhism in Southeast Asia during the twelfth and thirteenth centuries, women were drawn to maternal images conveyed as part of Theravada teaching, even though Theravada in principle regarded women as spiritually inferior. By the thirteenth century, Islam was becoming firmly implanted in Southeast Asia, and although Islam eventually influenced gender roles and family life, it did not dislodge women from their relatively strong position in Southeast Asian society.

Gender, family, and household in North America

The kinds of historical evidence we have to describe family and household vary as widely as do the concepts themselves: English parish registers recording births, marriages, and deaths; Islamic court records documenting marriages and divorces; Confucian family genealogies and guidebooks. In the absence of such records, the recovery of family history in the pre-Columbian Americas depends on a combination of oral, archaeological, and a few written sources.

A wide variety of different small-scale societies were scattered across the North American continent. Multifamily dwellings, or longhouses, were common to communities in the Pacific Northwest Coast region, the Great Plains, and among the Eastern Woodland Iroquois. At the beginning of the sixteenth century, one of the earliest European observers of native peoples in the Americas, Amerigo Vespucci, wrote of hundreds of persons sleeping in shared households. In some cases, multifamily dwellings were associated with the development of agriculture, since joint residency encouraged the cooperative labor required by intensive food production, although they were also characteristic of the non-agricultural Pacific Northwest. More commonly, shared kinship was the basis for establishing multifamily dwellings, with membership in a lineage determining joint residence. Matrilineal and patrilineal descent were recognized in different societies, and in some cases, bilateral descent was recognized.

Matriliny was characteristic of the Iroquois of the Eastern Woodlands. By around 1000, the Iroquois shifted from a way of life based on hunting, gathering, fishing, and subsistence agriculture to a more settled life dependent on agriculture. As the population grew, individual households began joining together and living in multifamily dwellings. Multifamily longhouses were probably occupied by matrilineal families, connected by kinship through women who traced their descent from a common ancestress. The new importance of agriculture reinforced the importance of women in subsistence and domestic affairs, and males had no authority in the household. The longhouse was dominated by a matron assisted by a council of women.

On the opposite side of the North American continent, the environmentally rich Northwest Coast was home to peoples such as the Tlingit, Haida, and Kwakiutl. Typically, Northwest Coast lineages or extended family groups lived in separate households, about 30 or so people in a longhouse made of cedar logs or planks. The basic social unit among Northwest Coast peoples was similar: politically autonomous groups of relatives, their spouses and children, aligned according to one of three methods. Some of them were based on matrilineal descent, wherein membership and inheritance came from the mother and her side of the family; others were patrilineal (wherein kinship, membership, and inheritance

were through the father); still others followed a bilateral reckoning of descent and membership.

The center of the North American continent was home to Plains peoples who banded together to hunt bison. Membership in the group was determined by residence. Later, by the Plains Village horticultural period, houses within villages were multifamily square or rectangular lodges, larger and more substantial than those seen earlier on the Plains. Membership in the community was fixed by heredity, which was achieved by consistently ignoring one side of the family and stressing the other. All persons of either sex descended from the male ancestor, through the male line only, formed a patrilineage community, or clan; all those descended from a female ancestor, through the female line only, formed a matrilineage community, or clan. Whereas each family unit recognized both parents, in determining membership, clans ignored one parent in favor of the other. This sort of organization meant that one-half of one's ancestors, either maternal or paternal, counted for certain purposes (admission to a ceremony or feast or the sharing of an inheritance), while for other matters the other half might be equally important. Clans bore names, usually of animal origin, such as Wolf, Eagle, Elk, and Beaver, and some of them had distinctive ceremonial and political functions.

By around 1000, the Pueblo peoples of the American Southwest lived in communal dwellings that consisted of contiguous flat-roofed stone or adobe houses, sometimes several stories high. Pueblo society was both matrilineal and matrilocal: when a woman married, her husband left his mother's house and came to live in her house, where he remained forever an outsider. The house and its possessions, the sacred objects and wealth, principally in the form of stored corn and access to the fields, belonged to the women who lived there. The typical household unit consisted of a grandmother and her husband, her sisters and their husbands, her daughters and their husbands, children, and perhaps an orphan or slave. While women remained attached to their natal homes throughout their lives, men moved according to their stage of life: in childhood a male lived with his mother; as a youth he moved to a *kiva* (male lodge and ritual chamber) to learn male ritual traditions; and then he took up residence in the home of his wife.

Family and household in Mesoamerica and South America

Written sources that reveal the nature of family and household in both Mexica-Aztec society in the Valley of Mexico and Incan society in the Andean highlands of South America are restricted for the most part to accounts recorded by Spanish scribes after the conquest. Archaeology and ethnography provide important supplements to these accounts.

Incas

Integrating territory and peoples across a vast terrain, the Incas established their empire in the Andes in the early fifteenth century. Changes in gender roles, family, and household accompanied territorial expansion. Men came to symbolize the conqueror and women, the conquered. As a result of the pervasive warfare, in which female enemies were incorporated into households as slaves and wives, and male enemies were killed, the status of Incan women was devalued and the power they had once held because of their economic and reproductive roles was diminished. Warfare became as important as childbirth in increasing populations.

The family or *ayllu* provided the basis of Inca social organization, and was regarded by the Incan state as a unit of economic production (see Chapter 6). Families were provided with land by the state, which claimed everything produced and had the power to move family members and households to wherever their labor was needed.

Men paid their tribute to the state through laboring on public works or in agriculture, or through military service; women spent much of their time weaving. Woven cloths had extraordinary ritual and ceremonial value. A special public building served as a convent for Chosen Women, brought to the Incan capital to weave cloth and participate in rituals. Male dominance was maintained in the patriarchal Incan society by treating women as property. Adultery was considered theft of the female involved, and the male was punished for having committed a crime against property. Boys and girls were educated in separate schools.

Mexica-Aztecs

Less is known of family and household in Mexica-Aztec society, which reached its peak in the fifteenth century, just before the European conquest. The complex tribute society of the Mexica-Aztecs centered around the city of Tenochtitlan, founded in 1325. From this center, the Mexica-Aztecs ruled through seven *calpulli*, or tribal-kinship units.

The cult of the warrior that dominated Mexica-Aztec culture and society was reflected in the beliefs and practices associated with childbirth and child rearing. The metaphor of battle was used for childbirth, and the infant was described as a "captive," won in battle. Women giving birth were possessed by the spirit of the Earth Mother. If a woman died in childbirth, the Earth Mother would have to be appeased. From birth, female infants were carefully distinguished from their male counterparts by differences in care and feeding, according to the roles that each would fulfill in society. The social duty of the male was to be a warrior; that of the female was to be a wife. Marriage was a secular rite that symbolized the transfer of a young male from the care of his mother to that of his bride.

Although women were restricted to the domestic sphere, some did have public roles – as healers and physicians, and especially as midwives. These

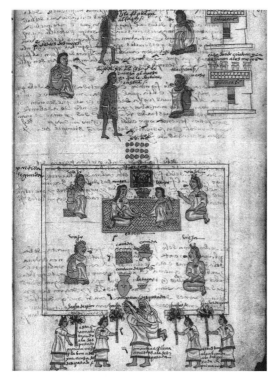

7.4 Mexica-Aztec marriage ceremony. The bride is carried to the groom's house (*bottom*) and their garments are ritually knotted (*top*) to signify the union.

occupations had spiritual dimensions. Whereas the constant marking of sexual differences and consideration of gender were central to the ordering of the world in Mexica-Aztec thought and culture, in the sacred realm sexual differences were often blurred. Many deities, in fact, had androgynous forms, and the gender of healers could be strategically ignored.

Summary

The private, daily realm of human activity has often been hidden by focus on large-scale political events so that the common human experiences of gender, family, and household have remained elusive. This chapter has sought to recover those experiences by looking beyond official records of

prescriptive behavior such as those found in law codes to less familiar kinds of historical sources such as literature and material evidence. A wide range of sources have been used to trace shifting constructions of gender, family, and household across cultures and over time as they were influenced by changes in ideology, religion, material conditions, and political orders.

Marriage can be seen as a thread linking gender, family, and household because in most societies some form of marriage established the foundations of family and household and reflected the basic assumptions about gender. Marriage was often an economic and political transaction, marking the transfer of wealth and creating political alliances between families. But it was also a cultural institution shaped by religious and social ideals. Ideology had as much impact on families and households as material conditions did. Religion, ranging from family veneration of ancestors to hierarchical institutions, helped to define families everywhere. In China, Confucianism provided the cementing ideology for patriarchy; in the Muslim world, Islam did. Laws sanctioned by religion, such as the Islamic *shari'a*, reinforced state controls over family, marriage, and inheritance. Similarly, European families after about the ninth century were strongly influenced by the Christian Church. But despite the regulation of gender roles, marriage, family, and household, practice frequently diverged from the ideals promoted by political and religious authorities.

Households reflected widely varying patterns of economic organization. Where a number of families resided together in larger common households, the household became a significant unit of production, as well as reproduction. In patriarchal societies, men controlled most of the household wealth and held greater access to political power than women did. Individual women of privilege – by virtue of circumstance, cunning, or their spiritual role – could and did circumvent the male-dominated hierarchies in many parts of the world, and they often acquired economic wealth alongside political power. Gender roles and families were equally shaped by shifting patterns of economic activity and changing modes of production. For example, the development of agriculture had an inevitable impact on foraging families. Because of the more intensive labor needs associated with agricultural production, families grew in size. Families also changed when they moved from farms into towns and cities, often becoming more limited in size, living in much more cramped conditions, and laboring in the marketplace or workshop rather than the fields.

As spheres of human interaction, families and households constitute the most basic threads in the social fabric, interwoven through marriage with gender and household patterns. Their differences over time and across cultures suggest the staggering range of significant variation in the human past. Transformations in gender, family, and household are as central to understanding world history as the rise and fall of empires.

Notes

1 Cicero, *Letters* (Harvard Classics, 1909), p14.
2 Alfred J. Andrea and James H. Overfield, eds, *The Human Record: Sources of Global History, Second Edition, Volume I: To 1700* (Boston, NY: Houghton Mifflin, 1998) p148.
3 Patricia B. Ebrey, *Chinese Civilization: A Sourcebook* (New York: The Free Press, 1993), pp125–26.
4 Paul Kahn, *The Secret History of the Mongols: An Adaptation of the Yuan Ch'ao Pi Shih Based Primarily on the English Translation by Francis Woodman Cleaves*, First Expanded Edition (Boston: Cheng and Tsui, 1998), p14.
5 Letter from the Cairo Geniza, cited in Andrea and Overfield, *The Human Record: Sources of Global History, Volume I: To 1700* (Boston, NY: Houghton Mifflin, 1998), p409.
6 Yossef Rapoport, *Marriage, Money, and Divorce in Medieval Islamic Society* (Cambridge: Cambridge University Press, 2005), pp64–68.

Suggested readings

Browning, Don S., et al. (2006) *Sex, Marriage, & Family in World Religions*, New York: Columbia University Press. Documents relating to marriage and family from Judaism, Christianity, Islam, Hinduism, Buddhism, and Confucianism, selected and introduced by scholars of these religious traditions.

Burguière, André, Christiane Klapisch-Zuber, Martine Segalen, and Françoise Zonabend, eds (1996 [original French edition 1986]) *A History of the Family, Vols 1 and 2*, Cambridge, MA: The Belknap Press of Harvard University Press. A collection of international scholarship on the family across the globe, with limited treatment of non-European societies.

Ebrey, Patricia B. (1993) *The Inner Quarters: Marriage and the Lives of Women in the Sung Period*, Berkeley, CA: University of California Press. An illuminating study of women's lives, marriage, family, and household in China during the tenth–thirteenth centuries.

Farah, Madelain (1984) *Marriage and Sexuality in Islam: A Translation of al-Ghazālī's book on the Etiquette of Marriage from the Ihyā*, Salt Lake City, Utah: University of Utah Press. A useful primary source translation of a classic work on Islamic views of marriage and sexuality.

Goitein, S.D. (1978) *A Mediterranean Society: The Jewish Communities of the Arab World as Portrayed in the Documents of the Cairo Geniza, Vol. III: The Family*, Berkeley, Los Angeles, London: University of California Press. A portrait of marriage and family life among Jewish, Christian, and Muslim families in medieval Cairo based on letters and other documents recovered from the Cairo Geniza, a repository of discarded pages of writing.

Hartman, Mary S. (2004) *The Household and the Making of History: A Subversive View of the Western Past*, Cambridge: Cambridge University Press. The author argues that a unique late-marriage pattern identifiable in European society from as early as the Middle Ages lies at the root of changes that usher in the modern world after about 1500.

Lynch, Katherine A. (2003) *Individuals, Families, and Communities in Europe, 1200–1500: The Urban Foundations of Western Society*, Cambridge Studies in Population, Economy, and Society in Past Time 37, Cambridge: Cambridge University Press. Integration of the history of the family with the history of public life, seeing the family at the center of "civil society," and emphasizing the relationship between kinship and larger voluntary, collective organizations in European urban society.

Rapoport, Yossef (2005) *Marriage, Money, and Divorce in Medieval Islamic Society*, Cambridge: Cambridge University Press. A richly detailed and documented study of the economic, legal, and social causes of Muslim divorce in Cairo, Damascus, and Jerusalem in the Mamluk period (1250–1517).

Seccombe, Wally (1992) *A Millennium of Family Change: Feudalism to Capitalism in Northwestern Europe*, New York: Verso. A long-term survey of structural changes in the western European family as they relate to economic transformations.

Online resources

Annenberg/CPB, *Bridging World History* (2004) <www.learner.org/channel/courses/worldhistory> Multimedia project with interactive website and videos on demand; see especially Unit 13 Family and Household.

Diotima <www.stoa.org/diotima/about.shtml> Collected resources, including primary sources in translation and weblinks, for the study of women and gender in the ancient world.

George Mason University, *Women in World History* <chnm.gmu.edu/wwh> A project of the Center for History and New Media, this website provides a wide range of resources on women in world history.

Study questions

1. How did Confucianism shape the Chinese family?

2. How did Christianity influence marriage and family in Europe through the institution of the Church?

3. In what ways did Islam influence the roles of women and the institutions of marriage, family, and household in West Asia?

4. In what ways is marriage an economic transaction?

5. How do families and households function as units of economic production?

6. How did political forces affect family life?

7. What impact did matrilineal customs have on gender relations, especially the position of women?

ca. 100 CE	ca. 300–602	ca. 490–600	794–1185	ca. 900	ca. 1000	916–1126
Book of Manu compiled in India with explanation of caste system	Lakmids of southern Mesopotamia	Ghassanids of Syria	Heian period in Japanese history	Flourishing of Igbo-Ukwu	Rulers of Yoruba and Kanem states in West Africa capture and control labor	Qidan Liao state in Northeast Asia

TIMELINE

8 Ties that bind

Lineage, clientage, and caste

Belonging to a group is a universal human social need. Creating a sense of belonging as part of a group is also key to the success of a community. As societies grew in size and complexity, the web of social relations securing individuals within the family and then the community was woven ever more tightly. The connecting link between family and community in many societies was the lineage, or descent group. Providing a primary source of identity, lineage has endured as a key building block of human communities throughout the world and has shaped large-scale political structures as well as individual destinies.

The Muslim historian Ibn Khaldun (1332–1406) understood well the importance of group identity embodied in the lineage-based societies of the world he knew best. The Arabic word that Ibn Khaldun used to refer to group identity, ***asabiya***, has been variously translated as "public spirit," "social solidarity," "group cohesion," or "group feeling." The root of the word means "to bind." Ibn Khaldun believed that group feeling

resulted from blood relationship – or something corresponding to it – and produced bonds of affection leading to mutual help and support. In the excerpt below, Ibn Khaldun described the cohesive community of the lineage-based society of fourteenth-century Bedouins in North Africa and recognized the group defined by common descent, or lineage, as a vital source of social support and identity:

The hamlets of the Bedouins are defended against outside enemies by a tribal militia composed of the noble youths of the tribe who are known for their courage. Their defense and protection are only successful if they are a closely-knit group of common descent. This strengthens their stamina and makes them feared, since everybody's affection for his family and his group is more important than anything else. Compassion and affection for one's blood relations and relatives exist in human nature as something

203

1115–1222	1038–1227	ca. 1100–1200	ca. 1122–1204	1192	1227	1185–1333
Jurchen Jin state in Northeast Asia	Tangut state in Inner Asia	Flourishing of feudalism in Europe	Life of Eleanor of Aquitaine	Minamoto Yoritomo named first shogun by Japanese emperor	Death of Chinggis Khan, founder of Mongol Empire	Era of Kamakura shogunate in Japan

God puts into the hearts of men. It makes for mutual support and aid (*asabiya*).

Source: Ibn Khaldun, *Muqaddimah*, quoted in Yves LaCoste, *Ibn Khaldun:The Birth of History and the Past of the Third World* (London: Verso, 1984), p105.

8.1 Muslim communal celebration of Ramadan feast. A cavalcade comes together to celebrate the feast at the end of Ramadan, the month of fasting. Flags bear religious inscriptions.

Such observations led Ibn Khaldun to theorize that the rise and fall of states were dependent as much on the interplay of lineage and other internal social factors as on military prowess, great leaders, or the power of gods. As he noted, the support and solidarity necessary for survival were dependent on ties of kinship. Lineage was the core of Bedouin identity, determining an individual's closest social bonds and place in Bedouin society.

By its very nature, a lineage – like any other group – creates exclusion in the process of establishing criteria of inclusion, such as blood ties. When lineages were the building blocks of a society such as that of the Bedouins, some lineages were considered to have a higher status than others, and lineages themselves were internally stratified by age and gender. By most accounts, early human societies were largely egalitarian, but with increasing complexity brought about by the development of agriculture and urbanization, social hierarchies began to emerge along with the concentration of political power in the formation of early states. Political orders – states, kingdoms, empires – and economic systems provided the contexts within which kinship bonds, gender identities, caste affiliations, and patronage–clientage ties shaped the lives of individuals. How did such categories of social identity reflect diverse cultural, political, economic, and religious traditions? How was social difference defined and then translated into hierarchies of inequality? How were inequalities in access to power and resources explained and justified?

ca. 1300	1325	1338–1573
Iroquoian villages show evidence of more permanent settlements	founding of Tenochtitlan as urban center of Mexica-Aztec	Ashikaga shogunate in Japan

Introduction to the theme of lineage, clientage, and caste

The most basic differences embedded in the human condition are the ones felt most personally – gender and age. What it means to be a child or an elder and how male and female identities are experienced over an individual's lifetime vary dramatically across cultures and from one period in human history to another. Distinct from biological sex, gender can be used to describe the socially and culturally constructed roles and identities associated with being male or female. Gender roles and identities are not independent of other social, political, and economic realities. For example, when gender differentiation was employed to subordinate women, biological explanations were often used to justify a gendered division of labor, construing menstruation or lactation as undesirable pollution or weakness. The biological fact of female reproduction, on the other hand, was a political and economic concern of states, which sought to exert control over the production of labor as a form of wealth.

Kinship provides a cultural framework for the construction of identity throughout world history, for a sense of belonging to and exclusion from groups. While the meanings ascribed to age and gender differences are constructed in a social context, these differences also interact with other social categories such as ethnicity, class, or social status. Kinship relations could be shaped by genealogical claims, descent patterns, age and gender. An individual's standing within a family

(for example, as a senior or junior member) or a family group's claims to land or rituals, rights and access to resources – all could give rise to inequalities in rank and status. The attainment of status as an elder conferred respect in many societies and, over time, could be translated into inherited status available to descendants across generations.

Basic forms of kinship organization, such as lineage, often served as a model for other patterns of social hierarchy with economic and political meaning: clientage and patronage. These terms describe patterns of power relations between and among individuals or groups in which someone, the patron, exercises power over someone else, the client. Within a lineage, for example, various kinds of power relations might appear, including patronage, in which the clients were the weaker, poorer, or more distantly related members of a large family group who served other family members who were wealthier or more powerful. "Patron-client" also describes the lord–**vassal** relationship of European and Japanese feudalism discussed in this chapter. Another form of social organization, caste, refers to inherited group membership in a society composed of hierarchically ranked groups or castes. Caste has been associated largely with South Asian society, although it is also found in some African societies and has sometimes been used to describe the inherited social status system of Tokugawa Japan (1600–1868).

Lineage, clientage, and caste were patterns of social organization based on the understanding and acceptance of social differences and the resulting unequal relationships that existed between individuals. Relationships defined by lineage, clientage, and caste were inherited, yet personal, and they provided a basis for the construction of both individual and social identity. Such relationships were also a means of distributing power in society. Together with religion and other forms of ideology, political structures, and economic systems, patterns of social organization helped to weave the fabric of human communities throughout the world. Exploiting and extending familiar social bonds, communities created the organization necessary to cement small polities and at times large empires. Tension between the forces of centralization that led to the growth of large-scale polities such as empires, and the decentralized patterns of political life characteristic of societies ordered by lineage, clientage, or caste, both fueled historical change and highlighted the powerful continuities of lineage, clientage, and caste.

Lineage societies in West Asia

Among the most enduring lineage-based societies were those found on the Arabian peninsula, traceable through both written and oral evidence to early human history in that region. With striking continuity to the present, these lineage societies were composed of urban dwellers and farmers, as well as pastoral nomads.

Reaching southward from Syria and the Mediterranean more than 3,000 kilometers (1,865 miles) to the mountains at the southern edge of the Arabian peninsula and the Indian Ocean, the Arab homeland included broad regions of flat dry desert in the north and high fertile lands in the south, where as much as a meter (40 inches) of rain fell per year. Because of its environmental diversity, many different economic systems and ways of life were found there. Nearly every individual, however, whether city trader, farmer, or nomad, lived either as a member (if related by

birth) or as a client (if adopted) of a lineage. All these groups were patrilineal, that is, they traced descent through the father's line, and they all claimed descent from one or two ancestors, which all the groups had in common.

The first of these common ancestors was Qahtan, the biblical Joktan, described in the Book of Genesis. The line he established was popularly believed to be the original genealogical line of the Arabs. Most of the hundreds of Qahtani lineages were found in southern Arabia, though some had scattered as far north as central Arabia and southern Iraq. The second genealogy was that of Adnan, son of Ishmael. His descendants were the hundreds of Arab lineage groups located in northern Arabia, Palestine, Syria, and northern Iraq.

Each of these two family trees was made up of eight or nine major branches, known as "tribes," and each of these branches in turn consisted of smaller lineage divisions. Further out on the branches were found hundreds of twigs, the family units. Although the Adnani–Qahtani division may indeed reflect real descent lines in the far-distant Arab past, it more likely reflects a myth built upon the cultural and economic differences between the well-watered southern and the dry northern Arab world. Whether or not the genealogical division was real, it functioned as if it were. In major crises, Adnanis supported Adnanis and Qahtanis supported Qahtanis.

Political as well as economic and social loyalties were attached first and foremost to the individual's lineage group. In times of personal trouble, individuals expected and gained support from their relatives, however distant. Wealth and power were held by the group (family, lineage branch, tribe), not the individual. A successful leader from the smaller family level up to that of the largest lineage network was judged by his ability to mediate in disputes between members and ensure distribution of wealth among all members of that lineage. A leader was also judged by his ability to defend the lineage against the aggression of others. Though the welfare of the community took precedence over that of its individual members, this lineage-based system of governance was both relatively decentralized and highly competitive.

Among Arab societies in both north and south, hierarchies of status existed. Especially in the north and center, nomadic camel-herding lineages carried the highest status even though they were the poorest in natural resources and wealth and probably represented no more than 25 percent of the population. Their status reflected their military abilities and their mobility in the arid environment, an asset that allowed them greater independence. Raiding one another for animals was an ongoing part of the lives of these nomadic peoples, since ownership of animals meant life to those who subsisted in the parched environment. Beneath the camel herders were the nomadic and semi-nomadic sheep and goat herders, and lower still in the status line were the sedentary farmers and townspeople. Even within each economic group, some lineages were thought to have more honor than others, honor being measured in terms of regional power, reputation for hospitality, and the security provided for members of the lineage. Within a lineage, certain families also had high status, and they usually provided perennial leadership to the lineage as a whole.

Honor and status could also be obtained in another way. Some towns, such as Mecca and Ta'if in western Arabia and San'a in the south, were the sites of sanctuaries for gods and goddesses identified with springs, trees, rocks, or other natural features. Certain families gained sacred status by maintaining those sanctuaries. Since warfare was forbidden around these sanctuaries, the families who had the maintenance rights held leverage in lineage politics and sometimes parlayed this into leadership.

The vast majority of the peninsula's population was Arab and fit into some niche or another in the prevalent lineage patterns. Some, however, were immigrants into the area, having come as either individuals or groups, typically from neighboring Africa or Persia. In any case, migrants could ill afford to be socially isolated and without protection or support. These people negotiated a client relationship with as powerful an Arab lineage as possible, thereby to gain both a functional membership in the lineage and the support of that lineage. Traditional laws within the lineages set out the respective responsibilities incumbent on both parties of the clientage relationship. Through marriage, clientage often became full lineage membership within a generation or two. The overall lineage system thus swallowed up immigrant groups and individuals, making them Arabs by declared kinship as well as by language and culture.

Two features of seventh-century life in Arabia created tension within its lineage society: urban life and the centralized governments that were being formed in the region. The small farm towns that dotted the landscape of central Arabia and the coastline presented no problem. The economics of pastoralism and sedentary agriculture blended easily with the needs of the neighboring non-Arab populations, who moved back and forth within the lineage system as clients. However, larger cities, such as Mecca, San'a, and the coastal towns of the Persian Gulf, based as they were on trade, industry, and the accompanying individual specialization of work, required a different, individualistic ethic that clashed with the group ethic of a lineage society.

In a period of change characterized by expanding, increasingly complex communities, the lineage societies of the Arabian peninsula were at a disadvantage. The Byzantine and Persian Empires caused particular tensions for Arabian lineages as they sought to co-opt the manpower and resources of Arabia by setting up and maintaining client states. These appeared superficially to be monarchies, but in fact they were lineage polities functioning as mercenary reserves or loosely organized buffer states protecting the empire's economic control over its territory while preserving the political and cultural independence of the lineages contained within the territory. The largest of such states were those of the Ghassanids of Syria (ca. 490–600), supported by the Byzantine Empire, and the Lakhmids (ca. 300–602) of southern Mesopotamia, allies of the Persians. Rather than conquering them, the Byzantine and Persian Empires dealt with their decentralized neighbors through a combination of co-option (threatening military force if cooperation was not gained), annual payoffs masquerading as salary for the lineage leaders, and the building of fortification lines along frontiers. When nothing else worked to bring them into the fold of the empire, intimidation by military campaigns was utilized in an attempt to secure political control.

These methods resulted in an unstable arrangement. The social, economic, and ideological systems of centralized empires and decentralized lineage polities were too different. The ideology of lineage politics required the sharing out of resources, rather than their centralization. The web of reciprocity and patronage demanded constant negotiation and consensus, which was impractical at the level of political strategy and control in a polity the size of an empire. Even the Islamic empires, which stressed faith over kinship, were unable to break down the Arabian lineage system. Tension between successive Islamic empires and lineage societies of the Arabian peninsula was characteristic of the relations between empires elsewhere and the lineage societies that bordered and interacted with them.

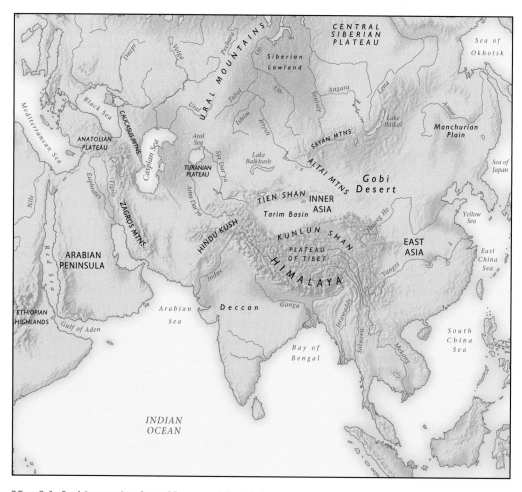

Map 8.1 Arabian peninsula and Inner and East Asia.

Lineage societies and states in East and Inner Asia

Like Islamic empires that encountered the strength of lineage-based societies on the Arabian peninsula, the history of the Chinese Empire was also marked by shifting relations between an imperial center and lineage societies on its borders. Chinese society from earliest recorded history in the Shang dynasty (1600–1045 BCE) was ordered by lineage, but with the first empires (Qin, 221–207 BCE, and Han, 206 BCE–220 CE) a centralized bureaucratic state was imposed over the patterns of lineage organization. Lineal descent determined inheritance of the throne through each dynasty, but imperial lineage could not transcend dynastic changes: each new dynasty set up its own line of descent. In contrast, the largely nomadic, pastoral peoples of Inner Asia were lineage-based societies that periodically united into centralized political orders under powerful leaders.

Lineages and the state in China

The noble lineages created by the Han founder to reward his supporters evolved into an aristocracy that competed with the emperor, considered themselves his social equals, and jealously guarded their claims to descent. Tang (618–907) society was dominated by great aristocratic lineages whose members inherited privileges, titles, and rank from generation to generation and whose status was largely independent of imperial authority. These aristocratic lineages belonged to a group of approximately 100 that practiced group endogamy (marriage within the group) and carefully preserved records of their descent lines to protect their social status. They excluded those who could not document, or in other ways substantiate, claims to aristocratic ancestry.

While lineage remained important as a fundamental organizing principle of Chinese society in later periods, the power of the state at least balanced that of the lineages so that political life was dominated by the bureaucratic state rather than by ties of descent. The domination of political life by the state and its power over lineage ties was expressed most vividly in the civil service examination system.

The civil service examination system, which would come to play a role of profound importance in the shaping of Chinese society and politics in the later imperial period, took root in the struggle between imperial authority and aristocratic privilege during the early Tang. As a means of reducing the power of a hereditary elite while recruiting talented officials, a policy of soliciting recommendations of good men for appointment to office in the imperial government began during the Han. Confucian ideology was used to sanction the adoption of an ostensibly meritocratic system of recruitment and selection of government officials. One of the hallmarks of Confucian thinking is the ideal of a meritocracy as a ruling elite, and the examination system can be seen as a means of implementing that ideal.

Beginning in the seventh century, the examination system gradually undermined the claims of aristocratic birthright by awarding status to those who demonstrated their merit by passing the examinations. In theory, and to a large extent in practice, talent or ability – defined by the state – mattered more than descent; in this way, the examination system subverted the claims of ancestry to power and status in Chinese society. Though lineage remained important as a source of identity in Chinese society and lineages provided support for education so that individual members could pass the examinations and thus bring rewards to the lineage as a whole, the power of the state to determine status was essentially unquestioned until the twentieth century.

Nomadic lineage societies and states in East and Inner Asia

The nomadic peoples who confronted the Chinese Empire across the Great Wall, traded with the Chinese, warred with them, and at times adopted Chinese political institutions came from societies organized by lineages into clans that extended into tribes. The great historian of the Han dynasty, Sima Qian (ca. 145–90 BCE), recorded his observations of the social and political organization of nomadic life among the Xiongnu, Turkic, and Mongolic peoples who formed a large confederation in the second century BCE that periodically threatened the Chinese Empire:

> They move about in search of water and grass [for their herds], having no cities, permanent dwellings, or agriculture . . . Their leaders have under them a few thousand to ten thousand horsemen. There are twenty-four chiefs altogether, each titled a "ten-thousand horsemen." All of the major offices are hereditary. The three clans of the Huyan, Lan, and later the Xubu are the nobility.
>
> Source: Patricia B. Ebrey, *Chinese Civilization: A Sourcebook* (New York: Free Press, 1993), p55.

Sima Qian's succinct description of these nomads reflects the concerns of the recently unified Chinese Empire's rulers, who viewed the unfamiliar customs of these nomads with a mixture of disdain and apprehension.

Heirs of the Xiongnu, the Tabgach Wei were a Mongolian-Turkic people who ruled much of north China from the fifth to the early sixth centuries. They adopted Buddhism and extended their patronage of that faith over the northern Chinese population. They adapted their nomadic way of life to rule the Chinese, as later nomadic peoples also learned to shift from tribal life on the steppes to ruling the sedentary agrarian population of China by adopting Chinese-style political institutions that centralized power in the hands of a ruler who distributed administrative authority to his subordinates.

The Qidan Liao (916–1126), a Mongolic people from the northeastern edges of China just beyond the Great Wall, rose as a power in the early tenth century. They claimed authority over other non-Chinese peoples in the region, including the Tungusic Jurchen people, who inhabited the forested river valleys of what was later known as Manchuria. Like other pastoral nomads, Qidan economic life was based on herding animals, and the control of the herds was assigned to Qidan males since Qidan society was both patrilineal and patriarchal. Qidan clans traced their descent to a common ancestor for a span of perhaps nine generations, after which they segmented into distinct lineages and marriages were then possible between members of these lineages. Women were relatively powerful in Qidan society because of their role in supervising the camps and herds during the frequent absence of males for hunting and warfare. Even after the Qidan transition to a Chinese-style state, Qidan empresses were far more powerful co-rulers than their Chinese counterparts.

The Jurchen people, who gradually gained power over their overlords, the Qidan, and established their own Chinese-style state in the early twelfth century, were accustomed to life in an environmentally diverse region where hunting, fishing, and agriculture were part of their subsistence, along with herding. Jurchen clans were patrilineal, with each clan consisting of several lineages. For example, the ruling clan that founded the Jurchen Jin state (1115–1222), the Wanyan, consisted of 12 lineages. The lineage was the basic organizational unit, and every lineage occupied a village or walled town under the control of a chief whose authority lay in acting as a military leader in the event of war.

The Mongols, who in turn defeated the Jurchen to control north China and finally conquered the Chinese Empire in the south in 1275, came from a generally arid environment that included grasslands, mountains, and desert. Theirs was a pastoral economy based on the sheep and horse, supplemented in the most arid regions by the camel. Herding and hunting were the primary occupations, and their social organization, like that of their predecessors, the Qidan and Jurchen, was based on common lineage, extending to clans and then to tribes. Loyalty to a leader was what held the tribes together, and personal bonds were the glue that cemented lineages, clans, and tribes. Common lineage operated even at the level of ruling the vast Eurasian empire created by the Mongols: the descendants of Chinggis Khan continued to rule after his death, though the "Great **Khan**" was selected by a convocation of representatives of noble clans.

Like other nomadic and semi-nomadic peoples of Central and East Asia, the Mongols practiced shamanism as their principal religion. They worshiped a sky god and an earth goddess, who was associated with fertility. But much of their religious belief and practice centered around worship of ancestors and on maintaining contact with spirits of the dead, which they did through shamans. Images of ancestors were kept in the tents of their descendants and carried around in wagons as the camps moved.

The Turkic Uighurs, who founded their own empire in Inner Asia contemporary with the Chinese Tang dynasty, were a lineage-based society organized into clans that coalesced into a tribal confederation. By the time of the Mongol rise to power in the thirteenth century, the Uighurs had abandoned the economy of pastoral nomadism and settled in the oasis regions of the Tarim basin, where they practiced agriculture. The Tangut people, a lineage-based society whose ruling clan claimed descent from the Tabgach Wei, dominated the Gansu corridor and surrounding areas from late Tang times and depended on a combination of pastoralism and agriculture for their economic base. For nearly two centuries, from 1038 to their conquest by the Mongols in 1227, the Tanguts adopted Buddhism as their state religion and ruled a region that encompassed parts of modern Tibet as well as northwestern China.

The Uighurs, Tanguts, Qidan, and Jurchen were nomadic or semi-nomadic peoples of mixed Turkic-Mongolic-Tungusic (Manchurian) ethnic background who formed tribal confederations, Sinified (Chinese-style) centralized states, and even empires in the case of the Uighurs and Tanguts, from the late Tang (ca. 750) through the Mongol conquest in the thirteenth century. Although these societies' nomadic or semi-nomadic way of life and their basic tribal and clan organization worked against the concentration of power characteristic of centralized states, the rise of a charismatic leader whose base of support through ties of personal allegiance was strong enough, could unite tribal leaders into a large confederation.

As the Mongols constructed their Eurasian empire in the thirteenth century, beginning with China, they encountered patterns of social organization that contrasted sharply with their own. Like China, the Indian subcontinent was the home of an ancient civilization with deeply entrenched ideas of how social life should be ordered, ideas that differed greatly from those of the Mongol and Turkic peoples who invaded India in the thirteenth century.

Caste and society in South Asia

The pattern of social organization encountered by Mongolian and Turkic conquerors as they invaded India in the thirteenth century was the caste system, a distinctive alternative to lineage as an approach to social organization and relations of power. The history of the caste system can be traced to the period of Indo-European migrations to the Indian subcontinent during the mid-second millennium BCE. By about 1000 BCE, the population of the Indus River Valley and the Ganges plain had been divided into four groups: priests, warriors, farmers, and servants or slaves. This division of society was justified and explained in the Vedic scriptures (the earliest surviving written literature of the region) as the result of the dismemberment of a cosmic being into four pieces. The system of castes, which became one of the key features of South Asian life, evolved from this four-part division of society.

Around the beginning of the first millennium CE, ideas about caste were codified in the Book of Manu, which explained the caste system as a result of *karma* (actions) accumulated in earlier incarnations. Priests, or *brahmans*, were at the top of the caste hierarchy, followed by warriors, then peasants (including both farmers and traders), and finally servants or slaves. There was a wide gap between the third and fourth castes, and outside this hierarchy entirely were the "untouchables," the lowest caste, with whom contact was strictly avoided.

The concept and practice of caste involved corporate membership, common descent, and endogamy: members of castes shared a common identity because they belonged to the same cultural and social group; they were descended from common ancestors; and their relatedness continued across generations through marriage practices restricting liaisons to others within the group. Three of the four initial groups were defined by occupation, although the fourth appears to have been an ethnic category.

Caste became a hereditary distinction that was demonstrated by rules forbidding marriage to outsiders, requiring that members eat together, and restricting other kinds of activities between members of different castes. Members belonging to one caste were believed to be ritually impure by members of other castes; contact between different castes resulted in contamination. Although such notions as ritual purity and pollution limited the contact between different caste groups and provided an ideological justification for caste, it is also likely that these practices resulted from the early social distinctions, rather than having generated them, and so helped maintain members and non-members in an orderly social and political structure.

The use of caste distinctions as a means of establishing social organization was neither rigid nor unchanging. Over time, caste divisions were further subdivided into increasingly complex occupational and ethnic groups, each with its own distinct rules of behavior. Breaking these rules would lead to social ostracism, while following them rigidly might allow one to be reborn into a higher caste. Thousands of subcaste distinctions based on geography and occupation, called *jatis*, were created as a result of intercaste and inter-*jati* marriages, which, while defying the caste system, also constantly redefined it. The *jati* categories were intimately linked in complex economic relationships of interdependency, including exchange of services, goods, and land-use rights.

Caste intersected with kingship and religion, as the priests of Brahmanism served the rulers of the north Indian kingdoms and established themselves at the pinnacle of the caste hierarchy of Indian society. Like kinship ties and systems of clientage, caste was a means of ordering society that expressed religious ideas and interacted with systems of political authority to shape power relations in South Asia. Like the lineage patterns of West Asia, caste has persisted through more than 2,000 years as the fundamental organizing principle of Indian society. The patterns and order created by caste remained, despite the challenges to Hinduism presented by other religions (Buddhism and Jainism) and through the rise and fall of numerous kingdoms and empires, including invasions from outside.

Lineage, clientage, and caste in Africa

The many forms of social organization found on the African continent have been better studied by anthropologists than by historians. With a few important exceptions, written historical documentation is recent. Yet until historians began to develop methodologies that utilized archaeological and oral or other ethnographic evidence (based on the study of living peoples), an understanding of the variety of African political experiences was incomplete. Discussion of lineage societies in Africa was confined to a substratum of anthropology, not history, with research demonstrating the political dimensions of contemporary kinship without reference to chronology or historical change. Kinship-based polities were significant in the past of many African societies, though the process of their historical reconstruction has differed markedly from that of the histories of literate societies.

The archaeological complex called Igbo-Ukwu (ca. 900), situated in a forested region of roughly 10,000 square kilometers (3,860 square miles), east of the Niger River in present-day southeastern Nigeria, provides evidence of an early lineage-based polity in West Africa. Despite the region's high population density, neither large cities nor centralized states or empires are known to have existed there. Evidence of the lineage-based society here is primarily archaeological. Excavations of three sites have produced an extraordinary array of technically complex bronze sculptures and objects, imported glass beads and textiles, and human remains. Among the objects excavated is a horseman's hilt, perhaps once attached to a staff of office and depicting a seated male astride a horse. The seated figure bears signs of deliberate facial scarring identical to face designs found among Ibo-speaking peoples in the same area in modern times. Ibo oral traditions similarly attest to a millennium of ethnic continuity in the region.

In more recent times, the Ibo have been studied by anthropologists as an example of a decentralized ("stateless") political system based on highly democratic, lineage-based connections. Unlike the hierarchical structure of highly centralized societies, the lineage-based society emphasized the common goals and achievements of the group. Membership in lineages was useful for settling disputes (since a member could be assured of the support and protection of other members) and redistributing wealth across generations.

Belonging to the same lineage also meant that members shared a common spiritual heritage,

central to which was the belief that ancestors were reborn again within the same lineage. The Ibo religion included a creator deity, as well as a component that provided each reincarnated person with a personal chi, or deity guide, from the spirit world. Political power was thus a worldly reflection of individual spiritual achievement.

The rule by a council of titled elders at Igbo-Ukwu provided members with opportunities to develop to their highest abilities and increasingly accumulate wealth and wield influence over others. Through their control over social relationships, council members made group decisions and received support in return. Their power and influence were developed gradually and relied on group consensus and the fruits of patronage. Both spiritual and political power were recognized in the award of titles and ranks. The excavator of Igbo-Ukwu has interpreted one of the sites as a possible burial of a priest-king figure, the highest-ranking person within Ibo titled society. Evidence from the site of Igbo-Ukwu also confirms the existence of long-distance trade in which horses, metals, and other goods were imported across the Sahara in pre-Islamic times (before the tenth century). Involvement in such trade networks did not invariably lead to the establishment of a centralized authority. The society's organizational complexity should not be confused with its physical size. Many decentralized societies were large, involving hundreds or thousands of people in voluntary, cooperative endeavors.

In other African societies, reliance on clientage, a relationship of dependence not necessarily based on kinship, was the essential cement for political systems. It was commonly said in the oral traditions of West and Central Africa that a king was his people. For example, in Dahomey, the metaphor of a perforated pot was used to describe the state: the king was like the pot's water, which everyone had to help keep inside. In other words, authority figures were necessary and existed to serve the essential needs of members of the social group, including protection and the extraction of labor for large social enterprises. Membership in such societies was based not on blood ties or genealogy but on service to the king, a dependency relationship in which the king was the patron and the people his clients.

The presence of clientage relationships in African societies reveals the social and political inequalities that brought them into being. Whereas in some parts of the world clientage involved landowners providing land to the landless, these relationships in Africa rarely involved land. They did sometimes involve the transfer of other forms of property, such as human beings and the value of their labor. For example, around 1000, the king at Ife (Yoruba, Nigeria) did not own the land surrounding the city, but he controlled the available labor and assigned persons to work the land surrounding the royal city. His counterpart to the north of Nigeria, the ruler of Kanem in the eleventh century, was celebrated in a song that commemorated his ability to capture and control labor:

> The best you took (and sent home) as the first fruits of battle,
> The children crying on their mothers you snatched away from their mothers,
> You took the slave wife from a slave, and set them in lands far removed from one another
> Source: N. Levtzion and J.F.P. Hopkins, eds, *Corpus of Early Arabic Sources for West African History* (Cambridge: Cambridge University Press, 1981), pp296–97.

In sub-Saharan Africa, where the population density remained low and land was valued less than people, authority was frequently expressed in personal rather than territorial terms. This was especially true in herding societies, where clientage was initiated by a cattle transaction between the owner of the cattle and the client herder: "Give milk, make me rich, be my father." In the Sena society of modern Mozambique, a pre-European system of clientage was the result of economic motives often arising during times of

drought and famine, when a desperate lineage group could temporarily pawn a member's labor to a larger, wealthier household. It also frequently indicated the need for protection and was initiated by the ritual act of "breaking the *mitate*," literally walking into the potential patron's household and smashing a clay pot, an act that created obligations and resulted in a period of servitude by the "offender."

The various means of establishing reciprocal relationships resulted in the accumulation of human resources by the larger and wealthier groups, which in turn derived greater political importance. The political and social order of the nearby fifteenth-century Mwenemutapa Empire in Southern Africa was built on relationships of personal dependency that successfully expanded over a large territory. Individuals owed allegiance, service, and agricultural labor to the ruler, who in turn provided protection and other benefits.

As elsewhere around the globe, in Africa the presence of clientage resulted in ties of obedience on the part of the client and obligation on the part of the patron. Reliance on clientage relations appears to occur when states are emerging or disappearing. The clientage system could be part of either the devolution of power (as in the breakup of polities) or of the evolution of highly centralized states (such as empires). The African examples indicate a variety of flexible polities in which inequalities based on inherited positions with differing access to wealth and influence were integrated in such a way as to enable all parties – both the more powerful and the less powerful – to sustain their common social fabric in the face of external threats. These various systems were temporary and indigenous solutions to the central problem of holding hierarchical power relations together amid great social inequality.

Social forms called "castes" also existed in parts of West Africa. These were primarily artisan and musician groups that practiced endogamy, marriage rules that restricted unions to those born within the defined group. These rules protected the proprietary knowledge contained within the

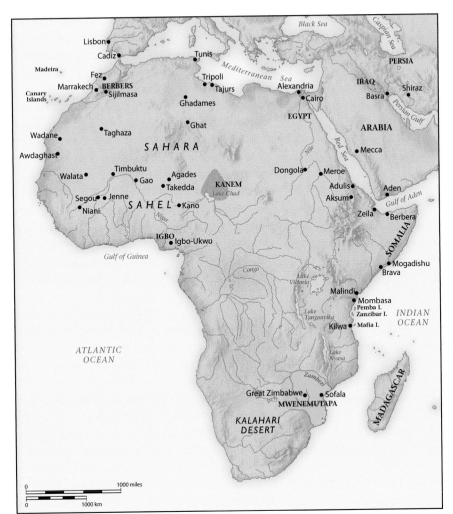

Map 8.2

Sites in West and Southern Africa.

group. Many of these castes appeared before 1300 and can be documented in part on the basis of historical linguistics and oral historical studies. Historians have shown that the West African castes were initially migratory groups of blacksmiths or other specialists who were foreigners, initially isolated as social groups and eventually adopted by their new communities.

Caste characteristics could and did change over time. For example, the defining occupations might alter, as in the case of iron smelters exhausting their fuel or ore supplies, and even strict marriage rules did not necessarily ensure that the populations remained isolated. Outsiders could,

for example, be adopted or captured. Among the Malinke, who founded the thirteenth-century empire of Mali, West Africa, the origin of some restrictions – exclusion from political office and prohibition of intermarriage – may have been instituted to ensure the creation of politically subordinate groups out of conquered specialists, who otherwise might have threatened the Malinke leadership. This example indicates that the defining features of social forms were not only reconstructed in response to changing political contours, such as the emergence of an empire or state, but were purposefully altered to serve the political interests of those in power.

Lineage and community in North America

The North American continent was home to an array of small-scale societies based on communities organized by lineage. Despite inhabiting diverse environments in the Eastern Woodlands, the Northwest Coast, and the Great Plains, these diverse peoples shared certain common features of social organization.

After about 1000, increased food supply through the intensification of agriculture resulted in population growth that led to changes in residence patterns as individual households joined together in multifamily dwellings. A second level of community change was the formation of villages, which occurred when multifamily houses began to be built next to others of the same type. Archaeological evidence suggests that each multifamily house in a village came to hold a lineage or a segment of one and bore an animal name, such as Bear, Turtle, and so on. Kinship relations were used to facilitate cooperative efforts (such as land clearing) and to maintain order in a society of increasing size and complexity. Councils of lineage heads were formed to manage village affairs.

Around 1300, villages that were stockaded and positioned on defensible hilltop locations began to be occupied on a more permanent basis. There are also indications of increased warfare that come from human burials, in which skeletal remains show a growing number of traumatic injuries. Archaeological excavations provide evidence of the increasing complexity. At the abandoned Iroquoian village site called the "Draper site," in southern Ontario, Canada, settlement pattern studies suggest that as the population increased between about 1450 and 1500, longhouses were added in clusters with a spatial orientation similar to pre-existing structures. It is likely that each set of houses represented a distinct social unit, perhaps a lineage or clan. Each expansion also created new plazas, places for village ceremonies and social activities that helped to integrate the larger community. In this way, lineage became the means by which Iroquois society organized its settlements and adapted to the challenges of social and political change.

Inhabitants of the Pacific Northwest Coast displayed some similarities to the Eastern Woodland Iroquois but also differed in important ways. Because of the plentiful natural food sources, these people did not develop agriculture yet evolved social systems characterized by elaborate ceremonialism, with an emphasis on material wealth and distinct social ranks based on wealth. Northwest Coast people's accumulation of wealth was well established by 500 BCE, as were social ranking and stratification, which were closely related to it. Elaborate material articles made from the bounty of the region – blankets made of mountain-goat hair; shell, copper, and bone pipes and spoons; baskets and other woven artifacts; elaborately decorated boxes, masks, and carved house posts – along with precious obsidian traded from afar were indications of wealth, supplementing food and gathered products and acting as symbols and currency of rank and social mobility. The eventual end product of this material accumulation was the potlatch (gifting) ceremony, which validated a person's rank in the community and featured extravagant gift-giving or even deliberate destruction of hoarded surpluses for the purpose of displaying rank. Vast quantities of goods and even human slaves were sometimes ritually destroyed when giving them away failed to be a sufficiently convincing statement of rank gauged by wealth.

The fundamental social unit of autonomous Northwest Coastal groups consisted of either a lineage, a group that could trace its descent to a common ancestor through either a male or female line, or an extended family, in which descent was treated less formally and rigidly. Second, social status, involving the system of rank, derived from neither heredity nor wealth alone, but from a combination of the two. Each longhouse dwelling was headed by a chief – any man who owned a house was a chief – and each had its clan insignia

8.2 Carved red cedar sea monster mask in the shape of a human face with a duck on top of the head. Three carved wooden fish are attached to the mask, one on each side and one hanging from the bottom. The lower jaw and the duck wings are movable. The mask has a plastic harness so it can be worn, and a piece of black cloth to cover the wearer. The mask has Northwest Coast Indian designs painted on it in black, red, and green. The overall dimensions are approximately 46 cm wide, 73 cm tall, and 18 cm deep. Kwakiutl, North Pacific Coast.

or crest, such as a bear, a whale, or a raven, often decorating a pole erected at the residence.

Chieftaincy was inherited both matrilineally and patrilineally, but chiefs were also dependent on wealth. The chief's wealth was the source of his independence and prestige and that of his lineage. The greater the collection of gifts accrued, the greater the potlatch (the manifestation of wealth) that could be created, and the more important the chief and his clan. Alliances were sometimes made with similar social groupings for purposes of common defense or for ceremonial ends, but groups never surrendered to one another certain highly individual and important rights, such as identity marker crests and ceremonial dances.

The center of the North American continent was dominated by temperate grasslands, home to a number of grazing and burrowing animal species that provided bounty for hunting peoples. It was also home to a variety of seeds, fruits, and tubers, but the Great Plains were so marginal for farming that horticultural practices developed elsewhere had to be introduced along river valleys by communities already adept at farming. Accordingly, the earliest Plains peoples were nomadic hunter-fisher-gatherers.

After about 900, during what is called the Plains Village period, influences and migrants from the east led to the development of substantial Plains Village communities that were comparatively permanent. Apart from social ties to family and clan, most Plains peoples belonged to organizations whose membership did not rest on kinship. Societies – military, dancing, spiritual – were far more frequently male in membership than female, but neither from these nor from any other aspect of Plains life were women sharply excluded. For example, the Blackfoot considered women's nature to be more innately religious. Women auxiliaries figured even in the military societies. These associations served a great many purposes, some religious and some secular. Visions, dreams, and the quest for a guardian spirit played a large role in Plains religion, especially for men in their desire to increase their own spirituality. Rituals such as the Sun Dance provided key roles for women, who had the sole power to move between the Holy People of the Above and the people below. Especially gifted visionaries became shamans and exercised an important role in Plains society.

Environmental diversity accounts in part for variations in the social organization of the peoples who inhabited the North American continent before 1500. By around 1000, the Eastern Woodland Iroquois had become dependent on agriculture, resulting in the concentration of population in villages, which enabled cooperative efforts in the practice of agriculture. Because of the rich natural sources of food, the Northwest Coast peoples were able to live in settled communities and subsist by gathering, fishing, and hunting. In contrast, before the beginning of the Plains Village period around 900, inhabitants of the Great Plains were nomadic hunter-fisher-gatherers who needed to move frequently to find new sources of food. All three examples increased in population and used wealth to distinguish families, their status and rank.

By around 1000, peoples in all three environmental zones – Eastern Woodlands, Northwest Coast, and Great Plains – lived in settled village communities made up of multifamily dwellings, or longhouses. Despite great variations in methods of tracing descent – patrilineal, matrilineal, or bilateral – the lineage or clan was consistently the primary organizational unit, and lineage heads jointly managed the affairs of village life. The use of material culture to mark identity was common to peoples in all three areas, as Iroquois, Northwest Coast Salish and others, and Plains peoples all traced their lineages to animal ancestors, such as the wolf, the eagle, or the raven. Commonalities can also be seen in religious beliefs and practices that provided inherited social references and promoted the welfare of the community.

Large-scale political structures characterized by the concentration of power at the center did not develop among the societies of North America before the coming of Europeans. Although trade was carried out among settled communities, it did not lead to large, centralized states. Social hierarchies and political influence derived from holding high rank or status within these hierarchies, such as those seen among Northwest Coast peoples, did not become manifestations of the large-scale institutionalization of power relations but

remained aspects of relatively small-scale communities that were sometimes connected by a common language and culture. Even in larger-scale societies of Central and South America, lineage relationships helped cement the ties between diverse populations.

Lineage and state in the Mexica-Aztec and Incan Empires

The complex tribute society of the Mexica-Aztecs centered around the city of Tenochtitlan, founded in 1325. From this center, the Mexica-Aztecs ruled through seven *calpulli*, or tribal-kinship units. Together the *calpulli* formed the *calpullec*, a council of elders who elected two chiefs. One was in charge of war and the other was in charge of religious functions. They were called "the father and mother of the people" and "the snake woman," suggesting that kinship and women were important in the organization of this large empire.

In both complex polities, the organization of state society relied on the familiar and local forms of kinship and lineage relations. Among the Incas, the *ayllu* provided the basis of social organization, allocating land to its members and joining with others to form a council whose powers included the election of the emperor. Brute force was not enough to bring together conquered peoples. Marriages helped build some alliances. By strategically selecting women of certain families to become "wives of the sun," the secondary wives of the emperor available for marriage to political allies, the Sapa Inca and his sister, the Coya (or "queen of women"), helped cement political ties. Manipulating marriages was not the only way kinship was used to enhance political power.

Both areas were also characterized by highly stratified societies that were increasingly marked by differences in wealth and power. These distinctions were expressed in the clothes and ornaments people wore, the food they ate, and their material possessions and houses. Social distinctions were inherited. For example, Mexica-Aztec lords dressed in fine cotton garments, ate venison, and resided in elaborate residences with servants, while commoners wore clothes made of coarse fibers, ate little meat, and lived in small adobe-and-stone structures. Keeping track of family lines was thus necessary for the organization of society. Over time, the importance of warriors increased, noble status could also be achieved, and the political roles of women were eliminated. The role of lineage faded in importance as the state grew in power.

"Feudalism" in Europe and Japan

Although its nature, duration – and even existence – is much debated by historians, none would deny that the basic components of what we call feudalism – lords, vassals, fiefs – existed for centuries in Europe following the fall of the Roman Empire. Similar features have also been identified in societies elsewhere, notably in Japan between about 1200 and 1800, although whether or not feudalism can appropriately be used to describe Japanese society in this era is also contested. The use of the term feudalism by Marxist historians to describe a particular stage of economic development prior to capitalism, focusing on the relationship between peasants and landlords, has also compromised the utility of the concept. For example, some scholars have argued that medieval India (600–1200 CE) was a feudal society. In its broadest definition, however, most would agree that the term feudalism may be used to describe a hierarchy of power in which land constitutes the principal form of wealth and provides the basis for the fusion of political, social, and economic organization through patron–client relationships. Europe and Japan are the two instances in world history where the contours of a feudal system have been most extensively defined and debated.

European feudalism

The institutions and practices of European feudalism developed after the power of a strong centralized state (the Roman Empire) had shifted onto local political units. Central to feudalism was the personal, specifically military, relationship between lord (patron) and vassal (client). The relationship was often perpetuated through family structures and in some cases actually reflected blood ties.

Feudalism in some parts of Europe developed when central government broke down and public functions, obligations, and privileges were taken over by individuals operating under a variety of private hierarchical arrangements created by personal obligation. Feudalism in its various forms was prevalent in western Europe from the ninth to thirteenth centuries, when private administrative structures – law, ideology, economic functions, and social relationships – assumed many of the attributes of centralized states. In parts of eastern Europe, feudalism was imposed later and lasted longer.

European feudalism is commonly considered to be two closely interdependent systems. Feudalism involved the relationship between landowners, in which the most powerful landowners provided aid and protection to less powerful landowners who had enough wealth to own horses and arms. The less powerful landowners, in turn, owed allegiance and military service to the most powerful. The vassal (or client) gradually became identified as a knight, a warrior around whom evolved a highly elaborate culture and lifestyle. The knight's prestige depended upon fighting, and knights justified their existence by waging wars. Many knights were descended from elites through the male line, and they maintained their power through kinship networks and alliances with other powerful lords. Because of the cultural and political significance of warfare among the elite, the status of women declined as they were culturally excluded from warfare in most cases.

The economic basis on which the feudal system rested, manorialism (see Chapter 6), was essentially a relationship of dominance and subordination between those who claimed authority over the land and those families who cultivated it. People and land, then, were the basic ingredients of feudalism. A fief, commonly a grant in the form of land, was presented by a lord to a vassal. The vassal accordingly became a land-holder, the lord of the fief. The land was organized into a manor or manors, which were worked by serfs, laborers with limited rights, whose labor and produce sustained the landlord and indeed the whole feudal-manorial system. Serfs were obligated to remain on the land and sometimes to give a portion of the annual harvest to the lord. Their claims to the land were more or less permanent and could be inherited by their children.

The practice of men without resources placing themselves under the protection of a wealthy, stronger patron dates from at least the eighth century. The following statement of obligation from that early time illustrates both the voluntary and reciprocal nature of entering into a formal contractual relationship between patron and client:

> Inasmuch as it is known to all and sundry that I lack the wherewithal to feed and clothe myself, I have asked of your pity, and your goodwill has granted to me permission to deliver and commend myself into your authority and protection . . . in return you have undertaken to aid and sustain me in food and clothing, while I have undertaken to serve you and deserve well of you as far as lies in my power. And for as long as I shall live, I am bound to serve you and respect you as a free man ought, and during my lifetime I have not the right to withdraw from your authority and protection, but must, on the contrary, for the remainder of my days remain under it. And in virtue of this action, if one of us wishes to alter the terms of the agreement, he can do so after paying a fine of

ten *solidi* [a Roman gold coin] to the other. But the agreement itself shall remain in force. Whence it has seemed good to us that we should both draw up and confirm two documents of the same tenor, and this they have done.

Source: Marjorie Rowling, *Life in Medieval Times* (New York: Perigee Books, 1979), p31–32.

As suggested here, the contractual relationship was a way for those in need of protection or sustenance to declare their dependence and obligation of service in return for which their needs were to be met.

The specific arrangements of the contract that were basic to the feudal relationship varied widely across Europe, although they often involved military protection and service. The individual gave up only enough freedom to ensure effective cooperation. When feudalism began to work on a local level to stabilize relations of power, kings and emperors also adopted it to strengthen monarchies. Feudalism flourished in the twelfth and thirteenth centuries as it spread across Europe from the areas between the Rhine and Loire Rivers.

The granting of rights over land in return for military or other services is the essence of the feudal system, but before this relationship could be firmly established, land had to be free or immune to possible intervention by the centralized authority. Immunity created a territory free from interference by the state, so that public functions, such as the administration of justice or protection, became the prerogative of private individuals. For example, the early Frankish kings granted churches and monasteries immunity for their lands and thus created a sort of religious state within their kingdom. Similarly, when fiefs – grants of land – were handed down by lords to vassals (and by inheritance to the vassal's heirs), local government functions, ranging from road building to administering justice, were assumed by the vassal to whom the fief had been given.

Fiefs were primarily pieces of land held on terms of personal obligation. There were three main varieties of such tenure (landholding): ecclesiastical (Church), military, and general. Ecclesiastical fiefs were those given to the Church, which provided spiritual benefits to the donor – and often nothing else – in return. There were two principal types of military tenure. Field service in the overlord's army, generally for up to 40 days a year (though the service might be shorter), was one type. The other main form of military tenure involved guard service at the overlord's residence.

Other forms of tenure also existed, and these involved general, rather than spiritual or military, services. Fiefs were granted to vassals for supplying overlords with goods (horses, equipment, provisions) or personal services (hospitality or comfort in sickness, or even holding their heads when they grew seasick crossing the English Channel). Toward the end of the feudal age, with the return of a money economy, these services were commuted into payments into the overlord's treasury.

Vassals who possessed extensive fiefs divided out portions of them in a process known as subinfeudation. The result of subinfeudation was that every landholder in the feudal system became both a vassal and an overlord, excepting (theoretically) the lord king and the lowliest vassal holding a single, indivisible fief. This arrangement grew unsystematically in western Europe in the tenth and eleventh centuries and so complicated tenure relationships that it carried with it the seeds of its own disintegration. In actuality, lords had little control over their lesser vassals. The descriptive phrase of the time, "The vassal of my vassal is not my vassal," describes the dissolution of the ability of the overlord to maintain effective authority over fiefs granted to vassals. Even kings "holding only from God" – who owed homage to no one and were purportedly above such fractionalizing involvements – became mere

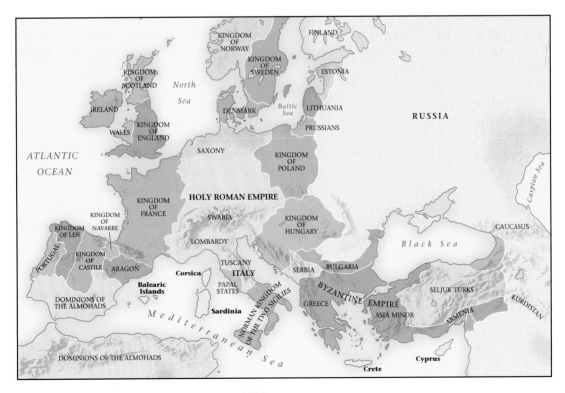

Map 8.3 Europe and the Mediterranean, ca. 1190.

landlords bound by feudal contracts to vassals who were their equals and sometimes their superiors in military strength and political power. The power of feudal monarchs was so limited by contracts to a position that they were little more than first among equals. The limitation of royal power, a striking feature of feudal society, was a result of such practices as subinfeudation. Attempts to end the erosion of the power of monarchies and to reestablish centralized sovereignty were the process by which feudal society in western Europe was ultimately transformed.

Under feudalism, control and inheritance of land passed from the hands of kings to those of families, and this tended to enrich women as well as men. The system of lineage accepted in some parts of western Europe, in which the line of descent of the familial surname was followed and recognized through female as well as male ancestors, guaranteed family control of land and allowed females, in the absence of male heirs, to inherit property. They held land in their own right and fulfilled the family obligations, including military ones, for the holding of fiefs. Probably the best-known example of this occurred in the twelfth century, when the vast fiefs of William X, Duke of Aquitaine, were bequeathed to his daughter Eleanor, who accordingly became the most important vassal of the king of France, possessing approximately one-third of that sovereign's territory. By the end of the thirteenth century, the rise of towns and the shift of economic and political forces away from the household toward the public sphere probably worked to undermine women's power as well as feudalism itself.

Japanese feudalism

As with European feudalism, Japanese feudalism was based on two institutions: the manor (*shōen*), to which was connected the idea of rights to the land, and the military power of a warrior elite. With the decline of Fujiwara power in the late twelfth century and the subsequent weakening of central authority, a new warrior elite, known as bushi or samurai, developed outside the capital. Samurai replaced the court aristocracy as a social and political elite whose power was consolidated through personal ties of loyalty and military service. As the military dictator, or *shogun*, rose to a position of political dominance in the twelfth century, Japan entered a long era of "feudalism," in which political power and authority were directly linked to landholding and the rights to land were conferred by "lords" on their "vassals" in return for military service.

The influence of Tang China as a model for centralized government declined as contact between Japan and China was severely curtailed for a century following the end of the Nara period in the late eighth century. The imperial army had dwindled to a force centered on the capital and was incapable of maintaining order in the provinces outside the capital. Tax collection had broken down as the imperial authority to back up officials responsible for collecting taxes weakened. Though in accord with the model of imperial authority derived from Tang China the Japanese emperor claimed all land as his own, to be distributed and utilized as he commanded, in fact privately held land existed from the foundation of the Japanese state in the pre-Nara period.

During the Heian period (794–1185), the authority of the imperial line was undermined by the indirect rule of a powerful family at the Japanese court, the Fujiwara. By serving as regents to young-adult emperors, who were often married to their daughters, the Fujiwara built their power at court and successfully subverted the emperors' authority. In addition to lands privately held by the imperial family, aristocratic families received grants of land from the emperor as rewards or as part of official ranks they held at court. The great Buddhist temples and Shinto shrines also received lands as a sign of court patronage. In the middle of the eighth century, in order to encourage the reclamation of uncultivated land, more or less permanent land rights were given to those who opened new fields to cultivation. Many of these landholdings enjoyed either temporary or permanent degrees of tax exemption.

By the tenth century, many large landholders sought and obtained immunity to tax payment as well as immunity from interference by local government officials, who were then prohibited to enter an estate or interfere with its administration. There were thus two kinds of land: public domain, which was taxed by the imperial government to fund the state treasury, and private land, which was largely immune to tax collection or other responsibility to the state. Small landholders sometimes commended their lands to a more powerful landholder, where they became part of a large estate protected from tax collection. The commender would then obtain the right to till the land in perpetuity for himself and his heirs, with obligations such as paying rent to the estate owner rather than paying taxes to the imperial government.

Land rights, the key to the economic base of feudalism, were defined in Japan by the term *shiki*, which originally meant "office" and implied certain duties toward the land. It eventually came to mean the "right to profit from the land." The estate protector, the proprietor, the local manager, and the peasant cultivator all held such rights to the land. The cultivator would have the right to till the land in return for payment of rent; the protector, often a member of the Heian nobility resident in the capital, would derive income from the estate and protect its immunity to taxation or other interference; the estate manager would receive a share of the harvest for managing the peasantry and sending rents to the proprietor. The proprietor had the most power: to survey the land, to keep land records, and to exercise control over estate residents. Like the protector, the proprietor was likely to be an absentee landholder who lived in the capital.

Japanese feudalism evolved from the reassertion during the Heian period of a lineage-based aristocratic social tradition in which patron–client relations were the basis of political organization and the means of governing the state, exemplified by the rule of the Fujiwara family during the ninth to eleventh centuries. The culture of the Heian nobility was far more sophisticated than that of the courts of the Franks, Germans, and Anglo-Saxons in Europe. The Heian nobility lived a life of great luxury and refinement, supported by the income from landed estates that lay outside the capital, often in provinces far distant from the center of cultural and political life at the Heian court. They were absentee landholders, dependent on estate managers to supervise their landholdings and secure their income. Control of the manors gradually slipped out of the hands of the court aristocrats and into those of the local managers and military men, who in the absence of imperial authority protected the manors from assault.

The wars that led to the final demise of the Heian originated with conflicts between two families, the Taira and the Minamoto, who were descended from ninth-century emperors and had been given aristocratic surnames and lucrative rewards in the form of lands or posts at the capital. In this way their lines had been removed from succession to the throne, but they became strong in their own right as they secured their positions: the Taira in the capital area and the Inland Sea, and the Minamoto in the Kanto region (the area surrounding modern Tokyo).

When the wars between the Taira and the Minamoto came to an end in 1185, Minamoto Yoritomo's **bakufu** (literally "tent government"), or shogunate, centered at his military base of power, Kamakura, became a military government that balanced and then dominated the civil government of the imperial court at Kyoto. In 1192, the title of *shogun* (military dictator) of all Japan was conferred by the emperor on Minamoto Yoritomo (1147–99).

Allegiance to Yoritomo by his vassals was based on his military strength and on personal loyalty. But the latter was also cemented by material rewards, which were enabled by Yoritomo's position as military protector of the emperor. One of the most important rights (*shiki*) the Minamoto conferred on their vassals was appointment to positions as land stewards on private estates, where the vassal had essentially the same duties as an estate manager and was similarly entitled to income from the estate. Yoritomo also appointed his vassals to official posts as provincial constables, responsible for maintaining order and able to derive income from this position.

After Yoritomo's death, the Kamakura shogunate (1185–1333) was under the control of his wife, Hojo Masako (1157–1225), and her father, brothers, and their descendants, who ruled as the Hojo regency. Emperors continued to reign as symbolic figures of authority from the old imperial capital at Heian, though two attempts to reassert imperial authority over the Hojo regency failed, in 1221 and again in 1333–36. The latter imperial rebellion brought about the collapse of the Kamakura shogunate and the founding of a new one (1338–1573) by the military leader Ashikaga Takauji (1305–58) centered at Kyoto (the old imperial capital of Heian).

In the Ashikaga period, as the personal ties that had existed between Minamoto Yoritomo and his vassals weakened under the Hojo and vassals no longer felt the bonds of loyalty and obligation that bound them to the shogun, a fuller form of feudalism began to flower. The single-lord (*shogun*)–vassal relationship exemplified by Minamoto Yoritomo and his heirs in the Kamukura shogunate evolved into many-lord (*daimyo*)–vassal relationships, with the *shogun* the symbolic apex of the feudal hierarchy. The key relationships, though, were those between the provincially based *daimyo* and their vassals, which remained personal and strong. By 1300, the warriors were in control of Japan and the estate system had collapsed, as most land became integrated into the domains or fiefs of the *daimyo*, supervised by their vassals. In contrast to Europe, where feudalism had all but disappeared by 1300, the full flowering of Japanese feudalism dates from the thirteenth century.

Both European and Japanese feudal institutions emerged from the crumbling of a centralized imperial government and its legal-administrative apparatus: the weakening of the Roman Empire and Roman law in the case of Europe and that of the Japanese state of the Nara and Heian periods (eighth to twelfth centuries), modeled on the imperial government of Tang China. The development of contractual relationships between patrons and clients in both cases rested on prior legal and administrative foundations, and evolved over time in response to changing economic and political conditions, such as the growing importance of commerce and the expansion of centralized states.

Slavery

Systems of slavery constitute a far more extreme form of human bondage than the contractual obligations incurred through feudalism, and slavery both predates feudalism and is found throughout the world. Historians do not always agree on when to apply the term slavery to systems of inequality, but slaves were found in large-scale polities in almost all parts of the ancient world. From Eurasia to the Americas and Africa, forms of coerced labor created a spectrum of intricate relationships of dependency and obligation. Beginning between about the middle of the first millennium BCE, systems of exploitation had begun to be built around unequal access to land and labor in larger states. All slave systems were characterized by the threat or actual use of violence to coerce labor for the benefit of others. Enslavement resulted in the total loss of personal rights.

Enslavement might be the consequence of capture in warfare or the internal processes of judicial judgment, punishment, or economic indebtedness. In Roman society, most slaves originated as war captives, whose lives were spared. They were legally defined as people who were owned by someone else. High-ranking slaves might self-select the status in order to be attached to the wealthy households of others. In ancient Greece, slaves attached themselves to larger households or to shrines in times of famine or debt through a ritual process. In some societies, domestic slavery might be temporary or could gain permanency through marriage into an adopted household. For example, Roman slaves in urban households were adopted as domestic servants. Slaves in many cultures provided labor in mining, domestic households, and in highly specialized crafts and trades.

Slave trading was a principle activity of states, which relied on military expansion. The cycle of imperial expansion resulted in war captives and was matched by increases in the slave population. Large-scale slave systems throughout world history supported the power and authority of rulers and enabled their extended access to labor. There was also an intimate link between land and the labor of the enslaved. As territorial conquests extended the control over land, conquered peoples were viewed as essential sources of labor or tribute.

The intersection of gender and other inequalities was dependent on complex cultural and social constructions that could and often did change over time. During the expansion of the Akan state (in West Africa) during and after the fourteenth and fifteenth centuries CE, neither women nor children gained position or power. The emphasis on warfare resulted in men gaining status, and the increased numbers of slaves available to perform household tasks generally devalued women's labor and diminished their influence even further. As Akan society became a slave society, dependent on slave labor, social classes became more entrenched and inequalities proliferated. The uncertainty and ambiguity inherent in the lack of ancestry and status are best exemplified by the fact that enemies captured by the expanding Akan state became permanent slaves unless they were integrated into an *abusua* through adoption or marriage (see Chapter 7).

A general feature of empires was the increased and more systematic exploitation of social inequality. An empire's territorial expansion ultimately relied on its increasing the supplies of food for its armies and other sources of wealth for trade. In addition to their reproductive role, women produced goods. Another important feature of imperial systems was the expansion of territorial control over land. The fourteenth-century Arab traveler Ibn Battuta described the extent of social inequality in Mali. One of the consequences of the expansion of empire through trade and military means was the capture of prisoners of war, who then became sources of male soldiers and female slaves. The Sahelian and Saharan towns of the Mali Empire (see Chapter 9) were organized as both staging posts in the long-distance caravan trade and trading centers for the various West African products. At Taghaza, for example, salt was exchanged; at Takedda, copper. Ibn Battuta observed the employment of slave labor in both towns. During most of his journey, Ibn Battuta traveled with a retinue that included slaves, most of whom carried goods for trade but would also be traded as slaves. On the return from Takedda to Morocco, his caravan transported 600 female slaves, suggesting that slavery was a substantial part of the commercial activity of the empire's fringes.

Imperial growth everywhere depended in part on women, the appropriation of female labor as well as the mechanisms for the exclusion of women from the sources of political and economic power. There were many more female slaves than male slaves traded in the empire, a fact that points out the inequality that existed between the genders. The variation in women's social positions increased with the growth of the empire's towns. Women, usually slaves, were valued porters in the trans-Saharan caravan trade. They sometimes served as concubines. Additionally, female labor produced salt, cloth for export, and most of the local foodstuffs essential to the provisions required by urban centers. Men were hunters, farmers, merchants, and specialists, in addition to frequently being conscripted as soldiers.

Whether or not a society's hierarchical structure monopolized labor, controlled access to strategic food or positions through farms, palaces, temples, or cities, power organized the relationships in society. The division of labor, ecological variability, and accumulation of material wealth resulted in the propensity for hierarchies to proliferate. The ability to appropriate labor and gain preferential access to strategic resources in turn created greater disparities. Enslavement was the most extreme form of social disempowerment and could result from the subjugation of labor, the transfer of rights over persons, or through sanctions that made an individual not only "unfree," but also kinless. Being made kinless was tantamount to denying an individual the right to belong to community.

Belonging to community was especially important in the world of Islam. By the fifteenth century CE, *dar al-Islam* (the territory where Islamic law prevails) stretched from the Arabian peninsula to the Iberian peninsula and North Africa, into sub-Saharan Africa, South and Southeast Asia. While the diverse peoples of *dar al-Islam* were spreading across three continents, land was not scarce. *Dar al-Islam* was a civilization of cities, where wealth and power were based on money and trade across vast reaches of land and sea. It was equally a system of interknit small communities in the hinterlands of those cities, hinterlands that provided townsfolk with essential food and the trade goods that sustained their commercial enterprises. Particularly in the more urban areas of Southwest Asia the common use for slave labor was in domestic situations and in the military. Islamic laws forbid the enslavement of fellow Muslims. To be Muslim was to be free. Therefore slaves could only be non-Muslims, and preferably not even "people of the book" (Christians and Jews).

An alternate form of enslavement occurred in societies in which slaves originated as persons disgraced or degraded in status. In Southeast Asia and some parts of Africa, slaves could be indigenous rather than perceived of as "others" (outside the social and kinship networks of familiar terrain). These societies were held together by vertical bonds of obligations between the elite and less powerful, and slavery was merely one of many options on a spectrum of obligation. Land was assumed to be abundant, and not therefore an index of power. Wealth and power lay in the dependent man-(and woman-)power one could gather. For the poor and weak, on the other hand, security and opportunity depended upon being bonded to somebody strong enough to look after them. Fundamental to success and wealth was the ability to succeed in gaining control over people not land.

The most common origin for this system of bondage was debt, although there were also war captives. When overwhelmed with debts (due to dowry payments, perhaps, or expensive rituals such as slaughtering a buffalo upon the death of a family member), a man could sell himself and/or his wife and children to the creditor. Most often, he became a domestic slave, much like a junior member of the household, doing all its most menial jobs, yet closely bound in intimacy to it and sharing its triumphs as well as its disasters. The slave owner was likewise expected to provide for his slave, even procuring a wife. The labor of the debt-bondsman had a definite value, however, and he could be sold, traded, and exchanged. Most importantly, the slave owner and ruler were tied directly or indirectly to the human drama of enslavement through various alliances and loyalties.

Although agriculture was by far the dominant activity in Southeast Asia, a slave mode of production did not seem to exist there: farm laborers owed a portion of their produce to their lord, but were not owned personally by the lord – even if they owed some form of tribute. The most characteristic roles for slaves were as domestics, entertainers, and as spinners and weavers of textiles. They also functioned as significant status symbols, and symbols of power. Kings and powerful nobles constantly struggled for control of men: the kings seeking to maximize the number of people obligated to him through corvée (unpaid state labor) and the nobles to withdraw men from the corvée for their own private uses. In the flour-

PRIMARY SOURCE: ZHOU DAGUAN ON SLAVES IN THE KHMER EMPIRE

Zhou Daguan (1266–1346) was sent as an envoy to the Khmer Empire (in present-day Cambodia) by the Mongol ruler Khubilai Khan. After his return to China in 1297, Zhou recorded his recollections of the customs of the Khmer people. The following excerpt concerns the status and role of slaves in Khmer society, who were largely drawn from prisoners of war and consequently viewed as less than human. This passage also reflects the effects of dehumanizing treatment, as the slaves are shown to respond submissively to their harsh treatment:

> Slaves are brought to do the work of servants. When they are young and strong, they fetch a hundred pieces of cloth; old and weak, from thirty to forty. Wealthy families may have more than a hundred; even those of modest means have ten or twenty; only the poor have none at all. The savages inhabit the wild mountains and belong to a different race; they are called *zhuangs*, thieves. If, in a quarrel, a man calls another a *zhuang*, it is a deadly insult, so despised are the savages, who are considered to be subhuman. Brought to the city, they never dare appear on the street. They are forced to live in the space under the houses which are built on stilts and when they come up to the house to do their work, they must first kneel and make the proper obeisance, prostrating themselves before they can advance. They call their owners "father" and "mother." If they make a mistake, they are beaten. They take their punishment with bent head and without making the slightest movement.

> Source: Alfred J. Andrea and James H. Overfield, eds, *The Human Record: Sources of Global History, Volume I: To 1700* (Boston, NY: Houghton Mifflin, 1998), p424.

ishing centers of Angkor, Ayudhuya, Melaka, Banten, Aceh, and Makassar, populations numbered up to 100,000 people each, and slaves were the single most important item of property. They symbolically conveyed status: it was important that the elite do no manual labor, and be seen always attended by a retinue of slaves. Likewise, foreign merchants could not function effectively unless they had men bonded to them. In these societies, the existence of slaves served to define the status of individuals and the bounds of community.

Summary

Social orders based on either genealogical ties or patron–client relationships can be found in most regions of the world, including Africa, the Americas, Asia, and Europe. In the exceptional case of the Mongols, a lineage-based society composed of different tribes united according to either real or fictive kinship ties coalesced to create probably the largest empire in world history (see Chapter 9). This was a temporary phenomenon, however, that demonstrated the capacity for large-scale action of such lineage-based societies given particular circumstances, rather than the logical outcome of such societies over time. The social and political complexity of Mexica-Aztec and Incan empires similarly was lineage-based. South Asia yields yet another, distinctive approach to the ordering of society in the evolution of the caste system. The West African examples illustrate that polities sometimes recognized the political utility of changing caste categories.

Societies organized on the principle of kinship ties, such as lineage societies in West Asia, did not show significant signs of disappearing until modern times. Lineage societies and neighboring centralized states developed strategies for dealing with one another based on the differing economic strengths and needs of both sides. Centralized states sometimes made insatiable demands on agrarian manpower and resources, and both nomadic and sedentary lineage societies worked out exchanges with empires that at least partially satisfied the needs of both, with less centralized groups receiving the protection of states when they needed it, while urban centers and large bureaucracies were supported by rural production. In this way, lineage-based polities played a major role in world history, though they were seldom understood and often attacked by their central-ized neighbors.

Despite the tensions and hostility between them, centralized and decentralized polities have consistently enjoyed an interdependent coexis-tence, a fact that was a major theme in the writings of Ibn Khaldun, who discussed the connection between decentralized, lineage-based and centralized polities in his *Muqaddimah*, a five-hundred-page introduction to the method-ology of history. Ibn Khaldun concluded that while all civilizations have risen and fallen because of socio-economic factors, the immediate agents of this cycle were the lineage groups of rural areas, pulled together by a charismatic leader offering a powerful religious ideology. Only armies such as those tied by kinship, the tightest bond of loyalty in society, had the strength to overwhelm the defenses of the centralized state. Ibn Khaldun's hypothesis, developed in great detail in the *Muqaddimah*, sheds useful light on the workings of lineage politics not only in West Asia but also wherever lineage-based societies have been found. In his discussion of the social, cultural, and economic bases of human behavior, Ibn Khaldun recognized the importance of forms of association based on both kinship and economic interest.

In other parts of the world, caste was a defining concept in establishing social hierarchies, which had both economic and political meanings. Although sometimes the boundaries between caste systems and slavery could be blurred, what distinguished slavery as a social system was its transformation of human beings into property, commercial commodities to be bought and sold, or, as Orlando Patterson has termed it, "social death." Before 1500, slavery was widely dispersed, found in societies across the globe, but after 1500, these systems would be bound together into global networks that intensified the meanings of "social death."

Suggested readings

Chatterjee, Indrani and Richard Maxwell Eaton (2006) *Slavery and South Asian History*, Bloomington: Indiana University Press. A study of slavery in South Asia, showing that slaves in this part of the world were largely military or domestic, not agricultural laborers.

Duby, Georges (1980) *The Three Orders: Feudal Society Imagined*, Chicago: University of Chicago Press. Classic, imaginative reconstruction of European feudal society by a French scholar.

Duus, Peter (1993) *Feudalism in Japan*, 3rd ed., New York: McGraw-Hill. Survey of evolution of feudal institu-tions in Japan from the sixth through the nineteenth centuries, with some comparative commentary.

Klein, Laura F. and Lillian A. Ackerman, eds (1995) *Women and Power in Native North America*, Norman, OK, and London: University of Oklahoma Press. Collected articles on gender issues in Native North American societies as they relate to lineage and tribal identities.

Mukhia, Harbans, ed. (1999) *The Feudalism Debate*, New Delhi: Manohar. A collection of articles by a variety of scholars debating the nature of, and the very existence of, feudalism on the Indian subcontinent, with particular attention to Marxist interpretations.

Reynolds, Susan (1994) *Fiefs and Vassals: The Medieval Evidence Reconsidered*, New York and Oxford: Oxford University Press. A provocative challenge to the concept of feudalism, supported by close exam-ination of the meaning of Latin terms usually translated as "fief" and "vassal."

Shaw, Thurstan (1970) *Igbo Ukwu: An Account of Archaeological Discoveries in Eastern Nigeria*, Evanston:

Northwestern University Press. Account of the archaeological evidence.

Online resources

Annenberg/CPB, *Bridging World History* (2004) Unit 14 Land and Labor Relationships <www.learner.org/courses/worldhistory/unit_main_14.html>

Study questions

1. In what ways were age and gender determinants of an individual's place in the social order?
2. What are lineage societies?
3. How did lineage societies interact with state power?
4. How did lineage-based societies create empires?
5. What is caste and how has it shaped Indian society?
6. Where else has caste been a significant marker of social identity?
7. Define feudalism and compare European and Japanese feudalism.
8. What forms did slavery take in different parts of the world?

670–1025 CE	711	770–834	802–1432	849–1287	1227	ca. 1220–1235
Srivijayan Empire	Muslim conquest of the Iberian peninsula, beginning of al-Andalus	Reign of Jayavarman II, ruler of the Khmer Empire	Khmer Empire	Pagan Burma	Death of Chinggis Khan, founder of the Mongol Empire	Reign of Sunjata, founder of Mali Empire

9 Early empires

In the thirteenth century, the Spanish Muslim writer Ibn Said summarized the history of the Muslim conquest of Spain, highlighting the struggles between Muslims and Christians that dominated the political history of this region from the eighth to the fifteenth centuries:

> Andalus [the Iberian peninsula], which was conquered in the year 92 of the Hijra [711 CE], continued for many years to be a dependency of the Eastern Khalifate, until it was snatched away from their hands by one of the surviving members of the family of Umeyyah [Umayyad], who, crossing over from Barbary, subdued the country, and formed therein an independent kingdom, which he transmitted to his posterity. During three centuries and a half, Andalus, governed by the princes of this dynasty, reached the utmost degree of power and prosperity, until civil war breaking out among its inhabitants, the Muslims, weakened by internal discord, became every where the prey of the artful Christians, and the territory of Islam was considerably reduced, so much so that at the present moment the worshipers of the crucified hold the greatest part of Andalus in their hands, and their country is divided into various powerful kingdoms, whose rulers assist each other whenever the Muslims attack their territories.

> Source: From Ibn Said, *Book of the Maghrib*, in Ahmed ibm Mohammed al-Makkari, *The History of the Mohammedan Dynasties in Spain*, translated by Pascuual de Gayangos, (London: Oriental Translation Fund, 1840), pp1, 95.

Ibn Said's account naturally favored Muslim control of the Iberian peninsula, an extension of the Arab Muslim empire that swept across the lands of the western end of the Mediterranean, through North Africa, to the shores of the Atlantic Ocean in the eighth century. His description illustrates not only the imperial expansion of Islam, but also political (and religious) resistance in the forms of Christian kingdoms. Empires brought together different peoples, cultures, and religions under an umbrella of authority frequently sanctioned by religion, as the *dar al-Islam* did through the rule of the caliphate from Umayyad Damascus and later Abbasid Baghdad. Imperial expansion was often a process of consolidation of previously independent kingdoms, which themselves were institutions that wielded

1260–94	ca. 1350	1336–1405	ca. 1230–1450	1428–1521	ca. 1438–1532
Reign of Khubilai Khan as Great Khan and emperor of the Yuan dynasty in China	Collapse of Mongol Empire	Lifetime of Tamerlane	Mali Empire in West Africa	Mexica-Aztec Empire	Inca Empire

9.1 Photo of the Alhambra, a fortified Moorish palace built between 1258 and 1354 near Granada, the last stronghold of Muslim rule in Spain.

power over cities, villages, rural hinterlands, coastlines, and islands. Just as in Ibn Said's account, empires were created, challenged, and collapsed, through both internal and external forces. How did empires forge new identities for the peoples they conquered, as in the Islamic Empire in al-Andalus, and in what ways did people resist the imposition of new identities? The history of empires is one of the most pervasive themes in world history, one that draws together dynamic patterns of political, economic, cultural, and religious history. What features did world empires have in common and how were they different?

Introduction to the theme of early empires

As peoples around the world began to practice agriculture and move into cities, growing populations living together expanded the scale of human activities and led to increasing social complexity. The unequal distribution of resources – and thereby power – intensified as agricultural villages became cities, city-states, kingdoms, and even empires. Accompanying the concentration of population and resources was the growth of military forces, to protect food stores, to defend territory, and eventually to expand control of both people (their labor) and land. Religious ideas and practices that had inspired and guided community life in earlier times were adapted to provide sanction for new rulers and forms of political organization, new social hierarchies, and new economic relationships.

Empires were the largest-scale polities and resulted from the expansion of one polity, such as a kingdom or city-state, at the expense of others. A succession of such empires emerged in the ancient Mediterranean world (see Chapter 4), unifying earlier city-states such as Uruk under their control. Beginning in the third millennium BCE, the Akkadian, Babylonian, Assyrian, and Hittite Empires rose and fell in this region of the world, invading and conquering territory and peoples only to be invaded and conquered in turn. Ancient Egypt exhibited features of an empire throughout its long history until it was brought under the imperial umbrella of Alexander the Great in the fourth century BCE. Alexander's empire was built on the conquest of the Persian Achaemenid Empire (550–334 BCE), and extended from the Balkans to the Hindu Kush as well as to Egypt in North Africa.

Alexander's Hellenistic Empire was contemporaneous with – and bordered – the Mauryan Empire in South Asia, whose ruler Ashoka converted to Buddhism and used his imperial power to spread the faith. Ashoka's promotion of Buddhism also supported his imperial authority, suggesting the complex dynamic at work in the interaction of religion and empire. Contemporary with Ashoka's reign, the Parthian Empire rose to dominate the regions of Persia and Mesopotamia for the next 400 years. The Mauryans fell to invading Kushans, a nomadic people who created a large empire in southwestern Asia and northwestern India in the first centuries CE. The Guptas (ca. 320–500 CE), who drew sanction for their rule from Hinduism, unified the northern part of India and followed a policy of religious tolerance toward Buddhism and other religions.

The first unification of China took place in the third century BCE, with the founding of the Qin (221–210 BCE). Short-lived though the Qin was, its successor, the Han dynasty (206 BCE–220 CE), spanned 400 years, building on the centralized political institutions of its predecessor and con-structing a new imperial cultural identity based on Confucianism. The cultural synthesis created by the Han established the foundations of the Chinese Empire for the next 2,000 years.

At the other end of the Eurasian continent, the Roman Empire at its peak in the first century CE ruled a vast area surrounding the Mediterranean, extending west and north to the Iberian peninsula and the isles of Britain and east to the edges of Central Asia. Roman legions policed this territory, and the Roman government exacted tribute from all over the empire to support its elite rulers, army, and administration. Roman emperors were eventually deified, deriving sanction to rule from association with Roman gods. Like the Han dynasty in China, Roman rule established a common culture throughout its empire and created institutions and laws that continued to exert a powerful influence long after its collapse.

The word "empire" in fact derives directly from the Latin *imperium*, and was used by the heirs of Rome to sanction their rule. Both the Holy Roman (Western) and Byzantine (Eastern) Empires were direct descendants of Rome, dividing much of the former territory of the Roman Empire between them as well as promoting different forms of Christianity (see Chapter 5). These Christian successor empires to Rome bordered the Zoroastrian Sassanian Empire, which dominated much of Southwest Asia from the third to the seventh centuries. The Holy Roman Empire, viewed by some as beginning with the crowning of Charlemagne in 800 by Pope Leo III, lasted in name and later primarily in its German incarnation for 1,000 years, until it was abolished by Napoleon in 1806. In a superficially similar way, the reunification of China under the Sui (589–617) and Tang (618–907) dynasties reclaimed the imperial legacy of the Han, promoting Buddhism, and expanding Chinese influence across East Asia. The reality of the Chinese Empire as a unified imperial power, however, stood in stark contrast to the shadowy presence of the Holy Roman Empire, an heir of Rome in name but not in power.

Religion was a key feature of these early empires, promoted by rulers to legitimize their authority or suppressed because of religion's potency as an agent of resistance to imperial rule. By far the most powerful symbiosis of religion and empire was in the Islamic empires, beginning in the seventh century (see Chapter 5). All these empires – Hellenistic, Chinese, Roman, Islamic – also were built by military power and controlled through administrative structures that enabled the assimilation of wealth through taxation and tribute (see Chapter 6). This chapter will pick up the theme of empires, beginning with the Mongol Empire in the thirteenth century, the West African Mali Empire in the fourteenth century, the Mughal Empire in South Asia, and concluding with the fifteenth-century Mexica-Aztec and Incan Empires in the Americas.

Empires have been defined in many different ways, and the processes that led to the formation of empires are equally varied. What all empires appear to have in common are control of a territorially extensive, multiethnic polity by a strong center, and the promotion of ideas or beliefs that sanction the exercise of imperial power. What factors were essential in the construction of empires? How did empires bridge cultural chasms, uniting different peoples through religious sanctions, as well as by military might? What forces eventually contributed to the disintegration and collapse of empires?

Maritime and mainland empires in Southeast Asia: Srivijaya and Khmer

Southeast Asia is a world of northern mountains and southern seas, of broad mainland river-delta plains and a profusion of large and small islands. Watered by the monsoons, heavy rains brought by winds that also moved sailing ships over the seas with great seasonal regularity, Southeast Asia shares the climate of the Indian subcontinent. In the early centuries of the first millennium, Southeast Asia sat astride an ancient maritime trade highway between West Asia and Africa on the one hand, and East Asia on the other. It was also the meeting place of local, as well as Indian and Chinese, cultures and belief systems.

Situated at the intersection of Indian and Chinese civilization, Southeast Asia has been seen either through an Indian lens stressing the Hindu influence on the formation of the first state, Funan (see Chapter 6), or through an equally distorting Chinese lens reflected in the Chinese accounts of Funan. In contrast to either of these perspectives, it seems better to conceptualize early Southeast Asian polities in terms of indigenous ideas and practices that emphasize a complex system of personal loyalties as the basis for power relations rather than to consider them as territories with defined boundaries administered by representatives of one or another ruler. The precise boundaries of the territory controlled by a ruler were not of primary concern; what mattered was the network of loyalties on which that ruler could depend. The mandala, a symbol drawn from early Indian cosmology, has been used to characterize the nature of political authority in early Southeast Asia. The mandala image, a sacred diagram of the cosmos constructed of concentric circles or rectangles, represents the ruler's personal charismatic authority radiating out from a center, in contrast to the vertically organized hierarchy of power directly exercised through the ruler's representatives.

Many polities rose and fell in Southeast Asia before 1500. The most impressive of these were empires that continued to influence regional traditions long after they had fallen. These empires were built on distinctive regional economic structures and created cultural and political foundations for their successors. The major polities of this period can be loosely categorized into two types: those of the mainland, based on intensive irrigated rice agriculture on river plains, and those of the islands, based on control of the river network and sea trade. Each economic system alone could support a strong regional polity. Only the two systems together, however, could provide sufficiently diversified material and human resources to maintain an empire. Here we will look at an empire that achieved such a linkage: Srivijaya. We will also consider the example of a strong regional polity, the mainland Khmer empire, which controlled and organized the redistribution of resources produced by wet-rice agriculture on the Mekong River delta through a network of Buddhist temples.

Srivijaya

The large Srivijayan island empire (ca. 670–1025) was built on the wealth produced by maritime trade (see Chapter 6), along with a combination of military force and the political acumen of the *datus* (chiefs or rulers) of the capital, Palembang, on the island of Sumatra. Given the fluctuations in international trade and variations in human abilities, military power and political skill alone were insufficient to ensure the survival of Srivijaya. The rulers also needed a belief system that could unite conquered regions with differing religious and ethnic groups under a common loyalty to Palembang. Srivijaya's rulers found such a unifying ideology in the universal religion of Buddhism. Srivijayan rulers used some of the profits of their empire to become patrons of Buddhism, dedicating temples as far away as Bengal and the southeast coast of India during the tenth and eleventh centuries.

The structure of the Srivijayan political order in the eighth century reflects its Malay *datu* (chief) origins. The king, who was in theory an absolute monarch, ruled nearby provinces through his sons and other royal family members. In more distant territories, however – on the Malay peninsula, for example, or to the south on Java – conquered *datus* were left in place to continue their family rule in the king's name. In one sense, the empire was an alliance system between one powerful *datu* and many others, among them the fleet captains who functioned in alliance with the

king, under whom they worked. In this system, Srivijaya's kings maintained their central position by carefully building alliances of regional leaders against rebels. Many of these leaders had private armies, the commanders of which were responsible to both the king and the local leader. Palembang's own royal army, paid for with imperial taxes and trade receipts, was large but not large enough to undertake major wars on its own. When the army of Srivijaya went on large campaigns, it did so as an organization of regional armies. It seemed a shaky system, yet by the beginning of the eighth century Palembang's *datu* was unmistakably the ruler of an empire, whose carefully planned succession reflects a well-established central government.

A structured court bureaucracy helped to maintain this imperial monarchy. One division of the bureaucracy was made up of the king's judges, who administered a common court law throughout the provinces. Another group was made up of priests, advisers on Indian court ritual, which remained important in legitimizing the ruler's authority, at the same time as Buddhism was being used to unify the realm and consolidate the ruler's control of the Srivijayan state. Still another category of official was that of market supervisor. Appearing deceptively low in the court hierarchy, this post was of key importance in an empire in which much of the surplus wealth came from international trade. The market inspector was responsible for setting and enforcing throughout Srivijaya's territories standard measures for gold and silver, the currency of trade, along with standard market weights and measures, and to some extent even standard prices for the main trade commodities. Market stability was of critical importance in attracting and holding foreign trade.

Srivijaya's success in maintaining law and order on the seas of the strait and in its markets brought an increase of shipping to its ports, which encouraged the empire to expand still further. Many of the goods sought by international traders originated in the islands to the south and east;

Srivijaya accordingly moved in that direction, taking over by force or agreement the main port towns of eastern Java. For example, the marriage of a Srivijayan princess into the Sailendra dynasty, which controlled the strongest state on Java during the eighth and ninth centuries, integrated that state into the Srivijayan sphere. Although the Sailendra continued to rule their central Javanese realm independently, the union meant that the Srivijayan Empire had little challenge to its dominance of Southeast Asian trade over the next 100 years.

The wealth the empire gathered produced not only better standards of living for the region's peoples but also large temple complexes, such as the great eighth-century Buddhist monument at Borobudur on the island of Java, which helped knit the people of the region together under a common religious ideology. Srivijaya's control of international trade through its ports along the Straits of Melaka enabled the Srivijayan ruler to send a costly mission to China as late as 1017, referring to himself as "king of the ocean lands." Yet, Srivijaya faced challenges from rulers in eastern Java and succumbed in 1025 to an attack by the Cholas from the Indian subcontinent. This attack dispersed the international trade that had been concentrated in Srivijayan ports. The empire weakened and collapsed when trade shifted and its balanced system of alliances between land and maritime interests crumbled, as it did during the late eleventh century.

During the same period, new powers were also emerging on the Southeast Asian mainland, in the areas of modern Burma, Sri Lanka, Cambodia, and Thailand. At a time when its control of the Melaka Strait trade was threatened by the Pagan (Burma) and the Ayudhya (Thai) monarchies, Srivijaya

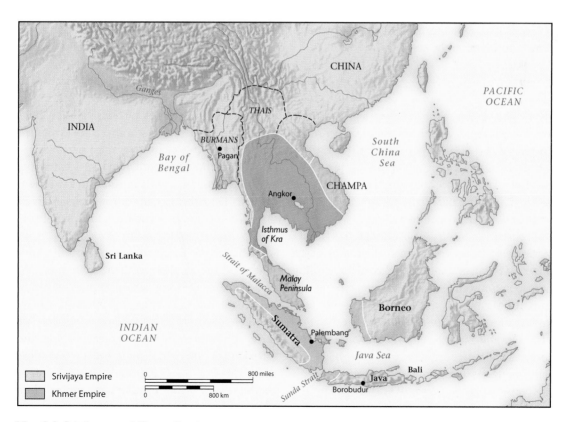

Map 9.1 Srivijayan and Khmer Empires.

was challenged by the advent of a new religion, Islam, and by merchants who were Muslim. It was unable to meet the dual challenge. Malay shipping in the region was replaced by Arab and Persian vessels, with owners and merchants who, given the opportunity, preferred to deal with Muslim harbormasters and ship chandlers. In some of the smaller ports of northern Sumatra, these Muslim port officers began to appear in increasing numbers. The Srivijayan Empire broke up into a collection of smaller independent city-states and trading confederations such as Majapahit, the clearest successor to Srivijaya. Several of these polities found their legitimacy in claims of descent from Srivijaya's ruling family. All used the administrative and ideological legacy of the old empire, including the established patterns of standardized weights and measures and coinage. As Funan's legacy in mainland Southeast Asia survived in its successor states, so too did the tradition of the Srivijayan Empire live on in polities that claimed legitimacy through links to the era of Srivijayan power.

Khmer

On the Southeast Asian mainland, the Khmer Empire (802–1432) at its height in the twelfth century controlled probably a million people in the area of modern Cambodia, Laos, Thailand, and parts of Burma, Vietnam, and the Malay peninsula. A network of canals used for both transportation and irrigation linked the Khmer state physically, and reservoirs helped control the uneven rainfall of a monsoon climate by storing monsoon rainwater for later use.

Both Hinduism and Buddhism provided sanction for the authority of rulers and the common cultural and religious bonds among the Khmer people (see Chapter 5). Their rulers initially blended Hinduism with indigenous beliefs to consolidate their power over their expanding territory, and the Sanskrit language was adopted by the Khmer court. Worship of the Hindu god Shiva, who was identified as the "Lord of the Mountain," was connected with indigenous beliefs in the sanctity of mountains, the home of ancestral spirits. Shiva worship was formalized in the *devaraja* (god-king) cult of the ruler Jayavarman II (ca. 770–834), who built the Khmer state through a combination of conquest and the formation of a network of personal alliances. Following Jayavarman, statues of gods were fused with the person of the ruler, symbolized by the merging of the monarch's personal title with the name of a god. After the twelfth century, at the capital city of Angkor Thom, Buddhist dominance was reflected in the Bayon temple complex façade, which portrayed the Buddhist deity Lokeshvara. This Buddhist deity was identified with the builder of Angkor Thom, Jayavarman VII (r. ca. 1181–1218), whose authority was reinforced through the new *Buddharaja* (Buddha-king) cult.

Massive public works projects carried out by the Khmer monarchy, such as the Hindu temple complex of Angkor Wat (*wat* means "temple") built in the twelfth century are testimony to the ability of the Khmer state to collect and redistribute economic resources on a huge scale. This was accomplished through a network of temples, which served as centers of redistribution from villages to local temples and on up through a hierarchy to the central temple in the king's capital. In this way both material wealth and symbolic capital, the cultural and religious symbols used to integrate Khmer society, were distributed through a complex temple network spread throughout the realm.

Although the Khmer did not control sea trade that would have allowed them to connect the agricultural hinterland with maritime commerce, as did Srivijaya, both empires controlled massive resources, incorporated different peoples and cultures within their realms, and created ideological foundations using both Hinduism and Buddhism that unified the region under their control. In both the Srivijayan and Khmer empires, new collective identities were constructed through religion and supported by economic wealth

9.2 Aerial view of Angkor Wat, early twelfth century CE.

produced by the labor of people who engaged in agriculture or both riverine and maritime trade. Temples and other religious monuments were vital expressions of collective identity as they manifested the material wealth commanded by rulers and sanctioned by religion. Personal alliances lay at the core of both empires, and no doubt at the local level where they were part of everyday life that remained unrecorded. People continued to identify closely with kin and village, even as they dwelt in the shadow of mighty empires.

Other mainland states, such as Pagan in Burma along the Irrawaddy River (mid-eleventh to late thirteenth centuries), were similarly based on irrigated rice agriculture and built religious monuments that both reflected the use of Hinduism and Buddhism to consolidate control over local communities and testified to the ability of their rulers to commandeer sufficient resources to construct such monuments to their own power and glory, often identifying themselves with Hindu or Buddhist deities. Wealthy and powerful though their rulers were, mainland states such as Pagan Burma could not control the sea trade that would

have allowed them to connect their agricultural hinterland with the maritime or riverine trade and expand into empires as Srivijaya and Khmer did.

Nomads and empire in Eurasia: The Mongol Empire

In the early thirteenth century, the foundations were laid for the largest contiguous land-based empire in human history. The Mongol Empire endured for only a century, but it had a profound impact on world history. Sometime around the close of the eleventh and the beginning of the twelfth centuries, Mongol clans began to organize into tribal collectives under the leadership of chieftains whose power was based on personal loyalty. By 1200, the Mongols had joined together in a large confederation. Under the leadership of Chinggis (ca. 1162–1227, also spelt Genghis), who was elected khan (chief) in 1206 by an assembly of tribal chieftains, they began to bring other peoples in the region, such as Turks and Uighurs, under their control. With this step, the Mongol conquest of Asia began. Chinggis was a charismatic political leader who organized the Mongol tribes, and a brilliant military strategist who led the Mongol armies to victory. Along with the military strength that made conquest possible, the Mongols were driven to conquest in part by the uncertain nature of their economic base, which depended to a degree on the fluctuating fortunes of trade. Their livelihood was made even more precarious by climatic change around 1200 in the form of colder weather, which caused them to seek pasturage for their animals farther south.

Religious sanction for the authority of Chinggis Khan and the conquest of the world came from the sky god, the principal deity of the steppe. Under Chinggis's leadership, a written script, adapted from the Uighur script, was created for the Mongol language, and a code of customary law was issued to provide guidance first for the administration of the Mongol tribes and later, as it was modified, for the governing of conquered lands and peoples. Succession to the position of khan, however, was not institutionalized, and at Chinggis' death, despite his stated will that he be succeeded by his third son, Ögödei (1186–1241),

there was no clear successor. In 1229, two years after Chinggis's death, the territories under Mongol control were divided among Chinggis's grandson Batu (d. 1255), who became the khan of the Qipchaq Khanate (the western lands, eventually including Russia); Chinggis's second son Chaghadai (ca. 1185–1242), who assumed control of central Asia (the Chaghadai Khanate); and Chinggis's youngest son, who was assigned responsibility for the Mongolian homeland and north China. In a gesture of compliance with Chinggis's will, Ögödei became the *khaghan*, or Khan of Khans, ruler over all Mongol domains.

Before his death in 1227, Chinggis's armies had swept across much of Eurasia, laying the foundations for later, extended assaults on Europe, Russia, the Middle East, and China. Europeans justified their failure to halt the Mongol invasion by attributing great savagery to the Mongol armies and by claiming that they were the "scourge of God" who had made an alliance with Satan. They were accused of cutting an ear off every Christian they killed. Following the initial success of their invasion in 1240, the Mongols settled down on

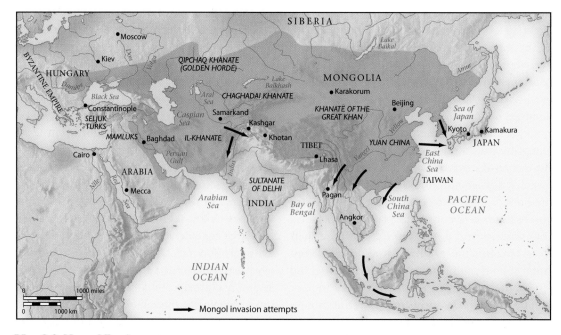

Map 9.2 Mongol Empire.

the Hungarian plain in the Danube Valley, where they established a government administration. They appointed judges and officials, placed Mongols in charge of towns, and proclaimed amnesty for any who would recognize Mongol authority. Then, just as the Mongol leaders were making plans to resume their assault and penetrate Europe further, in 1241 news came that Ögödei, the Khan of Khans, was dead. Mongol custom required that, after the death of the khan, all his heirs, wherever they might be, must return to Karakorum in Mongolia for the election of a new khan. The importance of this custom outweighed the potential conquest of Europe, and accordingly the Europeans were spared.

As the Mongols expanded into China, Russia, and Islamic lands in West Asia, they confronted vastly different political, religious, and social conditions in each region. Despite continuing conflicts among themselves over leadership, Mongol rulers in each Khanate (territory ruled by a khan) of the empire were able to implement an efficient administrative system that integrated Chinese, Muslim, Turkic, and native elements.

Mongol conquest of Islamic lands

Successive attacks on the realm of the Abbasid caliphate finally resulted in the fall of Baghdad in 1258 to the Mongol leader Hülegü, signaling the demise of the caliphate and the beginning of the Il-Khanate, Mongol rule of a territory that encompassed modern Iran, Turkmenistan, Iraq (plus trans-Euphrates Syria), and Azerbaijan, as well as much of the Caucasus, Turkey, and Afghanistan. The Mongol Il-khans used Persian advisers such as the famous Jewish physician and convert to Islam, the chronicler Rashid al-Din (1247–1318). They exacted tribute, but also used Persian methods of taxation indigenous to the territory. The Mongols were generally tolerant of Islam and other religions practiced in their realm, including Nestorian Christianity, Buddhism, and Judaism. They continued to practice their native shamanism, but gradually some Mongol leaders converted to Islam. Hülegü's wife was a Nestorian Christian, but his son Tegüder Ahmad (r. 1282–84) became a practicing Muslim and promoted Islam during his brief reign. His nephew, Arghun (r. 1284–91), who struggled for power with his uncle and criticized adherence to Islam on the part of the Il-Khanate, was married to a Byzantine Christian princess and during his own reign practiced tolerance toward all religions. In 1295 the Mongol Il-khan Ghazan (r. 1295–1304) publicly converted to Islam and encouraged other Mongols in the Il-Khanate to convert, too. Conversion to Islam by the Mongol conquerors facilitated rule of their largely Muslim subjects, but also set off massacres of Christians and Jews as Islam once again assumed its privileged position in the realm of the Il-Khanate.

Mongol rule of China

China under the Mongols shared some features of Mongol rule of the Il-Khanate, but also differed in significant ways. China was home to a population 60 times that of the entire Mongol population of Asia, with a rich agricultural economic base. Heir to a complex political and cultural tradition preserved by a highly educated elite, China presented a formidable challenge to its Mongol rulers.

Beijing, the capital of the Jurchen Jin state, was captured by the armies of Chinggis Khan in 1215. Before the conquest of the Jin was completed in 1234, an official of the Jin government had convinced Ögödei (r. 1229–41), against the advice of other Mongol leaders, not to turn north China into pasturage for the Mongols' herds but to utilize its agricultural productivity to enrich the Mongol rulers. When the Jin state was absorbed by the Mongols, the advanced iron technology and the skilled labor force of north Chinese ironworkers, developed during the Northern Song dynasty, also came under Mongol control. The Mongols' ability to make use of such resources, in

PRIMARY SOURCE: IBN AL-ATHIR ON THE MONGOL CONQUEST OF PERSIA

Ibn al-Athir (1160–1233) traveled widely throughout the Muslim world and wrote a history of the world. He accompanied Saladin and his army in Syria during the Crusades as Saladin attacked the Crusader states. Although he did not live to witness the fall of Baghdad to the Mongols in 1258, his description of the onslaught of the Mongol armies on Muslim lands in 1220–21 powerfully evokes the terror and devastation that accompanied these campaigns.

I say, therefore, that this thing involves the description of the greatest catastrophe and the most dire calamity (of the like of which days and nights are innocent) which befell all men generally, and the Muslims in particular; so that, should one say that the world, since God Almighty created Adam until now, has not been afflicted with the like thereof, he would but speak the truth. For indeed history does not contain anything which approaches or comes near unto it. . .

For even Antichrist will spare such as follow him, though he destroy those who oppose him, but these Tatars spared none, slaying women and men and children, ripping open pregnant women and killing unborn babes. Verily to God do we belong, and unto Him do we return, and there is no strength and no power save in God, the High, the Almighty, in face of this catastrophe, whereof the sparks flew far and wide, and the hurt was universal; and which passed over the lands like clouds driven by the wind. For these were a people who emerged from the confines of China, and attacked the cities of Turkestan, like Kashghar and Balasaghun, and thence advanced on the cities of Transoxiana, such as Samarqand, Bukhara and the like, taking possession of them, and treating their inhabitants in such wise as we shall mention; and of them one division then passed on into Khurasan, until they had made an end of taking possession, and destroying, and slaying, and plundering, and thence passing on to Ray, Hamadan and the Highlands, and the cities contained therein, even to the limits of Iraq, whence they marched on the towns of Adharbayjan and Arraniyya, destroying them and slaying most of their inhabitants, of whom none escaped save a small remnant; and all this in less than a year; this is a thing whereof the like has not been heard.

And when they had finished with Adharbayjan and Arraniyya, they passed on to Darband-i-Shirwan, and occupied its cities, none of which escaped save the fortress wherein was their King; wherefore they passed by it to the countries of the Lan and the Lakiz and the various nationalities which dwell in that region, and plundered, slew, and destroyed them to the full. And thence they made their way to the lands of Qipchaq, who are the most numerous of the Turks, and slew all such as withstood them, while the survivors fled to the fords and mountain-tops, and abandoned their country, which these Tatars overran. All this they did in the briefest space of time, remaining only for so long as their march required and no more.

Another division, distinct from that mentioned above, marched on Ghazna and its dependencies, and those parts of India, Sistan and Kirman which border thereon, and wrought therein deeds like unto the other, nay, yet more grievous. Now this is a thing the like of which ear has not heard; for Alexander, concerning whom historians agree that he conquered the world, did not do so with such swiftness, but only in the space of about ten years; neither did he slay, but was satisfied that men should be subject to him. But these Tatars conquered most of the habitable globe, and the best, the most flourishing and most populous part thereof, and that whereof the inhabitants were the most advanced in character and conduct, in about a year; nor did any country escape their devastations which did not fearfully expect them and dread their arrival.

Moreover they need no commissariat, nor the conveyance of supplies, for they have with them sheep, cows, horses, and the like quadrupeds, the flesh of which they eat, naught else. As for their beasts which they ride, these dig into the earth with their hoofs and eat the roots of plants, knowing naught of barley. And so, when they alight anywhere, they have need of nothing from without. As for their religion, they worship the sun when it rises, and regard nothing as unlawful, for they eat all beasts, even dogs, pigs, and the like; nor do they recognise the marriage-tie, for several men are in marital relations with one woman, and if a child is born, it knows not who is its father.

Therefore Islam and the Muslims have been afflicted during this period with calamities wherewith no people hath been visited. These Tatars (may God confound them!) came from the East, and wrought deeds which horrify all who hear of them, and which you shall, please God, see set forth in full detail in their proper connection. And of these was the invasion of Syria by the Franks (may God curse them!) out of the West, and their attack on Egypt, and occupation of the port of Damietta therein, so that Egypt and Syria were like to be conquered by them, but for the grace of God and the help which He vouchsafed us against them, as we have mentioned under the year 614 [1217–18 CE]. Of these, moreover, was that the sword was drawn between those who escaped from these two foes, and strife was rampant, as we have also mentioned: and verily unto God do we belong and unto Him do we return! We ask God to vouchsafe victory to Islam and the Muslims, for there is none other to aid, help, or defend the True Faith. But if God intends evil to any people, naught can avert it, nor have they any ruler save Him. As for these Tatars, their achievements were only rendered possible by the absence of any effective obstacle; and the cause of this absence was that Muhammad Khwarazmshah had overrun the lands, slaying and destroying their Kings, so that he remained alone ruling over all these countries; wherefore, when he was defeated by the Tatars, none was left in the lands to check those or protect these, that so God might accomplish a thing which was to be done.

Source: Edward G. Browne, *A Literary History of Persia*
(Cambridge: Cambridge University Press, 1902), pp427–31.

addition to the agricultural output of north China and eventually that of the fertile Yangzi delta, was a crucial factor in the continued expansion of the Mongol Empire in the decades after Chinggis's death. With the conquest of Jin, the Mongols were also able to make use of Jin institutions that had been adapted from Chinese models. The Mongol experience with the Jin state in north China made the transition to ruling over the entire population of China relatively smooth.

Chinese political ideology favored the adaptation of Mongol rule, in that the Mandate of Heaven in theory could be conferred on any ruler, and non-Chinese peoples, including most recently the Jurchen rulers of the Jin state in north China, had a long history of establishing states and kingdoms within China's borders. But many Confucian scholars nevertheless scorned serving their Mongol lords, regarding them as "barbarian" conquerors. While some members of the Chinese scholar-official elite served the Mongols as administrators, others withdrew from public life and refused to become officials in Khubilai Khan's administration. Khubilai and his successors did adopt Chinese institutions and practices to a considerable degree, including the renewal of the civil service examination system in 1315, although the Mongols instituted ethnic quotas for examination degrees that seriously disadvantaged Chinese in favor of Mongols and other non-Chinese peoples, such as the Uighurs. Khubilai built a new capital on the ruins of the Jurchen Jin capital, site of the modern capital of Beijing and the Chinese imperial capital without interruption from 1421 until the present.

Mongol rule of Russia

Mongol rule of the principalities of Rus' differed dramatically from that of both the Il-Khanate and China. As they advanced among the peoples of the southern Russian steppe during the winter of 1237–38, the conquerors were preceded by envoys demanding that the inhabitants of the steppe accept Mongol supremacy. Resistance led to the forceful taking of fortresses and occupation of territories, including the north Russian forest lands as well as the southern steppe. The invaders were determined to break the power of the Russian princes and to leave them no escape. By early 1238, the north Russian principalities had ceased to exist, and the Mongols turned south into the steppes to recuperate before undertaking new advances westward into Europe.

The Mongols controlled the Russian princes from the steppe lands of the Qipchaq Khanate, where the Mongols mixed together with Turkic tribes who had inhabited this territory long before the coming of the Mongols. Most of these Turkic peoples were Muslim, and gradually many Mongols converted to Islam. The Mongols

9.3 Khubilai Khan and his wife Chabi on a cookout. Detail of a Persian miniature in the Bibliothèque Nationale de France, Paris. Even after their successful empire-building, Mongol rulers tried to preserve aspects of their pastoral way of life, as portrayed in this depiction of Khubilai Khan and his wife cooking over a campfire beside their tents.

continued to pasture their herds on the steppe grasslands, while exacting tribute from the Russian principalities, which were largely Christian. Thus Mongol rule of Russia was indirect, unlike Mongol rule in the Il-Khanate and in China.

The fall and legacy of the Mongol Empire

The Mongols were defeated by a Russian army in 1380, the beginning of a process that was to drive them back into Asia. The princes of Muscovy (the region of modern Moscow) assumed leadership of this effort and accordingly gained control of the emerging Russian state. One of them, Ivan the Great (r. 1462–1505), who proclaimed himself czar (ruler) of all the Russias, succeeded in pushing the Mongols out of north Russia and drove them eastward beyond the Ural mountains.

Beginning in the 1350s, rebellions led by the Chinese against their Mongol conquerors gradually brought an end to Mongol rule there. The effects of these rebellions were exacerbated by power struggles among the Mongol leaders that seriously weakened their authority and control. When the Yuan (Mongol) dynasty fell in 1368 and the restoration of native Chinese rule under the Ming was declared, other Khanates of the Mongol Empire similarly began to crumble.

The Mongols had also moved into South Asia, where they established themselves in India. An enormous peninsula jutting out from the Eurasian landmass, divided from other lands by sea and by the mighty Himalayan mountains along its northern border, India is penetrable by only two corridors. The northeast one, through Burma, is long and difficult and not easily used. There are also a number of usable passes in the northwest corridor that link India, through Afghanistan, with Central Asia. These geographical features are significant to the movement of peoples into the relatively isolated subcontinent. Several different Central Asian peoples, who had come under the

sway of Chinggis Khan and his descendants, subsequently invaded India via the northwest corridor. The most famous of these was Tamerlane (1336–1405), who legitimized his rule by claiming descent from Chinggis Khan and created his own empire, from the former territory of the Golden Horde between the Caspian and Black Seas, to northwestern India, and westward to Syria, with his capital at Samarkand in present-day Uzbekistan.

Chinggis and his successors in the thirteenth and early fourteenth centuries had succeeded in creating a huge empire by their military prowess, discipline, and strength, and by their strategic and logistical skill at maneuvering large numbers of troops over long distances. Their military abilities were grounded in their superior horsemanship, honed in the course of Mongol life as nomadic herders and hunters. Their efficient communication network in the form of a courier system operated by riders on horseback was an essential part of their military operations. But their expansion and conquest of the Eurasian world would have stopped short of creating an empire had they not been able to successfully make use of the human and material resources of the lands they conquered to fuel the machinery of expansion and to provide the tools of empire.

Mongol armies linked vast areas of the Eurasian continent, bringing about an era known as the *pax Mongolica*, the "Mongolian peace." What is remarkable about the Mongol Empire is not that it was relatively short-lived but that an empire of such scale and complexity existed at all at a time when communication and transportation were largely dependent on the horse, donkey, and camel. The Mongol courier system was known for its speed and efficiency, and the effectiveness of this communication network, along with military skill and administrative ability, accounts in large part for the rise of the Mongols from a lineage-based society, to a tribal confederation, to one of the most powerful empires in world history. Its very size, however, also contributed to its fragility and brevity, since the Mongol empire incorporated so many different peoples, cultures, and ecologies that it was impossible to create a unitary collective identity with the technological limitations in communication and transportation of the time.

Trade, technology, ecology, and culture: The Mali Empire in West Africa

Mali was not the first empire to occupy the large grasslands region of West Africa that straddled the Sahara, the semi-arid edge of the desert known as the "Sahel" (literally the "shore" of the great ocean of sand, in Arabic) and the inland delta of the Niger River. The Mali Empire (ca. thirteenth–sixteenth centuries) developed from the conquest and union of several smaller states. At its height, Mali covered much of West Africa and incorporated into one polity hunters, herders, nomads, merchants and farmers from many different language groups. Oral traditions credit a single legendary and heroic figure with the final act of unification: Sunjata, the most powerful of the Mali rulers, finally subjected the Soso people to the authority of Mande languages and culture, with the ascendancy of the Keita clan. The praises of Sunjata today are sung by every griot, or Mande oral historian, on behalf of the royal clan. In this way, history was – and still is – used to legitimize the formation of empire.

The epic of Sunjata devotes a major portion of its tale to sorcery and its relationship to political power. All great exploits, including the founding of empires, require control of the supernatural, or **nyama**, which the Mande view as both natural and mystical energy. Access to sorcery is a component of political leadership and as such is needed to wage successful military campaigns, to subdue enemies, and even to protect one's personal fortune. One of the central battles in the history of the Mali Empire is a sorcery war between Sunjata and a rival. Calling on great powers, Sunjata obtained the formula for a substance called

nasi, "power of darkness, a thing used to harm someone." His **griot** poured it over the personal objects and sources of his rival's power, which were duly neutralized, and Sunjata triumphed.

Like many African divine rulers, Sunjata overcame obstacles, exile, and a physical handicap (the inability to walk from birth) in order to demonstrate his power (*nyama*). The griots generally attribute most of the empire's administrative structures and innovations to the reign of Sunjata, who was probably responsible for the division of the empire into two military regions and for the codification of hereditary craft clans. During and after his reign, blacksmithing, leatherworking, and other specialist activities became associated with statecraft. The products of such activities supported the expansion of trade and empire. While praise singers, oral historians who sang and performed the past, helped to spread the ideology, blacksmiths and others provided the tools of empire. Without iron weapons and leather and iron trappings for horses, military success would not have been possible.

Sunjata rebuilt his capital at Niani, where he ruled for about 25 years, until his death. The location of Niani was forgotten for many generations. Archaeologists recently located the probable site of the Malian capital of Niani on the Sankarani River, an area rich in iron and gold. It was well situated on the forest edge to become the intersection of extensive trade routes that linked the different ecological zones of the empire. Excavations have revealed an Arab quarter and a royal villa, as well as stone house foundations and a mosque. Not unlike other well-known West African trading centers, such as Jenné on the Niger, Niani's royal quarter was surrounded by dispersed quarters or villages organized for various trades: smithing, weaving, fishing, leatherworking. Such concentration of specialist activities and the consequent exchange of goods and services controlled by the centralized authority are classic features of most world empires. Their formation having resulted from conquest, their continued control of material wealth not only cements the incorporation of new territories into a single unity but also pays the costs of government.

Management of the trans-Saharan trade was a central feature of the Mali Empire, as well as of its predecessor (Ghana) and successor (Songhai). Mali was situated on an **ecotone**, an area that straddled the borders of desert, sahel, and savanna. The exchange between these regions, which supplied quite different products, also created a lucrative source of income. Internal trade and occasional tributary relations, with outlying regions being tapped for support, proved necessary to the functioning of the empire. Centers of trade such as Jenné, Gao, and Timbuktu were similarly situated on ecotones. However, exchange among zones was not the only way in which ecology played a role in the fortunes of the Mali Empire: much of the expansion of the Mali Empire was made possible by Mande military use of the horse, which made them dependent on certain ecological conditions for its breeding and survival,

and these conditions existed in the savanna grasslands of Mali.

Traders from Mali carefully controlled the breeding and use of horses in West Africa. Reportedly, they rarely traded mares south of the Sahara; therefore, despite their obvious value, horses remained rare items, connoting prestige and status outside the empire. The cavalry was extremely important in gaining a military advantage, particularly in the savanna grasslands. Although many towns in the Sahel had been walled before the introduction of the horse – probably to help control the influx of trade as early as the second-century CE introduction of camels – the number of settlements and villages surrounded by protective mud walls increased during the era of the Mali cavalry. The walls were necessary to stop sudden attacks by warriors on horseback. Here, as in other parts of the world where the horse was successfully exploited, the element of surprise was significant.

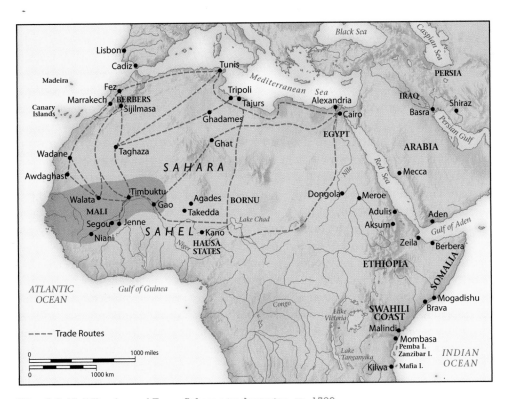

Map 9.3 Mali Empire and Trans-Saharan trade routes, ca. 1500.

Ecological factors played a paramount role in defining and limiting the extent of the spread of Mande culture and society. In tropical Africa, the humidity and presence of the tsetse fly limited the use of the horse. The tsetse fly thrived in damp and swampy conditions and spread diseases that were deadly to horses. Thus, the occurrence of a dry climatic period in West Africa between 1100 and 1500 was particularly significant. Horse breeders, warriors, and traders alike derived great advantage from that progressive dessication, which inhibited the spread of the tsetse fly. With the onset of a drier climate, expansion on horseback was favored over a much wider area. Sunjata's military success over his rival was closely associated with cavalry warfare. Also, the regions occupied by sahelian and savanna vegetation pushed southward at the expense of the southern forests, increasing the territory in which horses could survive. The elliptical lines of Mande expansion with the aid of their cavalry could then extend east and west. Only the rainforest zone, where other ethnic groups lived, remained inhospitable to the empire's warriors and their horses. Conversely, changing ecological conditions during the wet period between about 1500 and 1630 also influenced the fortunes of the empire, which had begun to collapse toward the end of the fifteenth century. Wetter conditions limited the use of cavalry and put the Mali military at a disadvantage.

The era of the Mali Empire was a classical period for Mande language and culture. The military, economic, and commercial relations that bound together the far-flung reaches of the empire were crucially cemented by the power of Mande cultural imperialism. How notions of Mande superiority were extended also helps explain the fluidity of the empire's internal relations. Central to the effective spread of the Mande cultural system and its worldview were power associations controlled by the empire's blacksmiths. The metallurgical skills of smiths were critically important to military success and agricultural operations. But Mande metalworkers were more than essential

9.4 Equestrian figure, Inland Niger Delta Style, Inland Niger Delta Region, Mali (thirteenth to fifteenth centuries). This depiction of horse and larger rider may have suggested the prestige associated with cavalries, either Mali's own warrior culture or those of smaller states and towns, resisting state expansion. Art was used in rituals to extend control over the environment. Source: Franco Khoury.

occupational specialists who followed behind the warriors. They constituted a caste that held *nyama*, the "energy of action" and supernatural power. Together with griots and leatherworkers (who supplied saddles, bridles, sword sheaths, garments, pouches for amulets, and so on), the blacksmiths provided necessary services of both a practical and a spiritual nature.

According to tradition, it was blacksmiths who were responsible for the founding of lodges, or centers for the transmission of Mande culture inside host communities, and they occupied the principal leadership roles within the lodges they established wherever they settled. The lodges were secret associations, that is, membership was limited to those initiated into the secrets of the craft. Like the later mosques of the Islamic era, they offered spiritual protection and moral leadership to the members of their community. They were where Mande speakers gathered. Lodges also maintained control over the physical roads and bridges that linked the empire's commercial realms, by repairing them and ensuring their safety. They protected trade and the trader, who enjoyed the professional affiliations and sense of common community provided to lodge members. While they were dependent on clients both inside the Mande associations and in the larger community, blacksmiths also maintained their separateness and control over the knowledge of smelting, metalworking, ritual, and healing powers that constituted the source of their power. Within the association and against the backdrop of host communities, the griots functioned as amplifiers of Mande superiority, articulating the claims of a heroic age.

The dessication of the first half of the millennium limited the extent of regions that could support iron-smelting activities. Both smelting and smithing required large quantities of wood to make charcoal for fuel. It is also likely, however, that the smiths helped extend the boundaries of their empire by moving further and further afield in search of wood to sustain their industry. The deforestation that resulted from extensive smelting and concentrated smithing opened up savanna woodland to their comrades on horseback. Thus, for many West African peoples, the era of the Mali Empire meant their first encounter with the economic, cultural, and ecological forces of imperialism.

The Mali Empire's fortuitous combination of technological skills, cultural control, and ecological circumstances came to an end in the late fifteenth century, but the legacy of the Mali Empire would be felt far and wide for centuries. Mande words that survive in the languages of forest regions are evidence of the empire's widespread linguistic influence and of the probable prestige associated with using the language of the elite trading culture. In Hausa, the language spoken in northern Nigeria, for example, the word for "Muslim" is *Imale*, which suggests that the Mali Empire may also be credited with the diffusion of Islam after the mid-fourteenth century. Through contact with Mande traders, items of technology were dispersed throughout the empire and southward into the West African forest towns and states. The evidence comes from the material culture of places distant from the empire: the use of the horizontal loom for weaving cloth spread from North Africa to the Niger and then southward, as evidenced by the spindle whorls excavated at sites along the Niger and south in the trading town of Begho in modern Ghana; the introduction of the horse-mounted cavalry in the Yoruba state of Oyo, in Nigeria, spread from the savanna through a gap in the forest; Arabic-inscribed brass vessels appear in the towns of the Akan (Ghana) forest. Long after the fall of Mali, the institutions of lodges remained in societies from the west Atlantic to the Niger, albeit reduced in power and influence. There remained as well the voices of the griots, whose ancestors had created the heroes of the Mande world and who continued to sing the praises of Sunjata, recalling the events of past centuries. In so doing, they breathed life into the history of the Mali Empire long after the walls of its palaces had crumbled.

Empires in the Americas

Earlier in this century, historians wrote of trade as "the great civilizer." Definitions of civilization aside, there is no doubt that trade has supported increasingly complex social and political orders throughout the world. As we have seen with the Southeast Asian empires of Khmer and Srivijaya, maritime and riverine trade was the basis of the knotting of political ties that bound diverse communities together under centralized rule. Though based on overland rather than maritime or riverine trade, both the Mexica-Aztec and Incan Empires of the fifteenth century were the culmination of empire-building based on complex systems of trade and tribute in central Mexico and in the Andean highlands of South America. As Hinduism, Buddhism, and Islam in Southeast Asian empires, and both Islam and indigenous beliefs in Mali, provided sanctions for rulers, for both the Mexica-Aztecs and the Incas, religion played a central role in legitimizing the power of ruling elites and in sanctioning warfare and the exaction of tribute from conquered territories.

The Mexica-Aztec Empire

With the demise of the great city of Teotihuacán in the Valley of Mexico (ca. 750 CE) and the abandonment of Mayan cities in the Yucatán peninsula by around 800 CE, the Toltecs rose to power. The Toltec Empire grew to be extensive, stretching over much of central Mexico and the former Mayan territories. Evidence of trade between the Toltecs and their neighbors to the north suggests that the Toltecs' influence reached far beyond the limits of their political control, perhaps even to regions as distant as the Mississippian culture in North America.

Following the collapse of the Toltecs in about 1150, city-states in the Valley of Mexico competed with one another to become the Toltecs' heirs. Known for their skill as warriors, the Mexica-Aztecs gradually established dominance over rival groups in the Valley of Mexico, where, in the aftermath of the Toltec collapse, the population was concentrated around a string of life-sustaining lakes. Claiming Toltec ancestry to legitimize their conquests, the Mexica-Aztecs continued the Toltec concerns with genealogy and militarism, along with religious rituals, including human sacrifice and ritual cannibalism.

The Mexica-Aztec religion drew on common Mesoamerican traditions, including those of the Olmecs, the Mayas, and the Toltecs, providing an identity rooted in the past that could be adapted to the needs of a new political order. The most important ideological change associated with the Mexica-Aztec transition from wandering warrior groups to empire was the elaboration of ancient Mesoamerican religious beliefs and practices relating warfare to human sacrifice. Combining the Mexica-Aztec patron god Huitzilopochtli (the sun) and their own military ambitions with an ancient vision of a constant struggle among the forces of the universe, Mexica-Aztec belief made the regular appearance of the sun dependent on the continuation of military exploits and human sacrifice. The sacrifice of humans was tied to the sun god's demand for ritual offerings, and war was necessary to provide sacrificial victims. Warfare was imagined as the earthly reenactment of the titanic battle waged across the skies, the sacred war of the sun, which daily had to fight evil to make its way from east to west. Only human sacrifice could assist in the positive outcome of this sacred event and thus ensure the daily rising of the sun.

The Mexica-Aztec ruler eventually became identified with both secular authority and divine power, a representative of the gods on Earth. In Mexica-Aztec theology, human sacrifice and wars of conquest were combined with the political authority of the ruler as aspects of a state cult. Mexica-Aztec rulers believed that two things were necessary to maintain the empire: tribute in food and raw materials from conquered peoples in outlying provinces, and sacrificial victims. Warfare provided both. The tribute gained was a major consequence of the warfare waged on behalf of the empire, which included most of Mesoamerica. It has been estimated that millions of pounds of maize, beans, and chocolate, and millions of cotton cloaks, war costumes, feathers, shields, and precious stones, were drawn to the Mexica-Aztec center at Tenochtitlán each year.

Mexica-Aztec society was profoundly urban. In the fifteenth century, approximately one-quarter of the population of the Valley of Mexico resided in cities and towns. The Mexica-Aztec capital of

Tenochtitlán, the site of modern Mexico City near the ancient center of Teotihuacán, was built on swampland in the Valley of Mexico. This and other urban centers were supported by the rural populations of the surrounding areas, who were required to pay tribute and engage in trade. A specialized class of long-distance traders functioned as "advance men," or merchant-spies, on behalf of the state. They would be followed by warriors whose military success ensured a steady flow of goods. The successful maintenance of the relationship between the urban center and the hinterland, compelled by military control exercised by Mexica-Aztec warriors, was essential to the empire's survival. The administration of the Mexica-Aztec Empire was carried out by an elaborate bureaucracy of officials, including tax collectors, judges, priests, ambassadors, treasurers, and a security force. Occupants of such positions were appointed by the Mexica-Aztec ruler from either the nobility or warrior classes. Each status carried with its title well-defined privileges, duties, and powers. They were distinguished by observable differences in dress, accommodation, diet, and the respect accorded them.

A good way of assessing the distribution of power and the allocation of social status is by comparing the tribute commitments of various groups. In Mexica-Aztec society, which can be visualized as a pyramidal structure, tribute was based on class affiliations and economic specialization. The nobility, at the apex of the pyramid, provided military service, as did the class of professional warriors, who could achieve a higher

Map 9.4 Mexica-Aztec and Incan Empires.

status through bravery than the one they had been born into. Further down the pyramid were commoners and farmers. Their labor and production supported those above. Merchants and craft specialists provided the goods that flowed through the arteries of the empire. In the more distant reaches of the empire, trade was conducted and tribute paid in regional specialties, such as feathers or obsidian. The much larger population at the pyramid's base was composed of persons with limited or almost no rights. Slavery existed as both a temporary condition, into which destitute individuals voluntarily sold themselves or their children to pay debts or were sent as punishment for crimes, and as the permanent status of prisoners of war. Prisoners of war often became the unfortunate victims of ritual torture and sacrifice by the state.

The rulers of the Mexica-Aztec Empire explained the need for wars as a means of obtaining slaves for sacrifice, rather than as an economic enterprise. A kind of circular logic maintained that sacrificial victims could be obtained through war, while war could be waged successfully only by sacrificing victims. Equally important were the complex systems of roads and waterways that brought goods and peoples to central markets. The complex tributary empire was a violent world in which war was deemed necessary and duly glorified.

The Incan Empire in South America

Like the Mexica-Aztecs in Mesoamerica, the Incan Empire in South America rose to power in the fifteenth century by building on earlier cultures in the region between the Pacific Ocean and the chain of Andes mountains extending along the western flank of the continent. The Incan Empire covered a highly diverse topographical area as it descended from mountains as high as 5–6.5 kilometers (three or four miles), down upland basins and plains, and across a narrow desert strip

transected by small rivers to the ocean shore. In the uplands, terraces and spillways were necessary for cultivation; in the desert, canals were essential. These differing environments required and enabled a variety of human activities and gave rise to the organized exploitation of these activities through a centralized political order. Systematic authority was essential for managing reciprocal production, and the movement and exchange of goods necessitated a hierarchical political organization.

Efforts by other Andean peoples to control the area of the Incan Empire, six times the size of modern France, were made as early as 800, but they were unsuccessful. The two centuries before the establishment of Incan dominance in the fifteenth century were, in fact, a period of political fragmentation. In 1400, the Incan state, one of several small states, was about 200 years old. During the reign of Pachacuti Inca (r. 1438–71), the expansion that created the Incan Empire began after a vision in which Pachacuti (whose name means "he who remakes the world") was told that he would conquer many peoples. The Incan Empire was vast but short-lived; it is considered to have ended with the Spanish conquest in 1536.

Expanding from their center, Cuzco, the Incas created a vast state spread along the western coast of South America for more than 4,300 kilometers (2,700 miles), from modern Colombia to modern Chile. The area contained an estimated 9–13 million inhabitants who, prior to the Incan conquest, had resided in agricultural communities under the leadership of local chieftains. The Incas' success in establishing control was only partially the result of their military prowess.

If the Incas' success at empire-building cannot be wholly explained by their military power, it can be understood in terms of their organizational skill and by the power of their religion. As they conquered, they co-opted, organized, and converted. They aimed to be beneficent, lenient conquerors, preferring peaceful incorporation of local communities to the destruction of those who resisted. Those who acquiesced to Incan control avoided being plundered. Chieftains of conquered areas who did not resist were adopted into the structure of the empire as it emerged. Some were co-opted by marriage into the royal family; blood and lineage ties were important. By contrast, those who resisted the Incas or rebelled were harshly dealt with and subject to severe penalties ranging from mass removal and redistribution to slaughter. The ideology of conquest claimed that Incan rule brought reason; that is, it saved people from themselves and lifted them out of savagery and war, out of the chaos that had existed before the conquest.

Those who accepted Incan conquest also adopted the cult connected with the Incan ruler, for the Incas propagated their religion as they conquered. The founders of the Incan Empire called their supreme god Viracocha ("Lord"), after an earlier ruler, and they considered him equivalent to the sun. According to the legends transmitted by the court historians, the first Inca was created to propagate and spread the cult of the sun. Pachacuti, who consolidated the empire, worked out a ceremonial order and theology that elevated Viracocha to a position of supremacy over other gods and that justified expansion in ways that appeared to serve the interests of both conqueror and conquered.

Like the Mexica-Aztec rulers, who claimed descent from the god Huitzilopochtli, the Sapa Inca, or "Sole Ruler," was believed to be a descendant of the sun god and his representative on Earth. Incorporating the Andean traditions of ancestor worship, the mummified bodies of dead kings became the tangible link between the Incan people and their pantheon. To preserve this link and to ensure the continuity of their own political order, the Incas had to maintain the royal dead in fitting splendor for perpetuity; thus a constant income was necessary, and this could be supplied only by continual conquests. Upon every conquest, the Incas made a thorough inventory of the people, land, and resources they had conquered, all of which accrued to the Sapa Inca.

The cult of the sun was an integral part of the imperial apparatus; it had elaborate ritual, a large priesthood, and many shrines. The Temple of the Sun built by the Inca Pachacuti at Cuzco was the center of state religion and housed the mummified bodies of former rulers. As a basis of imperial control, the Incan religion worked together with the all-encompassing bureaucracy, which the cult sanctioned and sustained. For example, Incan law, which was orally transmitted, was in the hands of judges. Breaking an Incan law was sacrilege, punishable by death. Priests, as guardians of morals, confessors, and imposers of penance, maintained the close connection of religion and law, of cult and state.

Such an empire was a theocracy, in which virtually everything belonged to the Sapa Inca, the personification of the state: all land, all gold and silver, all labor (a form of tax as well as a duty), all people. As in many other societies, women were considered a form of property. Adultery, therefore, was punished as a crime against property. Subjects of the Sapa Inca were all provided land, although they might be moved from place to place according to bureaucratic inventories of people and resources, as a guarantee against sedition and rebellion. The state did its best to keep people busy and well fed, storing large quantities of food and clothing against years of hardship and need. Administrative officials were held responsible if anyone went hungry.

Private property, with the possible exception of clothing and houses, did not exist. Taxes were levied in labor, and trade seems to have consisted largely of barter on the local level and a government monopoly over long distances. Indeed, for ordinary people, mobility was minimal; they were expected to stay at home and work. Guards controlled entry and exit to towns; crossing a bridge was allowed only when one was on official business.

The Sapa Inca's authority was maintained by an elaborate hierarchical administrative system, by blood lineage ties, and by his religious function. All his subjects were divided into groups, arranged in an orderly fashion of responsibility; for example, fathers were responsible for their children's actions. Another organizational pattern had to do with labor: all subjects had assigned tasks. The major labor obligation was cultivation of the land, which was divided into three types: what was necessary for the state, what was necessary for the cult of the sun, what was necessary for the people. Other general labor duties included keeping llama flocks, which were state-owned, and keeping up roads, bridges, and public monumental buildings.

The vast Inca state was spread over a mountainous territory of more than 4,830 kilometers (3,000 miles), linked together by an elaborate system of roads and bridges. It is possible that some of these roads date from the time of earlier Andean civilizations, perhaps even Chavín de Huántar, but under the imperial structure of the Incas these and other highways became a lifeline for the political and economic integration of the state.

Roads ranged from narrow footpaths to terraced and fortified structures with pavements, walls, and canals. Bridges were woven and sometimes suspended structures spanning rivers and mountainous chasms. Government messengers, armies, and trading caravans traveled their length, stopping at one or more of the several thousand roadside lodges or rest-stops that also served as local seats of government, spread along the imperial highway. Few Incas could have traveled all the roadways by foot in a single lifetime, but many journeys were no doubt facilitated by the use of the domesticated llama, which carried loads of 45 kilograms (100 pounds) at high altitudes.

Controlling this highly organized society required an elaborate bureaucracy, one that continued to grow as the empire expanded. Closest to the person of the Sapa Inca, at the center of power, was a council, though its somewhat vague authority decreased as the empire grew. Also important was a corps of learned men and poets whose regular responsibility was putting together

the official version of Incan history, an important task in maintaining authority. As there was no system of writing, these men memorized their political-historical accounts, which were modified when necessary to create versions effective for indoctrinating and controlling conquered peoples.

At its height, the Incan Empire was divided into four **viceroyalties** subdivided into provinces, each of which contained 40,000 families. Viceroys and provincial governors ranked with imperial court officials as the dominant aristocracy of the empire. These aristocrats had their own style of dress and their own language, but they were charged with imposing the ideology of Incan rule on their subjects. It was their duty to unite the remnants of earlier local cultures that functioned under the Incan imprint. Beneath the high aristocracy were intricate, hierarchically connected cadres of people, ending with family units. Fathers were responsible for their families and cadre leaders for their respective cadres. The empire remained an amalgam of different units, each contributing to the whole through tribute and trade.

Summary

Empires rose in regions of the globe with widely differing cultural and historical traditions, as well as geographical and environmental conditions. The examples presented here illustrate both the material conditions that led to the expansion of political orders and the concentration of power – geographical location and environmental changes – and the variety of ways in which religion was able to explain and sanction power. Beginning in the twelfth century, a drop in the mean annual temperature in the grasslands inhabited by Mongol peoples pushed them to seek pasturelands for their herds farther south, while the desiccation of West Africa between 1100 and 1500 enabled Mande horse-riders to expand their territorial claims. In both cases, environmental changes set the stage for the rise of empires. Equally important, once empires were built, ideologies that supported imperial rule were constructed from the joining of local community beliefs with either universal religions, as Buddhism in Southeast Asia and Islam in West Africa, or the absorption of local beliefs into a new complex structured by the beliefs of conquerors, as the Mexica-Aztecs and Incas in the Americas.

At the beginning of the first millennium CE, there were many different belief systems in Southeast Asia, all of which had some common elements: animism, ancestor worship, and a sacred role for mountains and the sea. Political leaders gradually adopted key features of Hinduism and Buddhism to sanction their rule and provide a unifying ideology for their states. Later, especially in the fourteenth and fifteenth centuries, Islam in turn was adopted by regional political leaders with much the same unifying results. In each case, foreign belief systems were grafted onto indigenous ones. Foreign religions initially penetrated along trade lines into parts of Southeast Asian society, and thus the demands of commerce and economic motives brought ideas that were then used to support the concentration of power. Nowhere was the role of religion as an aspect of political economy more sharply brought out than in the network of temples that provided the mechanism for the collection and redistribution of wealth in the Khmer state.

Empires such as Srivijaya and Khmer were constructed in part on the foundation of hinterland–port relationships: the hinterland needed the ports for its markets, and the ports depended on the production of the hinterlands for their livelihood. Both were dependent on technology and on the maintenance of sea routes, just as the Mali Empire was dependent on the horse and on caravan routes. Technology was important in the concentration of power in Southeast Asian and West African states: maritime technology in Southeast Asia and the horse and associated technologies of metalworking and leatherworking in both West Africa and Central Asia. Technology is closely related to trade, and empires as well as port city-states in both Southeast Asia and Africa were dependent on trade not only for the resources that sustained them but also, in the case of the Southeast Asian riverine and island empires and the West African empire of Mali, for providing ties that connected distant peoples and places to political centers.

The Mexica-Aztec and Inca Empires were constructed on trade and tribute networks. The Mexica-Aztec and Incan Empires relied on the supply of tribute goods from territories they conquered to support their ruling elites. Military expansion was dependent on both religious sanction and on the economic incentives provided by expanding population. As in Southeast Asian and West African examples, religious ideologies were crucial to the construction of the Mexica-Aztec and Incan Empires. However, religious ideologies that supported military expansion and economic exploitation in these Mesoamerican and Andean empires were based on shared traditions inherited from common predecessors, rather than from the integration of indigenous beliefs and practices with new ones imported from other cultures, such as Hinduism and Buddhism in Southeast Asia and Islam in West Africa.

In the Americas, Mexica-Aztec expansionism was fueled by the desire for goods to feed the growing needs of an increasingly complex culture and society, as well as an expanding population. The relatively loose, far-flung empire of the Mexica-Aztecs was well suited to their purpose of gaining captives for sacrificial purposes, since populations in outlying areas could be viewed as distinct and separate enough to fit the role of sacrificial victims. The Incas exacted tribute from territories they conquered not only to meet the demands of growing cultural complexity but also to sustain their religious ideology through the wealth necessary to support dead kings as links between the human and cosmic orders. The primary function of religious ideology in such highly stratified societies as those of the Mexica-Aztecs and Incas was to justify the existing order, including the unequal distribution of both power and property. Like the Mongols, who incorporated into their imperial administration leaders who submitted to them, the Incas also integrated local rulers who cooperated with them into their administrative hierarchy.

The Mongol Empire was constructed on the basis of military conquest that enabled the expropriation of resources from a vast range of ecological and cultural zones. Military strength honed in the inhospitable environment of the steppe, where horse-riding was a vital skill, was necessary for conquest; but military strength alone was insufficient to enable the Mongols to consolidate their hold over conquered territories. Sophisticated administrative ability was needed to govern and manage the human and material resources of peoples and lands in Central, East and West Asia, Russia, and eastern Europe, which included among their populations nomadic tribesmen, urban dwellers, and farmers. Territories conquered by the Mongols were the home of followers of virtually every major religion of the time, including Buddhism, Islam, Christianity, and Hinduism. Although Mongol religious beliefs originated in steppe shamanism and the Mongols eventually adopted a Tibetan form of Buddhism known as **lamaism**, the Mongol rulers were able to successfully integrate regions with vastly differing religious beliefs in part because they did not attempt to impose their own religion. In other empires, such as that of the Incas, religious ideology was a cornerstone of imperial rule, so local religious traditions had to be incorporated or obliterated by the imperial cult.

Suggested readings

Alcock, Susan, et al. (2001) *Empires: Perspectives from Archaeology and History*, Cambridge: Cambridge University Press. A collection of articles treating, among others, the Persian Achaemenid, Carolingian, Aztec, and Portuguese empires, illustrating different approaches through archaeological and text-based sources.

Conrad, David and Djanka Tassey Conde (2004) *Sunjata: A West African Epic*, Indianapolis: Hackett. A thorough study of this epic across time, as it has continued to evolve in changing historical contexts.

D'Altroy, Terence (2004) *The Incas*, Malden, MA: Blackwell. A comprehensive survey of the Incas by one of the foremost experts.

Dunn, Ross (2004) *The Adventures of Ibn Battuta: A Muslim Traveler of the 14th Century*, Berkeley, CA: University of California Press. New edition of biography of the famous Ibn Battuta, whose accounts of his travels through the Mali Empire remain one of the key sources for its history.

Fitzhugh, William, et al. (2009) *Genghis Khan and the Mongol Empire*, Seattle: University of Washington Press. A collection of articles by experts examining different aspects of the Mongol Empire, from the perspectives of archaeology, history, art, and literature.

Hall, Kenneth (2011) *A History of Early Southeast Asia: Maritime Trade and Societal Development, 100–1500*, Lanham, MD: Rowman & Littlefield. Update of classic study on relationship between trade and the development of early states and societies in Southeast Asia.

Lane, George (2006) *Daily Life in the Mongol Empire*, Westport, CT: Greenwod Press. A lively account of Mongol daily life, including such topics as family life, dwellings, food, and warfare.

Smith, Michael E. (2003) *The Aztecs*, Malden, MA: Blackwell. A lively survey of Aztec life and society by a well-known scholar.

Online resources

Annenberg/CPB, *Bridging World History* (2004) Unit 11 Early Empires <www.learner.org/courses/world history/unit_main_11.html>

The Mongols in World History <afe.easia.columbia.edu/mongols>

Study questions

1. What are the key features that define an empire?
2. What role does environment play in the formation of empires?
3. How do religion and empire reinforce each other?

4. In what ways might religion potentially play a dual role in the rise and fall of empires?

5. What are some of the factors that might precipitate the disintegration and collapse of empires?

6. How have different economies supported the formation of empires?

7. How do nomadic empires differ from other kinds of empires – or do they?

Part II Summary

Mapping order

This image of the African ruler Mansa Musa (r. ca. 1307–32) holding a gold nugget testifies to the reputation for the enormous wealth in gold of his realm, the Mali Empire. Mansa Musa was also famed for his 1324–25 pilgrimage to Mecca, where his lavish gifts of gold in Cairo and Medina as well as Mecca destabilized the economy of the region because of the enormous influx of gold. The portrayal of Mansa Musa shown here is part of the *Catalan Atlas* of 1375, so named because the Catalan (from the Spanish region of Catalonia) language is used for cosmographical, astronomical, and nautical information inscribed on it. The map has been attributed to a Jewish cartographer named Abraham Cresques from Palma, a seaport on the island of Majorca and a center of great cultural diversity as well as maritime trade, including relations with Africa and the Muslim East. Jewish and Muslim traditions converged there, a legacy of the era when Muslim, Christian, and Jewish traditions flourished in al-Andalus (Muslim Spain). Whoever the mapmaker was, the *Catalan Atlas* was undoubtedly influenced by European knowledge of Asia gleaned from the travel accounts of Marco Polo, and of North Africa from Ibn Battuta's writings.

The *Catalan Atlas* represents the peak of medieval cartography, combining innovations such as the first use of the compass rose (showing the cardinal directions) with features of the *mappamundi* tradition, circular maps based on Christian cosmology with Jerusalem at its center and the north at the bottom. It was painted on parchment attached to six wooden panels, a total of three meters (10 feet) in length and 65 centimeters (two feet) in width. The size and circular layout of the atlas suggest it was intended to be placed on a ship's table so that it could be viewed from all different angles and used as a kind of nautical chart.

Much as the *Catalan Atlas* represents the physical features of the known world at the time from the perspective of medieval mapmakers, the chapters of Part II map the ordering of human communities from different perspectives. The chapter on the spread of world religions mapped the movement of Buddhism, Christianity, and Islam across Afro-Eurasia, focusing on the first millennium CE. The next chapter highlighted the variety of economic orders that evolved in different parts of the globe, comparing diverse economic systems in relation to their environments and the kinds of political orders in which they were embedded. The following chapter moved from concerns of how people made their livings and survived to the ways that families sustained – and were sustained by – both communities and individuals. As diverse as family structures were, they were all shaped by religious ideals as promoted by both religious authorities and by states. Yet families were also embedded in larger social groups and intimately tied to ideals and practices of lineages, caste systems, and patron–client relationships, addressed in the next chapter. Finally, empires, the largest-scale political orders, were the subject of the last chapter in Part II. Empires encompassed ideology, economy, and social orders under their

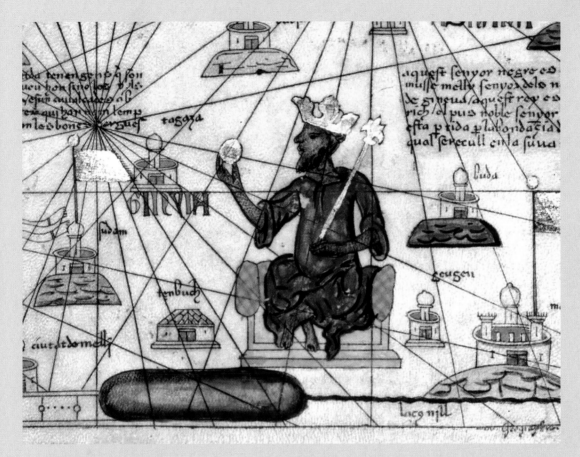

Portrayal of Mansa Musa on the Catalan Atlas, depicting him in the garb, crown, and scepter of a European monarch as he was imagined in the eyes of the mapmaker.

umbrella of political order, integrating the perspectives developed in each of the preceding chapters in this part. The Mali Empire under Mansa Musa exemplified the combination of ideological (Islamic religion and ethnic identity), economic (trade), social (kinship groups), and political tradition (centralized states under the rule of kings) that laid the foundation for empire in West Africa in the fourteenth century. The prominent portrayal of Mansa Musa in the *Catalan Atlas* suggests the wealth and power of this African empire at the time the atlas was made.

Part III

Connections

500–1600 CE

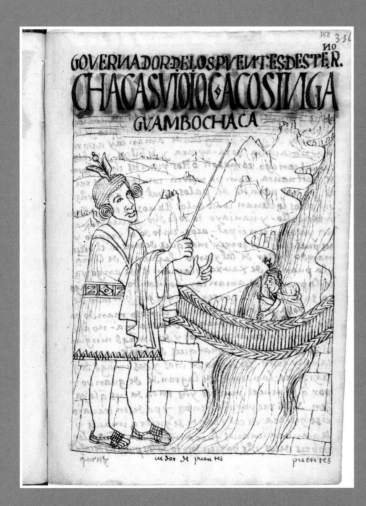

Governor of the bridges of this kingdom, by Guaman Poma (1615). The world history by Inca scholar Felipe Guaman Poma de Ayala, described pre-Columbian traditions and connected them to his own colonial observations after conquest.

Part III Introduction

Like many early states, the Inca of the Andean Highlands traced their political connections in visible lines upon the Earth. Bridges and roads traversed the mountainous terrain, deserts, and coastal regions alike, bringing the distant lands in consort with the central authority of the ruler. Merchants and rulers journeyed the realm, bringing goods and people back to the center. The rulers situated their seats of power within a visible distance from the bones of past rulers in order to emphasize their historical connectedness to their ancestors and a higher spiritual authority. The past was connected to the present and its tracings helped authenticate and legitimate the political and social orders and assured each individual a place in relation to the larger whole.

Part III explores both the variety of connections across space that linked peoples and cultures, and the construction of connections across generations that reflected attempts to interpret and transmit the past. Traditions across the globe were both transmitted and transformed as they encountered each other across geographical and political boundaries.

Chapter 10: Connections across land and sea explores the creation of empires and the spread of religion, which were, along with trade, the most important ways in which connections were established among peoples of the world before 1500. Expanding networks of military, political, economic, and religious ties created connections among cultures and societies in Eurasia, Africa, and within the Americas. This chapter highlights both maritime and land-based connections among societies across the globe before 1500, including the thirteenth-century Afro-Eurasian "world system." In **Chapter 11: Cultural memory: Transmitting traditions**, cultures and societies not only connected with each other across geographical space, they also connected over time with the past, through processes of knowledge transmission and systems of cultural memory. Making use of culturally specific ways of thinking, people across the globe interpreted their pasts and transmitted religious, philosophical, and technological knowledge. This chapter provides a global perspective on knowledge systems and their differing roles in societies, from Greek conceptions of history and Confucian textual traditions in East Asia to medieval theology in Europe and systems of oral transmission of knowledge in Africa. Technology is incorporated as a key aspect of the processes of transmission of traditions.

In **Chapter 12: Commerce and change: Creating a world system**, the emphasis is on how connections both maintain order and create change. Against the backdrop of a thirteenth-century Afro-Eurasian world system, this chapter moves from earlier commercial revolutions in China and Europe to predict the consequences of the rise of mercantilism and the expansion of Europe as the foundation of the sixteenth-century world system. We examine how this reorientation alters patterns and processes in world history.

All humans possess memories they both remember and forget. The task of world historians is to recover the processes and patterns of the past. Among the most important tracings left behind were the movements of people and objects through the establishment of political ties, the spread of religions, and the economics of trade. The theme of connections includes the links between people and place and between individuals and their identities. These are the links that forge the concrete and symbolic remains of the past. Connecting to the past may be inscribed boldly on the Earth or be invisible to the eye, but connections remain powerful testimony to both the commonalities and differences found in the human experience.

10 Connections across land and sea

Maps of Africa before 1500 CE invariably included an image of the king of Mali seated on his throne, holding a gold nugget nearly the size of his head. It was the fourteenth-century Malian ruler and his entourage who had given away so much gold while on hajj, or pilgrimage, to Mecca that the price of gold on the Cairo market had collapsed shortly thereafter. Egyptian chroniclers wrote about the event in the next century, and the traveler Ibn Battuta described the West African ruler around 1350: "[The sultan] has a lofty pavilion, of which the door is inside his house, where he sits for most of the time." His image of the gold-turbaned sultan under a silken dome stands in stark contrast to the vivid description of the desert caravans that actually carried goods such as highly prized salt and copper in exchange for gold. Ibn Battuta writes of the merchants of Sijilmasa that "they load their camels at late dawn, and march until the sun has risen, its light has become bright in the air, and the heat on the ground has become severe . . . When the sun begins to decline and sink in the west, they set off [again]." The caravans would reach Taghaza, a major salt-mining area, 25 days later. Describing

10.1 Pilgrimage caravan arriving at Mecca from the *Maqamat* by al-Hariri (twelfth century).

200 BCE–present	ca. 100 BCE–1200 CE	ca. 100 CE–1600	399–414	ca. 400–1100	900–1300
Silk Roads	Turquoise Roads	Gold Roads (trans-Saharan trade with camels)	Faxian, Buddhist pilgrim	Vikings	Mississippian trade

the enormous amounts of gold traded in the grim and perilous mining town, Ibn Battuta says: "This is a village with nothing good about it. It is the most fly-ridden of places."[1]

Long-distance trade and the ties that bound together the "abode of Islam" increasingly brought travelers such as the opinionated Ibn Battuta into contact with previously disconnected realms. These encounters were critical to the weaving of networks that interconnected key regions of the globe. In this chapter we focus on the spatial connections that bridged differences – among different environments, resources, ideas, beliefs, and peoples. What key commodities, diseases, and beliefs also traveled along the land, rivers, and oceanic networks of trade and exchange? How did societies interact through the circulation of people, goods, and ideas? How were world economies and societies knit together, connecting into regional and eventually global economic systems?

Introduction to the theme of connections

By the early first millennium CE, a regular pattern of relationships developed in many parts of the world between nomadic pastoral economies and sedentary agrarian ones, or between fishing and farming communities, or cities and their rural hinterlands. Across the frontiers that divided these different ways of life spanned trading relationships and warfare as common connections. Dwelling in the steppes of Mongolia during the early second millennium CE, the pastoral Mongols were dependent on trade in grain, textiles, tea, and other goods with their sedentary agricultural neighbors, particularly the Chinese. The Chinese likewise had need of goods from their nomadic neighbors, especially horses. The trade relations between the neighboring states periodically disintegrated into warfare, with Chinese raids on Mongol camps or Mongol raids on Chinese communities. In turn, the conflicts and even conquests also established new relations of exchange and trade, further leading to connected patterns and processes of historical change.

The Mongol Empire illustrates key aspects of connections in the life of world societies considered in this chapter: the role of environment and technology in shaping economic systems (agricultural communities and pastoralism); the control and distribution of material resources by rulers and states through tribute and taxation systems; the role of trade in connecting different economies and cultures. Although beyond the realm of the Mongol Empire, other parts of Asia, the Pacific, Africa, and the Americas experienced their own varieties of agriculture, pastoralism, and trade, and the rise and decline of regional economies. The networks of Afro-Eurasian, Pacific, and American connections were furthered by political expansion and the spread of religions. Vast and powerful as the Mongol Empire was, it extended across Eurasia, not the entire globe. Before about 1500, two vast oceans, the Atlantic and Pacific, limited the connections among world regions. In the chapter below, we explore the opportunities and limitations that determined the successful creation of connections among the world's societies.

Cowries, coins, and commerce

Although globalization may be a relatively recent phenomenon, the development of exchange networks is as old as human behavior itself. We know that between 1.9 and 1.6 million years ago, hominids carried prized stones from their quarry sites to distant places, where they were shaped into useful tools. Evidence of trade in stone tools, together with the specialized trade in **amber** and **obsidian**, hint at the extent of ancient exchange and early commercial interactions between cultures and regions. Prehistoric exchange networks in ores and precious commodities were among the first long-distance trade routes. Tin used in **bronze** was valued from the Mediterranean to Southeast Asia, and it has been speculated that the tin originated in Central Asian mines, suggesting an extensive exchange network that followed riverine routes.

Trade in precious metals and stones indicates extensive commercial contacts dealing in highly valued commodities. Although most early trade was carried out through the bartering of one good for another, there is evidence for the use of money, the earliest forms of which were materials that were rare, portable, and nearly impossible to counterfeit. **Cowry shells** fit this description. Cowry shells were a common form of currency in the Afro-Eurasian world from very early times until as late as 1800 CE. Cowry shells, actually several species including the *Cypraea moneta*, mined from the sea near the Maldives and with a limited distribution, were used in China for commercial purposes as early as the seventh century

10.2 Electrum 1/6 stater. Lydian, about 650–600 BCE. From western modern Turkey, one of the very earliest coins. The Greek historian Herodotus, writing in the fifth century BCE, stated that "the Lydians were the first people we know to have struck and used coinage of silver and gold." He is almost correct. The earliest coins were in fact made from electrum, an alloy of gold and silver. But, based on the evidence of their findspots, we can be fairly confident that the first coins were issued in the area of Lydia, today in western Turkey. These coins had a design on one side only – a result of the primitive method of manufacture. The coins were hand struck. A die with a design (in this case a lion's head) for the obverse (front) of the coin was placed on an anvil. A blank piece of metal was placed on top of the die, and a punch hammered onto the reverse. The result was a coin with an image on one side and a punch mark on the other. The device of the lion on these coins has often led to the assumption that they were issued by a royal power, the kings of Lydia. In truth, we cannot say for certain who minted these earliest coins.

BCE and even earlier as a sign of wealth. The tomb of one of the consorts of a king who lived around 1200 BCE contains more than 7,000 cowries. Even after the development of metal currencies, cowries continued to be used in some places. As late as the eighth-century CE, Arab gold traders in the western Sudan and ancient Ghana found that African merchants demanded cowries in payment. A cowry-based system of exchange prevailed in southwestern China's Yunnan region from the ninth through the seventeenth centuries.

Other kinds of shell currencies were also used elsewhere, even into more recent times, such as the **quiripa** (string of shells) used in the Orinoco basin of South America as late as the eighteenth century. In North America, *wampum* (derived from an Algonquian word **wampumpeag**, meaning "white strings [of beads]") was used to refer to many pre-Columbian currency systems. The Aztec relied on **cacao** beans (which today we know as "chocolate") as currency. Their conspicuous consumption by elites was in the form of a beverage *xocoatl*. Beans were used as weights in West African exchange systems. In Papua New Guinea, snail shells were collected and strung in specific lengths that corresponded to monetary values, and the *kina* (as the shell currency was known) is still used to refer to paper bank notes.

The first known coins were minted in the Anatolian kingdom of Lydia in about the mid-seventh century BCE. These coins were made of a naturally occurring alloy of gold and silver called electrum and described by the Greek historian Herodotus, who claimed: "Lydia does not have many marvelous things to write about . . . except for the gold dust that is carried down from Mount Tmolus." It is unknown whether the coins were weighed or counted. The use of electrum coinage spread to Greek cities. Not long after that, rulers of kingdoms in China cast their own bronze coinage in the shapes of shovels, knives, and shells. Both the metal itself and the symbolic objects into which it was cast contributed to the coinage's economic value, since iron tools were important in agriculture and shells had been in use as a form of currency. Like iron, other metals in relatively scarce supply, such as lead, tin, copper, or bronze (an alloy of tin, copper, and lead), were made into coins, along with the even rarer gold and silver. Copper currency was used in sub-Saharan Africa, where it was traded for gold at least as early as 950 CE. But for Africa, copper was the "red gold," a scarce metal that was highly prized locally. To those outside the continent, West Africa was known by the Arabic name *bilad al-tibr* ("land of gold"). West African gold provided the main source for the Mediterranean world during medieval times, when it formed the basis of complex weight systems.

The earliest Chinese imperial government, the Qin (221–210 BCE) minted round, bronze coins with a square hole in the center. Coins were strung together through the square holes to make a unit of currency called a "string of cash" (cash is the translation of the generic term for money). This practice continued under subsequent dynasties. Coins from the Tang (618–907) era, when China's power in East Asia was at its height, have been found in sites from the Arabian seacoast to Southeast Asia and Japan, indicating extensive commercial exchanges along the Silk Roads and maritime routes.

From the sixth to the twelfth centuries, the Byzantine gold coin, the **bezant**, was widely used throughout the Mediterranean as a medium of exchange. Following the Arab conquests of the seventh and eighth centuries that gave them access to rich sources of gold in Africa, the Arabic **dinar** was used in international trade throughout Afro-Eurasia. Eventually, however, both the *bezant* and the *dinar* declined in purity and weight and were replaced by gold coins of the Italian merchant city-states of Florence (the **florin** in 1252) and Venice (the **ducat** in 1284). It was the *ducat* that became the first true international coinage, maintaining its purity and thus its dominance in Eurasia for over 500 years.

Trade commodities

Salt

Until major improvements in production in the eighteenth century, governments commonly maintained monopolies on the production and trade of salt. Salt was a major source of governments' finances and both politically and economically important. In some parts of the world, government monopolization of major salt deposits and the trade lines associated with them provided the basis for large regional empires. As early as the second century BCE, the Chinese government instituted a controversial domestic salt monopoly to direct profits from the production and sale of salt into state coffers. Centuries later, a revival of the salt monopoly contributed substantially to the fiscal health of the Tang imperial house and thus to prolonging its rule after domestic rebellion and foreign losses in the mid-eighth century. The prosperity and vigor of the fifteenth-century sub-Saharan empire of Bornu was closely tied to its monopoly of the salt trade, which provided much of North Africa with its salt.

Horses

Everywhere, heavy and bulky items were generally confined to regional trade; only a few offered a large or certain enough profit to be moved regularly in long-distance trade. Governments' interest in trading such bulky items as horses, essential to effective cavalry in time of war, resulted in horse-trading over both middle and long distances. For example, India was a major importer of horses from Central and West Asia and by the third century, was regularly trans-shipping them to Indonesia. In the regions of West Africa where horses could survive, horse-mounted cavalry transformed states politically and economically. West African states were able to control and monopolize interregional trade from North Africa

by controlling the breeding of horses (they sold only stallions).

Grain and other foodstuffs

Throughout the first millennium CE, grain was a common middle-distance trading commodity. Because it was needed to feed the inhabitants of great cities such as second-century Rome, eighth-century Chang'an, and eleventh-century Cairo, each with a population of more than a million and without sufficient local access to grain supplies, the perishable food staple was intensively produced and traded from hinterlands of usually no more than one week's journey. The southern Mediterranean shores of North Africa were the initial granary for imperial Rome, while the Nile supplied Rome and later Constantinople and the Yangzi Valley provisioned Chang'an. Such products as grain and rice were useful in providing food provisions for armies and, along with other food products, the source of fermentation in wines and distilled alcoholic beverages that cemented social relations, provided political motivation for joining an imperial project, and invited loyal service thereafter. Much of the Mongol elite's success rested with their ability to acquire vast amounts of food and drink, making them available for feasts given to the armies and peasants by the (dozens of) wagon-loads. Similar efforts by the Inca elites resulted in the appropriation of foodstuffs that could be redistributed in times of hunger, thus establishing the legitimacy of political (imperial) control.

The luxury trade

While many traders dealt in bulk goods, traversing the continents in long caravans or sailing along their coasts in lumbering ships, others dealt in smaller quantities of more profitable luxury goods. Of these the most common were fine ceramics, jewelry, woven and embroidered silks and other hand-woven fabrics, incense, and spices. Manufactured goods originating in East, South, and Southeast Asia were traded into West Asia, Africa, and Europe in exchange for gold and silver. Caravan routes across the Sahara were established by African traders in salt, metals, and other commodities and across Central Asia by traders in silk, whose virtues were appreciated among Roman elites. Around the seas, from the first centuries CE, a string of ports of call marked routes from southern China down through the islands of Southeast Asia across the Indian Ocean and up the Red Sea to Africa and West Asia. In the Americas, a network of cloth, feathers, obsidian, and turquoise made its way from tropical Middle America northwards to the American Southwest region. Along West African Gold Roads went the most valuable commodities of all – books.

In preliterate societies, the acquisition of books was a visible sign of the arrival of Islam. The orthodox Sunni Muslim faith had spread across North Africa from Egypt, and Cairo was an important center of learning during the Mamluk dynasty (1250–1517 CE). Pilgrims such as Mansa Musa from Mali, West Africa, stopped in Cairo on their way to Mecca. They interacted with scholars and artisans, many of whom were imported to the centers of Timbuktu, Jenné, Bornu, and Hausaland. The traveler Leo Africanus (ca.1510) noted the popularity of merchants selling manuscripts and books as Islamic law and learning spread.

Early Christian, Hindu, and Jewish traditions also relied on a very few literate adults, who read the Bible, Mahabharata, or Torah aloud to the rest of the community. Books were copied, illustrated, and collected by a relatively small minority of wealthy elites. Prominent and powerful families had an increased impact on society by spending lavish sums on books and manuscripts made by renowned copyists and illuminators, whose works they may or may not have actually been able to read themselves.

The slave trade

Slaves were common to most large-scale, hierarchical societies engaged in long-distance and short-haul trading, from the Aztec to Zimbabwe. Only the wealthiest members of society could afford slaves. Enslavement originated in a variety of ways, including through pawning for debts and as victims, who were unfortunate war captives. Both men and women became enslaved and, especially in times of great famine, the enslaved were vulnerable to the whims of the most powerful parts of society. They could be traded and exchanged or held as laborers.

Slaves were so ubiquitous that their price often determined the price of other goods. In slave societies, where production depended upon investment in slave labor, the acquisition of slaves translated into higher social status for slave owners. Among the most valuable of captives were young women, who were valued for their productive and reproductive capacities, and the specialist craftsmen. Metallurgists, potters, tanners, cooks, and other artisans were valuable human commodities traveling the major trade routes of the ancient world.

The spice trade

Spices, arguably the most lucrative of the Afro-Eurasian global luxury trade in the period between 100 and 1450 CE, moved for the most part by sea. A world without refrigeration had powerful reasons to pay high prices for pepper, cloves, cumin, cinnamon, and nutmeg, all sources of strong flavors that occasionally masked the taste of overage meat and other perishables. Many spices were also considered advantageous to health (sugar was one such medicinal "spice"). Nearly all of the rare items originated in India and the islands of Southeast Asia. A few came from the Arabian peninsula and East African coast, including malagueta pepper, kola nuts, frankincense, and myrrh. Some were traded east and north to China for ceramics, silks, and other finished goods. Much of the spice trade throughout this period went as far west as the Mediterranean basin.

Merchants and international trade

International traders and travelers, appearing to local people as foreigners with strange languages, customs, and goods, nearly always lived apart when they were in foreign lands. Cities around the world, where trading took place, had neighborhoods occupied exclusively by foreign traders and their businesses. Arab merchants occupied special quarters in the medieval Chinese capital of Chang'an and in the southern port of Canton. Often the establishment of separate quarters was the result of a policy of the host government that was intended both to control the import and export of wealth and goods for its own benefit and to isolate new cultural ideas which might undermine the local belief system that legitimized government power. In western sub-Saharan Africa in the eleventh and twelfth centuries, cities such as Gao on the Niger River were constructed as double cities, one-half being for foreign traders. In fourteenth- and fifteenth-century Christian Ethiopia, Muslims engaged in international trade were forced by the government to live in entirely separate market towns, while Muslim governments across North Africa enforced foreign merchant quarters in every large city from Fez in Morocco to Cairo in Egypt.

Merchant associations

Merchant associations were another feature of Eurasian world trade before 1500 that maintained connections and encouraged commerce in the centers and along the routes of exchange. Based sometimes on common kinship ties or ethnic backgrounds and sometimes on a commonly held legal system or shared religious outlook, these associations provided financial, legal, and logistical support that facilitated the enterprise and helped protect the commercial monopolies of their members.

Even before the voyages of exploration that were to shift the center of commercial activity and power to the Atlantic, world trade had become so large-scale and risky that individual mercantile enterprise had given way to complicated multiparty arrangements. The most common of these arrangements were partnerships. Nearly all these partnership arrangements, whether in Africa, East Asia, or Europe, began as arrangements between family and lineage members. They continued up through the fifteenth century as a common form of business organization all along world trade routes.

Partnerships

The terms of partnerships, which proportionally strengthened the wealth, responsibilities, and liabilities of enterprises, were also shaped by regional legal systems or customs and enforced by government authorities or by merchants themselves through their professional associations. In West Asia, North Africa, northern India, and Spain, where **mudaraba** partnerships emerged, Islamic law was applied by state governments after the eighth century. The mudaraba and its variations provided a contractual means by which unrelated individuals could pool large amounts of capital to outfit and supply long-term, long-distance caravans and fleets and share out the risk. Whether influenced by Islamic practice or emerging out of indigenous practices, commenda and compagnia partnerships, which offered similar advantages, emerged in Europe by the twelfth century. Similar economically based power associations in West Africa helped unify the Mande-speaking peoples of Mali and contributed to the expansion of the Mali Empire in West Africa in the fourteenth century.

Lodges and brotherhoods

In thirteenth–fifteenth-century West Asia, the Muslim **futuwwa** lodge functioned like a modern businessmen's fraternal organization, complete with charitable activities. These organizations evolved from brotherhoods of men that sprang up in urban settings to provide protection for the interests of its members, who were often young and poor. By the thirteenth century, futuwwa lodges served the needs of the merchant class, especially in the Turkish and Persian territories of the Muslim world. A member merchant from western Anatolia could visit Aleppo or Baghdad and find a hostel there maintained by the lodge for its members; he would also find ready-made business connections among the local member-ship.

Similar lodges functioned in the same fashion in North and West Africa, where the **Karimi** merchant society, headquartered in Cairo, flourished as early as the eleventh to thirteenth centuries. *Karim* (meaning "great") was an Arabic term used to distinguish large-scale wholesale merchants from petty entrepreneurs. Karimi merchants rose to prominence in Cairo during the late thirteenth and early fourteenth centuries, just as Cairo came into its prime in international trade. Its membership was made up mostly of Jewish, but also of Muslim, long-distance traders who worked a commercial network that stretched from Spain to India. Arabic language and culture plus common business interests held this society together. Jewish members wrote their contracts in Arabic using Hebrew characters; among themselves they used Talmudic contract law, but with Muslim colleagues they practiced commonly accepted legal variations. Although spices were the primary commodities traded by Karimi merchants, cloth, porcelain, precious stones, silk, and slaves (non-Muslims) were among other goods traded. Some Karimi merchants were bankers or shipowners. Like their counterparts in Italian city-states such as Venice and Genoa, Karimi merchants formed partnerships for one overseas venture at a time in

which one partner put up two-thirds of the capital and the other contributed the remaining one-third, plus the labor to accompany the goods abroad. Profits were equally shared, once the transport and other costs of the venture were subtracted. This kind of partnership was known in Venice and Genoa as a **commenda** and was widely used by merchants there. In the fifteenth century, the practice was carried to West Africa, where the local coastal community became known as Komenda.

Money and international exchange

International merchants – Malayan, African, Chinese, Arab, or European – were all knowledgeable in world monies and their exchange rates, mostly relying on word of mouth and their own experiences. Most trade was carried out through the bartering of one good for another. Even so, internationally understood units of money were needed. One of the earliest international currencies was gold-based. We know that African gold was traded to Europe and beyond as early as the fifth century, as evidenced by the gold coinages struck by Vandals and later Byzantines. Cowries also linked Africa and the Indian Ocean.

Government and currency

By 1000 CE, gold and silver coins became more common as international currency than cowries. In some parts of the world, other metals – such as lead, tin, or copper – were more rare, and their scarcity permitted their use as forms of currency. By assuming monopolies over both the mining and the production of valuable metals and by establishing the weight, degree of adulteration, and value of metal coins, large and small states throughout the world began to mint and control currency. This intrusion of government into commerce served as proof and publicity of political legitimacy and power as well as a convenient means for governments to accumulate capital and simplify tax collection. Some state currencies quickly became accepted as units of exchange thousands of miles distant from their origins. At the height of Abbasid power in Baghdad (ninth to eleventh centuries), their *dinars* (minted from African gold) and *dirhems* were commonly accepted throughout the Mediterranean, as well as in Central and South Asia and eastern Europe. By the fifteenth century, Venetian *ducats* had become the basic international currency in Europe.

Diplomatic connections

Seeking to expand their bases of material and human resources, both large empires and smaller states sponsored missions to neighboring regions, sometimes to form military or trade alliances, sometimes to exchange gifts, but always to gather information about potential resources.

The Mexica-Aztec had a name for their professional class of merchant-spies, **pochteca**. *Pochteca* traded between the Mexica-Aztec heartland and distant areas, in search of rare items and goods used particularly in rituals. Agents for nobility, some *pochteca* venerated their own god Yacatecuhtli, "the Lord who guides." Trade and diplomacy tended to go hand in hand and the *pochteca* became economically wealthy and politically powerful over time.

Diplomatic communications were made difficult by each government's view of its own importance and by fundamental ideological as well as linguistic differences. To prevent the collapse of negotiations over misunderstandings, commonly accepted rules in matters of precedence and etiquette developed, as did formalities in the recording and documentation of transactions with foreigners. Every government developed its own protocol, the mastery of which was a prerequisite for any who wished to deal with

it successfully. In the absence of a bureaucracy specializing in foreign affairs, the business of diplomatic missions, which might nominally be headed by a highly placed government official or an aristocrat, was typically carried out by those involved in trade or in government postal, road, and harbor systems or by the military, those most likely to be familiar with foreign places and governments through experience.

Han Chinese diplomacy and exploration

Zhang Qian, a Han ambassador, traveling on missions which began in 139 BCE, not only developed military and political intelligence of great use to Han policy but also had an eye for commercial opportunities. While in Bactria about 128 BCE, Zhang Qian noticed for sale Chinese bamboo and textiles which came from southwest China by way of Bengal. This suggested to him the possibility of establishing safe roads from China to Bactria through India, thus protecting trade from the unfriendly peoples in Central Asia. His report on the famous horses of Ferghana inspired Han Wudi to send an expedition of 30,000 soldiers on a campaign to obtain them. Zhang Qian not only served Han diplomatic interests, he alerted Central Asian people to the possibilities of Chinese trade, and the resulting commercial relationships served to carry Chinese products west. The subsequent Western demand for Chinese silk and other products, and the Chinese interest in Western horses, had a powerful commercial and cultural impact on Eurasia.

Diplomatic accounts as historical sources

Accounts by envoys to foreign lands provide some of the most important historical sources we have today. Megasthenes (fourth century BCE) was posted by a successor of Alexander the Great,

Seleucus Nicator, as an envoy to the court of the Mauryan ruler, Chandragupta, at Pataliputra. The book he wrote detailing his observations of Mauryan India has been lost, but later Greek and Latin writers drew on it and it remains the earliest description of India by an outsider. The Chinese official Zhou Daguan was appointed by the Mongol ruler of China in the late thirteenth century to represent him in Cambodia, and Zhou's accounts of Cambodian society are a valuable historical source. The mission of Friar William of Rubruck to the Mongols in the fourteenth century provides a unique perspective on Mongol life at that time.

Diplomacy and culture

Diplomatic delegations linked one government to another. Their stays in a foreign land were normally brief; they traveled to initiate or confirm specific trade and political agreements between governments, although permanent embassies began to appear in the fifteenth century. For example, during the entire span of the Song dynasty (960–1275) in China, various diplomatic delegations were sent to negotiate with the rulers of border states that threatened the Song. The accounts of some of these delegations reveal much about how the Chinese viewed peoples they regarded culturally as "barbarians" but whose military strength seriously compromised the Song state. In Africa, the delegation of Mansa Musa, ruler of Mali (1307–32), served multiple purposes: it was a religious pilgrimage, a trading venture, and a diplomatic mission to lands beyond Mali's borders, namely Mecca and Cairo.

Religious connections

Traders and diplomats were by no means the only travelers maintaining international connections and cultural interchange in the centuries before European routes through the Americas to Asia

were established. Pilgrims were far more numerous than diplomats as long-distance travelers on the world's highways. They were drawn from all walks of life; everyone participated. To go on pilgrimage was to visit sacred places where the spiritual and material worlds touched. In such places, distinctions of social status disappeared. Kings and commoners, slaves and slave-owners, the poor and the rich were as one on pilgrimage. To emphasize this sense of commonality, many of the long-distance pilgrimages required standardized clothing.

Every culture in the world had its shrines, recognized and visited by its people as centers of power. Some were in sacred groves of trees, as in the case of Celtic Europe, or caves, as at Zimbabwe in Southern Africa. Others were on mountaintops, on seashores, or in towns. And as some religions stretched far beyond their original cultural boundaries, spread by political or economic pressures and sometimes by persuasion, pilgrims became world travelers.

Christian and Islamic pilgrimage

By the fourth century, Christian pilgrims were visiting Palestine from Africa, Europe, and West Asia. At shrines in Bethlehem, Nazareth, and Jerusalem they sought God's intervention for healing, children, and wealth. Some sought God's forgiveness for past sinful acts, and later, after the eleventh century, many came from Europe to fulfill a vow. In part because of the large numbers of homeless wanderers and pilgrims on the road, it was customary Christian practice to open one's door to strangers and provide them with food and drink. Any poor or homeless person had the right and privilege to find shelter in churches. In the tenth century, Christians also traveled to shrines in Europe, most of which were either tombs of saints or churches holding the bones or other relics of saints. By this time, towns had sprung up around the holy sites to provide services to the pilgrims. Guides knowing several languages, as well as restaurants and lodgings, were available in these towns. Downpatrick in Ireland, the site of a shrine to Saint Patrick, the patron saint of Ireland, was one such tenth-century resort town; similar towns could be found all over Europe. In eastern Europe, Christian pilgrims more often visited monasteries, seeking mediation with God by the holy men within.

Pilgrimage was more formally structured into Islam. By the tenets of the faith, all Muslims were expected to go on pilgrimage (hajj) to Mecca at least once in their lifetime. By the eighth century, that city was receiving thousands of pilgrims from all over West Asia during the month of pilgrimage each year. By the tenth century, still more arrived and from much farther afield: India, West and North Africa, and Spain. Mecca became the largest pilgrimage town site in the world. Muslim pilgrims also visited the tombs of prophets in Palestine and the tombs of saints elsewhere, but in smaller numbers.

The Crusades

The crusading expeditions by which Christians sought to recapture Palestine were in part an outgrowth of contacts between Muslims and Christian pilgrims visiting their "Holy Land." Beginning in 1095 CE, the pope and Christian monarchs launched a series of eight **Crusades** that were carried out over the next two centuries to restore Palestine to Christian control. They were initially successful and established Christian kingdoms in Palestine, but by the end of the thirteenth century, their kingdoms had been lost to the Muslims.

The long-term effects of the Crusades were undoubtedly greater on Europe than on the Muslim world. Through their experiences and contacts in the eastern Mediterranean, European Crusaders were able to regain from the Arabs much knowledge that had been lost after the fall of Rome. In addition to making much Greek knowledge available to the West, Arab mathematics, science, and medicine were more advanced than either knowledge or practice in western Eurasia, and trade and agriculture had much to learn from Arab business practices and horticulture. Common words such as "algebra", "alfalfa", and "alcohol", and agricultural products such as oranges, nectarines, and eggplants, are examples of what Arab contact provided Western Eurasia.

Pilgrimage in Asia: Hinduism and Buddhism

Pilgrimage was also an important religious practice throughout Asia. For Hindus, in addition to visits to temple shrines to Shiva, Vishnu, and other gods and goddesses, bathing in the seven main rivers of India, especially in the Ganges, was considered a means of sacred purification. Pilgrimage tours to several temples in succession, each of them located in different parts of India, were popular as well. Hindu pilgrimage, however, except for a few instances in Southeast Asia, was primarily limited to India proper.

Buddhists, on the other hand, took part in long-distance pilgrimages. By the first century CE, Buddhist pilgrims from Central and Southeast Asia, as well as from all over India, regularly visited places in northern India where the Buddha had lived. By the seventh century, the Buddhist pilgrimage network had been expanded to include China, Japan, and much of Southeast Asia. Pilgrims traveled not only to India but also to temples holding relics of the Buddha in such places as Sri Lanka and Burma.

All these long-distance pilgrims returned to their societies different people than when they had left. Having completed their pilgrimage brought them a higher status and more leverage in business and social affairs; they had a greater knowledge of other peoples and cultures, their ideas and practices. Like returning modern tourists, they passed such knowledge on to their neighbors.

Faxian, a Chinese Buddhist pilgrim, left for India in 399 by land and returned 15 years later by sea. His account of this journey, the *Record of the Buddhist Kingdoms*, is the oldest known travel book in Chinese literature and a valuable source of information on the political, social, and religious life of Central Asia, India, and the Indian Ocean lands Faxian visited. Another famous Chinese Buddhist pilgrim, Xuan Zang (600–664), journeyed to India via Central Asia in the mid-seventh century in search of Buddhist scriptures and left an account of his travels that reveals much about Indian life at that time. *Journey to the West*, the chronicle of his trip, later became the basis of one of the most popular novels of Chinese literature.

Xuan Zang served as an important conduit between Indian and Chinese cultures, translating not only Buddhist scriptures into Chinese but also, on the order of the Chinese emperor, Chinese works such as the Daoist classic, the *Daodejing*, into Sanskrit. During the eighth century, a Chinese Buddhist monk known best by his Japanese name, Ganjin, traveled to Japan and taught Buddhism to many disciples there. In the ninth century, the Japanese monk Ennin, like his Chinese predecessors who had journeyed to India in search of the true doctrines of Buddhism, traveled to China on a pilgrimage. The account he wrote of his travels in China provides a rich source of information on China during the waning days of the Tang dynasty.

Pilgrimage, government, and economy

Pilgrimage as a vehicle for connecting the world also had its effect on governments and economies. Major pilgrimages such as the Muslim hajj were big business. Ferrying Christian pilgrims from Europe to Palestine was important to the economies of Venice, Genoa, and other southern European port towns, especially after the crusading wars of the eleventh and twelfth centuries.

Governments along the routes took special interest in protecting – and taxing – the pilgrimage trade and services industry. They also identified themselves with the shrines within their territories and maintained old temples, churches, and mosques on the sites and built new ones. In the fifteenth century, Egypt's Mamluk government and the expanding Ottoman state in Anatolia fought over the right to claim primacy in defending Mecca and its pilgrimage. With that claim, it was felt, came ideological supremacy in the Muslim world.

Pilgrims commonly brought along small goods and traded them to pay their way on the lengthy journey. At established international shrines, annual markets developed which sometimes became more important for the region's economy than the pilgrimage business itself. Long-distance pilgrimages, finally, meant increased traffic along established highways and, in a few instances, the building of new roads. For example, before Islam, Mecca was a way station on the Red Sea trade line. After Islam, it became a terminus of world pilgrimage and new transregional roads were built to it. Overnight stopping stations were built at regular intervals on the caravan roads in the Arabian peninsula leading to Mecca.

Pilgrimage, trade, and diplomacy accounted for nearly all of the long-distance world travelers before the fifteenth century. Missionaries such as Buddhist monks and Muslim Sufis were added to these travelers. Both Buddhist and Muslim missionaries carried with them more than their faith: new technologies, different social and cultural customs, and a broader knowledge of the world were products of missionary activities. For example, the distribution of cotton and the horizontal weaving loom in West Africa follows the spread of Muslim merchant-clerics after the eighth century.

PRIMARY SOURCE: IBN BATTUTA, WORLD TRAVELER

World travelers have set out on journeys for many reasons, both personal and economic. Ibn Battuta began his journeys as a pious Muslim, who departed his home in Tangier in 1325 to make a pilgrimage to Mecca. This trek eventually became a tour of most of the Afro-Eurasian world known to him. He traveled by land and sea to Mesopotamia, Persia, India, the Maldive Islands, Ceylon, and China. He was a keen observer of local customs and cultures and was particularly interested in the impact of Islam on the lands he visited. Sometimes he settled for periods, and even assumed official roles, as he did when he became an envoy to China for a sultan of Delhi. Eventually he saw much of West and East Africa.

The early-fourteenth-century visit to Mogadishu by Ibn Battuta provides a rare eyewitness account of an East African coastal city. Battuta describes the procession of the local ruler through the town. Richly dressed and protected by a silk parasol which was carried over him, he was accompanied by an entourage with trumpets, drums, and pipes. Ibn Battuta found the inhabitants of Mogadishu obese, and he himself feasted to excess on a seasoned stew of meats and vegetables, served with rice cooked in ghee (clarified butter) and side dishes of bananas cooked in ginger and milk, peppers, and mangoes. The cosmopolitan character of coastal East Africa is illustrated by the various foods served to Ibn Battuta that were not indigenous to Africa: rice and bananas, for example, had been introduced to East Africa from India and Southeast Asia. In return, increasing quantities of indigenous African grains were exported to the drier regions of southern Asia.

Recent calculations suggest that Battuta set an early record for global travel: he visited the equivalent of 44 modern countries, traveling more than 117,500 kilometers (73,000) miles! Like other tourist-scholars before and after, he played a role in linking the world together. Both Marco Polo's and Ibn Battuta's odysseys transcended their original purposes. Their journeys of discovery not only expanded geographical knowledge in their own cultural contexts but also stimulated cultural and commercial connections between Asia, Africa, and Europe. Ibn Battuta's written descriptions of his travels from West Africa to China were circulated in numerous copies around West Asia. Similarly, although the Venetian traveler Marco Polo began his journey to China as a trading venture, it became a journey that linked western Europe with East Asia and helped to cement the ties of that world system.

Here begins Ibn Battuta's travels. . .

> I left Tangier, my birthplace, on Thursday, 2nd Rajab 725 [14 June 1325], being at that time twenty-two years of age [22 lunar years; 21 and 4 months by solar reckoning], with the intention of making the Pilgrimage to the Holy House [at Mecca] and the Tomb of the Prophet [at Medina]. . .
>
> I set out alone, finding no companion to cheer the way with friendly intercourse, and no party of travelers with whom to associate myself. Swayed by an overmastering impulse within me, and a long-cherished desire to visit those glorious sanctuaries, I resolved to quit all my friends and tear myself away from my home. As my parents were still alive, it weighed grievously upon me to part from them, and both they and I were afflicted with sorrow. . .

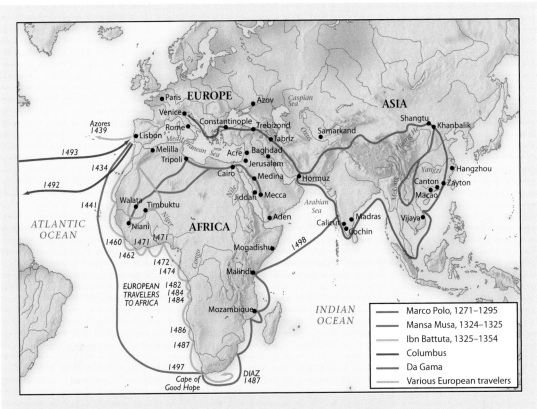

Map 10.1 Routes of selected travelers in Africa and Eurasia before 1500 CE.

At Bijaya I fell ill of a fever, and one of my friends advised me to stay there till I recovered. But I refused, saying, "If God decrees my death, it shall be on the road with my face set toward Mecca." "If that is your resolve," he replied, "sell your ass and your heavy baggage, and I shall lend you what you require. In this way you will travel light, for we must make haste on our journey, for fear of meeting roving Arabs on the way." I followed his advice and he did as he had promised – may God reward him!. . .

From Qusantinah we reached Bona [Bone] where, after staying in the town for several days, we left the merchants of our party on account of the dangers of the road, while we pursued our journey with the utmost speed. I was again attacked by fever, so I tied myself in the saddle with a turban-cloth in case I should fall by reason of my weakness. So great was my fear that I could not dismount until we arrived at Tunis.

Arrival at Alexandria [pp47–50]

At length on April 5th [1326] we reached Alexandria. It is a beautiful city, well-built and fortified with four gates and a magnificent port. Among all the ports in the world I have seen none to equal it except Kawlam [Quilon] and Calicut in India, the port of the infidels [Genoese] at Sudaq [Sudak, in the Crimea] in the land of the Turks, and the port of Zaytun [possibly Canton] in China, all of which will be described later. . .

Two holy men of the city

One of the learned men of Alexandria was the qadi, a master of eloquence, who used to wear a turban of extraordinary size. Never either in the eastern or the western lands have I seen a more voluminous headgear.

Another of them was the pious ascetic Burhan ad-Din, whom I met during my stay and whose hospitality I enjoyed for three days. One day as I entered his room he said to me "I see that you are fond of travelling through foreign lands." I replied "Yes, I am" (though I had as yet no thought of going to such distant lands as India or China). Then he said "You must certainly visit my brother Farid ad-Din in India, and my brother Rukn ad-Din in Sind, and my brother Burhan ad-Din in China, and when you find them give them greeting from me." I was amazed at his prediction and the idea of going to these countries having been cast into my mind, my journeys never ceased until I had met these three that he named and conveyed his greeting to them.

Source: Ibn Battuta, *Travels in Asia and Africa 1325–1354*, translated and edited by H.A.R. Gibb (London: Broadway House, 1929). Quoted in: Fordham University, Medieval Sourcebook <www.fordham.edu/halsall/source/1354-ibnbattuta.html>

Commercial connections

Traders made up the largest number of world travelers. By the second century, travel by ship and caravan was adequate for both regional and long-distance commerce. Trade moved steadily through a series of regional exchanges between West Africa and East Asia and culminated in large markets where both ordinary and exotic goods were traded. Along the lines of communication connecting Asia and Africa with the Mediterranean coast, basic types of ship and sail construction, as well as navigation and caravan routes and practices, were commonly known and used, regions borrowing from one another and each using what suited it best. In the Pacific Northwest coastal regions of North America, Chinookan canoes plied riverine and coastal waterways from at least the beginning of the first millennium CE. The largest seaworthy canoes held hundreds of sailors and fishermen onboard their provisioning vessels.

Between 100 and 500 CE, the camel, the "ship of the desert," was introduced to the Sahara from West Asia via Egypt. The use of the camel was an innovation in African overland trade equivalent to improvements in maritime technology. The camel led to faster, more frequent, and more regular commerce. Bred in different sizes and structures for different terrains, the standard one-hump camel could carry loads of up to 250 kilograms (550 pounds) while traveling more than a week without water. The relatives of the camel in South America (alpacas and llamas) were domesticated by about 6,000 years ago and mostly used by pre-Inca peoples for fiber and meat. Sometimes described as a difficult and disagreeable pack animal, the Afro-Eurasian camels received homage in poems and essays extolling their beauty, gentleness, speed, and patience or by comparing the human experience to that of the animals, as in this northeast African love poem by the Somali poet Axmed Maxamed Good:

> Unless I see you I never get nourishment from sleep
> Like a young camel I bellow out to you
> I am to you as a she-camel is to her adopted calf when her own has been killed.

Other poetry, such as this excerpt from a poem by the Somali poet Axmed Ismaaciil Diiriye, reveals the realities of desert journeys:

> The camels are packed and ready for the weary trek
> And men's thoughts dwell on distant destinations.

Camels were more than beasts of burden used in transport. They were prized for their milk and meat. They were nomadic companions, celebrated in religions and folklore. Camels carried exotic textiles, leatherwork, metals, spices, salt blocks, and other goods along the desert routes. Commodities in general demand, such as salt, which is essential to both humans and animals but is not readily available everywhere, were commonly traded in both regional and international commerce.

Merchants over land and sea: Ships of the desert and ocean

Although diplomats and pilgrims were important for the spread of ideas and beliefs, their efforts would not have been successful without the participation of merchants. The desire for exchange drove the development of currencies and led to the movement of people and expansion of governments, but exchange over long distances was made possible by merchants willing to take risks and by efficient transportation technologies.

From very early times, by both land and sea, merchants moved luxury goods and bulk commodities between towns, regions, and continents, delaying or changing their shipments according to shifting markets, wars, rumors, and weather. Driven by hopes of profit, they sought out trade items that might increase their wealth. Luxury goods such as silk and everyday commodities such as salt, were commonly traded in both regional and international commerce by interlocking overland and maritime routes. Merchants who took risks on trade and grew wealthy or became impoverished were not alone in their commercial ventures. Rulers also tied their fortunes to trade. They increased their power and expanded their states by knitting together agricultural hinterlands with strategically located commercial centers and maritime ports, and by taking advantage of shifting international trade routes.

From the first century CE, people, goods, and ideas moved over several well-known and long-established routes: the Indian Ocean route by sea and the Central Asian Silk Road by land, as well as the two established African connections, the trans-Saharan roads and the East African coastal system. Africa, at the far western end of the Silk Road and Indian Ocean routes, in addition to participating in the east–west exchange, provided a south–north connection, which added another dimension to established global commercial and cultural interaction. Across the huge continent, main highways were developed to link the inter-African markets and to connect them with Asia and Europe.

There were two major historical frontiers of global interconnection in Africa: the Red Sea and Indian Ocean frontier of East Africa, and West Africa's Sahara frontier. Although the commerce of the Red Sea–Indian Ocean frontier was maritime and that of the Sahara frontier was land-based, both seemed to border on oceans: the Sahara, a formidable desert some 7.7 million square kilometers (3 million square miles) in area, may be considered an ocean of sand. The Arabic word *sahel* translates as "coastline," and in the

Sahel region that borders the desert's southern edge were situated many "ports" of entry. Like the oceans of the East African frontier, the desert sands were not a barrier but rather a space to be regularly traversed, which Africans did along well-established trade routes beginning at least as early as the second century.

Silk Roads and Central Asian caravan routes

For 1,000 years before the Mongol conquest of Eurasia in the early thirteenth century, some of the most important east–west interconnections were the Silk Roads across Central Asia, created between the second century BCE and the second century CE. By the first century CE, large and wealthy market zones lay at the eastern and western ends of Asia: Han China to the east and, to the west, the Parthian Empire in Persia with its connections to the Roman Empire in Europe. Routes through Central Asia linked trade between these markets, but there was little guaranteed security to reassure cautious merchants.

Before the Silk Roads, goods moved sporadically and in small quantities. For 1,500 years following their establishment, the Silk Roads provided the main land connection over which people, technology, trade, and ideas moved between East and West Asia, Europe, and North Africa. As West Asian merchants and Roman soldiers reached eastward and Chinese merchants and Han armies stretched westward, Central Asian oasis states thrived along this caravan route. Gold was one of the most important items of trade, but spices, silks, and other luxury items were also traded.

Situated at the crossroads between an east–west lateral route and a north–south highway between India and Russia, Samarkand was one of the most ancient cities of Central Asia and played a major role in the caravan trade that traversed this region for more than 1,000 years. Samarkand was ruled successively by Turks, Arabs, and Persians and was conquered again by the Mongols in 1220. An account of Samarkand written shortly after this, portrays a garden-filled city surrounded by three concentric walls: an outer wall with 12 wooden gates, enclosing a second wall around the city itself, and an inner walled area that enclosed the main mosque and the walled citadel containing the ruler's palace. Samarkand and other oasis cities – such as Bukhara, Tabriz, or Turfan to the

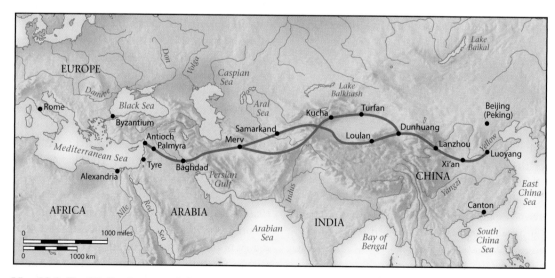

Map 10.2 The Silk Roads across Asia.

10.3 The Vow of the Merchant. Fresco detail from Turfan, Chinese Turkestan, ca. eighth century, showing the relationship between commerce and religion along the Silk Road. Uighur merchants are shown at the bottom paying homage to Buddhist deities.

northwest of China – were essential to the caravan trade across Central Asia that connected China to West Asia and Europe. They provided necessary stopping places for water and provisions for the great caravans that traversed the deserts and steppes of Central Asia.

There were unwanted voyagers on the Silk Roads. Disease spread from trading community to trading community, sometimes with devastating consequences. The fourteenth-century spread of the **bubonic plague** is now believed to have originated in China in the 1330s. Spread by rodents and also infected fleas along for the ride, the disease had reached Venetian merchants within a decade. Known as the Black Death, the plague decimated European populations and then spread to the West African oases of the trans-Saharan routes. Estimates of the death toll of the

fourteenth-century outbreak range as high as 75 million, more than one-third of the population of Europe.

Ideas and beliefs also traveled the Silk Roads between eastern Europe and the Pacific Ocean, making its largest cities both centers of trade and meeting places for the world's religions. Between the eleventh and thirteenth centuries, Christian, Jewish, and Muslim merchants intermingled in cities from Genoa to Persia. In areas under Mongol authority, Buddhism and Islam inspired the clothing, architecture, and other contemporary visual language of fourteenth-century multicultural Azerbaijan. In a compendium of world history, the *Jami al-Tavarikh* of Rashid al-Din, its complex social geography intermingled elements from Chinese, Abyssinian, and Persian sources. The manuscript's illustrations used elements of Buddhist beliefs to retell Islamic history in an era of cultural integration. The networks of religious affiliation had found that the Silk Roads under the Mongols provided new opportunities for the transmission of ideology and commodities.

Trans-Saharan caravans and commerce

The trans-Saharan gold trade predated the North African expansion of Islam in the seventh century CE. More than seven centuries later, gold was still being loaded and carried on the backs of camels along the centuries-old routes that crossed the great desert. Once the camel and wheeled vehicles were adopted along the trans-Saharan caravan routes in Roman times, the patterns of commercial growth remained technologically stable until the introduction of firearms and horseback cavalries in the sixteenth century. The desert routes rarely changed course since they relied on the navigational abilities of African merchant families familiar with the location of oases. The incorporation of early trade routes into the larger Islamic world commercial network occurred gradually and mostly peacefully as Muslim merchant-clerics traveled afar, engaging in trade and pilgrimage. There is no doubt that the increasing Islamization of West African societies furthered their participation in the land-based commercial world that stretched from the Atlantic to the Indian Ocean and beyond.

As essential as the trans-Saharan caravans were in the trading system of North and West Africa, caravans organized for the profit of North African merchants were only temporary associations of firms that happened to be bringing goods across the desert at the same time. Individual firms, not the caravans themselves, were the organizational core of the trans-Saharan caravan trade and these firms were joined together in the caravan enterprise by both formal and informal bonds. Islamic law provided the basis for drawing up written agreements of partnership in trading ventures or credit advances between independent merchants.

The trading city of Begho on the edge of the West African forest was strategically situated as an **entrepôt** (point of exchange or distribution) for the Akan goldfields, shipping gold north to the Mande world and beyond through the trans-Saharan caravan routes interconnecting the Mediterranean and Islamic worlds. At its height (thirteenth–sixteenth centuries), Begho was probably inhabited by some 15,000 people, including merchants from a vast number of cultural regions. Different language groups resided in distinct quarters of the town. Artisans lived and worked in a separate quarter, where they cast brass and bronze in crucibles, worked iron, steel, and ivory, and wove and dyed cotton cloth prized as far away as the Atlantic coast.

At Begho and other gold-trading cities, gold merchants used clay and brass goldweights. These weights, placed on counterbalance scales and in varying shapes and sizes, were used to weigh gold dust and nuggets. They conformed to an Islamic ounce system used in North Africa and across the western Sudan as early as the ninth century. The heaviest of the Islamic standards, the ounce of 31.5 grams, became known as the troy ounce in Europe. Gold traders traveled under the charge of a chief trader and often in large groups as a protection against thieves.

Journeys across the Sahara were filled with danger – as the bones and debris of lost caravans show – they could last for months, and oases could be as far as ten days apart. Even once tolls and duties were paid to local authorities to ensure safe passage, caravans were under constant danger of attack by thieves and bandits. Shifting dunes and blowing sands could confound even experienced guides. The hazards were great, but so were the potential fortunes to be made. Reliable estimates of Akan gold production, a major source of Saharan trade, suggest that during the 1400s, 5,000 to 22,000 ounces of gold were produced each year. This enormous wealth was supplemented by fortunes to be made in the trading of brass vessels, kola nuts (chewed as a stimulant), and salt mined in the Sahara desert. In addition, the Saharan commercial network served as a conduit for the transfer of technology and ideas. The great Saharan ports of Sijilmasa, Timbuktu, Gao, and others were the entry points for a lively exchange of peoples and cultures. Through these ports passed traders and travelers from Genoa, Venice, Ghana, Cairo, Morocco, and beyond.

In the centuries before 1500, trans-Saharan trade with Europe is documented by the regular appearance in European markets of such items as "Moroccan" leather, a product actually manufactured in the Sudanic region of present-day Nigeria. For centuries, no African goods captured the attention of world trade so much as West African gold. Like Siberian gold, that of Africa supported many contemporary European currencies. It was the rumor of gold, as well as other wealth on the African continent that inspired the Portuguese and later European sea voyages, which were to alter established global connections and significantly affect the global balance.

The Indian Ocean

The maritime routes of the Indian Ocean were established even earlier than the overland Eurasian Silk Roads and the trans-Saharan caravan routes in Africa. They were the primary competitors of these overland networks in east–west world trade. Sea routes were less subject to breakdowns of security and political disruptions than the overland routes were and consistently carried larger quantities of goods and people. Long-distance maritime trade in the western Indian Ocean existed from the third millennium BCE, and by the first century CE, the number of ports had significantly expanded.

Shipping linked Eastern Africa and Southwest Asia with India, Southeast Asia, and China. Ships that moved slowly, hugging the great northern loop of coastline between East and West, likely traced the earliest connections. Early in the first century CE, at both the eastern and western ends of this long, complex route, market conditions and political circumstances forced a change in the pattern of coastal trade: the Indian Ocean route became a maritime highway spanning the ocean between eastern and western ports. Southeast Asian ports served as a conduit for Chinese trade with Arab and African traders who sailed the Indian Ocean. Arabian frankincense, one of the main ingredients in incense used in religious ceremonies and also in many medicines, and African ivory, along with Southeast Asian spices, were among the staples of Indian Ocean trade destined for Chinese markets that passed through the ports of Southeast Asia. Chinese products in demand by its trading partners included silk, tea, and manufactured goods such as ceramics.

The seven voyages undertaken by the Chinese Muslim admiral Zheng He between 1407 and 1433 bore witness both to the seafaring capabilities of the Chinese navy and to the Ming court's desire to command the maritime frontier. The expeditions were huge in scale: 62 ships, more than 200 support vessels, and nearly 30,000 men made up the first contingent. The final voyage sailed more than 19,300 kilometers (12,000 miles), and altogether the series of expeditions visited at least 30 countries around the rim of the Indian Ocean. Financed and supported by imperial patronage, Zheng He's voyages were designed to display the power of Ming China and to confirm its place as the center of the world.

Unlike their European counterparts later in the century, however, the purpose of the voyages was not to establish a presence in foreign lands, nor to seek either goods or markets, but to confirm the basic order of tributary relations by taking gifts from the Chinese emperor to rulers of other lands and accepting tribute in return. When the winds shifted at court under a new emperor, funding for the voyages was halted because of their great expense and because of distrust of maritime commerce. The government's interest turned instead to the country's inland frontiers and to the consolidation of Chinese civilization in its land-based realm.

By the fifteenth century, there were three interlocking circuits of trade in the Indian Ocean: the Arabian Sea; the Indian Ocean; and the South China Sea. While Muslims dominated the first circuit, the second included Muslim merchants from coastal East Africa and Hindus from South and Southeast Asia, and the Chinese dominated the third. No single state, culture, or ethnic group dominated Indian Ocean trade as a whole; rather, it was a multiethnic world where Arab merchants resided in Chinese ports, East African merchants brought goods from the interior to Indian ports, and Indian merchants operated in East African and Chinese ports. Both goods and ideas – even languages – were exchanged in these encounters among merchants, and the seasonal monsoon winds determined when trade took place and how it was configured.

"Lands below the winds": Southeast Asia

The region we now know as Southeast Asia was shaped by the burgeoning east–west long-distance maritime trade through the Indian Ocean and beyond. Relying on the seasonal monsoon winds that brought heavy rains and regularized maritime commerce, Southeast Asia was known to its inhabitants – and to outsiders who plied the waters of the Indian Ocean for trade – as the "Lands below the winds." Both mainland and island Southeast Asia were dependent on the ocean-borne trade carried by the monsoon winds, and certain port cities, such as Malacca near the tip of the Malaysian peninsula, existed solely as a result of maritime commerce in the Indian Ocean.

From the thirteenth century on, Islamic influence grew steadily in the island world of Southeast Asia. The Muslim city-state of Melaka was founded in 1401. Melaka developed during the fifteenth century into a wealthy entrepôt, with a rapidly expanding volume of trade flowing through the strategically located port from north to south and south to north, through the narrow

Strait of Malacca. Indian, Arab, and Persian traders set up their trading headquarters at Melaka, and the Malay language became the principal language of trade throughout Southeast Asia. Indian cotton was one of the main goods that passed through the port of Melaka, where it was traded for East Indian spices destined for the European market. By 1500, Melaka was the largest and most populous commercial emporium in the international trade world of Southeast Asia.

Port cities, merchants, and maritime trade

Across the Indian Ocean, East African city-states also grew as centers for the administration of maritime trade. Situated on islands off present-day Kenya and Tanzania on the East African coast, complex urban societies such as Kilwa, Pemba, Lamu, and Pate emerged (after the second century

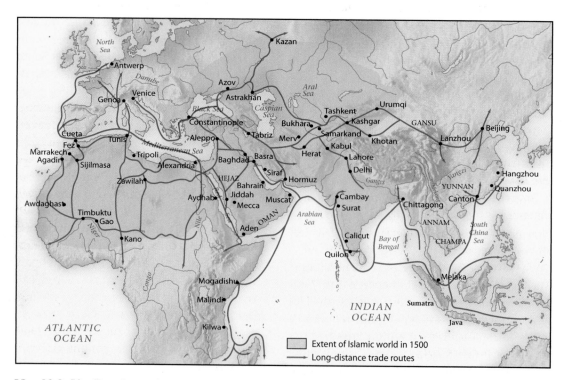

Map 10.3 Afro-Eurasian trade routes and centres 600–1500.

CE) from the background of early civilization on the African mainland. These coastal urban centers were the crucibles in which Swahili language (based on a local Bantu linguistic core with Arab elements added) and culture emerged by around 1100 CE. The wealth and political importance of the Swahili were based on their control of the extensive Indian Ocean trading networks. Trading gold, ivory, slaves, iron, rare woods, and other goods obtained from the African hinterland for Chinese porcelains, Islamic glazed wares, glass vessels, and beads, wealthy sultans built luxurious entrepôts, commercial centers for importing and exporting, with collection and distribution functions.

Three key areas on the subcontinent engaged in Indian Ocean trade: the Gujarat peninsula, the Malabar coast on the west, and the Coromandel coast on the east. Ibn Battuta praised the beautiful architecture of the city of Cambay, the major port of Gujarat, constructed by foreign merchants, who made up the majority of its inhabitants. Gujarati merchants played an important role in international shipping and commerce and were prominent in East African port cities as well. Far south of Cambay, along the Malabar coast, the city of Calicut was a commercial complex where Gujarati and Jewish merchants engaged in trade. Calicut rose in the mid-thirteenth century, when Baghdad fell to the Mongols and the Persian Gulf was eclipsed in importance as a trade route when the Karimi of Cairo took over the spice trade from the Indian Ocean.

At the end of the eleventh century, the First Crusade had inaugurated a process of trade revival that reconnected European economies to those of Asia and Africa, with the result that Italian cities became commercial centers of long-distance trade. The effort to recapture the Holy Land proved a boon to trade, and Italian merchants reaped vast profits. Genoa's strategy of developing ties in the western Mediterranean from Seville all the way to northern Europe proved to be momentarily advantageous. Further west, Venice came into its own during the first four Crusades, vanquishing its rivals, such as Genoa, dominating the eastern Mediterranean, and reaping the riches of the trade routes between Constantinople and western Europe.

Situated at the head of the Adriatic Sea, Venice grew up on mudflat islands located in brackish lagoons between the mainland and the banks formed by the debris of a number of rivers, notably the Po, which emptied into the sea there. Though Venetians had to collect rain for drinking water, the sea served them in almost every other way. The sea was the major source of food, since land on the islets was scarce and most of it was unsuitable for agriculture. From early trade with the mainland in fish and salt to the virtual monopoly of east–west trade that Venice achieved by the thirteenth century, maritime commerce enriched Venetians and made Venice an important European power. As Venice was becoming wealthy and powerful on the bounty of Mediterranean trade and profits connected with the Crusades, other people outside the setting of Eurasian port cities were similarly dependent on trade.

Connections in the Americas

Like the Venetians, the peoples of Mesoamerica were strategically located and played a key role in connecting continents via land and sea. Mesoamericans built intercontinental connections with both South and North America. The appearance of maize in agriculture along the Peruvian coast about 1500 BCE suggests early connections with Mesoamerica, where maize was first domesticated. Little is known about the nature of that contact or how it came about, but the appearance of maize and of a distinctly Mesoamerican style of figurine in Peru confirms an ancient connection. It is likely that the connections between Mesoamerica and South America were neither close nor continuous before Columbus, though there is evidence of Incan maritime contact with Mesoamerica.

South America

Regional connections in South America existed early, flourished, and were continuous. As early as the time of Chavín de Huántar (ca. 1000–1200 BCE), when the llama and alpaca (both **camelids**) were domesticated for transportation as well as wool, exchange routes were established along the west coast of South America. These were expanded by other cultures, such as the Chimu (ca. 800–1400), and were ultimately brought under the sway of the Incas (1438–1536), who organized control over some 3,700 kilometers (2,300 miles) of territory stretching along the western coast of South America from mid-Ecuador in the north to the upper half of Chile in the south.

The interweaving of the incredible range of ecological zones and altitudinal levels in Inca territories produced complex patterns of exchange and required concentrated authority to maintain routes and supervise trade. This may account for the special character of exchange during the period of Inca dominance. There was no private or open exchange; rather, goods, cultural influences, and the routes along which they moved were controlled by the hierarchically organized state. Highland basins traded produce and textiles to lowlands for the gold needed for ritual and conspicuous consumption. Connections were even established east of the Andes. Andean precious metals, copper, and produce passed east as far as the upper Paraguay River, and cotton cloth, feathers, jaguar skins, coca, fish poisons, and medicines returned from the trans-Andean lowlands. The elaboration of these regional networks for cloth, metals, and other goods later became an effective commercial highway and their maintenance was a signature feature of the fifteenth-century Inca Empire.

Ecuadorian voyages

Sedentary villages along the coast of present-day Ecuador date from about 4000 BCE, and archae-ologists have documented that the villagers relied heavily on marine resources for food. It appears that their Pacific connections also brought them wealth in the form of the Spondylus seashell. The shell, which is found only in the warmer waters of the Pacific near Mexico, was excavated in ritual contexts dating to around 3000 BCE After about 700 BCE, its use was more common; the shell had become an exchange currency. Ecuadorian voyagers used large, balsa wood sailing rafts with movable centerboards and rigged sails for their Pacific travels. The same sailing routes may also have permitted the diffusion of early metal-working technology from South America to Mesoamerica.

Trading networks cross the Americas

Long before the rise of the Inca Empire, like the Eurasian Silk Roads and trans-Saharan caravan routes, trading networks in the Americas linked peoples, cultures, and regional economies to each other. Longer-distance routes even connected the two continents of North and South America. Unlike the extensive web of Indian Ocean highways, in the Americas maritime coastal and riverine routes transported goods by water using smaller and lighter vessels.

In Mesoamerica, jade deposits in territory controlled by the Olmecs (fl. ca. 1000 BCE) contributed to far-flung trade, from modern Costa Rica and Guatemala in the south to the Mexico Valley in the north. Teotihuacán (ca. 100 BCE–650 CE) was involved in a wide trading network that probably linked all major contemporary Mesoamerican cultures. Teotihuacán obsidian, one of the most common materials used for weapons, has been found in widely distributed sites across the region.

The connections between Mesoamerica and North America are somewhat more clearly understood than those between Mesoamerica and South America. As early as Teotihuacán, there were northern routes that extended westward into Arizona and New Mexico to the Anasazi of the Colorado plateau, where Mesoamerican feathers, gold, and cacao beans (then the major medium of monetary exchange) were traded for **turquoise**. Other routes of trade and sociocultural influence extended eastward toward Oklahoma and Arkansas. Later Toltec (ca. 750–1150) traders and explorers in search of such things as alum, salt, incense, and raw copper also reached as far as the present-day southwestern United States, where they seem to have influenced the Anasazi. Much of the characteristic southwestern ceremonial art derives from the end of the Toltec period and may reflect a fusion of Mesoamerican rain god cults with local religious traditions.

Mesoamerican influence also spread north and eastward, to the area of the warm and wet woodlands around the confluence of the Mississippi, Missouri, and Ohio Rivers, the center of Mississippian culture. The routes of the Mississippian prototypes remain unknown, but the Mississippians' architectural styles, including temple-topped pyramids built around a central plaza, and their ceremonial art styles all show a generic relationship to Mesoamerican features. As in the case of the peoples of Andean highland South America, the heavy reliance of the Mississippians on maize, along with squash and beans, suggests early connections between North and South America, while copper seems to have been carried to South America from the eastern woodlands.

The Turquoise Roads

Archaeological evidence suggests that the cultural brilliance of Teotihuacán was known to the early Maya (ca. 300–900 CE) and was the result of trade conducted between these two cultures. Mayan regional trade in salt, hard stone, and pottery brought together outlying districts and may have been a major basis for the integration of Mayan society.

Between about 900 and 1200 CE, the use of turquoise became widespread throughout Mesoamerica. Since the source-mines containing this blue gem lie in North America, from California to Colorado, and turquoise objects have been found in many Mesoamerican sites, it is clear that turquoise was traded over long distances. Unlike the trade routes of Eurasia that ran between east and west, the roads that carried turquoise were constructed along a north–south corridor. Like gold in Africa and silk in Asia, turquoise was valued for its aesthetic appeal and rarity, but for Mesoamericans, it also had religious meaning. After it was mined and traded, it was worked into ceremonial objects and often placed in burial sites.

Mississippian regional connections in North America are better known. They focused on the great center at Cahokia (fl. ca. 900–1300), a city built by native North Americans. Through extensive trading connections, Cahokia was in constant contact with other communities scattered across nearly a third of the North American continent. The ruling elite at Cahokia controlled trade in raw materials, such as seashells, coppers, flint, and mica, which were drawn from a wide radius extending from north of Lake Superior to the Gulf Coast shoals of Florida and from the Appalachians as far west as the plains of North and South Dakota and Nebraska. In addition, the Cahokians manufactured a variety of goods for export: salt, tools, jewelry, and ceremonial goods.

The exports and imports – it took a steady flow of some 11,350–13,600 kilograms (25,000– 30,000 pounds) of food a day to feed the people of Cahokia – traveled mainly by water, since domesticated draft animals (other than dogs) were not in use. Much of the produce was transported on streams and lakes, perhaps linked by canals; the city may have been so interlaced with waterways that it would have resembled European Venice. Tons of goods carried in canoes up to 15 meters (50 feet) in length moved along water routes to satellite centers and outposts. These water-based connections were no less amazing than the links across the Pacific Ocean.

Pacific connections before 1500

Like the Americas, the thousands of islands that lay scattered over the face of Pacific Oceania remained isolated from the connections that had been established between Africans, Asians, and Europeans before 1500. Pacific Oceania is divided into Melanesia, Polynesia, and Micronesia. The peoples who inhabited these islands established their own regional connections across the Pacific as early as the first and second millennia BCE, when maritime traders identified with the Lapita cultural tradition began to settle in Melanesia, the islands south of the equator from Papua New Guinea to the west to Fiji to the east.

Lapita culture

The Lapita culture was probably an extension of much earlier migrations to Pacific Islands from Southeast Asia. Sedentary agriculturalists, the Lapita brought with them domesticated plants and animals along with a distinctive pottery style used to trace the movements and connections of its makers. They cultivated crops such as taro, yams, bananas, breadfruit, and coconuts, which were spread by occasional voyages among the islands. By 1300 BCE, these people had reached the outer boundary of Fiji and soon after made their way to Polynesia by way of Tonga and Samoa.

Melanesia: Vanuatu

One of the major island groups in central Melanesia, Vanuatu is a string of verdant volcanic islands. The archipelago of Vanuatu lies outside an ecological boundary at the Solomon Islands to

the northwest; beyond this boundary there are no native land mammals, and the vegetation and bird life on the islands is distinct from that on the other side of the boundary. The earliest evidence of human habitation dates to about 3,000 years ago and is consistent with the spread of Lapita culture from an early center northwest of the Solomons. In addition to pottery style, the spread of Lapita culture to Vanuatu is associated with the introduction of the pig, dog, and chicken, as well as evidence of stone tools and shell ornaments.

We can identify the spread of Lapita culture to Vanuatu with the expansion of regional exchange networks, and archaeological evidence of change about 2,000 years ago can be seen as the product of a process of diversification that took place in Lapita culture because of difficulties in maintaining regular contact among relatively distant island groups. This change indicates the constriction of regional exchange networks.

From about 750 years ago, archaeological sites suggest another major change in Vanuatu's connections with other South Pacific islands. Archaeologists who have excavated the grave of an individual known as Roy Mata, an important chief from "the south," suggest that he was a Polynesian immigrant and that his and other graves from this period and later show a wave of Polynesian migration to the Vanuatu chain. Whatever new discoveries yield about the past of Vanuatu and whatever new interpretations are shaped by them, it is clear that Vanuatu, like other islands in the Pacific was part of a complex and dynamic system of regional exchange networks and subject to changes brought about by fluctuations in contact as well as by migration of peoples across extensive sea routes.

Polynesia

Polynesians inhabited the group of islands within a triangle in the central Pacific bounded by Hawaii, New Zealand, and Easter Island. This area, along with Micronesia to the west of it, was among the latest to be occupied by humans, probably around 3,000 years ago. During the first millennium CE, trading relations established by the dispersal of peoples led to the transfer of crops, technology, and some aspects of a common culture. Around 300 CE, Samoans made their way by canoe eastward to the distant Marquesas Islands. Between 400 and 850, the Marquesas served as a primary center for the diffusion of a common culture – people, animals, plants, technology, and arts – across Polynesia, including the most distant corners of the Polynesian "triangle": the Hawaiian Islands; the Society Islands and Easter Island; the Southern Cooks and New Zealand.

Maori

Polynesians who settled in New Zealand, the Maori, provide a well-documented example of how Polynesians explored and settled the Pacific in decked vessels capable of carrying 100–200 persons, with water and stores sufficient for voyages of some weeks. They had knowledge of the stars and were able to determine favorable seasons for voyages. They were keen navigators, setting their courses from familiar landmarks and steering by the sun and stars and the direction of winds and waves.

Polynesian settlement of New Zealand presented an enormous ecological challenge, since most of the domesticated plants and animals from the Marquesas either failed to survive the long voyage or died out soon after in the different climate. Polynesian settlers adapted to the new environment by becoming hunter-farmers, which led to environmental changes and in turn to the necessity to adopt new strategies for survival that were no longer linked to Marquesan origins.

Megaliths of Easter Island

Formed of three extinct volcanoes, Easter Island, also known as Rapa Nui, lies about 3,700 kilometers (about 2,300 miles) off the west coast of modern Chile, at the outer edge of Polynesia. The fertile volcanic soil and year-round warm climate allow the cultivation of potatoes, sugar cane, taro, and tropical fruits. The earliest settlement of the island possibly took place about 1,200 years ago (800 CE), though some archaeologists believe its settlement was more recent, around 1200 CE. Strong trade winds brought early Polynesians to Easter Island. It is believed that people from the Marquesas Islands traveled in canoes and invaded Rapu Nui, taking over the island from any original inhabitants. Although overpopulation, deforestation, and environmental collapse was at one time blamed on human activities, it is also possible that earlier invaders – rats, who possibly arrived as stowaways – may have gnawed through local forests of palm trees, leading to devastating environmental degradation.

Since the arrival of a Dutch explorer on Easter Day in the early eighteenth century and later Chilean occupation of the island, archaeologists have puzzled over the large stone monuments (megaliths) found on the island. Ranging in height from 3 to 12 meters (10 to 40 feet), more than 200 of these statues – huge torsos and heads with elongated ears and noses – were transported to ceremonial sites that remain visible in the landscape. Large stone burial platforms called *ahus* support rows of statues; within the *ahus* are burial chambers for individuals or groups.

The burial platforms are located on bluffs overlooking the sea, and archaeologists have discovered nearly 1,000 statues thought to have been made by the Polynesians. Smaller sculptures of wood and wooden tablets have also been found on Easter Island. The tablets are inscribed with what appears to be a form of picture writing, providing the only evidence of a writing system in Polynesia, though it remains undeciphered.

Micronesia

To the west of Polynesia and the north of Melanesia lie the hundreds of islands of Micronesia, scattered over an ocean larger than the United States but containing a total of only 3,260 square kilometers (1,260 square miles) of land area. The most northerly and westerly Micronesian islands are the Marianas, the largest of which is Guam; also included are the southern chain called the Carolines, with the Marshalls to the east and the Kiribati to the southeast. Despite the great distances between the island groups and the fact that each inhabited island or the waters around it produced only the bare essentials for the peoples living on it, connections among the islands were maintained.

Overseas trade was a prominent feature of Micronesian life. Nearly every place produced a specialty – flat mats or baskets, unique dyes or special shell ornaments – that was exchanged for something unusual from another place. For example, Yap islanders sailed to Palau to quarry and carry back home the large disks of stone they used for a special kind of money. Fleets of atoll dwellers from the islands between Yap and Truk regularly sailed to Guam, and similar enterprises went on throughout Micronesia. Exploits over such distances produced daring sailors and skilled navigators. To maintain the connections among their islands, Micronesians mastered the intricacies of seasons, currents, and winds and even developed charts to guide them on their long voyages.

Although maritime connections initially had knit together a Pacific world, land routes were the important means by which people and commodities moved in the Americas. Similar in kind to those of Asia, Africa, and Europe, connections in the Americas bound two continents together and served as avenues for trade and cultural interchange. Extending over distances comparable to the east–west and north–south connections between Eurasia and Africa, they had unique features: for example, the lack of horses, donkeys, and camels as draft animals on overland routes and the differences in ships used for maritime and riverine passageways. They served the needs of peoples in the Americas before the European conquest and were reorganized and integrated into the shifting pattern of connections that underlay the establishment of European global dominance following 1500.

Northern Eurasian connections: The Vikings

While Pacific maritime connections may have been sporadic or accidental, they did not significantly alter the Americas prior to 1500 CE. From the opposite side of the continent, the Atlantic and North Seas became bases for constructing maritime connections that would eventually extend the global reach of Europe. Even in imperial Roman times, northwestern Eurasia was only partially connected with the rest of the world. Although they benefited from the flow of peoples and goods along the secure road systems the Romans constructed, the western European markets were too small to draw much business. After the fifth-century collapse of Roman imperial government in Western Eurasia, old connections were maintained along the Mediterranean coast through Venice and Constantinople, while in trans-Alpine regions, the dominance of a self-sufficient agriculture-based manorial system meant that the demand for imported goods nearly vanished. In the ninth and tenth centuries, Vikings from northern Eurasia built a sea-based empire on conquest and trade.

The Norse – or Viking – peoples of Scandinavia undertook the early steps in this direction. During the ninth century, the harshness of the Scandinavian environment and the pressure of an increased population on lands of limited productivity, along with the lure of profit and adventure, stimulated ambitious Viking rulers to set their people into motion. As immigrants, conquerors,

10.4 Viking ship from the Bayeux Tapestry. The nuns of Normandy embroidered this tapestry to commemorate the Norman conquest of England in 1066. Multicolored horses and men on Viking ships are among the scenes depicted.

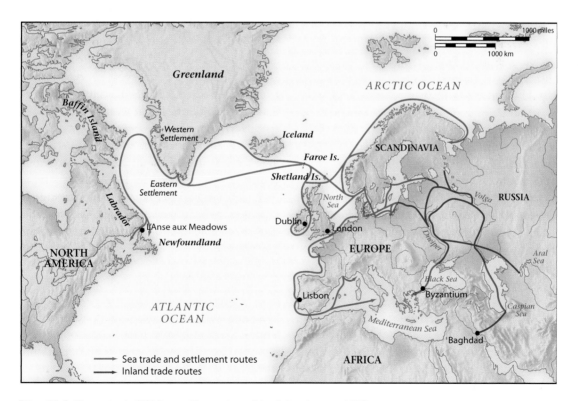

Map 10.4 The extent of Viking settlements and trade routes, ca. 1000.

and traders, Vikings left their northern homelands in open boats of 21–24 meters (70–80 feet) in length. Long and narrow, elegant and efficient, these were primarily rowed ships with a supplementary square sail, with high sides but a shallow draft. They could carry as many as 60 or 70 people across the open sea as well as down the quieter waters of inland rivers.

The Varangians: The eastern route

The Scandinavians took the eastern route that had been followed largely by Swedes. Crossing the Baltic, sailing down the Gulf of Finland, they used south-to-north-flowing rivers as aquatic highways for penetrating the plains of Russia. Indigenous people there called these Norse invaders "Varangians" or "Rus'" (from which was derived the name "Russia"). The Varangians first appeared as plunderers and adventurers; they stayed as traders and mercenaries. In their remarkable boats, they followed river routes further south to the Black Sea and imposed their control over the various disunited Slavic peoples among whom they appeared. By 850, they had gained control of Novgorod and soon thereafter Kiev.

Varangian Kiev

The traditional history of the origins of the Kievan state begins with its capture by the Rus' in 882, but almost everything connected with Varangian Kiev is subject to historiographical controversy. A Kievan state predated the arrival of the Rus', and there appears to be little basis for asserting a fundamental Scandinavian influence on Kievan culture. This does not negate a ninth-century Varangian presence there; indeed, archaeological, philological, and other evidence substantiates it. For example, the names of the ninth-century princes and the diplomats who negotiated treaties with Byzantium confirm a Varangian dynasty in Kiev.

From their base at Kiev, the Varangians maintained trade routes north to Scandinavia and south to Constantinople; indeed, Kiev was successful because of its position on the road "from the Varangians to the Greeks." Various Byzantine products found in Swedish tombs and graffiti that can still be seen on the columns of the great former cathedral and mosque of Hagia Sophia in Istanbul offer testimony to Varangian–Byzantine connection through Kiev. In addition, Kiev also traded with Central and West Asia, establishing commercial relations with the Islamic Empire, supplying slaves from Russia and Central Asia to the Abbasid caliphate in Baghdad.

The Vikings: Western routes

Other Vikings, principally from Norway and Denmark, went west and south. Before the end of the eighth century, they were skirting and raiding Scotland and Ireland. By 830, they were establishing villages there and on the offshore islands; they used these small colonies as bases from which to raid and plunder the rich monastic establishments on the fringes of Christian Europe. From their stations in Ireland and the North Sea islands, the Vikings sailed westward across the open North Atlantic.

Shortly after the middle of the ninth century, they reached Iceland and settled there permanently; from Iceland they were lured on to Greenland, where Erik the Red set up a colony in 981. Erik's son, Thorvald Eriksson, had been told about a place called "Vinland" (an Old Norse term for "grassland" or "pasture") by his brother Leif, who had reached this land (actually thought to be Nova Scotia) about the year 1000. Eriksson pushed westward to Labrador and southward to Newfoundland, on whose northernmost point, at L'Anse aux Meadows, the first known European colony in North America was established. Vikings may also have sailed further south to what today are Massachusetts and Martha's Vineyard, but their colony at L'Anse aux Meadows lasted scarcely a year and their connection with North America was not permanent.

The Vikings: Southern routes

Westward-moving Norse also turned south, to both Carolingian and Islamic Europe and North Africa, where they conquered lands and were successfully integrated into existing political systems in Spain and North Africa. By 1100, they had taken over southern Italy and all of Sicily. From this base, they became active participants and competitors in the political economy of the Mediterranean, the western terminus of the ancient east–west world trade routes.

As the Vikings moved into the Mediterranean, they came up against competition from Venice and the Byzantine Empire. These two experienced trading powers had achieved a successful relationship with the Africans and West Asians who controlled the east–west avenues of the world trade system before the Vikings appeared, and they concentrated their maritime energies on achieving a naval domination of the Mediterranean that would enable them to control the extraordinarily profitable trade connections between European and eastern and southern markets. From the twelfth century, the Mediterranean was increasingly a Venetian monopoly.

Summary

Despite the many connections before 1500, the two hemispheres remained mostly separated in the West. A few Viking settlements and the occasional Basque fishing vessel were the exceptions in the Atlantic. On the Pacific side of the hemispheric seams, where the roads of the Rus' ended and the boats of Eurasia's northern seas pushed eastwards across the Bering Strait into the Pacific reaches of North America, singularly important trading societies thrived in the Pacific Northwest of North America. The peoples of the Pacific Northwest Coast had enjoyed an abundant and lush environment of wild salmon, berries, and roots, alongside hunted game and whaling (from direct DNA evidence 1,300–1,600 years ago, but indirect evidence from bone harpoons is earlier), since at least 7800 BCE. They had no interest in agriculture, yet managed to produce large, affluent, and complex trading societies, rich in distinctive and expressive arts and spiritual beliefs, and settled in permanent houses by about 4000–3000 BCE. Some groups, such as the Columbia River Chinookans, were specialized in provisioning for long-distance travel and trade and they were acquainted with the accumulation of wealth. Their language became a widely influential language of trade and interaction. Like the traders of the Silk Roads, the Chinook met, gossiped, gambled, danced, and sang in large, vibrant communities. Like the neighboring Kwakwaka'wakw, they engaged in a distinctive Northwest Coast ceremony known as potlatch or give-aways, part feast and dramatic performance, in which wealth was given away in an attempt to win long-term social and political validation, together with increased status and recognition of genealogical rights. In the eighteenth century CE, their mighty Columbia River would in turn meet the ocean currents of globalization, devastating encounters that would forever alter their environment and lifestyle through new contacts and the spread of disease.

Whether traders were affluent foragers, successful pastoralists, or depended on the labor of agriculturalists, their essential contributions to the cultural encounters of the ancient world helped to create wealth and maintain elites, even while they negotiated the differences and disparities of a world subject to unbearable inequality and suffering. Not only merchants, but the missionaries, pilgrims, diplomats, and other travelers transcended their own places and times, connecting the world in dynamic patterns and processes on the way to the global network of our own lives. This chapter has suggested some of the ways in which societies managed to balance the accelerating integration of a world knit together by shared material concerns, even as they reeled apart through differences in cultural practices, from architecture to food tastes, beliefs, and ideas. In the next chapter, we examine the systems of cultural memory that helped to create coherence in the ever-changing landscapes of complexity.

Note

1   Ross E. Dunn, *The Adventures of Ibn Battuta: A Muslim Traveler of the 14th Century* (Los Angeles: University of California Press, 1989), pp302, 296–97.

Suggested readings

Barraclough, Geoffrey, ed. (1979) *The Times Atlas of World History*, London: Times Books, Ltd. Richly informative maps accompanied by concise summaries of key themes and events in world history.

Bentley, Jerry H. (1993) *Old World Encounters: Cross-Cultural Contacts in Pre-Modern Times*, New York: Oxford University Press. Excellent survey of world commercial, cultural, and political connections before Columbus.

Berrin, Kathleen and Esther Pasztory, eds (1993) *Teotihuacan: Art from the City of the Gods*, New York: Thames & Hudson.

Bonnemaison, Joel, Kirk Huffman, Christian Kaufmann, and Darrell Tryon, eds. (1996) *Arts of Vanuatu*, Honolulu: University of Hawaii Press. A beautifully illustrated collection of articles on the most recent archaeological and anthropological studies of this archipelago in the South Pacific.

Curtin, Philip D. (1984) *Cross-Cultural Trade in World History*, Cambridge: Cambridge University Press. Comparative approach to commercial links in world history.

Dunn, Ross E. (1989) *The Adventures of Ibn Battuta*, Berkeley and Los Angeles: University of California Press. Account of the fifteenth-century Muslim traveler's adventures.

Kratli, Graziano and Ghislaine Lydon (2010) *The Trans-Saharan Book Trade: Manuscript Culture, Arabic Literacy, and Intellectual History in Muslim Africa*, Leiden: Brill.

McNeill, William H. (1976) *Plagues and Peoples*, New York: Anchor Doubleday. Pathbreaking survey of
epidemiological connections in world history, especially the spread of the Black Death.

Online resources

Annenberg/CPB, *Bridging World History* (2004) <www.learner.org/channel/courses/worldhistory> Multimedia project with interactive website and videos on demand; see especially Unit 9 Connections Across Land and Unit 10 Connections Across Water.

NOVA online, *The Vikings* <www.pbs.org/wgbh/nova/vikings> Supporting resources from the PBS program.

Smithsonian Institution, *Vikings: The North Atlantic Saga* <www.mnh.si.edu/vikings/start.html> Online exhibition emphasizing the oceanic migrations of Viking voyagers.

University of Washington, *Silk Road Seattle Project* <depts.washington.edu/silkroad> Interactive website with maps and other visual resources.

Study questions

1. How are land and maritime connections different? How are they similar?

2. What was the impact of early currencies on commercial development? How can coins be used as historical evidence?

3. What were some of the unintended consequences of trade?

4. What do gold and turquoise share in common as early trade commodities?

5. Why did spices come to acquire such value in luxury trade?

6. What kind of connections do diplomats and pilgrims create? How do these connections differ from those forged by merchants?

7. Why does food become a key commodity in trade?

8. What is the role of environment in creating and sustaining connections among world regions?

9. Before 1500 CE, the two hemispheres remained largely separate. What were the obstacles and opportunities for connecting the world regions of Afro-Eurasia, Oceania, and the Americas? Why were few connections

built? Describe the potential for connections in the Pacific and Atlantic before 500 BCE and after 1000 CE.

10. Compare connections on the Mississippi, Columbia, Nile, Niger, Seine, Tiber, and Yangzi Rivers (see also earlier Chapters 3, 4, 5 and 6). How did geography and religion play a key role in furthering trade and influence for these regions?

TIMELINE

ca. 3500 BCE	3–2000	2900	2600	1600–1550	1500	1401
Quipu knotted strings at site of Caral	Mesopotamian cuneiform script	Egyptian hieroglyphics	Sphinx built	Shang China, oracle bones	Sanskrit alphabetic script	Sphinx restored

11 Cultural memory

Transmitting traditions

The colossal stone monument known as the Sphinx stands guard to the Giza plateau's greatest pyramids of ancient Egypt. Towering more than ten times the height of humans, the Sphinx – a sculpture that is part man, part god, and part animal – was built about 2600 BCE. It serves as a powerful reminder of Egypt's past. Although we tend to think of such monumental treasures as unchanging cultural memories, such is not the case. By the time of the Pharaoh Thutmose IV, living in 1401 BCE, the Sphinx was already ancient, already altered, and in need of major restoration. According to the inscriptions on a red granite slab erected in front of the statue, Thutmose cleared away the desert sand and restored the damaged lion body with large limestone blocks for protection against wind erosion.

After another 1,000 years, the Greeks and Romans visited and again restored the Sphinx. The Greek historian Herodotus (fifth century BCE) toured the valley and wrote the definitive tourist guide before the nineteenth century. Beginning with the Romans, visitors have also stolen smaller, more portable monuments, in attempts to

appropriate their power as historical icons. The appropriation of history, it seems, is as enduring as the monuments themselves. In the fifteenth century, Islamic leaders defaced the great sculpture, fearing that local Egyptians were still paying homage to its grandeur and durability. An Arab proverb claims that "man fears time, but time fears the pyramids." Perhaps the most blatant example of plunder was that of the French Emperor Napoleon, whose troops invaded the Nile in the late-eighteenth century CE, and uncovered the Sphinx again, followed by European explorers who began digging up hundreds of ancient treasures that eventually found their way into the museums and collections of the world.

Today, the Great Sphinx gazes on a transformed landscape marred by fast-food restaurants, polluted air, and tourists. The view behind remains the desert sands of the Sahara; like the sands of time they are constantly shifting. That the Sphinx and other Nile Valley monuments have survived the millennia was precisely the intent of the Egyptians, who built and painted them bright colors in antiquity. However, their

ca. 800	ca. 484–425	ca. 480–406	ca. 445–386	ca. 400 BCE–400 CE	300 BCE	ca. 100
Homer	Herodotus, who writes *The Histories*	Euripides	Aristophanes	Mahabharata epic constructed	Imperial University, China	Sima Qian, Chinese historian

intent was also that they not be entered ever again. While later generations have treated the great structures as human monuments, for the ancient Egyptians these were monuments to something cosmic and eternal. Yet, the deterioration of the stone surfaces of the Great Sphinx continues at an alarming rate. Perhaps one day, the hundreds of websites dedicated to ancient Egypt may be the only way to visit such monuments as the Great Sphinx.

Many historical memories are neither as durable nor as monumental as a pyramid. Ideas about the past can be embedded in the tall tales historians tell or in the songs children sing. They can be reflected in objects or in the technologies that create the material world. Their changing and sometimes enduring shape is the subject of this chapter.

Introduction to the theme of cultural memory

History is concerned not only with the products of the past but also with its processes: how we know what we know of the past, what the processes of remembering the past are, how they influence what is passed on, and how and by whom the processes of **historical memory** are controlled. What is passed on as history, what people remember and think it important to tell about the past, are the products of many complex

11.1 Image of the Great Sphinx.

ca. 0 CE	ca. 129–99	ca. 500	618–907	833	ca. 1000	ca. 1000
Paper invented, Han dynasty, China	Galen	Buddhist university at Nalanda, Bihar, India	Tang dynasty, examination system developed	Baghdad library founded	Movable type in China	Sei Shonagon writes *Pillow Book*

human processes. These processes involve not only collecting evidence about the past but also how and to what end that evidence is selected, arranged, and ordered so as to create a coherent and meaningful cultural memory.

Memory is not passive. It is embedded in specific cultures, the patterns of expression and behavior by which a community understands, uses, and survives in its environment. Not only is culture learned, it is malleable, changing over time. Changes in cultures are responses to material conditions – either natural or human in origin – such as environmental and climatic shifts or war and conquest, and the memory of change is preserved in cultural memory systems. Memory is a dynamic social process. Memory systems do not preserve or reproduce cultural knowledge without sometimes altering, shaping, or even inventing it, either consciously or unconsciously. Agents of the changes they record and preserve, memory systems exert powerful influence over the communities whose cultural experiences they record.

History is but one of the memory systems by which community is defined and cultural knowledge is transmitted. Among other domains of cultural memory are language, religion, architecture, dance, and music. These memory systems share with history the processes of shaping, defining, and perpetuating community cultural memory. Transmitters of community cultural knowledge, such as teachers and preachers, historians and dramatists, entrepreneurs and artisans, help define the identity of the community whose cultural memory they shape. Historians, artists, scientists, religious leaders, and philosophers all share responsibility for the cultural memory

systems of their communities, creating, propagating, and perpetuating communal culture over time and across spatial boundaries. Their role in transmitting and transforming cultural memory can either sustain, support, or challenge institutions of power and the authority of rulers and elites.

Though all members of a community shape culture, most humans individually have neither the power nor the ability to create cultural memory systems, which are often controlled by an institution or a group. Official forms of historical memory, such as that produced by governments or Churches, can impose a selective forgetting as well as a selective remembering. Popular cultural memory, however, manifested in a variety of forms such as performance art or literature, often provides a means of expressing resistance to official cultural memory and thus can function as an agency of cultural change, following its own principles of selective remembering and forgetting.

This chapter explores the theme of cultural memory and examines a variety of systems as they evolved around the globe up to about 1500 CE. We begin with consideration of the basic tools of cultural memory, the spoken and written word, and the institutions by which the word is perpetuated. This is followed by a discussion of other kinds of memory systems, among them technology and visual and performance arts, which rely primarily on image and practice. In particular, we examine the role of institutions and technologies in their transmission. Consideration of cultural memory systems in Asia, Africa, Europe, and the Americas leads to a discussion of

1037 CE	1058–1111	ca. 1100		1126–98	ca. 1214–92	ca. 1224–55
Death of Ibn Sina (Avicenna)	Al-Ghazzali	First European university, Bologna, Italy	Song of Roland epic	Ibn Rushd (Averroes)	Roger Bacon	Sunjata Epic

resistance to politically sanctioned cultural memory and its effect on changing historical consciousness: the process that transforms historical identity along the bridge between past and present.

Cultural memory systems: Oral traditions

The oldest system of cultural memory may be the spoken word. Written systems of cultural transmission are less than 6,000 years old, but oral traditions, orally transmitted cultural knowledge, date from the time the human species became capable of speech and communication. Since that time, human communities have transmitted their shared cultures orally. Even in the Digital Age of the computer, oral tradition remains an important means of preserving and transmitting cultural memory.

Oral tradition is a formal and highly ritualized system of cultural transmission, but it can also reflect change. As human agencies, oral memory systems are subject to revision. Some aspects of oral narratives conform with and support current political and social realities of their communities, while others resist revision and remain historically valid, fixed features of orally transmitted memory. The revised and fixed aspects of oral histories are not as oppositional as they might at first appear. They reflect the tendency of oral evidence to provide both immutable and historically dynamic cultural memory.

Oral traditions in Africa

Many oral cultures relied on specialists, who, like the scribes, priests, or scholars in literate societies, either themselves were elites (by virtue of the cultural information they controlled) or were connected intimately to elites through relations of patronage. Across much of West Africa, the oral historian known popularly as the **griot** held a position of power and importance as the individual responsible for preserving and transmitting the records of the past in oral form.

THE GRIOT IN MANDE SOCIETY   The historical role of the griot (*"jeliw"* in the Mande language) is described in the version of the Mande epic Sunjata, attributed to the griot Mamadou Kouyaté. He sums up the importance of oral memory, explaining his role as the agent of cultural transmission:

> [W]e are vessels of speech, we are the repositories which harbour secrets many centuries old. The art of eloquence has no secrets for us; without us the names of kings would vanish into oblivion, we are the memory of mankind; by the spoken word we bring to life the deeds and exploits of kings for younger generations.

In Mande society of the Mali Empire (ca. 1230–1600s CE), the griot (actually a later term widely applied to various oral historians) was often perceived to hold spiritual powers and played a key role in sanctioning leadership and maintaining political continuity. He was judge and counselor to kings as well as court historian, who, by knowing the past, was able to shape and control it. According to Mamadou Kouyaté, "history holds no mystery" and knowledge itself was a form of power. The influence and power of the griot was such as to make any modern-day historian envious. Their words not only brought to life the past but also profoundly affected the present course of events. Because they possessed and could shape knowledge of past events, griots could enhance the power of the king and his court and influence the cultural traditions they preserved.

Yoruba cultural memory systems

In another West African society, that of the ancestors of the Yoruba in southwestern Nigeria, those who preserved cultural memory were known as **arokin**. They were court functionaries, official historians who performed as bards and drummers. The Yoruba people also reenacted founding myths of lineages, quarters, towns, and kingdoms in annual festivals and installation ceremonies associated with chiefs and kings. The *arokin* performed royal and religious rituals that helped preserve myths. Yoruba cultural memory categorized the past in several different ways. Their view of the past consisted of immutable views of their world, which were publicly accepted, and of myths and rituals that were constantly subject to review and revision by contesting political and social forces in their community. There were also "deep truths," the knowledge of spiritual realms, that might subvert shifting myths and rituals and

thus were dangerous to the status quo because they undermined it and provided subversive resistance and opposition to those in authority, including those who controlled official Yoruba cultural memory.

Central Africa: Luba cultural memory systems

For the Luba of Central Africa (called "Kamilambian" and "Kisalian" from about 600 CE), a rich vocabulary of images and words exists to describe ideas about historical memory and connectedness, about remembering and forgetting as interdependent sides of memory. Luba officials still stage oral recitations of local history. Traditionally, state historians were rigorously trained men called *bana balute* ("men of memory"). They recited genealogies and king lists and recounted the founding charter of kingship. They traveled with kings and, like the griots, spread propaganda about the prestige and power of their patrons' culture. They used mnemonics, visual devices or objects that aid in and order remembering.

LUBA MEMORY BOARDS   The Luba world is quite literally strewn with mnemonic devices, images, and objects that are used to remember and reconfigure the past. These include royal emblems, shrines and grave markers, staffs, thrones, bead necklaces, and the object known as a **lukasa** (memory board). The *lukasa* is a hand-held wooden board covered with colored pins and beads; sometimes painted or incised geometric called a **quipu**, the colors and lengths of which recorded important numbers such as census figures, chronological data, and everyday transactions. Like the Luba's *lukasa*, the *quipu* seems to have functioned as a mnemonic device, a shorthand tool to aid in the memorization of large bodies of information.

The general history of the Inca Empire was secret and transmitted by specialists known by the term **amauta** and which were similar to the Yoruba *arokin*. The *amauta* taught in schools reserved for members of the elite who were given room and board by the state. Like Mali griots, Luba memory men, and Yoruba *arokin*, the Incan amauta ensured state control of cultural memory. By preserving those aspects of a ruler's exploits that he wished to be remembered and thus censoring the past, the *amauta* selectively reordered the past to serve present needs.

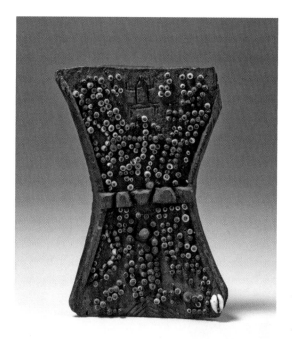

11.2 Luba memory board (lukasa), Zaire.

markings are added to evoke particular events, places, or names from the past. Such objects represent visually the vocabulary of memory, to be "read" only by those skilled and trained to convey the complexity of meaning encoded therein. The *lukasa* is used in initiation ceremonies to teach initiates the stories of culture heroes, clan migrations, and sacred lore. It also provides a visual mapping of the complicated political and social ordering of society, the natural world, and the world of the spirits.

Incan oral traditions

Like the traditional memory systems of the Luba, Mande, or Yoruba in Africa, that of the Incas in the central Andes of South America was oral. Incan oral traditions were organized in ways specific to their culture and transmitted with the help of mnemonic devices unique to it. Though their cultural memory system was fundamentally oral, Incan communities also used a knotted cord,

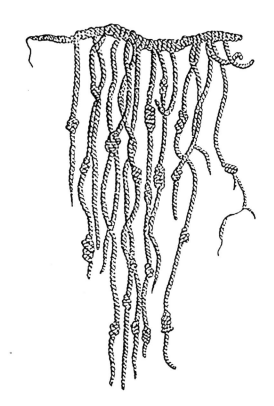

11.3 Quipu knotted cords aided Inca Empire specialists.

Cultural memory systems: Writing

From its beginnings, writing – like all memory systems – has served a variety of different purposes wherever it emerged in shaping and transmitting culture. Writing coexisted with other memory systems, which either supported or sometimes subverted written cultural memory. The interplay of written and non-written memory systems at times created significant political and social change.

The development of cuneiform script among the peoples of Mesopotamia in West Asia during the third millennium BCE, and the later evolution of an alphabetic script which was transmitted by Phoenician traders around the eastern shores of the Mediterranean, were related to the needs of commerce. Merchants needed a way of keeping inventories and financial records of transactions.

Writing and power

The development of writing was also associated with the exercise of power in early West Asian states, enabling scribes in service to rulers to record events, keep population records for taxation, and propagate and preserve law. Written law codes, such as that of the Babylonian ruler Hammurabi (r. 1795–1750 BCE), are examples of the lasting importance of written systems of cultural memory. The writing down of myths that supported royal power, such as those surrounding the god Marduk in Babylonia, contributed to the establishment of states and rulers and their continuity with earlier cultural traditions.

Sacred scripts

In early North Africa, Egyptian **hieroglyphics** ("priestly pictographs") were a sacred script under the control of a priesthood who served the pharaohs after about 2900 BCE. Later scripts include those developed during the second millennium BCE in the kingdom of Kush and at Axum, where sacred and secular powers were recorded on stone engravings and inscriptions. Other ritual and sacred traditions relied on scripts to record and control the transmission of information that supported and empowered priests and secular political rulers.

MAYAN SCRIPT   In the Americas, the Mayans created a script in the first millennium CE that was used in the keeping of historical and astronomical records. The Mayan script was a mixture of ideographic and phonetic elements, using graphic symbols or pictures to represent both objects and sounds. It included a complete syllabary, so theoretically everything could be written phonetically, as it sounded when spoken; however, the Mayan script was never used entirely to communicate phonetically since ideographs were considered to be religiously symbolic and thus to have great prestige. This probably reflects the desire of literate elites – priests and scribes – to maintain their monopoly of writing, knowledge of which gave them power. Scribes, who controlled astronomical, historical, and religious information, had their own patron deities, such as Itzamna, considered the creator and inventor of writing. Mayan hieroglyphics appeared on a variety of materials, including stone and bark paper, although relatively few manuscripts on paper have survived.

SANSKRIT AND INDO-EUROPEAN CULTURAL MEMORY   Sanskrit, the language of the Indo-Europeans who migrated into India in the mid-second millennium BCE, was transcribed in an alphabetic script and used to record religious texts of the Vedic tradition in early South Asia. The writing down of hymns to Indo-European gods, for example, helped to maintain Indo-Europeans' cultural memory and consolidate their power as they moved into the Indian subcontinent. Much later, in the third century BCE, inscriptions carved to proclaim the Indian ruler

11.4 Indian woman writing with a stylus. Sandstone sculpture, north India, eleventh century CE.

Ashoka's belief in Buddhism and to assert his claim to secular power further illustrate the utility of writing to preserve and transmit a politically useful message.

CHINESE WRITING AND RELIGION   While writing systems may be found in virtually every region of the world, nowhere was the written word endowed with greater power than in China. In Shang China (ca. 1600–1045 BCE) the development of the archaic script found on oracle bones was linked to divination practices. It was believed that the ancestors of the Shang kings, deities who could communicate with the supreme god, Di, would make their wishes known through the bones of animals used for sacrifice. To contact the spirits of these royal ancestors, a diviner would engrave a bone or turtle shell with written characters and then apply a heated bronze pin to them. Various lengths and patterns of cracks would appear on the shell or bone, and their relationship

to the written characters would be interpreted by the diviner as oracles and kept as records. The characters on oracle bones are archaic forms of the modern written script and thus provide evidence of the foundation of Chinese writing.

The practice of using oracle bones for prophecy and guidance, known as **scapulimancy**, also illustrates the role of a priestly elite in the creation and preservation of cultural memory. As in Egypt and among the Mayas, a scribal priesthood controlled a memory system and imbued it with a sacred quality and ritual character. The close association of the Chinese scribal elite with those who exercised political power provided the early Chinese state with religious underpinnings. Even the earliest oracle bone inscriptions – which recorded events such as battles, harvests, and royal marriages and births – can be seen as historical records, and the keeping of written accounts of the past became a central concern of those who held power in imperial China.

The transmission of culture through writing systems

More than 2,000 years later, the Chinese writing system spread to other parts of East Asia, primarily as a means of transmitting Chinese culture and Buddhism to Korea and Japan. Adapted by Koreans and Japanese to transcribe their own cultural memory, Chinese script was used by the emerging centralized states in Korea and Japan for the same purposes it served in China: the preservation of cultural memory to serve the interests of those in power. For example, the *Kojiki*, a record of myths and chronicles of the founding of Japan compiled under imperial sponsorship in 712 CE, was written using Chinese script in different ways, for both sound and meaning, an example of the process of adaptation. The writing down of myths that supported the claims of the imperial family to divine descent are a clear indication of the power of the written text as a cultural memory system.

Cultural memory systems: History

History began as an oral memory system, which became transformed into a written one wherever and whenever scripts were developed. For example, the Book of Deuteronomy in the Judeo-Christian Bible is history containing a law code embellished with legends and court records that validate the worship of Yahweh and explain the sacred role of the children of Israel. In early Judaism, Deuteronomy, learned by heart as a central act of religious faith, is an example of oral history that was eventually written down as a chapter of the Old Testament of the Bible.

Ancient Greece

The relationship between oral and written transmission of the past was close and complex, even in societies such as Greece, where written history developed early. By the late fifth century BCE, when the Greek scholar Herodotus, wrote his *Histories*, those who used writing to record their histories were designated chroniclers. But Herodotus himself gave oral performances of his works, either from memory as a recitation or reading from a written text. Herodotus sought a wider audience for his work by giving public readings, and his oral performances were the most effective way of gaining public recognition. Thus, even though writing was employed as a cultural memory system in fifth-century Greece, public and oral performances remained an important continuation from earlier traditions of the memorialist, a person who transmitted the past through memory and recitation.

While Herodotus was in West Asia and North Africa collecting information, he acquired long king lists and myths and legends from oral memory systems. Lengthy sections of his *Histories* existed in oral form before being written down by him. Herodotus's credo – "to say [in his writing] what is said" – reflects his use of oral sources,

11.5 Aristotle teaching from an early Arabic manuscript. The oral transmission of knowledge during Greek times was widely appreciated in the Islamic world.

which he would introduce in his text with a phrase such as "The Athenians say. . . " Herodotus heard different traditions recalled by different groups, and he saw his task as one of trying to verify and reconcile differing accounts. Herodotus's work is indicative of the transition from oral to written culture that was taking place during his lifetime. His *Histories* were written down and distinguished from other oral history because it came to be believed that the written word was less subject to alteration than the spoken one.

Early China

In China, where the written script early acquired a sacred character through the preservation of records of the past on oracle bones or bronze inscriptions, after the sixth century BCE, written historical texts attributed to Confucius (551–479 BCE) became the foundation of the Confucian canon (sacred or basic works). Confucius used the past to support his views of the ideal society. The *Book of Documents* (or History) is supposed to be a collection of documents from the first three dynasties (Xia, Shang, and Zhou), compiled and edited by Confucius to reveal his understanding of antiquity, which provided the model for rulers and for the ordering of society.

The *Spring and Autumn Annals*, also part of the written canon attributed to Confucius, is a chronicle of events in his home state of Lu, one of the states of the Warring States period (ca. 450–250 BCE). The terse entries in this chronicle, such as "The duke of Chao died," have been interpreted in later times as commentaries by Confucius on events and people through his careful use of particular terms such as "died" or "passed away" to reveal his judgment. Later embellishments, such as the "Traditions" (*zhuan*), date to the third century BCE and added accounts of intrigue, passion, and heroism to the terse recounting of events in the *Spring and Autumn Annals*. Like the written history of Herodotus's time, these works were probably meant to be read aloud, to be appreciated in a group setting through oral performance.

According to Confucian views, the historical record was thought to be the repository of "truth," the Confucian Way (*dao*) of humanity manifested in the pattern of the past. History was a mirror in which to reflect the present age against the exemplary model of antiquity. The historical record was thus a guide to political action and ethical behavior in the present. From earliest times in China, the writing of history was a moral obligation of those who ruled, and the historical record itself acquired a sacred quality.

Sima Qian (fl. ca. 100 BCE), who held the post of Grand Historian at the court of Emperor Wu of the Han dynasty (206 BCE–220 CE), wrote a history of the Chinese world up to his own time. He introduced a major innovation in the writing of history, as he shifted from an annalistic form exemplified by the *Spring and Autumn Annals* to a more sophisticated and complex thematic organization that included biographical accounts and topical treatises as well as court annals and imperial genealogies.

Although court historians who came after Sima Qian, such as Ban Gu (fl. ca. 100 CE), the author of the history of the Han dynasty, followed Sima Qian's model, their chronological coverage was limited to single dynasties. The dynastic histories, compiled by each dynasty in succession, reinforced the notion of the Mandate of Heaven as the principal agent of historical change, since each dynasty rose and fell according to the moral character of its rulers. The writing of history, dynasty by dynasty, also reinforced the cyclical model of historical change.

Cultural categories of knowledge: History, theology, and philosophy

The way in which cultures categorize knowledge structures the transmission of cultural memory and determines the culturally specific roles of memory systems such as history, **theology**, and philosophy. In early China and Greece, history and philosophy were the primary categories of cultural knowledge, transmitted in both oral and written forms, though the written text gained currency as the dominant mode of transmission. Whereas modern society may privilege history as a category of knowledge, people in other times or other cultures privileged theology, philosophy, literature, or technology. Such categories of knowledge are a primary, though intangible, means of control over cultural meaning.

Since the time of the Greeks, two distinct and parallel categories of knowledge had emerged: one, based on experience, was more inclusive; the other, based on representation, privileged the world of writing and scholarship. The world of books was like a photograph of knowledge, rather than a world lived. These two kinds of knowledge – represented and experienced – were not unique to the European world. There and elsewhere, the two were sometimes viewed as complementary systems; other times, they were perceived as sources of tension in relation to the institutional ordering of society.

Whatever categories of knowledge are privileged, the transmission of cultural memory seldom takes place without conflict. The debate between Christian faith and human reason in the medieval European world, between Islamic theology and Greek philosophy in medieval West Asia, or between Buddhism and Confucianism in medieval China are prime examples of conflicts between categories of knowledge that shape the transmission of cultural memory.

Christianity, history, and theology in medieval Europe

European historical writing during the 1,000 years following the establishment of Christianity as the official religion of the Roman Empire in 380 CE demonstrates the role of Christianity in the writing of history and thus in the shaping of cultural memory. In thirteenth-century Europe, the struggle between theology and philosophy, the product of human reason inherited from the Greeks, was reflected in attempts to reconcile Christian faith with reason. This struggle was resolved in a compromise satisfactory to the Church by Thomas Aquinas (1225–74), whose *Summa Theologica* was a synthesis of medieval learning that reconciled Christian theology and rational philosophy. By arguing for the acceptance of human reason while demonstrating its limits, Aquinas' work had a profound impact on

the relationship between religion and philosophy in medieval European thought and contributed to the undermining of Christianity's monopoly on knowledge.

Islam and cultural categories of knowledge in West Asia

In West Asia after the Arab conquest, knowledge was divided into discrete subjects, each of which was regarded as a separate field of knowledge (*ilm*, or "science"). The most important distinction was between the Muslim religious sciences – Qur'anic exegesis, the study of the Traditions of the Prophet, **jurisprudence**, speculative theology, and **mysticism** – and everything else, that is, the profane sciences. Though theology was the most important category of knowledge in Islamic societies, Islam shaped the writing of history much as Christianity did in Europe.

According to Islam, knowledge was believed to have several sources. The first and most important was the word of God as revealed to the Prophet Muhammad; this knowledge was recorded in the Qur'an and interpreted in seven traditions of recitation. The second source of knowledge was the collective memory of the sayings and doings of the Prophet known as the *sunna* (literally, the "beaten path" or "custom" of the Prophet). Individual statements of the sunna were known as **hadiths**, traditions attributed to particular individuals. One of the most esteemed early collections of *hadiths* was that of Bukhari (d. 870 CE), valued because of the careful manner in which Bukhari had culled through the thousands of *hadiths* to determine the reliability of each.

Muslim scholars were called *ulama*, or those with knowledge (*ilm*), and their scholarship was subject to the consensus of community. An important *hadith* said, "My community will never agree upon an error," suggesting the extent to which consensus was perceived to be a guide to truth. *Ulama* were found in almost every reach of the Islamic cultural world. In most communities, their main task was the transmission of formal legal knowledge or law (*shari'a*).

While Islamic culture placed a high value on the book and on written works, the emphasis remained on oral transmission. Muslims were fundamentally skeptical of the written word and questioned its reliability. According to the historian Ibn Khaldun: "When a student has to rely on the study of books and written material . . . he is confronted by . . . [a] veil . . . that separates handwriting and the form of the letter found in writing from the spoken words found in the imagination." The search for true meaning was to be conducted by reading a text out loud if it was written; students gained authority by oral transmission of a text to the satisfaction of the teacher who himself had gained authority from his teacher.

Theological disputes in Islam occupied many thinkers in medieval West Asia as they had in medieval Europe. The schism in Islam between Sunnism and Shi'ism began after the death of the Prophet Muhammad as the result of a dispute among the Arabs over his succession and hence the political leadership of Islam (see Chapter 5). From Egypt to Central Asia, the region was divided by both political and religious rivalries. Sunni (orthodox) Muslims, who tended to be in the majority, were often alarmed by the growth of political power in the hands of Shi'is.

ISLAMIC THEOLOGY AND SUFI MYSTICISM
Orthodox Sunnis faced not only the political and religious challenge of Shi'ism but also the popular mysticism of Sufism. Sufism coexisted uneasily with Sunni orthodoxy for several centuries after the rise of Islam. It had developed in response to the worldly power of Arab conquests that had reaped great material wealth. Whereas Islam relied on the word through reading, writing, and recitation, Sufi mysticism emphasized direct personal religious experience of the divine through the revelation of God's secrets hidden in the ordinary things, places, and circumstances of an individual's life. Not surprisingly, orthodox Sunni theologians regarded Sufism with suspicion, for they feared that popular mysticism would deprive them of their religious leadership and authority. Their attempts to suppress it, however, were futile.

AL-GHAZZALI, MUSLIM SCHOLAR   One of the most remarkable religious personalities in Islam was al-Ghazzali (1058–1111), who succeeded in reconciling orthodoxy with mysticism. Although al-Ghazzali was a master of both Sunni and Shi'i theology and philosophy, his greatest work, *The Revival of the Religious Sciences*, succeeded in bringing emotion back to religious life and in breaking the yoke of scholasticism that had stifled the feeling of personal relationship with God. He did this by reintroducing the fear of Hell to religious practice and by showing that mysticism was not only compatible with orthodox religious experience but could also amplify it. Al-Ghazzali's great work had a profound effect on the course of Islam and Islamic thought.

AVERROES   After al-Ghazzali's death, the few lights that shone in the Muslim world came chiefly from Spain and North Africa. Most noteworthy was Ibn Rushd (1126–98), known in Europe as Averroes. Trained in the Greek sciences and medicine, he believed that philosophy and religion were both true, and he wrote an important book to show that they were in harmony. Ibn Rushd even attempted to refute what al-Ghazzali had said about philosophy, but he did not convince the mainstream of Muslim opinion that there was a place for philosophy alongside theology. He was perhaps more successful in his serious commentaries on Aristotelian thought, which were translated into Latin and Hebrew and became the foundation of an important school of thought in medieval Europe. Though Ibn Rushd's works achieved harmony between unreasoned belief and human rationalism, Sufi mysticism became the preoccupation of devout Muslims and spread beyond the confines of West Asia.

Epic poetry and cultural memory

While world religions may use memory systems to extend their reach across time and space, other literary forms may be equally powerful in communicating ideas about more worldly (secular) power. Applied to both written and oral literary forms throughout much of the world, the term **epic** comes from Greek and refers to a long narrative poem about the deeds of a hero or heroes. Unlike other forms of poetry that may express emotion, make commentaries on society, or describe nature, epic poems by their very nature – recounting the feats of heroes – represent and transmit ideals that people were expected to admire, if not emulate. In Greece, the *Iliad* and the *Odyssey*, conventionally attributed to the blind Greek poet Homer (fl. ca. 800 BCE), are epic poems that became core works in the European literary canon. The wrath of the warrior Achilles in the Trojan Wars is the subject of the *Iliad*, in which gods play a role, but humans are responsible for their own fate. The adventures of Odysseus making his way home after the Trojan Wars are the subject of the *Odyssey*. Both preserve the cultural memory of early Greece, and have shaped European literary and cultural ideals. Many epics began as orally transmitted performances, sometimes spoken or sung, and then were later written down as literature.

The West African epic of Sunjata

In the epic of Sunjata, the hero begins his journey to greatness as a boy unable to walk. He eventually seizes an iron rod and using magic lifts himself upright, walks, and eventually conquers a kingdom. The act of relying on iron is a reference to the class of Mande artists and specialists called nyamakalaw, which includes blacksmiths, bards, leatherworkers, and potters, all occupations of questionable status and power. The traditional stories of the origin of this cultural category also refer to Sunjata, also known as Sundiata, founder of the thirteenth-century CE Mali Empire. They are told as stories, poetry, and sung to the accompaniment of a stringed instrument. Sunjata is credited with conquering Sumanguru, the king of the Soso. The praise songs originally attributed to Sumanguru were likely adopted by Sunjata to enhance and legitimize his own power in heroic terms. There is no single definitive version of the epic and historians have found that the multiple versions provide rich perspectives on how the Mande and their enemies viewed the events described in Mali's formation.

Epic poems in India

In India, the *Mahabharata*, the longest single epic poem in world literature with 90,000 stanzas in 18 books, was a product of continuous accretion over the centuries between about 400 BCE and 400 CE. The central story of this epic concerns a great battle fought by the descendants of a king. The *Mahabharata* was constructed from hero songs of ancient India and genealogical histories sung by bards who transmitted the oral traditions of the past. The *Ramayana*, an epic written down in the first century CE, concerns the exploits of Rama, an incarnation of Vishnu, one of the three principal Hindu deities. Both the *Mahabharata* and the *Ramayana* were originally secular, martial epics that became Hindu sacred texts when religious interpolations were added, an illustration of how cultural memory can be transformed in the process of transmission.

The epic in Iran

In Iran after its integration into the Islamic Empire, the epic became a means of preserving Persian culture despite the dominance of Arabic language and culture, a demonstration of how poetry as a memory system can preserve cultural identity against challenges that would transform it. Of all the countries that were conquered and held by Arabs in the seventh century, only Iran succeeded in preserving its own national language. By the ninth century, Persian reemerged to challenge Arabic as a great language of the Muslim world. Persian was the language of the *Shahnameh* ("Book of Kings") composed by Ferdowsi (d. ca. 1020 CE) in the early eleventh century. A history of Persia from the creation of the world to the Islamic conquest, this Iranian national epic preserved the cultural memory of pre-Islamic Iran by using collections of heroic tales and other documents and traditions. Dealing with battles, intrigues, and illicit love affairs, Ferdowsi's *Shahnameh*, like many other epics, was read aloud to musical accompaniment.

The epic in northern and western Europe

Like the use of the Persian language to preserve Persian culture within the Arab-dominated Islamic Empire, vernacular (spoken rather than literary) languages elsewhere were used to express the emergence of cultural differences. In northern Europe, the Latin epic of Roman times was replaced by epic literature in native dialects and languages such as Norse, German, Anglo-Saxon, and Old French vernaculars. Scandinavian epics wove together stories of gods and heroes to record Norse expansion, the chief cultural memory of which are the Icelandic (Old Norse) epics. Originally orally transmitted, Norse epics were written down in the thirteenth century. The best-known Anglo-Saxon epic is *Beowulf*, a fantastic story full of exceptionally valorous deeds against natural and supernatural foes. The tale of the struggle of the hero, Beowulf, with an evil monster, Grendel, *Beowulf* is based on popular stories that accumulated over centuries and suggests in epic form the memory of the triumph of Christianity over paganism.

In France, vernacular *chansons de geste* ("songs of mighty deeds") also preserved the memory of real events, generously embroidered with legend. The best known is the *Song of Roland* (ca. 1100 CE), which tells a heroic story of warfare between Christians and Muslims in Europe. It displays the military values of the feudal age, such as knightly loyalty and treason, death and honor, symbolized by the heroism of Roland, a knight of Charlemagne's court. Preserving the cultural memory of its time, the *Song of Roland* elevates a minor historical event into great literature. Epic poetry was a cultural memory system particularly suited to the deeds and legends of what has been remembered as a heroic age in European history. By preserving heroic deeds, epics helped to shape cultural memory of them.

The representation of cultural memory

Themes of the connection between the world of gods and the world of humans can be seen in such culturally diverse sources as Greek drama and the *Mahabharata*. As a cultural memory system, literature portrays the complex relationships between gods and humans, between individuals, families, or communities, and between different cultures. Literature can preserve cultural memory in the face of challenges that would erase it, such as the Arab conquest of Iran, or reflect emerging cultural differences, as in the vernacular epics of northern and western Europe or the court literature of Heian Japan. Literature inspired by individual experience, such as that of Rumi, can also be the agent of cultural memory for a community, as his *Mathnawi* became a classic of Persian literature.

Written and oral memory systems utilize both word and image to convey and remember the past. Equally important as a cultural memory system are the more material monuments of past cultures as well as the plastic and other representative arts such as painting. Buildings and monuments, sculpture and painting are tangible and visible means of maintaining cultural continuity across the centuries and also of engineering change. Like historians and poets, artists and artisans create works that reflect and help shape the culture of their times. And like the written (and orally transmitted) word, works in stone or paint – pottery and pictures, buildings and statues – are records of culture.

The architecture of cultural memory in Africa

Large buildings of permanent materials such as stone are among the oldest examples of cultural memory. By constructing buildings that reflect the needs and ideals of their times, architects and artisans embed the memory of those times in their work. For example, no record preserves the culture of ancient Egypt more clearly than the pyramid, a monumental stone form that represented the sun, a power nearly as important to the Egyptians as the Nile itself. Pyramids also intentionally commemorated the power of the pharaoh who ordered them built and, as one element of the royal burial complex, signified the survival of the ruler's power beyond his individual reign.

For nearly 4,000 years, the pyramid of Khufu at Giza was known as the tallest man-made structure in the world. It is recognized as an extraordinary achievement in workmanship, accuracy, and proportional beauty. The architects and artisans who built the temples and pyramids of ancient Egypt created monuments to their technical skill and artistic vision that are important repositories of cultural and historical information about Egyptian social and political practices and religious ideals.

Elsewhere on the African continent, monumental architecture appeared not only in stone but also in mud or other perishable materials where stone was not available. The mud walls surrounding West African urban centers such as Jenné-Jeno (before ca. 900 CE) or Benin (after ca. 900 CE) required an impressive organization of labor and indicate the defensive needs and commercial purposes of those cities, as great as the stone monuments of Egypt or Zimbabwe. Their maintenance was visible and ongoing, representative of the process of a centralized authority conscripting labor and thereby defining the limits of community.

Art and kingship in West African forest states

Much of the visual art of the West African forest states was associated with divine kingship. Because the succession of kings relied in theory at least on genealogical claims, the knowledge and control of history were used to validate power and authority. Within the palace of the **oba**, or king, of Benin, shrines and altars were built to remember past kings and their exploits. Linked by ritual and containing visual reminders such as ivory tusks carved with historical scenes of battles and cast bronze and brass memorial heads portraying specific kings and queen mothers, the shrines formed an important part of the extensive calendar of ritual life at the palace.

Another source of historical information in Benin was the collection of rectangular plaques cast in various copper alloys. Scholars believe that the plaques were attached to the pillars of the royal palace structure. Scenes on the plaques depicted events in the kingdom's history. They could be read like a history book of costume, technology, politics, and culture over time. The plaques were kept inside the palace, and their production was limited to members of the oba's guild of brass-casters. Within an oral culture, they also served as mnemonic devices enabling the recovery of past knowledge for the purpose of recitation and ritual.

Buildings such as the Egyptian pyramids and other monumental stone architecture preserve more than political power or civic pride. They constituted forms of religious cultural memory. Both architecture and visual arts around the world also strongly expressed the central role of religions such as Buddhism, Hinduism, and Christianity while making their ideas concrete and culturally relevant.

Religion and cultural memory

In India, the homeland of Buddhism, religion inspired monumental art, which was also influenced by invading foreign peoples. Following the death of the devout Buddhist ruler Ashoka and the collapse of his empire in the third century BCE, waves of migrating peoples – Greeks, Scythians, Central Asian Kushans – brought new and foreign influences into the subcontinent. By the first and second centuries CE, elaborations of Buddhist thought and doctrinal disputes led to the division of Buddhism into Mahayana and Theravada.

Buddhism in India

Mahayana doctrine, with its elaboration of Buddhas and bodhisattvas (enlightened beings) as deities, had a profound influence on Indian art. The Buddha Amitabha, who presides over the Western Paradise, his attendant bodhisattva Avalokitesvara, the compassionate "lord who looks down," and the historical Buddha, Sakyamuni, are widely represented in both sculpture and wall painting. Early Buddhist art, reflected in the Bamiyan caves (fourth to fifth centuries CE) in Afghanistan, shows the influence of Greek and Roman sculpture transmitted by the Kushans from Central Asia. The Ajanta caves on the Deccan plateau in south-central India contain extensive remains of Mahayana Buddhist wall paintings, dating from the fifth to the seventh centuries, many of which illustrate the Jataka tales of Buddha's previous incarnations.

Indian Buddhist temples, or **stupas**, which took their characteristic form between the third century BCE and the third century CE, were formal arrangements of gateways and stone railings that enclosed a burial shrine, or tumulus, of Buddhist

relics, such as a bone or other physical remains of the historical Buddha. The dome of the stupa that covered the tumulus was a symbol of the dome of Heaven, enclosing a world mountain. Worshipers walked around the circular terrace within the railings, which was a sacred space showing scenes from the life of Buddha as well as symbols of death and rebirth. Tactile sculptured frescoes adorn stupas in a continuous flow of images, somewhat like a narrative fresco painting. Many stupas are large, with domes raised on elaborate platforms.

Buddhism in China

The cave temples of Yun'gang and Longmen in north China are testimony to the powerful influence of Buddhism as it spread from India through Central and East Asia. Buddhist sculpture in China during the period when Buddhism spread (ca. third to sixth centuries) reflected both Indian and Central Asian influences. Giant images of Buddha and numerous smaller carvings at Yun'gang and Longmen display the devotion of wealthy and powerful believers, such as the Empress Wu (r. 690–705) in China, who commissioned the Longmen complex as an act of devotion. Religious art was produced under the patronage of Buddhist temples and monasteries as well as rulers throughout East Asia. Wall paintings from the excavations at Dunhuang in northwestern China dating to the sixth through eighth centuries illustrate Buddhist themes designed to appeal to a Chinese audience, but they are clearly influenced by Central Asian styles.

Buddhism spread from China through Korea and Japan, influencing architecture and plastic arts as well as religious beliefs. The tradition of Buddhist sculpture characteristic of eighth-century Japan, the era of intensive continental influence, shows close parallels with Chinese and Korean models. Korean artisans trained the Japanese in the sculptural styles they had adapted from China. Images of Buddhist deities became

11.6 Image of Vairocana (Universal) Buddha, surrounded by attendant bodhisattvas, at Longmen in North China, ca. 672–675. Carved into stone cliffs near the modern city of Luoyang, this Buddhist cave temple was built with the support of rulers who patronized such projects as an act of faith.

objects of worship in the Buddhist temples and monasteries that proliferated throughout Japan, symbolized by the erection of the statue of the Great Buddha at Nara in 752.

Hinduism in India

Under the Gupta (ca. 320–540) rulers of India, who were Hindu patrons of the cult of Vishnu, Buddhism declined as an independent faith and was reabsorbed into Hinduism. The great age of Indian Buddhist art ended, and Hinduism became the primary source of inspiration for South Asian artists, though Buddhist images by no means disappeared. With the rise in the seventh century of Hindu devotional (*bhakti*) cults, centered either on Shiva the Destroyer, or on Vishnu the Preserver and his incarnations Rama and Krishna, their images, both in round and in relief, joined figures of Buddhas and bodhisattvas as decorative art.

Hindu temple architecture and sculpture illustrate the unitary quality of Indian art, in which the erotic and the demonic are mutual expressions of cosmic unity. Sensuous sculptures showing such deities as Shiva and his wife, Parvati, locked in an erotic embrace manifest the erotic aspect of divinity, while portrayals of

Parvati as a fierce female brandishing weapons in preparation for battle illustrate its demonic side. By the ninth century, Hindu temples were covered with such relief carvings and sculptured patterns. There was a preference for human figures, though they usually represented gods or mythical beings, sometimes hybrid half-human half-animal, such as Ganesh, the son of Shiva, portrayed as a human body with the head of an elephant. Epic stories were also represented, and female figures, graceful nymphs and goddesses, were common.

Buddhism and Hinduism in Southeast Asia

The spread of Buddhism and Hinduism to Southeast Asia is exemplified by two impressive temple complexes, Borobudur in Java and Angkor Wat in Cambodia. Created in the eighth century, Borobudur is an artificial mountain that combines the concept of a Buddhist stupa with that of Mount Meru, the world mountain in early Indian cosmology. The entire complex represents a huge magic diagram of the cosmos. As pilgrims mounted the terraced sanctuary, they were believed to reenact symbolically the ascent of a soul from the world of desire to the world of spiritual perfection and ultimate union with the cosmic Buddha.

Angkor Wat, built by the Khmer rulers of Cambodia in the twelfth century, shows the powerful influence of Hinduism in Southeast Asia. Angkor Wat is a vast architectural complex serving simultaneously as a temple for Vishnu and a sanctuary for the *devaraja*, or "divine king," Khmer rulers who were believed to be earthly incarnations of Vishnu. The main sanctuary at Angkor Wat is 40 meters (130 feet) high and stands on a stone-encased platform 12 meters (40 feet) high and 46 meters (150 feet) square. Although it was abandoned as an active temple site in the fifteenth century, it remains an impressive record documenting the flow of Hinduism to Southeast Asia and the ability of Khmer rulers to mobilize artisans and workers sufficient to build a monument of such scale.

11.7 A Muslim and Christian perform the lute, thirteenth century.

Christianity in Europe

Religious themes similarly dominated European art in the medieval period (ca. 1000–1300 CE), when the Church was the dominant force in European society and the principal patron of the arts. Although religious themes dictated the subjects of painting and sculpture – such as figures of the Virgin Mary, Christ, and saints – religion inspired artistic genius most visibly in the architectural monument of the **cathedral**. As cities grew and flourished, their residents built handsome and impressive churches, which were as much monuments to urban wealth and pride as they were dwellings of the Christian divinity.

One of the most celebrated of these monuments was the French Cathédrale Saint Pierre in Beauvais, the vaulting of which exceeded 46 meters (150 feet), making it the highest of all Gothic churches. Cathedrals represent the unity of sacred and secular functions in other ways as well. They served their communities as refuges for the homeless and destitute, thus embodying the ethical virtues expected of the wider cultural community. Another example of the pinnacle of European architectural achievement, the Cathédrale Notre Dame de Paris, took nearly two centuries to complete. Its Gothic style of architecture was praised in the fourteenth century as shining "like the sun among stars."

Islam

In West Asia, the counterpart of the Buddhist and Hindu temples in South and East Asia and the cathedral in Europe was the Islamic **mosque**, characteristically a domed structure. Although the dome was in use in West Asia before the Arab conquest, the Muslims subsequently raised this architectural form to monumental proportions; mosque domes are evidence of the unequaled skills of West Asian engineers and architects. Hundreds of domed structures, above all mosques, were constructed throughout West Asia and beyond when Islam spread. There were several shapes: small or vast, squat or bulbous. Some were made of large blocks of stone, and others were made of bricks covered with dazzling colored tiles. As domes were introduced to parts of West Africa by the spread of Islam, they were constructed of indigenous materials following local traditions, which dictated their construction out of mud, requiring a constant cycle of devotional upkeep and repair.

The coming of the Turks to West Asia, symbolized by the eleventh-century conquest of Baghdad, inaugurated a cultural revolution in the Islamic world. Their arrival meant changes in artistic style and decoration; it also led to the introduction of architecture with entirely new functions. One such structure that rapidly spread under the Turks was the türbe, or "tower tomb," a tall building that was a popular burial place for Muslim rulers and religious mystics and often became an object of pilgrimage. Its shape may have originated in that of the Central Asian Buddhist stupas or in the circular tent houses, called yurts, of nomadic Turks.

Despite their monumental character, large religious structures could also be situated on contested terrain, their location within complex religious histories serving multiple purposes. The structure known as Hagia Sophia in Constantinople began as a church in 360 CE and was rebuilt in the sixth century, having been twice destroyed. In the third construction under the ruler Justinian I, a new Byzantine basilica was built in 532 CE and subsequently elaborated as a cathedral at the center of orthodox Christianity. From time to time, the building and its relics were vandalized and even partially destroyed by earthquakes. Eventually, after the capture of Constantinople in 1453, the domed structure was transformed into an Islamic mosque that blended the various original architectural elements into a culturally transformed space for practicing Muslims.

North America

The tangible remains of North American communities suggest a spiritual basis for culture that was as pervasive as Christianity was in Europe. The monumental remains from North American communities were dependent on agriculture and trade. Such peoples inhabited much of the Mississippi and Ohio River valleys and the south-eastern part of the United States. North American cultures known as Hopewell and Mississipian centered on towns and cities characterized by mounds and other urban features.

Earthworks, such as the Great Serpent Mound in Ohio, appear to have been designed to function as sacred effigies. Monumental mounds at Cahokia served political and religious purposes. Some were burial mounds, log tombs covered with earth piled up in various shapes (square, circular, rectangular, octagonal), often exceeding 500 meters (1650 feet) in diameter or length. Generally, the largest mounds are temple mounds. Monks Mound, at Cahokia was 360 by 241 meters (1181 by 790 feet) and contained 600,000 cubic meters (21 million cubic feet) of earth, all carried to the site in baskets filled with 18-kilogram (40-pound) loads. This, the largest earthen structure built in the Americas before the arrival of Europeans, was an engineering feat comparable to the stone pyramids of Egypt. Its massive structure altered the landscape and communicated ideas of power and belonging to those within its sight.

Mesoamerica

It is possible that the monumental traditions of North America were imported by immigrants from the south or at least inspired by earlier Mesoamerican architecture. There is general agreement that the Olmec culture (ca. 1500–400 BCE) provided a common foundation for the Mesoamerican cultures that came after it. Olmec art had a strong ritual aspect, focusing on a wide variety of supernatural combinations of animal and human features in bewildering complexity.

Olmec art objects and the influence of their style stretched by trade and conquest from Central America to Costa Rica. Later Mesoamerican cultures, such as that of the Maya, were once believed to descend directly from the Olmecs. Recent discoveries in the tropical forests of Guatemala and Belize now suggest local origins beginning around 300 BCE. Classic Mayan culture flourished in the Yucatán peninsula of modern Mexico between about 300 and 900 CE, and one of its best-known sites is Tikal. The monumental Mayan art reflects an environment in which stone was plentiful. Characteristic of Mayan remains are temple-pyramids made of stuccoed limestone, multiroomed "palaces," causeways connecting groups of structures in cities, and cities themselves, including stone monuments often inscribed with Mayan hieroglyphics. At Tikal, the buildings of a central acropolis were built over earlier tombs of elites cut into bedrock. The acropolis was for ceremonial purposes and was surrounded by substantial suburbs. Stone was the primary medium of Mesoamerican art and Tikal's monuments provide significant evidence of political complexity and cultural connections across the southern lowlands.

Andean South America

The earliest commonly occurring artistic and architectural remains in Andean South America are designated "Chavín," after the style of art centered at Chavín de Huántar, located in the highlands of modern Peru. The style of Chavín pottery art was uniform across northern Peru during the period 1000–1200 BCE, suggesting the possibility of intensive exchange, communication, and military competition between highland and coastal communities. Substantial stone buildings were erected for ritual and ceremonial purposes. As with Olmec culture in Mesoamerica, pre-Incan ceremonial centers were located in rural areas rather than being part of urban centers, with two important exceptions: Tihuanaco and Huari. The people of Chavín probably never numbered more than 2,000, but they built intricately terraced fields to make the steep slopes and hilly regions of the area more productive. They had highly developed weaving techniques and had sufficient metallurgical knowledge to be able to produce refined ornaments of copper and copper-gold alloys.

Most of the Chavín visual art can be explained in terms of religion, royal power, agriculture, or warfare. In general, the Chavín style, like that of the Olmecs in Mesoamerica, emphasized composite creatures, especially serpents and felines such as the jaguar, and Chavín sculpture portrayed the attributes of creatures in nature that suggest their supernatural qualities. Figures from the Chavín pantheon are depicted in Chavín pottery, painted cloth, worked metal, and small stone and bone objects, as well as in sculpture and temple carvings. Chavín styles and forms were later integrated into other Central Andean cultures. As was the case with the widespread Olmec style, adopting stylistic elements from Chavín de Huántar may have enhanced the cultural legitimacy of competing elites in other communities.

In the centuries between Chavín and the rise of the Incan culture in the fifteenth century, regional centers of culture, such as Chimu (ca. 750–1450 CE), dominate the central Andean area. On Peru's north coast, the giant pyramids at Moche (ca. 200 BCE–600 CE) provide even earlier evidence of political and artistic complexity. The pyramids were built of hundreds of millions of adobe bricks, each brick marked with a symbol pressed on its top surface. The symbols may represent their makers, thus recording the tribute provided as labor. A variety of styles, suggesting some influences inherited from Chavín, emerged during this period. The Moche society lasted as long as Rome and, while we may not know as much about the political impact, Moche elite culture used architecture as a unifying aspect of identity.

More than a millennium later, the Inca ruled the Andean highlands using a tribute-based empire. Incan culture was particularly noted for its fine stonework. Buildings in large cities, such as the Incan capital of Cuzco, showed impressive architectural skill. Public structures for religious or political use were constructed of mortar-less masonry. Large, irregular stones were fitted so closely that a knife blade could not pass between them. Equally amazing stonework went into elaborately engineered irrigation systems and agricultural terraces and the network of roads and bridges that bound the Incan Empire together. Machu Picchu, a complex of remarkable stone structures high in the Andes, is perhaps the best-known Incan remain. Machu Picchu was one of several royal estates built by Pachacuti (ca. 1440) to commemorate specific military exploits. Its temples and terraces bear dramatic witness to the power of the Incan Empire and its religious underpinnings.

Technology and cultural memory

Architectural and other aesthetic achievements relied on technological innovations. **Technology** itself can be a domain of cultural knowledge and, along with memory systems such as history, literature, and architecture, transmits essential cultural knowledge from generation to generation. Technology comprises tools and practices, as well as the ways in which people use tools to manipulate their environment and construct the physical world around them. Technology is a memory system, a cultural link that is as revealing of historical experience as art or literature.

Technological advancements were rarely documented before late medieval times. Even then, they were usually mentioned by accident, perceived to be merely incidental to historical narratives of great men and dramatic events. How and when a particular tool, device, or process came into being in a given region was almost never stated in historical sources. Moreover,

societies tended to adopt rather quickly anything that appeared to be to their immediate benefit or advantage, without showing much interest in its origin. Technologies were diffused via trade, war, and other means, perhaps from more than one source, over vast areas, while their origins were actually unknown or forgotten. For the most part, historians, archaeologists, and others must infer the origins and uses of technology from the physical remains of a culture or region.

Artisans and the transmission of cultural knowledge

Not only in Europe, but also in many other parts of the world, artisans were essential nodes in the transfer of ritual, technical skills, and keepers of important domains of cultural knowledge. Textile technology illustrates both the individuality and the interconnectedness of technology as a cultural memory system. Achievements in textile technology in different parts of the world made it possible for fabric and clothing, ranging from diaphanous gowns to thick felt cloaks, to became major items of international trade. The products of that technology carried distinct cultural messages. Textile patterns were equated with particular ethnic groups and sometimes illustrated ethnic identities, social categories, or even specific historical or cultural events.

Conquest as well as trade had effects on textile technology. One of the results of the tenth-century Turkish invasion of West Asia was the introduction and spread of carpet-weaving there. Persians rapidly adopted the art of carpet-making from the Turks and then made their own innovations, producing fine carpets that were in great demand. Since West Asian peoples sat on stools or sofas covered with textiles and ate and slept on the floor, making themselves comfortable with carpets, cushions, and mattresses, textile production provided important products for daily life. Carpets were as much functional as decorative art. They also became a significant trade item, as attested by their appearance in European paintings from the fifteenth and sixteenth centuries.

Iron technology as cultural memory

Technology can reveal cultural memory in profound and explicit ways. The technology of sub-Saharan African and many Asian societies before 1500 suggests that technology was not necessarily distinct from spirituality and material power. In sub-Saharan Africa, iron smelting was a cultural performance choreographed by the master smelter and smelting furnaces had both technological and spiritual functions. The smelter was typically a man with great knowledge and considerable political power who, in some societies, was also a spiritual leader. Among the Mashona in Southern Africa, knowledge of iron-making was claimed through contact with spirits and spirit-inspired dreams in which ancestors provided master craftsmen with the power to create. Such technological and spiritual skills were passed from one generation to the next through exclusive systems of apprenticeship and training. In ancient Japan, sword manufacture was similarly connected to ritual. The furnace was like a human being and so was fed charges of coal and iron. She (the furnace) digested the "food" in order to bear good iron.

Ironworking was linked similarly to other activities that the ancestors were also believed to have controlled, such as human reproduction. By the thirteenth century, the Bassari of Togo in West Africa smelted iron in what they considered to be gendered furnaces. The furnace was believed to be a woman who was impregnated by the smelter to "give birth" to red, glowing iron. Each furnace was constructed from pieces of an old furnace once used by the smelter's grandfather, thus supplying a physical genealogical link between past and present. According to the smelter: "It is not I who build this furnace, it is you [the ancestors and spirits] who build it."

While the repeated performance of past cultural traditions was not always so conscious, the reliance of cultural memory on practice was commonly a means of preserving information about the past. Through apprenticeship systems, patterned motor skills and the complex bodies of knowledge utilized in activities such as pottery making, metalworking, textile manufacturing, cooking, and other crafts became essential and familiar parts of cultural memory transferred from one generation to the next. The movement of knowledge through human migration also furthered the spread of technology and science before the rise of educational institutions, and in some parts of the world they continued to compete with the formalized systems of transmission.

Print technology and the transmission of cultural memory

Paper, which is essential to printing, was invented in several parts of the world, including in Mesoamerica (by the Maya before the fifth century CE) and in China early in the Han dynasty (206 BCE–220 CE). Professional scribes created Mayan folding books that contained hand-printed script and relied on glyphs. The earliest extant printed texts on paper were made in eighth-century Korea and Japan by carving text onto wooden blocks, which were then smeared with ink and covered with paper, producing an impression of the text. The earliest surviving Chinese text made by woodblock **printing** is a Buddhist sutra from the mid-ninth century. Woodblock printing became the favored method of reproducing texts throughout East Asia, in contrast to copying by hand using brush and ink. This method allowed fewer errors and omissions or other changes to creep into texts because the carved woodblock, though subject to deterioration over time, was a relatively permanent and unchanging means of reproducing texts. In addition to propagating religion and spreading culture through literature, printing was used to spread

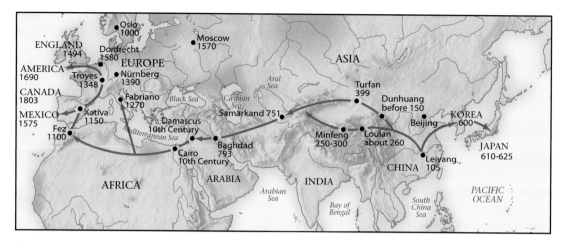

Map 11.1 The technology of papermaking spread from China to Europe.

new technologies for agriculture and silk production and in this way contributed substantially to the economic revolution of Song times.

In the eleventh century, movable type – in clay, wood, and metal – was invented in China, 400 years before its appearance in Europe. Ultimately, because of the use of an ideographic script with thousands of characters as opposed to an alphabetic one with fewer than 100 letters, movable type did not dominate printing in China because it was relatively more efficient to carve a woodblock page than to keep available the thousands of pieces of type necessary to set a page of text. Still, the development of a commercial printing industry in the Song period and the proliferation of printed books made learning and written culture more accessible to a wider population, aiding in the transmission of popular literature as well as the historical and philosophical texts used in studying for the civil service examinations.

By the seventh century, Buddhism had spread to and flourished in Korea, where it was accompanied by other Chinese cultural elements, including woodblock printing. Within a few centuries, the Buddhist canon had been carved into 6,000 wooden blocks for printing and dissemination to the Korean public. A movable type was made from metal molds and in the mid-fourteenth century, a local alphabet Han'gul

("The Great Letters") was simplified and eagerly adopted by illiterates and women, who had been excluded from formal education.

In contrast to China, where woodblock printing remained important despite the invention of movable type, the introduction of movable type in Europe in the fifteenth century brought about changes in the way cultural memory was shaped, transcribed, and transmitted, changes comparable to those resulting from the invention of writing in the third millennium BCE or the introduction of the word processor and computer in the late twentieth century. Although initially most works printed in Europe were in Latin, the language of the Church and state, increasing numbers of works in European vernacular languages were printed. By contributing to the expansion of vernacular and secular literatures, printing in Europe – as in China – made knowledge more widely and easily available to an increasingly literate audience.

The spread of papermaking technologies increased the impact of printing technologies in Europe, Asia, and Africa. Papermaking technologies made their way from China, where paper was invented in the first century CE, westward over the routes of commerce and conquest by the ninth century. In the twelfth century, papermaking spread from North Africa to Muslim Spain and

Sicily, then beyond to the European continent. Much cheaper than the Egyptian papyrus or the vellum (calf- or kidskin) used in Europe, paper made possible the development and widespread distribution of books, stimulating literacy and the expansion of an educated elite, while more generally spreading knowledge in Africa, Europe, and West Asia. In the Americas, paper was also manufactured from bark and animal skins, and used to produce and store knowledge. The accumulation of textual knowledge in the Americas did not survive the conquest. When Europeans eventually reached Mesoamerica in the 1500s, they recognized the power of the printed word and systematically destroyed nearly all the local Mayan texts (known as codices) replacing Mayan language and institutions with their own.

Institutions and the transmission of cultural memory

Systems of cultural memory may be private products of individual creation, patronage, and ownership or the results of public, community design and effort. Whatever the forms of cultural memory or the means by which they are created, the maintenance and transmission of cultural memory are often associated with institutions such as churches, schools, guilds, brotherhoods, libraries, and universities. In the process of preserving and transmitting cultural knowledge, institutions are agents of cultural memory, adding a distinctly social dimension to cultural knowledge. Such institutions can consolidate the authority of social and cultural elites, but they can also act as agents of change by expressing resistance to prevailing cultural norms and ideals.

Monasticism

Monasticism, the way of life of those who have taken religious vows to live apart from society,

fostered religious communities throughout the world. These religious communities, known as monasteries, were predominantly, though not exclusively, Christian or Buddhist; as institutions of cultural memory, they transmitted religious ideas through practice and sometimes became powerful agents in the political and social world outside the monastery. Monasteries adopted rules for living, encouraged the practice of religious vows, provided temporary refuges for laypeople, and often served the secular community through charitable activities in times of need.

Christian monasticism originated at the end of the fourth century in West Asia, where the first rules for governing a community, stressing prayer, work, and obedience, were written by Saint Basil (d. 379 CE). Monasticism was introduced to western Europe by the end of the fourth century and quickly spread from the Mediterranean northward and westward as far as Ireland, to which Saint Patrick (ca. 389–461) introduced an early form. Irish monasticism was responsible for extensive missionary efforts in northern Germany, and some Irish monasteries became prominent centers of learning and culture.

The rules established by Saint Benedict (ca. 480–543) for the monastery he founded on the heights of Monte Cassino, midway between Rome and Naples, became common to most religious communities in Europe. Benedict's rule swore monks to poverty, chastity, and obedience; they could possess no individual property and submitted their individual wills to that of the abbot, who headed the monastery. The individual lost his identity and became part of the whole, which was a strictly regulated community with a regimented routine of prayer, meditation, and works.

Religious communities for women appeared at the same time as those for men and were aided and encouraged by Church leaders. By the sixth century, major French cities had religious communities for women, and in the eighth century, Saint Boniface (ca. 680–754), an English missionary to the Germans, founded communities there for women as well as men.

Religious communities in medieval Europe attracted and supported women because they offered them opportunities not otherwise available. For example, Eleanor of Aquitaine (ca. 1122–1204), variously queen of France and England, gave money to and otherwise patronized monasteries. Other noblewomen founded convents, monasteries, and charitable institutions such as orphanages and hospitals. Women also continued to enter the cloistered life, which enabled them – no longer wives, mothers, daughters – to dedicate themselves, as men did, to study, good works, and spiritual growth.

In late medieval Europe, foundresses and abbesses were able to acquire religious and secular knowledge usually reserved for men. Hildegard of Bingen (1098–1179), founder and abbess of a convent in Germany, was widely known for her learning. The breadth and scope of her knowledge were extensive, ranging from music to theology to science. Popes and emperors, who believed her to be a prophetess, took her scientific and theological treatises seriously.

Though monks and nuns were removed from secular life, they also served lay society by providing hospices for the ill and hostels for travelers. But their main contribution lay in copying manuscripts and maintaining libraries, and monasteries thus served as a principal institution for the transmission of European cultural memory. Christian monasteries in Europe controlled the preservation and reproduction of cultural knowledge, much as Confucian institutions and ideas dominated this process in China, Buddhist and Hindu ones did in India, and Islamic ones did in West Asia.

Buddhist monasticism reached across Asia from India to China, Southeast Asia, and Japan. In China, independent Buddhist sects established networks of monasteries that housed hundreds of thousands of monks and nuns. By the Tang period (618–907), Buddhist monasteries were wealthy landowners and Buddhist abbots and priests socialized with the court aristocracy and were highly educated members of the literati

elite. Buddhist monasteries and temples also served as schools, providing primary education in Confucian texts as well as Buddhist ones. Buddhist monasteries, like their counterparts in Europe, often served as repositories of learning and also functioned as educational institutions that preserved and transmitted knowledge, including secular ideas such as Confucianism in East Asia.

In Heian Japan, an emperor might enter a cloistered life as a monk in order to avoid public ceremonial functions and thereby be able to operate more effectively as a political influence from behind the scenes. Noblewomen in Heian Japan similarly entered nunneries to preserve and protect their honor if their husbands were killed in battle or somehow dishonored, or to grieve. Buddhist monastic institutions in medieval Japan were centers of learning patronized by the military leaders of the time, much like monasteries in medieval Europe. Buddhist monasteries in both China and Japan served as sources of refuge for women who wanted to escape from miserable lives in the world because of marriage, politics, or both.

Education, universities, and schools

Many societies systematically developed means of acquiring and transmitting vital cultural knowledge through a variety of educational institutions, both religious and secular. Cathedral schools, along with the traditional monastic centers of learning, were the centers of education in Europe until the appearance of universities in the twelfth century. Students were considered clerks (clerics, clergy), even though they might never become priests. The earliest universities may be thought of as urbanized, expanded cathedral schools. The first appeared in Italy at Bologna in the late eleventh century, and the first north of the Alps was at Paris (ca. 1150). The University of Paris became the foremost center for theological and philosophical studies in Europe, an indication of its origins and the dominant role of the Church in education.

Buddhist and Hindu education in India

In India, the great Buddhist university at Nalanda in Bihar was founded in the sixth century CE and had an enrollment of around 5,000 students, including many foreign scholars and distinguished lecturers. Buddhist texts and the Vedas and Hindu philosophy were taught at this and other Buddhist universities. Caste divisions were reflected in other educational institutions, as brahman boys (and occasionally girls) were educated in the Vedic tradition; members of the warrior caste were educated largely by household tutors, who taught them reading, writing, military arts, dancing, painting, and music.

In contrast to China, where the written word was endowed with sacred power, there was far more regard for oral tradition in early India. Rote memorization of the Vedas was emphasized, although writing was eventually used as an aid to memorization. As in medieval Europe, libraries were found in monasteries and palaces. Manuscript copying was an industry involving professional scribes and was often considered a pious activity, also centered in monasteries and palaces.

Education and the examination system in China

In China, the Confucian notion that schools were a responsibility of the state persisted from antiquity. By the second century BCE, there was an "Imperial University" in the capital that taught the Confucian classics. Educational institutions were closely linked to the operation of the **examination system**. Based on the use of systematic recommendations of those judged suitable for government service as early as the Han dynasty

(206 BCE–220 CE), the examination system instituted in the Tang period (618–907) was designed to recruit and select men for office in the imperial government. Over time, it became the single most powerful mechanism for the reproduction of the cultural, social, and political elite in imperial China.

To acquire the vast learning necessary to pass the examinations, students would have to begin at an early age and work long hours for many years to master the entire corpus of the Confucian classics, the commentaries written on those classics, and historical works documenting the transmission of the scholarly tradition of Confucianism over time. Literary works, both poetry and essays, were included in this curriculum. Some early education took place in Buddhist monasteries, where Confucian texts were often transmitted along with Buddhist ones. The civil service examinations not only tested knowledge of the classics, their commentaries, and histories, but also required candidates to propose policies to deal with problems of government administration, such as fiscal matters. In addition, candidates were asked to write poems of a certain form on specified themes in order to demonstrate their abilities as men of culture.

Prospective candidates from families deeply entrenched in this cultural tradition or from those that aspired to status and power were educated by private tutors in their homes if they were wealthy, or through an extensive network of schools that radiated out from the capital to nearly every region of the empire by the twelfth century. These schools were not "public," in the sense of being open to everyone, but they were an important source of learning for the elite, whose sons filled these schools. Families sometimes endowed lands to provide income for a family school, and sometimes community leaders would promote joint efforts to establish a school to serve the sons of elite families. Private academies also began to proliferate by the twelfth century, and these academies were the seat of the new synthesis of classical learning called "Neo-Confucianism."

The Islamic madrasa

In Islamic West Asia, educational institutions (**madrasas**) arose mainly to provide religious and legal instruction according to the Qur'an and its interpreters. Arabic was the language of instruction in the madrasas, which were established to train orthodox Sunni theologians. One or more of these colleges were built in most of the major cities of the empire, where they eventually became an element in the Muslim definition of a town or city as a place where there was a mosque, a madrasa, a public bath, and a bazaar. Generally, a madrasa was a square building with one to four arched halls (classrooms) that opened onto a central arcaded courtyard and that had residential rooms for students and teachers.

Islamic libraries

Magnificent libraries were also established throughout West Asia in the ninth and tenth centuries. Although all kinds of books were collected, among the most important were those on the Greek sciences. The libraries served as academies where scholars of all faiths and origins came to study, discuss, and debate the hard sciences as well as other subjects. Libraries had a major influence on the transmission of ancient learning throughout the Islamic world and from there to Christendom. Among the most famous Muslim libraries were one founded in Baghdad in 833 and another founded in Cairo in 1005.

Islamic education in West Africa

Like its European, West Asian, and North African counterparts, the University of Timbuktu, on the banks of the great Niger River, witnessed the intellectual awakening across the Islamic societies of fifteenth-century West Africa. The university actually consisted of a constellation of nearly 200 small schools, mosques, and libraries, which together acquired and disseminated knowledge from the Arab world and various African oral traditions. Two famous tarikhs, or written histories, date from this period and were actually transcriptions in Arabic of local Sudanese traditions. For the most part, the university curriculum was controlled by the clerics, and it represented a privileged culture of elites that was reproduced through family ties. The curriculum included Muslim theology, jurisprudence, astronomy, geography, and history, subjects of interest to only a small minority of the urban elite.

Brotherhoods and guilds

Like the community of monks and nuns in Buddhist and Christian monasteries throughout Asia and Europe, in the Islamic world Sufi brotherhoods, called **tariqas** (paths to union with God), sprang up in the twelfth and thirteenth centuries and established networks of lodges throughout West Asia. These lodges were typically organized around an outstanding mystic, whose tomb was usually incorporated into the main lodge. Branch lodges were subsequently founded wherever groups of his disciples and adherents might meet. Each lodge had its own rituals and costume, and some were restricted to particular professions or strata of society. The brotherhoods in the cities, especially those associated with the professions, often adopted their own code of ethics, generally referred to as the futuwwa.

Tariqas played a major role in the spread of Islam. Each was in fact a popular movement that appealed to emotion rather than to rigid dogmatism. The emotional and syncretic nature of tariqa rituals and practices was something anyone could respond to. One of the most famous brotherhoods was inspired by Jalal ad-Din ar-Rumi (1207–73), a Sufi mystic and poet whose tomb at Konya in Anatolia became a site of pilgrimage for his disciples and their followers. Jalal ad-Din had used music and dance to help induce a mystical state, and dancing became the outstanding feature of religious rituals associated with Sufi brotherhoods.

The early Turkish brotherhoods had strong overtones of shamanism. The pagan Turks from Central Asia saw the leader (*shaik*) of a brotherhood as a shaman and his attempts to induce a mystical state by chanting, music, and dance as consistent with their traditional shamanistic ceremonies. By making conversion easier, the brotherhoods played an important role in the spread of Islam. Eventually tariqas of every description emerged, from the scholarly and contemplative to those whose followers babbled incoherently and handled poisonous snakes. Some brotherhoods exhibited a fanatical devotion to Islam, and their militancy was put to good use by the Turks in wars against Christian Byzantium. Tariqas were a critical factor in the Islamization of Anatolia (modern Turkey) by both peaceful and aggressive means.

Tariqas appeared in West Africa with the spread of Islam that accompanied the expansion of the Mali Empire (ca. thirteenth and fourteenth centuries). Muslim brotherhoods proved compatible with indigenous West African cultural institutions and made conversion to Islam easier. Among linguistically related West African peoples, secret men's and women's societies centering on commerce and its regulation existed among the merchant classes. Such urban lodges, scattered throughout the Mali Empire, increased cultural solidarity within the merchant community, defrayed the costs of individuals' trade and travel, and further enhanced the success of West African commercial and cultural connections within the Islamic world.

Counterparts to these Islamic lodges can be seen in the medieval European **guild** system. With the expansion of trade in Europe from about 1200 to 1500, associations for mutual aid and protection developed among town dwellers engaged in common pursuits. Known as "guilds," these societies were the urban counterparts of agrarian manorialism, the means by which manufacturing, trade, labor, and even government in towns and cities were regulated and protected. Like the urban lodges of West Africa, guilds provided a basis for the retention and transmission of specialist knowledge, offered community solidarity, and were among the agencies of political and cultural change in late medieval Europe. Guilds were among the most important institutions in medieval Europe.

There were almost as many guilds as there were different activities: there were guilds for bellringers, minstrels, candlemakers, masons, roadmenders, and weavers, to name but a few. Guilds assisted destitute or ill members and paid for the funeral Mass after death. Many guilds assumed judiciary roles, settled quarrels, and even investigated crimes. They also participated in public rituals and ceremonies, such as the celebration of the Doge (ruler) of Venice in 1268, a parade in which each of the city's guilds marched in bands, sumptuously dressed, carrying banners and flags, and heralded by musicians.

Cultural hegemony and resistance

By controlling the transmission and dissemination of cultural knowledge, institutions of cultural memory, such as monasteries, churches, universities, and brotherhoods, tend to reproduce the prevailing patterns of power relations and reinforce cultural **hegemony**, power or control exercised from above. Such institutions generate ideological authority that can sustain a social and political order as well as reinforce elite cultural ideals. At the same time, these institutions can be sources of dissent and contribute to the revision of cultural memory through challenging or resisting inherited cultural knowledge. In the process of transmission and reproduction, transformation can take place that fundamentally realigns power relationships or rejects the power of dominant elites by challenging the underpinnings of their authority.

The rise of the individual, secular scholar in western Europe served to extend the control of knowledge to a more diverse population – even to include exceptional women, such as the author Christine de Pisan (ca. 1364–1430) – thus also becoming part of the dialogue between experienced and represented knowledge. Finding herself without husband or father, Christine turned to her studies. In Christine de Pisan's *Le Livre de la Cité des Dames* (*The Book of the City of Ladies*), written in 1405, women are portrayed as actively constructing the ideal community and being essential contributors to the construction of knowledge. De Pisan criticized male authority and challenged the widely held views of male writers, who claimed that women were by nature weak and feeble-minded.

Tensions were resident in cultural settings in which both writing and experience served memory systems. They constituted an important source of resistance and transformation. For example, in Christianity and Islam, the experience of the divine or sacred was the means by which individuals might challenge or oppose the elite controls over written religious law and its interpretation. Mysticism, the direct experience of a spiritual dimension, was popular in Christian Europe and the Islamic world, but it was also looked upon with some fear by authorities simply because mystical experience evaded their controls. Mysticism generated movements in different religions, including Islam, Christianity, and Hinduism. Sufism in West Asia was a reaction to the rigidity of Islamic orthodoxy, which was protected by the legal scholars (*ulama*) who interpreted Islamic law based on the teachings of the Qur'an. In the same way, in South Asia, the *bhakti* movement was a reaction to the rigid ritualism of the brahmans in Hinduism. In both Islam and Christianity, the notions of orthodoxy, officially approved religious doctrine, and heterodoxy, doctrines regarded as incorrect or dangerous, caused deep divisions that often led to social, political, and even military conflict before they were resolved. At the most fundamental level, Judeo-Christianity and Islam can be seen as divisions that evolved out of the same West Asian

monotheistic tradition, but each in turn developed its own deep divisions.

Ritual and resistance

Even in memory systems where tensions between experience and written knowledge were absent, resistance could threaten the elite's control over knowledge. Popular and elite cultures sometimes served different populations and represented conflicting versions of cultural memory, just as family histories and court histories might differ vastly in their interest in and interpretation of the past. For example, the Yoruba conceive of rituals as both actual and virtual journeys. Transformation of cultural memory can take place whether rituals are performed as a procession or public parade, pilgrimage, masquerade, or possession trance.

Ritual performance can subvert the mundane order as easily as it can reinforce it. What may be more difficult to capture in this written description of ritual and other experienced performance is its simultaneous links to tradition or cultural memory and to impermanency and change. Although the Greeks relied on static written forms, the religion of the ancient Greeks was similarly focused on action: rituals, festivals, processions, athletic contests, oracles, sacrifices. The cult of Athena, goddess of wisdom, centered around splendid festivals rather than any fixed or written representation.

Summary

The Japanese drama form Noh can serve as a convenient metaphor for the theme of this chapter: the production and reproduction of culture and its transmission as cultural memory through distinctive memory systems. In the case of Noh, the retelling of a past event functions as a means of dramatic catharsis, a way of not only explaining the event but also commemorating and controlling it by recreating it. The point is not the objective recounting of the story but the assignment of meaning to it. In a similar way, as human cultures reproduce themselves over generations, they do so in part with intent. That is, people construct memories of the past embedded in cultural forms and practices through which they transmit that past in a purposeful way.

Some cultures stressed the keeping of formal historical records and transmitted the past in an explicit, conscious fashion through written texts, as the Chinese, or through oral traditions, as the Mande in West Africa. Other cultures paid greater attention to the transmission of religious ideas or cosmological conceptions, as those influenced by Hinduism and Buddhism in India and Southeast Asia. But all cultures, whether explicitly or implicitly, found ways to impart a particular understanding of their past through formal and informal means, through institutions and organizations, community rituals, and distinctive structures. In this way, they negotiated, produced, and reproduced culture in the very process of expressing and transmitting it. It is no accident that the words "memory" and "commemorate" are related. The institutionalization of memory through commemorative rituals of the past is an essential means of cultural reproduction and transmission.

In this chapter, we have emphasized the transmission of cultural memory through memory systems largely, though not exclusively, within cultures. This journey has provided a global perspective on knowledge systems and their differing roles in societies, from Greek conceptions of history and Confucian textual traditions in East Asia to medieval theology in Europe and systems of oral transmission of knowledge in Africa. We have seen that domains of knowledge can be danced or sung, built into monuments as well as written in books. We have also highlighted the transmission of ideas and practices across cultures as well as across time, such as the Arab transmission of Greek science and philosophy to medieval Europe. Cultures and societies not only connected with each other across geographical space. They also connected over time with the past, through processes of knowledge transmission and systems of cultural memory. Technology and performance were key aspects of the processes of transmission. Making use of culturally specific ways of thinking, people across the globe interpreted their pasts and transmitted religious, philosophical, and technological knowledge. The many systems for remembering the past were dynamic and changing, always subject to contending and competing ideas. In this way, they made history fundamental to the key parts of their identity as individuals and communities.

Suggested readings

Apter, Andrew (1992) *Black Critics and Kings: The Hermeneutics of Power in Yoruba Society*, Chicago and London: University of Chicago Press. Examines how Yoruba forms of ritual and knowledge shape history and resistance.

Connerton, Paul (2007) *How Societies Remember*, New York: Cambridge University Press.

Eisner, Lee (2003) *Sundiata: A Legend of Africa*, New York: Nantier Beall Minoustchine Publishing. A graphic novel version of the classic epic.

Lacoste, Yves (1984) *Ibn Khaldun: The Birth of History and the Past of the Third World*, London: Verso. Develops the historiographical importance of the Islamic scholar Ibn Khaldun.

Morris, Ivan (1964) *The World of the Shining Prince*, Oxford: Oxford University Press. A classic reconstruction of the world of the *Tale of Genji*, using literary sources to illuminate court life, culture, and society in eleventh-century Japan.

Roberts, Mary Nooter and Allen F. Roberts (1996) *Luba Art and the Making of History*, New York: The Museum for African Art. Brilliant consideration of art as cultural memory in Zaire.

Robinson, Francis (1996) *The Cambridge Illustrated History of the Islamic World*, Cambridge: Cambridge University Press. Comprehensive overview of Islamic history.

Rossington, Michael and Anne Whitehead (2007) *Theories of Memory: A Reader*, Baltimore: John Hopkins University Press.

Southern, R.W. (1990) *Western Society and the Church in the Middle Ages*, New York: Penguin. A useful survey of the Church's role in European society in the medieval period.

White, Lynn, Jr. (1966) *Medieval Technology and Social Change*, New York: Oxford University Press. Classic view of technology as a memory system.

Online resources

Annenberg Corporation and CPB, *Bridging World History* <www.learner.org/courses/worldhistory> Multimedia gallery of images, videos, and interactive website organized thematically, see Unit 2: History and Memory.

Patricia Ebrey, compiler, *A Visual Sourcebook of Chinese Civilization* <depts.washington.edu/chinaciv>

The Metropolitan Museum of Art, New York, *Heilbrunn Timeline of Art History* <www.metmuseum.org/toah> Overview of the history of world art represented by the Museum's collections.

Study questions

1. Compare and contrast the spoken and written word as memory systems.
2. How do memory systems intersect with institutions of power and authority in a given society? How do historians use memory systems?
3. Are technologies or performing arts more or less reliable as sources of information about the past? Why?
4. How does architecture convey cultural memory? Give examples from two parts of the world. What is the role of individuals in constructing memory and meaning? Why do societies attempt to construct enduring monuments?
5. What dimensions are added or changed when institutions are involved in transmitting cultural memory?
6. Has gender been a factor in the transmission of traditions?
7. What influences the ability of individuals or institutions to challenge cultural memory?
8. It is thought that the decline in letter-writing and use of the telephone combined with the rise of digital technology would lead to the loss of evidence for use by historians. What do you think will be the most important sources for recreating the history of the twenty-first century and why?

12 Commerce and change

Creating a world system

In 1571 CE, the famous Florentine goldsmith Benvenuto Cellini died. He left behind a legacy of magnificent gold creations, including a particularly stunning saltcellar commissioned by the King of France, Francis I (r. 1515–47). This precious storage container for salt depicted the gods as Europeans sitting languidly on top of the world, an intermingling of land and sea dominions.

In the same year as Cellini's death, the Ottoman Empire met a major defeat at the Battle of Lepanto, and soon after 1571, the Moroccan invasion of West Africa led to the fall of one of its greatest empires of gold, the likely source of Cellini's raw material. Halfway around the world, European silver merchants were founding the city of Manila, in the Philippines, in 1571. The Spanish fleets (of massive galleons) carried its silver bullion once or twice a year from mines in Peru and Mexico across the Pacific Ocean, ultimately destined for Ming China. While some of these events were perhaps fortuitous and only randomly related, they occurred at the same moment. Their narratives converged to shake apart the thirteenth-century world system and

12.1 Benvenuto Cellini, saltcellar of Francis I (1543).

replace it with a system of European-dominated global trade. Silver replaced gold as the world's precious metal and its engine of economic advancement altered the course of globalization.

1492–1503	1494	1494–1566	1513	1519–1522	1526	1545
Four voyages of Christopher Columbus	Treaty of Tordesillas	Sulayman the Magificent	Leo Africanus visits Timbuktu, Niger River	Voyage of Magellan	Mughal Empire founded	Potosi silver mines exploited

Introduction to the theme of commerce and change

In the Chinese language, the idea of critical juncture is represented by the combination of the characters for danger (*wei*) and opportunity (*ji*). History is filled with critical junctures, moments of crisis that can appear to determine the flow of events for centuries afterward. That crisis or danger is also opportunity is clear from the unfolding of world historical events around 1500 CE. Continuity as well as change is characteristic of history, but it truly seems that change has intensified in the last 500 years. Each generation, however, may feel that it is facing the most profound crises that humanity has ever confronted, so change is also a matter of perception.

The world faced a critical juncture in the sixteenth century with the expansion of Europe. It was a defining moment in global history, a critical juncture of danger and opportunity whose long-term impact would be profound and enduring. The forces of economic change propelled cultures and societies across the globe into collision with each other. Newer and more wide-ranging sea routes that marbled the world's oceans overtook the older conduits of both commercial and cultural exchange. The divergence of individual cultures linked by periodic trade or warfare shifted into a pattern of convergence shaped by intensified global connections. The potentially fruitful outcome and advantage for some involved in such encounters was balanced by the dangers of domination, struggle, and misunderstanding for others.

The success of the Mongols in their expansion across Eurasia in the thirteenth century relied heavily on the adaptation of the traditional technology of horse breeding to the environment. By unifying Eurasia, the Mongol conquest also facilitated trade along the Silk Roads and connected caravan routes. As Janet Abu-Lughod has argued, Mongol domination of Eurasia helped to bring about a "thirteenth-century world system," a network of trading ties that extended across the Eurasian continent and linked the economic, political, social, and cultural lives of peoples in places as distant from each other as Hangzhou and Venice or Cairo and Palembang. However, many scholars would argue that this thirteenth-century **world system** differed markedly from later world systems. Those merchants at the farthest reach from China had little recognition of Chinese domination and only a minor influence on a system of economic interconnectedness. Still, the actions of the Chinese emperor or Malian kings and Cairo merchants had a ripple effect on other world regions, suggesting that even if the ties were partly obscured by distance, they nonetheless constituted a shared experience of commercial destinies.

The achievement of this Afro-Eurasian world system was momentary. Following the fifteenth-century explorations of world oceans, European sailors, explorers, and merchants began to establish a competing network of truly global interconnections and dominance based on new maritime connections. These connections furthered the changing patterns of economic and cultural exchange on a much larger scale. It was

1542–1605	1571	1591	ca. 1602–1640
Akbar the Great	Death of Cellini; Founding of Manila; Defeat of Ottoman Empire in the Battle of Lepanto	Moroccan invasion of Songhay, West Africa	Dutch displace Portuguese in Southeast Asia and Brazil

Europeans who took the lead in this enterprise, linking together economies of Africa, the Americas, and Asia and ushering in a new age of globalization.

Competition among emerging European polities in the late fifteenth and early sixteenth centuries inspired the voyages of exploration that led to the shift of world trade and wealth, eventually to the Atlantic Ocean. Advances in maritime and commercial technology in Europe were as important for the creation of the new world system as the Mongol horsemanship had been for the old. Technological innovations were also essential to the development of capitalism and the economic expansion of Europe. By 1500, Europe was poised to reap, accumulate, and invest the profits of the developing capitalist economy of the new Atlantic frontier as the vital periphery to the expansion of the European core economy.

Finally, between about 1500 and 1800, following Columbus's voyages, the economic relationships and societies of the Americas and Europe, together with parts of Africa, Asia, and the Pacific were transformed through the creation of an Atlantic world economy that provided the means for subsequent European expansion into Asia and the Pacific. Voyages across the Pacific remained vital to the forging of new economic ties. Establishment of Atlantic connections had a profound impact on the lives and cultures of African peoples, particularly those of West and Central Africa, as well as those of the Americas. The new global connections upset the balance of the long-established relations among Asia, Africa, and Europe, replacing and redirecting their world systems of land-based and maritime, inter- and intraregional commerce.

Debating the rise of the West

Historians have put forward many reasons for the shifting centers of economic and commercial growth after the thirteenth century. Was the rise of Europe the consequence of convergence, divergence, or was it the inevitable consequence of superior advantages in technology, demography, and environment? Until recently, European dominance was viewed as the natural outcome of developments thought to be both technologically and philosophically based. However, modern theories of globalization suggest that the rise of capitalism and Western expansion were neither altogether positive nor beneficial, nor were they inevitable. When seen from a global perspective, European dominance did not occur until about 1800, when it arose as a consequence of industrialization. Before this time, commercial change was underway in many parts of the world. Many historians argue that the experience of Europeans was not a divergent or exceptional history. If anything, European demographic declines and the lack of sufficient resources of land and labor contributed equally to the revolutionary shift from one commercial center (China) to another (Europe). One could also argue that Europe had been preparing for an expansion that began centuries earlier.

The primacy of China between 1000 and 1500 CE was underappreciated until fairly recently. As a result of a series of poor harvests and the Black Death that had spread along the Silk Roads in the mid-fourteenth century, European populations – in some places reduced by about a third – were faced with crisis. Yet disease ravaged many parts of Afro-Eurasia, with various consequences including the disruption of existing patterns of trade and networks of common destiny. Anticipating the full portrait of an emerging world system, the fifteenth century witnessed a convergence of key innovations and changes. Importantly, the fifteenth century found a Europe primed for transformation and expansion.

Technology, commerce, and the expansion of Europe

Maritime and military technology played major roles in the development and expansion of European power both before and after the fifteenth century. Mediterranean maritime powers, such as Venice, did not adopt navigational innovations such as the compass until around 1000, in part because such innovations were of lesser importance to traffic on an inland sea such as the Mediterranean. From the twelfth century on, however, Venice actively pursued innovations in maritime technology as a means of maintaining dominance of trade in the Mediterranean between Europe and West Asia and enhancing profits. For example, the Venetians developed assembly-line techniques of shipbuilding based on the standardization of ship parts, which were warehoused in strategic ports around the Mediterranean. In this way and others, Venice became a sort of midwife to the transformation of European maritime technology that would enable the opening of the Atlantic frontier.

Maritime technology

Progress in improved ship design and construction was irregular and slow, but by the end of the fifteenth century, European ships, particularly those used in the Atlantic, attained the essential form they were to keep until the nineteenth century. The basic innovation was in ship construction, which enabled sails, essential for transoceanic commerce, to replace the oars that were suitable to travel on the inland Mediterranean. Improvements included such things as the construction of skeletons that were then covered with wood and pitch and the adoption of the square-rigged mainmast (after 1300); the use of several sails per mast; the transition from one-masted to three-masted ships; and the introduction of the sternpost rudder. These innovations increased speed, stability, and maneuverability.

12.2 Manuscript page (ca. 1540) from Michael of Rhodes's manuscript illustrating one of the signs of the Zodiac (Libra). Celestial events were essential for time reckoning and navigation, and their study encouraged a popular interest in astrology.

Michael of Rhodes and the nautical revolution

The remarkable writings of a fifteenth-century mariner Michael of Rhodes provide many details in Venice's maritime history. Michael himself was not a shipbuilder, but he had a keen interest in mathematics and his mathematical observations were detailed enough to permit the reconstruction of revolutionary shifts in shipbuilding technologies of the time. Beginning about 1401, as a humble oarsman on a Venetian galley, Michael documented more than 30 years of his life on the seas, recording his knowledge of shipbuilding, navigation, practical mathematics, and time reckoning. His writings reveal the marriage of Atlantic Coast and Mediterranean technology in the fifteenth century. During this period, private shipbuilders took the larger vessels of northern Europe (called cogs) with their stern rudders and shell-built style and applied the southern technique of frame-built, edge-to-edge planking (the carvel). In this way, the ships of Spanish and Portuguese mariners later adopting these innovations came to be known as "caravels." Not only the hulls, but also the sails of seaworthy European vessels underwent a revolutionary transformation. Again, the square sails of the north were combined with the lateen sails of the south, requiring a new and more complex system of rigging and allowing the captain to tack into the wind and change directions. These alterations permitted expanded opportunities for maneuverability and sealed the way for the maritime expansion of the following centuries.

By the fifteenth century, improvements in construction also resulted in ships of multiple decks and of noticeably increased tonnage. For example, the average tonnage of Portuguese ships doubled between 1450 and 1550. Innovations were not systematically adopted. Mediterranean shippers, for example, were reluctant to abandon old traditions, refusing to recognize the disadvantage of galleys dependent on oarsmen compared to sailing ships, and accordingly they lagged behind. Placing cannons on ships aided Europeans in opening the Atlantic frontier and extending their sea power around the world. Shipbuilders set about improving firepower as well as maneuverability. One innovation, introduced in 1501 and attributed to the French, was cutting portholes on decks below the upper deck so that cannons could be placed on them. This greatly increased ships' firepower.

Navigational aids

Equally important to European maritime progress was the adoption and general use of navigational aids. The magnetic **compass**, coming from China by way of the Arabs, reached Europe shortly after 1000 and was in general use by Europeans within a matter of decades. The Arabic **astrolabe**, an instrument used to observe and calculate the position of stars and planets, followed soon after the compass. Navigational charts, the "roadmaps" of maritime travel, facilitated and emboldened open-sea navigation. The first recorded use of a navigational chart by European sailors is in 1270, but it was not until the fifteenth century that the use of such charts was common.

European voyages of exploration

Voyages by western and northern European states were inspired by Italian commercial success and made possible by developments in maritime and business technology: the high prices and high profits that accrued to Italians as a result of their Mediterranean monopoly lured ambitious trans-Alpine Europeans to undertake voyages of exploration that sought alternative ways to trade and profit. The small Atlantic-facing kingdom of Portugal on the Iberian peninsula inaugurated these voyages.

Prince Henry the Navigator

Prince Henry the Navigator (1394–1460), who was in fact no navigator, is nonetheless credited with being the inspiration and enthusiastic patron and organizer of the Portuguese voyages, which were responses to the kingdom's poverty and exclusion from Mediterranean trade. The maritime voyages began, at least, as a latter-day "Crusade." The Portuguese, together with the Spanish, had for centuries engaged in wars (legitimized as "Crusades") to expel Muslims and Jews from the Iberian peninsula and to reduce the power and influence of both groups in surrounding areas. That task, during which centralized kingdoms were created in both Portugal and Spain, had been, for all intents and purposes, achieved by the fifteenth century.

In 1415, Prince Henry extended the Iberian "crusade" to North Africa, ordering an attack on the city of Ceuta, a Muslim strategic and commercial center. The acquisition of Ceuta gave the Portuguese access to African trade and became a base for further Portuguese expeditions southward. They sailed down the western coast of Africa to the Senegambian and then rounded the West and Central African coastlines between the 1430s and 1480s. They continued to the area of the Kongo, a major Central African kingdom, and on to the Cape of Good Hope, the southernmost point on the African continent, reached by the Portuguese in 1488. Although local groups of Khoikhoi pastoralists, using indigenous military techniques including having bulls charge into battle, expelled their Portuguese guests, other Europeans were not far behind.

From the cape, subsequent expeditions moved northward, attempting to replace centuries-old African and Arab merchant enterprises in port cities along the eastern coast of Africa. From East Africa, the Portuguese sailed across the Indian Ocean, reaching India in 1498. In their attempt to control the movement of goods, Portugal then built large fleets, which were used to conquer

12.3 Anonymous, a galleon sets sail to Venezuela (1560).

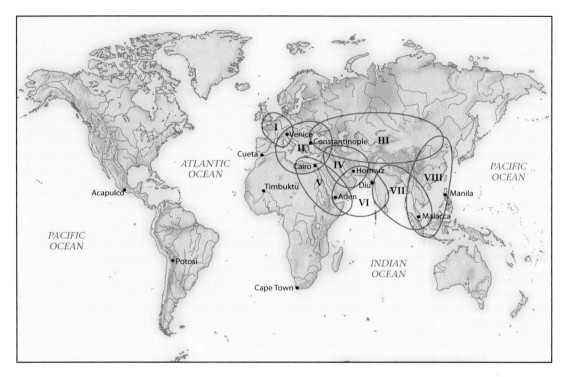

Map 12.1 Older circuits and new cities in the changing world systems, ca. 1350–1650.

Aden, Hormuz, Diu, and Malacca, key strategic ports on the established east–west Indian Ocean trade route. Here, as elsewhere, they were becoming successful interlopers in vast and ancient international commercial networks.

In this way, Portugal built a sixteenth-century commercial empire on the seas that, although it fell far short of global monopoly, was enormously profitable. By proving that Mediterranean trade was not the only way to commercial success, the Portuguese experience stimulated the eventual shift of European trade and wealth northward and westward to the Atlantic. The Portuguese success showed how profitable a seaborne empire could be, and later fifteenth- and sixteenth-century European explorations sought alternative routes to Asia. Within the half century following the death of Prince Henry, the world had been circumnavigated.

Commerce and change in the West African gold trade

Even before the maritime expansion of Europe, the international transfer of metals dominated world trade systems. Hungarian silver, West African gold, East African iron, and Asian copper all played a role in the establishment and growth of world commerce. From the time of Charlemagne (r. 786–814 CE), rulers attempted to standardize currency. A currency or money of account (a system for calculating value for trading purposes) eventually prevailed, based initially on the value of silver and later, by the fifteenth century, on gold.

International gold trade

Gold was the staple export item of the trans-Saharan caravan networks. Its supply supported the system of international currencies that linked Cairo, West Africa, and Europe. Gold sources attracted the attention of North Africans and Europeans alike. When Leo Africanus, a North African Arab traveler, visited Timbuktu on the Niger River in 1513, the large number of shops belonging to merchants and artisans impressed him. At the Niger city of Jenné, he found gold and local cloth traded for imported textiles, copper and brass vessels, iron, weapons, spices, and other exotic goods. Many of these goods were sold by weight. Throughout the fifteenth century, Europeans attempted to extend their trading ventures to reach the sources of gold directly. They established fortified bases on islands and coastal locations from which they might continue their search for gold and luxury items. At the island of Arguin off the northwest coast of Africa, a Venetian, Alvise da Cadamosto, witnessed the tight Portuguese control of trade in 1454:

> You should know that the said King of Portugal has leased this island to Christians for ten years, so that no one can enter the bay

to trade with the Arabs save those who hold the license. These have dwellings on the island and factories where they buy and sell with said Arabs who come to the coast to trade for merchandise of various kinds, such as woolen cloths, cotton, silver, and "alchezeli" [coarse cloth], that is, cloaks, carpets, and similar articles and above all, corn, for they are always short of food. They give in exchange slaves whom the Arabs bring from the land of the Blacks, and gold dust.

The Islamic world of the fifteenth and sixteenth centuries

Between the extreme ends of the old Afro-Eurasian world system, was an enormous Islamic world. Anchored by four major empires, the Ottoman, Safavid, Mughal, and Songhay, the regions of West and North Africa, southeastern Europe, the Black Sea, West Asia, and much of South Asia came under the control of powerful political units. Political unity in turn facilitated the maintenance of vast commercial connections. Overland routes in Central Asia, Europe, and in Southeast, West, and South Asia continued to transfer goods, people, ideas, and disease. This era has been called a second "flowering" of Islam.

This flowering took place in a diverse and commercially rich environment. After the Ottoman Turks conquered Constantinople in 1453, they fervently engaged in the expansion of roads and bridges, as well as constructing cultural monuments and institutions. By expanding their empire, the Ottomans confronted both Christianity and European states, all the while growing their commercial networks. Under the reign of Sulayman (r. 1522–66), the rich heritage of the Byzantine Empire was combined with that of the Abbasid caliphate in Baghdad. Eventually, the Sunni Ottomans were weakened by wars with Shi'i Safavids of Iran and revolts in Afghanistan. The Mughal Empire (1526–1858) incorporated elements of Hindu culture and language in their

12.4 Akan goldweight, Ghana (West Africa). Brass and bronze figurative weights were used as counterbalances on scales to weigh gold dust and nuggets. Once conforming to the Islamic weight system for trans-Saharan trade, the weights shifted to a system of European ounces as the coastal trade developed.

ethnically diverse territory that stretched to the Indian sub-continent. In West Africa, the Songhay Empire (ca. 1464–1591) found that trade was a double-edged sword, bringing wealth to the participants and unwanted interest by invaders seeking resources within their territories. The rising empire relied heavily on enslaved labor, supplying the Ottomans with an estimated 6,500 persons via the trans-Saharan trade through Libya. The competition to control and protect commercial connections led to increasingly militarized societies and ultimately undermined the stability of the regions they encompassed.

Merchants often became agents of imperial expansion. The Mughal emperor Babur defeated the Hindus in South Asia in 1526, but did not force conversion to his own Muslim faith. Less tolerant rulers were forced to expand trade to finance military campaigns. Eventually, desperate for commercial opportunities, they allowed European merchants to establish new enclaves and soon there were forts and castles in Bombay (today's city of Mumbai), Calcutta and other Indian Ocean ports. The same experience held an advantage for European commercial expansion in the Atlantic.

By the 1450s, Portuguese ships exploring the West African coast were trading along the frontiers of this Islamic world, including with Mande-speaking peoples for gold in the regions beyond the Senegambia. In 1471, vessels reached the Gold Coast, where Castilian mariners found Africans willing to trade gold nuggets for European goods. The gold supply was eventually so plentiful on the coast that the Portuguese named the place El Mina, "the Mine," and built a fort on land rented from the local African community.

Merchant communities

The gold traded directly to the early European sailors had been intended for different and more distant destinations accessible by land. Merchant communities engaged in the trans-Saharan trade were well organized. Among the most successful merchant organizations was that of the Mande speakers, whose system of lodges housed merchants across a vast territory and formed the basis of the political order that resulted in the Mali state in the thirteenth and fourteenth centuries. Mali's successor state, Songhay, was more precarious. Weakened by shifting trade routes and civil unrest, Songhay faced an invasion by Moroccan armies in 1591 that disrupted the security of commercial networks. Songhay had controlled salt from Taghaza to Awdaghust, gold from Bambuk, Bure and the Akan goldfields, and Saharan copper mines. Professional traders traveled thousands of miles from one end of the western Sudan to the other and crisscrossed the desert sands that led to other African societies, North Africa, the Mediterranean, and Asia.

Europeans and the gold trade

The Portuguese capture of Ceuta in the first quarter of the fifteenth century brought one of the terminal points in the trans-Saharan gold trade into European hands. Yet Europeans were still thousands of miles away from the Senegambian gold sources of Bambuk, Bure, and the Akan goldfields south of the Sahara that provided the foundation of their currencies, fully two-thirds of the world's gold supply. Although European merchants desired expansion across land to the mines and markets of Africa and Asia, Islamic empires in West Asia and in West and North Africa effectively blocked them. This massive Afro-Asian world system deflected European expansion from land and toward the sea routes around the African continent and eventually sent the Europeans westward across the Atlantic.

Commerce and change in China

At the same time that Europeans were seeking expansion from western Eurasia, the Chinese were becoming more interested in the commercial world beyond their borders. With the restoration of native Chinese rule in the fourteenth century under the Ming dynasty, the boundaries of Chinese civilization were redefined and two frontiers emerged: a maritime frontier and an inland frontier. The seven voyages undertaken by the Chinese Muslim admiral Zheng He between 1407 and 1433 bore witness both to the seafaring capabilities of the Chinese navy and to the Ming court's desire to command the maritime frontier.

prohibitions, however, private maritime trade continued to expand alongside state-controlled trade into the early 1600s, enriched by Spanish silver transported from Potosi and Acapulco to Manila, where Chinese merchants received payment in silver for silks, porcelains, and other luxury goods.

Zheng He's expeditions had stimulated the emigration of Chinese to all parts of Southeast Asia; by the sixteenth century, Chinese merchant communities were operating in port cities

Zheng He's voyages

Zheng He's Muslim background made him well suited for the task, since many of the countries visited by the expeditions were Muslim. Hailing from the southwestern province of Yunnan ("south of the clouds"), both Zheng He's father and brother were devout Muslims, who had made the pilgrimage to Mecca.

The expeditions were huge in scale and navigated the rim of the Indian Ocean. Financed and supported by imperial patronage, Zheng He's voyages were designed to display the power of Ming China and to confirm its place as center of the world, even though they discovered that the world beyond China was larger and more diverse than ever before imagined. Ma Huan (ca. 1380–1460), who accompanied Zheng He on the voyages, wrote an account of them to record information about the lands and peoples encountered, thus enriching Chinese knowledge of the world and establishing tribute relationships.

The Chinese diaspora

In the sixteenth century, the Ming government limited the size of seagoing vessels and declared harsh punishments for private traders who put to sea in defiance of imperial injunctions. One of the reasons for this was the activity of Sino-Japanese pirates along the southeast coast. Despite imperial

12.5 East African giraffe at the Emperor of China's court, 1415; painting by Shen Tu.

throughout Southeast Asia. Like the injunctions against engaging in maritime trade, prohibitions by the imperial government against emigration by and large failed. Those who sought profits from trade abroad or were lured by the promise of economic opportunities seldom heeded their prescriptions. Instead, the diaspora of Chinese merchants created new commercial frontiers that expanded far beyond China's territorial boundaries and brought Chinese into direct encounters with both Southeast Asians and Europeans.

Declining gold trade at Zimbabwe

There is considerable evidence that direct contact between African and Chinese merchants took place before the decline of the Afro-Eurasian world system. Diplomatic missions forged connections and exchanged gifts, as evidenced by the Chinese silk painting that records the gift to the emperor of an African giraffe. Moreover, Indian Ocean maritime commerce regularly connected the East African coastal towns, such as Sofala and Kilwa. Chinese silks and other textiles may have formed part of the exchange for African gold and ivory. Most of these products would have come from inland networks of trade, some of which were centered on metal sources more than a month's march from the coast. At the large urban site of Great Zimbabwe, thirteenth- and fourteenth-century Chinese celadon (a pale-green-glazed pottery), stoneware, and coins have been found. This long-distance trade extended regionally to West-Central Africa and also to the Persian Gulf, where the imported glass beads and glazed bowls originated. Sometime during the fourteenth century, owing perhaps to the declines that can be associated with the Black Death, the Indian Ocean trade declined. Certainly by the second half of the fifteenth century, a reduced demand for gold on the world market had begun to shift the commercial centers. Archaeologists have hypothesized that the decline of Great

Zimbabwe may have begun as early as this period, based on reduction in imported wealth, although even in the early sixteenth century, imported Chinese porcelain was still reaching Great Zimbabwe.

Silver's global connections

The increased Chinese demand for precious metal to back its currency originated in the disastrous experiment with paper currency before and during the Ming dynasty. Some of the first paper money (ca. 800 CE) was known as "flying cash," an apt tag for the speed of transactions enabled by the lightweight currency, when compared to copper-based coins or silver ingots, originating in Japan. However, during one period in the fourteenth century, too much paper currency was printed, devaluing the paper currency so as to make it almost worthless. The Chinese returned to the use of silver ingots for the payment of taxes and China became what economic historians have called the world's "silver sink." The traditional sources of silver were no longer sufficient to keep up with the increased demand. In response, huge amounts of silver mined in the Americas and transported by Europeans across the Pacific to Manila supplied the Chinese demand, which became the engine of a new era of **globalization**. Operating this world system were the European merchants of a newly transformed commercial landscape.

Mercantilism and the Atlantic world, ca. 1500–1750

Before Europeans would be able to undertake their role in creating a new world system, they too experienced a commercial revolution. The European economy began to be transformed when the self-sufficient feudal-manorial system of services and duties gave way to an urban economy based on money and trade and controlled by merchant-manufacturers. Because these merchant-manufacturers became very wealthy, rulers of city-states and monarchies – and even the pope – would turn to them and to their financiers for the cash wealth they needed to maintain and extend their power. In proportion to the princes' reliance on the wealthy merchant class, the political influence of this urban elite began to replace that of landholding feudal vassals. As their influence grew, the urban wealthy increasingly influenced state politics. What merchant-manufacturers needed and wanted most was freedom from the restrictions of a static medieval economy that was communal and largely self-sufficient, and in which production and trade for profit were constrained or limited by such regulations and restraints as tariffs, road duties, and the concepts of a just price and the prohibition of interest (usury). The demands of merchant-manufacturers and bankers to expand their enterprises and increase profits brought them into conflict with the norms of medieval agrarian society. In order to tap the growing wealth of the commercial elite, ambitious rulers increasingly supported their demands for changes in the economy. Use of political power to promote and protect trade was necessary to increase commercial wealth, which would benefit both prince and merchant alike.

The partnership that evolved between rulers and merchant-manufacturers enhanced the wealth and power of both. It also produced a set of doctrines and practices known as mercantilism, which aimed to enhance state power by increasing wealth. Mercantilism was based on the use of government intervention to promote the accumulation of profits, which, it was believed, would secure the prosperity and self-sufficiency of the state while benefiting those who contributed most to it, the urban commercial elite.

The voyages of Christopher Columbus illustrate the role of the prince in mercantilism and the mutual benefits to be derived by both prince and merchant. Although Columbus was a native of Genoa, he sought financial backing for his voyages first from the king of Portugal and then from Isabella of Castile and Ferdinand of Aragon in Spain. The Spanish monarchs retained Columbus in their service, but it took about five years to convince them to provide the 2,500 *ducats* for the voyage. The person who finally persuaded Ferdinand and Isabella of the financial potential of the venture was a banker and papal tax gatherer from Valencia, who had successfully raised a number of loans for them and who had himself amassed a fortune as a shrewd businessman. Merchants, whose power rested on their wealth, were as necessary to mercantilist enterprises as kings, and they derived great advantage from them, at least until the mid-eighteenth century, when merchants began to assert their independence from government support and protection.

One of the components of the theory and practice of European mercantilism was **bullionism**. For ambitious rulers, bullionism, the acquisition of surplus bullion (precious metals, specifically gold and silver ingots) meant that more ships could be built, larger fleets and armies equipped, and territorial expansion financed. One strong reason for the decision to back Columbus's voyage was the Spanish monarchy's acute lack of currency (especially gold); the possibility of enormous profits from an entirely new set of trading networks loomed large enough to overshadow the risks of Columbus's venture. Another component of mercantilism was the fervent hope that European voyages of exploration would lead to the establishment of colonies, the extension of European activities overseas. The Portuguese took the lead in accomplishing this in the east, while the Spanish looked westwards.

The Pacific world

The first documented link between the Americas and the islands of the Pacific was established by a Spanish expedition led by the Portuguese adventurer Ferdinand Magellan. Magellan's fleet sailed from Spain in the fall of 1519, wintered at Patagonia at the southern tip of South America, and then crossed into the Pacific through what is now known as the Strait of Magellan. After 100 days at sea, Magellan's fleet reached a group of islands that they claimed under the terms of the 1494 Treaty of Tordesillas that divided the world between Spain and Portugal. The Spanish finally secured their claim to the islands in 1542, renaming them "Islas Filipinas" (the Philippines). Spanish occupation of the Philippines was confirmed in 1571, when a third expedition took control of Manila, an important trading center that became the principal Spanish entrepôt in Asia.

By the second half of the sixteenth century, following the Spanish conquest of the Philippines, complicated patterns of both legitimate and contraband trade grew up around routes connecting the Spanish settlement of Acapulco in Mexico with Manila, from whence it reached China, principally through the Portuguese entrepôt of Macao. By the 1560s, Spanish "pieces of eight" had become the currency of expanding world trade, and Spanish galleons bearing goods, including silver bullion, became the object of piracy, either private or sponsored by Spain's European rivals and enemies. In 1573, the first galleon sailing eastward from Manila across the Pacific to Spanish America carried Chinese silks, satins, porcelains, and spices to Acapulco, from whence it returned to Manila with silver from Spanish-American mines. Potosi – more than 4,600 meters (15,000 feet) high in the Andes Mountains, ten weeks' journey from Lima – was the site of the richest silver mine in the history of the world. Founded in 1545, Potosi's mountain of silver funded the Spanish empire until about the middle of the seventeenth century.

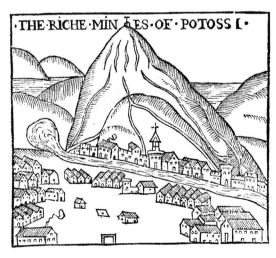

THE
DISCOVERIE AND CONQVEST
of the Prouinces of *PERV*, and
the *Nauigation in the South*
Sea, along that Coaſt.
And alſo of the ritche Mines
of *POTOSI.*

·THE·RICHE·MIN̄E̅S·OF·POTOSS I·

12.6 Anonymous, illustration town of Potosi in mountains (1581).

Potosi, the mountain that eats men

In the highlands of present-day Bolivia, Potosi became a celebrated treasure trove, yielding half the world's silver. Beginning in 1545 and continuing for more than two centuries, this *Cerro Rico* ("rich mountain") created a flow of wealth that financed the Spanish empire, influenced the course of European commercial expansion, and supported trade with Asia. Employing millions of Quechua in forced labor (under the **mit'a system**), the Spanish conquest had begun.

Potosi was both "the mountain that ate men" and the hemisphere's largest city. Within less than three decades, the city's population reached 120,000, equaling London. Silver flowed in the streets, covered the church altars, and was said to have been used to shoe horses. Silver ore was dug by forced labor from the bowels of the Earth, then processed and refined. In 1599, the Spanish friar Diego de Ocana wrote vividly of the commerce around the silver mining enterprises:

The Indian women look for the rocks that are discarded around the mouths of the mine, which is called *pallar*; that is, to break them up and choose those of value and separate them from the rest. And these are all sold at midday in Potosi. And before that hour, no Spaniard can buy anything from an Indian, and this is so that the Indians have a chance to buys these metals, as there are many Indians who buy them for their furnaces. And for this reason even kindling is very expensive, because of the [silver refinery] furnaces . . . And because of the rising cost of everything having to do with this, I say that even the excrement of people is worth money and is sold, and for this reason they have in Potosi some corrals where the Indians who walk the streets go to defecate; and these excrements are dried out in the sun and pressed together into large bulks and for a certain amount of this material they are paid eight *reales*, in order to burn the gray metal and refine it and enhance it with the opaque metal.

> Source: Quoted in Stephen Ferry, *I Am Rich Potosi: The Mountain that Eats Men* (New York: The Monacelli Press).

Despite the unpleasantness, relentless violence, and certain death to be found in the city, this urban society became a magnet for commercial growth and cultural transformation. At the end of the century, it contained equal numbers of magnificent churches and gambling houses. While exploiting indigenous labor through exploiting the traditional tribute system of the Incas, the city remained dependent on distant markets and rulers.

The flow of silver joins world commerce

By the end of the sixteenth century, the amount of bullion flowing from Acapulco to Manila surpassed the sum that was involved in transat-lantic shipments. Between 1570 and 1780, an estimated 4,000–5,000 tons of silver flowed to East Asia along the Acapulco–Manila route. As Spanish-American bullion flowed westward as well as eastward, both Asians and Europeans were enriched. This trade lasted until the first half of the nineteenth century, when Spanish rule in the Americas came to an end.

By the late sixteenth century, the Dutch had acquired the knowledge of navigation necessary to enter into world trade competition. Their initial target was the Portuguese-dominated spice trade in Southeast Asia. In 1602, the Dutch East India Company, a unified trading monopoly formed under state charter, began the administration of the Indonesian archipelago economy under Dutch control. By the 1640s, they had displaced the Portuguese and had consolidated their holdings across a vast sweep of islands from Ceylon in the west, through Malacca and Java (where they had an important administrative center at Batavia), to the Moluccas in the east. The Dutch had superior ships, arms, and organization, as well as more skilled merchants. They mixed piracy and missionary activities with trade.

Because of Dutch strength in Southeast Asia, British trade interests were diverted to South Asia, which became the base from which the British East India Company (1600) made inroads into Southeast and East Asia during the eighteenth century. In contrast to Spain, which reaped its wealth from the Americas, and Holland, which exploited the Indonesian archipelago, Britain concentrated, through its East India Company, on India and China, the heartlands of the two major Asian civilizations; the British government did not establish its ascendancy there until the nineteenth century, however. What all the seaborne European empires in Asia had in common by the eighteenth century was their starting point on the shores of the Atlantic.

The introduction of products from Asia created new tastes among Europeans that drove trade in the Pacific and had a global impact. Chinese tea was in great demand in European markets, when introduced by Dutch merchants; by 1664, tea reached England and quickly became the national beverage. Tea importing became a major enterprise under the monopoly of the British East India Company and an important source of government tax revenue. China demanded payment in silver for its tea, and most of the silver flowing to China from European trade originated in the Americas, the center of sugar production. In this way, the circle of global interconnectedness was completed.

The world economy, 1500–1800

As Europeans sailed into East Asian waters in the sixteenth century, they encountered a world dominated by China, a civilization more ancient and sophisticated than any in Europe. European expansion in East Asia was limited during the sixteenth century to peripheral missionary and mercantile contacts; not until the nineteenth century would European power erode the dominance of China and shatter the stability of the East Asian world order. Nonetheless, the expansion of Europe and the creation of a global economy through the opening of the Atlantic frontier had an impact on China, the core economy of the East Asian world.

With the growth of the Chinese economy following the end of Mongol rule and the restoration of a native Chinese dynasty, the Ming (1368–1644), merchants became prosperous, and even powerful, members of society. Foreign trade did match the growth of domestic commerce, however. Ming rulers generally followed policies designed to control foreign trade and bring it into the framework of the tributary system. Though the tributary system was conceived as a means of conducting diplomatic relations, trade was an important aspect of tribute relations. Tribute was paid in the form of gifts to the Chinese emperor from rulers of states surrounding China to express their homage to the Son of Heaven, the ruler of the center of the world. Return gifts from the Chinese court made tribute relations a kind of commodity exchange. Tribute missions in China from foreign countries were allowed to engage in trade as well. Merchants traveling with the tribute missions also conducted their own private trade. Despite the hostility of the Ming government to foreign trade, a substantial amount of such trade took place within the framework of the tributary system.

Ming prosperity was fueled by an agricultural revolution beginning around 1500 that saw the introduction of new crops from the Americas – corn, peanuts, and sweet potatoes – indirectly transmitted to Asia by Europeans through their voyages of exploration. These crops contributed significantly to an increase in the food supply since they could be cultivated in marginal soils unsuitable for other crops and provided substantial nutrition. Partly as a result of increased food supply, population swelled from 60–80 million (to which it had dropped as a result of the Mongol conquest) to at least 150 million by 1600.

The importation of new food crops was only one dimension of China's growing participation in a world economic system that would eventually be dominated by Europe. Though by the mid-fifteenth century, in contrast to European states' mercantilist policies, the Ming government had withdrawn its support from voyages of exploration, China could no longer remain entirely isolated from the world system being constructed through the expansion of Europe. By 1500, China was becoming part of a global monetary system through indirect links established by its Asian trading partners. East Asia in the age of European exploration and empire formed its own sector of the world economy, with silver flowing into Chinese coffers from Japan, Europe, and the Americas, often through intermediaries who used silver to pay for Chinese products, such as silks, spices, and porcelains, that were extremely profitable on the world market. The monetization of the Chinese economy that accompanied commercial growth during the Ming made China susceptible to shifts in the global economy and made even the poorest peasants in the most remote villages victims of inflation that pushed prices of goods beyond their reach, costing them more bronze cash in taxes to make up the equivalent value of silver, which had appreciated on the international market.

Between about 1500 and 1800, following Columbus's voyages, the economic relationships and societies of the Americas and Europe, as well as parts of Africa, Asia, and the Pacific were transformed through the creation of an Atlantic world economy that provided the means for subsequent European expansion into Asia and the Pacific. Establishment of Atlantic connections had a profound impact on the lives and cultures of African peoples, particularly those of West and Central Africa. The new global connections upset the balance of the long-established relations among Asia, Africa, and Europe, replacing and redirecting their world systems of land-based and maritime, inter- and intraregional commerce.

PRIMARY SOURCE: FERDINAND MAGELLAN'S VOYAGE AROUND THE WORLD, 1519–22

Born in about 1470, Ferdinand de Magellan probably spent his youth in the court of the queen of Portugal. He was also in the East India service, served in Morocco, and eventually enlisted as a captain under the Spanish king. Although credited with the first maritime circumnavigation of the globe, Magellan died in the Philippines and actually never completed the famous voyage. His crew did sail on to Spain, thus proving to the uneducated that the Earth is round, while establishing the new world system.

This account is from the paper-book of a Genoese pilot, "who came in the said ship, who wrote all the voyage as it is here. He went to Portugal in the year 1524 with Dom Amriqui de Menezes."

> Fernan de Magalhaes would not make any further stay, and at once set sail, and ordered the course to be steered west, and a quarter south-west; and so they made land [i.e., in the Phillippines], which is in barely eleven degrees. This land is an island, but he would not touch at this one, and they went to touch at another further on which appeared first. Fernando de Magelhaes sent a boat ashore to observe the nature of the island; when the boat reached land, they saw from the ships two paraos come out from behind the point; then they called back their boat. The people of the paraos seeing that the boat was returning to the ships, turned back the paraos, and the boat reached the ships, which at once set sail for another island very near to this island, which is in ten degrees, and they gave it the name of the island of Good Signs, because they found some gold in it. Whilst they were thus anchored at this island, there came to them two paraos, and brought them fowls and cocoa nuts, and told them that they had already seen there other men like them, from which they presumed that these might be Lequios or Magores; a nation of people who have this name, or Chiis; and thence they set sail, and navigated further on amongst many islands, to which they gave the name of the Valley Without Peril, and also St. Lazarus, and they ran on to another island twenty leagues from that from which they sailed, which is in ten degrees, and came to anchor at another island, which is named Macangor, which is in nine degrees; and in this island they were very well received, and they placed a cross in it.

This king conducted them thence a matter of thirty leagues to another island named Cabo, which is in ten degrees, and in this island Fernando de Magalhaes did what he pleased with the consent of the country, and in one day eight hundred people became Christian, on which account Fernan de Magalhaes desired that the other kings, neighbors to this one, should become subject to this who had become Christian: and these did not choose to yield such obedience. Fernan de Magalhaes seeing that, got ready one night with his boats, and burned the villages of those who would not yield the said obedience; and a matter of ten or twelve days after this was done he sent to a village about half a league from that which he had burned, which is named Matam, and which is also an island, and ordered them to send him at once three goats, three pigs, three loads of rice, and three loads of millet for provisions for the ships; they replied that of each article which he sent to ask them three of, they would send to him by twos, and if he was satisfied with this they would at once comply, if not, it might be as he pleased, but that they would not give it. Because they did not choose to grant what he demanded of them, Fernan de Magalhaes ordered three boats to be equipped with a matter of fifty or sixty men, and went against the said place, which was on the 28th day of April, in the morning; there they found many people, who might well be as many as three thousand or four thousand men, who fought with such a good will that the said Fernan de Magalhaes was killed there, with six of his men, in the year 1521.

Source: Oliver J. Thatcher, ed., *The Library of Original Sources, Vol V: 9th to 16th Centuries*, (Milwaukee: University Research Extension Co., 1907), pp41–57.

Triangular connections among societies in Africa, Europe, and the Americas revolved primarily around an expanding Atlantic trade, with its foundations mired in slavery and merchant capitalism. Soon after it was forged, the interconnected world of Atlantic commercial development was no longer a set of balanced relationships. European expansion into the Pacific added new global connections and constituted a westward shift of power away from earlier Afro-Eurasian centers such as the Indian Ocean trading world and the East Asian core economy of China. In the eighteenth century, new developments in Europe would provide the means to intensify European domination of the global economy.

Summary

Economic changes in both China and Europe were on such a large scale that they have been called "revolutionary." As commerce grew in importance, Europeans and Chinese experienced significant changes in the social order, particularly the growth of merchants as a social and economic class. The daily material lives of people were transformed by the expansion of commerce, which brought new goods and products to eat, wear, and use, and by developments in technology, such as printing and metalworking. These changes, however, took shape in different social and cultural settings and produced very different results in Europe and China. After the commercial revolution, which was followed by the Mongol conquest, China turned inward, rejecting the exploration of the rest of the world. In contrast, the combination of commercial growth and technological developments produced in Europe an outward expansion that sought to support and expand commerce through contacts with the rest of the world.

Beginning with commercial revolutions in Europe and China, these processes of transformation took place against the backdrop of the thirteenth-century world system. The shift of that world system increasingly to Europe as the core witnessed the impact of the new world system on the entire globe in the form of economic, cultural, social, and political changes. Earlier commercial developments in Europe, the desire for profit and power, and competition among emerging nation-states inspired the voyages of exploration that led to the shift of world trade and wealth – eventually to the Atlantic Ocean. Advances in maritime and commercial technology in Europe were essential to the development of capitalism and the expansion of Europe. Coupled with domestic political, economic, and social conditions that prompted expansion outward, improvements in navigation and shipping enabled western and northern Europeans to establish their preeminence over the world's seas, from the Indian to the Atlantic Oceans. Commerce in South and Southeast Asia, as well as coastal East Africa, was soon dominated by maritime Europe, and the great inland trans-Saharan and Central Asian caravan routes declined. In East Asia, the effects of Europe's expansion in the fifteenth and sixteenth centuries were felt primarily through the indirect impact of the formation of a world economy that would eventually transform China from an East Asian core to a European periphery. By 1500, Europe was poised to reap, accumulate, and invest the profits of the developing capitalist economy of the new Atlantic frontier as the vital periphery to the expansion of the European core economy. Although the idea of a world system may conjure up an image of the static machinery of economic relationships, the modern world system was dynamic and changing as soon as it was set into motion.

Suggested readings

Abu-Lughod, Janet D. (1989) *Before European Hegemony: The World System, AD 1250–1350*, New York: Oxford University Press. An ambitious study of the world system that predated the rise of Europe in the sixteenth century.

Braudel, Fernand (1981–84) *Civilization and Capitalism, 15th–18th Century, Vol 1: The Structures of Everyday Life; Vol 2: The Wheels of Commerce; Vol 3: The Perspective of the World*, New York: Harper & Row. The culminating works of a distinguished historian.

Chaudhuri, K.N. (1990) *Asia before Europe: Economy and Civilisation of the Indian Ocean from the Rise of Islam to 1750*, Cambridge: Cambridge University Press. An economic and cultural survey of the Indian Ocean world in the manner of Braudel's treatment of the Mediterranean.

Elvin, Mark (1973) *The Pattern of the Chinese Past*, Stanford, CA: Stanford University. A provocative argument concerning the commercial revolution of the Song period in China and subsequent developments.

Ferry, Stephen (1999) *I Am Rich Potosi: The Mountain that Eats Men*, New York: The Monacelli Press. An introductory text by Uruguayan historian Eduardo Galeano and moving photographs explore the complexity of cultural survivals on the mountain of silver.

Fischer, David Hackett (1996) *The Great Wave: Price Revolutions and the Rhythm of History*, New York and Oxford: Oxford University Press. A sweeping economic history of capitalism, proposing cycles of change, disequilibrium, and balance between the thirteenth and twentieth centuries.

Flynn, Dennis O. and Arturo Giráldez (1995) "Born with a 'Silver Spoon': The Origin of the World Trade in 1571." *Journal of World History*, vol 6, pp201–21.

Gilbert, Erik and Jonathan T. Reynolds (2004) *Africa in World History: From Prehistory to the Present*, New Jersey: Pearson Prentice Hall.

Wallerstein, Immanuel (2004) *World-Systems Analysis: An Introduction*, Durham, North Carolina: Duke University Press.

Yoshinobu, Shiba (1970) *Commerce and Society in Sung China*, Ann Arbor, MI: The University of Michigan Center for Chinese Studies. A detailed study of both social and economic changes in Sung China based on the close examination of multiple sources, including poetry.

Online resources

Annenberg/CPB, *Bridging World History* (2004) <www.learner.org/channel/courses/worldhistory> Multimedia project with interactive website and videos on demand; see especially Unit 9 Connections Across Land; Unit 10 Connections Across Water; and Unit 15 Early Global Commodities.

Museo Galileo, Institute and Museum of the History of Science (Florence), *Michael of Rhodes Project* <brunelleschi.imss.fi.it/michaelofrhodes/life.html> This website originated with a Dibner Institute for the Study of Science and Technology project and uses a recently uncovered manuscript written by the fifteenth-century mariner Michael of Rhodes, to explore the earliest surviving evidence on shipbuilding in the context of the astounding navigational revolution of the Middle Ages.

Study questions

1. Explain why historians might consider "the rise of the West" or European dominance to be inevitable.

2. Compare and contrast the history of European and Chinese voyages in the fifteenth century.

3. Define the characteristics of a world system.

4. What economic, social, and political factors provide fertile ground for European exploration and dominance after the fifteenth century?

5. What was the impact of the era's commerce and change on African societies? On South Asian societies? On indigenous societies of the Americas?

Part III Summary

In his beautifully sumptuous (ca. early 1440s) Renaissance painting, the artist Fra Filippo Lippi depicts the earliest double portrait known in Italian art. Thought to be the engagement portrait or even wedding image of the couple Angiola di Bernardo Sarpiti and Lorenzo di Ranieri Scolari, the pair is confined in a boxlike domestic space in which their gazes decidedly do not connect. Indeed, the man's image could almost be emerging from a mirror were it not for the slight extension of red cloth, hands holding a family crest, and his face's shadow cast on the wall as an allusion to the legend of the origin of painting itself by a woman, who traced her lover's shadow. The woman wears the "bling" of her time: pearls around the neck, gold bejeweled brooch and headdress, and gold metallic threads and studded pearls in her French gown that spell out the word "loyalty" in Italian in its folds around the wrist. Just as she looks past him, he looks beyond her in a strange dreamlike state of uneasy coexistence. Through the window is the outer world portrayed as a Dutch landscape artist might have rendered the scene. Like other works by this artist who was called by his contemporaries the most outstanding master of his time, this oil portrait was likely commissioned and possibly even executed by one of the several business partnerships (*compagnias*) in which he engaged in his career. In this way, as the figures in the painting suggestively move both backwards and forward, Lippi's painting suggests the primacy of economic relationships symbolized by artistic endeavors and

Filippo Lippi, *Portrait of a Woman with a Man at a Casement* (ca. 1440–1444). Metropolitan Museum of Art, Marquand Collection, Gift of Henry G. Marquand, 1889.

marriage itself. During and after the fifteenth century, the world increasingly became a space of interconnections woven through the movements of people and wealth across the globe.

The chapters in Part III have explored the themes of connections during the period from about 500 CE until 1500 CE, when cultures, economies, and hemispheres began to be integrated into a new global system. Both continuities and transformations were inevitable parts of the individual experience and identity. Yet the connectedness of local events to global patterns and processes could not be denied. The affluence depicted in Lippi's painting was an indication of portable possessions that would delight in their ostentatious advertisement of the commercial transactions they represented. Like other powerful people in cultures around the world, the art patron sought an enduring legacy in the midst of fleeting moments. Ultimately the connections among families, far-flung empires, transmitted ideas and traditions, and trading partners meeting in distant lands were among the myriad ways that world cultures negotiated the journeys between their present and their past.

Glossary

abusua The word for "family" among the West African Akan, a matrilineal descent group.

absolutism A form of government where absolute – complete and undiluted – authority vests in the sovereign.

agora In ancient Greece, the central gathering place or marketplace of a city or town.

agriculture The process of domesticating plants and animals for food production as well as useful crops for other purposes (such as cotton), involving soil cultivation, planting and harvesting. The gradual transition from foraging to agricultural production is sometimes known as the Neolithic Revolution.

akuaba One of the best-known sculptural traditions from the Akan region of West Africa, *akuaba* are fertility figures, small abstract carvings of a human figure.

al-Andalus The region of southern Spain which was under the control of Muslims after the Muslim conquests, ending about 730 CE.

alchemy A pseudo-science that aimed to transform metals such as lead or copper into silver or gold, considered by many the forerunner of modern chemistry and metallurgy.

altiplano The high plains running from Peru to Argentina.

amauta In Incan society, specialists known as *amauta* taught in elite schools, ensuring state control of cultural memory, selectively reordering the past to serve present needs.

amber A yellowish fossilized resin used for ornaments originating in many areas, but chiefly along the southern Baltic, found along ancient trade routes.

Amerindian A combination of "American" and "Indian," referring to the pre-Columbian native peoples of America.

Apartheid In South Africa, the 1948 policies that became a national guiding principle of segregation and oppression of black Africans, dictating where the majority African population could live, travel, and work.

archon The chief Greek magistrates in various Greek city states, such as Solon, who had authority to govern the Athenian republic, although later used to describe presiding officers in general.

areopagus A hill in Athens (the hill of Ares or Mars), which was the site of the highest court of law in Athens, often used to refer to the court itself.

arokin In West Africa, the court functionaries, official historians, and entertainers who preserved cultural memory for the ancestors of the Yoruba people.

asabiya An Arabic word, the root "to bind," used to refer to group identity, translated as "public spirit," "social solidarity," "group cohesion," or "group feeling."

astrolabe An instrument used to observe and calculate the positions of stars and planets, developed and transmitted by Arabs.

ayllu A kin group that formed the basic socio-political unit.

bakufu A Japanese term which may literally be translated as "tent government," generally a term for military headquarters, used to describe the government of Japan between 1192 and 1868; often Anglicized as "shogunate".

barrio A group of Mexica–Aztec households or villages – often built on kinship ties, but also on ethnicity, occupation, or patron–client relations – jointly obligated to pay tribute, providing a framework for administration.

BCE/CE BCE (Before the Common Era) and CE (Common Era) refer to the system of dating recent eras from the present (2012 CE) back 2,012 years to the "zero" of a timeline that then extends further back in time beginning in the year 1 BCE, 2 BCE, and so on.

bezant A Byzantine gold coin used widely as a medium of exchange throughout the Mediterranean from the sixth to the twelfth centuries.

bhakti A religious approach in Hinduism, the path of love or devotion to a god or an aspect of God; one of the three paths which also include *jnana* (the path of knowledge) and *karma* (the path of good works).

bioprospecting The colonizers' search for plants and animals around the world to be mined for knowledge and marketable products; called by some scholars "the global encounters of colonizers with new environments threatening those without power."

bipedal/bipedalism Moving about on two legs; characteristic of birds and humans, although some chimpanzees and apes can move bipedally for short distances.

boci Derived from the Fon words meaning "empowered" (*bo*) cadaver (*ce*); these are empowerment objects mostly present in the regions of the Guinea Coast, the Slave Coast, and the Bight of Benin.

bodhisattva In Buddhism, particularly the Mahayana tradition, a bodhisattva is one who after attaining enlightenment remains connected to the material world and continues altruistically aiding other beings in their quests for salvation and enlightenment.

Boers Dutch for countryman or farmer, used to describe the Afrikaans-speaking colonists in South Africa after about the seventeenth century.

Bolshevik The Russian Social-Democratic Party that came to power in the October Revolution of 1917, subsequently renamed the Russian Communist Party.

bracero A program that resulted in a series of laws and agreements initiated in August 1942 for the temporary immigration of contract workers from Mexico to the United States.

Brahman Although conceptualized somewhat differently by various Hindu groups, in Hinduism, Brahman is the supreme, all pervading, spiritual energy; the ultimate non-material source of everything. In priestly traditions, the Brahmanas are sacred utterances.

bridewealth Gifts of property or other valuable consideration paid by the groom or his family to the family of a woman upon their marriage.

bronze An alloy usually composed of copper and tin, harder than copper. In the ancient Mediterranean, the tin used in the alloy was a valuable trade item from Central Asian mines across the landmass.

bubonic plague A pandemic disease believed to have originated in China in the 1330s that spread along the Silk Road trade routes into Europe and Africa, resulting in a death toll of 75 million.

Buddharaja In Southeast Asia, the development of a cult of divine rule, the Buddha-kings.

bullion Precious metals, specifically gold and silver ingots.

bullionism The belief that acquiring surplus bullion (precious metals, primarily gold and silver) was the key to building and maintaining a strong state, a component of European mercantilism.

burakumin A Japanese social class of outcasts, the lowest level of society, officially abolished in 1871.

cacao A tropical tree originating in South America, the seeds of which – cocoa beans – are processed into chocolate, one of the major elements of monetary exchange in the pre-Colombian trade routes between Mesoamerica and North America.

calico An Indian printed cotton textile imported into England, the popularity of which aroused a strong hostility from the textile manufacturers and weavers of England.

calpullec In Mexica-Aztec society, the term refers to a council of elders who elected the chiefs described in *calpulli*.

calpulli In Mexica-Aztec society, the tribal-kinship units that formed the council of elders who elected chiefs, one in charge of war and the other in charge of religious functions.

camelids Members of the same family as camels, including llamas, alpacas and so forth. They are generally large animals with long legs, suitable for domestication as beasts of burden.

capitalism An economic system based on private ownership wherein capital (wealth not consumed or hoarded) is used for investments from which additional profit (capital) can be gained. At its essence, it is the use of wealth to create additional wealth.

cartographer One who makes maps or charts, of critical importance in the explorations of the early modern world.

cathedral In Western Christian churches, a cathedral is a church which is the official seat of a bishop; in Eastern Orthodox churches, the cathedral is the main church in a city, although ideally where a bishop would reside.

caudillos In Latin America, the independent politicians who relied on personal charisma and military force, defying both democratic politics and constitutional government, sometimes exercising power very much as imperial officials had.

CE see *BCE*

chakravartin In ancient India, the title *chakravartin* referred to a universal ruler, one "whose chariot wheels roll everywhere."

chinampas A Mesoamerican agricultural practice, these were raised fields in swampy land, sometimes referred to as floating fields, where the high water table could support multiple crops per year.

circum-Caribbean The zone along the Caribbean coast of Colombia, Venezuela, Guyana, Suriname, and French Guiana, which developed similar patterns of production as well as an economic dependency on Europe.

circumnavigation The act of sailing around something, an island, a continent (as in "circumnavigating Africa"), or the globe.

civilization A highly contested term which has been used to describe a complex society usually with monumental architecture, writing, a large bureaucracy, agricultural base, trade, and hierarchical systems of order. It has fallen from favor with many historians who believe that common use perpetuates the idea of a "natural progression" in the development of human societies.

coke A fuel derived from coal that has been distilled of its volatile components, having a more compact texture.

collectivization Policy of forcing peasants to give up privately owned farms and join collective farms in keeping with the nationalization of resources.

comfort women Women in Japanese colonies such as Taiwan and Korea who were forced to provide sexual services for Japanese troops.

commenda The name in Venice and Genoa for a type of partnership which merchants formed for overseas ventures, generally one at a time.

compass A navigational instrument that shows

direction, particularly the magnetic compass that aligns with the magnetic poles.

cosmology The fields of philosophy and science that are devoted to the study of the general laws of the universe as a whole and the role of human beings as a part of a unified whole.

cowry shell A common form of currency in the Afro-Eurasian world from very early times until as late as 1800 CE.

creole In Spanish America, a term which originally referred to Europeans born in the new world, and later those who were culturally and racially mixed.

crucible A vessel made to endure great heat; a place where different elements meet and may be changed in form and matter.

crusade Military expeditions of Europeans during the eleventh to thirteenth centuries in attempts to drive Muslims from the Holy Land.

culture The totality of the intellectual creations, beliefs and behaviors of a society, such as art, technology, philosophy, religion, political organization, etc., that are passed down from one generation to another (although often modified), providing social cohesion and environmental adaptation.

cuneiform A form of writing in ancient West Asia comprised of figures written by a wedge-shaped reed stylus on clay surfaces; it is at present considered the oldest script.

daimyo The regional lords of medieval and early modern Japan.

dao As a concept in Chinese philosophy, the term indicates a "way," meaning a road or path, a source (or the source) of the cosmos present both in and beyond the existing world, always present and in motion.

datu The chiefs or rulers of Southeast Asian island states.

deme A township or division of ancient Greece, distinct from the city-state or polis.

demesne The land granted by a king to nobles, forming a part of manorial holdings cultivated by peasants or serfs.

democracy Literally, rule by the people, derived from the Greek word demos (people) and kratos (rule); a form of government which appears to first emerged in ancient Greece.

demographic change Changes in a community's statistics pertaining to births, deaths, diseases, economic trends, etc.

demos Term used to describe the common class in ancient Greece, seen by sociologists as a group or unit.

desaparecidos In Argentina, the "disappeared ones," those who disappeared after criticizing or opposing government action. Women – often the mothers of those who disappeared – organized and protested in the Plaza de Mayo at the center of Buenos Aires against the government assaults on political opposition.

dessication The process by which something becomes extremely dry, especially drier environmental conditions caused by human or natural forces.

devaraja A "god-king" cult in eighth- and ninth-century Cambodia.

dharma A Hindu concept of right conduct or behavior befitting one's innate nature, caste or station in life; in Buddhism, the "law of the universe."

dhoti A long cloth wrapped around the body and through the legs, resembling knee-length pants, worn by Indian men, and adopted by Ghandi as a symbolic gesture.

dhyāna In Hinduism, the most advanced stage of meditation, leading to nirvana; in Buddhism, an awareness of ultimate reality brought about by meditation, used as the name for the Chinese Chan (Jpn. Zen) sect.

diaspora A movement or scattering of people away from their ancestral or traditional homeland; often used in connection with the Jewish Babylonian exile.

diet The Japanese parliament, composed of a House of Representatives and a House of Councilors, first convened in 1889 as a part of the Meiji constitution.

dinar An Arabic coin used in international trade throughout Afro-Eurasia, replaced by gold coins of the Italian merchant city-states in the thirteenth century.

divination The act of foretelling the future by supernatural means such as augury or prophecy, interpreting omens such as the effect of fire on shells or bones, the condition of entrails from a sacrificed animal, and so forth.

domus In ancient Rome and Pompeii, a private family residence, whether modest or palatial.

dual revolutions Refers to the interactions and interdependence between the economic revolutions (such as the Industrial Revolution) and political change.

ducat A coin issued by Venice in 1284 that became the first true international coinage, maintaining its purity and thus its dominance in Eurasia for over 500 years.

duma An elected Russian legislative body from 1906 until 1917.

ecology The term is used as a noun describing the relationship between living organisms and their surroundings. According to the *Oxford English Dictionary*, the term developed from a combination of the Greek word for dwelling and the German word for logic.

ecotone A transition zone between two or more ecological areas.

encomiendas Grants by the Spanish Crown to conquistadors or officials in the Americas of the right to the labor and taxation of a specific number of native peoples. Legally, it did not include a land grant, but in practice often extended to land.

endogamy The practice or custom of marrying within the limits of one's own tribe or social group.

entrepôt A trading post, point of exchange or distribution of goods to various parts of the world.

epic Term derived from Greek, refers to a long narrative poem about the deeds of heroes.

examination system The Chinese system initiated in the Tang period with the goal of assuring that the best men were selected for office in the imperial government. The examinations tested knowledge of the Confucian classics as well as their ability to deal with the problems of government administration.

familia Latin for "family," in its broadest usage, referring to all persons and property under the control of the head of the household (*see paterfamilias*)

fascism A political organization, the name of which was coined by Benito Mussolini in 1919, that called for the subjugation of the individual and society to the state under an all-powerful leader who embodied the people's will.

fief A tract of land or piece of property controlled by a lord to which a number of serfs were attached, ostensibly large enough to support the vassals as well as the landholder.

florin The gold coins issued in Florence in 1252 which, with the *ducat*, generally replaced the Arabic *dinar* in use for international trade.

futuwwa Fraternal organizations of merchants, particularly in the Turkish and Persian areas, that were organized in the Muslim world of West Asia to serve the needs of its members.

galleon Large sailing warships, probably of Spanish origin, developed in the fifteenth and sixteenth centuries, that allowed Iberian domination of the seas for decades.

genius In Latin, the term refers to a god or spirit who guides the life of an individual or family, determining their fate and fortune; a pagan concept of a controlling supernatural being associated with places or institutions.

genocide Deliberate policy of elimination of an ethnic or national group, defined by the United Nations as the physical destruction of a racial or national group.

gentile Pertaining to those of any people or nation other than Israelite; frequently used in connection with the discussions regarding the role of Judaism and Christianity.

geomancy The art of divination by means of signs derived from the earth; in early Chinese society, a belief in systems of correspondence between the human and natural worlds.

globalization The patterns and processes of economy, politics, and/or culture operating on a trans-regional or trans-national scale.

griot In North and West Africa, a resident traditionalist or traveling entertainer, poet, or musician whose duties include preservation and recitation of political and family histories.

guild European associations of those in the same profession or economic pursuit, providing a basis for the retention and transmission of specialist knowledge, forming community solidarity, and agents of political and cultural change.

gulag Soviet labor camps and prisons where political prisoners and criminals were housed, primarily from the 1920s to the 1950s.

hadith The Muslim oral traditions pertaining to Muhammad which are considered a supplement to the Qur'an called the Sunna.

hegemony The leadership or prevailing power of one source of authority over another; the term can refer to cultural power exercised from above or political power exercised by one state over another.

hejira The flight from Mecca of Muhammad and his followers to Medina in 622 CE.

hieroglyphics A form of writing, associated with ancient Egypt, wherein a character is a figure of an object representing a word.

Hispanismo A strong attachment to Spanish cultural and national identity; a nostalgic attachment to the Spanish past.

historical memory A collective memory adopted by a society, often consisting of stories that are repeated, with the backing of people in power, of historical events; a widely accepted, sanctioned memory.

Hominin Hominins are humans and their ancestors (as evidenced in the fossil record), part of the Homininae subfamily that also includes chimpanzees and gorillas. Used in place of the older term "hominid".

huangdi The pinyin (modern standard phonetic) romanization of the Chinese term for "emperor," derived in part from the ancient term for supreme deity, Shangdi, "lord on high."

Industrial Revolution The major changes in production beginning in eighteenth-century Great Britain, involving the use of mechanical power (the steam engine at first) and efficiencies in manufacturing, such as assembly lines and machines replacing or supplementing human labor. Production, however, was largely dependent on raw materials imported from less mechanized areas.

jia The modern Chinese word generally translated as "family," refers to a broader unit, a household, a corporate unit with a common residence and shared economy.

jihad In Islam, a war or crusade on behalf of Islam, a struggle for a doctrine.

jizya In Islamic states, a tax paid by non-Muslims – allowed to practice their own religion – in return for protection and a mark of submission to Islamic rule.

journées French for "days," used to denote the days of insurrection following the execution of Robespierre and other Jacobin leaders.

jurisprudence A body of law, knowledge and skill in the law; the study of laws.

karimi A society consisting of large-scale merchants, headquartered in Cairo, which flourished as early as the eleventh to the thirteenth centuries.

karma The Hindu concept of karma evolved from early texts, where it meant "ritually prescribed behavior" into the Buddhist concept of "cumulative causality determined by human actions."

Khan Turkish word for "supreme leader" used as a title for Chinggis, the founder of the Mongol Empire; his successors were titled by the related term, "qaghan", "Khan of Khans".

kshatriya The second of the varnas (castes), includes administrators and those in protective occupations, such as warriors.

kulaks In Russian history, wealthy or prosperous peasants who characteristically owned relatively large farms and played a prominent part in village affairs.

kunstkammer A treasure room filled with material objects designed to display the wealth and power of its owner.

lamaism In Tibetan Buddhism, the practice of placing emphasis on the spiritual teachings of the head of a monastery or great teacher.

lingam In Hinduism, a round, smooth rod-shaped object symbolizing the god Shiva, often paired with the *yoni*, a lipped, disk-shaped symbol of the goddess Shakti. The two together are sometimes conceptualized as the male and female sex organs.

lukasa Among the Luba of Africa, a lukasa is a wooden, handheld board covered with pins, beads, or sometimes painted or incised geometric markings used to evoke places, events, or names from the past.

ma'at Concept of order, fundamental to the ancient Egyptian worldview. It was the duty of the king, or pharaoh, to maintain the continuity between the secular and sacred worlds, assuring order and justice as well as the flooding of the Nile in appropriate seasons.

madlathule A famine that devastated Zululand from the 1790s until about 1810.

madrasa An Islamic institution of higher learning where students study the Muslim traditions (*hadith*), laws, literature, and other advanced studies.

Manichaeism A religious movement during the third century CE founded by the Persian priest, Mani. He developed a cosmology based on Zoroastrian concepts of a dichotomy between the forces of good and evil. Mani considered himself the final prophet of a long line, and believed that all humans had a divine spark.

manor An estate belonging to a lord, including both land and dwellings, generally farmed by serfs or peasant farmers.

maroons Communities of runaway Amerindians and escaped slaves living as freedom fighters in the inaccessible reaches of the Caribbean and Americas.

matrifocal A family unit centering on the mother as head of the household, also used to describe a society or culture that centers on a mother's authority.

matriliny A system of descent and kinship observed through the female line.

mayeque In Mexica–Aztec society, mayeque were the commoners, or serfs, who were attached to rural estates.

mercantilism Set of doctrines and practices which aimed to enhance the power of a state by increasing its wealth, based on the expectation of government intervention to protect and secure both the prosperity and self-sufficiency of the state and of the trading interests.

messiah Most commonly in reference to a promised deliverer of the Jewish people, considered by Christians to be Jesus, but regularly extended to refer to an anticipated savior in many different religious contexts.

Mestizos People of mixed Spanish and Indian ancestry.

Métis One of the peoples of Canada who trace descent to mixed European and Amerindian heritage.

metropole The parent state of a colony, or its primary city.

mfecane Time of widespread warfare, forced migrations, and turmoil in South Africa during 1820s and 1830s, exploited by the army of a Zulu leader, Shaka.

mit'a system Mandatory labor system under the Incas that was adapted and continued under the Spanish.

Mithra An important deity in the ancient Indo-Iranian pantheon, usually identified with the sun. The secret, male-oriented sect or cult spread across the Roman Empire as far as Great Britain.

monasticism The way of life of those who have taken a religious vow to live apart from society in religious communities throughout the world. They were predominately Christian or Buddhist, where they transmitted religious ideas and practices.

monumental architecture Large structures constructed by humans, usually made of clay, stone, or compacted earth. These are usually public buildings constructed for public purposes, such as protective gates or walls, burial mounds, or as religious sites. Their appearance in early societies is indicative of developing political and religious organization and economic specialization.

mosque An Islamic place of worship, characteristically, a domed structure.

mudaraba In Islamic economic law, a partnership; an agreement between an investor and a merchant which facilitated trade in the premodern Islamic world.

Mughal A dynasty that ruled much of India from the early sixteenth century until the mid-eighteenth century, although in nominal existence until 1857.

mysticism Religious practices or experiences that result in alternate states of consciousness or a direct experience of the sacred.

nasi A substance suspected of mystical power given credit for helping Sunjata to power, called a "power of darkness, a thing used to harm someone."

Nazi A political party in a German movement, National Socialism, which came to power in Germany in 1933 under the leadership of Adolf Hitler.

Nestorianism Adherents of the doctrine developed by the Patriarch of Constantinople, a Persian. Nestorius (ca. 386–451) believed that Christ was both fully human and fully divine, each existing fully, but joined in one body.

nirvana Literally translated as "becoming extinguished" or "blowing out," *nirvana* refers to the extinction of emotional and physical attachment to the material world, leading to the cessation of suffering caused by such attachment, and finally the achievement of a state of "enlightenment."

numina In early Roman religions, *numina* were divinities, gods, or powerful spirits (good or evil) occupying a home. They later became anthropomorphized into gods such as Jupiter and Juno.

nyama Mande term for "power," which may be derived from both natural and supernatural energy.

Oba The king of Benin, also sometimes used elsewhere in Africa.

obsidian A dark, very hard volcanic glass, which can be shaped to have extremely sharp edges, often rivaling even the most modern surgical implements.

one-child policy A policy introduced in China in 1979, in which, in most cases, families were allowed only one child. The purpose was to slow China's birth rate, which was increasing the population at an alarming rate.

oral tradition Formal and highly ritualized systems of cultural transmission through the spoken word.

papacy The office of the bishop of Rome, the pope, from the Latin word *papa*, or "father." The term was originally applied to all of the Western bishops but was restricted to the bishop of Rome by Pope Gregory VII in 1073.

paper Thin sheets of matted or felted materials, used for writing and art, generally essential for printing.

pastoralism An economic activity centering on tending flocks or herds of animals, such as sheep, cattle, swine, etc. In later usage, the term also referred to a form of art that celebrated the bucolic or rustic landscapes or ways of living.

paterfamilias In ancient Rome, the male head of the family or household, having complete legal authority over the members and property.

pax Mongolica A term meaning "Mongolian peace," referring to the period of relative tranquility when a wide swath of the Eurasian continent was under the control of the Mongol Empire, allowing caravans and traders to pass along the Silk Roads with little obstruction.

Pentecostals In Christianity, Pentecostals are persons believing in the individual experience of the Holy Spirit and in the power of faith for both physical and spiritual healing, emphasizing experience over doctrine.

pharaoh A ruler in ancient Egypt. The word means "Great House," but by the New

Kingdom in the fifteenth century BCE, it was used in reference to the ruler.

philosophia Literally "the love of wisdom," the origin of the modern English word "philosophy."

philosophes The intellectuals whose work and actions fueled the eighteenth-century period of the Enlightenment.

pochteca In the Mexica-Aztec economy, these were professional merchants, members of certain *barrios* who traveled outside the empire to maintain trade connections. They occupied a high status, just below the nobility.

polis The Greek term for "city," a basic political unit in ancient Greece.

polygyny A form of polygamy in which men have multiple wives.

printing A technique for replicating writing by pressing ink on paper using a surface with the images desired imprinted on them.

purdah From the Urdu word for "curtain," used to refer to the practice of concealing women from the view of males not of the woman's immediate family

pyrotechnology The science and technology of using fire as a resource, tool, or weapon. This skill set was the first known technological leap to have a profound impact on human life, resulting in more easily digested foods, sources of warmth in cold climates, etc.

qanat An underground irrigation in Eurasia system that taps mountain water and channels it through sloping tunnels.

quipu A knotted cord which records important numbers or chronological data by way of differentiated colors and knots.

quiripa Strings of shells used as currency in the Orinoco basin of South America.

realpolitik The politics of reality, used to describe politics based on the practical rather than ideology.

reconquista The campaigns of the Iberian Christian states between the eighth and fifteenth centuries to recapture the territory occupied by the Moors in the eighth century.

Renaissance A term meaning "rebirth" that carries with it the implication of a revival of past artistic and philosophical traditions.

Sahel A semi-arid region forming a transition zone between the Sahara desert and the humid savannas in sub-Saharan Africa.

samsara Literally translated as "wandering," *samsara* is the plane of existence manifested in the endless cycle of birth–death–rebirth, release from which can only be achieved by realizing the truth of impermanence and the state of *nirvana*.

sati Widow suicide by self-immolation (setting oneself on fire), a Hindu custom, practiced in varying degrees depending on region, caste, and economic conditions; widely criticized in the colonial period, and outlawed in modern times.

satyagraha Literally "truth force," the term refers to the peaceful non-cooperation and passive resistance espoused by Gandhi in his resistance to the British Raj.

scapulimancy The practice of using bones for prophecy and guidance.

sedentism The practice of staying in one place rather than moving from place to place in foraging activities. The practice of agriculture was conducive to sedentism, settling in an area for planting and harvesting and staying to tend the fields, which eventually led to larger-scale social organization.

serfdom An economic system that emerged in Europe from the collapse of the Roman Empire wherein a member of the military aristocracy or nobility provided protection in exchange for agricultural labor. In most instances, serfs could not be bought and sold as slaves, but were bound to the land and transferred when the land changed ownership.

servinakuy Among the Quechas of the Andean region of South America, a system of trial marriage in which betrothal involving cohabation was practiced to determine whether the couple fit well in the family structures.

shaik The title of the religious leaders in the Safavid empire.

Shakti Hindu female divine force; the mother goddess, became important ca. 400–800 CE.

Shari'a The body of Islamic law, the expression of Allah's requirements for Muslim society, the path of conduct to which Muslims are expected to adhere.

Shi'i One of the two major branches of Islam, Shi'i began as a political movement of those who believed the leader of Islam should be a member of the Prophet's family or their descendants.

shiki The Japanese term for land rights, the basic element of economic feudalism; the term originally meant "office," and implied duties related to the land, but eventually came to mean the "right to profit from the land."

shōen Japanese estates, generally found from about the eighth to the late fifteenth century, owned by the imperial family, aristocrats, or powerful religious institutions, often made up of scattered plots.

shogun A Japanese term for a military ruler, first used during the Heian period.

shogunate The government of the *shogun*, the military ruler of Japan from 1192–1867.

shudra One of the Vedic social divisions described in the Rig-Veda, the lowest of the varnas, including slaves and unskilled workers.

Silk Roads A network of trade routes connecting East and West Asia, Europe, and North Africa, established from the second century BCE to the second century CE, and still operating.

social democracy Parties organized in interwar Britain, France, and the United States engaged in the pursuit of socialism through democratic means, inspired by the ideas of Karl Marx.

stelae Plural for stela, carved or inscribed stone slabs or columns, generally tall and imposing, which are used to commemorate important events or the achievements of important people.

stupas Commemorative or religiously significant Hindu or Buddhist monuments.

Sufi An adherent of Sufism, the mystical branch of Islam, characterized by turning away from worldliness. Sufis believe that a spiritual union with God is possible through asceticism and an inward search.

sunna The body of law derived from the sayings and actions of the prophet Muhammad.

Sunni The larger of the two major branches of Islam. Sunnites believe that leadership of Islam is determined by political realities and accept leadership of any Muslims who rule in accordance with Islamic law and afford the proper exercise of religion while preserving order and stability.

sutra In Hinduism and Buddhism, a form of sacred writings or scripture.

swadeshi Literally Bengali for "of our own country," it was a strategy conceived by Indian nationalists with the goal of hurting Britain by not consuming British products and reviving Indian crafts and manufacturing.

swaraj Sanskrit term for self-rule, applied to the movement and agitation in favor of making India self-governing.

syncretism The selective integration of concepts, symbols, and practices drawn from different traditions.

tanzimat A reform movement in the Ottoman Empire between 1838 and 1876, influenced by European political organization and principles.

tariqa A term meaning "paths to union with God", brotherhoods that sprang up in the twelfth and thirteenth centuries throughout western Asia, typically organized around a mystic whose tomb was usually incorporated into the main lodge.

technology As pertains to early humans, it is the branch of human understanding that seeks to manipulate available materials in order to accomplish a practical purpose, such as adapting stone to be used as axes, or adapting natural materials in order to build a cooking hearth or a shelter.

theology The study that focuses on the nature of a deity and the deity's relationship with the world.

three-field system A medieval European pattern of cultivation where crops are rotated between two or three fields and one field is fertilized and left fallow in order to replenish the soil and maintain productivity.

totemistic Pertaining to a hereditary emblem or symbol of a tribe or other group, often a representation of an animal or other natural object, as a mark or emblem representing a mythical ancestor or friendly spirit.

trekboers People of Dutch descent, primarily farmers, who settled in coastal South Africa and migrated inland after the seventeenth century CE.

turquoise A blue-green mineral valued in the Americas for both its aesthetic appeal and religious significance, turquoise was exchanged along extensive trading connections, becoming widespread between about 900 and 1200 CE.

ulama Muslim scholars whose scholarship was important in preserving law, but whose orthodoxy was subject to community consensus.

ulgulan Meaning "great tumult", it was a popular resistance movement of 1899–1900 carried out by the Munda tribe on the Bengal–Bihar border, critical to the ultimate success of the Indian National Congress.

urbanism A term associated with the development of cities and the trend toward permanent settlement in relatively small areas and accompanied by more complex social, political, and economic structures than would be found in nomadic societies or villages.

vaishya The third of the four *varnas* (the social divisions of the Rig-Veda): the merchant caste (traditionally described as commoners).

vassal In feudal economies, the vassal held the role of client, to whom the lord or seignior owed the responsibility of protection in exchange for labor. The vassal's rights in their fiefs grew larger over time, eventually becoming hereditary.

vegeculture Cultivating vegetables and herbs as foodstuffs.

viceroyalty The area governed by a viceroy in the name of a king or by authority of a superior level of government.

Vodun A religion derived from the West African Yoruba, Ewe/Fon, and Central African Kongolese people introduced to Haiti and Louisiana.

Voortrekkers Afrikaans-speaking pioneers or any of the Boers who left the British Cape Colony after 1834 and migrated to the South African interior.

wampumpeag An Algonquian word meaning "white strings (of beads)" referred to many pre-Columbian currency systems.

waqf In Islamic societies, an endowment of land, the income of which was to be used for charitable purposes such as supporting schools, mosques, orphanages, hospitals, and so on.

wat The Khmer word for temple, such as Angkor Wat.

watanaki Another term for the Quecha practice of *servinakuy*.

world history A discipline of history that seeks to understand societies in context with the broader world. Those who identify themselves as "world historians" tend to focus on cross-cultural contacts, conflicts, or comparisons between societies. It differs from regional and national approaches in that it seeks a global perspective on the past, one that acknowledges and integrates the historical experiences of all of the world's peoples.

world system A network of ties and trading connections that extend across a region especially the one that began taking shape after the conquest of the Americas.

yoni In Hinduism, the symbol of the goddess Shakti, often conceptualized as a lipped dish. The *lingam* and *yoni* together represent creation and procreation, representations of male and female organs.

zakat A tithe or tax on livestock and agricultural production required of Muslims to be used by rulers as a source of state revenue.

Index